Land of the Long Horizons

AMERICAN VISTA SERIES:

Land of the

Edited, with introduction and commentary by

THE MIDWEST

Long Horizons

Walter Havighurst

fully illustrated

COWARD - McCANN INC. NEW YORK

ARRIVAL AND DEPARTURE: From *The Farm* by Louis Bromfield, published by Harper & Brothers. Copyright 1933, 1935, 1946 by Louis Bromfield. Reprinted by permission of the publishers.

WISCONSIN BOYHOOD: From *The Story of My Boyhood and Youth* by John Muir, published by Houghton Mifflin Company. Copyright 1941 by Wanda Muir Hanna. Reprinted by permission of the publishers.

RIDING THE SANGAMON CIRCUIT: From *The Autobiography of Peter Cartwright*, published by Abingdon Press and reprinted by their permission.

MAKING A MISSISSIPPI PANORAMA: From Henry Lewis' journal of 1848, edited by Bertha L. Heibron. Reprinted by permission of the Minnesota Historical Society.

THE TWO AKRONS: From *A Centennial History of Akron* by Herman Fetzer. Reprinted by permission of the Akron Beacon Journal.

WILDCAT MONEY, TOWNSITE FRAUD: From *Old Times on the Upper Mississippi* by George Byron Merrick published by The Arthur H. Clark Company. Copyright 1909, 1937—pp. 174-183, omitting plate pp. 177-8.

LAND OF THE CROOKED TREE: From *The Land of the Crooked Tree* by U. P. Hedrick. Copyright 1948 by Oxford University Press, Inc. Reprinted by permission.

UNLOCKING THE NORTH: From *Iron Brew* by Steward H. Holbrook, published by The Macmillan Company. Copyright 1939 by The Macmillan Company and used with the publishers' permission.

DISASTER IN THE WOODS: Reprinted by permission of the Michigan Historical Commission from *Reminiscences of the Big Fire of 1871* by Josephine Sawyer in *Michigan History Magazine,* 1932.

FIRST TRAIN ON THE PRAIRIE and CHICAGO IN ASHES: Reprinted by permission of R. R. Donnelley and Sons Company from *Growing Up With Southern Illinois* by Daniel Harmon Brush, and from *Reminiscences of Chicago During the Great Fire* by Horace White.

WORLD'S FAIR ON THE PRAIRIE: Reprinted from *The Tale of Chicago* by Edgar Lee Masters, published by G. P. Putnam's Sons, copyright 1933 by E. L. Masters. Used by permission of the publisher.

LOCAL HISTORY: Reprinted from *R. F. D.* by Charles Allen Smart. By permission of W. W. Norton & Company, Inc. Copyright 1938 by W. W. Norton & Company, Inc.

PORTAGE, WISCONSIN: From *Portage, Wisconsin* by Zona Gale, published by Alfred A. Knopf, Inc. Copyright 1928 by Zona Gale. Reprinted by permission of City Bank of Portage, Trustee U/W of Zona Gale Breese.

GOOD-BYE WISCONSIN: From *Good-bye Wisconsin* by Glenway Wescott. Copyright 1928 by Harper & Brothers. Copyright 1956 by Glenway Wescott. Reprinted by permission of Harper & Brothers.

ARRIVAL IN CHICAGO: From *An Autobiography* by Frank Lloyd Wright. Reprinted by permission of Duell, Sloan & Pearce, Inc. Copyright 1943 by Frank Lloyd Wright.

PRAIRIE TOWN: From *Always the Young Strangers* by Carl Sandburg, copyright 1952, 1953, by Carl Sandburg. Reprinted by permission of Harcourt, Brace and Company, Inc.

TIN LIZZIE: From *The Big Money* by John Dos Passos. Copyright 1930, 1932, 1933, 1934, 1935, 1936, 1937 by John Dos Passos. Published by Houghton Mifflin Company. Used by permission of the author.

WHAT IS OHIO? From *The Buckeye Country* by Harlan Hatcher. Reprinted by permission of the author and G. P. Putnam's Sons. Copyright 1940 by Harlan Hatcher.

INDIANA, HER SOIL AND LIGHT by Theodore Dreiser and MINNESOTA, THE NORSE STATE by Sinclair Lewis: From *These United States,* Edited by Charles Gruening, copyright (R) 1952. By permission of Liveright, Publishers, New York.

ILLINOIS, PRAIRIE PROVINCE: From *A Prairie Grove* by Donald Culross Peattie. Copyright, 1938, by Donald Culross Peattie. Reprinted by permission of Simon and Schuster, Inc.

THE REAL MICHIGAN by Bruce Catton. Reprinted by special permission of *Holiday,* copyright 1957, by The Curtis Publishing Company.

GHOSTS IN WISCONSIN by William Ellery Leonard: Reprinted by permission of the State Historical Society of Wisconsin from the *Wisconsin Magazine of History,* volume 6, 1922.

AMERICAN HUNGER, From *Tar* by Sherwood Anderson, published by Boni & Liveright. Copyright © 1926 by Eleanor Anderson. Reprinted by permission of Harold Ober Associates Inc.

MIDDLETOWN . . . IN TRANSITION: From *Middletown* by Robert S. Lynd and Helen Merrell Lynd, copyright, 1929, by Harcourt, Brace and Company, Inc.; renewed by Robert S. Lynd and Helen Merrell Lynd. Reprinted by permission of the publishers. From *Middletown in Transition* by Robert S. Lynd and Helen Merrell Lynd, copyright, 1937, by Harcourt, Brace and Company, Inc., and reprinted with their permission.

THE BIG ADVENTURE: Reprinted from *Midwest at Noon* by Graham Hutton by permission of The University of Chicago Press. Copyright 1946 by The University of Chicago.

Library of Congress Catalog Card Number: 60-11288

Designed by Ben Feder, Inc.

MANUFACTURED IN THE UNITED STATES OF AMERICA

Contents

Land of the Long Horizons

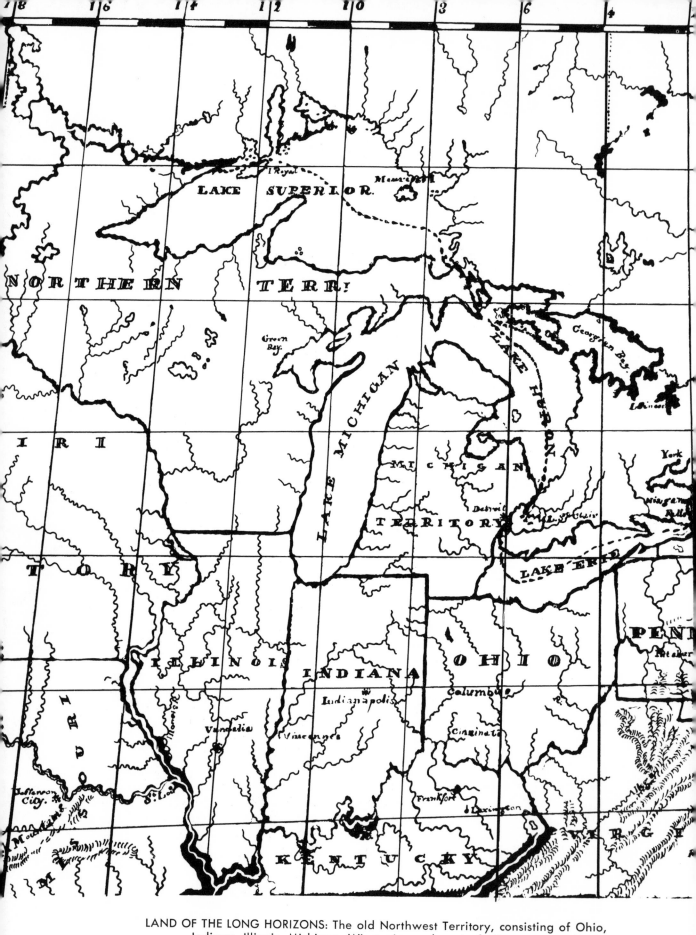

LAND OF THE LONG HORIZONS: The old Northwest Territory, consisting of Ohio, Indiana, Illinois, Michigan, Wisconsin, and part of Minnesota, as it appeared in a map of 1830.

INTRODUCTION

IN one of his early stories, nearly a century ago, Henry James told of an American artist who had fallen in love with Italy. As he walked the dim and echoing streets of Florence he felt the past around him, and thinking of his own country he lamented "our silent past, our deafening present."

Especially in the American interior the past has seemed thin and empty. Except for its border of great lakes and great rivers the Midwest landscape was undistinguished. Though immensely productive it appeared monotonous—no heights, no depths, no barriers, nothing hidden, few contrasts, no difficult or dangerous places. The level land cast no shadows. All its horizons looked alike.

Yet this was the land of America's longest warfare. It was fiercely fought for by the Indians, the French and the British, and by American soldiers and frontiersmen. For three generations, from the raid on Pickawillany to Black Hawk's brave and futile resistance, it was a disputed country.

This contested land was a realm of riches. French *émigrés* believed that candles grew in the Ohio marshes and custard hung from the trees. John Law's company advertised gold and silk as products of the Illinois prairie. On the upper Mississippi, Peter Pond of Connecticut caught catfish that weighed a hundred pounds. Simon Kenton counted a file of a thousand buffalo pacing toward salt licks on the Ohio. When he arrived in 1820, Noah Major found twenty thousand deer in a single county of Indiana. Near the Sangamon River an Irish immigrant farmed 640 acres which produced "forty bushels of wheat to the second crop without sowing." Wrote John Eyre of England in 1832: ". . . the fame of Ohio having gone into every nation upon earth."

This fabulous country was also accessible, a land of promise lying just beyond the Allegheny ridges. In two post-Revolutionary generations multitudes of settlers took possession. With prodigious energy they cleared the forest and plowed the wild prairie. Towns sprang up at the crossroads and cities grew beside the lake harbors and river landings. The voices of its past were lost in its strident present.

In America the past is brief. Farmers still turn up Indian flints in their fields, and it is only a short way back to prehistory. But a past that is short is also recoverable. In the "old" logging town of Bemidji, far up the dwindling Mississippi, I once asked about early newspapers. "Yes," said the editor of the Bemidji *Pioneer*, "we have some papers that are really old. They go all the way back to 1901." That was the time of Bemidji's beginning.

Everywhere in the Midwest we can go back to the beginnings, to the first landfall, the first river passage, the first ax thudding in the woods. Who discovered the Rhine, the Elbe and the Danube?—there are no Marquettes and Jolliets in Old World history. The literature of Europe has no "landlookers," no search for a Northwest Passage, no trail breaking in the wilderness. The Old World past fades back, through layers of culture and tradition, into unknown distance. But in America we can know where every name came from and how it got there. Shawneetown, Vincennes, Fort Defiance, Mackinac, Prairie du Chien—they gleam on the map like sinking campfires. We can recall the first blacksmith in a township, the first circuit rider in the forest, the first pedlar on the roads. None of our past is lost.

Since Henry James made his regretful observation, American history has grown longer and it has become more vocal. In the past thirty years, since the great depression, a regional literature has developed in America, focusing upon place and the life that has evolved there. It is a new literature, resting upon an older one.

The record of the Midwest begins with the long, arduous and dramatic narratives of the French missionaries—the seventy-three volumes of the *Jesuit Relations*. It continues with laconic accounts of danger and promise, written by the light of campfires on an upturned canoe or a bulging packsaddle. After the explorers' and traders' narratives come the letters of pioneer settlers, the memories of river captains, the diaries of surveyors, land colonizers, and frontier travelers. The record adds up to a vivid, immediate, many-paneled picture of a new land and its people.

This anthology is chiefly a collection of personal experience. The narratives make up a sequence, tracing the Midwest from its first exploration and discovery to its complex civilization three hundred years later. A spacious story, it comprises a great social drama, greater than most of its participants could comprehend. It is the drama of a people finding, winning, developing a new land, and in that process evolving a new society. They write of danger and hardship, of toil and struggle, of hope and failure and fulfillment, and so they provide a many-voiced autobiography of the region.

These segments of experience suggest that the Midwest has been marked by the variety of its people as well as by their energy, and that it has sought spiritual as well as mundane goals. Its past is an earnest, arduous, eventful, amusing, restless, persistent record of aspiration. It embraces within a few generations the greatest changes: industry lining the Detroit River where Indian campfires twinkled, an atomic plant where boatmen poled up the Scioto, Chicago rising on the site of a trading hut at the mouth of a marshy river.

To its own and other people the Midwest has sometimes seemed colorless and prosaic. (The first thing observed in any prosperous country is prosperity.) But a second look reveals that its horizons are not all alike. The Midwest is an inland region with a 4,000-mile seacoast, now emphasized by the St. Lawrence Seaway. It had a "grand prairie" extending from the Wabash to the Mississippi, and its northern woods comprised the greatest pine forest in the world. It is a level country, but Mark Twain never forgot the lift of hills along the Mississippi and Abraham Lincoln lies buried on a knoll above the Sangamon prairie. It is a rural region dominated by restless cities. It is the American heartland and yet it is marked with names from all the nations of Europe. It is an unfinished country, still stirring and stretching and changing, while memories lengthen in the land.

I

Discoverers

NEW England was a coastal colony, a few clusters of settlements clinging to the shores of America, but New France was an empire. In the 1630's, while Salem and Boston were planted on the broken coast of Massachusetts, French explorers were pushing their canoes into the heart of the continent. They learned the interior by their own groping voyages and from the tales of the Indians. The St. Lawrence waterway led them a thousand miles into the wilderness—up the Ottawa River, through Lake Nipissing and French River and into Lake Huron's Georgian Bay.

In our time the St. Lawrence Seaway links the lower Great Lakes to the Atlantic, but history came first to the northern waters. The French were blocked off from the Ohio country by two barriers: the hostile Iroquois nations and the thunderous falls of the Niagara River. They learned Lake Huron first, and from its North Bay they groped into the vast, cold Lake Superior and the mysterious Lake Michigan, which they knew as the Lake of the Illinois.

From Green Bay, on the far side of Lake Michigan, the Fox River led inland to an Indian portage path. A mile of carrying ended at another river, rolling westward. This was the Wisconsin, which flowed into the Old Big Deep Strong River, the Mississippi.

Nicolet, the discoverer of Green Bay and the Fox River, was a forerunner of other explorers who would map the northern lakes and rivers. He died believing there were but four "seas of sweet water" in the interior. Lake Erie was unknown to the French when Nicolet drowned in 1642 in the numbing waters of the St. Lawrence.

In 1654 Pierre Radisson, a hardy youth of eighteen, set out with his brother-in-law Groseilliers on a 2,000-mile canoe trip. They explored the dark country between the Wisconsin River and Lake Superior, and it is possible that they touched the Mississippi. But the first mention of the great river by name was recorded by the Jesuit missionary Claude Allouez, who went to the Northwest in 1665. He established a mission on Chequamegon Bay of Lake Superior, where some wandering Indians told him of the river "Messipi." To find that river became the dream of French explorers.

The coveted opportunity fell to a weathered *voyageur*, Louis Jolliet, and a princely priest, Father Jacques Marquette. Their discovery of the Mississippi on a June day in 1763 is one of the great moments in the history of man's knowledge of the earth.

An imperial-minded Frenchman, Robert Cavelier, Sieur de la Salle, had come to the St. Lawrence in 1666. He dreamed of finding an inland route to China, and in derision his neighbors called his estate on the St. Lawrence "La Chine." In 1669 he led a party of French and Indians over Lake Ontario and to the headwaters of the Allegheny River. He descended the Ohio, perhaps as far as the falls, the site of present Louisville. Back on the St. Lawrence, while his countrymen were exploring the Mississippi, he dreamed of a great commerce with the interior tribes. In 1679 he built on the Niagara River, below the falls, a ship of forty tons burden and sailed it west to Green Bay. The vessel was lost, with all its peltry, on the return voyage, while La Salle and two memorable colleagues, Hennepin and Tonty, were scouting the Illinois country. Hennepin explored the upper Mississippi, fell captive to Sioux Indians and was rescued by another Frenchman, Duluth, who had ranged the wilderness around Lake Superior. La Salle and Tonty established a trade among the Illinois tribesmen. Seeking a southern outlet for this commerce, La Salle was killed by one of his own men near the shore of the Gulf of Mexico. Tonty died of yellow fever, in 1704, in the gulf port of Mobile.

By that time the French had mapped the interior waterways. No trace of their trade or evangelism remains, but they left a ring of French names on the western waters. Detroit, Sault Ste. Marie, St. Croix, La Crosse, Prairie du Chien, Dubuque, St. Louis, Vincennes—these began as stations in the wilderness, with the flag of France beside a trading hut and a bark chapel lifting a cedar cross.

NICOLET'S LANDFALL

FATHER VIMONT'S ACCOUNT OF
THE JOURNEY OF JEAN NICOLET, 1634

The first white man to pass through the Straits of Mackinac was Jean Nicolet, who had come to New France as an adventurous youth of twenty. For sixteen years he lived among the tribes, learning their lore and their languages. In 1634 Governor Champlain ordered him to go farther west than any white man had ever been. Beyond a great water, Champlain had been told, lived a hairless people whose villages looked eastward across the sea. This sounded like the Chinese, and Champlain hoped his voyageur *would find the way to the Orient.*

From the Straits of Mackinac Nicolet peered westward. Beyond the narrows the seas opened grandly. He thought he was looking toward the coast of China. In his canoe, manned by seven Huron paddlers, he carried a robe of Chinese damask, embroidered with poppies and birds of paradise. He was prepared to meet the merchants of Cathay.

Instead, landing on the shores of Green Bay, he found half-naked Winnebago Indians. He made peace with them, feasted on roast beaver and heard of a great river in the West. He had not found the way to China but he had found the way by which his countrymen, a generation later, would discover the Mississippi.

Nicolet left no record of his adventurous life, but on his return to the St. Lawrence he told his story to the priests. One of them, Father Vimont, recorded it in the series of missionary reports called the Jesuit Relations. *This brief account of an epic journey is taken from the* Jesuit Relations, *in the Thwaites edition, Vol. XXIII.*

I WILL now speak of the life and death of Monsieur Nicolet, interpreter and agent for the Gentlemen of the Company of New France. He died ten days after the Father, and had lived in this region twenty-five years. What I shall say of him will aid to a better understanding of the country. He came to New France in the year 1618; and forasmuch as his nature and excellent memory inspired good hopes of him, he was sent to winter with the Island Algonquins, in order to learn their language. He tarried with them two years, alone of the French, and always joined the barbarians in their excursions and journeys, undergoing such fatigues as none but eyewitnesses can conceive; he often passed seven or eight days without food, and once, full seven weeks with no other nourishment than a little bark from the trees. He accompanied four hundred Algonquins, who went during that time to make peace with the Hyroquois, which he successfully accomplished; and would to God that it had never been broken, for then we should not now be suffering the calamities which move us to groans, and which must be an extraordinary impediment in the way of converting these tribes. After this treaty of peace, he went to live eight or nine years with the Algonquin Nipissiriniens, where he passed for one of that nation, taking part in the very frequent councils of those tribes, having his own separate cabin and household, and fishing and trading for himself. He was finally recalled, and appointed agent and interpreter. While in the exercise of this office, he was delegated to make a journey to the nation called People of the Sea, and arrange peace between them and the Hurons, from whom they are distant about three hundred leagues westward. He embarked in the Huron country, with seven savages; and they passed by many small nations, both going and returning. When they arrived at their destination, they fastened two sticks in the earth, and hung gifts thereon, so as to relieve these tribes from the notion of mistaking them for enemies to be massacred. When he was two days' journey from that nation, he sent one of those savages to bear tidings of the peace, which word was especially well received when they heard that it was a European who carried the message; they despatched several young men to meet the Manitouiriniou—that is to say, "the wonderful man." They meet him; they escort him, and carry all his baggage. He wore a grand robe of China damask, all strewn with flowers and birds of many colors. No sooner did they perceive him than the women and children fled, at the sight of a man who carried thunder in both hands—for thus they called the two pistols that he held. The news of his coming quickly spread to the places round about, and there assembled four or five thousand men. Each of the chief men made a feast for him, and at one of these banquets they served at least sixscore beavers. The peace was concluded; he returned to the Hurons, and some time later to the Three Rivers, where he continued his employment as agent and interpreter, to the great satisfaction of both the French and the savages, by whom he was equally and singularly loved.

DISCOVERY OF THE MISSISSIPPI
THE VOYAGE OF JOLLIET AND MARQUETTE, 1673

Long before they dipped their paddles in the Mississippi, the French explorers dreamed of finding the great river of the western wilderness. From descriptions of the Indians they knew of the fabled river, and they restlessly awaited its discovery. Chosen for the undertaking were two men of different natures. The rugged Louis Jolliet was the son of a Quebec wagonmaker; the gentle Jacques Marquette belonged to the most ancient family of the stately city of Laon. By 1673 both were veterans of the wilderness.

In two bark canoes with five Indian paddlers they set out from St. Ignace on the Straits of Mackinac. They traveled south to Green Bay and up the dwindling Fox River, where an easy portage brought them to the broad Wisconsin. On the 17th of June they saw the majestic Mississippi rolling its flood toward an unknown sea. It was the supreme moment of their lives.

For a thousand miles they descended the Mississippi, passing the mouths of the unnamed Missouri and the Ohio rivers. At the mouth of the Arkansas they turned back. They knew now that the great river emptied into the Gulf of Mexico, and they did not care to risk encounter with the Spanish at the river mouth. On their return they paddled up the Illinois River, made the prairie portage from the Des Plaines to the Chicago, and followed the western shore of Lake Michigan to the mission house at De Pere.

Jolliet's journal of the voyage was lost when a canoe overturned in the rapids above Montreal. The following account is Marquette's record. It is taken from the Jesuit Relations, *Vol. LIX.*

THE feast of the Immaculate Conception of the Blessed Virgin—whom I have always invoked since I have been in this country of the Outaouacs, to obtain from God the grace of being able to visit the nations who dwell along the Missisipi River—was precisely the day on which Monsieur Jollyet arrived with orders from Monsieur the Count de Frontenac our governor, and Monsieur Talon, our intendant, to accomplish this discovery with me. I was all the more delighted at this good news, since I saw that my plans were about to be accomplished; and since I found myself in the blessed necessity of exposing my life for the salvation of all these peoples, and especially of the Ilinois, who had very urgently entreated me, when I was at the Point of St. Esprit, to carry the word of God to their country.

We were not long in preparing all our equipment, although we were about to begin a voyage, the duration of which we could not foresee. Indian corn, with some smoked meat, constituted all our provisions; with these we embarked—Monsieur Jollyet and myself, with five men—in two bark canoes, fully resolved to do and suffer everything for so glorious an undertaking.

Accordingly, on the 17th day of May, 1673, we started from the mission of St. Ignace at Michilimakinac, where I then was. The joy that we felt at being selected for this expedition animated our courage, and rendered the labor of paddling from morning to night agreeable to us. And because we were going to seek unknown countries, we took every precaution in our power, so that, if our undertaking were hazardous, it should not be foolhardy. To that end, we obtained all the information that we could from the savages who had frequented those regions; and we even traced out from their reports a map of the whole of that new country; on it we indicated the rivers which we were to navigate, the names of the peoples and of the places through which we were to pass, the course of the great river, and the direction we were to follow when we reached it.

Above all, I placed our voyage under the protection of the Blessed Virgin Immaculate, promising her that, if she granted us the favor of discovering the great river, I would give it the name of the Conception, and that I would also make the first mission that I should establish among those new peoples, bear the same name. This I have actually done, among the Ilinois.

With all these precautions, we joyfully plied our paddles on a portion of Lake Huron, on that of the Ilinois and the Bay des Puants.

The first nation that we came to was that of the Folle Avoine. I entered their river, to go and visit these peoples to whom we have preached the Gospel for several years, in consequence of which, there are several good Christians among them.

The wild oat, whose name they bear because it is found in their country, is a sort of grass, which grows naturally in the small rivers with muddy bottoms, and in swampy places. It greatly resembles the wild oats that grow amid our wheat. The ears grow upon hollow stems, jointed at intervals; they emerge from the water about the month of June, and continue growing until they rise about two feet above it. The grain is not larger than that of our oats, but it is twice as long, and the meal therefrom is much more abundant. The savages gather and prepare it for food as follows. In the month of September, which is the suitable time for the harvest, they go in canoes through these fields of wild oats; they shake its ears into the canoe, on both sides, as they pass through. The grain falls out easily, if it be ripe, and they obtain their supply in a short time. But, in order to clean it from the straw, and to remove it from a husk in which it is enclosed, they dry it in the smoke, upon a wooden grating, under which they maintain a slow fire for some days. When the oats are thoroughly dry, they put them in a skin made into a bag, thrust it into a hole dug in the ground for this purpose, and tread it with their feet—so long and so vigorously that the grain separates from the straw, and is very easily winnowed. After this, they pound it to reduce it to flour, or even, without pounding it, they boil it in water, and season it with fat. Cooked in this fashion, the wild oats have almost as delicate a taste as rice has when no better seasoning is added.

I told these peoples of the Folle Avoine of my design to go and discover those remote nations, in order to teach them the mysteries of our holy religion. They were greatly surprised to hear it, and did their best to dissuade me. They represented to me that I should meet nations who never show mercy to strangers, but break their heads without any cause; and that war was kindled between various peoples who dwelt upon our route, which exposed us to the further manifest danger of being killed by the bands of warriors who are ever in the field. They also said that the great river was very dangerous, when one does not know the difficult places; that it was full of horrible monsters, which devoured men and canoes together; that there was even a demon, who was heard from a great distance, who barred the way, and swallowed up all who ventured to approach him; finally that the heat was so excessive in those countries that it would inevitably cause our death.

I thanked them for the good advice that they gave me, but told them that I could not follow it, because the salvation of souls was at stake, for which I would be delighted to give my life; that I scoffed at the alleged demon; that we would easily defend ourselves against those marine monsters; and, moreover, that we would be on our guard to avoid the other dangers with which they threatened us. After making them pray to God, and giving them some instruction, I separated from them. Embarking then in our canoes, we arrived shortly afterward at the bottom of the Bay des Puants, where our Fathers labor successfully for the conversion of these peoples, over two thousand of whom they have baptized while they have been there.

This bay bears a name which has a meaning not so offensive in the language of the savages; for they call it la Baye Sallee rather than Bay des Puans, although with them this is almost the same and this is also the name which they give to the sea. This led us to make very careful researches to ascertain whether there were not some salt-water springs in this quarter, as there are among the Hiroquois, but we found none. We conclude, therefore, that this name has been given to it on account of the quantity of mire and mud which is seen there, whence noisome vapors constantly arise, causing the loudest and most continual thunder that I have ever heard.

The bay is about thirty leagues in depth and eight in width at its mouth; it narrows gradually to the bottom, where it is easy to observe a tide which has its regular ebb and flow, almost like that of the sea. This is not the place to inquire whether these are real tides; whether they are due to the wind, or to some other cause; whether there are winds, the precursors of the moon and attached to her suite, which consequently agitate the lake and give it an apparent ebb and flow whenever the moon ascends above the horizon. What I can positively state is, that, when the water is very calm, it is easy to observe it rising and falling according to the course of the moon; although I do not deny that this movement may be caused by very remote winds, which, pressing on the middle of the lake, cause the edges to rise and fall in the manner which is visible to our eyes.

We left this day to enter the river that discharges into it; it is very beautiful at its mouth, and flows gently; it is full of bustards, ducks, teal, and other birds, attracted thither by the wild oats, of which they are very fond. But, after ascending the river a short distance, it becomes very difficult of passage, on account of both the currents and the sharp rocks, which cut the canoes and the feet of those who are obliged to drag them, especially when the waters are low. Nevertheless, we successfully passed those rapids; and on approaching Machkoutens, the Fire Nation, I had the curiosity to drink the mineral waters of the river that is not far from that village. I also took time to look for a medicinal plant which a savage, who knows its secret, showed to Father Alloues with many ceremonies. Its root is employed to counteract snake-bites, God having been pleased to give this antidote against a poison which is very common in these countries. It is very pungent, and tastes like powder when crushed with the teeth; it must be masticated and placed upon the bite inflicted by the snake. The reptile has so great a horror of it that it even flees from a person who has rubbed himself with

Above: Marquette and Jolliet at Chicago, August 1673. Courtesy State Historical Society of Wisconsin

Below: The landfall of Jean Nicolet in Wisconsin, 1634, painted by Edwin Willard Deming. Courtesy State Historical Society of Wisconsin

it. The plant bears several stalks, a foot high, with rather long leaves; and a white flower, which greatly resembles the wallflower. I put some in my canoe, in order to examine it at leisure while we continued to advance toward Maskoutens, where we arrived on the 7th of June.

Here we are at Maskoutens. This word may, in Algonquin, mean "the Fire Nation," which, indeed, is the name given to this tribe. Here is the limit of the discoveries which the French have made, for they have not yet gone any farther.

This village consists of three nations who have gathered there—Miamis, Maskoutens, and Kikabous. The former are the most civil, the most liberal, and the most shapely. They wear two long locks over their ears, which give them a pleasing appearance. They are regarded as warriors, and rarely undertake expeditions without being successful. They are very docile, and listen quietly to what is said to them; and they appeared so eager to hear Father Alloues when he instructed them that they gave him but little rest, even during the night. The Maskoutens and Kikabous are ruder, and seem peasants in comparison with the others. As bark for making cabins is scarce in this country, they use rushes; these serve them for making walls and roofs, but do not afford them much protection against the winds, and still less against the rains when they fall abundantly. The advantage of cabins of this kind is, that they make packages of them, and easily transport them wherever they wish, while they are hunting.

When I visited them, I was greatly consoled at seeing a handsome Cross erected in the middle of the village, and adorned with many white skins, red belts, and bows and arrows, which these good people had offered to the great Manitou (this is the name which they give to God). They did this to thank him for having had pity on them during the winter, by giving them an abundance of game when they most dreaded famine.

I took pleasure in observing the situation of this village. It is beautiful and very pleasing; for, from an eminence upon which it is placed, one beholds on every side prairies, extending farther than the eye can see, interspersed with groves or with lofty trees. The soil is very fertile, and yields much Indian corn. The savages gather quantities of plums and grapes, wherewith much wine could be made, if desired.

No sooner had we arrived than we, Monsieur Jollyet and I, assembled the elders together; and he told them that he was sent by Monsieur our governor to discover new countries, while I was sent by God to illumine them with the light of the holy Gospel. He told them that, moreover, the sovereign Master of our lives wished to be known by all the nations; and that in obeying His will I feared not the death to which I exposed myself in voyages so perilous. He informed them that we needed two guides to show us the way; and we gave them a present, by it asking them to grant us the guides. To this they very civilly consented; and they also spoke to us by means of a present, consisting of a mat to serve us as a bed during the whole of our voyage.

On the following day, the tenth of June, two Miamis who were given us as guides embarked with us, in the sight of a great crowd, who could not sufficiently express their astonishment at the sight of seven Frenchmen, alone and in two canoes, daring to undertake so extraordinary and so hazardous an expedition.

We knew that, at three leagues from Maskoutens, was a river which discharged into Missisipi. We knew also that the direction we were to follow in order to reach it was west-southwesterly. But the road is broken by so many swamps and small lakes that it is easy to lose one's way, especially as the river leading thither is so full of wild oats that it is difficult to find the channel. For this reason we greatly needed our two guides, who safely conducted us to a portage of 2,700 paces, and helped us to transport our canoes to enter that river; after which they returned home, leaving us alone in this unknown country, in the hands of Providence.

Thus we left the waters flowing to Quebeq, four or five hundred leagues from here, to float on those that would thenceforward take us through strange lands. Before embarking thereon, we began all together a new devotion to the blessed Virgin Immaculate, which we practised daily, addressing to her special prayers to place under her protection both our persons and the success of our voyage; and, after mutually encouraging one another, we entered our canoes.

The river on which we embarked is called Meskousing. It is very wide; it has a sandy bottom, which forms various shoals that render its navigation very difficult. It is full of islands covered with vines. On the banks one sees fertile land, diversified with woods, prairies, and hills. There are oak, walnut, and basswood trees; and another kind, whose branches are armed with long thorns. We saw there neither feathered game nor fish, but many deer, and a large number of cattle. Our route lay to the southwest, and, after navigating about thirty leagues, we saw a spot presenting all the appearances of an iron mine; and, in fact, one of our party who had formerly seen such mines, assures us that the one which we found is very good and very rich. It is covered with three feet of good soil, and it quite near a chain of rocks, the base of which is covered by very fine trees. After proceeding 40 leagues on this same route, we arrived at the mouth of our river; and, at 42 and a half degrees of latitude, we safely entered Missisipi on the 17th of June, with a joy that I cannot express.

Here we are, then, on this so renowned river, all of whose peculiar features I have endeavored to note carefully. The Missisipi River takes its rise in various lakes in the country of the northern nations. It is narrow at the place where Miskous empties; its current, which flows southward, is slow and gentle. To the right is a large chain of very high mountains, and to the left are beautiful lands; in various places, the stream is divided by islands. On sounding, we found ten brasses of water. Its width is very unequal; sometimes it is three-quarters of a league, and sometimes it narrows to three arpents. We gently followed its course, which runs toward the south and southeast, as far as the 42nd degree of latitude. Here we plainly saw that its aspect was completely changed. There are hardly any woods or mountains; the islands are more beautiful, and are covered with finer trees. We saw only deer and cattle, bustards, and swans without wings, because they drop their plumage in this country. From time to time, we came upon monstrous fish, one of which struck our canoe with such violence that I thought that it was a great tree, about to break the canoe to pieces. On another occasion, we saw on the water a monster with the head of a tiger, a sharp nose like that of a wildcat, with whiskers and straight, erect ears; the head was gray and the neck quite black; but we saw no more creatures of this sort. When we cast our nets into the water we caught sturgeon, and a very extraordinary kind of fish. It resembles the trout, with this difference, that its mouth is larger. Near its nose, which is smaller, as are also the eyes, is a large bone shaped like a woman's busk, three fingers wide and a cubit long, at the end of which is a disk as wide as one's hand. This frequently causes it to fall backward when it leaps out of the water. When we reached the parallel of 41 degrees 28 minutes, following the same direction, we found that turkeys had taken the place of game; and the pisikious, or wild cattle, that of the other animals.

We call them "wild cattle," because they are very similar to our domestic cattle. They are not longer, but are nearly as large again, and more corpulent. When our people killed one, three persons had much difficulty in moving it. The head is very large; the forehead is flat, and a foot and a half wide between the horns, which are exactly like those of our oxen, but black and much larger. Under the neck they have a sort of large dewlap, which hangs down; and on the back is a rather high hump. The whole of the head, the neck, and a portion of the shoulders, are covered with a thick mane like that of horses; it forms a crest a foot long, which makes them hideous, and, falling over their eyes, prevents them from seeing what is before them. The remainder of the body is covered with a heavy coat of curly hair, almost like that of our sheep, but much stronger and thicker. It falls off in summer, and the skin becomes as soft as velvet. At that season, the savages use the hides for making fine robes, which they paint in various colors. The flesh and the fat of the pisikious are excellent, and constitute the best dish at feasts. Moreover, they are very fierce; and not a year passes without their killing some savages. When attacked, they catch a man on their horns, if they can, toss him in the air, and then throw him on the ground, after which they trample him under foot, and kill him. If a person fire at them from a distance, with either a bow or a gun, he must, immediately after the shot, throw himself down and hide in the grass; for if they perceive him who has fired, they run at him, and attack him. As their legs are thick and rather short, they do not run very fast, as a rule, except when angry. They are scattered about the prairie in herds; I have seen one of four hundred.

We continued to advance, but, as we knew not whither we were going, for we had proceeded over one hundred leagues without discovering anything except animals and birds, we kept well on our guard. On this account, we make only a small fire on land, toward evening, to cook our meals; and, after supper, we remove ourselves as far from it as possible, and pass the night in our canoes, which we anchor in the river at some distance from the shore. This does not prevent us from always posting one of the party as a sentinel, for fear of a surprise. Proceeding still in a southerly and south-southwesterly direction, we find ourselves at the parellel of 41 degrees, and as low as 40 degrees and some minutes, —partly southeast and partly southwest,— after having advanced over 60 leagues since we entered the river, without discovering anything.

Finally, on the 25th of June, we perceived on the water's edge some tracks of men, and a narrow and somewhat beaten path leading to a fine prairie. We stopped to examine it; and, thinking that it was a road which led to some village of savages, we resolved to go and reconnoitre it. We therefore left our two canoes under the guard of our people, strictly charging them not to allow themselves to be surprised, after which Monsieur Jollyet and I undertook this investigation—a rather hazardous one for two men who exposed themselves, alone, to the mercy of a barbarous and unknown people. We silently followed the narrow path, and, after walking about two leagues, we discovered a village on the bank of a river, and two others on a hill distant about half a league from the first. Then we heartily commended ourselves to God, and, after imploring His aid, we went farther without being perceived, and approached so near that we could even hear the savages talking. We therefore decided that it was time to reveal ourselves. This we did by shouting with all our energy, and stopped, without advancing any farther. On hearing the shout, the savages quickly issued from their cabins, and having probably recognized us as Frenchmen, especially when they saw a black gown—or, at least, having no cause for distrust, as we were only two men, and had given them notice of our arrival—they deputed four old men to come and speak to us. Two of these bore tobacco-pipes, finely ornamented and adorned with various feathers. They walked slowly, and raised their pipes toward the sun, seemingly offering them to it to smoke, without, however, saying a word. They spent a rather long time in covering the short distance between their village and us. Finally, when they had drawn near, they stopped to consider us attentively. I was reassured when I observed these ceremonies, which with them are performed only among friends; and much more so when I saw them clad in cloth, for I judged thereby that they were our allies. I therefore spoke to them first, and asked them who they were. They replied that they were Ilinois; and, as a token of peace, they offered us their pipes to smoke. They afterward invited us to enter their village, where all the people impatiently awaited us. These pipes for smoking tobacco are called in this country calumets. This word has come so much into use that, in order to be understood, I shall be obliged to use it, as I shall often have to mention these pipes.

At the door of the cabin in which we were to be received was an old man, who awaited us in a rather surprising attitude, which constitutes a part of the ceremonial that they observe when they receive strangers. This man stood erect, and stark naked, with his hands extended and lifted toward the sun, as if he wished to protect himself from its rays, which nevertheless shone upon his face through his fingers. When we came near him, he paid us this compliment: "How beautiful the sun is, O Frenchman, when thou comest to visit us! All our village awaits thee, and thou shalt enter all our cabins in peace." Having said this, he made us enter his own, in which were a crowd of people; they devoured us with their eyes, but, nevertheless, observed profound silence. We could, however, hear these words, which were addressed to us from time to time in a low voice: "How good it is, my brothers, that you should visit us."

After we had taken our places, the usual civility of the country was paid to us, which consisted in offering us the calumet. This must not be refused, unless one wishes to be considered an enemy, or at least uncivil; it suffices that one make a pretense of smoking. While all the elders smoked after us, in order to do us honor, we received an invitation on behalf of the great captain of all the Ilinois to proceed to his village where he wished to hold a council with us. We went thither in a large company, for all these people, who had never seen any Frenchmen among them, could not cease looking at us. They lay on the grass along the road; they preceded us, and then retraced their steps to come and see us again. All this was done noiselessly, and with marks of great respect for us.

When we reached the village of the great captain, we saw him at the entrance of his cabin, between two old men, all three erect and naked, and holding their calumet turned toward the sun. He harangued us in a few words, congratulating us upon our arrival. He afterward offered us his calumet, and made us smoke while we entered his cabin, where we received all their usual kind attentions.

Seeing all assembled and silent, I spoke to them by four presents that I gave them. By the first, I told them that we were journeying peacefully to visit the nations dwelling on the river as far as the sea. By the second, I announced to them that God, who had created them, had pity on them, inasmuch as, after they had so long been ignorant of Him, He

AN INDIAN COUNCIL.

AN INDIAN WIGWAM.

MARQUETTE'S CANOE IN A RAPID.

Birch-bark drawings by Marquette. *Courtesy State Historical Society of Wisconsin*

wished to make himself known to all the peoples; that I was sent by Him for that purpose; and that it was for them to acknowledge and obey Him. By the third, I said that the great captain of the French informed them that he it was who restored peace everywhere; and that he had subdued the Iroquois. Finally, by the fourth, we begged them to give us all the information that they had about the sea, and about the nations through whom we must pass to reach it.

When I had finished my speech, the captain arose, and, resting his hand upon the head of a little slave whom he wished to give us, he spoke thus: "I thank thee, black gown, and thee, O Frenchman," addressing himself to Monsieur Jollyet, "for having taken so much trouble to come to visit us. Never has the earth been so beautiful, or the sun so bright, as today; never has our river been so calm, or so clear of rocks, which your canoes have removed in passing; never has our tobacco tasted so good, or our corn appeared so fine, as we now see them. Here is my son, whom I give thee to show thee my heart. I beg thee to have pity on me, and on all my nation. It is thou who knowest the great Spirit who had made us all. It is thou who speakest to Him, and who hearest His word. Beg Him to give me life and health, and to come and dwell with us, in order to make us know Him." Having said this, he placed the little slave near us, and gave us a second present, consisting of an altogether mysterious calumet, upon which they place more value than upon a slave. By this gift, he expressed to us the esteem that he had for Monsieur our governor, from the account which we had given of him; and, by a third, he begged us on behalf of all his nation not to go farther, on account of the great dangers to which we exposed ourselves.

I replied that I feared not death, and that I regarded no happiness as greater than that of losing my life for the glory of Him who has made all. This is what these poor people cannot understand.

The council was followed by a great feast, consisting of four dishes, which had to be partaken of in accordance with all their fashions. The first course was a great wooden platter full of sagamite, that is to say, meal of Indian corn boiled in water, and seasoned with fat. The master of ceremonies filled a spoon with sagamite three or four times, and put it to my mouth as if I were a little child. He did the same to Monsieur Jollyet. As a second course, he caused a second platter to be brought, on which were three fish. He took some pieces of them, removed the bones therefrom, and, after blowing upon them to cool them, he put them in our mouths as one would give food to a bird. For the third course, they brought a large dog, that had just been killed; but, when they learned that we did not eat this meat, they removed it from before us. Finally, the fourth course was a piece of wild ox, the fattest morsels of which were placed in our mouths.

After this feast, we had to go to visit the whole village, which consists of fully three hundred cabins. While we walked through the streets, an orator continually harangued to oblige all the people to come to see us without annoying us. Everywhere we were presented with belts, garters, and other articles made of the hair of bears and cattle, dyed red, yellow, and gray. These are all the rarities they possess. As they are of no great value, we did not burden ourselves with them.

We slept in the captain's cabin, and on the following day we took leave of him, promising to pass again by his village, within four moons. He conducted us to our canoes, with nearly six hundred persons who witnessed our embarkation, giving us every possible manifestation of the joy that our visit had caused them. For my own part, I promised, on bidding them adieu, that I would come the following year, and reside with them to instruct them.

FATE OF THE "GRIFFIN"

FRANCIS PARKMAN

The first commercial vessel to sail the Great Lakes was built by La Salle at Niagara in 1679. The Griffin, *45 tons burden, could bring back a fortune in furs from the upper lakes. On its voyage to the Straits of Mackinac the vessel carried three men of destiny: La Salle, Tonty, and Hennepin.*

On the far shore of Lake Michigan, which Nicolet had thought to be China, La Salle loaded his ship with peltry and sent it back to Niagara in charge of the pilot. The Griffin *sailed away on September 18, 1679—and was never seen again. Its fate has been a subject of speculation ever since. All that is known is that the Lakes claimed the first cargo ship, as they would claim hundreds of vessels in the years to come.*

This narrative is taken from Parkman's vivid account of La Salle and the Discovery of the Great West.

THE "Griffin" had lain moored by the [Niagara] shore, so near that Hennepin could preach on Sundays from the deck to the men encamped along the bank. She was now forced up against the current with tow-ropes and sails, till she reached the calm entrance of Lake Erie. On the seventh of August, La Salle and his followers embarked, sang *Te Deum*, and fired their cannon. A fresh breeze sprang up; and with swelling canvas the "Griffin" ploughed the virgin waves of Lake Erie, where sail was never seen before. For three days they held their course over these unknown waters, and on the fourth turned northward into the Strait of Detroit. Here, on the right hand and on the left, lay verdant prairies, dotted with groves and bordered with lofty forests. They saw walnut, chestnut, and wild plum trees, and oaks festooned with grape-vines; herds of deer, and flocks of swans and wild turkeys. The bullwarks of the "Griffin" were plentifully hung with game which the men killed on shore, and among the rest with a number of bears, much commended by Hennepin for their want of ferocity and the excellence of their flesh. "Those," he says, "who will one day have the happiness to possess this fertile and pleasant strait, will be very much obliged to those who have shown them the way." They crossed Lake St. Clair, and still sailed northward against the current, till now, sparkling in the sun, Lake Huron spread before them like a sea.

For a time they bore on prosperously. Then the wind died to a calm, then freshened to a gale, then rose to a furious tempest; and the vessel tossed wildly among the short, steep, perilous waves of the raging lake. Even La Salle called on his followers to commend themselves to Heaven. All fell to their prayers but the godless pilot, who was loud in complaint against his commander for having brought him, after the honor he had won on the ocean, to drown at last ignominiously in fresh water. The rest clamored to the saints. St. Anthony of Padua was promised a chapel to be built in his honor, if he would but save them from their jeopardy; while in the same breath La Salle and the friars declared him patron of their great enterprise. The saint heard their prayers. The obedient winds were tamed; and the "Griffin" plunged on her way through foaming surges that still grew calmer as she advanced. Now the sun shone forth on woody islands, Bois Blanc and Mackinaw and the distant Manitoulins,—on the forest wastes of Michigan and the vast blue bosom of the angry lake; and now her port was won, and she found her rest behind the point of St. Ignace of Michilimackinac, floating in that tranquil cove where crystal waters cover but cannot hide the pebbly depths beneath. Before her rose the house and chapel of the Jesuits, enclosed with palisades; on the right, the Huron village, with its bark cabins and its fence of tall pickets; on the left, the square compact houses of the French traders; and, not far off, the clustered wigwams of an Ottawa village. Here was a centre of the Jesuit missions, and a centre of the Indian trade; and here, under the shadow of the cross, was much sharp practice in the service of Mammon. Keen traders, with or without a license, and lawless *coureurs de bois*, whom a few years of forest life had weaned from civilization, made St. Ignace their resort; and here there were many of them when the "Griffin" came. They and their employers hated and feared La Salle, who, sustained as he was by the governor, might set at nought the prohibition of the King, debarring him from traffic with these tribes. Yet, while plotting against him, they took pains to allay his distrust by a show of welcome.

The "Griffin" fired her cannon, and the Indians yelped in wonder and amazement. The adventurers landed in state, and marched under arms to the bark chapel of the Ottawa village, where they heard mass. La Salle knelt before the altar, in a mantle of scarlet bordered with gold. Soldiers, sailors, and artisans knelt around him,—black Jesuits, gray Récollets, swarthy *voyageurs*, and painted savages; a devout but motley concourse.

As they left the chapel, the Ottawa chiefs came to bid them welcome, and the Hurons saluted them with a volley of musketry. They saw the "Griffin" at her anchorage, surrounded by more than a hundred bark canoes, like a Triton among minnows. Yet it was with more wonder than good-will that the Indians of the mission gazed on the "floating fort," for so they called the vessel. A deep jealousy of La Salle's designs had been infused into them. His own followers, too, had been tampered with. In the autumn before, it may be remembered, he had sent fifteen men up the lakes to trade for him, with orders to go thence to the Illinois and make preparation against his coming. Early in the summer, Tonty had been despatched in a canoe from Niagara to look

after them. It was high time. Most of the men had been seduced from their duty, and had disobeyed their orders, squandered the goods intrusted to them, or used them in trading on their own account. La Salle found four of them at Michilimackinac. These he arrested, and sent Tonty to the Falls of Ste. Marie, where two others were captured, with their plunder. The rest were in the woods, and it was useless to pursue them.

Anxious and troubled as to the condition of his affairs in Canada, La Salle had meant, after seeing his party safe at Michilimackinac, to leave Tonty to conduct it to the Illinois, while he himself returned to the colony. But Tonty was still at Ste. Marie, and he had none to trust but himself. Therefore, he resolved at all risks to remain with his men; "for," he says, "I judged my presence absolutely necessary to retain such of them as were left me, and prevent them from being enticed away during the winter." Moreover, he thought that he had detected an intrigue of his enemies to hound on the Iroquois against the Illinois, in order to defeat his plan by involving him in the war.

Early in September he set sail again, and passing westward into Lake Michigan, cast anchor near one of the islands at the entrance of Green Bay. Here, for once, he found a friend in the person of a Pottawattamie chief, who had been so wrought upon by the politic kindness of Frontenac that he declared himself ready to die for the children of Onontio ["The Great Mountain"—Indian name for the governor of Canada]. Here, too, he found several of his advance party, who had remained faithful and collected a large store of furs. It would have been better had they proved false, like the rest. La Salle, who asked counsel of no man, resolved, in spite of his followers, to send back the "Griffin" laden with these furs, and others collected on the way, to satisfy his creditors. It was a rash resolution, for it involved trusting her to the pilot, who had already proved either incompetent or treacherous. She fired a parting shot, and on the eighteenth of September set sail for Niagara, with orders to return to the head of Lake Michigan as soon as she had discharged her cargo. La Salle, with the fourteen men who

"The Sailing of the *Griffon*," painted by H. T. Koerner. *Courtesy Buffalo Historical Society*

remained, in four canoes deeply laden with a forge, tools, merchandise, and arms, put out from the island and resumed his voyage.

The parting was not auspicious. The lake, glassy and calm in the afternoon, was convulsed at night with a sudden storm, when the canoes were midway between the island and the main shore. It was with difficulty that they could keep together, the men shouting to each other through the darkness. Hennepin, who was in the smallest canoe with a heavy load, and a carpenter for a companion who was awkward at the paddle, found himself in jeopardy which demanded all his nerve. The voyagers thought themselves happy when they gained at last the shelter of a little sandy cove, where they dragged up their canoes, and made their cheerless bivouac in the drenched and dripping forest. Here they spent five days, living on pumpkins and Indian corn, the gift of their Pottawattamie friends, and on a Canada porcupine brought in by La Salle's Mohegan hunter. The gale raged meanwhile with relentless fury. They trembled when they thought of the "Griffin." When at length the tempest lulled, they re-embarked, and steered southward along the shore of Wisconsin; but again the storm fell upon them, and drove them for safety to a bare, rocky islet. Here they made a fire of drift-wood, crouched around it, drew their blankets over their heads, and in this miserable plight, pelted with sleet and rain, remained for two days.

At length they were afloat again; but their prosperity was brief. On the twenty-eighth, a fierce squall drove them to a point of rocks covered with bushes, where they consumed the little that remained of their provisions. On the first of October they paddled about thirty miles, without food, when they came to a village of Pottawattamies, who ran down to the shore to help them to land; but La Salle, fearing that some of his men would steal the merchandise and desert to the Indians, insisted on going three leagues farther, to the great indignation of his followers. The lake, swept by an easterly gale, was rolling its waves against the beach, like the ocean in a storm. In the attempt to land, La Salle's canoe was nearly swamped. He and his three canoemen leaped into the water, and in spite of the surf, which

nearly drowned them, dragged their vessel ashore with all its load. He then went to the rescue of Hennepin, who with his awkward companion was in woeful need of succor. Father Gabriel, with his sixty-four years, was no match for the surf and the violent undertow. Hennepin, finding himself safe, waded to his relief, and carried him ashore on his sturdy shoulders; while the old friar, though drenched to the skin, laughed gayly under his cowl as his brother missionary staggered with him up the beach.

When all were safe ashore, La Salle, who distrusted the Indians they had passed, took post on a hill, and ordered his followers to prepare their guns for action. Nevertheless, as they were starving, an effort must be risked to gain a supply of food; and he sent three men back to the village to purchase it. Well armed, but faint with toil and famine, they made their way through the stormy forest bearing a pipe of peace, but on arriving saw that the scared inhabitants had fled. They found, however, a stock of corn, of which they took a portion, leaving goods in exchange, and then set out on their return.

Meanwhile, about twenty of the warriors, armed with bows and arrows, approached the camp of the French to reconnoitre. La Salle went to meet them with some of his men, opened a parley with them, and kept them seated at the foot of the hill till his three messengers returned, when on seeing the peace-pipe the warriors set up a cry of joy. In the morning they brought more corn to the camp, with a supply of fresh venison, not a little cheering to the exhausted Frenchmen, who, in dread of treachery, had stood under arms all night.

This was no journey of pleasure. The lake was ruffled with almost ceaseless storms; clouds big with rain above, a turmoil of gray and gloomy waves beneath. Every night the canoes must be shouldered through the breakers and dragged up the steep banks, which, as they neared the site of Milwaukee, became almost insurmountable. The men paddled all day, with no other food than a handful of Indian corn. They were spent with toil, sick with the haws and wild berries which they ravenously devoured, and dejected at the prospect before them. Father Gabriel's good spirits began to fail. He fainted several times from famine and fatigue, but was revived by a certain "confection of Hyacinth" administered by Hennepin, who had a small box of this precious specific.

At length they descried at a distance, on the stormy shore, two or three eagles among a busy congregation of crows or turkey buzzards. They paddled in all haste to the spot. The feasters took flight; and the starved travellers found the mangled body of a deer, lately killed by the wolves. This good luck proved the inauguration of plenty. As they approached the head of the lake, game grew abundant; and, with the aid of the Mohegan, there was no lack of bear's meat and venison. They found wild grapes, too, in the woods, and gathered them by cutting down the trees to which the vines clung.

While thus employed, they were startled by a sight often so fearful in the waste and the wilderness,—the print of a human foot. It was clear that Indians were not far off. A strict watch was kept, not, as it proved, without cause; for that night, while the sentry thought of little but screening himself and his gun from the floods of rain, a party of Outagamies crept under the bank, where they lurked for some time before he discovered them. Being challenged, they came forward, professing great friendship, and pretending to have mistaken the French for Iroquois. In the morning, however, there was an outcry from La Salle's servant, who declared that the visitors had stolen his coat from under the inverted canoe where he had placed it; while some of the carpenters also complained of being robbed. La Salle well knew that if the theft were left unpunished, worse would come of it. First, he posted his men at the woody point of a peninsula, whose sandy neck was interposed between them and the forest. Then he went forth, pistol in hand, met a young Outagami, seized him, and led him prisoner to his camp. This done, he again set out, and soon found an Outagami chief,—for the wigwams were not far distant,—to whom he told what he had done, adding that unless the stolen goods were restored, the prisoner should be killed. The Indians were in perplexity, for they had cut the coat to pieces and divided it. In this

dilemma they resolved, being strong in numbers, to rescue their comrade by force. Accordingly, they came down to the edge of the forest, or posted themselves behind fallen trees on the banks, while La Salle's men in their stronghold braced their nerves for the fight. Here three Flemish friars with their rosaries, and eleven Frenchmen with their guns, confronted a hundred and twenty screeching Outagamies. Hennepin, who had seen service, and who had always an exhortation at his tongue's end, busied himself to inspire the rest with a courage equal to his own. Neither party, however, had an appetite for the fray. A parley ensued: full compensation was made for the stolen goods, and the aggrieved Frenchmen were farther propitiated with a gift of beaver-skins.

Their late enemies, now become friends, spent the next day in dances, feasts, and speeches. They entreated La Salle not to advance farther, since the Illinois, through whose country he must pass, would be sure to kill him; for, added these friendly counsellors, they hated the French because they had been instigating the Iroquois to invade their country. Here was another subject of anxiety. La Salle was confirmed in his belief that his busy and unscrupulous enemies were intriguing for his destruction.

He pushed on, however, circling around the southern shore of Lake Michigan, till he reached the mouth of the St. Joseph, called by him the Miamis. Here Tonty was to have rejoined him with twenty men, making his way from Michilimackinac along the eastern shore of the lake; but the rendezvous was a solitude,—Tonty was nowhere to be seen. It was the first of November; winter was at hand, and the streams would soon be frozen. The men clamored to go forward, urging that they should starve if they could not reach the villages of the Illinois before the tribe scattered for the winter hunt. La Salle was inexorable. If they should all desert, he said, he, with his Mohegan hunter and the three friars, would still remain and wait for Tonty. The men grumbled, but obeyed; and, to divert their thoughts, he set them at building a fort of timber on a rising ground at the mouth of the river.

They had spent twenty days at this task, and their work was well advanced, when at length Tonty appeared. He brought with him only half of his men. Provisions had failed; and the rest of his party had been left thirty leagues behind, to sustain themselves by hunting. La Salle told him to return and hasten them forward. He set out with two men. A violent north wind arose. He tried to run his canoe ashore through the breakers. The two men could not manage their vessel, and he with his one hand could not help them. She swamped, rolling over in the surf. Guns, baggage, and provisions were lost; and the three voyagers returned to the Miamis, subsisting on acorns by the way. Happily, the men left behind, excepting two deserters, succeeded, a few days after, in rejoining the party.

Thus was one heavy load lifted from the heart of La Salle. But where was the "Griffin"? Time enough, and more than enough, had passed for her voyage to Niagara and back again. He scanned the dreary horizon with an anxious eye. No returning sail gladdened the watery solitude, and a dark foreboding gathered on his heart. . . .

Her safety was vital to his enterprise. She had on board articles of the last necessity to him, including the rigging and anchors of another vessel which he was to build at Fort Crèvecœur, in order to descend the Mississippi and sail thence to the West Indies. But now his last hope had well-nigh vanished. Past all reasonable doubt, the "Griffin" was lost; and in her loss he and all his plans seemed ruined alike.

Nothing, indeed, was ever heard of her. Indians, fur-traders, and even Jesuits, have been charged with contriving her destruction. Some say that the Ottawas boarded and burned her, after murdering those on board; others accuse the Pottawattamies; others affirm that her own crew scuttled and sunk her; others, again, that she foundered in a storm.

CAPTIVE OF THE SIOUX

FATHER HENNEPIN'S NARRATIVE, 1680

On its first and only voyage the historic Griffin *carried a company of thirty-four men. Three of them became immortal: Robert Cavelier de La Salle, the imperial merchant and explorer of New France; Henry de Tonty, who had worn an iron hand since being maimed on a battlefield in Spain; and an adventurer in the gray robes of a Récollet friar, Louis Hennepin. After a winter in Illinois, Hennepin, with two companions, went north to explore the upper Mississippi. Captured by the Sioux, he was finally released at the intercession of Daniel de Grosolon, Sieur Dulbut—whom Hennepin had first met on a battlefield in Belgium five years earlier.*

Back in France after his sojourn in the wilderness, Hennepin wrote the story of his travels in North America. An unreliable historian given to exaggerating his own accomplishments, he yet conveyed the excitement of discovery. His books were read in several languages.

The following narrative finds Hennepin ascending the Mississippi, which he calls the River Colbert, for Jean Baptiste Colbert, Minister of Finance under Louis XIV. It is from his Description of Louisiana.

WE scrupulously said our morning and evening prayers every day on embarking, and the Angelus at noon, adding some paraphrases on the Response of St. Bonaventure in honor of St. Anthony of Padua. In this way we begged of God to meet these Indians by day, for when they discover people at night, they kill them as enemies, to rob those whom they murder secretly of some axes or knives which they value more than we do gold and silver; they even kill their own allies, when they can conceal their death, so as afterward to boast of having killed men, and so pass for soldiers.

We had considered the river Colbert with great pleasure, and without hindrance, to know whether it was navigable up and down. We were loaded with seven or eight large turkeys, which multiply of themselves in these parts. We wanted neither buffalo nor deer, nor beaver, nor fish, nor bear meat, for we killed those animals as they swam across the river.

Our prayers were heard when, on the 11th of April, 1680, about two o'clock in the afternoon, we suddenly perceived thirty-three bark canoes, manned by a hundred and twenty Indians, coming down with extraordinary speed, to make war on the Miamis, Islinois, and Maroa. These Indians surrounded us, and while at a distance, discharged some arrows at us; but as they approached our canoe the old men seeing us with the calumet of peace in our hands, prevented the young men from killing us. These brutal men leaping from their canoes, some on land, others into the water with frightful cries and yells, approached us, and as we made no resistance, being only three against so great a number, one of them wrenched our calumet from our hands, while our canoe and theirs were tied to the shore. We first presented them a piece of French tobacco, better for smoking than theirs, and the eldest among them uttered the words Miamiha, Miamiha. As we did not understand their language, we took a little stick, and by signs which we made on the sand, showed them that their enemies, the Miamis whom they sought, had fled across the river Colbert to join the Islinois; when they saw themselves discovered and unable to surprise their enemies, three or four old men, laying their hands on my head, wept in a lugubrious tone.

With a wretched handkerchief I had left, I wiped away their tears, but they would not smoke our peace-calumet. They made us cross the river with great cries, which all shouted together with tears in their eyes; they made us row them, and we heard yells capable of striking the most resolute with terror. After landing our canoe and goods, part of which had been already taken, we made a fire to boil our kettle; we gave them two large wild turkeys that we had killed. These Indians having called an assembly to deliberate what they were to do with us; the two head-chiefs of the party approaching, showed us, by signs, that the warriors wished to tomahawk us. This compelled me to go to the war chiefs with one of my men, leaving the other by our property, and throw into their midst six axes, fifteen knives, and six fathom of our black tobacco, then bowing down my head, I showed them, with an axe, that they might kill us, if they thought proper. This present appeased many individual members, who gave us some beaver to eat, putting the three first morsels in our mouth according to the custom of the country, and blowing on the meat which was too hot, before putting their bark dish before us, to let us eat as we liked. We spent the night in anxiety, because before retiring at night, they had returned us our peace-calumet. Our two boatmen were, however, resolved to sell their lives dearly, and to resist if attacked. Their arms and swords were ready. As for my own part, I determined to allow myself to be killed without any resistance, as I was going to announce to them a God, who had been falsely accused, unjustly condemned, and cruelly crucified, without showing the least aversion to those who put him to death. We watched in turn in our anxiety so as not to be surprised asleep.

In the morning April 12th, one of their captains named Narrhetoba, with his face and bare body smeared with paint, asked me for our peace-calumet, filled it with tobacco of his country, made all his band smoke first, and then all the others who plotted our ruin. He then gave us to understand that we must go with them to their country, and they all turned back with us; having thus broken off their voyage, I was not sorry in this conjuncture to continue our discovery with these people.

But my greatest trouble was, that I found it difficult to say my office before these Indians many of whom seeing me move my lips said, in a fierce tone, Ouackanche; and as we did not know a word of their language, we believed that they were angry at it. Michael Ako, all out of countenance, told me, that if I continued to say my breviary we should all be killed, and the Picard begged me at least to pray apart, so as not to provoke them. I followed the latter's advice, and the more I concealed myself, the more I had the Indians at my heels, for when I entered the wood, they thought I was going to hide some goods under ground, so that I knew not on what side to turn to pray, for they never let me out of sight. This obliged me to beg pardon of my two canoemen, assuring them that I could not dispense with saying my office, that if we were massacred for that, I would be the innocent cause of their death, as well as of my own. By the word Ouakanche, the Indians meant that the book I was reading was a spirit; but by their gesture they nevertheless showed a kind of aversion, so that to accustom them to it, I chanted the litany of the Blessed Virgin in the canoe with my book open. They thought that the breviary was a spirit which taught me to sing for their diversion, for these people are naturally fond of singing.

The outrages done us by these Indians during our whole route was incredible, for seeing that our canoe was much larger and more heavily laden than theirs (for they have only a quiver full of arrows, a bow, and a wretched dressed skin, to serve too as a blanket at night, for it was still pretty cold at that season, always going north), and that we could not go faster than they, they put some warriors with us to help us row, to oblige us to follow them. These Indians sometimes make thirty or forty leagues, when at war and pressed for time, or anxious to surprise some enemy. Those who had taken us were of various villages and of different opinions as to us; we cabined every night by the young chief who had asked for our peace-calumet, and put ourselves under his protection; but jealousy arose among these Indians, so that the chief of the party named Aquipaguetin, one of whose sons had been

killed by the Miamis seeing that he could not avenge his death on that nation as he had wished, turned all his rage on us. He wept through almost every night him he had lost in war, to oblige those who had come out to avenge him, to kill us and seize all we had, so as to be able to pursue his enemies; but those who liked European goods were much disposed to preserve us, so as to attract other Frenchmen there and get iron, which is extremely precious in their eyes; but of which they knew the great utility only when they saw one of our French boatmen kill three or four bustards or turkeys at a single shot, while they can scarcely kill only one with an arrow. In consequence, as we afterward learned, that the words Manza Ouackange, mean "iron that has understanding," and so these nations call a gun which breaks a man's bones, while their arrows only glance through the flesh they pierce, rarely breaking the bones of those whom they strike, and consequently producing wounds more easily cured than those made by our European guns, which often cripple those whom they wound.

We had some design of going to the mouth of the river Colbert, which more probably empties into the gulf of Mexico than into the Red sea; but the tribes that seized us, gave us no time to sail up and down the river. . . .

Having arrived on the nineteenth day of our navigation five leagues below St. Anthony's falls, these Indians landed us in a bay and assembled to deliberate about us. They distributed us separately, and gave us to three heads of families in place of three of their children who had been killed in war. They first seized all our property, and broke our canoe to pieces, for fear we should return to their enemies. Their own they hid in some alders to use when going to hunt; and though we might easily have reached their country by water, they compelled us to go sixty leagues by land, forcing us to march from daybreak to two hours after nightfall, and to swim over many rivers, while these Indians, who are often of extraordinary height, carried our habit on their head; and our two boatmen, who were smaller than myself, on their shoulders, because they could not swim as I could. On leaving the water, which was often full of sharp ice, I could scarcely stand; our legs were all bloody from the ice which we broke as we advanced in lakes which we forded, and as we eat only once in twenty-four hours, some pieces of meat which these barbarians grudgingly gave us, I was so weak that I often lay down on the way, resolved to die there, rather than follow these Indians who marched on and continued their route with a celerity which surpasses the power of the Europeans. To oblige us to hasten on, they often set fire to the grass of the prairies where we were passing, so that we had to advance or burn. I had then a hat which I reserved to shield me from the burning rays of the sun in summer, but I often dropped it in the flames which we were obliged to cross.

As we approached their village, they divided among them all the merchandise of our two canoemen, and were near killing each other for our roll of French tobacco, which is very precious to these tribes, and more esteemed than gold among Europeans. The more humane showed by signs that they would give many beaver-skins for what they took. The reason of the violence was, that this party was made up from two different tribes, the more distant of whom, fearing lest the others should retain all the goods in the first villages which they would have to pass, wished to take their share in advance. In fact, some time after they offered peltries in part payment; but our boatmen would not receive them, until they gave the full value of all that had been taken. And in course of time I have no doubt they will give entire satisfaction to the French, whom they will endeavor to draw among them to carry on trade.

These savages also took our brocade chasuble, and all the articles of our portable chapel, except the chalice, which they durst not touch; for seeing that glittering silver gilt, they closed their eyes, saying that it was a spirit which would kill them. They also broke a little box with lock and key, after telling me, that if I did not break the lock, they would do so themselves with sharp stones; the reason of this violence was that from time to time on the route, they could not open the box to examine what was inside, having no idea of locks and keys; besides, they did not care to carry the box, but only the goods which were inside, and which they thought considerable, but they found only books and papers.

After five days' march by land, suffering hunger, thirst, and outrages, marching all day long without rest, fording lakes and rivers, we descried a number of women and children coming to meet our little army. All the elders of this nation assembled on our account, and as we saw cabins, and bundles of straw hanging from the posts of them, to which these savages bind those whom they take as slaves, and burn them; and seeing that they made the Picard du Gay sing, as he held and shook a gourd full of little round pebbles, while his hair and face were filled with paint of different colors, and a tuft of white feathers attached to his head by the Indians, we not unreasonably thought that they wished to kill us, as they performed many ceremonies, usually practised, when they intend to burn their enemies. The worse of it was, too, that not one of us three could make himself understood by these Indians; nevertheless, after many vows, which every Christian would make in such straits, one of the principal Issati chiefs gave us his peace-calumet to smoke, and accepted the one we had brought. He then gave us some wild rice to eat, presenting it to us in large bark dishes, which the Indian women had seasoned with whortleberries, which are black grains which they dry in the sun in summer, and are as good as currants. After this feast, the best we had had for seven or eight days, the heads of families who had adopted us, instead of their sons killed in war, conducted us separately each to his village, marching through marshes knee deep in water, for a league, after which the five wives of the one who called me Mitchinchi, that is to say, his son, received us in three bark canoes, and took us a short league from our starting place to an island where their cabins were.

On our arrival, which was about Easter, April 21st, 1680, one of these Indians who seemed to me decrepit, gave me a large calumet to smoke, and weeping bitterly, rubbed my head and arms, showing his compassion at seeing me so fatigued that two men were often obliged to give me their hands to help me to stand up. There was a bearskin near the fire, on which he rubbed my legs and the soles of my feet with wild-cat oil.

Aquipaguetin's son, who called me his brother, paraded about with our brocade chasuble on his bare back, having rolled up in it some dead man's bones, for whom these people had a great veneration. The priest's girdle made of red and white wool, with two tassels at the end, served him for suspenders, carrying thus in triumph what he called Pere Louis Chinnien, which means "the robe of him who is called the sun." After these Indians had used this chasuble to cover the bones of their dead, they presented it to some of their allies, tribes situated about five hundred leagues west of their country, who had sent them an embassy and danced the calumet.

The day after our arrival, Aquipaguetin, who was the head of a large family, covered me with a robe made of ten large dressed beaver-skins, trimmed with porcupine quills. This Indian showed me five or six of his wives, telling them, as I afterward learned, that they should in future regard me as one of their children. He set before me a bark dish full of fish, and ordered all those assembled, that each should call me by the name I was to have in the rank of our near relationship; and seeing that I could not rise from the ground but by the help of two others, he had a sweating cabin made, in which he made me enter naked with four Indians. This cabin he covered with buffalo-skins, and inside he put stones red to the middle. He made me a sign to do as the others before beginning to sweat, but I merely concealed my nakedness with a handkerchief. As soon as these Indians had several times breathed out quite violently, he began to sing in a thundering voice, the others seconded him, all putting their hands on me, and rubbing me, while they wept bitterly. I began to faint, but I came out, and could scarcely take my habit to put on. When he had made me sweat thus three times a week, I felt as strong as ever.

I often spent sad hours among these savages; for, besides their only giving me a little wild rice and smoked fish roes five or six times a week, which they boiled in earthen pots, Aquipaguetin took me to a neighboring island with his wives and children to till the ground, in order to sow some tobacco seed, and seeds of vegetables that I had brought, and which this Indian prized extremely. Sometimes he assembled the elders of the village, in whose presence he asked me for a compass that I always had in my sleeve; seeing that I made the needle turn with a key, and believing justly that we Europeans, went all over the habitable globe, guided by this instrument, this chief, who was very eloquent, persuaded his people that we were spirits, and capable of doing anything beyond their reach. At the close of his address, which was very animated, all the old men wept over my head, admiring in me what they could not understand. I had an iron pot with three lion-paw feet, which these Indians never dared touch, unless their hand was wrapped up in some robe. The women hung it to the branch of a tree, not daring to enter the cabin where it was. I was some time unable to make myself understood by these people, but feeling myself gnawed by hunger, I began to compile a dictionary of their language by means of their children, with whom I made myself familiar, in order to learn.

As soon as I could catch the word Taketchiabihen, which means in their language, "How do you call that," I became, in a little while, able to converse with them on familiar things. At first, indeed, to ask the word run in their language, I had to quicken my steps from one end of their large cabin to the other. The chiefs of these savages seeing my desire to learn, often made me write, naming all the parts of the human body, and as I would not put on paper certain indelicate words, at which they do not blush, it afforded them an agreeable amusement. They often put me questions, but, as I had to look at my paper, to answer them, they said to one another: "When we ask Pere Louis (for so they had heard our two Frenchmen call me), he does not answer us; but as soon as he has looked at what is white (for they have no word to say paper), he answers us, and tells us his thoughts; that white thing," said they, "must be a spirit which tells Pere Louis all we say." They concluded that our two Frenchmen were not as great as I, because they could not work like me on what was white. In consequence the Indians believed that I could do everything; when the rain fell in such quantities as to incommode them, or prevent their going to hunt, they told me to stop it; but I knew enough to answer them by pointing to the clouds, that he was great chief of heaven, was master of everything, and that they bid me to do, did not depend on me.

These Indians often asked me how many wives and children I had, and how old I was, that is, how many winters, for so these nations always count. These men never illumined by the light of a faith were surprised at the answer I made them; for pointing to our two Frenchmen whom I had then gone to visit three leagues from our villages, I told them that a man among us could have only one wife till death; that as for me, I had promised the Master of life to live as they saw me, and to come and live with them to teach them that he would have them be like the French; that this great Master of life had sent down fire from heaven, and destroyed a nation given to enormous crimes, like those committed among them. But that gross people till then, lawless and faithless, turned all I said into ridicule. "How," said they, "would you have those two men with thee have wives? Ours would not live with them, for they have their hair all over the face, and we have none there or elsewhere." In fact, they were never better pleased with me, than when I was shaved; and from a complaisance certainly not criminal, I shaved every week. All our kindred seeing that I wished to leave them, made a packet of beaver-skins worth six hundred livres among the French. These peltries they gave me to induce me to remain among them, to introduce me to strange nations that were coming to visit them, and in restitution of what they had robbed me of; but I refused these presents, telling them that I had not come among them to gather beaver-skins, but only to tell them the will of the great Master of life, and to live wretchedly with them, after having left a most abundant country. "It is true," said they, "that we have no chase in this part, and that thou sufferest, but wait till summer, then we will go and kill buffalo in the warm country." I should have been satisfied had they fed me as they did their children, but they eat secretly at night unknown to me. Although women are, for the most part, more kind and compassionate than men, they gave what little fish they had to their children, regarding me as a slave made by their warriors in their enemies' country, and they reasonably preferred their children's lives to mine.

There were some old men who often came to weep over my head in a sighing voice, saying, "Son," or "Nephew, I feel sorry to see thee without eating, and to learn how badly our warriors treated thee on the way; they are young braves, without sense, who would have killed thee, and have robbed thee of all thou hast. Hadst thou wanted buffalo or beaver-robes, we would wipe away thy tears, but thou wilt having nothing of what we offer thee."

Ouasicoudé, that is, the Pierced-pine, the greatest of all the Issati chiefs, being very indignant at those who had so maltreated us, said, in open council, that those who had robbed us of all we had, were like hungry curs that stealthily snatch a bit of meat from the bark dish, and then fly; so those who had acted so toward us, deserved to be regarded as dogs, since they insulted men who brought them iron and merchandise, which they had never had; that he would find means to punish the one who had so outraged us. This is what the brave chief showed to all his nation, as we shall see hereafter.

As I often went to visit the cabins of these last nations, I found a sick child, whose father's name was Mamenisi; having a moral certainty of its death, I begged our two Frenchmen to give me their advice, telling them I believed myself obliged to baptize it. Michael Ako would not accompany me, the Picard du Gay alone followed me to act as sponsor, or rather as witness of the baptism. I christened the child Antoinette in honor of St. Anthony of Padua, as well as from the Picard's name which was Anthony Auguelle. He was a native of Amiens, and a nephew of Mr. de Cauroy, procurator-general of the Premonstratensians, both now at Paris. Having poured natural water on the head of this Indian child, and uttered these words: "Creature of God, I baptize thee in the name of the Father, and of the Son, and of the Holy

Ghost," I took half an altar cloth which I had wrested from the hands of an Indian who had stolen it from me, and put it on the body of the baptized child; for as I could not say mass for want of wine and vestments, this piece of linen could not be put to a better use, than to enshroud the first Christian child among these tribes. I do not know whether the softness of the linen had refreshed her, but she was the next day smiling in her mother's arms, who believed that I had cured her child, but she died soon after to my great consolation.

During our stay among the Issati or Nadouessiou, we saw Indians who came as embassadors from about five hundred leagues to the west. They informed us that the Assenipoualacs were then only seven or eight days distant to the northeast of us; all the other known tribes on the west and northwest inhabit immense plains and prairies abounding in buffalo and peltries, where they are sometimes obliged to make fires with buffalo dung for want of wood. . . .

All the Indian women hid their stock of meat at the mouth of Buffalo river, and in the islands, and we again went down the Colbert about eighty leagues to hunt with this multitude of canoes. From time to time the Indians hid their canoes on the banks of the river and in the islands. They then struck into the prairies seven or eight leagues beyond the mountains, where they took, at different times, a hundred and twenty buffaloes. They always left some of their old men on the tops of the mountains to be on the lookout for their enemies. One day when I was dressing the foot of one who called himself my brother, and who had run a splinter deep into his foot, an alarm was given in the camp. Two hundred bowmen ran out, and that brave Indian, although I had just made a deep incision in the sole of his foot to draw out the wood, left me and ran even faster than the rest, not to be deprived of the glory of fighting. But instead of enemies, they found only a herd of about eighty stags, who took flight. The wounded man could scarcely regain the camp. During this alarm, all the Indian women sang in a lugubrious tone. The Picard left me to join his host, and I remain-

ing with one called Otchimbi, had to carry in the canoe an old Indian woman of over eighty. For all her great age, she threatened to strike with her paddle three children who troubled us in the middle of our canoe. The men treated me well enough, but as the meat was almost entirely at the disposal of the women, I was compelled, in order to get some, to make their children's tonsures, about as large as those of our religious, for these little savages wear them to the age of fifteen or sixteen, and their parents make them with red hot stones.

We had another alarm in our camp. The old men on duty on the top of the mountains announced that they saw two warriors in the distance. All the bowmen hastened there with speed, each trying to outstrip the others, but they brought back only two of their own women, who came to tell them that a party of their people were hunting at the extremity of Lake Condé [Superior], had found five spirits (so they call the French), who, by means of a slave, had expressed a wish to come on, knowing us to be among them, in order to find out whether we were English, Dutch, Spaniards or Frenchmen being unable to understand by what roundabout we had reached those tribes.

On the 25th of July, 1680, as we were ascending the river Colbert after the buffalo-hunt, to the Indian villages we met the sieur de Luth, who came to the Nadouessious, with five French soldiers. They joined us about two hundred and twenty leagues distant from the country of the Indians who had taken us. As we had some knowledge of their language, they begged us to accompany them to the villages of those tribes, to which I readily agreed, knowing that these Frenchmen had not approached the sacraments for two years. The sieur de Luth, who acted as captain, seeing me tired of tonsuring the children, and bleeding asthmatic old men to get a mouthful of meat, told the Indians that I was his elder brother, so that, having my subsistence secured, I labored only for the salvation of these Indians.

We arrived at the villages of the Issati on the 14th of August, 1680. I there found our chalice and books which I had hidden in the ground. The tobacco which I had planted had been choked by the weeds. The turnips, cabbages and other vegetables were of extraordinary size. The Indians durst not eat them. During our stay, they invited us to a feast where there were more than a hundred and twenty men all naked. The first chief, a relative of the one whose body I had covered with a blanket, brought me a bark dish of food which he put on a buffalo-robe, dressed, whitened, and trimmed with porcupine quills on one side, and the curly wool on the other. He afterwards put it on my head, saying: "He whose body thou didst cover, covers thine. He has borne tidings of thee to the land of souls. Brave was thy act in his regard. All the nation praises thee for it." He then reproached the sieur de Luth, for not having covered the deceased's body, as I did. He replied that he covered only those of captains like himself. But the Indian answered, "Pere Louis is a greater captain than thou for his robe (meaning our brocade chasuble), which we have sent to our allies, who dwell three moons from this country, is more beautiful than that which thou wearest."

Toward the end of September, having no implements to begin an establishment, we resolved to tell these people, that for their benefit, we would have to return to the French settlements. The grand chief of the Issati, or Nadouessiouz, consented, and traced in pencil on a paper I gave him, the route we should take for four hundred leagues. With this chart, we set out, eight Frenchmen, in two canoes, and descended the rivers St. Francis and Colbert. Two of our men took two beaver-robes at St. Anthony of Padua's falls, which the Indians had hung in sacrifice on the trees.

We stopped near Ouisconsin river to smoke some meat. Three Indians coming from the nations we had left, told us that their great chief named Pierced-pine, having heard that one of the chiefs of the nation wished to pursue and kill us, had entered his cabin and tomahawked him, to prevent his pernicious design. We regaled these three Indians with meat, of which we were in no want then.

Two days after, we perceived an army of one hundred and forty canoes, filled with about two hundred and fifty warriors. We thought that those who brought the preceding news were spies, for instead of descending the river on leaving us, they ascended to tell their people; however, the chiefs of the little army visited us and treated us very kindly, and the same day descended the river as we did to the Ouisconsin. We found that river as wide as the Seignelay [Illinois], with a strong current. After sailing up sixty leagues, we came to a portage of half a league, which the Nadouessiouz chiefs had marked for us. We slept there to leave marks and crosses on the trunks of the trees. The next day we entered the river which winds wonderfully, for after six hours sailing, we found ourselves opposite the place where we started. One of our men wishing to kill a swan on the wing, capsized his canoe, fortunately not beyond his depth.

We passed four lakes, two pretty large, on the banks of which the Miamis formerly resided, we found Maskoutens, Kikapous, and Outaougamy there, who sow Indian corn for their subsistence. All this country is as fine as that of the Islinois.

We made a portage at a rapid called Kakalin, and after about four hundred leagues sail from our leaving the country of the Issati, and Nadouessiouz, we arrived safely at the extremity of the bay of the Fetid, where we found Frenchmen trading contrary to orders with the Indians. They had some little wine in a tin flagon which enabled me to say mass. I had then only a chalice and altar stone, but Providence supplied me with vestments of the chapel of Father Zenobius Membre Recollect, who was with the Islinois in their flight. They gave me all they took, except the chalice, which they promised to give back in a few days for a present of tobacco.

I had not celebrated mass for over nine months for want of wine. I had still some hosts. We remained two days to rest, sing the Te Deum, high mass, and preach. All our Frenchmen went to confession and communion, to thank God for having preserved us amid so many wanderings and perils.

One of our Frenchmen gave a gun for a canoe larger than ours, with which, after sailing a hundred leagues, we reach Missili-mackinac, where we were obliged to winter. To employ the time usefully, I preached every holyday, and on the Sundays of Advent and Lent. The Ottawas and Hurons were often present, rather from curiosity than from any inclination to live according to Christian maxims. These last Indians said, speaking of our discovery, that they were men, but that we Frenchmen were spirits, because, had they gone so far, the strange nations would have killed them, while we went fearlessly everywhere.

During the winter, we took whitefish in Lake Orleans [Huron] in twenty or twenty-two fathoms water. They served to season the Indian corn, which was our usual fare. Forty-two Frenchmen trading there with Indians begged me to give them all the cord of St. Francis, which I readily did, making an exhortation at each ceremony.

We left Missilimackinac in Easter week, 1681, and were obliged to drag our provisions and canoes on the ice, more than ten leagues on Lake Orleans; having advanced far enough on this fresh-water sea, and the ice breaking, we embarked after Low Sunday, which we celebrated, having some little wine which a Frenchman had fortunately brought, and which served us quite well the rest of the voyage. After a hundred leagues on Lake Orleans, we passed the strait [Detroit], for thirty leagues and Lake St. Clair, which is in the middle and entered Lake Conty, where we killed, with sword and axe, more than thirty sturgeon which came to spawn on the banks of the lake. On the way we met an Ottawa chief called Talon, six persons of whose family had died of starvation, not having found a good fishery or hunting-ground. This Indian told us that the Iroquois had carried off a family of twelve belonging to his tribe, and begged us to deliver them, if yet alive.

We sailed along Lake Conty, and after a hundred and twenty leagues we passed the strait of the great falls of Niagara and Fort Conty, and entering Lake Frontenac, coasted along the southern shore. After thirty leagues from Lake Conty, we reached the great Seneca village about Whitsunday, 1681. We entered the Iroquois council and asked them, why they had enslaved twelve of our Ottawa allies, telling them that those whom they had taken, were children of the governor of the French, as well as the Iroquois, and that by this violence, they declared war on the French. To induce them to restore our allies, we gave them two belts of wampum.

The next day the Iroquois answered us by two belts, that the Ottawas had been carried off by some mad young warriors; that we might assure the governor of the French, that the Iroquois would hearken to him in all things; that they wished to live with Onontio like real children with their father (so they call the governor of Canada), and that they would restore those whom they had taken.

A chief named Teganeot, who spoke for his whole nation in all the councils, made me a present of otter and beaver-skins, to the value of over twenty-five crowns. I took it with one hand, and gave it with the other to his son, telling him that I gave it to him to buy goods of the other Frenchmen; that as for us, Barefeet, as the Iroquois called us, we would not take beaver or peltries; but that I would report their friendly feeling to the governor of the French. This Iroquois chief was surprised at my refusing his present, and told his own people that the other French did not do so. We took leave of the chief men, and after sailing forty leagues on the lake, reached Fort Frontenac, where the dear Recollect Father Luke was greatly surprised to see me, as for two years it had been reported that the Indians had hung me with our Franciscan cord. All the inhabitants, French and Indians, whom we had gathered at Fort Frontenac, welcomed me with extraordinary joy at my return; the Indians calling me Atkon, and putting their hand to their mouth, which means, Barefeet is a spirit to have travelled so far. At the mouth of Lake Frontenac the current is strong, and the more you descend the more it increases; the rapids are frightful. In two days and a half we descended the river St. Lawrence so rapidly that we reached Montreal (sixty miles from the fort), where the count de Frontenac, governor-general of all New France then was. This governor received me as well as a man of his probity can receive a missionary. As he believed me killed by the Indians, he was for a time thunderstruck believing me to be some other religious. He beheld me wasted, without cloak, with a habit patched with pieces of buffalo-skin. He took me with him for twelve days to recover, and himself gave me the meat I was to eat, for fear I should fall sick by eating too much after so long a diet. I rendered him an exact account of my voyage, and represented to him the advantage of our discovery.

II

The Disputed Country

FOR certain luxuries in the Old World—a lady's fur piece and a gentleman's felt hat—and for the profit of the French and English merchants, armies clashed in the wilderness of America. The French carried their trading system deep into the interior. From a chain of posts on the Great Lakes and the Mississippi canoe caravans brought baled peltry to the St. Lawrence. New France was an enterprise flung over the waterways from the Gulf of the St. Lawrence to the Gulf of Mexico, arced around the coastal colonies of the English.

It was a thin French line that ringed the West, so thin that one looks hard to trace it through the wilderness. At a dozen stations, hundreds of miles apart, were a few French troops, some *voyageurs* with Indian women, a priest, and a trader or two. In 1700 there were but 12,000 Frenchmen in all New France, while ten times that many English were enlarging their colonies.

From the Mississippi the French traders pushed eastward, planting stations on the Wabash and in the Ohio country. Meanwhile British traders were reaching west, over the Alleghenies to the Ohio valley. In an exchange of empty gestures the French warned off the English and the English menaced the French. England and France were two old enemies, finding a new battleground. They made alliances with native tribes. Soon Mohawks were fighting Ottawas to determine whether France or England should possess their country.

The French had the advantage of strategic possession and long experience in the wilderness. And they had support of the western tribes; by mission labors and intermarriage they were close to the Indians. But the British had overwhelming numbers, an alliance with the powerful Iroquois, and control of the seas. The French won early victories, defeating Braddock's army and holding Forts Niagara and Duquesne. But the British won the war. At the Treaty of Paris, in 1763, New France passed into history and Britain came into possession of all the territory east of the Mississippi.

The Indians were still there, and though they sometimes dreamed of the uncorrupted life of their fathers they had become dependent on the white man. When the British took over Detroit the tribes demanded ammunition for hunting, a better payment for their peltries and a lower price on knives, traps and blankets. The British were inconsiderate, and the savages rebelled.

Pontiac gathered an intertribal army to seize Detroit. From there the "conspiracy" quickly spread through the interior. In a few spring weeks of 1763 the warriors, by stealth, treachery and daring, captured all the western posts from Fort Mackinac to Fort Ouitenon on the Wabash and Fort Venango on the Allegheny. But it was an empty victory. With the campaigns of Bouquet and Bradstreet the British quickly recovered their stations from a savage people who could not live without, nor with, the white man's trade.

SIX LEAD PLATES

CÉLERON'S EXPEDITION TO THE OHIO, 1749

While British traders were enlarging their traffic with the Ohio tribes, the French considered the entire Ohio valley a part of the Province of Quebec. In the citadel above the St. Lawrence sat a brooding, humpbacked man who had been a naval officer before coming to the New World. In 1749 the Marquis de la Galissonnière, governor of New France, sent an expedition to the Ohio valley. Céleron de Blainville with a company of 250 French and Indians was instructed to warn off the English traders and assert French property rights over the area.

Céleron, who had served as commandant at Detroit, knew the western country and the Indians. In a fleet of birch canoes his big party left Montreal in June, 1749. They paddled over Lake Ontario to the Niagara portage, crossed Lake Erie and portaged to Conewango Creek, one of the headwaters of the Ohio. Then it was good paddling, with the steady June current through the great green valley of the West.

In Céleron's own canoe was a box packed with lead plates bearing a declaration of possession ". . . of said river Ohio, and of all those that therein empty; and of all the land on both sides of said river." At the mouth of each important tributary to the Ohio the company drew up in military ranks on the shore and buried a lead plate in the ground. Then to a tree, like a NO TRES-PASSING *sign, Céleron nailed a tin plaque inscribed with the arms of France. When his last plate was buried at the mouth of the Great Miami, he had posted the Ohio country like a game preserve. But the English traders came in growing numbers.*

Years after the French-British rivalry was forgotten, a group of Marietta boys playing at the mouth of the Muskingum found a piece of metal protruding from the riverbank. They had stumbled onto history. That lead plate, declaring French possession of the Ohio country, is now in the museum of the American Antiquarian Society at Worcester, Massachusetts.

The following excerpt from Céleron's narrative finds him in the heart of the Ohio valley late in the summer of 1749.

ON August 25th I assembled all the chiefs, and made them a present, on the part of the General, and asked them to keep the promise which they had given me. A little while after, I made the traders come to me, and summoned them to retire, making them feel that they have no right of commerce or anything else in the Belle Rivière.

I wrote to the Governor of Carolina, whom I have well warned of the risks which their traders will run if they return here. That was enjoined on me in my instructions, and even to pillage the English, but I was not strong enough for that—these traders being established in the village, and well sustained by the savages. I would have made an attempt, which might not have succeeded, and would have turned against the French. The Ottawas sent by Mr. de Sabrevois arrived, and brought me letters by which advice was given to me, which was no more than that which Mr. La Naudière had told me—of the disposition of the savages of Detroit—and, besides that, that some efforts which Mr. de Longueil had made to engage them to march they had constantly refused. I gave provision to these couriers, although I was very short; and I wrote to Mr. de Sabrevois, and asked him to keep twenty canoes below Detroit, with provisions for my establishment, at the commencement of October.

Aug. 26th, I departed, at 10 o'clock in the morning, from St. Yotoc. All the savages were under arms, and saluted when I passed before the village.

Aug. 27th, I arrived at the Rivière Blanche [the little Miami] at 10 o'clock in the evening. I knew that, three leagues in the country, there were six cabins of the Miamis, which induced me to sleep at this place. The 28th, I sent Mr. de Villiers and my son to these cabins, to tell these savages to come to speak to me. They brought them, and I engaged them to come with me to the village of the Demoiselle, where I was going to carry the words of their Father Onontio ["the Great Mountain," Iroquois name for the Governor of Canada]. They consented, asking me to wait until the next day, to give them time to go for their equipage. There are in this village two Sonontonane cabins. The policy of these nations is to have some of them with them who are like protectors. I engaged one of the Sonontonanes, who speaks Miami well, to come with me to the home of the Demoiselle. I needed him, not having an interpreter of this language, and I had some affairs of consequence to treat with them.

Aug. 29th, I wrote to Mr. Raimond, Captain and Commandant at the Miamis, and asked him to send to me the one named "King's Interpreter," with as many horses as possible, to make the transport of our baggage at a portage of fifty leagues.

Aug. 30th, The savages of the Rivière Blanche having arrived, I embarked to gain the Rivière A la Roche, and at the entrance I buried a plate of lead, and attached to a tree the arms of the king—of which I drew up a Procès Verbal.

Procès Verbal of the Sixth Plate of Lead, buried at the entrance of the River à la Roche [the Great Miami], August 31, 1749

"The year 1749, I, Celeron, Chevalier of the Order Royal and Military of St. Louis, Captain Commanding a Detachment sent by the orders of the Marquis de la Galissonnière, Commanding General in Canada, in the Belle Rivière (otherwise the Ohio), accompanied by the principal officers of our detachment, have buried on the point formed by the right shore of the Ohio, and the left of the River la Roche, a plate of lead, and attached to a tree the arms of the king. In faith of which we have drawn up and signed with the officers the present Procès Verbal."

September.—That done, I embarked; the little water which I found in this river made me take thirteen days to ascend it.

The 12th, The Miamis of the village of the Demoiselle, having learned that I was about to arrive at their home, sent four chiefs to me with calumets of peace for me to smoke, as I had invited them to my people on land, not having water enough in the river to draw the loaded canoes through. I was informed by Mr. Courtmanche, an officer of the detachment, of the arrival of these envoys. I disembarked at the place where they were, and, when we were all seated, they commenced their ceremonies, presenting to me the calumet. I accepted it. They then carried it to Mr. de Contrecoeur, second captain of the detachment, and to all the officers, and to the Canadians, who, famished for a smoke, wished that the ceremony had lasted a long time. The hour having arrived to encamp, we slept at this place. The messengers rested with us. I was obliged, notwithstanding the little provision we had, to give them supper.

13th, I arrived at the village de la Demoiselle, and I placed my camp and arranged the sentries and waited for the arrival of the interpreter, which I had demanded from Mr. de Raimond. During this time I sounded their minds to learn if they were willing to return to Kiskakon. This is the name of their ancient village. It appeared to me that they had not a great repugnance. They had two English workmen in their village, whom I made leave; those who had passed the summer there trading, had retired with their effects by land. They have roads communicating from one village to the other.

NIGHT OVER DETROIT

FRANCIS PARKMAN

The British won the French and Indian War, but they did not win the Indians. Resistance to the new regime was led by Pontiac, a chief of the Ottawas, who united the western tribes in a bold plan of action. According to tradition the warriors agreed upon an Uprising Day, when they would fall upon every British post and annihilate every Englishman in the western country. Actually the "conspiracy" was not so fully planned. But in a series of uprisings in the late spring of 1763 the tribes seized all the western posts except Detroit, where Pontiac himself was in charge of the rebellion.

At Detroit the maneuver was plotted carefully. Pontiac and his chiefs, with weapons concealed in their blankets, would ask the commander for an interview. Inside the fort, at Pontiac's signal, they would strike down the British officers, and at the sound of their war cries Indians outside would overpower the sentries.

It would probably have succeeded, except for a chance warning that came to the British commander. The alerted garrison was not overwhelmed, and the best Pontiac could do was to subject the fort to a five-month siege. When at last Colonel Bradstreet, arriving from Lake Erie, dispersed the Indians, Pontiac was not there. He had fled west where, six years later, he was killed by an Illinois warrior. According to a dubious tradition the assassin had been hired by an English trader, and the price was a barrel of rum.

This account is taken from The Conspiracy of Pontiac *(1851), the first volume in the great series that reviewed the New World contest between France and England—a drama that Parkman regarded as "the history of the American forest."*

TO the credulity of mankind each great calamity has its dire prognostics. Signs and portents in the heavens, the vision of an Indian bow, and the figure of a scalp imprinted on the disk of the moon, warned the New England Puritans of impending war. The apparitions passed away, and Philip of Mount Hope burst from the forest with his Narragansett warriors. In October, 1762, thick clouds of inky blackness gathered above the fort and settlement of Detroit. The river darkened beneath the awful shadows, and the forest was wrapped in double gloom.

Drops of rain began to fall, of strong, sulphurous odor, and so deeply colored that the people, it is said, collected them and used them for writing. A literary and philosophical journal of the time seeks to explain this strange phenomenon on some principle of physical science; but the simple Canadians held a different faith. Throughout the winter, the shower of black rain was the foremost topic of the fireside talk; and forebodings of impending evil disturbed the breast of many a timorous matron.

La Mothe-Cadillac was the founder of

Detroit. In the year 1701, he planted the little military colony, which time has transformed into a thriving American city. At an earlier date, some feeble efforts had been made to secure the possession of this important pass; and when La Hontan visited the lakes, a small post, called Fort St. Joseph, was standing near the present site of Fort Gratiot. The wandering Jesuits, too, made frequent sojourns upon the borders of the Detroit, and baptized the savage children whom they found there.

Fort St. Joseph was abandoned in the year 1688. The establishment of Cadillac was destined to a better fate, and soon rose to distinguished importance among the western outposts of Canada. Indeed, the site was formed by nature for prosperity; and a bad government and a thriftless people could not prevent the increase of the colony. At the close of the French war, as Major Rogers tells us, the place contained twenty-five hundred inhabitants. The center of the settlement was the fortified town, currently called the Fort, to distinguish it from the straggling dwellings along the river banks. It stood on the western margin of the river, covering a small part of the ground now occupied by the city of Detroit, and contained about a hundred houses, compactly pressed together, and surrounded by a palisade. Both above and below the fort, the banks of the stream were lined on both sides with small Canadian dwellings, extending at various intervals for nearly eight miles. Each had its garden and its orchard, and each was enclosed by a fence of rounded pickets. To the soldier or the trader, fresh from the harsh scenery and ambushed perils of the surrounding wilds, the secluded settlement was welcome as an oasis in the desert.

The Canadian is usually a happy man. Life sits lightly upon him; he laughs at its hardships, and soon forgets its sorrows. A lover of roving and adventure, of the frolic and the dance, he is little troubled with thoughts of the past or the future, and little plagued with avarice or ambition. At Detroit, all his propensities found ample scope. Aloof from the world, the simple colonists shared none of its pleasures and excitements, and

were free from many of its cares. Nor were luxuries wanting which civilization might have envied them. The forest teemed with game, the marshes with wild fowl, and the rivers with fish. The apples and pears of the old Canadian orchards are even to this day held in esteem. The poorer inhabitants made wine from the fruit of the wild grape, which grew profusely in the woods, while the wealthier class procured a better quality from Montreal, in exchange for the canoe loads of furs which they sent down with every year. Here, as elsewhere in Canada, the long winter was a season of social enjoyment; and when, in summer and autumn, the traders and *voyageurs*, the *coureurs de bois* and half-breeds, gathered from the distant forests of the northwest, the whole settlement was alive with dancing and feasting, drinking, gaming, and carousing.

Within the limits of the settlement were three large Indian villages. On the western shore, a little below the fort, were the lodges of the Pottawattamies; nearly opposite, on the eastern side, was the village of the Wyandots; and on the same side, five miles higher up, Pontiac's band of Ottawas had fixed their abode. The settlers had always maintained the best terms with their savage neighbors. In truth, there was much congeniality between the red man and the Canadian. Their harmony was seldom broken; and among the woods and wilds of the northern lakes roamed many a lawless half-breed, the mongrel offspring of the colonists of Detroit and the Indian squaws.

We have already seen how, in an evil hour for the Canadians, a party of British troops took possession of Detroit, towards the close of the year 1760. The British garrison, consisting partly of regulars and partly of provincial rangers, was now quartered in a well-built range of barracks within the town or fort. The latter, as already mentioned, contained about a hundred small houses. Its form was nearly square, and the palisade which surrounded it was about twenty-five feet high. At each corner was a wooden bastion, and a block-house was erected over each gateway. The houses were small, chiefly built of wood, and roofed with bark or a thatch of

Above: The unveiling of the conspiracy at Detroit, painted by John Mix Stanley.
Courtesy Burton Historical Collection, Detroit

Below: Indians leaving the fort at Detroit, painted by Frederic Remington. *Courtesy*
William L. Clemens Library

straw. The streets also were extremely narrow, though a wide passage way, known as the *chemin du ronde,* surrounded the town, between the houses and the palisade. Besides the barracks, the only public buildings were a council-house and a rude little church.

The garrison consisted of a hundred and twenty soldiers, with about forty fur-traders and *engagés;* but the latter, as well as the Canadian inhabitants of the place, could little be trusted, in the event of an Indian outbreak. Two small, armed schooners, the *Beaver* and the *Gladwyn,* lay anchored in the stream, and several light pieces of artillery were mounted on the bastions.

Such was Detroit,—a place whose defenses could have opposed no resistance to a civilized enemy; and yet, far removed as it was from the hope of speedy succor, it could only rely, in the terrible struggles that awaited it, upon its own slight strength and feeble resources.

Standing on the water bastion of Detroit, a pleasant landscape spread before the eye. The river, about half a mile wide, almost washed the foot of the stockade; and either bank was lined with the white Canadian cottages. The joyous sparkling of the bright blue water; the green luxuriance of the woods; the white dwellings, looking out from the foliage; and, in the distance, the Indian wigwams curling their smoke against the sky,— all were mingled in one broad scene of wild and rural beauty.

Pontiac, the Satan of this forest paradise, was accustomed to spend the early part of the summer upon a small island at the opening of the Lake St. Clair, hidden from view by the high woods that covered the intervening Isle-au-Cochon. "The king and lord of all this country," as Rogers calls him, lived in no royal state. His cabin was a small, oven-shaped structure of bark and rushes. Here he dwelt, with his squaws and children; and here, doubtless, he might often have been seen, lounging, half-naked, on a rush mat, or a bear-skin, like any ordinary warrior. We may fancy the current of his thoughts, the turmoil of his uncurbed passions, as he revolved the treacheries which, to his savage mind, seemed fair and honorable. At one moment, his fierce heart would burn with the anticipation of vengeance on the detested English; at another, he would meditate how he best might turn the approaching tumults to the furtherance of his own ambitious schemes. Yet we may believe that Pontiac was not a stranger to the high emotion of the patriot hero, the champion not merely of his nation's rights, but of the very existence of his race. He did not dream how desperate a game he was about to play. He hourly flattered himself with the futile hope of aid from France, and thought in his ignorance that the British colonies must give way before the rush of his savage warriors; when, in truth, all the combined tribes of the forest might have chafed in vain rage against the rock-like strength of the Anglo-Saxon.

Looking across an intervening arm of the river, Pontiac could see on its eastern bank the numerous lodges of his Ottawa tribesmen, half hidden among the ragged growth of trees and bushes. On the afternoon of the fifth of May, a Canadian woman, the wife of St.-Aubin, one of the principal settlers, crossed over from the western side, and visited the Ottawa village, to obtain from the Indians a supply of maple sugar and venison. She was surprised at finding several of the warriors engaged in filing off the muzzles of their guns, so as to reduce them, stock and all, to the length of about a yard. Returning home in the evening, she mentioned what she had seen to several of her neighbors. Upon this, one of them, the blacksmith of the village, remarked that many of the Indians had lately visited his shop, and attempted to borrow files and saws for a purpose which they would not explain. These circumstances excited the suspicion of the experienced Canadians. Doubtless there were many in the settlement who might, had they chosen, have revealed the plot; but it is no less certain that the more numerous and respectable class in the little community had too deep an interest in the preservation of peace, to countenance the designs of Pontiac. M. Gouin, an old and wealthy settler, went to the commandant, and conjured him to stand upon his guard; but Gladwyn, a man of fearless temper, gave no heed to the friendly advice.

In the Pottawattamie village, if there be

truth in tradition, lived an Ojibwa girl, who could boast a larger share of beauty than is common in the wigwam. She had attracted the eye of Gladwyn. He had formed a connection with her, and she had become much attached to him. On the afternoon of the sixth, Catharine—for so the officers called her —came to the fort, and repaired to Gladwyn's quarters, bringing with her a pair of elk-skin moccasins, ornamented with porcupine work, which he had requested her to make. There was something unusual in her look and manner. Her face was sad and downcast. She said little, and soon left the room; but the sentinel at the door saw her still lingering at the street corner, though the hour for closing the gates was nearly come. At length she attracted the notice of Gladwyn himself; and calling her to him, he pressed her to declare what was weighing upon her mind. Still she remained for a long time silent, and it was only after much urgency and many promises not to betray her, that she revealed her momentous secret.

To-morrow, she said, Pontiac will come to the fort with sixty of his chiefs. Each will be armed with a gun, cut short, and hidden under his blanket. Pontiac will demand to hold a council; and after he has delivered his speech, he will offer a peace-belt of wampum, holding it in a reversed position. This will be the signal of attack. The chiefs will spring up and fire upon the officers, and the Indians in the street will fall upon the garrison. Every Englishman will be killed, but not a scalp of a single Frenchman will be touched.

Such is the story told in 1768 to the traveler Carver at Detroit, and preserved in local tradition, but not sustained by contemporary letters or diaries. What is certain is, that Gladwyn received secret information, on the night of the sixth of May, that an attempt would be made on the morrow to capture the fort by treachery. He called some of his officers, and told them what he had heard. The defenses of the place were feeble and extensive, and the garrison by far too weak to repel a general assault. The force of the Indians at this time is variously estimated at from six hundred to two thousand; and the commandant greatly feared that some wild impulse might precipitate their plan, and that they might storm the fort before the morning. Every preparation was made to meet the sudden emergency. Half the garrison were ordered under arms, and all the officers prepared to spend the night upon the ramparts.

The day closed, and the hues of sunset faded. Only a dusky redness lingered in the west, and the darkening earth seemed her dull self again. Then night descended, heavy and black, on the fierce Indians and the sleepless English. From sunset till dawn, an anxious watch was kept from the slender palisades of Detroit. The soldiers were still ignorant of the danger; and the sentinels did not know why their numbers were doubled, or why, with such unwonted vigilance, their officers repeatedly visited their posts. Again and again Gladwyn mounted his wooden ramparts, and looked forth into the gloom. There seemed nothing but repose and peace in the soft, moist air of the warm spring evening, with the piping of frogs along the river bank, just roused from their torpor by the genial influence of May. But, at intervals, as the night wind swept across the bastion, it bore sounds of fearful portent to the ear, the sullen booming of the Indian drum and the wild chorus of quavering yells, as the warriors, around their distant camp-fires, danced the war-dance, in preparation for the morrow's work.

A BALL GAME AND A MASSACRE

ALEXANDER HENRY AT MICHILIMACKINAC

In 1763 the turtle-shaped Michilimackinac was still an Indian island, and the Fort stood on the mainland directly across the strait. This was the capital of the whole north country, a meeting place of merchants and missionaries, traders from the East and tribesmen from the wild north country. At this remote, romantic point a garrison of British soldiers lived a satisfying life until a dire June day in 1763.

Two years earlier Alexander Henry had left his home in New Jersey for the West. With defeat of the French the western fur trade was passing into British hands and this young adventurer wanted to have a share in the rich enterprise. He was the first British trader to reach Michilimackinac. In fact he arrived before the English garrison, and he passed for a French voyageur until the British troops arrived.

Henry soon became an established trader. He made trips by canoe and on snowshoes all around the straits. He liked the country, he got on easily with the Indians, he enjoyed the orderly little British world within the stockade walls. He was pleased with all his prospects when, suddenly, on the King's birthday, that world came to an end.

In May of 1763 after the ports on the lower lakes had been assaulted by Pontiac's warriors, remote Michilimackinac remained at peace, with no knowledge of the Indian unrest. But the chiefs had not chosen to spare this northern outpost; they were merely waiting.

Among the swift assaults by Pontiac's conspirators, one was more crafty, merciless and dramatic than all the rest. On a serene June morning at Fort Mackinac, twenty-one Britishers were killed and seventeen were captured. Among the captives was Alexander Henry, and because he wrote it down while it was still etched in his memory, we have the whole startling story of the massacre at the romantic station beside the Straits of Mackinac.

THE morning was sultry. A Chipewa came to tell me that his nation was going to play at baggatiway with the Sacs or Saakies, another Indian nation, for a high wager. He invited me to witness the sport, adding that the commandant was to be there, and would bet on the side of the Chipewa. In consequence of this information I went to the commandant and expostulated with him a little, representing that the Indians might possibly have some sinister end in view; but the commandant only smiled at my suspicions.

Baggatiway, called by the Canadians *le jeu de la crosse*, is played with a bat and ball. The bat is about four feet in length, curved, and terminating in a sort of racket. Two posts are planted in the ground at a considerable distance from each other, as a mile or more. Each party has its post, and the game consists in throwing the ball up to the post of the adversary. The ball, at the beginning, is placed in the middle of the course and each party endeavors as well to throw the ball out of the direction of its own post as into that of the adversary's.

I did not go myself to see the match which

was now to be played without the fort, because there being a canoe prepared to depart on the following day for Montreal I employed myself in writing letters to my friends; and even when a fellow trader, Mr. Tracy, happened to call upon me, saying that another canoe had just arrived from Detroit, and proposing that I should go with him to the beach to inquire the news, it so happened that I still remained to finish my letters, promising to follow Mr. Tracy in the course of a few minutes. Mr. Tracy had not gone more than twenty paces from my door when I heard an Indian war cry and a noise of general confusion.

Going instantly to my window I saw a crowd of Indians within the fort furiously cutting down and scalping every Englishman they found. In particular I witnessed the fate of Lieutenant Jemette.

I had in the room in which I was a fowling piece, loaded with swan-shot. This I immediately seized and held it for a few minutes, waiting to hear the drum beat to arms. In this dreadful interval I saw several of my countrymen fall, and more than one struggling between the knees of an Indian, who, holding him in this manner, scalped him while yet living.

At length, disappointed in the hope of seeing resistance made to the enemy, and sensible, of course, that no effort of my own unassisted arm could avail against four hundred Indians, I thought only of seeking shelter. Amid the slaughter which was raging I observed many of the Canadian inhabitants of the fort calmly looking on, neither opposing the Indians, nor suffering injury; and from this circumstance I conceived a hope of finding security in their houses.

Between the yard door of my own house and that of M. Langlade, my next neighbor, there was only a low fence, over which I easily climbed. At my entrance I found the whole family at the window, gazing at the scene of blood before them. I addressed myself immediately to M. Langlade, begging that he would put me into some place of safety until the heat of the affair should be over; an act of charity by which he might perhaps

preserve me from the general massacre; but while I uttered my petition M. Langlade, who had looked for a moment at me, turned again to the window, shrugging his shoulders and intimating that he could do nothing for me:— "Que voudriez-vous que j'en ferais?"

This was a moment for despair; but the next a Pani woman, a slave of M. Langlade's, beckoned me to follow her. She brought me to a door which she opened, desiring me to enter, and telling me that it led to the garret, where I must go and conceal myself. I joyfully obeyed her directions; and she, having followed me up to the garret door, locked it after me and with great presence of mind took away the key.

This shelter obtained, if shelter I could hope to find it, I was naturally anxious to know what might still be passing without. Through an aperture which afforded me a view of the area of the fort I beheld, in shapes the foulest and most terrible, the ferocious triumphs of barbarian conquerors. The dead were scalped and mangled; the dying were writhing and shrieking under the unsatiated knife and tomahawk; and from the bodies of some, ripped open, their butchers were drinking the blood, scooped up in the hollow of joined hands and quaffed amid shouts of rage and victory. I was shaken not only with horror, but with fear. The sufferings which I witnessed I seemed on the point of experiencing. No long time elapsed before every one being destroyed who could be found, there was a general cry of "All is finished!" At the same instant I heard some of the Indians enter the house in which I was.

The garret was separated from the room below only by a layer of single boards, at once the flooring of the one and the ceiling of the other. I could therefore hear everything that passed; and the Indians no sooner came in than they inquired whether or not any Englishman were in the house. M. Langlade replied that he could not say—he did not know of any—answers in which he did not exceed the truth, for the Pani woman had not only hidden me by stealth, but kept my secret and her own. M. Langlade was therefore, as I presume, as far from a wish to destroy me as he was careless about saving me, when he added to these answers that they might examine for themselves, and would soon be satisfied as to the object of their question. Saying this, he brought them to the garret door.

The state of my mind will be imagined. Arrived at the door some delay was occasioned by the absence of the key and a few moments were thus allowed me in which to look around for a hiding place. In one corner of the garret was a heap of those vessels of birch bark used in maple sugar making as I have recently described.

The door was unlocked, and opening, and the Indians ascending the stairs, before I had completely crept into a small opening, which presented itself at one end of the heap. An instant later four Indians entered the room, all armed with tomahawks, and all besmeared with blood upon every part of their bodies.

The die appeared to be cast. I could scarcely breathe; but I thought that the throbbing of my heart occasioned a noise loud enough to betray me. The Indians walked in every direction about the garret, and one of them approached me so closely that at a particular moment, had he put forth his hand, he must have touched me. Still I remained undiscovered, a circumstance to which the dark color of my clothes and the want of light in a room which had no window, and in the corner in which I was, must have contributed. In a word, after taking several turns in the room, during which they told M. Langlade how many they had killed and how many scalps they had taken, they returned down stairs, and I with sensations not to be expressed, heard the door, which was the barrier between me and my fate, locked for the second time.

There was a feather bed on the floor, and on this, exhausted as I was by the agitation of my mind, I threw myself down and fell asleep. In this state I remained till the dusk of the evening, when I was awakened by a second opening of the door. The person that now entered was M. Langlade's wife, who was much surprised at finding me, but advised me not to be uneasy, observing that the Indians had killed most of the English,

but that she hoped I might myself escape. A shower of rain having begun to fall, she had come to stop a hole in the roof. On her going away, I begged her to send me a little water to drink, which she did.

As night was now advancing I continued to lie on the bed, ruminating on my condition, but unable to discover a resource from which I could hope for life. A flight to Detroit had no probable chance of success. The distance from Michilimackinac was four hundred miles; I was without provisions; and the whole length of the road lay through Indian countries, countries of an enemy in arms, where the first man whom I should meet would kill me. To stay where I was threatened nearly the same issue. As before, fatigue of mind, and not tranquillity, suspended my cares and procured me further sleep.

The game of baggatiway, as from the description above will have been perceived, is necessarily attended with much violence and noise. In the ardor of contest the ball, as has been suggested, if it cannot be thrown to the goal desired, is struck in any direction by which it can be diverted from that designed by the adversary. At such a moment, therefore, nothing could be less liable to excite premature alarm than that the ball should be tossed over the pickets of the fort, nor that having fallen there, it should be followed on the instant by all engaged in the game, as well the one party as the other, all eager, all struggling, all shouting, all in the unrestrained pursuit of a rude athletic exercise. Nothing could be less fitted to excite premature alarm —nothing, therefore, could be more happily devised, under the circumstances, than a stratagem like this; and this was in fact the stratagem which the Indians had employed, by which they had obtained possession of the fort, and by which they had been enabled to slaughter and subdue its garrison and such of its other inhabitants as they pleased. To be still more certain of success they had prevailed upon as many as they could by a pretext the least liable to suspicion to come voluntarily without the pickets, and particularly the commandant and garrison themselves.

The respite which sleep afforded me

during the night was put an end to by the return of morning. I was again on the rack of apprehension. At sunrise I heard the family stirring, and presently after, Indian voices informing M. Langlade they had not found my hapless self among the dead, and that they supposed me to be somewhere concealed. M. Langlade appeared from what followed to be by this time acquainted with the place of my retreat, of which no doubt he had been informed by his wife. The poor woman, as soon as the Indians mentioned me, declared to her husband in the French tongue that he should no longer keep me in his house, but deliver me up to my pursuers, giving as a reason for this measure that should the Indians discover his instrumentality in my concealment, they might revenge it on her children, and that it was better that I should die than they. M. Langlade resisted at first this sentence of his wife's; but soon suffered her to prevail, informing the Indians that he had been told I was in his house, that I had come there without his knowledge, and that he would put me into their hands. This was no sooner expressed than he began to ascend the stairs, the Indians following upon his heels.

I now resigned myself to the fate with which I was menaced; and regarding every attempt at concealment as vain, I arose from the bed and presented myself full in view to the Indians who were entering the room. They were all in a state of intoxication, and entirely naked, except about the middle. One of them, named Wenniway, whom I had previously known, and who was upward of six feet in height, had his entire face and body covered with charcoal and grease, only that a white spot of two inches in diameter encircled either eye. This man, walking up to me, seized me with one hand by the collar of the coat, while in the other he held a large carving knife, as if to plunge it into my breast; his eyes, meanwhile, were fixed steadfastly on mine. At length, after some seconds of the most anxious suspense, he dropped his arm, saying, "I won't kill you!" To this he added that he had been frequently engaged in wars against the English, and had brought away many scalps; that on a certain occasion he had lost a brother whose name was Musinigon, and that I should be called after him.

A reprieve upon any terms placed me among the living, and gave me back the sustaining voice of hope; but Wenniway ordered me downstairs, and there informing me that I was to be taken to his cabin, where, and indeed everywhere else, the Indians were all mad with liquor, death again was threatened, and not as possible only, but as certain. I mentioned my fears on this subject to M. Langlade, begging him to represent the danger to my master. M. Langlade in this instance did not withhold his compassion, and Wenniway immediately consented that I should remain where I was until he found another opportunity to take me away.

Thus far secure I reascended my garret stairs in order to place myself the furthest possible out of the reach of insult from drunken Indians; but I had not remained there more than an hour, when I was called to the room below in which was an Indian who said that I must go with him out of the fort, Wenniway having sent him to fetch me. This man, as well as Wenniway himself, I had seen before. In the preceding year I had allowed him to take goods on credit, for which he was still in my debt; and some short time previous to the surprise of the fort he had said upon my upbraiding him with want of honesty that he would pay me before long. This speech now came fresh into my memory and led me to suspect that the fellow had formed a design against my life. I communicated the suspicion to M. Langlade; but he gave for answer that I was not now my own master, and must do as I was ordered.

The Indian on his part directed that before I left the house I should undress myself, declaring that my coat and shirt would become him better than they did me. His pleasure in this respect being complied with, no other alternative was left me than either to go out naked, or to put on the clothes of the Indian, which he freely gave me in exchange. His motive for thus stripping me of my own apparel was no other as I afterward learned than this, that it might not be stained with blood when he should kill me.

I was now told to proceed; and my driver followed me close until I had passed the gate of the fort, when I turned toward the spot where I knew the Indians to be encamped. This, however, did not suit the purpose of my enemy, who seized me by the arm and drew me violently in the opposite direction to the distance of fifty yards above the fort. Here, finding that I was approaching the bushes and sand hills, I determined to proceed no farther, but told the Indian that I believed he meant to murder me, and that if so he might as well strike where I was as at any greater distance. He replied with coolness that my suspicions were just, and that he meant to pay me in this manner for my goods. At the same time he produced a knife and held me in a position to receive the intended blow. Both this and that which followed were necessarily the affair of a moment. By some effort, too sudden and too little dependent on thought to be explained or remembered, I was enabled to arrest his arm and give him a sudden push by which I turned him from me and released myself from his grasp. This was no sooner done than I ran toward the fort with all the swiftness in my power, the Indian following me, and I expecting every moment to feel his knife. I succeeded in my flight; and on entering the fort I saw Wenniway standing in the midst of the area, and to him I hastened for protection. Wenniway desired the Indian to desist; but the latter pursued me round him, making several strokes at me with his knife, and foaming at the mouth with rage at the repeated failure of his purpose. At length Wenniway drew near to M. Langlade's house; and, the door being open, I ran into it. The Indian followed me; but on my entering the house he voluntarily abandoned the pursuit.

Preserved so often and so unexpectedly as it had now been my lot to be, I returned to my garret with a strong inclination to believe that through the will of an overruling power no Indian enemy could do me hurt; but new trials, as I believed, were at hand when at ten o'clock in the evening I was roused from sleep and once more desired to descend the stairs. Not less, however, to my satisfaction than surprise, I was summoned only to meet Major Etherington, Mr. Bostwick, and Lieutenant Lesslie, who were in the room below.

These gentlemen had been taken prisoners while looking at the game without the fort and immediately stripped of all their clothes. They were now sent into the fort under the charge of Canadians, because, the Indians having resolved on getting drunk, the chiefs were apprehensive that they would be murdered if they continued in the camp. Lieutenant Jemette and seventy soldiers had been killed; and but twenty Englishmen, including soldiers, were still alive. These were all within the fort, together with nearly three hundred Canadians.

These being our numbers, myself and others proposed to Major Etherington to make an effort for regaining possession of the fort and maintaining it against the Indians. The Jesuit missionary was consulted on the project; but he discouraged us by his representations, not only of the merciless treatment which we must expect from the Indians should they regain their superiority, but of the little dependence which was to be placed upon our Canadian auxiliaries. Thus the fort and prisoners remained in the hands of the Indians, though through the whole night the prisoners and whites were in actual possession, and they were without the gates.

That whole night, or the greater part of it, was passed in mutual condolence, and my fellow prisoners shared my garret. In the morning, being again called down, I found my master, Wenniway, and was desired to follow him. He led me to a small house within the fort, where in a narrow room and almost dark I found Mr. Ezekiel Solomons, an Englishman from Detroit, and a soldier, all prisoners. With these I remained in painful suspense as to the scene that was next to present itself till ten o'clock in the forenoon, when an Indian arrived, and presently marched us to the lakeside where a canoe appeared ready for departure, and in which we found that we were to embark.

Our voyage, full of doubt as it was,

would have commenced immediately, but that one of the Indians who was to be of the party was absent. His arrival was to be waited for; and this occasioned a very long delay during which we were exposed to a keen northeast wind. An old shirt was all that covered me; I suffered much from the cold; and in this extremity M. Langlade coming down the beach, I asked him for a blanket, promising if I lived to pay him for it at any price he pleased; but the answer I received was this, that he could let me have no blanket unless there were some one to be security for the payment. For myself, he observed, I had no longer any property in that country. I had no more to say to M. Langlade; but presently seeing another Canadian, named John Cuchoise, I addressed to him a similar request and was not refused. Naked as I was, and rigorous as was the weather, but for the blanket I must have perished. At noon our party was all collected, the prisoners all embarked, and we steered for the Isles du Castor [Beaver Islands] in Lake Michigan.

THE PIPES OF PEACE

GEORGE CROGHAN'S
JOURNAL OF A TOUR TO ILLINOIS, 1765

To the English the huge interior basin beyond the Allegheny ridges was known as the Black Forest. It was a big, dim, silent country, with a web of tracks leading between the waterways. It remained a mysterious realm for many years. But one British name was known in every village from Fort Pitt to the Wabash. George Croghan, Irish-born trader and diplomatist, had taken the Black Forest for his province.

In the gloom of the Ohio woods he occasionally met his friends—Conrad Weiser, trader, translator and negotiator with the tribes; Christopher Gist, an explorer and landlooker for Virginia speculators; and the roving half-breed Andrew Montour. These were the first agents of English colonial interests to penetrate the interior.

A year after Céleron's expedition, Croghan made a long tour of the western country, carrying presents to tribes where he was already known and erasing Céleron's influence in the Black Forest. But his most important mission came in 1765, at the end of the French and Indian War, when Pontiac and his followers had fled to Illinois and were there defying the approach of British traders.

When his flatboats had dropped down the Ohio, word went over the mountains to Philadelphia that Croghan and his men were captured and burned at the stake. Actually Croghan did lose a few of his men and "got the stroke of a hatchet" on his own head. But he persuaded his captors to release him. In a diplomatic triumph he met Pontiac and won that somber chief to his terms. So he opened the Illinois country to British traders.

The following account is taken from Croghan's Journal of the eventful summer of 1765.

MAY 15th, 1765.—I set off from Fort Pitt with two batteaux, and encamped at Chartier's Island, in the Ohio, three miles below Fort Pitt.

May 16th.—Being joined by the deputies

of the Senecas, Shawnesse and Delawares, that were to accompany me, we set off at seven o'clock in the morning, and at ten o'clock arrived at the Logs Town, an old settlement of the Shawnesse, about seventeen miles from Fort Pitt, where we put ashore, and viewed the remains of that village, which was situated on a high bank, on the south side of the Ohio river, a fine fertile country round it. At 11 o'clock we re-embarked and proceeded down the Ohio to the mouth of Big Beaver Creek, about ten miles below the Logs Town: this creek empties itself between two fine rich bottoms, a mile wide on each side from the banks of the river to the highlands. About a mile below the mouth of Beaver Creek we passed an old settlement of the Delawares, where the French, in 1756, built a town for that nation. On the north side of the river some of the stone chimneys are yet remaining; here the highlands come close to the banks and continue so for about five miles. After which we passed several spacious bottoms on each side of the river, and came to Little Beaver Creek, about fifteen miles below Big Beaver Creek. A number of small rivulets fall into the river on each side. From thence we sailed to Yellow Creek, being about fifteen miles from the last mentioned creek; here and there the hills come close to the banks of the river on each side, but where there are bottoms, they are very large, and well watered; numbers of small rivulets running through them, falling into the Ohio on both sides. We encamped on the river bank, and found a great part of the trees in the bottom are covered with grape vines. This day we passed by eleven islands, one of which being about seven miles long. For the most part of the way we made this day, the banks of the river are high and steep. The course of the Ohio from Fort Pitt to the mouth of Beaver Creek inclines to the north-west; from thence to the two creeks partly due west.

May 17th.—At 6 o'clock in the morning we embarked: and were delighted with the prospect of a fine open country on each side of the river as we passed down. We came to a place called the Two Creeks, about fifteen miles from Yellow Creek, where we put to shore; here the Senecas have a village on a high bank, on the north side of the river; the chief of this village offered me his service to go with me to the Illinois, which I could not refuse for fear of giving him offence, although I had a sufficient number of deputies with me already. From thence we proceeded down the river, passed many large, rich, and fine bottoms; the highlands being at a considerable distance from the river banks, till we came to the Buffalo Creek, being about ten miles below the Seneca village; and from Buffalo Creek, we proceeded down the river to Fat Meat Creek, about thirty miles. The face of the country appears much like what we met with before; large, rich, and well watered bottoms, then succeeded by the hills pinching close on the river; these bottoms, on the north side, appear rather low, and consequently subject to inundations, in the spring of the year, when there never fail to be high freshes in the Ohio, owing to the melting of the snows. This day we passed by ten fine islands, though the greatest part of them are small. They lay much higher out of the water than the main land, and of course less subject to be flooded by the freshes. At night we encamped near an Indian village. The general course of the river from the Two Creeks to Fat Meat Creek inclines to the south-west.

May 18th.—At 6 o'clock, A.M. we set off in our batteaux; the country on both sides of the river appears delightful; the hills are several miles from the river banks, and consequently the bottoms large; the soil, timber, and banks of the river, much like those we have before described; about fifty miles below Fat Meat Creek, we enter the long reach, where the river runs a straight course for twenty miles, and makes a delightful prospect; the banks continue high; the country on both sides, level, rich, and well watered. At the lower end of the reach we encamped. This day we passed nine islands, some of which are large, and lie high out of the water. . . .

June 7th.—We stayed here and despatched two Indians to the Illinois by land, with letters to Lord Frazer, an English officer, who had been sent there from Fort Pitt, and Monsieur St. Ange, the French commanding officer

all along the Ouabache, and too far for the Indians, which reside hereabouts, to go either to the Illinois, or elsewhere, to fetch their necessaries.

June 16th.—We were obliged to stay here to get some little apparel made up for us, and to buy some horses for our journey to Ouicatonon, promising payment at Detroit, for we could not procure horses from the French for hire; though we were greatly fatigued, and our spirits much exhausted in our late march, they would lend us no assistance.

June 17th.—At mid-day we set out; traveling the first five miles through a fine thick wood. We traveled eighteen miles this day, and encamped in a large, beautiful, well watered meadow.

June 18th and 19th.—We traveled through a prodigious large meadow, called the Pyankeshaw's Hunting Ground: here is no wood to be seen, and the country appears like an ocean: the ground is exceedingly rich, and partly overgrown with wild hemp; the land well watered, and full of buffalo, deer, bears, and all kinds of wild game.

June 20th and 21st.—We passed through some very large meadows, part of which belong to the Pyankeshaws on Vermilion River; the country and soil much the same as that we traveled over for these three days past, wild hemp grows here in abundance; the game very plenty: at any time, in half an hour we could kill as much as we wanted.

June 22nd.—We passed through part of the same meadow as mentioned yesterday; then came to a high woodland, and arrived at Vermilion River, so called from a fine red earth found here by the Indians, with which they paint themselves. About half a mile from the place where we crossed this river, there is a village of Pyankeshaws, distinguished by the addition of the name of the river. We then traveled about three hours, through a clear high woody country, but a deep and rich soil; then came to a meadow, where we encamped.

June 23rd.—Early in the morning we set out through a fine meadow, then some clear woods; in the afternoon came into a very large bottom on the Ouabache, here I met several chiefs of the Kickapoos and Musquattimes, who spoke to their young men who had taken us, and reprimanded them severely for what they had done to me, after which they returned with us to their village, and delivered us all to their chiefs.

The distance from port Vincent to Ouicatanon is two hundred and ten miles. This place is situated on the Ouabache. About fourteen French families are living in the fort, which stands on the north side of the river. The Kickapoos and the Musquattimes, whose warriors had taken us, live nigh the fort, on the same side of the river, where they have two villages; and the Ouicatanons have a village on the south side of the river. At our arrival at this post, several of the Wawcottonans, (or Ouicatonans) with whom I had been formerly acquainted, came to visit me, and seemed greatly concerned at what had happened. They went immediately to the Kickapoos and Musquattimes, and charged them to take the greatest care of us, till their chiefs should arrive from the Illinois, where they were gone to meet me some time ago, and who were entirely ignorant of this affair, and said the French had spirited up this party to go and strike us.

The French have a great influence over these Indians, and never fail in telling them many lies to the prejudice of His Majesty's interest, by making the English nation odious and hateful to them. I had the greatest difficulties in removing these prejudices. As these Indians are a weak, foolish, and credulous people, they are easily imposed on by a designing people, who have led them hitherto as they pleased. The French told them that as the southern Indians had for two years past made war on them, it must have been at the instigation of the English, who are a bad people. However I have been fortunate enough to remove their prejudice, and, in a great measure, their suspicions against the English. The country hereabouts is exceedingly pleasant, being open and clear for many miles; the soil very rich and well watered; all plants have a quick vegetation, and the climate very temperate through the winter. This post has always been a very considerable trading place. The great plenty of furs taken in this country, induced the French to establish this post, which was the first on the Ouabache, and by a very advantageous trade they have been richly recompensed for their labor.

On the south side of the Ouabache runs a big bank, in which are several fine coal mines, and behind this bank, is a very large meadow, clear for several miles. It is surprising what false information we have had respecting this country: some mention these spacious and beautiful meadows as large and barren savannahs. I apprehend it has been the artifice of the French to keep us ignorant of the country. These meadows bear fine wild grass, and wild hemp ten or twelve feet high, which, if properly manufactured, would prove as good, and answer all the purposes of the hemp we cultivate.

July 1st.—A Frenchman arrived from the Illinois with a pipe and speech from thence to the Kickapoos and Musquattamies, to have me burned, this speech was said to be sent from a Shawanese Indian who resides at the Illinois, and has been during the war, and is much attached to the French interest. As soon as this speech was delivered to the Indians by the French, the Indians informed me of it in council, and expressed their great concern for what had already happened, and told me they then set me and my people at liberty, and assured me they despised the message sent them, and would return the pipe and belt to their fathers the French, and enquire into the reason of such a message being sent them by one of his messengers, and desired me to stay with them until the deputies of the Six Nations, Shawanese and Delawares arrived with Pondiac at Ouiatonon in order to settle matters, to which I consented.

From July 4th to the 8th.—I had several conferences with the Wawiotonans, Pyankeeshas, Kickapoos and Musquatamies in which conferences I was lucky enough to reconcile those nations to His Majesty's interest and obtain their consent and approbation to take possession of any posts in their country which the French formerly possessed and an offer of their service should any nation oppose our taking possession of it, all which they confirmed by four large pipes.

July 11th.—Mr. Maisonville arrived with an interpreter and a message to the Indians to bring me and my party to the Illinois, till then I had no answer from Mr. St. Ange to the letter I wrote him on the 16th June, as I wanted to go to the Illinois, I desired the Chiefs to prepare themselves and set off with me as soon as possible.

July 12th.—I wrote to General Gage and Sir William Johnson, to Col. Campbell at Detroit, and Major Murray at Fort Pitt and Major Firmer at Mobiel or on his way to the Mississippi, and acquainted [them with] everything that had happened since my departure from Ft. Pitt.

July 13th.—The chiefs of the Twightwees came to me from the Miamis and renewed their ancient friendship with His Majesty and all his subjects in America and confirmed it with a pipe.

July 18th.—I set off for the Illinois with the Chiefs of all those Nations when by the way we met with Pondiac together with the deputies of the Six Nations, Delawares and Shawanese, which accompanied Mr. Frazier and myself down the Ohio and also deputies with speeches from the four Nations living in the Illinois country to me and the Six Nations, Delawares and Shawanese, on which we returned to Ouiatonon and there held another conference, in which I settled all matters with the Illinois Indians—Pondiac and they agreeing to everything the other nations had done, all which they confirmed by pipes and belts, but told me the French had informed them that the English intended to take their country from them, and give it to the Cherokees to settle on, and that if ever they suffered the English to take possession of their country they could make slaves of them, that this was the reason of their opposing the English hitherto from taking possession of Fort Chartres and induced them to tell Mr. La Gutrie and Mr. Sinnott that they would not let the English come into their country. But being informed since Mr. Sinnott had retired by the deputies of the Six Nations, Delawares and Shawanese, that every difference subsisting between them and the English was now settled, they were willing to comply as the other nations their brethren had done and desired that their father the King of England might not look upon his taking possession of the forts which the French had formerly possessed as a title for his subjects to possess their country, as they never had sold any part of it to the French, and that I might rest satisfied that whenever the English came to take possession they would receive them with open arms.

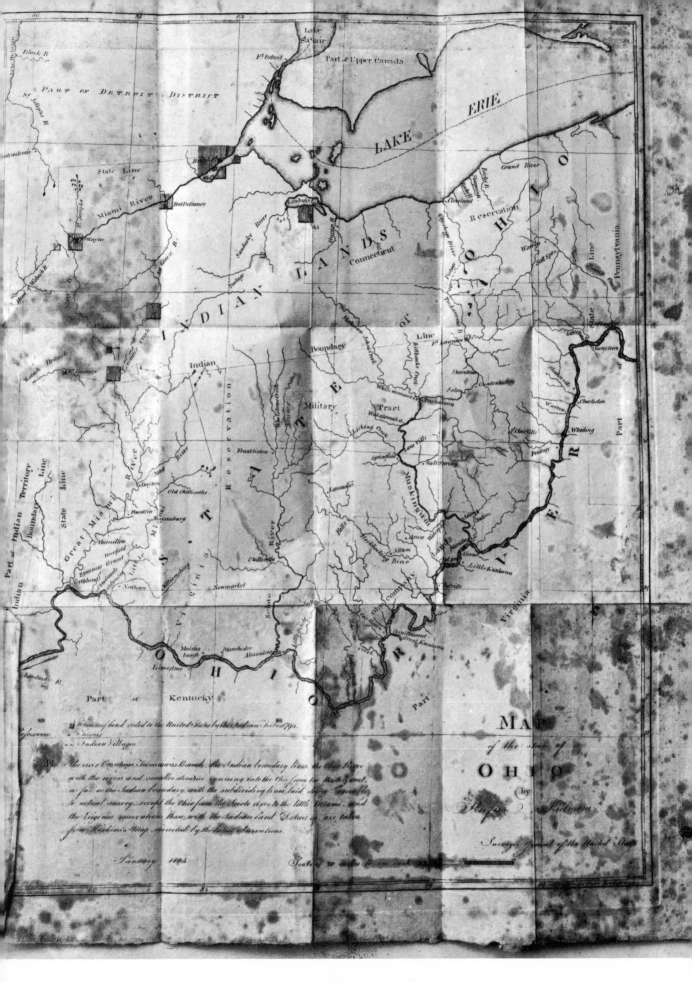

Map of Ohio by Rufus Putnam

III

The American West

ON English maps the Province of Quebec extended to the Ohio and Mississippi rivers, but the Proclamation Act of 1763 forbade purchase or settlement of any lands beyond the Alleghenies. A king could draw a Proclamation Line, like a fence at the edge of luring country, but he could not keep people from looking over it. There were four horizons in America, but it was the West that tugged the mind and the imagination. The eastern colonists had a western future, as ineluctable as the ocean tide.

Virginia's charter described the colony as extending to the western sea, and Virginia men pushed into the western country. One of them went West at nineteen, walking to Pittsburgh and paddling down the Ohio in a big canoe hollowed from a poplar log. With him were three leathery boatmen and a young Welsh preacher who wanted to win some Indians for the Welsh Tract Baptist Church. So George Rogers Clark first saw the interior valley.

In 1774 under the British colonial governor, Lord Dunmore, Virginia militiamen defeated Cornstalk's warriors at Point Pleasant, and so kept the way open for increasing settlement of Kentucky. The militia were still on the frontier when they had word of the forming of the Continental Congress in Philadelphia. Here was a new issue. The Virginians were British subjects, but they were also American. They declared allegiance to the king—as long as he should reign over a free people. A new struggle, with the British, was about to begin.

From Detroit the British sent Indian war parties against the Kentucky settlements. During 1777—"year of the bloody sevens"—young George Rogers Clark saw that the only defense of the frontier was to attack the British posts. He asked the Virginia authorities for an "army" of 500 troops; he got 175. With that file of men he captured Kaskaskia and Vincennes, and so won the Northwest Territory for the American nation. But it was still the Indians' country.

To open the territory to survey and settlement, American forts were built on the Ohio, first at Marietta, then at Cincinnati, and the border wars began. Two expeditions marching north from Cincinnati were driven back by the allied warriors. Then, in 1794, Anthony Wayne built a chain of strongholds up the Miami valley and defeated the tribes at Fallen Timbers. At the Treaty of

Greene Ville the chiefs ceded two thirds of present Ohio, and the doors of the country were open.

In Indiana Territory in the early 1800's Governor William Henry Harrison won large cessions of land from the demoralized tribes. But the Indians, urged by the British in Canada, made a final resistance under Tecumseh. The War of 1812 began with American defeats in the West, where Detroit was surrendered to the British and Indians burned Fort Dearborn on the Chicago River. The next year, 1813, Commodore Perry won control of Lake Erie and General Harrison drove a combined force of British and Indians across the Detroit River.

The Peace of Ghent, on the day before Christmas, 1814, settled the war with England, but more important for the frontier was another treaty, a few months earlier, in the forests of Ohio. At Greenville, the site of Wayne's famous treaty, chiefs of the Indian nations renounced their alliance with the British and ceded lands to the United States. More cessions would follow. Piece by piece the Indian hunting grounds were surveyed into the white man's townships.

SALVATION AND RUM

THE REV. DAVID JONES

In 1761 the Rev. David Jones became minister of the Welsh Tract Baptist Church at Freehold, New Jersey. A few years later he felt impelled to visit and to evangelize the Indians in the little-known Ohio country. In this endeavor he made two trips west. On his first journey, in the summer of 1772, he went down the Ohio River with a nineteen-year-old Virginian whose name would become history—George Rogers Clark.

The missionary efforts of Mr. Jones met with small success, but his journal provides a fresh account of the upper Ohio wilderness and of the Shawnee and Delaware Indians.

During the Revolution Jones served as a chaplain under General St. Clair, and when Wayne conducted his campaign against the Indians in the Ohio country Jones went West again, as chaplain to the troops. He became one of the signers of the Treaty of Greene Ville in 1795.

The following narrative is his account of his first journey west, in 1772.

TUESDAY June 9, left Fort Pitt in company with Mr. George Rogers Clark, and several others, who were disposed to make a tour through this new world. We travelled by water in a canoe, and as I laboured none, had an opportunity of observing the course of the river. It would be too tedious to give a particular account; it may suffice to be more general, and refer the curious reader to a map expected soon to be published by Messrs. Hutchins and Hooper. It may be expected that this performance will be accurate, as greatest part will be done by actual survey. As Mr. Hooper favoured me with the distances of places, the calculations are theirs. From Fort Pitt the river Ohio runs about fifteen miles near a N. W. course; thence near N. about 14 miles; then it makes a great bent for about 20 miles running a little S. of W. thence for near 20 miles S. E. to the place called the Mingo town, where some of that nation yet reside. Some of this town were wont to plunder canoes, therefore we passed them as quietly as possible; and were so happy as not to be discovered by any of them. From this town to Grave Creek is about thirty miles, and the river, taking the meanders of it, may be said

to run a little W. of S. Met here with my interpreter, who came across the country from the waters of Monongehela, and with him some Indians, with whom I had a little conversation. This night my bed was gravel stones by the river side. From Fort Pitt to this creek we were only in one house inhabited by white people. All the way our lodging was on the banks of the river, which at first did not suit me, but custom made it more agreeable.

Saturday June 13, moved to a creek by the Indians called Caapteenin, i.e. Captains Creek. This creek comes into the river from the west side, and is supposed to be about 75 miles E. S. E. from Newcomer's town, which is the chief town of the Delaware Indians. We encamped opposite to Caapteenin on the east side of Ohio. Here were some families of Indians—we went over and conversed with them, and in the evening some of them returned the visit. Mr. Owens was well acquainted with some of them, and let them know what sort of a man I was. They all shewed respect to me; even when some of them afterwards were drunk, they were civil to me, and would take me by the hand and say, "You be minsta." Here we spent the Lord's day: in the evening instructed what Indians came over. The most intelligent auditor is called Frank Stephens. He could speak no English but in this point, was at no loss when Mr. Owens was with me. In this interview, spoke on many subjects, and asked several questions, among others, whether he believed that after death there is a state of eternal happiness and of misery? he replied, this he believed—he proceeded and said, "he considered God as the Giver of all good things; if he killed a deer he thought God gave him that good luck." What he said on this subject raised my expectation, for we know that man is more prone to forget the providence of God, than his existence. While many things were said concerning God, he gave great attention. At this time I felt myself much distressed how to speak so as to make him sensible of the way and manner that we received the scriptures from God. At last these ideas arose in my mind, which were communicated in words to this effect, viz. "Long ago, oh! very long ago: sometimes at one time, and sometimes at another time, God had good men on the earth; and by his great power, God did so confine the imagination of these good men, that at that time they could think nothing but what God would have them think. And while they were thus under this great power of God, they wrote the scriptures, which tell us all things that we should believe concerning God, and all things that we should do to please him. This was the same as if God had spoken himself." This I must say, though I have firmly for many years past believed that the holy scriptures were given by inspiration of God, yet never had before a deeper sensation of their exalted dignity. What a mercy is it that we are thus directed of God! how awful must the case of such be, who either despise or neglect instructions from heaven itself!—What was said on this subject much affected Frank, who replied, "that he believed long ago Indians knew how to worship God, but as they had no writings they had lost all knowledge of him: yet sometimes some of them tried to worship him, but knew not whether their services were pleasing to him or not;" and indeed this must have been the case with all, had not God been pleased to reveal his will to us; for no man hath seen him; but says the Evangelist, "the only begotten Son," which is in the bosom of the Father, he hath "declared him." This brought to mind, what formerly had been quoted in conversation from a certain author, viz. "a philosopher was demanded by an emperor to give an answer to two questions; the first was, whether there is a God? having proper time given to ruminate on the subject, returned an answer in the affirmative: the second was, how to worship God acceptably? after due deliberation answered, that this never could be known, except God is pleased to reveal it himself." Seeing that this is the case, from hence it appears, how exact we should be in all our religious obedience to God; and never deviate from the directions given us in the holy scriptures: for all additions, though under the specious name of decency and order, must be an abomination in the sight of God.

By this time we were surrounded by the evening shades, and repose demanded an end to the present interview—informed Frank, that it was the custom of good white folks to pray to God, before they went to sleep—that we were now going to pray, and would pray for him—and tho' he understood not what was said, yet may be God would give him good thoughts while I was speaking. With this we all rose up to pray; the Indians rose likewise, being previously informed by the interpreter. With a solemn heart and voice addresses were made to God.—Was informed that during the time the Indians looked very seriously at me. When prayer was ended, Frank told my interpreter, that my voice affected his heart; that he thought I spoke the same way that our Saviour did when he was on earth. It is likely that this Indian had heard of our Saviour from the Moravians or their Indians. It was said by Mr. Owens, that it was common among the Delawares, to mention the name of our Saviour: but the case is otherwise among the Shawannees. An answer was expected here by the ambassador sent to the chief town of the Delaware Indians: but a trader having brought rum, all prospects of doing good by any longer continuance, were at an end; and the ambassador delaying his return, concluded to go down to the Little Canhawa, to view the land. This was near 70 miles below, and from

Grave Creek to the Little Canhawa, the river Ohio may be said to run S. W. but it is very crooked, turning to many points of compass.

Tuesday 16, set out for the Little Canhawa, and arrived to it on Thursday 18. This stream comes from the E. and is near 150 yards wide at the mouth. Went up this about ten miles; found, though it was deep at the mouth, that the falls were so shallow, that our canoes were prevented passing further. Went out to view the land on each side, and to kill provisions. Mr. Owens killed several deer, and a stately buffalo bull. The country here is level, and the soil not despisable, though not equal in quality to some other places. It is not well watered, consequently not the most promising for health. In several places the highest land is well adorned with stately pine trees; and yet the soil did not appear too poor to produce good wheat.

Wednesday 24, set out for Caapteenin again. On our way had some bad weather; viewed the land in many places; soil generally good; level land but narrow; good settlements may be made on several creeks; some were well watered; fish in great abundance; some of which we were so happy as to take.

Tuesday 30, came safe to Caapteenin. Here was an Indian sent to me from the Delaware's town, who gave intelligence that their council were not all at home—that they were considering the matter, and in a little time should hear from them again. This answer would have been better understood, had I known them as well then as now. Being indisposed in stomach, which frequently occasioned vomiting after eating meat, and this being our chief sustenance, was reduced to great weakness and was in much need of nourishment better adapted to my condition; therefore moved up to Grave Creek, leaving there our canoes; crossed the desart to Ten Mile Creek, which empties into Monongehela. It was thought the way we travelled made our journey between 50 and 60 miles before we came to the house of Mr. Owens. The season was very warm; all except myself had loads to carry, so that on the 2d day of July with much fatigue, we arrived to the inhabitants, faint, weak, weary and hungry—especially Mr. Clark and myself. No victuals was ever more acceptable than some buttermilk given by the kind inhabitants, which greatly raised my esteem of cows. Stayed at Mr. Owens's over the Lord's day, and preached to a small congregation. To recruit strength, remained in the settlement, and preached next Lord's day near George's Creek on Monongehela to about two hundred hearers.

About this time a second messenger came from the Indians, giving intelligence that some of the chiefs would soon be at Fort Pitt, where a more particular account would be given, &c. At this time many of the inhabitants were near a famine, occasioned by the multitudes lately moved into this new country; so that it was only through favour that supplies were obtained to make another tour of the wilderness.

Tuesday July 14, in company with Messrs. Clark, Higgins and my interpreter, set out for Fort Pitt; and as it was some time before the Indians would be at Fort Pitt, took another tour through the desarts to Ohio. Preached on the Lord's day in a cabin near to a creek called Weeling, to about 15 auditors. In the afternoon having sent word, a few Indians met me, one of which was Frank Stephens. Having all set down on deerskins presented to us for that purpose by the Indians, addressed them on these subjects, viz. 1. The state in which God created man. 2. His fall. 3. The promise of a Saviour; his coming and sufferings. 4. The work of God in renewing our souls to qualify us for heaven, and enabling us to believe on the Saviour. On this occasion was very sensible of the great difficulties of speaking on such important subjects to these poor heathens, who were strangers even to the historical accounts thereof. After due deliberation spoke to this effect, viz. "You see, my brothers, that man is now very bad; he does many bad things; he has a wicked and bad heart: but when God made him at first he was all good, all love. Then he loved God, and loved one another. God said to him, if you will only obey me, you shall always live in a happy state; but if you disobey, you shall surely die, and be miserable. But afterwards man thought, may be, he might be happy and not die, even if he disobeyed God. Then he did that which God told him he should not do. But oh! immediately he lost all his good, and became very bad, having no love to God, nor to one another. In this state God looked on him and said, ah! you have disobeyed, and would not believe me: you must now die, and you deserve to suffer forever: yet I have compassion on you, though you do not deserve it, and will send you a Redeemer. After a long time the Redeemer came, and so great was his love for us, that he himself in our stead endured all the punishment due to our transgressions, in order to make peace between God and us. Now God saith that all that believe on this Saviour shall be happy forever. And to prepare us for that happiness, God by his great power changes the temper of the hearts of all that believe: then they love God and one another. God takes delight in them, and when they die he takes them up into heaven to be forever with himself." Some white people besides my own company were present: it was observable that some of them were more affected than when they had been more immediately addressed. By what appeared expectations were raised; but these Indians had no further opportunities, being in time of the second visit down Ohio with my interpreter.

Monday July 20, set out for Fort Pitt; had a small path called Catfish's Road, which led us through the country between Ohio and Monongehela; had the pleasure of seeing a large extent of good land, but few inhabitants; it is somewhat uneven, but most part habitable. —Came to Fort Pitt on Wednesday July 22; remained about six days; had an opportunity of conversing with several principal Indians of different nations: they all spoke very agreeably, and seemed pleased with my intentions of instructing them. It is possible that these men were honest; but am now so well acquainted with Indian deceit as to know, that when they are among us, to pretend to love what will best recommend them, is their common practice. Being informed that it was some time before any further intelligence could be had respecting my visit: therefore wrote another letter to the Delaware king and chiefs of the nation, informing them, that I had been long from home; could stay no longer at present; but they might expect me out again in the fall.

GAUNT VICTORY

GEORGE ROGERS CLARK AT VINCENNES, 1779

America has always been a restless land, a country of change. But no other period was so changing as the Revolutionary years, when thirteen seaboard colonies became a nation extending to the Mississippi. One man's shadow falls across the whole interior country, the great valley of the Ohio. He saw it first as a youth of nineteen, steering down the wilderness river. He claimed wild land and surveyed the sites of future cities. As a political delegate from Kentucky he voiced the hopes of the frontier in the Virginia Assembly. As a commander he defended it from Indian attack and captured the British strongholds north of the Ohio. In a few momentous years he won the Old Northwest for the new nation.

In the summer of 1778 Clark led a tiny army, 170 men, into the British-held Illinois country. By stealth and daring they took the town of Kaskaskia without a gunshot. When news of this invasion reached Detroit, General Hamilton marched seven hundred British troops and Indians down the Wabash to Fort Sackville at Vincennes. With such a force he could drive the Americans out of the country. But autumn rains had flooded the prairie, and Hamilton waited for good weather.

At Kaskaskia Clark had barely a hundred and fifty men, but an audacious plan gave him confidence. No one would suppose that a weak force would cross a flooded country to attack a stronghold. Clark wrote to Governor Patrick Henry of Virginia: "Great things have been affected by a few men well conducted. Perhaps we may be fortunate."

They were hardly fortunate—marching through waist-deep floodlands, shaking with chills and fever, gaunt with privation—but they succeeded. After a stealthy invasion came the bedlam of battle. Clark kept his men shifting, whooping, firing, until the bewildered British surrendered. The scarlet ranks marched out and the mud-stained men moved in. Clark had won a western empire for the new American nation.

This narrative is from General Clark's Memoir, *the last and longest account of his campaign against the British posts north of the Ohio.*

ON the 29th of January, 1779, Mr. Francis Vigo, a Spanish merchant, who had been at St. Vincennes, arrived and gave the following information:

That Governor Hamilton, with thirty regulars, fifty French volunteers, Indian agents, interpreters, boatmen, etc., that amounted to a considerable number, and about four hundred Indians, had, in December last, taken that post, and as the season was so far advanced, it was thought impossible to reach the Illinois. He sent some of the Indians to Kentucky to watch the Ohio, disbanding of others, etc., the whole to meet again in spring, drive us out of the Illinois and attack the Kentucky settlements, in a body, joined by their southern friends; that all the goods were taken from the merchants of St. Vincent for the king's use; that the troops under Hamilton were repairing the fort, and expected a reinforcement from Detroit in the spring; that they appeared to have plenty of all kinds of stores; that they were strict in their discipline, but that he didn't believe they were under much apprehension of a visit, and believed that, if we could get there undiscovered, we might take the place. In short, we got every information from this gentleman that we could wish for, as he had had good opportunities, and had taken great pains to inform himself, with a design to give intelligence.

We now viewed ourselves in a very critical situation—in a manner cut off from any intercourse between us and the United States. We knew that Governor Hamilton, in the spring, by a junction of his northern and southern Indians, which he had prepared for,

would be at the head of such a force, that nothing in this quarter could withstand his arms; that Kentucky must immediately fall, and well if the desolation would end there. If we could immediately make our way good to Kentucky, we were convinced that before we could raise a force even sufficient to save that country it would be too late, as all the men in it, joined by the troops we had, would not be sufficient, and to get timely succor from the interior frontiers was out of the question. We saw but one alternative, which was to attack the enemy in their quarters. If we were fortunate, it would save the whole; if otherwise it would be nothing more than what would certainly be the consequence if we should not make the attempt.

Encouraged by the idea of the greatness of the consequences that would attend our success—the season of the year being also favorable—as the enemy could not suppose that we should be so mad as to attempt to march eighty leagues through a drowned country in the depths of winter; that they would be off their guard and probably would not think it worth while to keep our spies; that, probably, if we could make our way good, we might surprise them, and [if] we fell through, the country would not be in a worse situation than if we had not made the attempt. These, and many other similar reasons, induced us to resolve to attempt the enterprise, which met with the approbation of every individual belonging to us.

Orders were immediately issued for preparations. The whole country took fire at the alarm and every order was executed with cheerfulness by every description of the inhabitants—preparing provisions, encouraging volunteers, etc.—and, as we had plenty of stores, every man was completely rigged with what he could desire to withstand the coldest weather.

Knowing that the Wabash, at this season of the year, in [all] probability, would be overflowed to five or six miles wide, and to build vessels in the neighborhood of the enemy would be dangerous, to obviate this and to convey our artillery and stores, it was concluded to send a vessel round by water so strong that she might force her way, as she could not be attacked only by water, without she chose it, as the whole of the low lands was under water, and of course she might keep off any heights that were on the rivers.

A large Mississippi boat was immediately purchased and completely fitted out as a galley, mounting two four-pounders and four large swivels and forty-six men, commanded by Captain John Rogers. He set sail on the 4th of February, with orders to force his way up the Wabash as high as the mouth of White river, and to secrete himself until further orders, but if he found himself discovered to do the enemy all the harm he could without running too great a risk of losing his vessel, and not to leave the river until he was out of hope of our arrival by land; but, by all means, to conduct himself so as to give no suspicion of our approach by land. We had great dependence on this vessel. She was far superior to anything the enemy could fit out without building a new one, and, at the worse, if we were discovered, we could build a number of large pirogues, such as they possessed, to attend her, and with such a little fleet, perhaps, pester the enemy very much, and if we saw it our interest, force a landing. At any rate, it would be some time before they would be a match for us on the water.

As we had some time past been in a state of suspense, we had partly prepared for some such event as this. Of course, we were soon complete. The inhabitants of Kaskaskia, being a little cowed since the affair of the supposed intended siege, nothing was said to them on the subject of volunteers until the arrival of those [from] Kohokia, to whom an expensive entertainment, to which they invited all their acquaintances of Kaskaskias, all little differences made up, and by twelve o'clock the next day application was made to raise a company at Kaskaskia, which was granted and completed before night—the whole of the inhabitants exerting themselves in order to wipe off past coolness.

Everything being now ready, on the 5th of February, after receiving a lecture and absolution from the priest, etc., we crossed the Kaskaskia river with one hundred and seventy men; marched about three miles and encamped, where we lay until the 8th (refer to Major Bowman's journal for the particulars of this march), and set out, the weather wet, but, fortunately, not cold for the season, and a great part of the plains under water several inches deep. It was difficult and very fatiguing marching. My object now was to keep the men in spirits. I suffered them to shoot game on all occasions, and feast on it like Indian war-dancers—each company, by turns, inviting the others to their feasts—which was the case every night, as the company that was to give the feast was always supplied with horses to lay up a sufficient store of wild meat in the course of the day, myself and principal officers putting on the woodsmen, shouting now and then, and running as much through the mud and water as any of them. Thus, insensibly, without a murmur, were those men led on to the banks of the Little Wabash, which we reached on the 13th, through incredible difficulties, far surpassing anything that any of us had ever experienced. Frequently the diversions of the night wore off the thoughts of the preceding day. This place is called the two Little Wabashes. They are three miles apart, and from the heights of the one to that of the other, on the opposite shore, is five miles—the whole under water, generally about three feet deep, never under two, and frequently four.

We formed a camp on a height which we found on the bank of the river, and suffered our troops to amuse themselves. I viewed this sheet of water for some time with distrust, but, accusing myself of doubting, I immediately set to work, without holding any consultation about it, or suffering anybody else to do so in my presence, ordered a pirogue to be built immediately and acted as though crossing the water would be only a piece of diversion. As but few could work at the pirogue at a time, pains were taken to find diversion for the rest to keep them in high spirits, but the men were well prepared for this attempt, as they had frequently waded further in water, but, perhaps, seldom above half-leg deep. My anxiety to cross this place continually increased, as I saw that it would at once fling us into a situation of a forlorn hope, as all ideas of retreat would, in some measure, be done away with; that if the men began, after this was accomplished, to think seriously of what they had really suffered, that they prefer risking any seeming difficulty that might probably turn out favorable, than to attempt to retreat, when they would be certain of experiencing what they had already felt, and if [the] weather should but freeze, altogether impracticable, except the ice would bear them.

In the evening of the 14th, our vessel was finished, manned and sent to explore the drowned lands on the opposite side of the Little Wabash with private instructions what report to make, and, if possible, to find some spot of dry land. They found about half an acre and marked the trees from thence back to the camp, and made a very favorable report.

Fortunately the 15th happened to be a warm, moist day for the season. The channel of the river where we lay was about thirty yards wide. A scaffold was built on the opposite shore which was about three feet under water, and our baggage ferried across and put on it; our horses swam across and received their loads at the scaffold, by which time the troops were also brought across, and we began our march through the water. Our vessel [was] loaded with those who were sickly, and we moved on cheerfully, every moment expecting to see dry land, which was not discovered until [we came] to the little dry spot mentioned. This being a smaller branch than the other, the troops immediately crossed and marched on in the water, as usual, to gain and take possession of the nighest height they could discover. Our horses and baggage crossed as they had done at the former river, and proceeded on, following the marked trail of the troops. As tracks could not be

seen in the water, the trees were marked.

By evening we found ourselves encamped on a pretty height in high spirits, each party laughing at the other in consequence of something that had happened in the course of this ferrying business, as they called it. A little antic drummer afforded them great diversion by floating on his drum, etc. All this was greatly encouraging, and they really began to think themselves superior to other men, and that neither the rivers nor the seasons could stop their progress. Their whole conversation now was concerning what they would do when they got about the enemy. They now began to view the main Wabash as a creek, and made no doubt but such men as they were could find a way across it. They wound themselves up to such a pitch that they soon took St. Vincent, divided the spoil, and before bedtime were far advanced on their route to Detroit.

All this was no doubt pleasing to those of us who had more serious thoughts. We were now, as it were, in the enemy's country —no possibility of a retreat if the enemy should discover and overpower us, except by the means of our galley, if we should fall in with her.

We were now convinced that the whole of the low country on the Wabash was drowned, and that the enemy could easily get to us, if they discovered us and wished to risk an action; if they did not, we made no doubt of crossing the river by some means or other. Supposing Captain Rogers had not got to his station, agreeable to his appointment, that we would, if possible, steal some vessels from houses opposite the town, etc. We flattered ourselves that all would be well, and marched on in high spirits.

On the 17th, dispatched Mr. Kennedy and three men off to cross the river Embarrass (this river is six miles from St. Vincennes), and, if possible, to get some vessels in the vicinity of the town, but principally if he could get some intelligence. He proceeded on, and getting to the river found that the country between that and the Wabash overflowed. We marched down below the mouth of the Embarrass, attempting, in vain, to get to the banks of the Wabash. Late in the night, find-

Above, left: The surrender of Fort Sackville, Vincennes, painted by Ezra Winter. Courtesy Indiana State Library   Above, right: George Rogers Clark. Courtesy Anthony Wayne Pkwy Bd

ing a dry spot, we encamped, and were aroused, for the first time, by the morning gun from the garrison. We continued our march, and about two o'clock, 18th, gained the banks of the Wabash, three leagues below the town, where we encamped; dispatched four men across the river on a raft to find land, if possible, march to the town, if possible, and get some canoes privately. Captain W. McCarty with a few [men] set out the next [day] in a little canoe he had made, for the same purpose. Both parties returned without success. The first could not get to land, and the captain was driven back by the appearance of a camp. The canoe was immediately dispatched down the river to meet the galley, with orders to proceed day and night; but, determined to have every string to my bow I possibly could, I ordered canoes to be built in a private place, not yet out of hopes of our boat arriving—if she did, those

canoes would augment our fleet; if she did not before they were ready they would answer our purpose without her.

Many of our volunteers began, for the first time, to despair. Some talked of returning, but my situation now was such that I was past all uneasiness. I laughed at them, without persuading or ordering them to desist from any such attempt, but told them that I should be glad they would go out and kill some deer. They went, confused with such conduct. My own troops I knew had no idea of abandoning an enterprise from the want of provisions, while there was plenty of good horses in their possession; and I knew that, without any violence, the volunteers could be detained for a few days, in the course of which time our fate would be known. I conducted myself in such a manner that caused the whole to believe that I had no doubt of success, which kept their spirits up.

On the 20th the water guard decoyed on shore a boat with five Frenchmen and some provisions on board, they on their way to join a party of hunters down the river. . . . Early of the 21st the crossing of our troops commenced. . . . This last march through the water was so far superior to anything the Frenchmen had an idea of that they were backward in speaking, said that the nearest land to us was a small league called the sugar camp, on the bank of the river. A canoe was sent off and returned without finding that we could pass. I went in her myself and sounded the water; found it deep as to my neck.

I returned with a design to have the men transported on board the canoes to the sugar camp, which I knew would spend the whole day and ensuing night, as the vessels would pass but slowly through the bushes. The loss of so much time to men half starved was a matter of consequence. I would have given now a great deal for a day's provision or for one of our horses. I returned but slowly to the troops, giving myself time to think. On our arrival all ran to hear what was the report. Every eye was fixed on me. I unfortunately spoke in a serious manner to one of the officers. The whole were alarmed without knowing what I said. They ran from one to another, bewailing their situation. I viewed their confusion for about one minute, whispered to those near me to do as I did, immediately put some water in my hand, poured on powder, blackened my face, gave the war-whoop and marched into the water, without saying a word, like a flock of sheep. I ordered those near me to begin a favorite song of theirs. It soon passed through the line and the whole went on cheerfully.

I now intended to have them transported across the deepest part of the water, but when about waist deep one of the men informed me that he thought he felt a path— a path is very easily discovered under water by the feet. We examined and found it so, and concluded that it kept on the highest ground, which it did, and, by taking pains to follow it, we got to the sugar camp without the least difficulty (and what gave the alarm at the former proved fortunate), where there was about half an acre of dry ground, at least not under water, where we took up our lodging.

The Frenchmen we had taken on the river appeared to be uneasy at our situation. They begged that they might be permitted to go in the two canoes to town in the night. They said that they would bring from their own houses provisions without a possibility of any person knowing it; that some of our men should go with them, as a surety of their good conduct; that it was impossible that we could march from the place until the water fell; that [would not be] for a few days, for the plain, for upward of three miles, was covered two [feet] deep.

Some of the selected believed that it might be done. I would not suffer it. I never could well account for this piece of obstinacy and give satisfactory reasons to myself or anybody else why I denied a proposition apparently so easy to execute and of so much advantage, but something seemed to tell me that it should not be done, and it was not.

The most of the weather that we had on this march was moist and warm for the season. This was the coldest night we had. The ice, in the morning, was from one-half to three-quarters of an inch thick near the shores and in still waters. The morning was the finest we had on our march. A little after sunrise I lectured the whole. What I said to them I forget, but it may be easily imagined by a person who could possess my affections for them at that time. I concluded by informing them that surmounting the plain, that was then in full view, and reaching the opposite woods, would put an end to their fatigue; that in a few hours they would have a sight of their long wished for object, and immediately stepped into the water without waiting for any reply. A huzza took place. We generally marched through the water in a line; it was much easiest. Before a third entered, I halted, and, further to prove the men, having some suspicion of three or four, I hallooed to Major Bowman, ordering him to fall in the rear with twenty-five men and put to death any man who refused to march, as we wished to have no such person among us. The whole gave a cry of approbation that it was right, and on we went. This was the most trying of all the difficulties we had experienced. I generally kept fifteen or twenty of the strongest men next myself, and judging from my own feelings what must be that of others. Getting about the middle of the plain, the water about knee deep, I found myself sensibly failing, and as there were [here] no trees nor bushes for the men to support themselves by, I doubted that many of the most weak would be drowned. I ordered the canoes to make the land, discharge their loading, and play backward and forward, with all diligence, and pick up the men, and to encourage the party; sent some of the strongest men forward with orders when they got to a certain distance to pass the word back that the water was getting shallow, and when getting near the woods to cry out "land." This stratagem had its desired effect. The men, encouraged by it, exerted themselves almost beyond their abilities—the weak holding by the stronger, and frequently one with two others' help, and this was of infinite advantage to the weak. The water never got shallower, but continued deepening—even [when] getting to the woods, where the men expected land. The water was up to my shoulders, but gaining the woods was of great consequence. All the low men, and the weakly, hung to the trees and floated on the old logs until they were taken off by the canoes. The strong and tall got ashore and built fires. Many would reach the shore, and fall with their bodies half in the water, not being able to support themselves without it.

This was a delightful, dry spot of ground, of about ten acres. We soon found that the fires answered no purpose, but that two strong men taking a weaker one by the arms was the only way to recover him, and, being a delightful day, it soon did. But fortunately, as if designed by Providence, a canoe of Indian squaws and children was coming up to town, and took through part of this plain as a nigh way. It was discovered by our canoes as they were out after the men. They gave chase and took the Indian canoe, on board of which was near half a quarter of buffalo, some corn, tallow, kettles, etc. This was a grand prize and was invaluable. Broth was immediately made and served out to the most weakly

with great care; most of the whole got a little, but a great many gave their part to the weakly, jocosely saying something cheering to their comrades. This little refreshment and fine weather, by the afternoon, gave new life to the whole.

Crossing a narrow, deep lake in the canoes and marching some distance, we came to a copse of timber called the Warrior's Island. We were now in full view of the fort and town, not a shrub between us, at about two miles' distance. Every man now feasted his eyes and forgot that he had suffered anything, saying that all that had passed was owing to good policy and nothing but what a man could bear, and that a soldier had no right to think, etc., passing from one extreme to another, which is common in such cases. It was now we had to display our abilities. The plain between us and the town was not a perfect level. The sunken grounds were covered with water full of ducks. We observed several men out on horseback, shooting of them, within a half mile of us, and sent out as many of our active young Frenchmen to decoy and take one of these men prisoner in such a manner as not to alarm the others, which they did. The information we got from this person was similar to that which we got from those we took on the river, except that of the British having that evening completed the wall of the fort, etc., and that there were a good many Indians in town.

Our situation was now truly critical—no possibility of retreating in case of defeat—and in full view of a town that had, at this time, upward of six hundred men in it, troops, inhabitants and Indians. The crew of the galley, though not fifty men, would have been now a reinforcement of immense magnitude to our little army (if I may so call it), but we would not think of them. We were now in the situation that I had labored to get ourselves in. The idea of being made prisoner was foreign to almost every man, as they expected nothing but torture from the savages if they fell into their hands. Our fate was now to be determined, probably in a few hours. We knew that nothing but the most daring conduct would insure success. I knew that a number of the inhabitants wished us well; that many were lukewarm to the interest of either; and I also learned that the grand chief, the Tobacco's Son, had, but a few days before, openly declared, in council with the British, that he was a brother and friend to the big knives. These were favorable circumstances, and as there was but little probability of our remaining until dark undiscovered as great numbers of fowlers go out in the day, and that we now see and hear them through the plains around us, I determined to begin the career immediately, and wrote the following placard to the inhabitants and sent it off by the prisoner just taken, who was not permitted to see our numbers:

To the Inhabitants of Post Vincennes:

Gentlemen—Being now within two miles of your village with my army, determined to take your fort this night, and not being willing to surprise you, I take this method to request such of you as are true citizens and willing to enjoy the liberty I bring you, to remain still in your houses; and that those, if any there be, that are friends to the king of England, will instantly repair to the fort and join his troops and fight like men. And if any such as do not go to the fort should hereafter be discovered that did not repair to the garrison, they may depend on severe punishment. On the contrary, those who are true friends to liberty may expect to be well treated as such, and I once more request that they may keep out of the streets, for every person found under arms, on my arrival, will be treated as an enemy.
(Signed)   G. R. Clark.

I had various ideas on the supposed results of this letter. I knew that it could do us no damage, but that it would cause the lukewarm to be decided, encourage our friends and astonish our enemies; that they would, of course, suppose our information good, and our forces so numerous that we were sure of success—and this was only a piece of parade; that the army was from Kentucky and not from the Illinois, as it would be thought quite impossible to march from thence, and that my name was only made use of. This they firmly believed until the next morning, when I was shown to them by a person in the fort who knew me well—or that we were a flying party that only made use of this stratagem to give ourselves [a chance] to retreat. This latter idea I knew would soon be done away with. Several gentlemen sent their compliments to their friends, under borrowed names, well known at St. Vincent, and the persons supposed to be at Kentucky. The soldiers all had instructions that their common conversation, when speaking of our numbers, should be such that a stranger overhearing must suppose that there were near one thousand of us.

We anxiously viewed this messenger until he entered the town, and in a few minutes could discover by our glasses some stir in every street that we could penetrate into, and great numbers running or riding out into the commons, we supposed to view us, which was the case. But what surprised us was, that nothing had yet happened that had the appearance of the garrison being alarmed—no drum nor gun.

We began to suppose that the information we got from our prisoners was false, and that the enemy already knew of us and were prepared. Every man had been impatient—the moment had now arrived. A little before sunset we moved and displayed ourselves in full view of the town, crowds gazing at us. We were flinging ourselves into certain destruction—or success: there was no midway thought of. We had but little to say to our men, except in calculating an idea of the necessity of obedience, etc. We knew they did not want encouraging, and that anything might be attempted with them that was possible for such a number—perfectly cool, under proper subordination, pleased with the prospect before them, and much attached to their officers. They all declared that they were convinced that an implicit obedience to orders was the only thing that would ensure success, and hoped that no mercy would be shown the person who should violate them, but should be immediately put to death. Such language as this from soldiers to persons in our station must have been exceedingly agreeable. We moved on slowly in full view of the town; but, as it was a point of some consequence to us to make ourselves appear as formidable [as possible], we, in leaving the covert that we were in, marched and counter-marched in such a manner that we appeared numerous.

In raising volunteers in the Illinois, every person who set about, the business had a set of colors given him, which they brought with them to the amount of ten or twelve pairs. These were displayed to the best advantage; and as the low plain we marched through was not a perfect level, but had frequent raisings in it seven or eight feet higher than the common level, which was covered with water, and as these raisings generally ran in an oblique direction to the town, we took the advantage of one of them, marching through the water under it, which completely prevented our men being numbered. But our colors showed considerably above the heights, as they were fixed on long poles procured for the purpose, and at a distance made no despicable appearance; and as our young Frenchmen had, while we lay on the Warrior's Island, decoyed and taken several fowlers, with their horses, officers were mounted on these horses and rode about, more completely to deceive the enemy. In this manner we moved, and directed our march in such a [manner] as to suffer it to be dark before we had advanced more than half way to the town. We then suddenly altered our direction, and crossed ponds where they could not have suspected us, and about eight o'clock gained the heights back of the town. As there was yet no hostile appearance, we were impatient to have the cause unriddled.

Lieutenant Bailey was ordered, with fourteen men, to march and fire on the fort. The main body moved in a different direction and took possession of the strongest part of the town. The firing now commenced on the fort, but they did not believe it was an enemy until one of their men was shot down through a port as he was lighting his match, as drunken Indians frequently saluted the fort after night. The drums now sounded and the business fairly commenced on both sides. Reinforcements were sent to the attack of the garrison, while other arrangements were making in town, etc.

We now found that the garrison had known nothing of us; that, having finished the fort that evening, they had amused themselves at different games, and had retired just before my letter arrived, as it was near roll-call. The placard being made public, many of the inhabitants were afraid to show themselves out of the houses for fear of giving offense, and not one dare give information.

Our friends flew to the commons and other convenient places to view the pleasing sight, which was observed from the garrison and the reason asked, but a satisfactory excuse was given; and, as a part of the town lay between our line of march and the garrison, we could not be seen by the sentinels on the walls. Captain W. Shannon and another being some time before taken prisoner by one of their [raiding parties] and that evening brought in, the party had discovered at the sugar camp some signs of us.

They supposed it to be a party of observation that intended to land on the height some distance below the town. Captain Lamothe was sent to intercept them. It was at him the people said they were looking when they were asked the reason of their unusual stir. Several suspected persons had been taken to the garrison. Among them was Mr. Moses Henry. Mrs. Henry went, under the pretense of carrying him provisions, and whispered him the news and what she had seen. Mr. Henry conveyed it to the rest of his fellow-prisoners, which gave them much pleasure, particularly Captain Helm, who amused himself very much during the siege, and, I believe, did much damage.

Ammunition was scarce with us, as the most of our stores had been put on board of the galley. Though her crew was but few, such a reinforcement to us at this period would have been invaluable in many instances. But, fortunately, at the time of its being reported that the whole of the goods in the town were to be taken for the king's use, for which the owners were to receive bills, Colonel Legras, Major Bosseron and others had buried the greatest part of their powder and ball. This was immediately produced, and we found ourselves well supplied by those gentlemen.

The Tobacco's Son being in town with a number of warriors, immediately mustered them, and let us know that he wished to join us, saying that by the morning he would have a hundred men. He received for answer that we thanked him for his friendly disposition, and, as we were sufficiently strong ourselves, we wished him to desist and that we would counsel on the subject in the morning; and, as we knew that there were a number of Indians in and near the town who were our enemies, some confusion might happen if our men should mix in the dark, but hoped that we might be favored with his counsel and company during the night, which was agreeable to him.

The garrison was now completely surrounded, and the firing continued without intermission, except about fifteen minutes a little before day until about nine o'clock the following morning. It was kept up by the whole of the troops—joined by a few of the young men of the town, who got permission —except fifty men kept as a reserve in case of casualty happening, which was many and diverting in the course of the night. I had made myself fully acquainted with the situation of the fort, town, and the parts relative to each. The gardens of St. Vincent were very near, and about two-thirds around it; the fencing of good pickets, well set, and about six feet high where those were watching. Breast-works were soon made by tearing down old houses, gardens, etc., so that those within had very little advantage to those without the fort, and not knowing the number of the enemy, thought themselves in a worse situation than they really were.

The cannons of the garrison were on the upper floors of strong block-houses, at each angle of the fort, eleven feet above the surface, and the ports so badly cut that many of our troops lay under the fire of them within twenty or thirty yards of the walls. They did no damage, except to the buildings of the town, some of which they much shattered, and their musketry, in the dark, employed against woodsmen covered by houses, palings, ditches, the banks of the river, etc., was but of little avail and did no damage to us, except wounding a man or two, and as we could not afford to lose men, great care was taken to preserve them sufficiently covered and to keep up a hot fire in order to

intimidate the enemy as well as to destroy them. The embrasures of their cannons were frequently shut, for our riflemen, finding the true direction of them, would pour in such volleys when they were open that the men could not stand to the guns—seven or eight of them in a short time got cut down. Our troops would frequently abuse the enemy in order to aggravate them to open their ports and fire their cannons, that they might have the pleasure of cutting them down with their rifles, fifty of which, perhaps, would be leveled the moment the port flew open, and I believe that if they had stood at their artillery the greater part of them would have been destroyed in the course of the night, as the most of our men lay within thirty yards of the wall, and in a few hours were covered equally to those within the walls and much more experienced in that mode of fighting. The flash of our guns detected them, perhaps, the instant the man moved his body. The moment there was the least appearance at one of their loop-holes, there would probably be a dozen guns fired at it.

Sometimes an irregular fire, as hot as possible, was kept up from different directions for a few minutes, and then only a continual scattering fire at the ports as usual, and a great noise and laughter immediately commenced in different parts of the town by the reserved parties, as if they had only fired on the fort a few minutes for amusement, and as if those continually firing at the fort were only regularly relieved. Conduct similar to this kept the garrison eternally alarmed. They did not know what moment they might be stormed or [blown up?], as they could plainly discover that we had flung up some entrenchments across the streets, and appeared to be frequently very busy under the bank of the river, which was within thirty feet of the walls.

The situation of the magazine we knew well. Captain Bowman began some works in order to blow it up in case our artillery should arrive, but as we knew that we were daily liable to be overpowered by the numerous bands of Indians on the river, in case they had again joined the enemy (the certainty of which we were unacquainted with), we resolved to lose no time but to get the fort in our possession as soon as possible. If [our] vessel did not arrive before the ensuing night, we resolved to undermine the fort, and fixed on the spot and plan of executing this work, which we intended to commence the next day.

The Indians of different tribes that were inimical had left the town and neighborhood. Captain Lamothe continued to hover about it, in order, if possible, to make his way good into the fort. Parties attempted in vain to surprise him. A few of his party were taken, one of which was Maisonville, a famous Indian partisan. Two lads, who captured him, tied him to a post in the street, and fought from behind him as a breastwork—supposing that the enemy would not fire at them for fear of killing him, as he would alarm them by his voice. The lads were ordered, by an officer who discovered them at their amusement, to untie their prisoner and take him off to the guard, which they did, but were so inhuman as to take part of his scalp on the way. There happened to him no other damage. As almost the whole of the persons who were most active in the department of Detroit were either in the fort or with Captain Lamothe, I got extremely uneasy for fear that he would not fall into our power, knowing that he would go off if he could not get into the fort in the course of the night.

Finding that, without some unforeseen accident, the fort must inevitably be ours, and that a reinforcement of twenty men, although considerable to them, would not be of great moment to us in the present situation of affairs, and knowing that we had weakened them by killing or wounding many of their gunners, after some deliberation we concluded to risk the reinforcement in preference of his going again among the Indians. The garrison had at least a month's provisions, and if they could hold out, in the course of that time he might do us much damage. A little before day the troops were withdrawn from their positions about the fort, except a few parties of observation, and the firing totally ceased. Orders were given, in case [of Lamothe's approach], not to alarm or fire on him without a certainty of killing or taking the whole. In less than a quarter of an hour he passed within ten feet of an officer and a party who lay concealed. Ladders were flung over to them, and as they mounted them our party shouted. Many of them fell from the top of the walls— some within and others back; but as they were not fired on they all got over, much to the joy of their friends, which was easily discovered by us; but, on considering the matter, they must have been convinced that it was a scheme of ours to let them in, and that we were so strong as to care but little about them or the manner of their getting into the garrison, our troops hallooing and diverting themselves at them while mounting, without firing at them, and being frequently told by our most black-guard soldiers of the scheme, and reason for suffering them to get into the fort—which on reflection they must have believed—but we knew that their knowledge of it could now do us no damage, but rather intimidate them. However, the garrison appeared much elated at the recovery of a valuable officer and party.

The firing immediately commenced on both sides with double vigor, and I believe that more noise could not have been made by the same number of men—their shouts could not be heard for the firearms; but a continual blaze was kept around the garrison, without much being done, until about daylight, when our troops were drawn off to posts prepared for them, from about sixty to a hundred yards from the garrison. A loophole then could scarcely be darkened but a rifle-ball would pass through it. To have stood to their cannon would have destroyed their men without a probability of doing much service. Our situation was nearly similar. It would have been imprudent in either party to have wasted their men, without some decisive stroke required it.

Thus the attack continued until about nine o'clock on the morning of the 24th. Learning that the two prisoners they had brought in the day before had a considerable number of letters with them, I supposed it an express that we expected about this time, which I knew to be of the greatest moment to us, as we had not received one since our arrival in the country; and, not being fully acquainted with the character of our enemy, we were doubtful that those papers might be destroyed, to prevent which I sent a flag, with a letter, demanding the garrison and desiring Governor Hamilton not to destroy them, with some threats of what I would do in case that he did if the garrison should fall into my hands. His answer was that they were not disposed to be awed into anything unbecoming British subjects.

The firing then commenced warmly for a considerable time, and we were obliged to be careful in preventing our men from exposing themselves too much, as they were now much animated, having been refreshed during the flag. They frequently mentioned their wishes to storm the place and put an end to the business at once. This would at this time have been a piece of rashness. Our troops got warm.

The firing was heavy, through every crack that could be discovered in any part of the fort, with cross shot. Several of the garrison got wounded, and no possibility of standing near the embrasures. Towards the evening a flag appeared, with the following proposition:

Governor Hamilton proposes to Colonel Clark a truce for three days, during which time he proposes there shall be no defensive work carried on in the garrison, on condition that Colonel Clark shall observe, on his part, a like cessation of any offensive work. That is, he wishes to confer with Colonel Clark as soon as can be, and promises, that, whatever may pass between these two and another person, mutually agreed upon to be present, shall remain secret till matters be finished, as he wishes that, whatever the result of their conference, it may be to the honor and credit of each party. If Colonel Clark makes a difficulty of coming into the fort, Lieutenant-Governor Hamilton will speak to him by the gate.

(signed)   Henry Hamilton.
24th February, 1779.

I was greatly at a loss to conceive what reason Governor Hamilton could have for wishing a truce of three days on such terms as he proposed. Numbers said it was a scheme to get me into their possession. I had a differ-

ent opinion and no idea of his possessing such sentiments, as an act of that kind would infallibly ruin him, but was convinced that he had some prospect of success, or otherways, of extricating himself. Although we had the greatest reason to expect a reinforcement in less than three days that would at once put an end to the siege, I yet did not think it prudent to agree to the proposals, and sent the following answer:

Colonel Clark's compliments to Governor Hamilton, and begs leave to inform him that he will not agree to any other terms than that of Mr. Hamilton surrendering himself and garrison prisoners at discretion. If Mr. Hamilton is desirous of a conference with Colonel Clark, he will meet him at the church, with Captain Helm, 24th February, 1779.

G. R. Clark.

We met at the church, about eighty yards from the fort—Lieutenant-Governor Hamilton, Major Hay, superintendent of Indian affairs; Captain Helm, their prisoner; Major Bowman and myself. The conference began. Governor Hamilton produced articles of capitulation, signed, that contained various articles, one of which was that the garrison should be surrendered on their being permitted to go to Pensacola on parole. After deliberating on every article, I rejected the whole. He then wished that I would make some proposition. I told him that I had no other to make than what I had already made—that of his surrendering as prisoners at discretion. I said that his troops had behaved with spirit, that they could not suppose they would be worse treated in consequence of it, with their viewing us as savages; that if he chose to comply with the demand, though hard, perhaps the sooner the better; that it was in vain to make any proposition to me; that he, by this time, must be sensible that the garrison would fall; that both of us must [view?] that all blood spilled for the future by the garrison as murder; that my troops were already impatient, and called aloud for permission to tear down and storm the fort; if such a step was taken, many, of course, would be cut down, and the result of an enraged body of woodsmen breaking in must be obvious to him—it would be out of the power of an American officer to save a single man.

Various altercations took place for a considerable time. Captain Helm attempted to moderate our fixed determination. I told him he was a British prisoner, and it was doubtful whether or not he could, with propriety, speak on the subject. Governor Hamilton then said that Captain Helm was from that moment liberated, and might use his pleasure. I informed the captain that I would not receive him on such terms; that he must return to the garrison and await his fate. I then told Governor Hamilton that hostilities should not commence until fifteen minutes after the drums gave the alarm. We took our leave and parted but a few steps when the governor stopped, and, politely, asked me if I would be so kind as to give him my reasons for refusing the garrison on any other terms than those I had offered. I told him I had no objections in giving him my real reasons, which were simply these: That I knew the greater part of the principal Indian partisans of Detroit were with him; that I wanted an excuse to put them to death, or otherwise treat them, as I thought proper; that the cries of the widows and the fatherless on the frontiers, which they had occasioned, now required their blood from my hands, and that I did not choose to be so timorous as to disobey the absolute commands of their authority, which I looked upon to be next to divine; that I would rather lose fifty men than not to empower myself to execute this piece of business with propriety; that if he chose to risk the massacre of his garrison for their sakes, it was at his own pleasure, and that I might, perhaps, take it into my head to send for some of the widows to see it executed.

Major Hay paying great attention, I had observed a kind of distrust in his countenance, which, in a great measure, influenced my conversation during this time. On my concluding, "Pray, sir," said he, "who is that you call Indian partisans?" "Sir," I replied, "I take Major Hay to be one of the principals." I never saw a man in the moment of execution so struck as he appeared to be—pale and trembling, scarcely able to stand. Governor Hamilton blushed, and, I observed, was much affected at his behavior in [our] presence! Major Bowman's countenance sufficiently explained his disdain for the one, and his sorrow for the other. I viewed the whole with such sentiments as I supposed natural to some men in such cases. Some moments elapsed without a word passing, as we could now form such disposition with our troops as render the fort almost useless. To deface that then could be no danger of course; supposed it prudent to let the British troops remain in the fort until the following morning. We should not have had [such] suspicions as to make so much precaution, but I must confess that we could not help doubting the honor of men who would condescend to encourage the barbarity of the Indians, although almost every man had conceived a favorable opinion of Governor Hamilton. I believe what affected myself made some impression on the whole, and I was happy to find that he never deviated, while he staid with us, from that dignity of conduct that became an officer in his situation. The morning of the 25th approaching, arrangements were made for receiving the garrison (which consisted of seventy-nine men), and about ten o'clock it was delivered in form, and everything was immediately arranged to the best advantage on either side. From that moment my resolutions changed respecting Governor Hamilton's situation. I told him that we would return to our respective posts; that I would reconsider the matter, and that I would let him know the result. If we thought of making any further proposals [than] that of [his] surrendering at discretion, he should know it by the flag—if not, to be on his guard at a certain beat of the drum. No offensive measures should be taken in the meantime. Agreed to, and we parted.

What had passed being made known to our officers, it was agreed that we should moderate our resolutions. The following articles (Major Bowman's MS. journal) were signed and the garrison capitulated:

1. Lieutenant-Governor Hamilton engages to deliver up to Colonel Clark Fort Sackville, as it is at present, with all the stores, etc.

2. The garrison are to deliver themselves as prisoners of war and march out, with their arms and accoutrements, etc.

3. The garrison to be delivered up at ten o'clock tomorrow.

4. Three days' time to be allowed the garrison to settle their accounts with the inhabitants and traders of this place.

5. The officers of the garrison to be allowed their necessary baggage, etc.
Signed at Post St. Vincent (Vincennes), 24th February, 1779.

Agreed, for the following reasons: The remoteness from succor, the state and quantity of provisions, etc.; unanimity of officers and men in its expediency, the honorable terms allowed, and, lastly, the confidence in a generous enemy.
(Signed)   Henry Hamilton,
Lieutenant-Governor and Superintendent.

The business being now nearly at an end, troops were posted in several strong houses around the garrison and patroled during the night to prevent any deception that might be attempted. The remainder, off duty, lay on their arms, and, for the first time for many days past, got some rest.

A LADY AND A BLOCKHOUSE

JACOB BURNET

Upon graduation from Princeton, Jacob Burnet went West in 1796 and became a leader in the social and political life of early Cincinnati. His first friend on the frontier was a young army officer, Lieutenant William Henry Harrison, commandant at Fort Washington. Forty years later at the Harrisburg Convention, Burnet made the speech which nominated Harrison for the nation's presidency.

Burnet's Notes on the Settlement of the North-Western Territory *is a vividly detailed account of the development of western Ohio through the Territorial period. The following passage, describing the beginnings of settlement in the Cincinnati district, discloses the highly personal reasons that led an army officer to choose Cincinnati as the site of Fort Washington—a choice which soon made it the emporium of the West.*

THREE parties were formed to occupy and improve separate portions of Judge Symmes' purchase, between the Miami rivers. The first, led by Major Benjamin Stites, consisted of eighteen or twenty, who landed in November, 1788, at the mouth of the Little Miami river, within the limits of a tract of ten thousand acres, purchased by Major Stites, from Judge Symmes. They constructed a log fort, and laid out the town of Columbia, which soon became a promising village. Among them were Colonel Spencer, Major Gano, Judge Goforth, Francis Dunlavy, Major Kibbey, Reverend John Smith, Judge Foster, Colonel Brown, Mr. Hubbell, Captain Flinn, Jacob White, and John Riley.

They were all men of energy and enterprise, and were more numerous than either of the parties who commenced their settlements below them on the Ohio. Their village was also more flourishing, and for two or three years contained a larger number of inhabitants than any other in the Miami purchase. This superiority, however, did not continue, as will appear from the sequel.

The second party destined for the Miami, was formed at Limestone, under Matthias Denman and Robert Patterson, amounting to twelve or fifteen in number. After much difficulty and danger, caused by floating ice in the river, they landed on the north bank of the Ohio, opposite the mouth of Licking, on the 24th of December, 1788. Their purpose was to establish a station, and lay out a town according to a plan agreed on, before they left Limestone. The name adopted for the proposed town was Losanteville, which had been manufactured by a pedantic foreigner, whose name, fortunately, has been forgotten. It was formed, as he said, from the words *Le os ante ville*, which he rendered "the village opposite the mouth." Logicians may decide whether the words might not be rendered more correctly, the mouth before the village. Be that as it may, the settlement then formed was immediately designated by the name adopted for the projected town—though the town itself never was laid out, for reasons which will be explained hereafter. Yet, from the facts stated, a very general belief has prevailed that the original name of the town of Cincinnati was Losanteville, and that through the influence of Governor St. Clair and others, that name was abandoned, and the name of Cincinnati substituted. This impression, though a natural one, under the circumstances of the case, was nevertheless incorrect.

It is impossible to say what influence operated on the minds of the proprietors, to induce them to adopt the name of Cincinnati, in preference to the one previously proposed. Judge Symmes, being on the spot, might have advised it; but it is not probable that Governor St. Clair had any agency in it, as he was at the time negotiating a treaty with the north-western Indians, at Marietta, between which place and Cincinnati, there was then but very little intercourse. The truth may be gathered from the facts of the case, which are these.

Matthias Denman, of Springfield, New Jersey, had purchased the fraction of land on the bank of the Ohio, and the entire section adjoining it on the north, which, on the survey of Symmes' grant should be found to lie opposite the mouth of Licking river. In the summer of 1788, he came out to the west to see the lands he had purchased, and to examine the country. On his return to Limestone, he met among others, Colonel Patterson, of Lexington, and a surveyor by the name of Filson. Denman communicated to them his intention of laying out a town on his land, opposite Licking; and, after some conversation, agreed to take them in as partners, each paying a third of the purchase-money; and, on the further condition, that Colonel Patterson should exert his influence to obtain settlers, and that Filson, in the ensuing spring, should survey the town, stake off the lots, and superintend the sale. They also agreed on the plan of the town, and to call it Losanteville. This being done, Patterson and Filson, with a party of settlers, proceeded to the ground, where they arrived late in December. In the course of the winter, before any attempt had been made to lay out the town, Filson went on an exploring expedition, with Judges Symmes, and others, who had it in contemplation to become purchasers, and settle in the country. After the party had proceeded some thirty or forty miles into the wilderness, Filson, for some cause not now known, left them, for the purpose of returning to the settlements on the Ohio; and in that attempt, was murdered by the Indians. This terminated his contract with Denman, as no part of the consideration had been paid, and his personal services, in surveying the town, and superintending the sale of the lots, had become impracticable.

Mr. Denman, being yet at Limestone, entered into another contract with Colonel Patterson and Israel Ludlow, by which Ludlow was to perform the same services as were to have been rendered by the unfortunate Filson, had he lived to execute his contract. A new plan of a town was then made, differing, in many important respects, from the former,—particularly as to the public square, the commons, and the names of the streets. The whimsical name which had been adopted for the town to be laid out under the first contract, was repudiated, and Cincinnati selected, as the name of the town, to be laid out under the new contract. Late in the succeeding fall, Colonel Ludlow commenced a survey of the town which has since become the Queen City of the West. He first laid off the lots, which, by previous agreement, were to be disposed of as donations to volunteer

Above: Fort Washington. *Courtesy Anthony Wayne Pkwy Bd*   Below: Cincinnati in 1800; Fort Washington in middle distance at right. *Courtesy Historical and Philosophic Society of Ohio*

CINCINNATI-1800.

settlers, and completed the survey at his leisure.

A misapprehension has prevailed, as appears from some recent publications, in regard to the price paid by the proprietors for the land on which the city stands. The original purchase by Mr. Denman, included a section and a fractional section, containing about eight hundred acres; for which he paid five shillings per acre, in Continental Certificates, which were then worth, in specie, five shillings on the pound—so that the specie price per acre was fifteen pence. That sum multiplied by the number of acres, will give the original cost of the plat of Cincinnati.

The third party of adventurers to the Miami Purchase, were under the immediate care and direction of Judge Symmes. They left Limestone on the 29th of January, 1789, and on their passage down the river, were obstructed, delayed, and exposed to imminent danger from floating ice, which covered the river. They, however, reached the Bend, the place of their destination, in safety, early in February. The first object of the Judge was to found a city at that place, which had received the name of North Bend, from the fact that it was the most northern bend in the Ohio river below the mouth of the Great Kanawha.

The water-craft used in descending the Ohio, in those primitive times, were flat-boats, made of green oak plank, fastened by wooden pins to a frame of timber, and caulked with tow, or any other pliant substance that could be procured. Boats similarly constructed on the northern waters, were then called *arks*, but on the western rivers, they were denominated *Kentucky boats*. The materials of which they were composed, were found to be of great utility in the construction of temporary buildings for safety, and for protection from the inclemency of the weather, after they had arrived at their destination.

At the earnest solicitation of the Judge, General Harmar sent Captain Kearsey with forty-eight rank and file, to protect the improvements just commencing in the Miami country. This detachment reached Limestone in December, 1788, and in a few days after, Captain Kearsey sent a part of his command in advance, as a guard to protect the pioneers under Major Stites, at the Little Miami, where they arrived soon after. Mr. Symmes and his party, accompanied by Captain Kearsey, landed at Columbia, on their passage down the river, and the detachment previously sent to that place joined their company. They then proceeded to the Bend, and landed about the first or second of February. When they left Limestone it was the purpose of Captain Kearsey to occupy the fort built at the mouth of the Miami, by a detachment of United States' troops, who afterwards descended the river to the Falls.

That purpose was defeated by the flood in the river, which had spread over the low grounds and rendered it difficult to reach the fort. Captain Kearsey, however, was anxious to make the attempt, but the Judge would not consent to it; he was of course much disappointed, and greatly displeased. When he set out on the expedition, expecting to find a fort ready built to receive him, he did not provide the implements necessary to construct one. Thus disappointed and displeased, he resolved that he would not attempt to construct a new work, but would leave the Bend and join the garrison at Louisville.

In pursuance of that resolution, he embarked early in March, and descended the river with his command. The Judge immediately wrote to Major Willis, commandant of the garrison at the Falls, complaining of the conduct of Captain Kearsey, representing the exposed situation of the Miami settlement, stating the indications of hostility manifested by the Indians, and requesting a guard to be sent to the Bend. This request was promptly granted, and before the close of the month, Ensign Luce arrived with seventeen or eighteen soldiers, which, for the time, removed the apprehensions of the pioneers at that place. It was not long, however, before the Indians made an attack on them, in which they killed one soldier, and wounded four or five other persons, including Major J. R. Mills, an emigrant from Elizabethtown, New Jersey, who was a surveyor, and an intelligent and highly respected citizen. Although he recovered from his wounds, he felt their disabling effects to the day of his death.

The surface of the ground where the Judge and his party had landed, was above the reach of the water, and sufficiently level to admit of a convenient settlement. He therefore determined, for the immediate accommodation of his party, to lay out a village at that place, and to suspend, for the present, the execution of his purpose, as to the city, of which he had given notice, until satisfactory information could be obtained in regard to the comparative advantages of different places in the vicinity. The determination, however, of laying out such a city, was not abandoned, but was executed in the succeeding year on a magnificent scale. It included the village, and extended from the Ohio across the peninsula to the Miami river. This city, which was certainly a beautiful one, on paper, was called Symmes, and for a time was a subject of conversation and of criticism; but it soon ceased to be remembered—even its name was forgotten, and the settlement continued to be called North Bend. Since then, that village has been distinguished as the residence and the home of the soldier and statesman, William Henry Harrison, whose remains now repose in a humble vault on one of its beautiful hills.

In conformity with a stipulation made at Limestone, every individual belonging to the party received a donation lot, which he was required to improve, as the condition of obtaining a title. As the number of these adventurers increased in consequence of the protection afforded by the military, the Judge was induced to lay out another village, six or seven miles higher up the river, which he called South Bend, where he disposed of some donation lots; but that project failed, and in a few years the village was deserted and converted into a farm.

During these transactions, the Judge was visited by a number of Indians from a camp in the neighborhood of Stites' settlement. One of them, a Shawnee chief, had many complaints to make of frauds practised on them by white traders, who fortunately had no connection with the pioneers. After several conversations, and some small presents, he professed to be satisfied with the explanation he had received, and gave assurances that the Indians would trade with the white men as friends.

In one of their interviews, the Judge told him he had been commissioned and sent out to their country, by the thirteen fires, in the spirit of friendship and kindness; and that he was instructed to treat them as friends and brothers. In proof of this, he showed them the flag of the Union, with its stars and stripes, and also his commission, having the great seal of the United States attached to it; exhibiting the American eagle, with the olive branch in one claw, emblematical of peace, and the instrument of war and death in the other. He explained the meaning of those symbols to their satisfaction, though at first the chief seemed to think they were not very striking emblems either of peace or friendship; but before he departed from the Bend, he gave assurances of the most friendly character. Yet, when they left their camp to return to their towns, they carried off a number of horses belonging to the Columbia settlement, to compensate for the injuries done them by wandering traders, who had no part or lot with the pioneers. These depredations having been repeated, a party was sent out in pursuit, who followed the trail of the Indians a considerable distance, when they discovered fresh signs, and sent Captain Flinn, one of their party, in advance, to reconnoitre. He had not proceeded far before he was surprised, taken prisoner, and carried to the Indian camp. Not liking the movements he saw going on, which seemed to indicate personal violence, in regard to himself, and having great confidence in his activity and strength, at a favorable moment, he sprang from the camp, made his escape, and joined his party. The Indians, fearing an ambuscade, did not pursue. The party possessed themselves of some horses belonging to the Indians, and returned to Columbia. In a few days, the Indians brought in Captain Flinn's rifle, and begged Major Stites to restore their horses—alledging that they were innocent of the depredations laid to their charge. After some further explanations, the matter was amicably settled, and the horses were given up.

The three principal settlements of the Miami country were commenced in the manner above described; and although they had one general object, and were threatened by one common danger, yet there existed a strong spirit of rivalry between them—each feeling a pride in the prosperity of the little colony to which he belonged. That spirit produced a strong influence on the feelings of the pioneers of the different villages, and produced an *esprit du corps*, scarcely to be expected under circumstances so critical and dangerous as those which threatened them. For some time it was a matter of doubt, which of the rivals, Columbia, Cincinnati, or North Bend, would eventually become the chief seat of business.

In the beginning, Columbia, the eldest of the three, took the lead, both in the number of its inhabitants, and the convenience and appearance of its dwellings. It was a flourishing village, and many believed it would become the great business town of the Miami country. That delusion, however, lasted but a short time. The garrison having been established at Cincinnati, made it the head-quarters, and the depot of the army. In addition to this, as soon as the County Courts of the Territory were organized, it was made the seat of justice of Hamilton county. These advantages convinced every body that it was destined to become the emporium of the Miami country.

At first, North Bend had a decided advantage over it; as the troops detailed by General Harmar for the protection of the Miami pioneers were landed there, through the influence of Judge Symmes. That consideration induced many of the first adventurers to plant themselves at the Bend, believing it to be the place of the greatest safety. But, as has been stated, that detachment soon took its departure for Louisville. It appears also that Ensign Luce, the commandant of the party which succeeded it, did not feel bound to erect his fort at any particular place, but was at liberty to select the spot best calculated to afford the most extensive protection to the Miami settlers. Viewing his duty in that light, he put up a small temporary work, sufficient for the security of his troops, regardless of the earnest entreaty of the Judge, to proceed at once to erect a substantial, spacious, block-house, sufficient for the protection of the inhabitants of the village.

The remonstrances and entreaties of the Judge had but little influence on the mind of this obstinate officer; for, in despite of them all, he left the Bend, and proceeded to Cincinnati with his command, where he immediately commenced the construction of a military work. That important move was followed by very decided results—it terminated the strife for supremacy, by removing the only motive which had induced former emigrants to pass the settlements above, and proceed to the Bend. As soon as the troops removed from that place to Cincinnati, the settlers of the Bend, who were then the most numerous, feeling the loss of the protection on which they had relied, became uneasy, and began to follow; and ere long the place was almost entirely deserted, and the hope of making it, even a respectable town, was abandoned.

In the course of the ensuing summer, Major Doughty arrived at Cincinnati, with troops from Fort Harmar, and commenced the construction of Fort Washington, which was the most extensive and important military work in the Territory belonging to the United States.

About that time there was a rumor prevailing in the settlement, said to have been endorsed by the Judge himself, which goes far to unravel the mystery, in which the removal of the troops from the Bend was involved. It was said and believed, that while the officer in command at that place was looking out very leisurely for a suitable site, on which to build the block-house, he formed an acquaintance with a beautiful black-eyed female, who called forth his most assiduous and tender attentions. She was the wife of one of the settlers at the Bend. Her husband saw the danger to which he would be exposed, if he remained where he was. He therefore resolved at once to remove to Cincinnati, and very promptly executed his resolution.

As soon as the gallant commandant discovered that the object of his admiration had changed her residence, he began to think that the Bend was not an advantageous situation for a military work, and communicated that opinion to Judge Symmes, who strenuously opposed it. His reasoning, however, was not as persuasive as the sparkling eyes of the fair dulcinea then at Cincinnati. The result was a determination to visit Cincinnati, and examine its advantages for a military post, which he communicated to the Judge, with an assurance that if, on examination, it did not prove to be the most eligible place, he would return and erect the fort at the Bend.

The visit was quickly made, and resulted in a conviction that the Bend could not be compared with Cincinnati as a military position. The troops were accordingly removed to that place, and the building of a blockhouse commenced. Whether this structure was on the ground on which Fort Washington was erected by Major Doughty, cannot now be decided.

That movement, produced by a cause whimsical, and apparently trivial in itself, was attended with results of incalculable importance. It settled the question whether North Bend, or Cincinnati, was to be the great commercial town of the Miami Country. Thus we see what unexpected results are sometimes produced by circumstances apparently trivial. The incomparable beauty of a Spartan dame, produced a ten year's war, which terminated in the destruction of Troy; and the irresistible charms of another female, transferred the commercial emporium of Ohio from the place where it had been commenced, to the place where it now is. If this captivating American Helen had continued at the Bend, the garrison would have been erected there—population, capital, and business, would have centered there, and there would have been the Queen City of the West.

ST. CLAIR'S DEFEAT

JOHN A. McCLUNG

On a raw winter day in 1790 a tall, solid-striding man arrived in Cincinnati. From the river landing he carried his papers up the steep road that would become Broadway and took up quarters in the blockhouse of Fort Washington. With the arrival of Governor Arthur St. Clair the log fort became the capital of the West.

As a colonel in the Revolutionary army St. Clair had been dogged by misfortune. Now, in the West, he had the Indian Wars on his hands. While he waited at Fort Washington, General Josiah Harmer marched north against marauding Indians. Two months later his tattered army limped back to Cincinnati, leaving the tribes unchecked in the interior.

The next year St. Clair took to the field himself. Marching his men northward in September, 1791, he built Fort Hamilton and Fort Jefferson and pushed on to the upper Wabash. There, on the third of November, the Indians under Chief Little Turtle struck with stunning surprise. In the old frontier ballad of "Sainclaire's Defeat" it is reported:

> *We charged again with courage firm,*
> *But soon again gave ground;*
> *The war-whoop then redoubled,*
> *As did the foes around.*

On that gray morning 37 officers and 593 men were slaughtered. Back to Fort Washington St. Clair brought his survivors; they got away when the Indians turned back to capture his four hundred horses and plunder his abandoned camp. In the blockhouse, with portholes looking out at the cold river and the bleak November hills, St. Clair wrote his report to the Secretary of War. "Yesterday afternoon the remains of the army under my command got back to this place, and I now have the painful task to give you an account. . . ." The next attempt against the tribes would be made by Anthony Wayne.

The following narrative is taken from John A. McClung's Sketches of Western Adventure. *It is based on memories which the author heard recounted by participants in St. Clair's sorry campaign.*

WE now come to one of the heaviest disasters which occurs in the annals of Indian warfare. The failure of Harmer made a deep impression upon the American nation, and was followed by a loud demand for a greater force, under the command of a more experienced general. General Arthur St. Clair was, at that time, governor of the northwestern territory, and had a claim to the command of such forces as should be employed within his own limits. This gentleman had uniformly ranked high as an officer of courage and patriotism, but had been more uniformly unfortunate than any other officer in the American service. He had commanded at Ticonderoga in the spring of 1777, and had conducted one of the most disastrous retreats which occurred during the revolutionary war. Notwithstanding his repeated misfortunes, he still commanded the respect of his brother officers, and the undiminished confidence of Washington. He was now selected as the person most capable of restoring the American affairs in the North West, and was placed at the head of a regular force, amounting to near fifteen hundred men, well furnished with artillery, and was empowered to call out such reinforcements of militia as might be necessary. Cincinnati, as usual, was the place of rendezvous.

In October, 1791, an army was assembled at that place, greatly superior, in numbers, officers, and equipments, to any which had yet appeared in the west. The regular force was composed of three complete regiments of infantry, two companies of artillery, and one of cavalry. The militia who joined him at Fort Washington, amounted to upwards of six hundred men, most of whom had long been accustomed to Indian warfare. The general

commenced his march from Cincinnati on the — of October, and following the route of Harmer, arrived at Fort Jefferson without material loss, although not without having sustained much inconvenience from scarcity of provisions. The Kentucky rangers, amounting to upwards of two hundred men, had encountered several small parties of Indians, but no serious affair had as yet taken place. Shortly after leaving Fort Jefferson, one of the militia regiments, with their usual disregard to discipline, determined that it was inexpedient to proceed farther, and detaching themselves from the main body, returned rapidly to the fort on their way home. This ill-timed mutiny, not only discouraged the remainder, but compelled the general to detach the first regiment in pursuit of them, if not to bring them back, at least to prevent them from injuring the stores, collected at the fort for the use of the army. With the remainder of the troops, amounting in all to about twelve hundred men, he continued his march to the great Miami villages.

On the evening of the 3d of November, he encamped upon a very commanding piece of ground, upon the bank of one of the tributaries of the Wabash, where he determined to throw up some slight works for the purpose of protecting their knapsacks and baggage, having to move upon the Miami villages, supposed to be within twelve miles, as soon as the first regiment should rejoin them. The remainder of the evening was employed in concerting the plan of the proposed work with Major Ferguson of the engineers, and when the sentries were posted at night, everything was as quiet as could have been desired. The troops were encamped in two lines, with an interval of seventy yards between them, which was all that the nature of the ground would permit. The battalions of Majors Butler, Clarke, and Patterson, composed the front line, the whole under the orders of Major General Butler, an officer of high and merited reputation. The front of the line was covered by a creek, its right flank by the river, and its left by a strong corps of infantry. The second line was composed of the battalions of Majors Gaither and Bedinger, and the second regiment under the command of Lieutenant Colonel Darke. This line, like the other, was secured upon one flank by the river, and upon the other by the cavalry and pickets. The night passed away without alarm. The sentinels were vigilant, and the officers upon the alert.

A few hours before day, St. Clair caused the reveillie to be beaten, and the troops to be paraded under arms, under the expectation that an attack would probably be made. In this situation, they continued until daylight, when they were dismissed to their tents. Some were endeavoring to snatch a few minutes' sleep, others were preparing for the expected march, when suddenly the report of a rifle was heard from the militia a few hundred yards in front, which was quickly followed by a sharp irregular volley in the same direction. The drums instantly beat to arms, the officers flew in every direction, and in two minutes the troops were formed in order of battle. Presently the militia rushed into the camp, in the utmost disorder, closely pursued by swarms of Indians, who, in many places, were mingled with them, and were cutting them down with their tomahawks.

Major Butler's battalion received the first shock, and was thrown into disorder by the tumultuous flight of the militia, who, in their eagerness to escape, bore down everything before them. Here Major General Butler had stationed himself, and here St. Clair directed his attention, in order to remedy the confusion which began to spread rapidly through the whole line. The Indians pressed forward with great audacity, and many of them were mingled with the troops, before their progress could be checked. Major General Butler was wounded at the first fire, and before his wound could be dressed, an Indian who had penetrated the ranks of the regiment, ran up to the spot where he lay, and tomahawked him before his attendants could interpose. The desperate savage was instantly killed. By great exertions, Butler's battalion was restored to order, and the heavy and sustained fire of the first line compelled the enemy to pause and shelter themselves.

This interval, however, endured but for a moment. An invisible but tremendous fire, quickly opened upon the whole front of the encampment, which rapidly extended to the rear, and encompassed the troops on both sides. St. Clair, who at that time, was worn down by a fever, and unable to mount his horse, nevertheless, as is universally admitted, exerted himself with a courage and presence of mind worthy of a better fate. He instantly directed his litter to the right of the rear line, where the great weight of fire fell, and where the slaughter, particularly of the officers, was terrible. Here Darke commanded, an officer who had been trained to hard service, during the revolutionary war, and who was now gallantly exerting himself to check the consternation which was evidently beginning to prevail. St. Clair ordered him to make a rapid charge with the bayonet, and rouse the enemy from their covert.

The order was instantly obeyed, and, at first, apparently with great effect. Swarms of dusky bodies arose from the high grass, and fled before the regiment with every mark of consternation; but as the troops were unable to overtake them, they quickly recovered their courage, and kept up so fatal a retreating fire, that the exhausted regulars were compelled, in their turn, to give way. This charge, however, relieved that particular point for some time; but the weight of the fire was transferred to the centre of the first line, where it threatened to annihilate everything within its range. There, in turn, the unfortunate general was borne by his attendants, and ordered a second appeal to the bayonet. This second charge was made with the same impetuosity as at first, and with the same momentary success. But the attack was instantly shifted to another point, where the same charge was made and the same result followed. The Indians would retire before them, still keeping up a most fatal fire, and the continentals were uniformly compelled to retire in turn. St. Clair, brought up the artillery in order to sweep the bushes with grape, but the horses and artillerymen were destroyed by the terrible fire of the enemy, before any effect could be produced. They were instantly manned afresh from the infantry, and again swept of defenders.

The slaughter had now become prodigious. Four-fifths of the officers and one half of the men were either killed or wounded. The ground was covered with bodies, and the little ravine which led to the river was running with blood. The fire of the enemy had not in the least slackened, and the troops were falling in heaps before it in every part of the camp. To have attempted to have maintained his position longer, could only have led to the total destruction of his force, without the possibility of annoying the enemy, who never showed themselves, unless when charged, and whose numbers (to judge from the weight and extent of the fire,) must have greatly exceeded his own. The men were evidently much disheartened, but the officers, who were chiefly veterans of the revolution, still maintained a firm countenance, and exerted themselves with unavailing heroism to the last. Under these circumstances, St. Clair determined to save the lives of the survivors if possible, and for that purpose collected the remnants of several battalions into one corps, at the head of which he ordered Lieutenant Colonel Darke to make an impetuous charge upon the enemy, in order to open a passage for the remainder of the army. Darke executed his orders with great spirit, and drove the Indians before him to the distance of a quarter of a mile. The remainder of the army instantly rushed through the opening, in order to gain the road! Major Clarke, with the remnant of his battalion, bringing up the rear, and endeavoring to keep the Indians in check.

The retreat soon degenerated into a total rout. Officers who strove to arrest the panic, only sacrificed themselves. Clarke, the leader of the rear guard, soon fell in this dangerous service, and his corps were totally disorganized. Officers and soldiers were now mingled without the slightest regard to discipline, and "devil take the hindmost," was the order of the day. The pursuit, at first, was keen; but the temptation afforded by the plunder of the camp, soon brought them back, and the wearied, wounded and disheartened fugitives, were permitted to retire from the field unmolested. The rout continued as far as Fort Jefferson, twenty-nine miles from the scene of action. The action lasted more than three hours, during the whole of which time, the fire was heavy and incessant.

The loss, in proportion to the number engaged, was enormous, and is unparalleled, except in the affair of Braddock. Sixty-eight officers were killed upon the spot, and twenty-eight wounded. Out of nine hundred privates who went into action, five hundred and fifty were left dead upon the field, and many of the survivors were wounded. General St. Clair was untouched, although eight balls passed through his hat and clothes, and several horses were killed under him. The Indian loss was reported by themselves at fifty-eight killed and wounded, which was probably not underrated, as they were never visible after the first attack, until charged with the bayonet. At Fort Jefferson, the fugitives were joined by the first regiment, who, as noticed above, had been detached in pursuit of the deserters. Here a council of war was called, which terminated in the unanimous opinion, that the junction with the first regiment did not justify an attempt upon the enemy in the present condition of affairs, and that the army should return to Fort Washington without delay. This was accordingly done, and thus closed the second campaign against the Indians.

Above, left: St. Clair's defeat. Courtesy Anthony Wayne Pkwy Bd Above, right, and below: The Battle of Fallen Timbers. Courtesy Ohio Historical Society and Anthony Wayne Pkwy Bd

BIG WIND AT THE COUNCIL FIRE

GENERAL WAYNE'S SPEECH TO THE CHIEFS
AT GREENE VILLE, 1795

General Anthony Wayne's victory over the tribes at Fallen Timbers in 1794 was followed by a great treaty council at Fort Greene Ville. In June, 1795, after four years of forest warfare, the chiefs and warriors of twelve tribes came afoot and on horseback to the rugged palisade bordered by Greenville and Mud creeks. This remote fort was the strongest station in the West, and in this historic summer it was the most populous place in the western country. General Wayne's headquarters faced the artillery park and the trampled parade. Ten rows of log huts housed the troops, a regiment to a row. On a big meadow under the blockhouse cannon eleven hundred tribesmen, some limping from wounds received at Fallen Timbers, pitched their camps. They raced their ponies over the pasture. They engaged in feats of strength and skill with Wayne's soldiers. At dusk fires twinkled over the meadow. The warriors feasted on the white man's beef and pork, brown sugar and coffee. They smoked his tobacco and gulped his whiskey. On the night wind, with the drifting smoke of the cooking fires, came the sounds of bark whistles and cane flutes and a chorus of savage cries.

In the big log council house a fire smoldered. General Wayne in blue coat, cocked hat, crossed sword belt and silver-mounted sword, puffed the feathered ceremonial pipe and passed it around the circle of chiefs. For seven weeks the treaty council proceeded, with formal speeches by the great soldier and responses by the chiefs of twelve nations. At last the treaty terms were drawn, and when the two large sheets of parchment were signed—by ninety-two chiefs and twenty-seven white men—twenty million acres were surrendered to the United States and the doors of the mid-Ohio valley were open to the future. In the shortening days of August the Indians went home to their shrunken hunting grounds.

To the tribesmen Wayne was the "Big Wind" who brought destruction to their camps and villages. Here is his summarizing speech, in which he reminds the chiefs of the domain which they have given up to "the fifteen fires"—the United States—and predicts a lasting peace between the Indian and white nations.

"BROTHERS of the three great fires! You say you thought you were the proper owners of the land, that was sold to the fifteen fires, at the treaty of Muskingum; but you say also, that you never received any compensation for those lands. It was always the wish and intention of the fifteen fires, that the true owners of those lands should receive a full compensation for them. If you did not receive a due proportion of the goods, as original proprietors, it was not the fault of the United States; on the contrary, the United States have paid twice for those lands; first at the treaty of McIntosh, ten years ago, and next at that of Muskingum, six years since.

"*Younger brothers!* Notwithstanding that these lands have been twice paid for, by the fifteen fires, at the places I have mentioned, yet such is the justice and liberality of the United States, that they will now, a third time, make compensation for them." [A large string to the three fires.]

"*Brothers, the Miamies!* I have paid attention to what the Little Turtle said, two

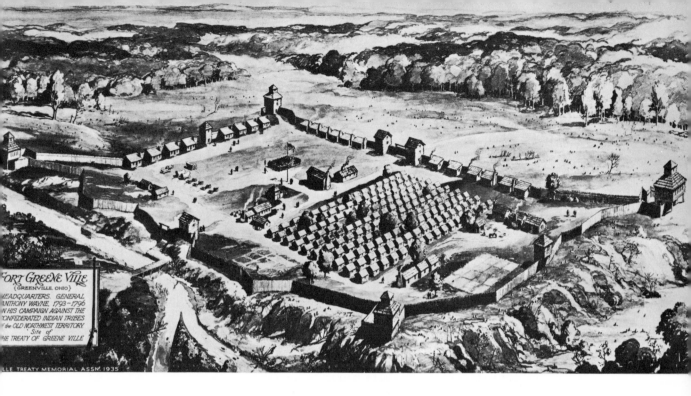

Above: Fort Greene Ville. *Courtesy Anthony Wayne Pkwy Bd*   Below: The Treaty of Greene Ville, 1795, by Howard Chandler Christy. *Courtesy Anthony Wayne Pkwy Bd*

days since, concerning the lands which he claims. He said his father first kindled the fire at Detroit, and stretched his line from thence to the head waters of Scioto; thence down the same to the Ohio; thence down that river to the mouth of the Wabash, and from thence to Chicago, on the south west end of lake Michigan; and observed that his forefathers had enjoyed that country, undisturbed, from time immemorial.

"*Brothers!* These boundaries enclose a very large space of country indeed; they embrace, if I mistake not, all the lands on which all the nations now present live, as well as those which have been ceded to the United States. The lands which have been ceded have within these three days been acknowledged by the Ottawas, Chippeways, Pottawattamies, Wyandots, Delawares, and Shawanees. The Little Turtle says, the prints of his forefathers' houses are everywhere to be seen within these boundaries. *Younger brother!* it is true these prints are to be observed, but at the same time we discover the marks of French possessions throughout this country, which were established long before we were born. These have since been in the possession of the British, who must, in their turn, relinquish them to the United States, when they, the French and the Indians, will be all as one people. [A white string.]

"I will point out to you a few places where I discover strong traces of these establishments; and first of all, I find at Detroit, a very strong print, where the fire was first kindled by your forefathers; next at Vincennes on the Wabash; again at Musquiton, on the same river; a little higher up on that stream, they are to be seen at Ouitanon. I discover another strong trace at Chicago; another on the St. Joseph's of lake Michigan. I have seen distinctly, the prints of a French and of a British post, at the Miami villages, and of a British post at the foot of the Rapids, now in their possession. Prints, very conspicuous, are on the Great Miami, which were possessed by the French, forty-five years ago; and another trace, is very distinctly to be seen at Sandusky.

"It appears to me, that if the Great Spirit, as you say, charged your forefathers to pre-serve their lands entire, for their posterity, they have paid very little regard to the sacred injunction, for I see they have parted with those lands to your fathers the French—and the English are now, or have been, in possession of them all: therefore, I think the charge urged against the Ottawas, Chippeways and other Indians, comes with a bad grace indeed, from the very people who, perhaps, set them the example. The English and French both wore hats; and yet your forefathers sold them, at various times, portions of your lands. However, as I have already observed, you shall now receive from the United States, further valuable compensation for the lands you have ceded to them by former treaties.

"*Younger brothers!* I will now inform you who it was who gave us these lands in the first instance;—it was your fathers the British, who did not discover that care for your interests which you ought to have experienced. This is the treaty of peace, made between the United States of America and Great Britain, twelve years ago, at the end of a long and bloody war, when the French and Americans proved too powerful for the British: on these terms they obtained peace. [Here part of the treaty of 1783 was read.]

"Here you perceive, that all the country south of the great lakes has been given up to America; but the United States never intended to take that advantage of you, which the British placed in their hands; they wish you to enjoy your just rights, without interruption, and to promote your happiness. The British stipulated to surrender to us all the posts on this side of the boundary agreed on. I told you some days ago, that treaties should ever be sacredly fulfilled by those who make them; but the British, on their part, did not find it convenient to relinquish those posts as soon as they should have done; however, they now find it so, and a precise period is fixed for their delivery. I have now in my hand the copy of a treaty, made eight months since, between them and us, of which I will read you a little. [First and second articles of Mr. Jay's treaty read.]

"By this solemn agreement they promise to retire from Michilimackinac, Fort St. Clair, Detroit, Niagara, and all other places on this side of the lakes, in ten moons from this period, and leave the same to the full and quiet possession of the United States.

"*Brothers!* All nations present, now listen to me!

"Having now explained those matters to you, and informed you of all things I judged necessary for your information, we have nothing to do but to bury the hatchet, and draw a veil over past misfortunes. As you have buried our dead, with the concern of brothers, so I now collect the bones of your slain warriors, put them into a deep pit which I have dug, and cover them carefully over with this large belt, there to remain undisturbed. I also dry the tears from your eyes, and wipe the blood from your bodies, with this soft white linen. No bloody traces will ever lead to the graves of your departed heroes; with this, I wipe all such away. I deliver it to your uncle, the Wyandot, who will send it round amongst you. [A large belt, with a white string attached.]

"I now take the hatchet out of your heads, and with a strong arm, throw it into the centre of the great ocean, where no mortal can ever find it; and I now deliver to you the wide and straight path to the fifteen fires, to be used by you and your posterity, forever. So long as you continue to follow this road, so long will you continue to be a happy people. You see it is straight and wide, and

they will be blind indeed, who deviate from it. I place it also, in your uncle's hands, that he may preserve it for you. [A large road belt.]

"I will, the day after to-morrow, show you the cessions which you have made to the United States, and point out to you the lines which may, for the future, divide your lands from theirs; and, as you will have to-morrow to rest, I will order you a double allowance of drink, because we have now buried the hatchet, and performed every necessary ceremony, to render propitious, our renovated friendship."

Tarkee, chief of the Wyandots, arose, and spoke as follows:

"*Brothers, the fifteen fires, listen!* and all you chiefs and warriors present. This is a day appointed by the Great Spirit above, for us; he has taken pity on us all, and disposed us to perfect this good work. You have all heard what our elder brother has said on these two belts. We will all now return thanks to this great chief, and to the great chief of the fifteen fires, for their goodness towards us; and we will, at the same time, offer our acknowledgements to the Great Spirit, for it is he alone, who has brought us together, and caused us to agree in the good works which have been done. My thanks are also due to you, chiefs and warriors present." Council adjourned.

VIOLENCE AT VINCENNES

WILLIAM HENRY HARRISON

In 1800 Congress passed a bill which divided the Northwest Territory. Ohio, with a population of 45,000 and aspiring to statehood, was split off from the rest of the western domain, which became Indiana Territory. It had a total white population of some five thousand. Indiana Territory comprised the present states of Indiana, Illinois, Michigan and Wisconsin—nearly all of it owned by the Indians. The old French town of Vincennes on the Wabash became the capital of that huge territory. Harrison was appointed governor.

In January, 1801, he arrived at Vincennes, a village of four hundred log and clapboard houses between the curving river and uplands of prairie and forest. This was an old French settlement, a year older than Philadelphia, where the Indians had brought peltry to French traders. Then the trade was in the hands of French traders. Now the trade was in the hands of Americans, and the French villagers lived on in their whitewashed cottages, sitting on their galleries on summer evenings, playing their fiddles by the chimney fire on winter nights. They wanted no more land than their orchards, gardens and a tag of pasture; they had no interest in government or trade. In 1801 the old habitants watched a young American, lean as a roof pole, arrive in their little town that had become the capital of a territory as big as all of France. He would have his hands full of threatening and wheedling chiefs, of lawless squatters, of traders who took the Indians' catch of furs in return for rum and whiskey.

HARRISON TO THE SECRETARY OF WAR
July 15th, 1801
Dawson, *Harrison*, 10-11

SIR

For the last ten or twelve weeks I have been constantly engaged in receiving visits from the Chiefs of most of the Indian nations which inhabit this part of the Territory. They all profess and I believe that most of them feel a friendship for the United States—but they make heavy complaints of ill treatment on the part of our Citizens. They say that their people have been killed—their lands settled on—their game wontonly destroyed—& their young men made drunk & cheated of the peltries which formerly procured them necessary articles of Cloathing, arms and ammunition to hunt with. Of the truth of all these charges I am well convinced. The Delaware Chiefs in their address to me mentioned the loss of six persons of their nation, since the treaty of Greenvill having been killed by the White people—& I have found them correct as to number. In one instance however the White boy who killed the Indian was tried and acquitted as it was proved that it was done in self defence. In another instance the Murderer was tried and acquitted by the Jury, altho it was very evident that it was a cruel and unprovoked murder. About twelve months ago a Delaware was killed in this Town by a Citizen of the Territory against whom a bill has been found by the grand. He has however escaped and it is reported that he has gone to Natchez or New Orleans. But the case which seems to have affected the Indians more than any other is the murder of two men and one woman of this same nation about three years

ago. This cruel deed was perpetrated on this side of the Ohio, forty or fifty miles below the falls & is said to have been attended with circumstances of such atrocity as almost to discredit the whole story—were it not but too evident that a great many of the Inhabitants of the Fronteers consider the murdering of Indians in the highest degree meritorious—the story is this. About three years ago two Delaware men and a woman were quietly hunting in the neighbourhood of the Ohio—I believe on the waters of Blue river their Camp was discovered by two men I think of the name of Williams—brothers—and these Williams mutually determined to murder them for the purpose of possessing themselves of about fifty dollars worth of property and the trifling equipage belonging to the hunting Camp of a Savage. They thought it too dangerous to attack them openly as one of the Indians well known to the white people by the name of Jim Galloway or Gilloway—was remarkable for his strength and bravery. They approached the camp as friends & as I am toled they have since confessed asked leave to stay at the Indians Camp and hunt for a few days. Their request was granted & they remained until a favorite opportunity offered to carry their design into effect—& the then Indians were murdered. Altho they were missed by their friends it was a long time before their fate was ascertained. The murderers thinking themselves safe from the length of time which has elapsed, now begin to talk of the affair, and one of them is said to have declared that he was very nearly over-powered by the Indian after he had wounded him—that he had closed in with him and the Indian was on the point of getting the better of him when his brother to whom the murder of the other Indian had been committed came to his assistance. Altho I am convinced that the facts above stated are all true—yet so difficult is it to get testimony in a case of this kind, that I have not as yet been able to get the necessary depositions on which to ground an application to the Executive of Kentucky for the delivery of these people to Justice. Whenever I have ascertained that the Indian boundary line has been encroached on by the white people I have caused the Intruders to withdraw. But as the boundary line seperating the Indian land from that to which the title has been extinguished has not been run—nor the manner in which it is to run precisely ascertained either at this place or in the country on the Mississippi called the Illinois—it is impossible to tell when encroachments are made on the Indians at those two places. As this is an object of considerable importance to the Citizens of the Territory I must beg you Sir to obtain the directions of the President to have it done as soon as possible. The people have been about petitioning Congress on this subject—Untill it was observed that the President was authorized by law to cause all the boundaries between the lands of the U.N. States & the Indian tribes to be ascertained and marked—Untill their boundaries are established it is almost impossible to punish in this quarter the persons who make a practice of Hunting on the lands of the Indians in violation of law and our Treaty with that people. This practice has grown into a monstrous abuse. Thousands of the wild animals from which the Indians derive their subsistance have been distroyed by the white people. They complain in their speeches to me that many parts of their Country which abounded with game when the general peace was made in 1795 now scarcely contains a sufficiency to give food to the fiew Indians who pass through there. The people of Kentucky living on the Ohio from the mouth of the Kentucky river down the Mississippi make a constant practice of crossing over on the Indian lands opposite to them every fall to kill deer, bear, and buffaloe—the latter from being a great abundance a few years ago is now scarcely to

be met with, in that whole extent. One white hunter will distroy more game than five of the common Indians—the latter generally contenting himself with a sufficiency for present subsistance—while the other eager after game hunt for the skin of the animal alone. All these Injuries the Indians have hitherto borne with astonishing patience but altho they discover no disposition to make war upon the United States at present—I am confident that most of the tribes would eagerly seize any favorable opportunity for that purpose—& should the United States be at war with any of the European nations who are known to the Indians there would probably be a combination of nine tenths of the Northern Tribes against us —Unless some means are made use of to conciliate them. The British have been unremitted in their exertions to preserve their influence over the Indians resident within our Territory ever since the surrender of the Forts upon the Lake—& those exertions are still continued —last year they delivered a greater quantity of goods to their Indians than they have been ever known to do—and I have been lately informed that talks are now circulating amongst them, which are intended to lesten the small influence we have over the Indians—I cannot vouch for the truth of this report—but I think it very probable that the British will redouble their efforts to keep the Indians in their Interest as a mean of assisting them in any designs they may form against Louisiana which it is said will be shortly delivered up to the French.

I have had much difficulty with the small tribes in this immediate Neighbourhood—viz. —the Peankashaws, Weas & Eel river Indians, these three tribes form a body of the greatest Scoundrels in the world—they are dayly in this town in considerable numbers and are frequently intoxicated to the number of thirty or forty at once—they then commit the greatest disorders—drawing their knives and stabing every one they meet with—breaking open the Houses of the Citizens killing their Hogs and cattle and breaking down their fences. But in all their frolicks they generally suffer most severely themselves they kill each other without mercy, some years ago as many as four were found dead in the morning—& altho these murders are actually committed in the streets of the town, yet no attempt to punish them has ever been made. This forbearance has made them astonishingly insolent & on a late occasion (within 8 weeks) when one of these rascals had killed without provocation two of the Citizens in one of the Traders Houses in this place, & it was found impossible to apprehend him alive, he was put to death. This peice of Justice so exasperated those of his tribe in the neighbourhood that they actually assembled in the borders of the town with a design to seize some favourable opportunity of doing mischief—the Militia were ordered out and their resentment has subsided.

Should you think proper to garrison Fort Knox with a small body of troops it will be the means of keeping the Indians under much better controle when they come here to trade —& would enable the civil Magistrats to punish those who violate the laws. Inded I do not think that a military force is so necessary on any part of the fronteers as at this place—the inhabitants tho fully able to repulse them when aware of their designs are constantly in danger from their treachery. Five Hundred Warriers might introduce themselves into the settlement undiscovered by the White people —& after doing all the mischief in their power might make—their escape with as much facility. I do not indeed apprehend in the least that the neighbouring tribes have any inclination to make open war upon us—I fear only the effect of some sudden resentment arrising from their constant intercourse with the people of this town. In this intercourse causes of irritation are constantly produced twice within a few weeks an appeal was made to arms by both parties—one occasioned by some drunken Indians attempting to force a House in which one was killed and an other wounded. The other at the time when the two white men were killed as above mentioned. Luckily however no other mischief was done in either instance.

The Indian Chiefs complain heavily of the mischiefs produced by the enormous quantity of Whiskey which the Traders introduce into their Country. I do not believe there are more than six Hundred Warriers upon this River (the Wabash) and yet the quantity of whiskey brought here annually for their use is said

to amount to at least six thousand Gallons. This poisonous liquor not only incapasitates them from obtaining a living by Hunting but it leads to the most attrocious crimes—killing each other has become so customary amongst them that it is no longer a crime to murder those whom they have been most accustomed to estem and regard. Their Chiefs and their nearest relations fall under the strokes of their Tomhawks & Knives. This has been so much the case with the three Tribes nearest us—the Peankashaws, Weas, & Eel River Miamis that there is scarcely a Chief to be found amongst them.

The little Beaver a Wea Chief of note well known to me was not long since murdered by his own son. The Little Fox another Chief who was always a friend to the white people was murdered at mid day in the Streets of this by one of his own nation. All these Horrors are produced to these Unhappy people by their too frequent intercourse with the White people. This is so cirtain that I can at once tell by looking at an Indian whom I chance to meet whether he belong to a Neighbouring or a more distant Tribe. The latter is generally well Clothed healthy and vigorous the former half naked, filthy and enfeebled with Intoxication, and many of them without arms except a Knife which they carry for the most vilanous purposes. The Chiefs of the Kickapoos, Sacks, & Patawatimies, who lately visited me are sensible of the progress of these measures, and their Views amongst themselves —which they are convinced will lead to utter exterpation—and earnestly desire that the introduction of such large quantities of Whiskey amongst them may be prevented.

Whether some thing ought not to be done to prevent the reproach which will attach to the American Character by the exterpation of so many human beings, I beg leave most respectfuly to submit to the Consideration of the President—That this exterpation will happen no one can doubt who knows the astonishing annual decrease of these unhappy beings. The Delawares are now making an other attempt to become agriculturists—they are forming settlements upon the White river a branch of the Wabash under the conduct of two Missionaries of the Society of "The United Brethren for propogating the gospel amongst the Heathens" otherwise Meravians. To assist them in this plan the Chiefs desire that one half of their next annuity may be laid out in impliments of agriculture, and in the purchase of some domestic animals as Cows and Hogs. The Kaskaskeas & Peankashaws request the same thing and the Patawatimies wish a few corse hoes may be sent with their goods. The sun a great Chief of the last mentioned Nation requests that a Coat and Hat of the Uniform of the United States & to prevent Jealousy a few more may be aded for the other Chiefs, of his nation. Indeed I am convinced that nothing would please the Chiefs of all the Nations so much as a distinction of this kind. It was a method always persued by the British and nothing did more to preserve their Influance. I therefore take the liberty of recommending that about a half dozen Coats made in the uniform of the United States and ordinary Cocked Hats may be sent for each of the nations who have an annuity of one thousand dollars, and Half that number for the Nations who receive 500 dollars—the expence to be taken from the allowance of each nation. The Kickapoos who are a strong and warlike Nation have not a proper proportion of goods allowed them by the United States their annuity is 500 dollars only, which is the sum allowed to the remnant of the Kaskaskias which have only fifteen or twenty warriors. The Kickapoos of the Priaria a large branch of that nation never receive any part of the goods. They frequently steal Horses which are never returned because they do not fear the withholding of their annuity. The Sacks a very large nation which Inhabit the Waters of the Illinois River are not bound by any treaty—and will not deliver up horses or prisones in their possession. I have reason to believe that there are several persons still with them which were taken during the late war. They say they are very willing to treat if they are put upon the same footing that the rest of the Indian Nations are.

The contractor to the army had untill lately an agent at this place—from whom I had procured the provisions which were necessary in the Councils I have had with Several nations which have visited me. I have signed an abstract for the quantity furnished. In their issues I have been as economical as possible—perhaps more so than was proper—the whole amount of Issues under my direction until this—amounted only to 13 rations.

PROCLAMATION: FORBIDDING TRADERS FROM SELLING LIQUOR TO INDIANS IN AND AROUND VINCENNES

July 20, 1801
Executive Journal, 4

This day the Governor Issued a proclamation expressly forbidding any Trader from selling or giving any Spirituous Liquors to any Indian or Indians in the Town of Vincennes and ordering that the Traders in future when they sold Liquor to the Indians should deliver it to them at the distance of at least a mile from the village or on the other side of the Wabash River. And Whereas certain evil disposed persons have made a practice of purchasing from the Indians (and giveing them Whiskey in exchange) articles of Cloathing, Cooking, and such other articles as are used in hunting, viz; Guns powder, Ball &c. he has thought proper to publish an Extract from the Laws of the United States, that the persons offending against the Law may know the penalties to which they are subject. he also extorts [exhorts] and requires all Magistrates and other Civil officers vigilantly to discharge their duties, by punishing, as the Law directs, all persons who are found drunk, or rioting in the streets or public houses; and requests and advises, the good Citizens of the Territory to aid and assist the Magistrates, in the execution of the Laws by Lodgeing information against, and by assisting to apprehend the disorderly and rioutuos persons, who constantly infest the streets of Vincennes and to inform against all those who violate the Sabbath by selling or Bartering Spirituous Liquors or who pursue any other unlawful business on the day set apart for the service of God. [Abstract]

WAR CRIES AT TIPPECANOE

WILLIAM HENRY HARRISON

For sixty years, from the rout of Chief Cornstalk on the upper Ohio to Black Hawk's defeat in Wisconsin, American troops contested with the tribesmen for the Midwest country. Point Pleasant, Fallen Timbers, Tippecanoe, Bad Axe Bottoms— these are names for war cries and gunfire and the driving of the tribes from their ancestral lands.

The most resounding name is Tippecanoe, and it calls to mind the clash of two leaders of their people, the Shawnee chief Tecumseh and the Indian fighter and brief-term President, William Henry Harrison. Tecumseh, a later-day Pontiac, dreamed of a united Indian nation, strong enough to drive the white men out. With his twin brother, the one-eyed Prophet, he roamed from tribe to tribe, picturing a bright future in which the Indians would regain their surrendered land, game would multiply in the forest, and thickets would close over the roads that white men had slashed through the woods. The tribesmen listened gladly and allied themselves in this future.

In 1808 the Shawnee brothers set up a new town where Tippecanoe Creek joins the Wabash River. Called Prophet's Town, this settlement soon became the Indian capital of the Northwest. When word of intertribal gatherings reached Vincennes, Governor Harrison was alarmed.

Three times between 1808 and 1811 Harrison summoned Tecumseh to Vincennes for council. With their escorts of troops and warriors, they met under the trees at Grouseland, the governor's mansion, while Harrison's seven children peered from the porch and windows. Each time Tecumseh was dignified and defiant, and after each meeting, he ranged the western country, cementing new alliances of the tribes. Meanwhile Indians were attacking surveying crews and frontier settlers.

At last in the fall of 1811, Harrison felt it was time to move. Sixty miles above Vincennes, at the site of present Terre Haute, he built a blockhouse. From there he marched his army of nearly a thousand men to Tippecanoe. This account of the battle is General Harrison's official report to the Secretary of War.

VINCENNES, 18th November, 1811.

SIR:—In my letter of the 8th inst., I did myself the honor to communicate the result of an action between the troops under my command and the confederation of Indians under the control of the Shawanee Prophet. I had previously informed you in a letter of the 2d inst., of my proceedings previous to my arrival at the Vermillion river, where I had erected a block house for the protection of the boats which I was obliged to leave, and as a depository for our heavy baggage, and such part of our provisions as we were unable to transport in wagons.

On the morning of the 3d inst., I commenced my march from the block house. The Wabash, above this, turning considerably to the eastward, I was obliged to avoid the broken and woody country, which borders upon it, to change my course to the westward of north, to gain the prairies which lie to the back of those woods. At the end of one day's march, I was enabled to take the proper direction, (N. E.) which brought me, on the evening of the 5th, to a small creek, at about eleven miles from the Prophet's town. I had, on the preceding day, avoided the dangerous pass of Pine creek, by inclining a few miles to the left, where the troops and wagons were crossed with expedition and safety. Our route on the 6th, for about six miles, lay through prairies, separated by small points of woods.

My order of march hitherto had been similar to that used by General Wayne; that is, the infantry were in two columns of files on either side of the road, and the mounted rifle men and cavalry in front, in the rear and on the flanks. Where the ground was unfavorable for the action of cavalry, they were placed in the rear; but where it was otherwise, they were made to exchange positions with one of the mounted rifle corps.

Understanding that the last four miles were open woods, and the probability being greater that we should be attacked in front, than on either flank, I halted at that distance from the town, and formed the army in order of battle. The United States infantry placed in the centre, two companies of militia infantry, and one of mounted riflemen, on each flank, formed the front line. In the rear of this line was placed the baggage, drawn up as compactly as possible, and immediately behind it, a reserve of three companies of militia infantry. The cavalry formed a second line, at the distance of three hundred yards in the rear of the front line, and a company of mounted riflemen, the advanced guard at that distance in front. To facilitate the march, the whole were then broken off into short columns of companies—a situation the most favorable for forming in order of battle with facility and precision.

Our march was slow and cautious, and much delayed by the examination of every place which seemed calculated for an ambuscade. Indeed the ground was for some time so unfavorable, that I was obliged to change the position of the several corps three times in the distance of a mile. At half past two o'clock, we passed a small creek at the distance of one mile and a half from town, and entered an open wood, when the army was halted, and again drawn up in order of battle.

During the whole of the last day's march,

parties of Indians were constantly about us, and every effort was made by the interpreters to speak to them, but in vain. New attempts of the kind were now made, but proving equally ineffectual, a Captain Dubois, of the spies and guides, offering to go with a flag to the town, I dispatched him with an interpreter, to request a conference with the Prophet. In a few moments a messenger was sent by Captain Dubois, to inform me that in his attempts to advance, the Indians appeared on both his flanks, and although he had spoken to them in the most friendly manner, they refused to answer, but beckoned to him to go forward, and constantly endeavored to cut him off from the army. Upon this information I recalled the captain, and determined to encamp for the night, and take some other measures for opening a conference with the Prophet.

Whilst I was engaged in tracing the lines for the encampment, Major Daviess, who commanded the dragoons, came to inform me that he had penetrated the Indian fields; that the ground was entirely open and favorable; that the Indians in front had manifested nothing but hostility, and had answered every attempt to bring them to a parley with contempt and insolence. I was immediately advised by all the officers around me to move forward; a similar wish, indeed, pervaded all the army. It was drawn up in excellent order, and every man appeared eager to decide the contest immediately.

Being informed that a good encampment might be had upon the Wabash, I yielded to what appeared the general wish, and directed the troops to advance, taking care, however, to place the interpreters in front, with directions to invite a conference with any Indians they might meet with. We had not advanced above four hundred yards, when I was informed that three Indians had approached the advanced guard, and had expressed a wish to speak to me. I found, upon their arrival, that one of them was a man in great estimation with the Prophet. He informed me that the chiefs were much surprised at my advancing upon them so rapidly; that they were given to understand, by the Delawares and Miamies, whom I had sent to them a few days before,

Fort Harrison on the Wabash. *Courtesy Anthony Wayne Pkwy Bd*

that I would not advance to their town, until I had received an answer to my demands made through them; that this answer had been dispatched by the Pottawattamie chief, Winnemac, who had accompanied the Delawares and Miamies, on their return; that they had left the Prophet's town two days before, with a design to meet me, but had unfortunately taken the road on the south side of the Wabash.

I answered that I had no intention of attacking them, until I discovered that they would not comply with the demands that I had made; that I would go on, and encamp at the Wabash; and in the morning would have an interview with the Prophet and his chiefs, and explain to them the determination of the President; that in the meantime, no hostilities should be committed. He seemed much pleased with this, and promised that it should be observed on their part. I then resumed my march. We struck the cultivated ground about five hundred yards below the town, but as these extended to the bank of the Wabash, there was no possibility of getting an encampment which was provided with both wood and water.

My guides and interpreters being still with the advanced guard, and taking the direction of the town, the army followed, and had advanced within about one hundred and fifty yards, when fifty or sixty Indians sallied out, and with loud acclamations called to the cavalry and to the militia infantry, which were on our right flank, to halt. I immediately advanced to the front, caused the army to halt, and directed an interpreter to request some of the chiefs to come to me.

In a few moments, the man who had been with me before, made his appearance. I informed him that my object for the present was to procure a good piece of ground to encamp on, where we could get wood and water; he informed me that there was a creek to the north-west, which he thought would suit our purpose. I immediately dispatched two officers to examine it, and they reported the situation was excellent. I then took leave of the chief, and a mutual promise was again made for a suspension of hostilities until we could have an interview on the following day.

I found the ground destined for the encampment not altogether such as I could wish it—it was indeed admirably calculated for the encampment of regular troops, that were opposed to regulars, but it afforded great facility to the approach of savages. It was a piece of dry oak land, rising about ten feet above the level of a marshy prairie in front, (toward the Indian town,) and nearly twice that height above a similar prairie in the rear, through which, and near to this bank, ran a small stream, clothed with willows and brushwood. Toward the left flank, this bench of high land widened considerably, but became gradually narrow in the opposite direction, and at the distance of one hundred and fifty yards from the right flank, terminated in an abrupt point.

The two columns of infantry occupied the front and rear of this ground, at the distance of about one hundred and fifty yards from each other on the left, and something more than half that distance on the right flank—these flanks were filled up, the first by two companies of mounted riflemen, amounting to about one hundred and twenty men, under the command of Major-General Wells, of the Kentucky militia, who served as a major; the other by Spencer's company of mounted riflemen, which amounted to eighty men.

The front line was composed of one battalion of United States infantry, under the command of Major Floyd, flanked on the right by two companies of militia, and on the left by one company. The rear line was composed of a battalion of United States troops, under the command of Captain Bean, acting as major,

and four companies of militia infantry, under Lieutenant-Colonel Decker.

The regular troops of this line joined the mounted riflemen, under General Wells, on the left flank, and Col. Decker's battalion formed an angle with Spencer's company on the left.

Two troops of dragoons, amounting to, in the aggregate, about sixty men, were encamped in the rear of the left flank, and Captain Parke's troop, which was larger than the other two, in the rear of the front line. Our order of encampment varied little from that above described, excepting when some peculiarity of the ground made it necessary.

For a night attack, the order of encampment was the order of battle, and each man slept immediately opposite to his post in the line. In the formation of my troops, I used a single rank, or what is called Indian file—because in Indian warfare, where there is no shock to resist, one rank is nearly as good as two, and in that kind of warfare, the extension of line is of the first importance. Raw troops also maneuver with much more facility in single than in double ranks.

It was my constant custom to assemble all the field officers at my tent every evening by signal, to give them the watchword, and their instructions for the night—those given for the night of the 6th were, that each troop which formed a part of the exterior line of the encampment, should hold its own ground until relieved.

The dragoons were ordered to parade in case of a night attack, with their pistols in their belts, and to act as a corps de reserve. The camp was defended by two captains' guards, consisting each of four non-commissioned officers and forty-two privates; and two subalterns' guards, of twenty non-commissioned officers and privates. The whole under the command of a field officer of the day. The troops were regularly called up an hour before day, and made to continue under arms until it was quite light.

On the morning of the 7th, I had risen at a quarter after four o'clock, and the signal for calling out the men would have been given in two minutes, when the attack commenced. It began on our left flank—but a signal gun was fired by the sentinels, or by the guard in that direction, which made not the least resistance, but abandoned their officer, and fled into camp, and the first notice which the troops of that flank had of the danger, was from the yells of the savages within a short distance of the line—but even under those circumstances the men were not wanting to themselves or the occasion.

Such of them as were awake, or were easily awakened, seized their arms, and took their stations; others which were more tardy, had to contend with the enemy in the doors of their tents. The storm first fell upon Captain Barton's company of the 4th United States regiment, and Captain Geiger's company of mounted riflemen, which formed the left angle of the rear line. The fire upon these was exceedingly severe, and they suffered considerably before relief could be brought to them.

Some few Indians passed into the encampment near the angle, and one or two penetrated to some distance before they were killed. I believe all the other companies were under arms, and tolerably formed before they were fired on.

The morning was dark and cloudy; our fires afforded a partial light, which, if it gave us some opportunity of taking our positions, was still more advantageous to the enemy, affording them the means of taking a surer aim; they were therefore extinguished. Under all these discouraging circumstances, the troops (nineteen-twentieths of whom had never been in action before,) behaved in a manner that can never be too much applauded. They took their places without noise, and less confusion than could have been expected from veterans placed in the same situation.

As soon as I could mount my horse, I rode to the angle that was attacked—I found that Barton's company had suffered severely and the left of Geiger's entirely broken. I immediately ordered Cook's company and the late Captain Wentworth's, under Lieutenant Peters, to be brought up from the center of the rear line, where the ground was much more defensible, and formed across the angle in support of Barton's and Geiger's.

My attention was then engaged by a heavy firing upon the left of the front line, where were stationed the small company of United States' riflemen, (then, however, armed with muskets) and the companies of Bean, Snelling, and Prescott, of the 4th regiment. I found Major Daviess forming the dragoons in the rear of those companies, and understanding that the heaviest part of the enemy's fire proceeded from some trees about fifteen or twenty paces in front of those companies, I directed the major to dislodge them with a part of the dragoons.

Unfortunately the major's gallantry determined him to execute the order with a smaller force than was sufficient, which enabled the enemy to avoid him in front and attack his flanks. The major was mortally wounded, and his party driven back. The Indians were, however, immediately and gallantly dislodged from their advantageous position, by Captain Snelling, at the head of his company.

In the course of a few minutes after the commencement of the attack, the fire extended along the left flank, the whole of the front, the right flank, and part of the rear line. Upon Spencer's mounted riflemen, and the right of Warwick's company, which was posted on the rear of the right line, it was excessively severe. Captain Spencer and his first and second lieutenants, were killed, and Captain Warwick was mortally wounded— those companies, however, still bravely maintained their posts, but Spencer had suffered so severely, and having originally too much ground to occupy, I reinforced them with Robb's company of riflemen, which had been driven back, or by mistake ordered from their position on the left flank, toward the center of the camp, and filled the vacancy that had been occupied by Robb with Prescott's company of the 4th United States regiment.

My great object was to keep the lines entire, to prevent the enemy from breaking into the camp until daylight, which should enable me to make a general and effectual charge. With this view, I had reinforced every part of the line that had suffered much; and as soon as the approach of morning discovered itself, I withdrew from the front line, Snelling's, Posey's (under Lieutenant Albright,)

Above: Meeting of William Henry Harrison and Tecumseh at Vincennes, 1810. *Courtesy Indiana Historical Society Library*   Below: The Battle of Tippecanoe. *Courtesy Indiana Historical Society Library*

and Scott's, and from the rear line, Wilson's companies, and drew them up upon the left flank, and at the same time, I ordered Cook's and Bean's companies, the former from the rear, and the latter from the front line, to reinforce the right flank; forseeing that at these points the enemy would make their last efforts.

Major Wells, who commanded on the left flank, not knowing my intentions precisely, had taken command of these companies, and charged the enemy before I had formed the body of dragoons with which I meant to support the infantry; a small detachment of these were, however, ready, and proved amply sufficient for the purpose.

The Indians were driven by the infantry, at the point of the bayonet, and the dragoons pursued and forced them into a marsh, where they could not be followed. Captain Cook

and Lieutenant Larabee had, agreeable to my order, marched their companies to the right flank, had formed them under the fire of the enemy, and being then joined by the riflemen of that flank, had charged the Indians, killed a number, and put the rest to precipitate flight. A favorable opportunity was here offered to pursue the enemy with dragoons, but being engaged at that time on the other flank, I did not observe it till it was too late.

I have thus, sir, given you the particulars of an action, which was certainly maintained with the greatest obstinacy and perseverance, by both parties. The Indians manifested a ferocity uncommon even with them—to their savage fury our troops opposed that cool, and deliberate valor, which is characteristic of the Christian soldier.

THE PALMY DAYS OF MACKINAC
JULIETTE KINZIE

In September, 1830, Juliette Kinzie visited the storied island of Michilimackinac, then the headquarters of the American Fur Company and the commercial capital of the whole Northwest. The wife of John Kinzie, pioneer fur trader at Chicago, she saw many changes come to the frontier country. She left a classic record of her life in Wau-Bun: The "Early Day" in the Northwest, *from which the following excerpt is taken.*

MICHILIMACKINAC! That gem of the Lakes! How bright and beautiful it looked as we walked abroad on the following morning. The rain had passed away, but had left all things glittering in the light of the sun as it rose up over the waters of Lake Huron, far away to the east. Before us was the lovely bay, scarcely yet tranquil after the storm, but dotted with canoes and the boats of the fishermen already getting out their nets for the trout and whitefish, those treasures of the deep. Along the beach were scattered the wigwams or lodges of the Ottawas who had come to the island to trade. The inmates came forth to gaze upon us. A shout of welcome was sent

forth as they recognized Shaw-nee-aw-kee, who, from a seven years' residence among them, was well known to each individual.

A shake of the hand, and an emphatic "*Bon-jour—bon-jour,*" is the customary salutation between the Indian and the white man.

"Do the Indians speak French?" I inquired of my husband.

"No; this is a fashion they have learned of the French traders during many years of intercourse."

Not less hearty was the greeting of each Canadian *engagé* as he trotted forward to pay his respects to "Monsieur John," and to utter a long string of felicitations, in a most incom-

Old Fort Mackinac. *Courtesy Michigan Historical Commission Archives*

prehensible *patois*. I was forced to take for granted all the good wishes showered upon "Madame John," of which I could comprehend nothing but the hope that I should be happy and contented in my *"vie sauvage."*

The object of our early walk was to visit the Mission-house and school which had been some few years previously established at this place by the Presbyterian Board of Missions. It was an object of especial interest to Mr. and Mrs. Stuart, and its flourishing condition at this period, and the prospects of extensive future usefulness it held out, might well gladden their philanthropic hearts. They had lived many years on the island, and had witnessed its transformation, through God's blessing on Christian efforts, from a worldly, dissipated community to one of which it might almost be said, "Religion was every man's business." This mission establishement was the beloved

child and the common center of interest of the few Protestant families clustered around it. Through the zeal and good management of Mr. and Mrs. Ferry, and the fostering encouragement of the congregation, the school was in great repute, and it was pleasant to observe the effect of mental and religious culture in subduing the mischievous, tricky propensities of the half-breed, and rousing the stolid apathy of the genuine Indian.

These were the palmy days of Mackinac. As the headquarters of the American Fur Company, and the entrepot of the whole Northwest, all the trade in supplies and goods on the one hand, and in furs and products of the Indian country on the other, was in the hands of the parent establishment or its numerous outposts scattered along Lakes Superior and Michigan, the Mississippi, or through still more distant regions.

Probably few are ignorant of the fact that all the Indian tribes, with the exception of the Miamis and the Wyandots, had, since the transfer of the old French possessions to the British Crown, maintained a firm alliance with the latter. The independence achieved by the United States did not alter the policy of the natives, nor did our government succeed in winning or purchasing their friendship. Great Britain, it is true, bid high to retain them. Every year the leading men of the Chippewas, Ottawas, Pottowattamies, Menomonees, Winnebagoes, Sauks and Foxes, and even still more remote tribes, journeyed from their distant homes to Fort Malden in Upper Canada to receive their annual amount of presents from their Great Father across the water. It was a master-policy thus to keep them in pay, and had enabled those who practiced it to do fearful execution through the aid of such allies in the last war between the two countries.

The presents they thus received were of considerable value, consisting of blankets, broadcloths or *strouding*, calicoes, guns, kettles, traps, silver-works (comprising armbands, bracelets, brooches and ear-bobs) looking-glasses, combs, and various other trinkets distributed with no niggardly hand.

The magazines and storehouses of the Fur Company at Mackinac were the resort of all the upper tribes for the sale of their commodities, and the purchase of all such articles as they had need of, including those above enumerated, and also ammunition, which, as well as money and liquor, their British friends very commendably omitted to furnish them.

Besides their furs, various in kind and often of great value—beaver, otter, marten, mink, silver-gray and red fox, wolf, bear, and wild-cat, musk-rat, and smoked deerskins—the Indians brought for trade maple-sugar in abundance, considerable quantities of both Indian corn and beans and wild rice; while the squaws added to their quota of merchandise a contribution in the form of moccasins, hunting-pouches, mococks, or little boxes of birch-bark embroidered with porcupine quills and filled with maple-sugar, mats of a neat and durable fabric, and toy-models of Indian cradles, snowshoes, canoes, etc., etc.

It was no unusual thing at this period to see a hundred or more canoes of Indians at once approaching the island, laden with their articles of traffic; and if to these we add the squadrons of large Mackinac boats constantly arriving from the outposts, with the furs, peltries, and buffalo-robes collected by the distant traders, some idea may be formed of the extensive operations and important position of the American Fur Company, as well as of the vast circle of human beings either immediately or remotely connected with it.

It is no wonder that the philanthropic mind, surveying these races of uncultivated heathen, should stretch forward to the time when, through an unwearied devotion of the white man's energies, and an untiring sacrifice of self and fortune, his red brethren might rise in the scale of social civilization,—when Education and Christianity should go hand in hand to make "the wilderness blossom as the rose."

Little did the noble souls of that day rejoicing in the success of their labors at Mackinac, anticipate that in less than a quarter of a century there would remain of all these numerous tribes but a few scattered bands, squalid, degraded, with scarce a vestige remaining of their former lofty character—themselves chased farther and farther towards the setting sun, until they were literally grudged a resting-place on the face of the earth.

I V

Land Seekers

ONE of Francis Parkman's great passages described La Salle at the mouth of the Mississippi taking possession, in the name of the King of France and of Navarre, of all the territory drained by the river and its tributaries. This vast realm of savannahs and forests, of sun-cracked deserts and grassy prairies, watered by a thousand rivers, ranged by a thousand warlike tribes, passed beneath the scepter of Louis the Fourteenth—"all," remarked Parkman, "by virtue of a feeble human voice, inaudible at half a mile."

When the Northwest Territory became American there was no king to claim possession. There were only the people. "The public lands," carefully explained James Flint, a visitor from Scotland, "are in reality the property of the people."

The first settlers beyond the mountains were squatters who went ahead of surveying crews and government land agents. They lived in the wilds without purse or scrip, wanting nothing but freedom and their own footpath to the hillside spring. One of them, John Amberson, squatting in "Amberson's Bottom" on the upper Ohio in 1785, declared that all men "have undoubted right to pass into every vacant country . . . and Congress is not empowered to forbid them." He spoke for the generations of men who would go into wild land, ahead of legalized settlement, all the way from the forks of the Ohio to the coast of Oregon.

The Ordinance of 1785 called for a survey, into townships and sections, of the Northwest Territory. The first district to be surveyed was the Seven Ranges, just beyond the Pennsylvania line, and the surveyors brought back glowing reports of that country. In 1787 a band of Revolutionary army officers in Boston organized the Ohio Company to purchase a large tract and make a settlement. So began the historic town of Marietta. Linked with the Ohio Company's contract with Congress was the purchase by the Scioto Company of a river-front tract below the Marietta site. This land, strenuously advertised in revolution-torn France, became the goal of five hundred French émigrés who formed the ill-starred colony of Gallipolis.

One other large transaction was made by Congress in a contract with Judge John Cleves Symmes of New Jersey. The Symmes Purchase comprised a million acres between the two Miami rivers, fronting on the Ohio. Its chief settlement became Cincinnati, a city with an assured future when Fort Washington was erected there.

The first federal land law was designed to raise revenue to pay the national debt. It called for minimum purchase of one section, 640 acres, at $2 an acre, half the sum to be paid within thirty days. Few frontier farmers could count out that much money, and land sales were almost nil. In 1800 William Henry Harrison, Congressional delegate from the Northwest Territory, convinced Congress that the West must offer a future to poor and ambitious men. The resulting Harrison Land Act provided for sale of 320-acre lots, to be paid in installments over four years. In 1804 the minimum purchase was reduced to 160 acres. Under the new law, land offices were established all the way to the Mississippi. Their activity gave to the American language a new phrase: they did a land-office business.

LANDLOOKER FROM VIRGINIA

GEORGE WASHINGTON'S
JOURNAL OF A TOUR TO THE OHIO, 1770

The first detailed and accurate account of the Ohio valley was written by George Washington in 1770. In a diary now preserved in the Library of Congress, the veteran surveyor and Indian fighter records his excitement as a landlooker in the virgin valley beyond the mountains.

Washington had a material interest in the West because of Governor Dinwiddie's offer in 1754 of bounty lands along the Ohio to Virginia soldiers of the French and Indian War. Two hundred thousand acres of the "King of Great Britain's Lands" were designated as military bounty. In addition to his own bounty claim Washington acquired other land by purchase.

In the fall of 1770 he made his western tour, wanting to secure bounty lands for the men of his Virginia regiment and to look at tracts along the Ohio for personal purchase. In a canoe he drifted three hundred miles down the Ohio and then paddled up the Great Kanawha. After marking out his corners on 41,000 acres of river-front land, he returned on horseback to Fort Pitt. The tour occupied the months of October and November, 1770.

MONDAY [November] 5th. I set of the Canoe with our Baggage & Walkd across the Neck on foot with Captn Crawford distance according to our Walking about 8 Miles as we kept a strait course under the Foot of the Hills which ran about S^o E^t & was two hours & an half walking of it

This is a good Neck of Land the Soil being generally good; & in places very rich — their is a large proportion of Meadow Ground, and the Land as high, dry & Level as one coud wish — the growth in most places is beach intermixd with Walnut &c^a but more especially with Poplar (of which there are numbers very large) ———— the Land towards the upper end is black Oak, & very good — upon the whole a valuable Tract might be had here, & I judge the quantity to be about 4000 Acres

After passing this Bottom & the Rapid, as also some Hills wch jut pretty close to the River, we came to that Bottom before remarkd the 29th Ult^o; which being well describd, there needs no further remark except that the Bottom within view appears to be exceeding rich; but as I was not out upon it, I cannot tell how it is back from the River ————

a little above this Bottom, we Incampd — the Afternoon being Rainy & night wet —

Tuesday 6$^{th.}$ We left our Incampment a little after day light, & in about 5 Miles we came to Kiashute Hunting Camp which was now removed to the Mouth of that Creek noted Oct^o 29 for having fallen Timber at the Mouth of it, in a bottom of good land ———— between the Bottom last describd, & this bottom, there is nothing but Hills on the East side; except a little flat of a 100 Acres or so, between — this Bottom thro which the Creek comes may be about 4 or 5 Miles in length & tolerably wide. ———— grown up pretty much with Beach tho the Soil is good ————

By the kindness, and Idle ceremony of the Indians, I was detained at Kiashutas Camp all the remain^g part of this day; and having a good deal of conversation with him on the Subject of Land, He informed me that, it was further from the Mouth of the Great Kanhawa to the Fall of that River than it was between the two Kanhawas — that the Bottom on the West side (which begins near the Mouth of the Kanhawa) continues all the way to the Falls without the Interposition of Hills, and widens as it goes, especially from a pretty large Creek that comes in ab^t 10 or 15 Miles higher up than where we were ———— that in the Fork there is a body of good Land ———— and at some pretty considera[ble] distance above this, the River forks again at an Island, & there begin the Reed or Cain to grow — that the Bottoms on the East side of the River are also very good, but broken with Hills, and that the River is easily passd with Canoes to the Falls wch cannot be less than 100 Mil but further it is not possible to go with them and that there is but one ridge fr thence to the Settlements upon the [New] River above, that it is possible for a Man to travel; the Country betw[een] being so much broken with steep Hills & precipices

[At this point the manuscript is mutilated —apparently damaged by mud and water—and the record from November 6th to 17th is illegible. The journey continued, however, up the rain-swollen Ohio River, and the record resumes on November 17th.]

Saturday 17th. By this Morning the River had fallen (in the whole) 2 or 3 & twenty feet, & was still lowering ———— Ab^t 8 Oclock we set out, & passing the lower cross Creeks we came to a pretty long, & tolerable wide & good bottom on the East side the River; then comes in the Hills, just above which, is Buffalo Creek (a Creek I neither see nor remarkd in going down) upon which, and above it, between y^t & the cross Creeks near the Mingo Town (distant 3 or 4 Miles) is a Bottom of exceeding fine Land, but not very large, unless it extends up the Creek.

About 3 Oclock we came to the Town without seeing our Horses the Indian (which was sent express for them) having passd through only the morning before (being de-taind by the Creeks which were too high to ford; without going high up them) ———— here we resolvd to wait there arrival which was expected to morrow & here then will end our water Voyage along a River the general course of which from Bever Creek to the Kanhawa is about S W^t (as near as I coud determine); but in its winding thro a narrow Vale, extreamly serpentine; forming on both sides the River alternately, Necks of very good (some exceeding fine) Bottoms; lying for the most part

in the shape of a half Moon, & of various sizes — there is very little difference in the gen^l width of the River from Fort Pitt to the Kanhawa; but in the depth I believe the odds is considerably in favour of the lower parts; as we found no shallows below the Mingo Town, except in one or two places where the River was broad; & there, I do not know but there might have been a deep Channel in some part of it ———— every here and there are Islands, some larger, & some smaller, which operating in the nature of Locks, or steps, occasion pretty still water above but for the most part strong & rapid water along side of them — however there is none of these so swift but that a Vessel may be Rowed or set up with Poles — When the River is in its Natural State, large canoes that will carry 5 or 6000 weight & more, may be workd against stream by 4 hands 20 & 25 Miles a day; & down, a good deal more — The Indians who are very dexterous (even there women) in the management of Canoes have there Hunting Camp's & Cabins all along the River for the convenience of transporting their Skins by water to Market ———— In the Fall, so soon as the Hunting Season comes on, they set out with their Familys for this purpose; & In Hunting will move there Camps from place to place till by the Spring they get 2 or 300 or more Miles from there Town's; Then Bever catch it in there way up which frequently brings them into the Month of May, when the Women are employd in Plant^g ———— the Men at Market & in Idleness, till the Fall again; when they pursue the same course again ———— during the Summer Months they live a poor & perishing life ————

The Indians who live upon the Ohio (the upper parts of it at least) are composed of Shawnas, Delawares, & some of the Mingos, who getting but little part of the consideration that was given for the Lands Eastward of the Ohio, view the settlement of the People upon this River with an uneasy & jealous Eye; & do not scruple to say that they must be compensated for their Right if the People settle thereon, notwithstanding the Cession of the Six Nations thereto ———— On the other hand, the People from Virginia & elsewhere, are exploring and Marking all the Lands that are valuable not only on Redstone & other Waters

The Ohio River at Marietta, by Charles Sullivan. *Courtesy Ohio Historical Society*

of Monongehela but along down the Ohio as low as the little Kanhawa; & by next Summer I suppose will get to the great Kanhawa, at least; how difficult it may be to contend with these People afterwards is easy to be judgd of from every days experience of Lands actually settled, supposing these to be made; than which nothing is more probable if the Indians permit them, from the disposition of the People at present. ——— A few Settlements in the midst of some of the large Bottoms, woud render it impracticable to get any large q^{ty} of Land Together; as the Hills all the way down the River (as low as I went) come pretty close and are steep & broken incapable of settlements tho some of them are rich and only fit to support the Bottoms with Timber and Wood ———

The Land back of the Bottoms, as far as I have been able to judge, either from my own observations or from information, is nearly the same, that is exceeding uneven & Hilly; & I do presume that there is no body's of Flat rich Land to be found one gets far enough from the River to head the little run & drains that come through the Hills; & to the Sources (or near it) of the Creeks & there Branches ——— this it seems is the case of the Lands upon Monongahela and Yaugh^a & I fancy holds good upon this River till you get into the Flat Lands (or near them) below the Falls —

The Bottom Land differs a good deal in quality ——— that highest up the River in general is richest; tho the Bottoms are neither so wide or long, as those below ——— Walnut, H[ickory] Cherry, & some other Woods that grow snarly, & neither Tall nor large, but coverd with Grape Vines (with the Fruit of which this Country at this Instant abounds) are the growth of the richest Bottoms, but on the other hand these Bottoms appear to me to be the lowest and most subject to Floods. Sugar Tree and Ash, mixd with Walnut &ᶜᵃ compose the growth of the next richest low grounds —— and Beach Poplar Oaks &cᵃ the last —— the Soil of this is also good but inferior to either of the other kinds & beach Bottoms are excepted against on acct of the difficulty of clearing them there Root's spreading over a large surface of ground & being hard to kill.

Sunday, 18th. Agreed with two Delaware Indians to carry up our Canoe to Fort Pitt for the doing of which I was to pay 6 Dollars & give them a Quart Tinn Can ——

Monday 19th. The Delawares set of with the Canoe — and our Horses not arriving, the day appeard exceeding long & tedious. Upon conversing with Nicholson, I found he had been two or three times to Fort Chartres at the Illinois, and got from him the following Acct of the Lands between this & that; & upon the Shawna River [Cumberland River]; on which he had been a Hunting.

The Lands down the Ohio grow more and more level as you approach the Falls and about 150 Miles below them, the Country appears quite Flat, & exceeding rich, —— On the Shawna River (which comes into the Ohio 400 Miles below the Falls & about 1100 from Pittsburg) up which he had hunted 300 & more Miles the Lands are exceeding Level, rich, & fine, but a good deal intermixed with Cain or Reed, which might render them difficult to clear; that game of all kinds was to be found here in the greatest abundance, especially Buffalo —— That from Fort Chartres to Pittsburg by Land, is computed 800 Miles; & in travelling thro the country from that place he found the soil very rich —— the Ground exceeding level to OPost [Vincennes] (a French Settlement & from Opost to the Lower Shawna Town on Scioto equally flat —— that he passd through large Planes 30 miles in length without a Tree except little Islands of Wood —— that in these Planes thousands & 10,000 of Buffalo may be seen feeding —— That the distance from Fort Chartres to Opost is about 240 Miles & the Country not very well waterd —— from Opost to the lower Shawna Town about 300 more abounding in good Springs & Rivulets —— that the remainder of the way to Fort Pitt is Hilly; and the Hills larger as you approach the Fort tho the Lᵈ in general is also good.

"CUTLER'S PARADISE"

MANASSEH CUTLER'S
SKETCH OF THE OHIO COUNTRY

In 1787, when the Continental Congress was debating the ordinance which would open the Ohio country to sale and settlement, eleven men met at the Bunch of Grapes tavern in Boston. They formed the Ohio Company of Associates, planning to purchase land and locate a settlement on the Ohio. One of the Associates was the Rev. Manasseh Cutler, botanist, lawyer, merchant, and Congregational minister. A big, buoyant man, he went to New York to lobby for the project. On July 13, 1787, the ordinance was enacted, and Cutler then urged approval of the Ohio Company's purchase. Congress wanted a million dollars for a million acres, payable in three months. Cutler could not agree, and the prospect dimmed.

Then Cutler was approached by Colonel William Duer, Secretary of the Board of the Treasury, who proposed that the "Scioto Project," hastily organized by a group of speculators, be added to the Ohio Company's contract. Cutler agreed. Accordingly he enlarged his application to four million acres, of which three million would be assigned to the Scioto Company.

Four months later, at Ipswich, Massachusetts, with a cold wind blowing from the ocean, twenty-two men listened to Manasseh Cutler's farewell words. They cracked their ox whips and started west, striding beside a wagon covered with canvas and lettered in Cutler's bold hand FOR THE OHIO COUNTRY. These were the vanguard of the Marietta settlement.

Meanwhile Cutler had written a luring description of the Ohio country, to interest settlers and speculators. In 1789 the pamphlet, translated into French, was used by the Scioto Company to promote emigration from France, an effort which resulted in the settlement of five hundred French émigrés at Gallipolis on the Ohio River in 1790.

Manasseh Cutler drove a horse and buggy to Ohio in the summer of 1788, but he had not yet seen the western country when he wrote his rosy pamphlet. His extravagant description led Yankees to refer ironically to the Ohio Purchase as "Cutler's Indian Haven" and "Cutler's Paradise." Though its statements were extravagant—including a prediction that the national capital would be located on the Ohio—it was based on reports from explorers and surveyors on the upper Ohio.

The original text of Cutler's pamphlet was lost. The following version is a translation from a French copy which belonged to one of the first settlers at Gallipolis. Its title: "A Description of the Soil, Productions, etc., of that Portion of the United States Situated between Pennsylvania and the Rivers Ohio and Scioto and Lake Erie."

THE great river Ohio is formed by the confluence of the Monongahela and the Alleghany in Pennsylvania. It flows from about 290 miles west of the city of Philadelphia, and about 20 miles west of the western boundary of Pennsylvania. In following the ordinary route the 290 miles are increased to 320, and the windings of the Ohio increase the 20 miles to about 42.

These two sources of the Ohio are both great navigable rivers; the first flows from the southeast, and there is, between it and the navigable waters of the Potamac, in Virginia, a portage of only about 30 miles; the latter opens a passage to the northeast, and rises not far from the source of the Susquehanna.

The State of Pennsylvania has already adopted the plan of opening a navigation from the Alleghany River to Philadelphia by way of the Susquehanna and the Delaware. In following this route there will be only a transit by land, or portage, of 24 miles.

At the junction of these two rivers, or at the source of the Ohio, we find Fort Pitt, which gives its name to the city of Pittsburgh, a flourishing settlement in the vicinity of the fortress. From this city the Ohio pursues its way to the southwest for 1188 miles (including the windings of the river) and empties into the Mississippi, after traversing for this prodigious distance a most fertile and agreeable country, and having increased its waters by those of several other navigable rivers: the Muskingum, the Hockhocking, the Scioto, the Miami, and the Wabash from the northwest; the Kanawha, the Kentucky, the Buffaloe, the Shawnee, and the Cherokee from the southwest; all these rivers, navigable for a distance of from 100 to 900 miles, fall into the Ohio, and it is this river that furnishes a great part of those united waters which flow into the ocean through the bed of the Mississippi.

The Ohio, from Pennsylvania to the Mississippi, separates the State of Virginia from other domains of the United States, or in other words, from the territory not comprised within the limits of any particular State. This territory extends westward to the Mississippi, and north to the frontiers of the United States. Commencing at the meridian which forms the western boundary of Pennsylvania they have laid off a space sufficient for seven ranges of *municipalities* (townships). As a north and south line extends along the Ohio in a very oblique direction, the western boundary of the seventh range strikes the Ohio nine miles above the Muskingum, which is the first large river which empties into the Ohio. Their junction is 172 miles below Fort Pitt, following the winding of the Ohio, but in a straight line little more than 90 miles.

The Muskingum is a river which flows slowly, and has banks high enough to prevent all inundation. It is 250 yards wide at the place where it enters the Ohio, and is navigable for large vessels and bateaux as far as Tree Legs, and for small boats to the lake at its source. From thence by means of a transit by land of about one mile, communication is opened with Lake Erie by means of the Cuyahoga, which is a river of great value, navigable through its whole length, without any cataracts to obstruct its course. The passage from Lake Erie to the Hudson, through the State of New York, is well known. The longest transit by land on this route is that which is caused by the falls of Niagara, which interrupts the communication between Lakes Erie and Ontario. After that, one passes by the River Oswego, Oneida Lake, Woods Creek (the bay of the woods), and by means of a short portage, enters the Mohawk; another portage occasioned by the cataract near the confluence of the Mohawk, and the Hudson brings the voyager to Albany.

The Hockhocking is somewhat like the Muskingum, but not so large. It is navigable for large vessels for about seventy miles, and much further for small ones. On the banks of this much frequented river are inexhaustible quarries of building stone, great beds of iron ore, and some rich mines of lead. We find also, very frequently in the neighborhood of this river, coal mines and salt springs, which abound in this Western country. The salt which is obtained from these springs furnishes a never-failing abundance of this article of prime necessity. Beds of clay, both white and blue, of an excellent quality, are met with also throughout this region. This clay is adapted for the manufacture of glass, of pottery, and all kinds of brick. Armenian clay, and several other useful deposits, have also been discovered along the different branches of this river.

The Scioto is a river longer than either of those of which we have thus far spoken, and furnishes a navigation much more considerable. For an extent of two hundred miles large vessels can navigate it. Then there is a passage to be made by land of four miles only to the Sandusky, a river also easily navigable, which enters into Lake Erie. It is by the Sandusky and Scioto that they pass generally in going from Canada to the Mississippi. This route is one of the most considerable and most frequented found in any country. By it are united some of the most extensive territories, and when we consider the rapidity with which settlements are made in the Western part of Canada, upon Lake Erie, and in Kentucky, we may predict that there will be an immense commerce between these people. It is certain that the lands which border upon, and which lie near these rivers, will be of the greatest value from their situation alone, and quite apart from their natural fertility. There can be no doubt that the flour, wheat, hemp, etc., exported from the extensive regions surrounding Lakes Huron and Ontario would have an easier transit by means of Lake Erie and the neighboring rivers than by any other route. The merchant who shall in future inhabit the banks of the Ohio will be able to pay more for these commodities than the merchant of Quebec, by reason of these advantages, because they can be transported from the former of these countries to Florida and the West India Islands with much less expense and risk, and at a much lower rate of insurance than from the latter. In fact, the transportation of these productions of the soil, the expenses upon the Ohio included, would not amount to more than a fourth part of what it would cost from Quebec, and it will be still cheaper than it is by way of Lake Oneida.

The Scioto has a gentle current, which is interrupted by no cataracts. Sometimes in the spring it overflows its banks, which are covered by vast fields of rice, which nature here produces spontaneously. For the rest, we find in abundance in the country which borders upon this river, salt springs, coal mines, deposits of white and blue clay and of free stone.

The general expressions of admiration

Manasseh Cutler. *Courtesy Ohio Historical Society*

which are commonly made use of in speaking of the natural fertility of the countries watered by these western rivers of the United States render difficult the description one would wish to make, unless one takes particular pains to mark on the map the places which merit especial attention, or unless he gives an exact description of the territory in general without regard to the risk he runs of being charged with exaggeration. But upon this point we are able to say that we have with us the unanimous opinion of geographers, of surveyors and of all those travelers who have collected precise information concerning the characteristics of the country, and who have observed with the most scrupulous exactitude all the remarkable objects which nature there displays. They all agree that no part of the ter-

ritory belonging to the United States combines in itself so many advantages, whether of salubrity, fertility or variety of productions, as that which extends from the Muskingum to the Scioto and the Great Miami.

Colonel Gordon speaking of his travels through a country much more extensive in which this is included and of which it is indubitably the most beautiful part, makes the following observations: "The country along the Ohio is extremely agreeable, filled with great plains of the richest soil and exceedingly salubrious. One remark of this kind suffices for all that region bounded by the western slope of the Allegheny Mountains and extending to the southwest a distance of five hundred miles down the Ohio, thence to the north as far as the source of the rivers that empty into the Ohio, and thence eastward along the hills which separate the lakes from the river Ohio as far as French creek. I can, from the perfect knowledge which I have of it, affirm that the country which I have just described is the most salubrious, the most agreeable, the most advantageous, the most fertile land which is known to any people of Europe, whatsoever."

The lands which are watered by the different rivers emptying into the Ohio, of which we have just spoken, are, since the time of Col. Gordon, better known, and can be described with more precision and in a manner which ought to inspire confidence.

They are remarkable for their variety of soil from which results everything which can contribute to the advantages due to their local position and which promise the success and the riches which ought to burst forth among every agricultural and manufacturing people.

The great level plains which one meets with here and which form natural prairies, have a circumference of from twenty to fifty miles, they are found interspersed almost everywhere along the rivers. These plains have a soil as rich as can be imagined and which with very little labor can be devoted to any species of cultivation which one wishes to give it. They say that in many of these prairies one can cultivate an acre of land per day and prepare it for the plough. There is no undergrowth on them and the trees which grow very high and become very large only need to be deprived of their bark in order to become fit for use.

The kinds of timber fit for the purposes of the joiner which grow most abundantly in this country and the most useful of trees which are found here are the sugar-maple, the sycamore, black and white mulberry, and black and white walnut, the chestnut, oaks of every kind, the cherry tree, beech tree, the elm, the cucumber tree, ironwood, the ash tree, the aspen, the sassafras, the wild apple tree, and a great number of other trees of which it is impossible to express the names in French.

General Parsons has measured a black walnut near the Muskingum, of which the circumference, five feet above the ground, was twenty-two feet. A sycamore measured in the same way had a circumference of forty-four feet. One finds on the heights white and black oaks as well as the chestnut, and nearly all the trees we have just named, which grow there, very large and to a proportionate height. One finds both on the hills and on the plains a great quantity of grapes growing wild, and of which the inhabitants make a red wine, which suffices for their own consumption. They have tried the experiment of pressing these grapes at the settlement of Saint Vincent, and the result is a wine which, by keeping a little while, becomes preferable to the many wines of Europe. Cotton of an excellent quality is also a product of the country.

The sugar-maple is of great value to a region situated as this is in the interior of the country. It furnishes enough sugar for the use of a large number of people, and for this purpose a small number of trees are usually kept by each family. A maple tree will produce about ten pounds of sugar per year, and it is produced with little difficulty. The sap of the tree flows in the months of February and March; it becomes crystalized after being boiled, and the sugar is equal in flavor and whiteness to the best Muscavado.

All parts of this country are abundantly supplied with excellent springs, and one finds everywhere both small and large creeks, on which mills may be established. These brooks, useful for so many purposes, have the appearance of being disposed by the hand of art in such a manner as to contribute toward procuring every advantage which can make life desirable.

There is a very little bad land in this territory, and no marsh. There are plenty of hills; their position is agreeable, and they are not high enough to interfere with their cultivation. Their soil is deep, rich, covered with trees of good growth, and adapted to the cultivation of wheat, rye, indigo, tobacco, etc.

The communication between this territory and the ocean is principally by the four following routes:

First: The route by the Scioto and Muskingum to Lake Erie, and thence by the River Hudson, we have already described.

Second: The passage by the Ohio and

Monongahela to the transit by land already mentioned, which leads to navigable waters of the Potomac. This land transit is about thirty miles, but it will very probably be diminished in a little while, by means of the plan which is actually in contemplation for opening a communication between these rivers.

Third: The Great Kanawha which empties into the Ohio toward the confines of Virginia, between the Hockhocking and Scioto, affords a very ready navigation toward the Southeast, and requires but a short portage to reach the navigable waters of the James River in Virginia. This communication, useful to the settlements between the Muskingum and Scioto, will very probably be the most frequented for the exports of the manufactures of the country, and still more for the importation of foreign goods, because they can be carried more cheaply from the Chesapeake to the Ohio, than they now are from Philadelphia to Carlisle and the other counties situated in the lower parts of Pennsylvania.

Fourth: But above all, it is upon the Ohio and Mississippi that there can be transported a great number of things necessary for the markets of Florida and the West Indies, such as wheat, flour, beef, bacon, timber for joinery and ship-building, etc, that they will be more frequented than any river upon the earth. The distance from the Scioto to the Mississippi is eight hundred miles, thence to the ocean nine hundred; all this journey can be easily made in fifteen days, and the voyage in reascending these rivers is not so difficult as one would suppose. Experience has demonstrated that one can make great use of sails on the Ohio.

Here again is a fortunate circumstance; it is that the Ohio Company is on the point of establishing its settlements, and it is making them in a manner alike, systematic and judicious. Its operations will serve as a useful model for all the settlements which will be found in the future in the United States. Add to this that this new colony is established so near the Western boundary of Pennsylvania as to appear to be only a continuation of the older settlements, by reason of which there will no longer be reason to fear that these unsettled regions may be occupied by the savages, as

has too frequently happened in situations very far removed from the seat of government.

The intention of Congress, and that of the inhabitants, is that these settlements shall be made in a regular manner; that they shall follow the course of the Ohio, and that they shall commence by occupying the northern part of the country toward Lake Erie. And it is hoped that not many years will probably elapse until the whole country above the Miami will be raised in value to such a point that the advantages which travelers have celebrated will be seen in their true light, and it will be admitted that they spoke nothing but the truth when they called this country the garden of the universe, the center of wealth, a place destined to be the heart of a great Empire.

The following reflections will not escape either the philosopher or the statesman, who shall see this delightful part of the United States settled upon a wise system and in a well ordered manner:

1. The labors of the agriculturist will here be rewarded by productions as useful as, and more varied than in any part of America; the advantages which are generally found divided in any other climate are here united; and all the advantages which other parts of the United States present, are here combined in the highest perfection. In all parts the soil is deep, rich, producing in abundance wheat, rye, corn, buckwheat, barley, oats, flax, hemp, tobacco, indigo, the tree that furnishes the food for the silk-worm, the grape-vine, cotton. The tobacco is of a quality much superior to that of Virginia, and the crops of wheat are much more abundant here than in any other part of America. The ordinary crop of corn is from sixty to eighty English bushels per acre. The bottom lands are especially adapted to the production of all the commodities we have just enumerated. There where the vast plains, which are met with in this territory, are intersected with little brooks, the land is suitable for the culture of rice, and it grows here abundantly. Hops also are produced spontaneously in this territory, and there are also the same peaches, plums, pears, melons, and in general, all the fruits which are produced in the temperate zone.

There is no country more abounding in game than this. The stag, fallow deer, elk, buffalo and bears fill the woods and are nourished on these great and beautiful plains, which are encountered in all parts of these countries, an unanswerable proof of the fertility of the soil; wild turkeys, geese, ducks, swans, teal, pheasants, partridges, and so forth, are here found in greater abundance than our domestic fowls in all the older settlements of America. The rivers are well stocked with fish of different kinds, and several of these fish are of an exquisite quality. In general, they are large, the cat-fish (*poisson-chat*) has an excellent flavor and weighs from twenty to eighty pounds.

One will find here provisions for several years, and the borders of each one of these rivers will serve for a long time in place of a market. When inhabitants shall come here from all parts of the world nature will have provided for them, at least for one year, all they need, without the necessity of making any purchases.

2. There is no place more suitable from its situation and productions for the establishment of manufactures than this. The necessaries of life are abundant and cheap. The raw material for all things necessary for clothing and personal adornment are here found in quantities. Silk, flax and cotton bring a good price here; but these articles, being manufactured and being adapted for the different purposes of use and luxury, would still be cheap here by reason of the small amount of freight necessary to pay for their transportation. The United States, and perhaps other countries beside, will be replaced, or superseded in the market, by the competition of the inhabitants of the interior parts of America.

The construction of vessels will be one of the most considerable branches of business on the Ohio River and its tributaries. In the lowest stage of water in the Ohio we find a depth of four fathoms from the mouth of the Muskingum to its junction with the Mississippi. In only one part is it very rapid, and there the navigation is interrupted for about one mile. Elsewhere throughout its whole extent the fall is not more than fifteen feet, and the bed of the river, which has a breadth

of two hundred and fifty rods, has never less than five feet of water. In winter it increases to thirty feet. The river can be ascended not only by means of oars, but they readily surmount the current by means of sails only. Geographers and others who have seen the locality are of the opinion that if a canal were dug at a little less than half a mile south of the river, at a point where a low prairie is found, the current could be avoided and navigation thus be without interruption the whole year round.

Hemp, iron and ship timber are abundant and of good quality here. During the highest stage of water, which is from February to April, and frequently in October and November, vessels can easily pass the rapids with their cargoes to the sea even in the present condition of the river.

An English engineer, who has made a thorough examination of the western country, has communicated the following observations to Lord Hillsborough in 1770. This nobleman was the Secretary of State for the Department of America at the time when we were colonists of Great Britain, and when our country was regarded solely, as it could be made available for a market for English fabrics.

"No part of North America has less need for encouragement in order to furnish rigging for ships, and the raw material destined for Europe, and to furnish to the West India Islands building material, provisions, etc., than the Ohio country, and that for the following reasons:

"1. The country is excellent, climate temperate; grapes grow without cultivation; silk worms and mulberry trees abound everywhere; hemp, hops and rice grow wild in the valleys and low lands; lead and iron abound in the hills; salt springs are innumerable; and there is no country better adapted to the culture of tobacco, flax and cotton than that of the Ohio.

"2. The country is well watered by several navigable rivers, which communicate with each other, and by means of which, with a very short transport by land, the productions of the Valley of the Ohio can even at this moment be conveyed at a much lower price to the seaport of Alexandria on the River

Potomac, where General Braddock landed his troops, than merchandise can be carried from Northampton to London.

"3. The Ohio River is navigable at all seasons of the year for large boats, and during the months of February, March and April it is possible to construct large vessels upon it and send them to the ocean loaded with hemp, iron, flax, silk, tobacco, cotton, potash, etc.

"4. Flour, wheat, beef, planks for ship-building and other things not less useful can descend the Ohio to Western Florida and go thence to the West India Islands more cheaply and in better condition than the same merchandise can be sent from New York or Philadelphia to the same islands.

"5. Hemp, tobacco, iron and similar bulky articles can descend the Ohio to the ocean at least 50 per cent. cheaper than the same articles have ever been transported by land in Pennsylvania over a distance no greater than sixty miles, although the expense of carriage there is less than in any part of North America.

"6. The freight for transporting goods manufactured in Europe from the sea-board to the Ohio, will not be so considerable as it now is, and always will be, to a great part of the counties of Pennsylvania, Virginia and Maryland. When the farmers or merchants who dwell upon the Ohio set about providing for transportation they will build vessels of all kinds suited for commerce with the West India Islands and Europe, or, as they will have black walnut, cherry, oak, etc., sawed ready for foreign commerce, they will make of them rafts in the same manner as is practiced by those who live about the headwaters of the Delaware in Pennsylvania, on which they will put their hemp, their iron, their tobacco, etc., and with which they will go to New Orleans.

"The following observations should not be omitted: They manufacture a great quantity of flour in the region situated in the west of Pennsylvania, and they send it by land to Philadelphia, which costs a great deal, and thence they send it by sea to South Carolina and Eastern and Western Florida, where they grow little or no grain. One may say that nature herself has designed the Ohio to be the river by which the two Floridas may be supplied with flour, and that not only for the consumption of these two provinces, but still more for a considerable commerce which they carry on in that article with Jamaica and the Spanish settlements of Mexico. Quantities of mill-stones may be procured from the hills which border the Ohio, and the country everywhere abounds with water-courses suited to the construction of mills of every kind. The passage from Philadelphia to Pensacola is rarely made in less than a month, and they ordinarily pay fifty shillings a ton freight (a ton consists of sixteen barrels) for transportation that far. Boats carrying from 500 to 1000 barrels of flour go in nearly the same time from Pittsburgh to Pensacola as from Philadelphia to Pensacola, and at half the expense. Merchants on the Ohio can furnish flour on better terms than Philadelphia, and without running the risk of damage by sea or the delays of transportation on that element; and besides, without paying insurance, advantages which can not be enjoyed in the case of goods shipped from Philadelphia to Pensacola. And let no one imagine that this is a supposition merely; it is the constant experience. About the year 1746 there was a scarcity at New Orleans, and the French settlements on the banks of the Illinois, feeble in number as they were, sent thither in one winter alone 800,000 weight of flour." So that, in place of furnishing other nations with raw materials, some company of manufacturers might be introduced and established in these countries, so attractive by their situation, under the direction of men thoroughly competent to the task. Such an establishment would produce a considerable augmentation of population and wealth to these new settlements and would set a useful example to other parts of the United States.

3. The measures which have been taken by the act of Congress, providing for the disposition of the lands west of the Ohio as far down as the Scioto for the establishment and maintenance of schools, and of a University shed an especial lustre on these settlements and inspire the hope that by the particular attention which has been given to education, the fields of science will be extended, and that the means of acquiring

useful knowledge will be placed on a more respectable footing in this country than in any other part of the world. Without speaking of the advantages of discovering in this new country species hitherto unknown in natural history, botany and medical science, it cannot be questioned that in no other part of the habitable globe can there be found a spot where, in order to begin well, there will not be found much evil to extirpate, bad customs to combat, and ancient systems to reform. Here there is no rubbish to clear away before laying the foundations. The first commencement of this settlement will be undertaken by persons inspired with the noblest sentiments, versed in the most necessary branches of knowledge, acquainted with the world and with affairs, as well as with every branch of science. If they shall be so fortunate as to have at first the means of founding on an advantageous plan these schools and this University, and of sustaining them in such a manner that the professors may be able to commence without delay the different labors to which they may be called, they will, in the infancy of the colony, have secured to themselves advantages which will be found nowhere else.

4. In the ordinance of Congress for the government of the territory northwest of the Ohio it is provided that when the territory shall have acquired a certain amount of population it may be divided into several States. The most eastern of these (this is already provided for) is bounded by the Great Miami on the west, and by Pennsylvania on the east. The centre of this State will be between the Scioto and the Hockhocking. The seat of government of one of these States will very probably be at the mouth of one of these two rivers. And if we may be permitted to forecast the future, we may imagine that when the United States of America, composed of an intelligent and renowned people, shall have greatly extended the boundaries of their dominions the general government will establish itself upon the banks of the Ohio. This country is at the centre of the whole Nation, it is a place the most convenient for all, the most agreeable and probably the most healthy.

It is undoubtedly of the greatest importance that the Congress should soon fix the place of its residence; nevertheless, in the present state of the country it is possible, some may think it not expedient to fix it immovably. Take the chain of the Alleghany Mountains from north to south, it is probable that twenty years will not elapse before there will be more of the inhabitants of the United States living on the banks of the Western than on the Eastern rivers. The Western people ought now to understand that the government is disposed to favor them as much as their brethren who inhabit the Eastern part of the country. It is even necessary that they should have this feeling in order that they may not cherish dreams of independence, that they may not seek for other alliances, and that they may not take steps with especial view to their own welfare. As it is indisputable that it ought to be the principal object of the Legislature, and the one dearest to its heart to unite as great a number of people as possible, and render them happy under one government, every step which Congress may take toward this new constitution will have this object in view; and, we will hope, will promote the success of the plan, and cause it to be regarded as inviolably established. There is no doubt, whatever, that sooner or later the government will either reserve to itself or purchase a suitable site on which to build *the city of the confederation*, which will be at the center of the whole country; and that it will make known its intentions in this regard as soon as circumstances, such as an equal population in the new State, etc. will permit.

Such a determination, taken in advance, will give to the older States the power of carrying it into execution without causing any disturbance or dissatisfaction to any person, whilst it would inspire the new States with the hope of some day seeing the plan realized.

NATHANIEL MASSIE, SURVEYOR

JOHN McDONALD

Before relinquishing its claim on the Northwest Territory, Virginia reserved a tract of Military Lands north of the Ohio, extending between the Scioto and Little Miami rivers. In 1790 the Virginia Military Tract was opened to claimants. Immediately the eyes of warrant holders and of land speculators turned toward the Scioto.

Into this wild country came Nathaniel Massie, already, at twenty-six, a veteran Kentucky surveyor and landlooker. Late in 1790 he chose a site on the north bank of the Ohio and laid out the town that is now called Manchester. Originally it was Massie's Station, the first settlement in the Virginia Military District and the fourth town in Ohio. "The inhabitants," wrote Massie's chairman, John McDonald, "were generally as playful as kittens, and as happy in their way as the heart could wish. The men spent most of their time in hunting and fishing, and almost every evening the boys and girls footed merrily to the tune of the fiddle."

But they had strenuous seasons in the field, surveying a big country of tangled hillsides, rich river bottoms, deep and sudden gorges, and streams as sinuous as the great serpent mound above Bush Creek. Between 1790 and 1801 Massie and his men (one of them, the burly Duncan McArthur, later became Governor of Ohio) surveyed 750,000 acres of Military Lands.

The following account of the hazards of surveying in the wilderness is taken from a sketch of Nathaniel Massie by his woodsman-colleague, John McDonald of Poplar Ridge, Ross County, Ohio.

THE plan adopted by Massie, in his various surveying excursions at that time, was such as to secure safety to the party. Three assistant surveyors, with himself making the fourth, were generally engaged at the same time in making surveys. To each surveyor was attached six men, which made a mess of seven. Every man had his prescribed duty to perform. Their operations were conducted in this manner:—In front went the hunter, who kept in advance of the surveyor two or three hundred yards, looking for game, and prepared to give notice should any danger from Indians threaten. Then followed, after the surveyor, the two chain-men, marker, and pack-horse men with the baggage, who always kept near each other, to be prepared for defence in case of an attack. Lastly, two or three hundred yards in the rear, came a man, called the spy, whose duty it was to

keep on the back trail, and look out lest the party in advance might be pursued and attacked by surprise. Each man (the surveyor not excepted) carried his rifle, his blanket, and such other articles as he might stand in need of. On the pack-horse was carried the cooking utensils, and such provisions as could be conveniently taken. Nothing like bread was thought of. Some salt was taken, to be used sparingly. For subsistence, they depended alone on the game which the woods afforded, procured by their unerring rifles. In this manner was the largest number of surveys made in the district. But to return.

In the fall of the year 1793, Massie determined to attempt a surveying tour on the Scioto river. This, at that time, was a very dangerous undertaking; yet no danger, unless very imminent, could deter him from making the attempt. For that purpose, he employed about thirty men, of whom he choose three as assistant surveyors. These were John Beasley, Nathaniel Beasley, and Peter Lee. It was in this expedition, Massie employed, for the first time, a young man by the name of Duncan McArthur as a chain-man or marker. This man had distinguished himself remarkably on several occasions, and particularly in Harmer's unfortunate expedition. He was one of the best woodsmen of his age. He was a large, strong, and muscular man, capable of enduring fatigue and privations, equal to the best trained Indians. His courage was unquestioned, to which was added an energetic mind, which soon displayed its powers. He afterwards became a surveyor, and was one of the most acute land speculators in the western country. Such a man Massie desired to have on an expedition of this character.

In the month of October, some canoes were procured, and Massie and his party set off by water. They proceeded up the Ohio to the mouth of the Scioto, thence up the Scioto to the mouth of Paint creek. While meandering the Scioto, they made some surveys on the bottoms. After reaching the mouth of Paint creek, the surveyors went to work. Many surveys were made on the Scioto, as far up as Westfall. Some were made on Main, and others on the North Fork of Paint creek, and the greatest parts of Ross and Pickaway counties in the district were well explored and partly surveyed. Massie finished his intended work without meeting with any disturbance from the Indians. But one Indian was seen during the excursion, and to him they gave a hard chase. He, however, escaped. The party returned home delighted with the rich country of the Scioto valley, which they had explored.

During the winter of 1793-4, Massie, in the midst of the most appalling dangers, explored the different branches to their sources, which run into the Little Miami river, and thence passed in a northestern direction to the heads of Paint and Clear creeks, and the branches that form those streams. By these expeditions he had formed from personal observation, a correct knowledge of the geographical situation of the country composing the Virginia military district.

During the winter of 1794-5, Massie prepared a party to enter largely into the surveying business. Nathaniel Beasley, John Beasley, and Peter Lee were again employed as the assistant surveyors. The party set off from Manchester well equipped to prosecute their business, or should occasion offer give battle to the Indians. They took the route of Logan's trace, and proceeded to a place called the deserted camp, on Tod's fork of the Little Miami. At this point, they commenced surveying, and surveyed large portions of land on Tod's fork, and up the Miami to the Chillicothe town, (now in Clark county) thence up Massie's creek and Cæsar's creek nearly to their heads. By the time the party had progressed thus far, winter had set in. The ground was covered with a sheet of snow, from six to ten inches deep. During the tour, which continued upwards of thirty days, the party had no bread. For the first two weeks, a pint of flour was distributed to each mess once a day, to mix with the soup, in which the meat had been boiled. When night came, four fires were made for cooking, that is, one for each mess. Around these fires, till sleeping time arrived, the company spent their time in the most social glee, singing songs and telling stories. When danger was not apparent or immediate, they were as merry a set of men as ever assembled. Resting time arriving, Massie always gave the signal, and the whole party would then leave their comfortable fires, carrying with them their blankets, their firearms, and their little baggage, walking in perfect silence two or three hundred yards from their fires. They would then scrape away the snow, and huddle down together for the night. Each mess formed one bed, they would spread down on the ground one half of the blankets, reserving the other half for covering. The covering blankets were fastened together by skewers to prevent them from slipping apart. Thus prepared, the whole party crouched down together with their rifles in their arms, and their pouches under their heads for pillows; laying spoon-fashion, with three heads one way and four the other, their feet extending to about the middle of their bodies. When one turned, the whole mess turned, or else the close range would be broken and the cold let in. In this way, they lay till broad day light; no noise and scarce a whisper being uttered during the night. When it was perfectly light, Massie would call up two of the men in whom he had the most confidence, and send them to reconnoiter, and make a circuit around the fires, lest an ambuscade might be formed by the Indians to destroy the party as they returned to the fires. This was an invariable custom in every variety of weather. Self-preservation required this circumspection. If immortality is due to the names of heroes who have successfully labored in the field of battle, no less honors are due to such men as Massie, who ran equal risk of life from danger with less prospect of eclat, and produced more lasting benefit to the country.

Massie proceeded to survey up Cæsar's creek, nearly to where its waters interlock with the waters of Paint creek. Late one evening, he came upon the tracks of Indians in the snow. Some of his men were despatched to search out the Indian encampment, while others were sent in pursuit of the assistant surveyors, in order to collect the force into one body, that he might be prepared to attack or defend as circumstances might direct. A short time before sun-down, his force was collected. In a few minutes after, the two men returned who had been sent to discover the Indian camp. They reported, that they had proceeded as near the Indian encampment as they could with safety, and that it consisted of eight or ten tents, and that from the noise about the camp, they had no doubt but that there was a large number of Indians. Massie, thereupon, concluded that it would be too hazardous to attack them while the snow was on the ground, believing it would endanger the whole party if they would be compelled to retreat, encumbered with any wounded. He therefore resolved to desist from surveying, and make a rapid retreat to his own station, not doubting but that he would be pursued, as the Indians would have no difficulty in tracking them through the snow. The line of march was formed for home by the party, who traveled until ten or eleven o'clock at night, when they halted and remained until morning, when they again resumed their march, moving

in a southern direction. About twelve o'clock, they came to a fresh trail, which was made by four horses and eight or ten footmen. This trail was crossed diagonally, and was again struck upon after traveling a few miles. After a consultation with some of the most experienced of his men, Massie concluded the Indians, whose trail had been crossed, knew nothing of them, and determined to pursue them so long as they kept the direction in which they appeared then to be going. The pursuit of the Indians was kept up as fast as the men could walk, until dusk without overtaking them. The party then halted to consult as to their future operations. In a few minutes, the Indians were heard at work with their tomahawks, cutting wood and tent poles, within a few hundred yards of the place where the party had halted. It was put to vote, whether the Indian camp should be attacked immediately, or whether they should postpone it to day-light. A majority were for lying by and attacking them in day-light. Two or three men were then sent to reconnoiter their camp and bring away their horses. The horses were brought away, and preparations made to lie by for the night. Massie, who was more thoughtful than the rest of the company, began to reflect on the critical situation of the party. He told them, he did not approve of the idea of lying by until morning, as there was no doubt they were rapidly pursued by the Indians from the head of Cæsar's creek, and that by waiting until morning, the pursuing Indians might come up in the course of the night, and when day-light appeared, they would find themselves between two fires. He said it was true the Indians might be destroyed more effectually in day-light, but that it was dangerous to loiter away their time on a retreat, and advised that whatever they did to the Indians should be done quickly, and the march continued towards home. It was resolved to follow his advice.

It was about two hours in the night when this occurred. The day had been warm, and had melted the snow which was eight inches deep, and quite soft on the top. At night it began to freeze rapidly, and by this time there was a hard crust on the top. In this situation, the crust when broken by a man walking on a calm night could be heard at the distance of three hundred yards. Massie, under these circumstances prepared to attack the Indians forthwith. The men were formed in a line, in single file, with their wiping sticks in their hands, to steady them when walking. They then commenced moving towards the Indian camp in the following manner:—the foremost would walk about twenty steps, and halt; then the next in the line would move on, stepping in the tracks of the foremost, to prevent any noise when breaking the crust of the snow. In this cautious and silent manner, they crept within about twenty-five yards of the Indian encampment, when an unexpected interruption presented itself; a deep ravine was found between Massie and the camp which was not perceived by the reconnoitering party. The Indians had not as yet laid down to rest, but were singing and amusing themselves round their fires, in the utmost self-security, not dreaming of danger in their own country, in the depth of winter. The bank of the ravine concealed Massie and his men, who were on low ground, from the light of the Indian fires. After halting a few minutes on the bank of the ravine, Massie discovered, a few paces above him, a large log which had fallen across the ravine. On this log he determined to cross the gully. Seven or eight of the men, on their hands and knees, had crossed, and were within not more than twelve or fifteen paces of the Indians, crouching low, and turning to the right and left, when too many men at the same time got on the log; and as it was old and rotten, it broke with a loud crash. This started the Indians. The whites, who had crossed over before the log broke, immediately fired into the Indian camp, shouting as they run. The Indians fled, naked, and without their arms. No Indian was killed in the camp, although their clothing and blankets were found stained with blood. No attempt was made to pursue them. Their camp was plundered of the horses and arms, making altogether considerable booty. The party traveled that night and until noon the next day, when they halted to cook some provisions, and rest their wearied limbs. After taking some refreshments, they loitered about the fires a short time, and again commenced

their march through snow and brush, and about midnight of the second day, arrived at Manchester, after a fatiguing march of two days and nights from the head of Cæsar's creek.

On the last day of their march, about a mile north of where West Union now stands, one of the men who carried a bag of Indian plunder, and rode one of the horses, dropped the bag, and did not miss it until they arrived at Manchester. Sometime in the succeeding day, two of the men took fresh horses, and rode back on the trail, to look for the bag. They found the bag some distance south of the brow of the hill, and concluded they would go to the brow and look over for deer. When they reached it, they were astonished to find the spot where a large party of Indians had followed the trail to the top of the hill, and there stopped to eat their breakfast, leaving some bones and sinewy jirk, that was too hard to eat. Had the Indians pursued the trail one hundred yards farther, they would have found the bag, and laid in ambush for the whites to return, and would doubtless have killed or taken the men who returned for the bag. This was truly a narrow escape.

The winter of 1794-95 was attended by no disturbances from the Indians, as the defeat they had sustained the summer before from General Wayne, had completely checked them in their depredations. In the spring of 1795, Massie again prepared a party to return to the waters of the Little Miami, Paint creek, and the Scioto, for the purpose of surveying. He employed three assistant surveyors, with the usual complement of men. Every man carried, as usual in these surveying tours, his own baggage on his back. No one, indeed, was exempt from this service; and when the weight is taken into consideration, and the encumbrance from it, there seems to be little ground for the complaints, which have latterly been made, about the inaccuracies of early surveys. Indeed, it is really astonishing, how they could be made so accurate as they are found to be.

Early in March the party set off from Manchester. The weather was fine, and the spring appeared to have commenced in ear-

Above: The Ohio River above Madison.   *Below:* Dalzell's Clearing, near Piqua, Ohio.
Both drawings by Thomas K. Wharton. *Courtesy New York Public Library and Ohio Historical Society*

nest. Massie commenced surveying on the west fork of Ohio Brush creek. The woods then furnished game in great abundance, such as turkeys and bears, of the finest quality. A description of the method in which bears were taken, although familiar to the old backwoodsmen, will be perhaps interesting to their descendants, as these animals have become scarce since the settlement of the country. It is well known that bears retire to the hollows of rocks or trees, about the last of December, and remain in a dormant state until the winter breaks, be it early or late. When the weather becomes warm, they will bustle out of their holes to the nearest water, once in two or three days. In walking from their holes to the water, they are careful to step in the same track; and as the earth at that season of the year is soft and spongy, the feet of the bear, in passing and repassing, make a deep impression. These impressions are called by the old hunters, "the bear's stepping-place." When the hunter finds the stepping-place, he can easily follow the track, until he finds the tree in the hollow of which, or in some cave or hole in the rocks, the animal lies at ease. They are then, by various means used, driven from their holes, and shot. During this expedition, a young man, by the name of Bell, who was very active in climbing trees, exhibited great boldness in driving them from their holes. When a bear was tracked to a tree, this man, when the tree was not very large and smooth, would climb up and look into the hole, and punch the bear with a sharp stick until it would come out. Bears at this season are very lazy and difficult to move. By punching them, however, for some time, they will move heavily to their holes, and slowly drag themselves out. As soon as they were clear of their holes, some one or two picked marksmen would shoot them. Bell, so soon as he would provoke the bears to come out, would slip out on a limb, and wait with perfect composure until the marksmen would shoot them. These feats are specimens of Bell's daring. He was, altogether, one of the most hardy, fearless, and thoughtless men of danger, I ever saw. In this way numerous bears were found and killed. The fat part of the meat, boiled or roasted with turkey or venison, makes a very luxurious repast. But to return.

The weather, for some time, continued quite pleasant, while the party surveyed towards the head waters of Brush creek. They thence passed to the Rocky and Rattlesnake forks of Paint creek; thence crossing Main Paint, they passed up Buckskin, and across to "the old town," on the north point of Paint creek. While surveying in this section of the country, the weather became cloudy, and commenced snowing and hailing. The snow continued to fall and drift for two days and nights; and when it ceased, the ground was covered between two and three feet deep. The camp was on the ground, at this time the farm of Colonel Adam Mallow, four miles above Old town (or Frankfort, as it is now called.) About the time it ceased snowing, the weather became warm, and a soft rain fell for a short time. Suddenly it became intensely cold, accompanied by a frost, which soon formed a strong crust on the snow, which had been previously softened by the rain. The snow, although somewhat settled by the rain, was at least two feet deep, with a crust that would bear about half the weight of a man. This was the deepest snow I ever saw, before or since, in the western country. The turkeys, and other small game, could run on the crust of snow, which disabled the hunters from pursuing and killing game; and as the party had no provisions with them, the doleful prospect of death by starvation stared them in the face.

This tour was subsequently called the starving tour; and the remnant of those who are on this side of the grave, yet remember with horror their situation at that time. The prudence exercised by them heretofore, of sleeping away from their fires, was not attended to. The party lay around their fires by day and night, anxiously praying for a change in the weather. Some of the strongest and most spirited among the party, several times made ineffectual attempts to kill game. Among these hunters, General Duncan McArthur, of Fruit hill, near Chillicothe, and William Leedom, of Adams county, were conspicuous. On the third day of the storm, they killed two turkeys. They were boiled, and divided into twenty-eight shares or parts, and given equally to each man. This little food seemed only to sharpen their appetites. Not a particle of the turkeys was left. The heads, feet, and entrails, were devoured, as if most savory food.

The fourth morning of the continuance of the snow, Massie, with his party, turned their faces homeward. The strongest and most hardy of the men were placed in front, to break through the snow. This was a fatiguing and laborious business, and was performed alternately by the most spirited and strongest of the party. They thus proceeded in their heavy and disconsolate march the whole day, and at night reached the mouth of the Rattlesnake fork of Paint creek, a distance of about ten miles. In the course of that day the sun shone through the clouds, for the first time since the storm commenced, and by its warmth softened the crust on the snow. This rendered the traveling less laborious. As the party descended the sloping ground towards the bank of Paint creek, they came across a flock of turkeys, and killed several. These were cooked, and equally divided among the men. That night the party lay by their fires without guards or sentinels; and as the night was warm, the snow gradually melted. Early next morning the most of the party turned out to hunt, and killed a number of turkeys, some deer, and a bear. When these were brought to camp, a feast ensued, which was enjoyed with a zest and relish, which none can properly appreciate, but those who have been so unfortunate as to be placed in a similar situation.

The writer of this narrative accompanied General Massie on this tour, and had previously passed through many trying and distressing scenes; but the hardships and privations of this tour were the most trying to the firmness, resolution, and fortitude of men, he ever saw or experienced. Only reflect, reader, on the critical situation of twenty-eight men, exposed to the horrors of a terrible snow-storm in the wilderness, without hut, tent, or covering, and, what was still more appalling, without provision, without any road or even a track to retreat on, and nearly one hundred miles from any friendly aid or place of shelter, exposed to the truly tremendous and pitiless peltings of a storm of four days continuance, and you can fancy to yourself some faint idea of the sufferings of this party.

Although more than forty years have passed, I can scarcely think of our sufferings, even at this length of time, without shuddering. The people of the present time, who now inhabit our western country, and are sheltered from tempestuous storms in comfortable and elegant mansions, and are blessed with peace and plenty, can scarcely appreciate the sufferings and privations of those who led the way in settling our western country. Under all the hardships of this tour, Massie always showed a cheerful face, and encouraged his men to hope for better times. Nothing like despondency ever clouded his brow, nor did his good humor forsake him during the gloom and despair of this trying occasion.

The storm being passed, fine weather and plenty ensued, and the party again went cheerfully to work. Massie surveyed all the land he at first designed, and returned to Manchester without any adventure worthy of relation.

Above: A Western clearing. Courtesy Ohio Historical Society   Below: Map by Seth
Pease of the Connecticut Western Reserve. Courtesy Edmondson Studio

PROSPECTS IN NEW CONNECTICUT

MOSES CLEAVELAND and CHARLES WHITTLESEY

The charter of Connecticut, granted by Charles II in 1662, described the colony as extending from Narragansett Bay to "the South Seas." That gave Connecticut a Pacific coast line, though no one knew of a "Pacific Ocean" in 1662, or even of a river called the O-hy-o. In 1787 when the new American boundary extended to the Mississippi, Connecticut insisted on its claim to western lands. Under pressure of the other states, that claim was finally surrendered to the federal government, but Connecticut reserved a tract bordering on Lake Erie and extending 120 miles west from the Pennsylvania line. This Western Reserve was bought from the state, for forty cents an acre, by thirty-five shareholders in the Connecticut Land Company. In 1795 they sent a surveying crew, under General Moses Cleaveland, to explore the country.

The following excerpts are taken: 1) from the field diary of General Cleaveland; and 2) from the writings of Colonel Charles Whittlesey, pioneer resident of Cleveland and historian of the Western Reserve.

DIARY OF MOSES CLEAVELAND

ON this creek ["Conneaught"] in New Connecticut land, July 4th, 1796, under General Moses Cleaveland, the surveyors, and men sent by the Connecticut Land Company to survey and settle the Connecticut Reserve, and were the first English people who took possession of it. The day, memorable as the birthday of American Independence, and freedom from British tyranny, and commemorated by all good freeborn sons of America, and memorable as the day on which the settlement of this new country was commenced, and in time may raise her head amongst the most enlightened and improved States. And after many difficulties perplexities and hardships were surmounted, and we were on the good and promised land, felt that a just tribute of respect to the day ought to be paid. There were in all, including men, women and children, fifty in number. The men, under Captain Tinker ranged themselves on the beach, and fired a Federal salute of fifteen rounds, and then the sixteenth in honor of New Connecticut. We gave three cheers and christened the place Port Independence. Drank several

toasts, viz:

1st. The President of the United States.
2d. The State of New Connecticut.
3d. The Connecticut Land Company.
4th. May the Port of Independence and the fifty sons and daughters who have entered it this day be successful and prosperous.
5th. May these sons and daughters multiply in sixteen years sixteen times fifty.
6th. May every person have his bowsprit trimmed and ready to enter every port that opens.

Closed with three cheers. Drank several pails of grog, supped and retired in remarkable good order.

THE SURVEYS OF 1796
Col. Charles Whittlesey

While the four parties were engaged in running up the first four meridians, Cleaveland, after conciliating the Indians, made an excursion to the site of the future city, which should bear his name. He reached here on the 22d of July. All of the party must have felt unusually interested, as they approached the spot. Not one of them had seen the place.

As they coasted close along the shore, overhung by a dense green forest, mirrored in the waters over which they were passing, the mouth of the river disclosed itself, as a small opening, between low banks of sand. The man who controls the party, is seated in the stern, steering his own craft; which is gracefully headed into the stream.

His complexion was so swarthy, his figure so square and stout, and his dress so rude; that the Indians supposed some of the blood of their race had crept into his veins.

Joshua Stow was probably at this time in this pioneer boat. As they passed into the channel, and the broad river unfolded itself to their view; bordered by marshes, reeds, and coarse grass; their anticipations must have been somewhat moderated. The flats on the west side, and the densely wooded bluffs on the east, did not present a cheerful prospect for a city. They were confined to the eastern shore, by their agreement with the Indians at Buffalo, and at Conneaut.

It was necessary to proceed some distance along this shore, before there was solid ground enough to effect a landing. As the Indians had, from generation to generation, kept open a trail along the margin of the lake, it is probable that Cleaveland's party, scanning with sharp eyes every object as they rowed along the river, saw where the aboriginal highway descended the hill, along what is now Union lane. Here they came to the bank, and scrambling out, trod for the first time the soil of the new city. While the boat was being unloaded, the agent had an opportunity to mount the bluff, and scan the surrounding land. This view must have revived his enthusiasm, more than the swamps along the river had depressed it. A young growth of oaks, with low bushy tops, covered the ground. Beneath them were thrifty bushes, rooted in a lean, but dry and pleasant soil, highly favorable to the object in view. A smooth and even field sloped gently towards the lake, whose blue waters could be seen extending to the horizon. His imagination doubtless took a pardonable flight into the future, when a great commercial town, should take the place of the stinted forest growth, which the northern tempests had nearly destroyed. But whatever may have been his

anticipations, the reality has outstripped them all. . . .

It is not certainly known, but probably Stiles, and perhaps his wife, were of this party. Enough men were left to put up a store house for the supplies, and a cabin for the accommodation of the surveyors. These rude structures were located a short distance south of St. Clair street, west of Union Lane, at a spring on the side hill, in rear of Scott's warehouse. During the season, a cabin was put up for Stiles, on Lot 53, east side of Bank street, north of the Herald Building, where Morgan & Root's Block is now being erected. Thus was the settlement of the city commenced.

By authorities, which will be given hereafter, it will be seen, that houses had before this been built by white people, near the mouth of the river; but not for the purpose of permanent settlement. Col. James Hillman avers, that he put up a small cabin on the east side of the river in 1786, near the foot of Superior street, of which, however, nothing further is known. Sometime previous to 1787, a party who were wrecked, upon a British vessel, between one and two miles east of the river, built an hut, large enough to shelter themselves, through one winter. On the west side of the river, a log store house was erected, prior to 1786, to protect the flour which was brought here from Pittsburg, on the way to Detroit. This building, in a dilapidated state, was standing in 1797, when it was occupied awhile by James Kingsbury and his family.

Some cabins were erected during the summer near the shore, beyond Euclid creek, which are noticed in the journals of Holley and Pease. The design and origin of this embryo settlement, is not yet well understood. No one is known to have remained there during the winter of 1796–97.

A Frenchman is reported to have been at Sandusky, not as a settler but a trader. At that time proceeding west of Buffalo; the first white inhabitants on the south shore of Lake Erie were located at Erie, Pa.; the next, the families of Gun and Kingsbury, at Conneaut; and the last and only other settlers, on this bleak wilderness coast were Stiles and his wife, at Cleveland, with whom Edward Paine was domiciled as a boarder.

A YEAR IN GALLIPOLIS

H. M. BRACKENRIDGE

In Paris in the revolutionary summer of 1789 the agents of the Scioto Company were selling American real estate. They distributed Manasseh Cutler's alluring pamphlet and an engraved map of the favored region in the Ohio valley. The empty Ohio acres seemed a haven to French refugees, and soon Paris merchants, artists and tradesmen were clamoring for Scioto lands. Said the philosopher Volney: "Nothing was talked of, in every social circle, but the paradise that was opened for Frenchmen in the western wilderness, the free and happy life to be led on the blissful banks of the Scioto." King Louis himself, according to his barber, observed that all Paris was talking about the Scioto lands.

In January, 1790, five hundred French émigrés embarked for America. Some were men of rank; some were professional men; many were artisans—jewelers, watchmakers, gardeners, wood carvers, wigmakers. None were prepared for life on the frontier. From Alexandria on the Potomac they were escorted over the Alleghenies and then by boat to the Première Ville which had been built for them two miles beyond the mouth of the Great Kanawha. What they found there was a square of stumpland framed in forest gloom. In the clearing crouched four rows of log barracks, each divided into twenty one-room dwellings. This was the New World paradise. They named it Gallipolis—City of the French.

The trials and privations and the cheerful spirit of the French colony at Gallipolis have been fully recorded. One of the freshest accounts is that of H. M. Brackenridge, who by an odd chance spent the year 1794 among the émigrés. Suffering from ague on a river journey, ten-year-old Henry Brackenridge was brought ashore at Gallipolis. While his father went on trading down the valley, the boy lived at the house of sprightly Dr. Saugrain. In his later years Brackenridge became a noted frontier lawyer and an explorer of the Far West. But he never forgot his boyhood season at Gallipolis.

This narrative is taken from his vivid Recollections of Persons and Places in the West.

BEHOLD me once more in port, and domiciliated at the house, or inn, of Monsieur, or rather Dr. Saugrain, a cheerful, sprightly little Frenchman, four feet six English measure, and a chemist, natural philosopher, and physician, both in the English and French signification of the word. I was delighted with my present liberation from the irksome thraldom of the canoe, and with the possession of the free use of my limbs. After wrapping my blanket round me, which was my only bedding, I threw myself into a corner for a couple of hours, during the continuance of the fever and ague, and then rose up refreshed, with the lightness of spirits which I possessed in an unusual degree. I ran out of the house, and along the bank, where I met a boy about my own size; I laid hold of him in mirth, but he, mistaking my vivacity, gave me a sound beating.

The next day the doctor tried his skill upon me, or rather upon my ague, and pretty much on the plan of that other celebrated physician, whose name begins with the letter S; whether on the principle of the *solviente universal*, I do not so well know, but certain it is, he repeated the very words recorded by Gil Blas, *"bebe agua, hijo mio, bebe agua in abundancia,"*—drink water, my son, drink plenty of water. I drank a gallon or two of tepid water, and threw it up again, thus rinsing out the stomach as one might rinse a bottle; but the ague was not to be shaken off so easily; it still continued to visit me daily, as usual, all that winter and part of the next spring.

I was but poorly clad, and was without hat or shoes, but gradually became accustomed to do without them: like the Indian, I might in time have become *all face*. My guardian left no money, perhaps he had none to leave; M. Saugrain had none to spare, and, moreover, had no certainty that he would be reimbursed; besides, as this was the period when the French Revolution was at its height, *sans culottism* was popular with those who favored that breaking up of all social economy. Dr. Saugrain, however, and many others in Gallipolis were not of that party; they were royalists who bitterly lamented the condition of their native country.

Gallipolis, with the exception of a few straggling log-houses, of which that of Dr. S. was one, consisted of two long rows of barracks built of logs, and partitioned off into rooms of sixteen or twenty feet wide, with what is called a cabin roof and wooden chimneys. At one end there was a larger room than the rest, which served as a council chamber and ball-room. This singular village was settled by people from Paris and Lyons, chiefly artisans and artists, peculiarly unfitted to sit down in the wilderness and clear away forests. I have seen half a dozen at work in taking down a tree, some pulling ropes fastened to the branches, while others were cutting round it like beavers. Sometimes serious accidents occurred in consequence of their awkwardness. Their former employments had only been calculated to administer to the luxury of highly polished and wealthy societies. There were carvers and gilders to the king, coachmakers, frizeurs and perukemakers, and a variety of others, who might have found employment in our larger towns, but who were entirely out of their place in the wilds of the Ohio. Their means by this time had been exhausted, and they were beginning to suffer from the want of the comforts and even necessaries of life. The country back from the river was still a wilderness, and the Gallipolitans

did not pretend to cultivate anything more than small garden spots, depending for their supply of provisions on the boats which now began to descend the river; but they had to pay in cash, and that was become scarce. They still assembled at the ball-room twice a week; it was evident, however, that they had felt disappointment, and were no longer happy. The predilections of the best among them being on the side of the Bourbons, the horrors of the Revolution, even in their remote position, mingled with their private misfortunes, which had at this time nearly reached their acme, in consequence of the discovery that they had no title to their lands, having been cruelly deceived by those from whom they had purchased. It is well known that Congress generously made them a grant of twenty thousand acres: from which, however, but few of them derived any advantage.

As the Ohio was now more frequented, the house was occasionally resorted to, and especially by persons looking out for land to purchase. The doctor had a small apartment which contained his chemical apparatus, and I used to sit by him as often as I could, watching the curious operations of his blowpipe and crucible. I loved the cheerful little man and he became very fond of me in turn. Many of my countrymen used to come and stare at his doings, which they were half inclined to think had too near a resemblance to the black art. The doctor's little phosphoric matches, igniting spontaneously when the glass tube was broken, and from which he derived some emolument, were thought by some to be rather beyond mere human power. His barometers and thermometers, with the scale neatly painted with the pen, and the frames richly carved, were objects of wonder, and some of them are probably still extant in the West. But what most astonished some of our visitors was a large peach in a glass bottle, the neck of which could only admit a common cork; this was accomplished by tying the bottle to the limb of the tree, with the peach when young inserted into it. His swans, which swam round basins of water, amused me more than any of the wonders exhibited by the wonderful man.

The doctor was a great favorite with the Americans, as well for his vivacity and sweetness of temper which nothing could sour, as on account of a circumstance which gave him high claims to the esteem of the backwoodsmen. He had shown himself, notwithstanding his small stature and great good nature, a very hero in combat with the Indians. He had descended the Ohio in company with two French philosophers, who were believers in the primitive innocence and goodness of the children of the forest. They could not be persuaded that any danger was to be apprehended from the Indians: as they had no intention to injure that people, they supposed, of course, that no harm could be meditated on their part. Dr. Saugrain was not altogether so well convinced of their good intentions, and accordingly kept his pistols loaded. Near the mouth of Big Sandy, a canoe with a party of warriors approached the boat; the philosophers invited them on board by signs, when they came rather too willingly. The first thing they did on entering the boat was to salute the two philosophers with the tomahawk; and they would have treated the doctor in the same way, but that he used his pistols with good effect: killed two of the savages, and then leaped into the water, diving like a dipper at the flash of the guns of the others, and succeeded in swimming to shore, with several severe wounds whose scars were conspicuous.

The doctor was married to an amiable young woman, but not possessing as much vivacity as himself. As Madame Saugrain had no maid to assist in household work, her brother, a boy of my age, and myself, were her principal helps in the kitchen. We brought water and wood, and washed the dishes. I used to go in the morning about two miles for a little milk, sometimes on the frozen ground, barefoot. I tried a pair of sabots, or wooden shoes, but was unable to make any use of them, although they had been made by the carver to the king. Little perquisites sometimes, too, fell to our share, from blacking shoes and boots: my companion generally saved his, while mine would have burnt a hole in my pocket if it had remained there. In the spring and summer, a good deal of my time was passed in the garden, weeding the beds. While thus engaged, I formed an acquaintance with a young lady of eighteen or twenty, on the other side of the palings, who was often similarly occupied. Our friendship, which was purely Platonic, commenced with the story of Blue Beard, recounted by her, and with the novelty and pathos of which I was much interested. This incident may perhaps remind the reader of the story of Pyramus and Thisbe, or perhaps of the hortical eclogue of Dean Swift, "Dermot and Shela."

Connected with this young lady, there is an incident which I feel a pleasure in relating. One day, while standing alone on the bank of the river, I saw a man who had gone in to bathe, and who had got beyond his depth without being able to swim. He began to struggle for life, and in a few seconds would have sunk to rise no more. I shot down the bank like an arrow, leaped into a canoe, which fortunately happened to be close by, pushed the end of it to him, and as he rose, perhaps for the last time, he seized it with a deadly convulsive grasp, and held so firmly, that the skin afterward came off the parts of his arms which pressed against the wood. I screamed for help; several persons came, and took him out perfectly insensible. He afterward married the young lady, and they raised a numerous and respectable family. One of his daughters married a young lawyer, who now represents that district in Congress. Thus at eight years of age I earned the civic crown by saving the life of a human being.

If my occupations were of a menial character, they were not rendered, or received, as such; for I was treated as if I were the child or brother of my landlord and landlady. Money had been sent for my keeping, but unfortunately it never reached its destination. The doctor once took me with him to a small town at the mouth of the Kenawha River, where we were treated in a very hospitable manner by Colonel Lewis. It was here that for the first time I tasted wine, and I confess that I have liked it ever since, while, in an equal degree, it created a dislike to brandy, rum, and whisky. I saw a venerable-looking man of the name of Vanbiber, with a long snow-white beard, and

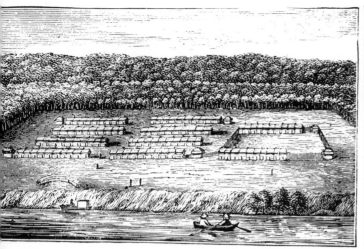

Above: Gallipolis as the French settlers found it in 1790. *Right:* Settlers from Paris, France, felling trees in Gallipolis. From Howe, *Historical Collections of Ohio*

deprived of sight, who related the manner in which he and his family had been saved by the fidelity of a negro man, who had repelled an attack made by a party of Indians; I have forgotten the circumstances, but they were thought very extraordinary. By this time I had learned to speak my native tongue; we soon regain what has been once known and forgotten; it was a long time, however, before I was entirely freed from my French idiom.

Toward the latter part of summer, the inhabitants suffered severely from sickness and want of provisions. Their situation was truly wretched. The swamp in the rear, now exposed by the clearing between it and the river, became the cause of a frightful epidemic, from which few escaped, and many became its victims. I had recovered from my ague, and was among the few exempted from the disease; but our family, as well as the rest, suffered much from absolute hunger, a most painful sensation, as I had before experienced. To show the extremity of our distress, on one occasion the brother of Madame Saugrain and myself pushed a light canoe to an island above the town, where we pulled some corn, took it to floating mill, and, excepting some of the raw grains, had had nothing to eat from the day before, until we carried home the flour and

made some bread, but had neither milk nor meat. I have learned to be thankful when I had a sufficiency of wholesome food, however plain, and was blessed with health; and I could put up with humble fare without a murmur, although accustomed to luxuries, when I have seen those, who had never experienced absolute starvation, turn up their noses at that which was very little worse than the best they had ever known. Such are the uses of adversity.

I had been nearly a year at Gallipolis when Captain Smith of the United States Army came along, in advance of the barge of General Wilkinson, and, according to the request of my father, took me into his custody for the purpose of bringing me once more to my native place. He remained two or three days, waiting for the general, and in the mean while procured me hat, shoes, and clothes befitting a gentleman's son, and then took me on board his boat. Shortly after the general overtook us, and I was transferred on board of the barge as a playmate and companion for his son Biddle, a boy of my own age. The general's lady, and several ladies and gentlemen were on board of the boat, which was fitted up in a style of convenience, and even magnificence, scarcely surpassed by the present steamboats. It was propelled against the stream by twenty-five or thirty men, sometimes with the pole, by the cordelle, and often by the oar. There was also a band of musicians, and the whole had the appearance of a mere party of pleasure. My senses were overpowered—it seemed an Elysium! The splendor of the furniture—the elegance of the dresses—and then the luxuries of the table, to a half-starved creature, produced an effect which cannot be easily described. Every repast was a royal banquet, and such delicacies were placed before me as I had never seen, and in sufficient abundance to satiate my insatiable appetite. I was no more like what I had been, than the cast off skin of the black snake resembles the new dress in which he glistens in the sunbeam. The general's countenance was continually lighted up with smiles, and he seemed *faire le bonheur* of all around him,—it seemed to be his business to make every one happy. His countenance and manners were such as I have rarely seen, and, now that I can form a more just estimate of them, were such as better fitted him for a court than a republic. His lady was truly a most estimable person, of the mildest and softest manners. She gave her son and me a reproof one day, which I never forgot. She saw us catching minnows with pin hooks—made us desist, and then explained, in the sweetest manner, the cruelty of taking away life, wantonly, from the humblest thing in the creation.

Our arrival at Pittsburg was announced by the thunder of artillery, many times repeated by the echoes of the surrounding hills. I trembled at the thought of appearing before the being whom I held in so much awe—my father! The boy who had taken care of me in childhood, and of whom I have already spoken, watched the landing of the boat, immediately took me in his arms, and then led me home. We found my father sitting in his office, unmoved by the uproar which had disturbed the whole village. I thought he looked more severe than ever. Raising his spectacles from his clear and polished forehead, he accosted me as follows: "Well, boy, can you read French?" Then taking down a copy of Telemachus, put it into my hands. I stammered, perhaps a little rusty from my residence at Gallipolis, where there was no school—perhaps my faculties were benumbed with fear. "Sir," said he, "your progress does not equal my expectations;" then, turning round, said, "Joe, take him to Fenemore, the tailor, to get a suit of clothes, and then to Andrew Willocks, to have his measure for a pair of shoes."

I was now in the tenth year of my age.

BLENNERHASSETT'S ISLAND

S. P. HILDRETH

Of all the land seekers in the Ohio valley, none came like Harmon Blennerhassett. Squatters arrived on rafts and shanty boats, burdened only with an ax, a rifle and a bag of seed corn. Settlers steered a flatboat, its deck space taken up by a plow and a team of oxen, a brood sow and a spinning wheel. But Blennerhassett came in a keelboat with his pretty wife and an English manservant. He bought an island, built a stately mansion, and talked all night with Aaron Burr about a treasonous empire beyond the Mississippi. After ten years in paradise he fled down the river and was overtaken by the United States militia.

Now the island is tranquil, with cornfields rustling in the summer sun. Under a forked maple tree is the cool well that Burr and Blennerhassett drank from. Nearby lie a few cut stones—all that is left of the mansion that became a legend.

This account is from Dr. Hildreth's Lives of the Early Settlers of Ohio.

HIS stay in New York was of only a few months' continuance; when, hearing of the rich valleys and beautiful country on the Ohio river, he crossed the mountains, and after spending a few weeks in Pittsburg, took passage for Marietta, in the fall of the year 1797. Here he passed the winter, examining the vicinity of that place for a spot on which to make his permanent residence. He finally decided on purchasing a plantation on an island in the Ohio river, fourteen miles below the mouth of the Muskingum, within the jurisdiction of the state of Virginia. The situation was wild, romantic, and beautiful; and as it was chiefly in a state of nature, a few acres only being cleared, he could reclaim it from the forest, adorn and cultivate it to his own taste. Its location also gave him the privilege of holding colored servants as his own property, which he could not do in the Northwest Territory. The island was, moreover, near the settlement of Belpre, composed chiefly of very intelligent and well-educated men, disbanded officers of the American army, whose society would at any time relieve him of ennui. The island itself was a picture of beauty, as well as all of its kind, at that early day, before the hand of man had marred its shores. The drooping branches of the willow laved their graceful foliage in the water, while the more lofty sycamore and elm, with their giant arms, protected them from the rude blasts of the storm, and gave a grandeur and dignity to these primitive landscapes, now only to be seen in the remoter regions of the west.

The island at present known as "Blennerhassett's," was then called "Backus's," who had owned it since 1792. It is said to have been located by Gen. Washington, as he owned a large tract of land immediately below, called "Washington's bottom," entered by him in the year 1770. It was first surveyed in May, 1784, on a land warrant, issued in 1780, and a patent made out by Patrick Henry, governor of Virginia, in 1786, to Alexander Nelson, of Richmond, Va., who was a member of a mercantile firm in Philadelphia. By a bill in chancery, of the High Court of Virginia, procured by Mr. Blennerhassett, to perfect his title, it appears that Elijah Backus, of Norwich, Conn., bought of James Herron, of Norfolk,

Va., in the year 1792, two islands in the Ohio river; the principal one being the first below the mouth of the Little Kenawha, then in the county of Monongalia, containing two hundred and ninety-seven acres, for the sum of two hundred and fifty pounds, Virginia currency, or about eight hundred and eighty-three dollars and thirty-three cents. This island is of a very peculiar form, narrow in the middle, and broad at both extremities.

In March, 1798, Mr. Blennerhassett purchased the upper portion, containing about one hundred and seventy acres, for the sum of four thousand, five hundred dollars, and soon after moved, with his wife and one child, on to his new purchase, living in a large old block-house, standing about half a mile below the upper end of the island, built in the time of the Indian war, by Capt. James. Here he resided while conducting the improvements near the upper end of the island, and building his island mansion, which was completed in 1800. A good deal of labor and heavy expense was necessary in preparing the ground for his buildings and the gardens. It was covered, at this spot, with forest trees, which had to be removed, and stumps eradicated, so as to leave a smooth, level surface, with extensive landings up and down the banks on both sides of the river, for convenient access to and from the island. Boats of various sizes were also to be procured, and a company of eight or ten black servants purchased, as waiters, grooms, watermen, etc. His outlays, when the improvements were completed, amounted to more than forty thousand dollars. This sum, expended chiefly amongst the mechanics, laborers, and farmers of this new region, where money was scarce, and hard to be obtained, was of very great advantage to their interests; and Mr. Blennerhassett may be considered as the greatest benefactor, in this respect, that had ever settled west of the mountains.

The island mansion was built with great taste and beauty; no expense being spared in its construction, that could add to its usefulness or splendor. It consisted of a main building, fifty-two feet in length, thirty in width, and two stories high. Porticoes, forty feet in length, in the form of wings, projected in front, connected with offices, presenting each a face of twenty-six feet, and twenty feet in depth, uniting them with the main building; forming the half of an ellipsis, and making, in the whole, a front of one hundred and four feet. The left-hand office was occupied for the servant's hall; and the right for the library, philosophical apparatus study, etc. . . .

A handsome lawn of several acres occupied the front ground; while an extended opening was made through the forest trees, on the head of the island, affording a view of the river for several miles above, and bringing the mansion under the notice of descending boats. Nicely graveled walks, with a carriage-way, led from the house to the river, passing through an ornamental gateway, with large stone pillars. A fine hedge, of native hawthorn, bordered the right side of the avenue to the house, while back of it lay the flower garden, of about two acres, inclosed with neat palings, to which were traced gooseberry bushes, peaches, and other varieties of fruit-bearing trees, in the manner of wall fruits. The garden was planted with flowering shrubs, both exotic and native; but especially abounding in the latter, which the good taste of the occupants had selected from the adjacent forests, and planted in thick masses, through which wandered serpentine walks, bordered with flowers, imitating a labyrinth. Arbors and grottoes, covered with honeysuckles and eglantines, were placed at covenient intervals, giving the whole a very romantic and beautiful appearance. On the opposite side of the house was a large kitchen garden, and back of these, orchards of peach and apple trees of the choicest varieties, procured from abroad, as well as from the Belpre nurseries. Lower down on the island was the farm, with about one hundred acres under the nicest cultivation; the luxuriant soil producing the finest crops of grain and grass. For the last three or four

years of his residence, a large dairy was added to his other agricultural pursuits, under the management of Thomas Neal, who also superintended the labor of the farm. The garden was conducted by Peter Taylor, a native of Lancashire, England, who was bred to the pursuit, but under the direction of Mr. Blennerhassett, whose fine taste in all that was beautiful, ordered the arranging and laying out the grounds.

The mansion and offices were frame buildings, painted with the purest white, contrasting tastefully with the green foliage of the ornamental shade trees, which surrounded it. An abundance of fine stone for building, could have been quarried from the adjacent Virginia shore, but he preferred a structure of wood, as less liable to be damaged by earthquakes. The finishing and furniture of the apartments were adapted to the use for which they were intended. The hall was a spacious room; its walls painted a somber color, with a beautiful cornice of plaster, bordered with a gilded molding, running round the lofty ceiling; while its furniture was rich, heavy, and grand. The furniture of the drawing-room was in strong contrast with the hall; light, airy, and elegant; with splendid mirrors, gay-colored carpets, rich curtains, with ornaments to correspond, arranged by his lady with the nicest taste and harmonious effect. A large quantity of massive silver plate ornamented the sideboards, and decorated the tables. Yet they had not entirely completed their arrangements, when the destroyer appeared, and frustrated all their designs for comfort and future happiness. The whole establishment was noble, chastened by the purest taste, without that glare of tinsel finery, too common among the wealthy.

Their style of living was in unison with the house and furniture, elegant, easy, and comfortable.

THE GIFT OF JOHNNY APPLESEED

HENRY HOWE

Multitudes of land seekers found farms for themselves, but Johnny Apple-seed looked only for places to plant orchards for people yet to come. He was a kind of St. Francis of the frontier, one of the few legends in a busy, practical country. He never fought a battle or founded a town, but people remembered the ragged man who planted apple trees and talked of the road to heaven.

Born John Chapman, at Leominster, Massachusetts, in 1774, he came west in 1801, floating down the Ohio with two canoes lashed together and laden with apple pulp from the cider mills of Pennsylvania. For forty years he wandered the western country with a deerhide sack of apple seeds over his shoulder. Wherever he went he made friends and preached his simple gospel—the oneness of all things, the kinship of all men, the nearness of God. The settlers gave him a name and kept it warm in their memory. He died near the site of the Battle of Fallen Timbers and was buried, on the first day of spring, 1845, under a budding apple tree.

Like Blennerhassett and the French at Gallipolis, Johnny Appleseed has ap-pealed to poets and novelists as well as to historians. The literature of Johnny Appleseed is extensive, and much of it is fanciful. One of the first characteriza-tions of him is the plain, unvarnished portrait which Henry Howe included in his Historical Collections of Ohio.

AT an early day, there was a very eccentric character who frequently was in this region, well remembered by the early settlers. His name was John Chapman, but he was usually known as *Johnny Appleseed*. He came origi-nally from New England.

He had imbibed a remarkable passion for the rearing and cultivation of apple trees from the seed. He first made his appearance in western Pennsylvania, and from thence made his way into Ohio, keeping on the outskirts of the settlements, and following his favorite pursuit. He was accustomed to clear spots in the loamy lands on the banks of the streams, plant his seeds, enclose the ground, and then leave the place until the trees had in a measure grown. When the settlers began to flock in and open their "clearings," Johnny was ready for them with his young trees, which he either gave away or sold for some trifle, as an old coat, or any article of which he could make use. Thus he proceeded for many years, until the whole country was in a measure settled and supplied with apple trees, deriving self-satisfaction amounting to almost delight, in the indulgence of his engrossing passion. About 20 years since he removed to the far west, there to enact over again the same career of humble usefulness which had been his occupation here.

His personal appearance was as singular as his character. He was quick and restless in his motions and conversation; his beard and hair were long and dark, and his eye black and sparkling. He lived the roughest life, and often slept in the woods. His clothing was mostly old, being generally given to him in exchange for apple trees. He went bare-footed, and often travelled miles through the snow in that way. In doctrine he was a follower of Swedenborg, leading a moral, blameless life, likening himself to the primitive Christians, literally taking no thought for the morrow. Wherever he went he circulated Swedenborgian works, and if short of them would tear a book in two and give each part to different persons. He was careful not to injure any animal, and thought hunting morally wrong. He was welcome everywhere among the settlers, and was treated with great kindness even by the Indians. We give a few anecdotes, illustrative of his character and eccentricities.

On one cool autumnal night, while lying by his camp-fire in the woods, he observed that the mosquitoes flew in the blaze and were burnt. Johnny, who wore on his head a tin utensil which answered both as a cap and a mush pot, filled it with water and quenched the fire, and afterwards remarked, "God forbid that I should build a fire for my comfort, that should be the means of destroying any of His creatures." Another time he made his camp-fire at the end of a hollow log in which he intended to pass the night, but finding it occupied by a bear and cubs, he removed his fire to the other end, and slept on the snow in the open air, rather than disturb the bear. He was one morning on a prairie, and was bitten by a rattlesnake. Some time after, a friend inquired of him about the matter. He drew a long sigh and replied, "Poor fellow! he only just touched me, when I, in an ungodly passion, put the heel of my scythe on him and went home. Some time after I went there for my scythe, and there lay the poor fellow dead." He bought a coffee bag, made a hole in the bottom, through which he thrust his head and wore it as a cloak, saying it was as good as anything. An itinerant preacher was holding forth on the public square in Mansfield, and exclaimed, "Where is the bare-footed Christian, travelling to heaven!" Johnny, who was lying on his back on some timber, taking the question in its literal sense, raised his bare feet in the air, and vociferated *"Here he is!"*

FIRST TOUR IN MICHIGAN

CAPTAIN HERVEY PARKE

Thousands of government surveyors left field notes of the Midwest wilderness, but only a few left records of experience. One of the articulate surveyors was Captain Hervey Parke of Pontiac, Michigan, whose writings recall the wild and lonely country which lies behind the farms and cities of today.

Tired of a schoolmaster's life in Oneida County, New York, Parke walked to Michigan Territory in 1821 and joined a surveying crew running section lines between the Flint and Cass rivers. During the next sixteen years Parke walked twenty thousand miles in unmapped country, laying out townships all the way to the Mississippi.

In 1837 Captain Parke settled on a farm near Pontiac, in the once-wild ranges where he had marked the witness trees. He lived to be eighty-nine. During his last twelve years he was chained with paralysis, but in his memory he was afield again—as this vivid reminiscence shows.

IN February, 1821, while returning to my home one evening from the school I was teaching in Camden, Oneida county, New York, the thought of going to Michigan and engaging in government land surveying first occurred to my mind, and in a few minutes I decided I would go. Before leaving my home in Middle Haddam, Connecticut, at the age of eighteen, I had studied surveying in accordance with my father's wishes, who, although an old sea captain, opposed my desire to study navigation, and after coming into the State of New York I continued the study under a competent surveyor. In those days newspapers were few and far between, and comparatively nothing was known of the Territory, and I had not heard of the unfavorable report of the deputy surveyors made in the autumn of 1815.

One of my neighbors said he was in Detroit, and saw one of the deputy surveyors, who assured him Michigan was a poor, miserable country, filled with swamps and marshes, and where potatoes could not be raised. This was not encouraging, I am willing to admit. But I remained firm in my resolution; my friends all opposed my going; my wife only favored the project. Desiring further information, I corresponded with Henry R. Schoolcraft, the historian who had accompanied Governor Cass on an expedition to the upper lakes; but he could give no information in regard to the interior of the country.

However, on the 21st of March, 1821, in company with Samuel Treat Bryant and John Simons, I started on my journey of 500 miles through Canada, carrying a knapsack of over forty-five pounds weight, including surveying instruments. After sixteen days' faithful travel through mud and water, often knee deep, we reached Detroit river, and crossed over to the city in a row-boat, landing at the foot of Woodward avenue. I remember the old market house in the center of the street, which we passed just before reaching Jefferson avenue, at King's clothing store. Passing up the avenue to the stone council house, between which and the street near the river stood the Steamboat hotel, kept by Benjamin Woodworth, crossing Jefferson avenue from the council house, down the avenue, passing Peter Desnoyer's brick two-story store, and at the corner of Jefferson avenue and Bates street a little farther down was the store of Oliver Newberry, in whose employ as clerk I first met our late townsman, Elisha Beach. A little way below was the residence of Governor Cass. The buildings were few on the street; the brick buildings less than one-half dozen. A short distance up Woodward avenue was Major Larnard's cottage residence, near the pickets of the old fort; replaced, probably, since the city was laid in ashes in 1805.

From this point to the north and northwest the commons appeared like an extensive pasture field, with now and then a shade tree. About a half-mile from the present opera house stood a building appearing like

a common barn on the farm of General J. R. Williams; from this point to the northwest no buildings were to be seen. In the vicinity of the barn before mentioned I observed four upright large stones of quarried granite, placed in form of a square, five or six rods from each other, said to be for the purpose of starting points for measurements on the angle for the streets. The manner in which the city is laid out was said to have been suggested by Judge Woodward.

On the line of the road as we passed through the wilderness to the interior, we passed three small houses, the last about nine miles from Detroit, and occupied by Mrs. Chappel, more familiarly known as Mother Handsome. Here we found shelter for the night, and slept soundly on a blanket on the floor. About a half mile beyond we reached the causeway built by the troops under Colonel Leavenworth in 1818. The causeway was a little less than a mile in length, and was the worst ever built, as no regard was had to equalizing the size of the logs—the largest and the smallest lying side by side. At the angle of the road, twelve miles from Detroit, we passed the Royal Oak tree, which had nothing remarkable in its appearance, but was known as the point from which Horatio Ball had started the line when surveying the road to Pontiac, known as the Ball line road. This angle also was the point of intersection of Paint Creek road; a Mr. Woodford lived on section —— about a mile beyond. A little south of the line between the towns of Bloomfield and Royal Oak, two families by the name of Keyser and Thurber had settled. Reaching the beautiful table-land where is now situated the village of Birmingham, we found four families; Elisha Hunter, his son John W. Hunter, John Hamilton, and Elijah Willetts—the latter innkeeper. Here I got my first glimpse of the lovely land of Oakland county. Three-fourths of a mile this side of Hunter's lived Dr. Swan and his son-in-law, Sidney Dole, who was justice of the peace, register of deeds, and county clerk. The next house was Deacon Elijah Fish, and on the hill just south of where now is Bloomfield Centre, resided Amasa Bagley and his son-in-law, William Morris, the latter being sheriff of the county.

The next settler was —— Ferguson, whose neighbors, if living, may remember him from the remark he made after the nomination of Austin E. Wing as delegate to Congress in 1824 or 1825. Ferguson was a whig, and disputing with a democrat who asserted Wing could never be elected, replied: "He will surely be elected, for the very whippoorwills sing 'vote for Wing, vote for Wing.' " Well, Wing was elected, and took his seat in Congress, and performed his duty nobly for the young territory. Major Joseph Todd lived on the farm since known as the Elliott farm, and near by Asa B. Hadsel. The next house a half-mile further, was Colonel David Stanard, in a small framed house, being the same Joseph J. Todd occupied about forty-five years, having added to its length and height. About one and a half miles through the woods we approached the village of Pontiac, where we found a small framed house on the west side of Saginaw street, nearly opposite where the Methodist church now stands, occupied by Mr. Terry. Crossing the bridge, on the corner of Saginaw and Water streets, was a small log house, the first erected in the village, and a little beyond, and on the east side of Saginaw street (if my memory serves me), O. Bartlett lived in a small framed house. These were the only buildings at this time, June 1, 1821, on Saginaw street. This street being well filled with hazel brush, Water street received the travel to Perry street. On the west side of the latter street, between Pike and Lawrence, were three houses, one occupied by Deacon Orison Allen, and a little beyond and on the east side of Perry street, and nearly opposite the grist mill, stood a double log house called the "Company house," and occupied by Colonel Stephen Mack, agent of the Pontiac company. In addition to the grist mill there was a saw-mill and work shop. On the first Monday in June, my first visit to the village, a militia training was in full blast; John W. Hunter commanded the one and only company north of the base line in Michigan territory. On this day the company was divided, and a new company formed by electing the late Colonel Calvin Hotchkiss captain. Proceeding northwest on the road occasionally traveled to Saginaw, distant about a mile from the village, Captain Stanley lived on what has

more recently been known as the Pier farm, on the present White Lake road.

The Indian trail from Detroit to Saginaw, which decided the location of Pontiac, crossed the Clinton at the same point as the present bridge on Saginaw street; turned northerly toward the company house, then bore northwesterly keeping east to the extensive marsh just beyond the residence of the late Governor Wisner, then turned in a northwesterly direction, crossing the Pontiac Creek a few rods northwest of the present crossing on the Saginaw road. Oliver Williams on the southwest side of Silver lake was the next home, three and one-half miles from Pontiac. He had removed to this place from Detroit in 1818; he built the first farm barn in the county, the lumber for enclosing it being manufactured by a couple of Frenchmen from Detroit, with a whip saw. Mr. Wisner kept open house, and in passing and re-passing to Flint river in 1821 I invariably called. He was a real gentleman, social, good natured, remarkably generous and hospitable, and fond of a good story. I well remember late one evening in December, 1821, in returning with our surveying party from Flint, after fording the Clinton at the little pinery, with the thermometer at zero, when nearly off our legs, we reached and were most kindly cared for in this most hospitable home. During one of my calls I inquired if there were many fish in Silver lake; he replied he could not say in regard to numbers, but he once hauled out a mullet that weighed 140 pounds. This rather surprised me, and while reflecting, not wishing to dispute his veracity, he observed my embarrassment as to the remark being somewhat fishy, and explained that a brother of John Mullett, the surveyor, was once fishing there, and falling into the lake was rescued by Mr. Williams. In those days of easy familiarity, he was known by the cognomen of Major Togee, and once at a social party at Dr. Chipman's, Mrs. Chipman desiring to address him by his title, and in the excitement of the occasion becoming forgetful of the same, said: "Major Hot Toddy, Major Hot Toddy!" About four miles beyond O. Williams, and at the crossing of the Indian trail on the Clinton, resided Alpheus Williams and Captain Archibald Phillips, where a saw-mill had been erected, and at this time was in operation.

But I will now return to my temporary home at Captain John Hunter's, of whose kindness, together with that of his excellent wife, long since gone to her reward, I cannot too highly speak. Here I made the acquaintance of Horatio Ball, son of Daniel Ball, who lived three-fourths of a mile southwest of Hunter's. He had received a contract for subdividing ten townships of land between Flint and Cass rivers. I arranged to accompany him as assistant, to carry the compass half of the time. He was waiting for the completion of the town lines, which had been assigned to a young man by the name of Hester. We were soon informed he had done nothing after having discovered an Indian wigwam, near a small lake, and as he was accompanied by his dogs, and was otherwise prepared for a winter's hunt, had decided to pass the winter in this pleasant locality and avoid the swamps. In a week's time every man of his party had left him while he was taking lessons of the Indians in hunting, and of the squaws in moccasin making. Here he remained during the winter. The next June he was seen passing through Pontiac on horseback, accompanied by about a dozen natives, of both sexes, to make his report to the surveyor general, at Chillicothe, and also to his father for $600 cash advanced. Hester having thus failed in fulfilling his contract the work was assigned to Joseph Wampler, of Ohio (the surveyor who subdivided ranges ten and eleven in Oakland county). We set off for our work on the 13th of June, arriving at Flint river before Wampler returned from Saginaw bay. The heavy rains had swollen the river to nearly full banks, and as there was no way of crossing we started up the river to the Kearsley, where we felled a suitable pine, about sixteen feet of which we removed from the main body of the tree and shaped it canoe-like, digging out the same, so far as could be done with axes, and made it answer our purpose, and we floated it down the river and landed it on the north side, where the city of Flint is now located. Here we found Jake Smith, called "Wabaseis" by the Indians, who had been Indian trader for several years, and who had recently received the

appointment of Indian farmer. He had built a comfortable log house a few rods below the present railroad bridge. This was occupied by Smith, a white man, with his mother and sister. Also by a man by the name of Doane. The two men at this time (the middle of June) were hoeing corn, with veiled faces on account of the mosquitoes.

After waiting about a week we were furnished with the field notes, and commenced our work in town seven north, of range seven east. After a week's work we returned to the trading house, when soon after Wampler and his party came in, the men utterly refusing to continue longer on account of the suffering they had endured from the mosquitoes, both men and horses being weak from loss of blood and want of rest. Owing to the continuance of the township lines survey, we were compelled to discontinue our work, and we decided to accompany Wampler's party to Pontiac. During the remainder of the season I made my home with Mr. Hunter, and occasionally accompanied a land-looker. I also assisted him in securing his winter's supply of marsh hay, among the massasaugas, where they appeared in great abundance.

Early in autumn Wampler returned to Flint river to finish his work, and our party followed for the purpose of finishing our work, in October.

This occupied about sixty days, and from the inexperience of Ball, and the miserable outfits, we suffered both from hunger and cold. We had no tents, only an old second-hand tarpaulin, which had been laid aside as useless for hatchway service. In the absence of a kneading trough, our cook made use of this piece of canvas to mix his bread. This was unfortunate, for on our first visit to the trading-house some swine, attracted by the adhering dough, nearly devoured and entirely destroyed it, and we had now no cover besides our blankets. Our provisions were inadequate; we were frequently reduced to a short allowance of only buggy peas, and at one time, when weak from want of food, we found a wigwam where a squaw was cooking succotash, which she kindly divided with us. This occurred on the last day of our survey, while meandering the river. Closing our work on the line of the reserve at sunset and following up the river, forcing our way through thick beds of rushes knee high, at about nine o'clock we reached Smith's trading-house, so hungry from several days' short allowance, that we took the potatoes from the kettle half boiled. I must not forget to mention the names of the men who formed this surveying party. Besides Ball and myself, there were Rufus Stevens, Michael Beach, Chester Webster, and a young man from the Emerald Isle, named Pool.

During the sub-division of town nine north, of range six east, we encountered the most terrific gale of wind I ever witnessed in the woods of Michigan. The trees crackled and fell in all directions close around us. It was on the same night the "Walk-in-the-Water" lay off Buffalo, deeply laden for Detroit. When Captain Rodgers, after discovering the open seams of the steamer, and realizing the impending danger, very properly gave the order to slip the cables, releasing her, and she went on shore.

We finished our work on the last of December, and I decided to accompany Mr. Ball to Chillicothe, Ohio, where he made his returns to the surveyor general's office. In addition to letters I already possessed from Governor Clinton, of New York, and from Judge Wright, chief engineer of the Erie canal, I had procured one from Governor Cass, who recommended me from the fact I intended making Michigan my home. Starting on our journey, when a little way below Detroit, we were fortunate in obtaining a passage with an Ohio farmer, who had just made sale of his butter and cheese in Detroit. Landing at Sandusky, we footed it to Chillicothe. Presenting my letters, which proved satisfactory, he promised me future work. The purpose of my visit to Michigan being accomplished, and arrangements for future employment as government surveyor perfected, I immediately returned to my home, where I arrived on the 14th of February, having been absent eleven months.

NOTES FROM SHAWNEETOWN

MORRIS BIRKBECK

A spare little Englishman with lighted eyes, a wind-burned face, and a bald head fringed with rumpled hair, Morris Birkbeck was the most ardent spokesman for Illinois in the years of its first settlement. "No man since Columbus," a traveler wrote, "has done so much toward peopling America as Mr. Birkbeck; and if all could have settled in Illinois whom he had tempted across the Atlantic and the mountains, it had now been the most populous state in the Union."

In London in 1816 Birkbeck had chanced to meet the American diplomat Edward Coles, and his future swung in a new direction. Hearing of vast empty lands in Illinois, for sale at two dollars an acre, Birkbeck began dreaming of a colony for depressed English country laborers. This bright project he shared with his friend George Flower, and the two joined in the undertaking.

Bringing his family to America in 1817, Birkbeck led them west on horseback. Beyond the Wabash, in the wild Illinois territory, they found the land of his dream. "We are so taken with the prairie," he wrote, "that no timbered land can satisfy our present views." So they rode fifty miles south to the District Land Office at Shawneetown on the Ohio. In a Shawneetown tavern, with boat-

men's voices ringing from the mile-wide river, Birkbeck wrote some pages for his Notes on a Journey in America, which would soon go through eleven editions on both sides of the Atlantic.

SHAWNEE Town. This place I account as a phenomenon evincing the pertinacious adhesion of the human animal to the spot where it has once fixed itself. As the lava of Mount Etna cannot dislodge this strange being from the cities which have been repeatedly ravaged by its eruptions, so the Ohio with its annual overflowings is unable to wash away the inhabitants of Shawnee Town.—Once a year, for a series of successive springs, it has carried away the fences from their cleared lands, till at length they have surrendered, and ceased to cultivate them. Once a year, the inhabitants either make their escape to higher lands, or take refuge in their upper stories, until the waters subside, when they recover their position on this desolate sand-bank.

Here is the land office for the south-east district of Illinois, where I have just constituted myself a land-owner by paying seven hundred and twenty dollars, as one fourth of the purchase money of fourteen hundred and forty acres: this, with a similar purchase made by Mr. Flower, is part of a beautiful and rich prairie, about six miles distant from the Big, and the same from the Little Wabash.

The land is rich natural meadow, bounded by timbered land, within reach of two navigable rivers, and may be rendered immediately productive at a small expence. The successful cultivation of several prairies has awakened the attention of the public, and the value of this description of land is now known; so that the smaller portions, which are surrounded by timber, will probably be settled so rapidly as to absorb, in a few months, all that is to be obtained at the government rate, of two dollars per acre.

Sand predominates in the soil of the south-eastern quarter of the Illinois territory: —the basis of the country is sand-stone, lying, I believe, on clay-slate. The bed of the Ohio, at Shawnee Town is sand-stone: forty miles north-east, near Harmony, is a quarry of the same stone, on the banks of the Big Wabash.

The shoals of the Little Wabash and the Skillet-fork, twenty, forty, and sixty miles up, are of the same formation. No lime-stone has yet been discovered in the district. I have heard of coal in several places, but have not seen a specimen of it. Little, however, is yet known with precision of the surface of many parts of the country; and the wells, though numerous, rarely reach the depth of thirty feet, below which, I presume, the earth has in no instance been explored.

The geographical position of this portion of territory promises favourable for its future importance. The Big Wabash, a noble stream, forming its eastern boundary, runs a course of about four hundred miles, through one of the most fertile portions of this most fertile region. It has a communication well known to the Indian traders, with lake Huron and all the navigation of the north, by means of a portage of eight miles to the Miami of the lakes. This portage will, probably, be made navigable in a few years. Population is already very considerable along this river, and upon White River, another beautiful and navigable stream, which falls into the Wabash from the east. The Little Wabash, though a sluggish stream, is, or may become a navigable communication extending far north, I am *informed* four hundred miles.

The prairies have been represented as marshes, and many of them are so. This is not, however, the case with all. Our prairie rises at its northern extremity to a commanding height, being one of the most elevated portions of the country, surmounting and overlooking the woodlands to the south and west, to a great distance. There are also many others to the northward on lands of the same eligible character, high and fertile, and surrounded by timbered lands. These are unsurveyed, and of course are not yet offered to the public.

Nothing but fencing and providing water for stock is wanted to reduce a prairie into the condition of useful grass land; and from that state, we all know, the transition to arable is through a simple process, easy to perform, and profitable as it goes on. Thus no addition, except the above on the score of improvement, is to be made to the first cost, as regards the land. Buildings, proportioned to the owner's inclination or purse, are of course requisite on every estate.

The dividing a section (six hundred and forty acres) into inclosures of twenty-five acres each, with proper avenues of communication, each inclosure being supplied with water, in the most convenient manner, and live hedges planted, or sown, will cost less than two dollars per acre. This, added to the purchase money, when the whole is paid, will amount to eighteen shillings sterling, per acre, or five hundred and seventy-six pounds for six hundred and forty acres.

Calculations on the capital to be employed, or expended on buildings, and stock alive and dead, would be futile, as this would be in proportion to the means. The larger the amount, within the limits of utility, the greater the profit: but, as the necessary outgoings are trifling, *a small sum will do.* Two thousand pounds sterling for these purposes would place the owner in a state of comfort, and even affluence.

I conclude from these data, that an English farmer possessing three thousand pounds, besides the charges of removal, may establish himself *well* as a proprietor and occupier of such an estate. The folly or the wisdom of the undertaking I leave among the propositions which are too plain to admit of illustration.

In their irregular outline of woodland and their undulating surface, these tracts of natural meadow exhibit ever beauty, fresh from the hand of nature, which art often labours in vain to produce; but there are no organs of perception, no faculties as yet prepared in this country, for the enjoyment of these exquisite combinations.

The grand in scenery I have been shocked to hear, by American lips, called disgusting, because the surface would be too rude for the plough; and the epithet of *elegant* is used on every occasion of commendation but that to which it is appropriate in the English language.

An elegant improvement, is a cabin of rude logs, and a few acres with the trees cut down to the height of three feet, and surrounded by a worm-fence, or zig-zag railing. You hear of an *elegant* mill, an *elegant* orchard, an *elegant* tanyard, &c. and familiarly of *elegant* roads,—meaning such as you may pass without extreme peril. The word implies eligibility or usefulness in America, but has nothing to do with taste; which is a term as strange to the American language, where I have heard it spoken, as comfort is said to be to the French, and for a similar reason:— the idea has not yet reached them. Nature has not yet displayed to them those charms of distant and various prospect, which will delight the future inhabitants of this noble country.

Scientific pursuits are also, generally speaking, unknown where I have travelled. Reading is very much confined to politics, history and poetry. Science is not, as in England, cultivated for its own sake. This is to be lamented the more, on account of the many heavy hours of indolence under which most people are doomed to toil, through every day of their existence. What yawning and stretching, and painful restlessness they would be spared, if their time were occupied in the acquisition of useful knowledge!

There is a sort of covetousness which would be the greatest of blessings, to those Americans whose circumstances excuse them from constant occupation for a subsistence,— that is, to the great majority of the people,— the covetousness of time, from a knowledge of its value.

The life and habits of the great Franklin, whose name, I am sorry to say, is not often heard here, would be a most profitable study. He possessed the true Philosopher's stone; for whatever he touched became gold under his hand, through the magical power of a scientific mind. This lamentable deficiency in science and taste, two such abundant sources of enjoyment, must not be attributed to a want of energy in the American character:— witness the spirit and good sense with which

Fording the Wabash. *Courtesy Indiana Historical Society Library*

men of all ranks are seen to engage in discussions on politics, history, or religion; subjects which have attracted, more or less, the attention of every one. Nature has done much for them, and they leave much to Nature: but they have made *themselves* free; —this may account for their indifference to science, and their zeal in politics.

ARRIVAL AND DEPARTURE

LOUIS BROMFIELD

In The Farm *(1933) Louis Bromfield chronicled a century of life in rural Ohio, on the edge of the Western Reserve. "The story of a way of living which has largely gone out of fashion," the narrative portrays a family that is nourished by a deeply rooted attachment to the land.*

This excerpt pictures the symbolic meeting of three men in a blockhouse at the close of the War of 1812. The Jesuit priest is leaving the Northwest country; the Maryland settler and the Yankee merchant are arriving. The French missions to the Indians are of the past; the future belongs to the farmer and the trader. This episode gathers up the significant strands of social life in the early frontier.

THE Colonel came to the Midland County in the spring of the year 1815, arriving in sight of the blockhouse just at twilight. He rode a mare called Belle, and with him there rode a guide called Hallie Chambers, who had a thin tough horse and wore buckskin pants, a jacket of bottle-green woolen stuff, fastened with brass buttons, and a beaver cap. Hallie Chambers could not read or write and a great many people thought him half-witted, but he had the sense of an animal and could find his way anywhere in the Western Reserve and he knew how to get on with the Shawnees, the Wyandots, and the Delawares. He had a way of telling long stories from which he always drew a moral, and he carried a Bible with him, though he could not read a word of it, and prayed every evening, kneeling down unashamed in the mud or the dust or the snow. For fifteen days they had been on the way north from Marietta and the Colonel was bored with Hallie Chambers. In the beginning Hallie had seemed a strange and interesting character, and the Colonel thought that at last he had discovered Jean Jacques' "natural man," for had not Hallie been born and brought up in the wilderness, simple and pure and uncorrupted by the civilization which lay east of the mountains? The Colonel had wanted to like him. He had felt a desire to attach Hallie to him so that he might study a simple man who knew nothing of Hamilton or politics or banks and bargaining or New England business men. But after a week, while the Colonel lay on his back, sleepless, under one of the ox-carts, he admitted to himself that Hallie Chambers was all surface and had no more depth than a friendly dog. Being a child of nature had given him nothing but simplicity, and the Colonel saw that simplicity unadorned might have a deadly lack of interest. Hallie Chambers had not even a natural sense of God, for somewhere corruption had been carried over the mountains, perhaps by Hallie's mother, and his God was simply the commonplace, somewhat crude God of the Methodists who kept shops and bartered horses back in Maryland.

The Colonel's mare, Belle, was a thoroughbred chestnut with a white star on her forehead, and as they halted in sight of the Pentland settlement, until the ox-carts caught up with them, her pretty head drooped a little after the long ride. It was not the Colonel's weight which wearied her, but the long, heavy going. He was a spare man, with a small bony head and a hawklike nose. But for his eyes and the gentleness of his mouth, which drew in at the corners into small, humorous wrinkles, he would have been a man of fierce appearance. His brow was square and his jaw set at a sharp angle. The Colonel was fifty-two, but he had the appearance of a man ten years younger, for he had always lived well and sensibly, neither crucifying the flesh nor plunging it into debauchery and excess. He had eaten good food and drunk fine wines and loved now and then when love had offered itself pleasantly. Behind him lay an easy life, a big house, and broad rich fields, but as he sat on the weary Belle, looking across the marshes toward Pentland he knew there was small chance of his ever seeing Maryland and those fields again. At fifty-two he was beginning life over again, with a young wife left behind in Maryland in her first pregnancy, to join him when the baby was born and a decent house built to shelter her in the wilderness. In spite of the youth in the blue eyes, something inside the Colonel was dead. He was sick of the old life and the politicians and the bankers. He was sick of dishonesty and corruption and intolerance and all the meanness of civilization and of man himself. Because something deep inside him was dead, he had begun to seek peace in a dream. It was the dream of his time, for he belonged to the Eighteenth Century and in it he remained until he died, when the Nineteenth Century was half way to its end.

While they waited for the carts, he asked Hallie Chambers about the two low mounds which rose out of the flat marshes. They were not large and irregular like the hills through which they had been riding all day, but small and perfectly symmetrical and so beautifully molded beneath their blanket of dogwood and sassafras that they aroused his curiosity.

"Indian mounds," said Hallie. "Some say they're tombs of Indian kings, but the Wyandots and Delawares won't go near them. They won't shoot deer or pigeons when they're on those mounds. The pigeons know it, too." And while he spoke a great flock of wood-pigeons rose and circled about them, to settle once more on the mounds.

"I've seen flocks that hid the sun," said Hallie.

But the Colonel wasn't listening to any more of Hallie's fabulous stories of the game in this new country. He was tired and he was listening to the shouts which came distantly toward them, "Heigh, Buck! Ho, Berry!" as his men encouraged the oxen dragging the heavy carts through the mud of the marshes. Before him against the sunset he saw the settlement, a long blockhouse and a stockade surrounded by a cluster of cabins. From the chimneys the smoke curled upward and lost itself in the mist of the spring evening. A golden light fell on the surface of the little sluggish stream which meandered through the marshes.

"What's it called—the brook?" asked the Colonel.

"Toby's Run. It's called for an old Delaware chief who got drunk one night in the blockhouse and fell into the branch on his way home to his camp. He was so drunk he couldn't get up. The water ain't deep, but he drownded."

The ox-carts creaked up through the dusk and the Colonel pulled up Belle's head and set on his way again. After a hundred yards, the little procession reached the ford over the creek and the oxen moved reluctantly, belly deep, through the muddy stream. On the other side, just beyond a thicket of sassafras, there was a clearing, and in the clearing stood the settlement. Already there were lights in the windows of the cabins. The carts drew up under the shadow of the blockhouse and the Colonel swung down from his mare and tossed the reins to one of his men. He was at the end of his journey. This was the wilderness where he was to live the rest of his life and to die, where one could begin life over again and find a new and decent world. As the night fell, it grew colder and the wind rose, and, listening to it, the Colonel felt weary and a little afraid. He might never see Maryland again and never again would he see London and Scotland, nor talk with the men and women he had known in Paris in his youth when there

was no Bonaparte and Voltaire had come home from Ferney to die.

In the little cluster of houses, the first citizens of Pentland had been awaiting the Colonel's party, for he was a man of importance and news of his coming had preceded him. They knew that he was the last man out of Washington the day the British burned the White House, and that he had a ball in his thigh, and that Congress had awarded him a sword and the rank of Colonel and a grant of land in the Western Reserve. And they had heard that before he set out for the West he had given all his slaves their freedom and sent them into the world with new clothes and money in their pockets.

That night when the oxen had been turned loose and the Colonel had eaten and drunk the wine he brought with him in one of the carts, the "citizens" gathered round the big fire in the ground floor of the blockhouse. There were seven of them in all, not counting the lieutenant and the four soldiers who garrisoned the blockhouse. There were the two traders, one like Hallie Chambers, born on the Kentucky frontier, and the other a Canuck, half-Indian, half-French, who came from the Lakes; and there were the two surveyors who were blocking out the County, and a young Swiss, named Weiler, who was big and blond. He had come to make his fortune as a tavern-keeper in the new country and brought his wife with him. As yet there was no need for a real tavern, but Weiler and his wife Marie were young and strong and they thought about the future. They had a piece of land along the creek and the biggest log house in the settlement. In front of it hung a sign with the legend "Weiler's Tavern." There were only two rooms, but it served as a tavern for guides and surveyors and an occasional wanderer. It was in Weiler's Tavern that the Colonel and his men and Hallie Chambers were lodged for the night.

Just inside the door, seated on the earthen floor of the blockhouse, was the Indian woman, called Mary, who lived with the fur-traders and followed them wherever they went. She was fat and untidy, with long greasy black hair half-hidden by a cap made of skins.

She wore a calico dress and over it a man's torn threadbare jacket. While the men talked in the firelight she kept dozing and waking, starting up suddenly to mumble to herself. She was drunk and now and then when she mumbled too loudly the lieutenant swore at her in crude French and she became silent once more.

The other man in the room was neither a settler nor a surveyor, a trapper or a soldier. He wore the dress of a Jesuit, and the Colonel addressed him as Father Duchesne. He had a lean, hard body and a lean, gentle face, cut with deep lines on each side of the big mouth. His hair was cut short and was grizzled. The Colonel and the priest knew each other. A dozen times they had met in Washington, and once the priest had come to pass ten days with the Colonel at his place on the shores of Chesapeake Bay. It was a miracle now that they should meet here by chance in the wilderness.

"Not altogether a miracle," Father Duchesne had said, "because I heard you were coming here and I've been waiting four days for you to arrive. I was on my way to Sandusky."

"Alone?" the Colonel had asked.

"Alone. It's a journey I've made many times."

"Some day you'll meet a drunken Indian."

"That is in the hands of God."

While they sat by the fire, the men asked the Colonel and Hallie Chambers for news, but they had little which the Jesuit had not already given them. There was only the tragedy of a family near Chillicothe who had been tomahawked in their lone cabin by some wandering Indians. One of the soldiers cursed at the news and said the sooner the Indians were all wiped out the better, because they were a drunken lot of animals, and the Jesuit said: "There aren't many left. It won't be long until they're all gone."

And then Weiler said he had seen the Dauphin. And all of them listened while he told of the young man called Lazare who lived with the Indians but was white and remembered mobs and torches and the Revolution, and then for a long time they argued about him and whether the Dauphin had really died

in the Temple or been carried off to Canada. Father Duchesne had seen him twice, but did not believe he was the Dauphin. "Nobody knows who he is. The Indians tell one story and then another."

The lieutenant said that all Indians were liars, and Father Duchesne looked at him but said nothing, perhaps because he knew that his time was at an end in this part of the wilderness.

Then the Indian woman, Mary, was sick and the Canuck trapper rose and crossed the room and pushed her out of the door, and Weiler rose, yawning, and said he must go to bed, and the little party broke up and one by one climbed the ladder into the loft above or went toward Weiler's Tavern until only the Colonel and the Jesuit were left sitting before the fire, and in the shadows the soldier who was on guard.

When all the others had gone save the sleepy soldier the Colonel and the Jesuit looked at each other and smiled. It was a smile of understanding which came from the secret parts of their souls. By the smile they told each other that they had been waiting all the evening for this moment when, alone, they might relax and reveal themselves. For the Jesuit the moment was one of luxury and it was a luxury which the Colonel had come to understand after the long journey into the wilderness. The smile, so subtle and quiet, betrayed the two men—that the Jesuit was less a man of God than an intellectual, and the Colonel less of a Democrat and philosopher than he had believed himself, and much more of an aristocrat. In his soul the Colonel was weary of the constraint of those long weeks spent in journeying through forest and by river, always in the company of his two men and Hallie Chambers, when he found himself forced always to speak with simplicity and even to think with childishness that he might not puzzle his companions or disturb their simple beliefs. For more than six long weeks he had not been alive at all, save for those brief interludes when a strange tree or a new kind of rock or the call of an unknown bird roused his curiosity for a moment. He was weary and a little homesick, and the disillusionment he found in that child of nature,

Hallie Chambers, troubled him, because it concerned not only Hallie Chambers, but all the future of the Colonel and the dream which had caused him to sell everything he had and go into the West.

But now, sitting opposite the lean Jesuit, life seemed to flow back into his veins. The gray look went out of his face and fire returned to the blue eyes. He lighted his pipe and refilled the glasses of himself and his friend, and then he asked Father Duchesne his plans.

The priest sighed and told him that this was probably the last time they would ever meet. He was going to Mexico. The mission at Sandusky was finished. Times had changed. The wilderness was vanishing. The government was unsympathetic to Jesuit missions, and fanatics accused them of being centers of intrigue and Indian plots.

"That is not true," said the priest, gravely. "The Indians have been friendly to us because we have been friendly."

And there were the settlers. They were fiercely Protestant. They came, nearly all of them, from Massachusetts and Connecticut. They were Puritan and New England. They suspected and hated Jesuits.

At the mention of New England, the Colonel gave a grunt of disapproval. He cherished New Englanders less than Father Duchesne himself. They were tradespeople and shopkeepers, interested only in making money and swindling one another and the rest of the country. Was it not the Essex Junto and the noble New Englanders who, aided by that scoundrel Hamilton, had swindled the old soldiers and speculated on the rewards of the men who had fought to free their country and establish a democratic republic?

At the word "democratic" the priest smiled but said nothing. After a little silence he put down his glass and said, thoughtfully, "I'm not going to Mexico because new settlers hate me nor because the government is determined to force me out. Those things are nothing to a Jesuit. It is because I am left in a barren spot, like a seed lodged in a rock from which the hurricane has torn all the soil. Who am I to defeat a whole race, a whole civilization? I am a Latin. This new country is lost to us. In a little while there will be no more

redskins, no Delawares, no Wyandots—only shopkeepers where God is a tradesman's god. In Mexico, it is different."

The Colonel did not answer him and presently the priest, smiling, asked: "And what of your wilderness? What do you think of it?"

"It is a fine country. It is fresh and new."

The gray eyes of the priest twinkled, "And the children of nature—Hallie Chambers and Mary?"

"Mary?"

"The Indian woman who was squatting by the door."

"She has been corrupted."

"The soldiers and the lieutenant?"

The Colonel gave a scornful snort, "They are merely soldiers. One doesn't count them."

"And the trappers? *Voilà!*—children of nature."

"They seem not a bad sort."

"It is they who corrupted Mary. They carry her about with them. She lives with both of them."

The Colonel did not answer him.

"And the innkeeper, Weiler?"

"He seems an honest, wholesome fellow."

"Shrewd and thrifty. He will succeed in your Utopia."

The Colonel put down his pipe. "It is easy to mock."

"No, my friend, your 'children of nature' are too much like the noble savages in the plays of Voltaire who never saw a redskin and could not himself live without an excellent cook and a house filled with civilized people."

Again the Colonel was silent, and the Jesuit said, "There is the Kingdom of God and the kingdom of man. The kingdoms of men are alike, whether they be republics or tyrannies."

Without thinking of it they had fallen into speaking French. The sleepy soldier could understand them now even less than he had understood them before when they talked of nature and civilization and God. It was a tongue which the Colonel spoke easily, for in his youth there had always been a French Jesuit in the big house on the shores of the Chesapeake. The first MacDougal in the Colonies was a Jacobite, and the Colonel was

A rail splitter's home, c. 1820. *Courtesy Illinois State Historical Library*

brought up as a Roman Catholic, but since his childhood he had wandered a long way. At twenty he had been a Deist, and now, if he believed in God at all, it was in the vague romantic God of Jean Jacques.

While they talked there grew up about the two of them a strange atmosphere of elegance, as if, instead of sitting in the log blockhouse with only good earth beneath them for a floor, their chairs rested upon a floor of nutwood and the crude mugs which held their wine were of delicate crystal. Presently in his corner the guard began to snore, for he, like the priest, knew that there were really no dangers against which a sentinel was needed. Since the Battle of Fallen Timbers the menace of Indians was over and their power gone.

The candles burned out and at last there was only the firelight, but the two men stayed, sometimes talking, sometimes silent. When one of them made a speech which failed to take fire, kindling the mind of the other, there were no dull phrases uttered, without meaning, for both men were of mature years and long ago they had learned to scorn the talk which begins and ends in nothing. But even in their silence there was a kind of melancholy communication as if the two minds were aware of a common sadness. The Jesuit knew what it was that troubled him, but of the two he was the happier because beneath the shining surface of his intellect he really believed in a God who could serve as a refuge from his disillusionment. The mind of the Colonel, less clear and realistic than that of the Frenchman, neither accepted his disillusionment nor found a refuge in God.

At last the fire, too, began to die away and shyly, as if he did it as a suggestion, the Colonel rose and threw more logs into the cavernous fireplace and as he turned away he stopped abruptly, listening.

"A man calling. Did you hear him?"

The priest listened, "No, but my ears are no longer good."

Again the call was repeated, and this time Father Duchesne heard the distant "Halloo" and, rising, went to the door, where he took down the lantern meant for the sleeping sentinel. Opening the door, he stepped outside and held the lantern high above his head. The Colonel followed him and stood at his side, peering across the clearing.

It was a chill night with a bright clear moon, and underfoot the mud was frozen now, so that when the Colonel stepped out of the door the crust broke beneath his square-toed riding-boots. They waited, listening, but for a long time the cry was not repeated and they heard only the hooting of an owl somewhere in the forest nearby. Then quite suddenly, near at hand, the "Halloo" rose again and out of the forest into the moonlit clearing they saw the figure of a tall, lean man approaching. He was leading a mule so heavily laden that there was no place left for the man to ride. He saw the lantern and came toward them. When he reached the light they saw that he was dressed in homespun, with a leather jacket and a top hat. Over his shoulders he wore a shabby bearskin. Coming out of the wall of forest into the wilderness clearing, he was a moonlit scarecrow. Even the Jesuit seemed less strange. As the priest held the lantern high, the two friends saw that the newcomer was a youngish man. His face was long, with a long nose and a lantern jaw and a hard mouth.

He said, "Good evening, gentlemen. I take it this is Pentland blockhouse. My name is Silas Bentham. I'm from Massachusetts. From Worcester, to be exact."

The man held out his hand and the Colonel took it, but the faintest shadow of a frown crossed his face as if he had said again, "shopkeepers and tradesmen, intended only to swindle one another." It was as if he had encountered a ghost in paradise.

The stranger asked for shelter for his mule, and the Colonel showed him the shed where his mare and the four oxen were stabled, going with the man while he swung the pack down from the back of the tired animal.

"I'd 'a' been lost but for the bright moon," he said. "I calculated to reach here before dark." He had a dry voice, not unpleasant, but curiously flat and empty of feeling.

"I suppose you know the trail," said the Colonel.

"Never been in these parts before," said the man.

"It's dangerous without a guide."

The man grunted as he swung down the second pack. "Guides cost money. A man setting up a business can't spend good money on a guide. Anyway, I been lost a couple of times, but I just turned in an' slept against the mule. He's right well trained for that."

Something in the tough indifference of the man roused a flicker of amusement in the Colonel. There was something comical about the lean, weatherbeaten fellow in his shopkeeper's clothes which made mock of the big stories of frontiermen like Hallie Chambers. The man was not boasting. He made the statement flatly, like a man who was the prey of a fixed idea so strong that hardships and perils were a matter of indifference.

The Jesuit never spoke at all, but stood silently in his rusty black, like a grave bird, yet in his silence and concentration there was a curious air of hostility and contempt.

When the mule had been bedded down with oak leaves, the three of them turned and in silence crossed the frozen, trampled mud and entered the blockhouse. The fire was blazing now, and in his corner the sentinel still snored. The stranger put down the pack he had brought with him and turned to fetch the second.

"It's safe in the shed," said the priest, but the man opened the door and went out, and when he returned he said: "You never can tell. Things disappear sometimes like as if there was magic about it."

He shivered and went over to the fire, standing with his lank figure silhouetted against the flames.

"Have you supped?" asked the Colonel.

"Yes. I always calculate to be independent."

The Colonel picked up the jug of wine. "A drink will warm you."

"No. Thanks just the same."

"It's good wine. . . . Maybe some brandy." The Colonel spoke graciously, as if the blockhouse were his own dwelling and he were entertaining a chance guest.

But the man refused: "No, thanks. I'm a teetotaler. A man can spend a pretty penny on drink once he gets started. I never got started yet. But if there's some good spring water."

The manner of the Colonel chilled a little. He pointed to the iron pail with the handle of a gourd visible in it. The man called Bentham refreshed himself, and then, as if the water had been something stronger, he began to talk and the small blue eyes set a little too close together in the long face lighted up.

He told them that he had come into the West because it was a new country where a man had a chance to begin life over again and make a fortune. Times were hard back East. A fellow couldn't make a living as a peddler in New England. Farmers and village people hadn't any money. People in this new country hadn't any money, either, but it was different here. People *had* to buy things, because they needed them—thread, and buttons and pewterware and calico, and the market was growing all the time instead of getting smaller. By the time the country was pretty well settled he'd have enough to set up a good business. Did they know how much could be made on twelve dozen bone buttons in a country where buttons were a necessity?

He went on talking like one hypnotized by visions of profits, but the Colonel and the priest scarcely heard him. Now and then the Colonel pulled himself up with a start and feigned a semblance of interest, as if he still had the illusion that this was his house and this man his guest, but he really heard nothing the man said. Father Duchesne made no pretense of interest, but simply stared into the fire, never troubling to look at the man.

"I calculate that if things go right I ought to be a rich man by the time I'm fifty. It's a wonderful new country."

The Jesuit rose slowly and said, "I'll be moving soon," and at the sound of his voice the stranger said, "French, ain't you?"

"Yes."

"Catholic?"

"Yes."

"I reckoned so. It's hard luck for you, losing a fine country like this."

The Jesuit did not answer him, and as the Colonel rose the peddler stepped forward quickly, moving in front of them, "Wait a minute, gentlemen. I've some things to show you. Silver buttons for your waistcoat. Fine silk for your neckerchief. Handkerchiefs . . . fine things such as befits gentlemen like you."

With miraculous speed he had one of the packs open and was ready to spread his wares.

"Don't trouble," said the Colonel. "There's nothing I need."

The priest passed him on his way to the door, and Bentham, looking up from his pack, said: "You'll regret it, gentlemen, if you miss this chance. See this fine bit of silk—just the thing for a gentleman like you."

The Colonel turned, "If you're going to the tavern we'll show you the way."

"You'll regret it, gentlemen." Then suddenly his instinct told him that there was no business to be done, and he stood up once more, his great length unfolding joint by joint like a carpenter's rule. "I don't count on sleeping in a tavern. I've got my jacket and packs. I'll make up a bed right here. Many a time I've slept that way without a roof over my head. Thank you, gentlemen." He moved toward the door, "Good night to you."

"Good night," said the Colonel.

The door closed behind them and in silence they set out over the frozen mud to the log house with the crude little sign, "Weiler's Tavern." In the brilliant moonlight they walked in silence to the door. The magic of the evening was gone now and suddenly they were both tired.

The Colonel pushed open the door of the tavern and stepped into the common room, where his two men, the surveyor, the trappers, and Hallie Chambers were snoring. There was no light, but the dying fire cast a glow over the room. When the priest had closed the heavy door, they stood looking at each other in silence and presently the Colonel said, "You'll be off early, no doubt."

"Soon after sunup. I want to ride to Frémont by sundown."

"I'll ride with you a part of the way." He began unbuttoning the tobacco-colored jacket, and presently he said, "I wish I was a young man again."

"All of us wish that."

"I'd go with you to Mexico."

· · · · · · ·

At dawn they rose and ate the smoking breakfast which Weiler's wife cooked for them. The priest saddled his old horse, and one of the Colonel's men brought up Belle, freshened by rest and corn and water, and the two set out through the opening in the clearing where the trail led to the north.

It was a brilliant spring morning, with the nip of the frost still in the air, and as they rode the vague sense of depression flowed away from the Colonel. It was beautiful, mellow country, all low hills and pleasant wooded valleys, and the little swollen streams flowed between banks where the pussywillows were in flower and the tropical green of the skunk cabbages pushed through the brown of last year's leaves. They did not talk much, but the Colonel saw that his companion was sad and he fancied he knew the reason.

" 'Tis true it's a fine brave country," he said. "But I've read that the Mexican country is all red and gold and purple." And when the Jesuit did not answer he said, again, "I wish that I was young again, that I might go with you." But now in the brilliance of the fine morning the words were insincere and he was troubled lest his friend should sense their falseness. And in his heart he knew that for all its newness, this was the kind of country to which he belonged—a country, gentle, smiling, well-watered and fertile, out of which man might make a new paradise if he were good and wise enough. In that other country, for all its purple and golden deserts, he would be forever lost and uneasy.

Thrushes ran across the trampled path and twice they started rabbits from beneath the very hoofs of the horses. The squirrels chattered in the sunlight and once a deer crossed the trail, and then presently they came to the top of a low hill, and then the Colonel drew up his mare and the Jesuit reined in his old horse so that the two animals stood close together. The Colonel held out his hand and the priest took it, and then suddenly, as if the thought had come to them at the same instant, the two men put their arms about each other and embraced in the French fashion.

"*Bon voyage*," said the Colonel, "*Écris moi de temps en temps.*"

"*Bonne chance*," said Father Duchesne, and for a moment a shadow of irony crossed his lean face. "Good luck with your new paradise."

Then without looking back the two men parted, aware that they would never meet again. They knew too that this parting was far more than a farewell between two friends. Each of them had said farewell to a life which in their hearts they loved.

V

The Great Migration

OF all the "thousand rivers" that make the Mississippi system, one flows westward from the Alleghenies. For multitudes of emigrants the broad Ohio was in just the right place and it moved toward the right destination. For nearly a hundred years it carried a strong current of western history.

From the beginning of its commerce, the Ohio drew men of many nations. In the summer of 1791 John Pope floated west from Pittsburgh on a flatboat. Taking turns at the long steering oar were six men—a Kentuckian, a Virginian, a German, a Frenchman, a Welshman, and a man born at sea. In 1802 the French naturalist François Michaux made an exploring trip down the river. He was a good observer, despite a blind left eye, and as he drifted west his notebook filled with observations of the frontier country. On river landings, in boatyards, blacksmith shops and taverns, he heard the repeated greeting: " 'What part of the world do you come from?'—as if those immense and fertile regions were to be the asylum common to all the inhabitants of the globe."

There were four ways to the western country—the Genesee Road through the Mohawk valley to Buffalo, Forbes' Road from Philadelphia over the mountains to Pittsburgh, the Cumberland Road from Baltimore, and the Wilderness Road down the great valley of Virginia over Cumberland Gap and through the woods and barrens of Kentucky. Four roads fanning into the valley brought the future to the West. In the 1820's the Genesee Road became the route of the Erie Canal and a decade later the Cumberland Pike was extended through Ohio and Indiana as the National Road. The great migration filled them all with an urgent stream of life.

"The old America seems to be breaking up and moving West," said Morris Birkbeck in 1817. Population was growing in the older states, and the "Ohio fever" went like a contagion through New England. There was room in the West, a new chance over the mountains. The empty lands drew immigrants from the Old World; Birkbeck himself was seeking a site for an English colony in Illinois. No dukedom in France or England lay open to discontented yeomen, but millions of acres waited for settlement in America.

For half a century migration surged into the midlands with a tidal rhythm and power. The first big wave swept in following the Harrison Land Act of 1800.

The War of 1812 checked the movement, which rose to a flood in the five years following 1814. This settlement came by the Ohio River, and it peopled the southern counties of Ohio, Indiana and Illinois while their northern reaches remained wild and empty. After the Erie Canal was opened in 1825, an endless stream of Yankee farmers and European immigrants left the canal barges at Buffalo and crowded the harbor wharves. They saw lake schooners, three, four, five abreast, heaped to the hatches with golden wheat. Men waded knee-deep in that cargo, scooping it up with shovels, careless of what they spilled, as though there were unmeasured harvests where it came from.

With that picture in their minds the emigrants boarded the steamers that would take them to the land of plenty.

THE NAVIGATOR

In 1801 Zadok Cramer of Pittsburgh published the first edition of The Navigator, *a pilot's manual which became indispensable for every boatman on the river. Even the emigrant drifting down the Ohio with his family and a team of oxen in a flatboat depended on Cramer's mileage list of landmarks, islands, creeks, camps and settlements from Pittsburgh to the mouth of the Ohio. "On approaching the Mississippi," Cramer wrote, "the current naturally throws you over towards the willow point, from which, inclining downwards without difficulty (except the application of the oars and steerage, the better to keep the boat under headway, which ought to be done uniformly where two currents meet, there always being in such places more or less of a counter current) you enter the union of two of the most noble rivers in the universe." This is the halfway point in his manual, which goes on to guide boatmen all the way down the Mississippi to New Orleans.*

As the river channel changed with every spring flood, the publication of a river guide was a self-perpetuating business. A new edition of The Navigator *was brought out each year. The following excerpt is taken from the tenth edition, published in 1811, when the first steamboat on the western waters was building at Pittsburgh. The "Mr. Rosewalt" of Cramer's reference was Nicholas James Roosevelt, a partner of Livingston and Fulton, who took the historic* New Orleans *down the Ohio and Mississippi in the fall of 1811.*

THE Ohio has been described, as "beyond all competition, the most beautiful river in the universe, whether we consider it for its meandering course through an immense region of forests, for its clean and elegant banks, which afford innumerable delightful situations for cities, villages, and improved farms: or for those many other advantages, which truly entitle it to the name originally given it by the French, of 'La Belle Riviere,' that is, 'the Beautiful river.' " This description was penned several years since, and it has not generally been thought an exaggerated one. Now the immense forests recede, cultivation smiles along its banks, towns every here and there decorate its shores, and it is not extravagant to suppose, that the day is not very far distant when its whole margin will form one continued village.

The reasons for this supposition are numerous—the principal ones are, the immense tracts of fine country that have communication with the Ohio by means of the great number of navigable waters that empty into it; the extraordinary fertility, extent, and beauty of the river bottoms, generally high, dry, and with few or no exceptions, remarkably healthy, and the superior excellence of its navigation, through means of which, the various productions of the most extensive and fertile parts of the United States must eventually be sent to market.

For 80 miles below Pittsburgh it takes a N. W. course, then turns gradually to the W. S. W. and pursuing that course for about 500 miles, turns to the S. W. for nearly 170 miles, then it turns westward 280 miles, thence S. W. 180 miles, and empties itself into the Mississippi, in a flat and swampy country, where there are no hills to variegate the scene, nor mountains to overtop the union of these two noble streams.

The numerous islands that are interspersed in this river in many instances, add much to the grandeur of its appearance, but they embarrass the navigation considerably particularly in low water, as they occasion a great many shoals and sandbars. The soil of the islands for the most part is rich, timber luxuriant, and the extent of many of them considerable. Fruit is raised to great perfection on them, and seldom fail of a crop, as is generally the case in all the river bottoms.

In low water the navigation of the Ohio is difficult to the old Mingo town, about 75 miles below Pittsburgh; from thence to the Mississippi it is good for keelboats or barges carrying from 100 to 200 tons burden; up from thence it may be navigated with smaller crafts. In times of high water, vessels of 400 tons burden can descend with ease, except the difficulty arising from managing so unwieldy a bulk at the points of islands and short turns in the channel of the river. Vessels of this tonnage have descended from Pittsburgh to Orleans in safety, but the chance of good water renders the undertaking a little hazardous. The Falls, however, are much the greatest impediment, for unless vessels happen to hit the time of the highest stage of water, they are either detained, perhaps the next season, or, if they attempt a passage over them, a wreck in part or in whole may be the consequence, in either case, putting in jeopardy property to an amount that few individuals can bear the loss of. A lock-canal round the Falls would remove this difficulty, and be of an immense advantage to the Ohio trade, and to the people on or near the river from the Falls up to the head of the Allegheny and Monongahela rivers.—There has been some talk of attempting the commencement of this lock-canal. What jarring and clashing interests prevent the undertaking, are not easily to be found out. It can scarcely be supposed to be a want of public spirit in the Kentuckians or their legislature.

There are many smaller impediments, however in the river from Pittsburgh to the Mingo-town, which may be as long getting removed as even the Falls themselves: these consist of rocks that might be blown to pieces, and ripples that might be easily cleared out in such a way as to make the channel good through them. This is certainly an important

national concern, but the people must begin to act first, before their representatives will bring the thing forward in the house of general assembly. It must be done by grants of monies from the state, aided by subscriptions from the people; both must be liberal and vigilant, or the object will never be accomplished.

The consideration for opening the navigation of the Ohio, has become a matter of greater importance and necessity for the interest of Pennsylvania now than ever before. The United States' road from Cumberland on the Potomack, to Wheeling on the Ohio, when completed, will naturally draw a great deal of the trade of the northern states to the states of Ohio, Kentucky, Tennessee, and to Louisiana, through that channel, thereby abridging very much the trade from those states through Pennsylvania. Therefore if Pennsylvania looks closely to her own interests, she will find that the completing of the turnpike road from Harrisburgh to Pittsburgh, and opening the navigation of the Ohio, are the two principal objects which will tend to secure to her, her usual commercial, foreign and domestic advantages. Exclusive of the probability of the United States' road drawing the trade to the south of Pennsylvania, New York state, on the north, is pushing her inland navigation, and opening easy communications from one end of the state to the other, by way of turnpikes, canals, &c. to an extent unparalleled in any other state in the Union. The spirit of the people in the back part of the state of New York is peculiarly turned to this point, and no exertions seem to be lacking in the industry of the one class; or money wanting from the other. The purses of the one, and the labour of the other seem to be happily united for the good of the whole. When this is the case, a state must flourish in her internal improvements, and of course advance to wealth and independence.

The Ohio river has on its left in descending, Pennsylvania as far as the mouth of Mill creek; Virginia to the mouth of Big Sandy river; and the state of Kentucky, about 60 miles below the mouth of the Ohio. On the right, Pennsylvania to the line crossing just below the mouth of Little Beaver; the state of

Ohio from thence to the mouth of the Great Miami; and below this the Indiana to the mouth of the Wabash; thence to the Mississippi, the Illinois territory.

It receives in its course many large and navigable streams, the principal of which are; on the right, Big and Little Beaver, Muskingum, Sciota, Little and Great Miami, and the Wabash. On the left, Little and Great Kenhawa, Sandy, Licking, Kentucky, Green, Cumberland and Tennessee rivers:—These will be more particularly mentioned as we go on with directions for navigating the Ohio.

The fish of the Ohio are numerous and of various kinds: the black and yellow cat, weighing from 3 to 100 pounds; the buffalo, from 5 to 30 pounds; the pike from 4 to 15 pounds; the sturgeon from 4 to 40; the perch from 3 to 12 pounds; the sucker from 1 to 6 pounds; a few herrings sometimes, and in the spring of 1805, several shad were caught and sold in the Pittsburgh market, weighing about two pounds; eels and soft shelled turtles are sometimes caught.—These ascend the Allegheny and Monongahela rivers, and their principal branches, and are caught in seines, baskets, pots, and with trot-lines, hooks and lines, &c. The different species of the wild duck are numerous, and a few geese, brant, &c. are seen on the river, and the swan has sometimes been seen stemming the current. Turkies, pheasants and partridges are numerous on its banks; these, with the opportunity of sometimes shooting bears and deer swimming across the river, afford much pleasure to the navigator, and form sumptuous meals to the boat's crew. Boats to take advantage of this profitable amusement, are generally well provided with ammunition and fire-arms.

The principal articles constituting loading for the boats trading on the Ohio and Mississippi, are: flour, whiskey, apples, cider, peach and apple brandy, bar iron and castings, tin and copperwares, glass and cabinet work, windsor chairs, mill stones, grind stones, nails, &c. &c. And the principal articles brought up the Ohio in keel boats, are, cotton, lead, furs and peltry, and hemp and tobacco from Kentucky. This traffic is carried on briskly at this time, and no doubt a few years will greatly increase it, and much to the advantage of the adventurers.

Exclusive of the trading boats, there are many loaded altogether with merchandise of foreign importation, destined to Kentucky, Tennessee, Ohio, Indiana and the territories. Many others are family boats, seeking places of settlement in these new countries, where their posterity may rest in safety, having plenty of all the necessaries, and many of the luxuries of life, where their children's children may enjoy the rich and prolific productions of the land, without an over degree of toil or labour, where the climate is mild and the air salubrious, where each man is a prince in his own kingdom, and may without molestation, enjoy the frugal fare of his humble cot; where the clashing and terrific sounds of war are not heard; where tyrants that desolate the earth dwell not; where man, simple man, is left to the guidance of his own will, subject only to laws of his own making, fraught with mildness, operating equally just on all, and by all protected and willingly obeyed.

The hills on both sides of the Ohio, as low as Grave creek, below Wheeling, are filled with excellent coal. Below this, coal grows scarce, and what is found, is not of so good a quality. Coal has been boated down from Grave creek to Marietta, Limestone, falls of the Ohio, &c. where it sells for 12 cents per bushel. Even at this price, it is not a very advantageous article of trade. It is also boated to Natchez from mines above the falls, and sells in that market to the blacksmiths at from 25 to 37½ cents per bushel, and is preferred at that advanced price to the charcoal of that country. A mine of mineral coal has been observed lately at the Yellow Banks on the Ohio. The hills of the Allegheny and Monongahela rivers are also filled with good coal mines up to their head waters; and in some places valuable iron ores are found in them.

The lands of the Ohio and its branches, are differently timbered according to their quality and situation. The high and dry lands are covered with red, white and black oak, hickory, walnut, red and white mulberry, ash, poplar, dogwood, some yellow pine, cucumber tree, sassafras, chestnut, and patches of grapevines are sometimes to be found on the south

Flatboat on the Ohio. From Croft, *Pioneers in the Settlement of America*

side of the hills. The low and bottom lands produce butter-nut, tulip tree, papaw, black willow, locust, honey-locust, buck-eye, cherry, mulberry, beech, elm, aspen, maple, or sugar tree, plum tree, hickory, walnut, grapevine, remarkably large, spice wood, black alder, &c. And below or southwardly of the Falls, are several cedar and cypress swamps, where the cedar and cypress trees grow remarkably large, and where also are a great abundance of canes, such as grow in South Carolina, and on the Mississippi.

The *Sycamore* seems to be the king of the forest on the banks of the Ohio. Their monstrous growth, towering height, and extended branches really fill the beholder with awe and astonishment. Between Wheeling and Marietta I measured several from 10 to 16 feet over, four feet above ground, and this seems to be but their common size. A gentleman of Marietta told me he knew of one 60 feet in circumference, and that in the hollow of another he had turned himself around with a ten foot pole in his hands, sweeping it at

right angles with himself. And there is one of these huge trees in Sciota county, Ohio, on the land of a Mr. Abraham Miller, into whose hollow thirteen men rode on horse back, June 6, 1808, the fourteenth did not enter, his horse being skittish and too fearful to advance into so curious an apartment, but there was room enough for two more.

In the fall of the leaf, and when the years growth of bark begins to peal off these trees, the rays of the bright moon playing through their white branches, form a scene uncommonly brilliant, and quite cheering and amusing to the nightly traveller.

The growth of the grapevines on the banks of the Ohio astonish the beholder not less than that of the sycamores. It is not uncommon to find them measure from seven to eleven inches over, and so numerous, that in many places for 250 yards in circuit they form a complete canopy or covering of a great body and thickness, in which the tops of the trees are left in the entwining branches of the umbrageous vine leaves. The number and manner of their hanging 60 or 80 feet from the tops of the tallest trees without touching the trunk, rather puzzels the spectator how they could thus fix themselves. A sailor might say they were first planted in the tops of the trees, as he first fastens his ropes to the mast head, and then grew downwards and fastened into the ground at their leisure; they have this appearance but the principle does not answer the order of nature.

There is now on foot a new mode of navigating our western waters, particularly the Ohio and Mississippi rivers. This is with boats propelled by the power of steam. This plan has been carried into successful operation on the Hudson river at New York, and on the Delaware between New Castle and Burlington.—It has been stated that the one on the Hudson goes at the rate of four miles an hour against wind and tide on her route between New York and Albany, and frequently with 500 passengers on board. From these successful experiments there can be but little doubt of the plan succeeding on our western waters, and proving of immense advantage to the commerce of our country. A Mr. Rosewalt, a gentleman of enterprize, and who is acting it is said in conjunction with Messrs. Fulton and Livingston of New York, has a boat of this kind now (1810) on the stocks at Pittsburgh, of 138 feet keel, calculated for 300 or 400 tons burthen. And there is one building at Frankfort, Kentucky, by citizens who no doubt will push the enterprise. It will be a novel sight, and as pleasing as novel to see a huge boat working her way up the windings of the Ohio, without the appearance of sail, oar, pole, or any manual labour about her—moving within the secrets of her own wonderful mechanism, and propelled by power undiscoverable!—This plan, if it succeeds, must open to view flattering prospects to an immense country, an interior of not less than two thousand miles of as fine a soil and climate, as the world can produce, and to a people worthy of all the advantages that nature and art can give them, a people the more meritorious, because they know how to sustain peace and live independent, among the crushing of empires,

the falling of kings, the slaughter and bloodshed of millions, and the tumult, corruption and tyranny of all the world beside. The immensity of country we have yet to settle, the vast riches of the bowels of the earth, the unexampled advantages of our water courses, which wind without interruption for thousands of miles, the numerous sources of trade and wealth opening to the enterprising and industrious citizens, are reflections that must rouse the most dull and stupid. Indeed the very appearance of the placid and unbroken surface of the Ohio invite to trade and enterprise, and from the canoe, which the adventurer manages with a single pole or paddle, he advances to a small square ark boat, which he loads at the head waters with various wares, liquors, fruits, dry goods and small groceries, and starts his bark for the river traffic, stopping at every town and village to accommodate the inhabitants with the best of his cargo. —This voyage performed, which generally occupies three months, and the ark sold for half its first cost, the trader returns doubly invigorated, and enabled to enlarge his vessel and cargo, he sets out again; this is repeated, until perhaps getting tired of this mode of merchandising, he sets himself down in some town or village as a wholesale merchant, druggist or apothecary, practising physician, or lawyer, or something else, that renders him respectable in the eyes of his neighbors, where he lives amidst wealth and comforts the remainder of his days—nor is it by any known that his fortune was founded in the paddling of a canoe, or trafficking in apples, ciderroyal, peach brandy, whiskey, &c. &c. &c. From the canoe, we now see ships of two or three hundred tons burden masted and rigged, descending the same Ohio, laden with the products of the country, bound to New Orleans, thence to any part of the world.—Thus, the rise and progress of the trade and trader on the western waters; thus, the progress of our country from infancy to manhood; and thus, the flattering prospects of its future greatness through the channels of the Ohio and Mississippi rivers.

MIKE FINK, THE LAST BOATMAN

MORGAN NEVILLE

In 1811 the first steamboat churned the Ohio, and by 1825 steamboats car-
ried the bulk of the trade. Though keelboats were still used on tributary rivers
and a few were towed behind steamboats on the Ohio, their day was past. With
them went the formidable keelboatmen. But one of that lusty breed lived on in
memory. Like the later Paul Bunyan of the woods and Buffalo Bill of the plains,
Mike Fink, king of the rivermen, became a frontier hero and a frontier myth.

Morgan Neville (1783–1840) was a frontier editor at Pittsburgh and Cin-
cinnati. His sketch of Mike Fink appeared in James Hall's The Western Souvenir,
1829, one of the first of the western miscellanies.

I EMBARKED a few years since, at Pitts-burg, for Cincinnati, on board of a steam boat—more with a view of realising the possibility of a speedy return against the current, than in obedience to the call of either business or pleasure. It was a voyage of speculation. I was born on the banks of the Ohio, and the only vessels associated with my early recollections were the canoes of the Indians, which brought to Fort Pitt their annual cargoes of skins and bear's oil. The Flat boat of Kentucky, destined only to float with the current, next appeared; and after many years of interval, the Keel boat of the Ohio, and the Barge of the Mississippi were introduced for the convenience of the infant commerce of the West.

At the period, at which I have dated my trip to Cincinnati, the steam boat had made but few voyages back to Pittsburg. We were generally skeptics as to its practicability. The mind was not prepared for the change that was about to take place in the West. It is now consummated; and we yet look back with astonishment at the result.

The rudest inhabitant of our forests;—the man whose mind is least of all imbued with a relish for the picturesque—who would gaze with vacant stare at the finest painting—listen with apathy to the softest melody, and turn with indifference from a mere display of ingenious mechanism, is struck with the sublime power and self-moving majesty of a steam

boat;—lingers on the shore where it passes—and follows its rapid, and almost magic course with silent admiration. The steam engine in five years has enabled us to anticipate a state of things, which, in the ordinary course of events, it would have required a century to have produced. The art of printing scarcely surpassed it in its beneficial consequences.

In the old world, the places of the greatest interest to the philosophic traveller are ruins, and monuments, that speak of faded splendour, and departed glory. The broken columns of Tadmor—the shapeless ruins of Babylon, are rich in matter for almost endless speculation. Far different is the case in the western regions of America. The stranger views here, with wonder, the rapidity with which cities spring up in forests; and with which barbarism retreats before the approach of art and civilization. The reflection possessing the most intense interest is—not what has been the character of the country, but what shall be her future destiny.

As we coasted along this cheerful scene, one reflection crossed my mind to diminish the pleasure it excited. This was caused by the sight of the ruins of the once splendid mansion of Blennerhasset. I had spent some happy hours here, when it was the favorite residence of taste and hospitality. I had seen it when a lovely and accomplished woman presided—shedding a charm around, which made it as inviting, though not so dangerous, as the island of Calypso;—when its liberal and polished owner made it the resort of every stranger, who had any pretensions to literature or science.—I had beheld it again under more inauspicious circumstances:—when its proprietor, in a moment of visionary speculation, had abandoned this earthly paradise to follow an adventurer—himself the dupe of others. A military banditti held possession, acting "by authority." The embellishments of art and taste disappeared beneath the touch of a band of Vandals: and the beautfiul domain which presented the imposing appearance of a palace, and which had cost a fortune in the erection, was changed in one night, into a scene of devastation. The chimneys of the house remained for some years—the insulated monument of the folly of their owner, and pointed out to the stranger the place where once stood the temples of hospitality. Drift wood covered the pleasure grounds; and the massive, cut stone, that formed the columns of the gateway, were scattered more widely than the fragments of the Egyptian Memnon.

When we left Pittsburg, the season was not far advanced in vegetation. But as we proceeded the change was more rapid than the difference of latitude justified. I had frequently observed this in former voyages: but it never was so striking, as on the present occasion. The old mode of traveling, in the sluggish flat boat seemed to give time for the change of season; but now a few hours carried us into a different climate. We met spring with all her laughing train of flowers and verdure, rapidly advancing from the south. The buck-eye, cottonwood, and maple, had already assumed, in this region, the rich livery of summer. The thousand varieties of the floral kingdom spread a gay carpet over the luxuriant bottoms on each side of the river. The thick woods resounded with the notes of the feathered tribe —each striving to outdo his neighbor in noise, if not in melody. We had not yet reached the region of paroquets; but the clear toned whistle of the cardinal was heard in every bush; and the cat-bird was endeavouring, with its usual zeal, to rival the powers of the more gifted mockingbird.

A few hours brought us to one of those stopping points, known by the name of "wooding places." It was situated immediately above Letart's Falls. The boat, obedient to the wheel of the pilot, made a graceful sweep towards the island above the chute, and rounding to, approached the wood pile. As the boat drew near the shore, the escape steam reverberated through the forest and hills, like the chafed bellowing of the caged tiger. The root of a tree, concealed beneath the water, prevented the boat from getting sufficiently near the bank, and it became necessary to use the paddles to take a different position.

"Back out! Mannee! and try it again!" exclaimed a voice from the shore. "Throw your pole wide—and brace off!—or you'll run against a snag!"

This was a kind of language long familiar to us on the Ohio. It was a sample of the slang of the keel-boatmen.

The speaker was immediately cheered by a dozen of voices from the deck; and I recognised in him the person of an old acquaintance, familiarly known to me from my boyhood. He was leaning carelessly against a large beech; and, as his left arm negligently pressed a rifle to his side, presented a figure, that Salvator would have chosen from a million, as a model for his wild and gloomy pencil. His stature was upwards of six feet, his proportions perfectly symmetrical, and exhibiting the evidence of Herculean powers. To a stranger, he would have seemed a complete mulatto. Long exposure to the sun and weather on the lower Ohio and Mississippi had changed his skin; and, but for the fine European cast of his countenance, he might have passed for the principal warrior of some powerful tribe. Although at least fifty years of age, his hair was as black as the wing of the raven. Next to his skin he wore a red flannel shirt, covered by a blue capot, ornamented with white fringe. On his feet were moccasins, and a broad leathern belt, from which hung, suspended in a sheath, a large knife, encircled his waist.

As soon as the steam boat became stationary, the cabin passengers jumped on shore. On ascending the bank, the figure I have just described advanced to offer me his hand.

"How are you, Mike?" said I.

"How goes it?" replied the boatman—grasping my hand with a squeeze, that I can compare to nothing, but that of a blacksmith's vise.

"I am glad to see you, Mannee!"—continued he in his abrupt manner. "I am going to shoot at the tin cup for a quart—off hand—and you must be judge."

I understood Mike at once, and on any other occasion, should have remonstrated, and prevented the daring trial of skill. But I was accompanied by a couple of English tourists, who had scarcely ever been beyond the sound of Bow Bells; and who were travelling post over the United States to make up a book of observation, on our manners and customs. There were, also, among the passengers, a few bloods from Philadelphia and Baltimore, who could conceive of nothing equal to Chestnut or Howard streets; and who expressed great disappointment, at not being able to find terrapins and oysters at every village—marvellously lauding the comforts of Rubicum's. My tramontane pride was aroused; and I resolved to give them an opportunity of seeing a Western Lion—for such Mike undoubtedly was—in all his glory. The philanthropist may start, and accuse me of want of humanity. I deny the charge, and refer for apology to one of the best understood principles of human nature.

Mike, followed by several of his crew, led the way to a beech grove, some little distance from the landing. I invited my fellow passengers to witness the scene.—On arriving at the spot, a stout, bull-headed boatman, dressed in a hunting shirt—but bare-footed—in whom I recognised a younger brother of Mike, drew a line with his toe; and stepping off thirty yards—turned round fronting his brother—took a tin cup, which hung from his belt, and placed it on his head. Although I had seen this feat performed before, I acknowledge, I felt uneasy, whilst this silent preparation was going on. But I had not much time for reflection; for this second Albert exclaimed—

"Blaze away, Mike! and let's have the quart."

My "compagnons de voyage," as soon as they recovered from the first effect of their astonishment, exhibited a disposition to interfere. But Mike, throwing back his left leg,

levelled his rifle at the head of his brother. In this horizontal position the weapon remained for some seconds as immovable, as if the arm which held it, was affected by no pulsation.

"Elevate your piece a little lower, Mike! or you will pay the corn," cried the imperturbable brother.

I know not if the advice was obeyed or not; but the sharp crack of the rifle immediately followed, and the cup flew off thirty or forty yards—rendered unfit for future service. There was a cry of admiration from the strangers, who pressed forward to see if the foolhardy boatman was really safe. He remained as immovable, as if he had been a figure hewn out of stone. He had not even winked, when the ball struck the cup within two inches of his skull.

"Mike has won!" I exclaimed; and my decision was the signal which, according to their rules, permitted him of the target to move from his position. No more sensation was exhibited among the boatmen, than if a common wager had been won. The bet being decided, they hurried back to their boat, giving me and my friends an invitation to partake of "the treat." We declined, and took leave of the thoughtless creatures. In a few minutes afterwards, we observed their "Keel" wheeling into the current,—the gigantic form of Mike, bestriding the large steering oar, and the others arranging themselves in their places in front of the cabin, that extended nearly the whole length of the boat, covering merchandize of immense value. As they left the shore, they gave the Indian yell; and broke out into a sort of unconnected chorus—commencing with—

"Hard upon the beech oar!—
    She moves too slow!
All the way to Shawneetown,
    Long while ago."

In a few minutes the boat "took the chute" of Letart's Falls, and disappeared behind the point, with the rapidity of an Arabian courser.

Our travellers returned to the boat, lost in speculation on the scene, and the beings they had just beheld; and, no doubt, the circumstance has been related a thousand times with all the necessary amplifications of finished tourists.

Mike Fink may be viewed, as the correct representative of a class of men now extinct; but who once possessed as marked a character, as that of the Gypsies of England, or the Lazaroni of Naples. The period of their existence was not more than a third of a century. The character was created by the introduction of trade on the Western waters; and ceased with the successful establishment of the steam boat.

There is something inexplicable in the fact, that there could be men found, for ordinary wages, who would abandon the systematic, but not laborious pursuits of agriculture, to follow a life, of all others, except that of the soldier, distinguished by the greatest exposure and privation. The occupation of a boatman was more calculated to destroy the constitution and to shorten life, than any other business. In ascending the river, it was a continued series of toil, rendered more irksome by the snail like rate, at which they moved. The boat was propelled by poles, against which the shoulder was placed; and the whole strength, and skill of the individual were applied in this manner. As the boatmen moved along the running board, with their heads nearly touching the plank on which they walked, the effect produced on the mind of an observer was similar to that on beholding the ox, rocking before an overloaded cart. Their bodies, naked to their waist for the purpose of moving with greater ease, and of enjoying the breeze of the river, were exposed to the burning suns of summer, and to the rains of autumn. After a hard day's push, they would take their "fillee," or ration of whiskey, and having swallowed a miserable supper of meat half burnt, and of bread half baked, stretch themselves without covering, on the deck, and slumber till the steersman's call invited them to the morning "fillee." Notwithstanding this, the boatman's life had charms as irresistible, as those presented by the splendid illusions of the stage. Sons abandoned the comfortable farms of their fathers, and apprentices fled from the service of their masters. There was a captivation in the idea of "going down the river"; and the youthful

boatman who had "pushed a keel" from New Orleans, felt all the pride of a young merchant, after his first voyage to an English sea port. From an exclusive association together, they had formed a kind of slang peculiar to themselves; and from the constant exercise of wit, with "the squatters" on shore, and crews of other boats, they acquired a quickness, and smartness of vulgar retort, that was quite amusing. The frequent battles they were engaged in with the boatmen of different parts of the river, and with the less civilized inhabitants of the lower Ohio, and Mississippi, invested them with that ferocious reputation, which has made them spoken of throughout Europe.

On board of the boats thus navigated, our merchants entrusted valuable cargoes, without insurance, and with no other guarantee than the receipt of the steersman, who possessed no property but his boat; and the confidence so reposed was seldom abused.

Among these men, Mike Fink stood an acknowledged leader for many years. Endowed by nature with those qualities of intellect, that give the possessor influence, he would have been a conspicuous member of any society, in which his lot might have been cast. An acute observer of human nature has said—"Opportunity alone makes the hero. Change but their situations, and Caesar would have been but the best wrestler on the green." With a figure cast in a mould that added much of the symmetry of an Apollo to the limbs of a Hercules, he possessed gigantic strength; and accustomed from an early period of life to brave the dangers of a frontier life, his character was noted for the most daring intrepidity. At the court of Charlemagne, he might have been a Roland; with the Crusaders, he would have been the favourite of the Knight of the Lion-heart; and in our revolution, he would have ranked with the Morgans and Putnams of the day. He was the hero of a hundred fights, and the leader in a thousand daring adventures. From Pittsburg to St. Louis, and New Orleans, his fame was established. Every farmer on the shore kept on good terms with Mike—otherwise, there was no safety for his property. Wherever he was an enemy, like his great prototype, Rob Roy, he levied the contribution of Black Mail for the use of his boat. Often at night, when his tired companions slept, he would take an excursion of five or six miles, and return before morning, rich in spoil. On the Ohio, he was known among his companions by the appellation of the "Snapping Turtle"; and on the Mississippi, he was called "The Snag."

At the early age of seventeen, Mike's character was displayed, by enlisting himself in a corps of Scouts—a body of irregular rangers, which was employed on the Northwestern frontiers of Pennsylvania, to watch the Indians, and to give notice of any threatened inroad.

At that time, Pittsburg was on the extreme verge of white population, and the spies, who were constantly employed, generally extended their explorations forty or fifty miles to the west of this post. They went out, singly, lived as did the Indian, and in every respect, became perfectly assimilated in habits, taste, and feeling, with the red men of the desert. A kind of border warfare was kept up, and the scout thought it as praiseworthy to bring in the scalp of a Shawnee, as the skin of a panther. He would remain in the woods for weeks together, using parched corn for bread, and depending on his rifle for his meat—and slept at night in perfect comfort, rolled in his blanket.

In this corps, whilst yet a stripling, Mike acquired a reputation for boldness, and cunning, far beyond his companions. A thousand legends illustrate the fearlessness of his character. There was one, which he told himself, with much pride, and which made an indelible impression on my boyish memory. He had been out on the hills of Mahoning, when, to use his own words, "he saw signs of Indians being about."—He had discovered the recent print of the moccasin on the grass; and found drops of fresh blood of a deer on the green bush. He became cautious, skulked for some time in the deepest thickets of hazel and briar; and, for several days, did not discharge his rifle. He subsisted patiently on parched corn and jerk, which he had dried on his first coming into the woods. He gave no alarm to the settlements, because he discovered with perfect certainty, that the enemy consisted of a small hunting party, who were receding from the Alleghany.

As he was creeping along one morning, with the stealthy tread of a cat, his eye fell upon a beautiful buck, browsing on the edge of a barren spot, three hundred yards distant. The temptation was too strong for the woodsman, and he resolved to have a shot at every hazard. Re-priming his gun, and picking his flint, he made his approaches in the usual noiseless manner. At the moment he reached the spot, from which he meant to take his aim, he observed a large savage, intent upon the same object, advancing from a direction a little different from his own. Mike shrunk behind a tree, with a quickness of thought, and keeping his eye fixed on the hunter, waited the result with patience. In a few moments, the Indian halted within fifty paces, and levelled his piece at the deer. In the meanwhile, Mike presented his rifle at the body of the savage; and at the moment the smoke issued from the gun of the latter, the bullet of Fink passed through the red man's breast. He uttered a yell, and fell dead at the same instant with the deer. Mike re-loaded his rifle, and remained in his covert for some minutes, to ascertain whether there were more enemies at hand. He then stepped up to the prostrate savage, and having satisfied himself, that life was extinguished, turned his attention to the buck, and took from the carcass those pieces, suited to the process of jerking.

In the meantime, the country was filling up with a white population; and in a few years the red men, with the exception of a few fractions of tribes, gradually receded to the Lakes and beyond the Mississippi. The corps of Scouts was abolished, after having acquired habits, which unfitted them for the pursuits of civilized society. Some incorporated themselves with the Indians; and others, from a strong attachment to their erratic mode of life, joined the boatmen, then just becoming a distinct class. Among these was our hero, Mike Fink, whose talents were soon developed; and for many years, he was as celebrated on the rivers of the West, as he had been in the woods.

I gave to my fellow travellers the substance of the foregoing narrative, as we sat on deck by moonlight and cut swiftly through the magnificent sheet of water between Letart and the Great Kanhawa. It was one of those beautiful nights, which permitted every thing to be seen with sufficient distinctness to avoid danger;—yet created a certain degree of illusion, that gave reins to the imagination. The outline of the river hills lost all its harshness; and the occasional bark of the house dog from the shore, and the distant scream of the solitary loon, gave increased effect to the scene. It was altogether so delightful, that the hours till morning flew swiftly by, whilst our travellers dwelt with rapture on the surrounding scenery, which shifted every moment like the capricious changes of the kaleidoscope—and listening to the tales of border warfare, as they were brought to mind, by passing the places where they happened. The celebrated Hunter's Leap, and the bloody battle of Kanhawa, were not forgotten.

The afternoon of the next day brought us to the beautiful city of Cincinnati, which, in the course of thirty years, has risen from a village of soldiers' huts to a town,—giving promise of future splendour, equal to any on the sea-board.

Some years after the period, at which I have dated my visit to Cincinnati, business called me to New Orleans. On board of the steam boat, on which I had embarked, at Louisville, I recognised, in the person of the pilot, one of those men, who had formerly been a patroon, or keel boat captain. I entered into conversation with him on the subject of his former associates.

"They are scattered in all directions," said he. "A few, who had capacity, have become pilots of steam boats. Many have joined the trading parties that cross the Rocky mountains; and a few have settled down as farmers."

"What has become," I asked, "of my old acquaintance, Mike Fink?"

"Mike was killed in a skrimmage," replied the pilot. "He had refused several good offers on steam boats. He said he could not bear the hissing of steam, and he wanted room to throw his pole. He went to the Missouri, and about a year since was shooting the tin cup, when he had corned too heavy. He elevated too low, and shot his companion through the head. A friend of the deceased, who was present, suspecting foul play, shot Mike through the heart, before he had time to reload his rifle."

With Mike Fink expired the spirit of the Boatmen.

THE FIRST WESTERN STEAMBOATS

JAMES HALL

The year 1811 was a time of marvels in the West. Floods marked the spring; a "cold plague" chilled the country in midsummer; in September an eclipse darkened the sun and the night sky showed a comet trailing fire; November brought the Battle of Tippecanoe and the beginning of war with England. The year ended with shuddering earthquakes throughout the Ohio and Mississippi valleys. But to the western rivermen the greatest wonder was the passing of a steamboat from Pittsburgh to Natchez.

After the success of the New Orleans, *other steamboats followed. They had, as a rule, short lives, ending in collision, explosion or fire. But more were coming. By 1837 three hundred steamboats kept the frontier commerce moving and carried multitudes of emigrants to new lands in the West.*

James Hall, a pioneer lawyer and editor in Illinois, moved in 1832 to Cincinnati where he issued the Western Monthly Magazine *and reported in several books on the history and society of the West. The following excerpt, beginning with a reference to John Fitch, is taken from* The West: Its Commerce and Navigation.

THIS ingenious man, who was probably the first inventor of the steamboat, wrote three volumes, which he deposited in manuscript, sealed up, in the Philadelphia library, to be opened thirty years after his death. When, or why, he came to the west we have not learned; but it is recorded of him, that he died and was buried near the Ohio. His three volumes were opened about five years ago, and were found to contain his speculations on mechanics. He details his embarrassments and disappointments, with a feeling which shows how ardently he desired success, and which wins for him the sympathy of those who have heart enough to mourn over the blighted prospects of genius. He confidently predicts the future success of the plan which, in his hands, failed only for the want of pecuniary means. He prophesies that, in less than a century, we shall see our western rivers swarming with steamboats; and expresses a wish to be buried on the shores of the Ohio, where the song of the boatman may enliven the stillness of his resting place, and the music of the steam engine soothe his spirit. What an idea! Yet how natural to the mind of an ardent projector, whose whole life had been devoted to one darling object, which it was not his destiny to accomplish! And how touching is the sentiment found in one of his journals:—"The day will come when some more powerful man will get fame and riches from my invention; but nobody will believe that *poor John Fitch* can do any thing worthy of attention." In less than thirty years after his death, his predictions were verified. He must have died about the year 1799.

"The first steamboat built on the western waters," says a writer in the Western Monthly Magazine, "was the Orleans, built at Pittsburgh in 1811; there is no account of more than seven or eight, built previously to 1817; from that period they have been rapidly increasing in number, character, model, and style of workmanship, until 1825, when two or three boats built about that period were declared by common consent to be the finest in the world. Since that time, we are informed, some of the New York and Chesapeake boats rival and probably surpass us, in richness and beauty of internal decoration. As late as 1816, the practicability of navigating the Ohio with steamboats was esteemed doubtful; none but the most sanguine augured favorably. The writer of this well remembers that in 1816, observing, in company with a number of gentlemen, the long struggles of a stern wheel boat to ascend Horse-tail ripple, (five miles below Pittsburgh) it was the unanimous opinion, that 'such a contrivance' might conquer the difficulties of the Mississippi, as high as Natchez, but that we of the Ohio must wait for some 'more happy century of inventions.' "

We can add another anecdote to that of our friend which we have quoted. About the time that Fulton was building his first boat at Pittsburgh, he traveled across the mountains in a stage, in company with several young gentlemen from Kentucky. His mind was teeming with those projects, the successful accomplishment of which has since rendered his name so illustrious—and his conversation turned chiefly upon steam, steamboats, and facilities for transportation. Upon these subjects he spoke frankly, and his incredulous companions, much as they respected the genius of the projector, were greatly amused at what they considered the extravagance of his expectations. As the journey lasted several days, and the party grew familiar with each other, they ventured to jest with Mr. Fulton, by asking if he could do this, and that, by steam; and a hearty laugh succeeded whenever the single-minded and direct inventor asserted the power of his favorite element. At length, in the course of some conversation on the almost impassable nature of the mountains, over which they were dragged with great toil, upon roads scarcely practicable for wheels, Mr. Fulton remarked, "the day will come, gentlemen—I may not live to see it, but some of you, who are younger, probably will—when carriages will be drawn over these mountains by steam engines, at a rate more rapid than that of a stage upon the smoothest turnpike." The apparent absurdity of this prediction, together with the gravity with which it was uttered, excited the most obstreporous mirth in this laughter loving company, who roared, shouted, and clapped their hands, in the excess of their merry excitement. This anecdote was repeated to us by one of that party; who, two years ago, on finding himself rapidly receding from Baltimore in a railroad car, recollected the prediction of Fulton, made twenty years before.

The improvement in steamboats has been so rapid, and the incidents attending them so interesting, that we shall, at the hazard of rendering the subject tedious, give a particular history of a few of the earliest that were built.

1. The *Orleans*, four hundred tons, the first boat built at Pittsburgh, was owned and constructed by Mr. Fulton. Sailed from Pittsburgh in December, 1812, and arrived at New Orleans about the 24th of the same month. She continued to run between New Orleans and Natchez, making her voyages to average seventeen days, and was wrecked near Baton Rouge, in 1813 or 14, by striking a snag, on an upward bound passage.

2. The *Comet*, twenty-five tons, owned by Samuel Smith; built at Pittsburgh by D. French; stern wheel, and vibrating cylinder, on French's patent, granted in 1809. Made a voyage to Louisville in the summer of 1813, descended to New Orleans in the spring of 1814, made two voyages thence to Natchez, and was sold,—and the engine put up in a cotton gin.

3. The *Vesuvius*, three hundred and forty tons, built at Pittsburgh, by Mr. Fulton, and owned by a company at New York and New Orleans. Sailed for New Orleans in the spring of 1814, commanded by Captain Frank Ogden. She sailed from New Orleans for Louisville, about the 1st of June following; grounded on a sandbar, seven hundred miles up the Mississippi, where she lay until the 3d of December following, when the river rose, and floated her off. She returned to New Orleans, where she run aground a second time on the Batture, where she remained until March 1st, when a rise of water set her afloat.

She was then employed some months, between New Orleans and Natchez, under the command of Captain Clemment, who was succeeded by Captain John De Hart; shortly after, she took fire near the city of New Orleans and burned to the water's edge, having a valuable cargo on board. Her hull was afterwards raised and built upon, at New Orleans. She was since in the Louisville trade, was sold to a company at Natchez, and condemned in 1819.

4. The *Enterprise*, forty-five tons, built at Brownsville, Pa., on the Monongahela, by Daniel French, under his patent, and owned by a company at that place. She made two voyages to Louisville in the summer of 1814, under the command of Captain J. Gregg. On the 1st of December, she took in a cargo of ordnance stores at Pittsburgh, and sailed for New Orleans, commanded by Captain Henry M. Shreve, and arrived at New Orleans on the 14th of the same month. She was then despatched up the river in search of two keel boats, laden with small arms, for General Jackson's army, which had been delayed on the way; and returned with the cargoes of these after an absence of six days and a half, in which time she ran six hundred and twenty-four miles. For some time after, she was actively engaged in transporting troops. She made one voyage to the Gulf of Mexico as a cartel, one voyage to the rapids of Red river with troops, and nine voyages to Natchez. She set out for Pittsburgh on the 6th of May, 1817, and arrived at Shippingsport, (Louisville) on the 30th, twenty-five days out, being the first steamboat that ever arrived at that port from New Orleans. The citizens of Louisville gave a public dinner to Captain Shreve for having accomplished, in twenty-five days, a trip which previous to that time had never been accomplished, by the barges and keel boats, in less than three months. The *Enterprise* proceeded to Pittsburgh, the command was then given to Captain D. Worley, who lost her in Rock Harbor, Shippingsport.

5. The *Ætna*, three hundred and forty tons, built at Pittsburgh, and owned by the same company as the *Vesuvius*. Sailed from Pittsburgh for New Orleans in March, 1815, under the command of Captain A. Gale; made

the voyage, and then went into the Natchez trade—was commanded by Captain R. De Hart, who made six voyages in her, and then again by Captain Gale.

6. The *Despatch*, twenty-five tons, built at Brownsville, in 1817, on French's patent, and owned by the same company as the *Enterprise*. She made several voyages from Pittsburgh to Louisville, and one from New Orleans to Shippingsport, where she became a wreck in 1820, and her engine was taken out.

7. The *Buffalo*, three hundred tons, was built at Pittsburgh, by Mr. Latrobe.

8. The *James Monroe*, one hundred and twenty tons, was built at Pittsburgh, by Mr. Latrobe.

9. The *Washington*, four hundred tons, built at Wheeling; contracted and part owned by Captain H. M. Shreve; her engine was made at Brownsville under the immediate direction of Captain Shreve. Her boilers were on the upper deck, and she was the first boat on that plan, since so generally in use. The *Washington* crossed the falls, September, 1816, under Captain Shreve, went to New Orleans, and returned to Louisville in the winter. In March, 1817, she went from Louisville to New Orleans and returned in forty-five days. This was the trip that first convinced the despairing public that steamboat navigation would succeed on the Western waters.

10. The *Franklin*, one hundred and twenty-five tons, built at Pittsburgh, by Messrs. Shiras and Cromwell; engine made by George Evans. She sailed from Pittsburgh in December, 1816, was sold at New Orleans, went into the Louisville and St. Louis trade, and was sunk near St. Genevieve, in 1819.

11. The *Oliver Evans*, seventy-five tons, was built at Pittsburgh, by George Evans; engine his patent. Left Pittsburgh, December, 1816, for New Orleans. Burst one of her boilers in April, 1817, at Point Coupee, by which eleven men, chiefly passengers, were killed. Never did much business afterwards.

12. The *Harriet*, forty tons, built at Pittsburgh, owned and constructed by Mr. Armstrong, of Williamsport, Pa. She sailed from Pittsburgh, October, 1816, for New Orleans, crossed the falls in March, 1817, made one voyage to New Orleans, and then run

between that place and the Muscle shoals.

We shall not proceed any further with this list, as it would occupy more room than could be usefully devoted to such a purpose. Our object in giving the particulars of the history of a few of the first boats, in their regular order, is to show the progress that was made in the first years of the introduction of steamboats, and the difficulties which frowned upon the enterprise. The first advance was slow, and the prospects very discouraging. The *fourth* boat that descended the river, was the *first* to reascend as far as Louisville, and even then it was considered doubtful whether steamboats could be rendered useful as a mode of navigation for the ascending trade. It was not until 1816, when the boat, which was about the *ninth* in the order of building, having been conducted from Louisville to New Orleans and back in forty-five days, by Captain Henry M. Shreve, the question of practicability was considered as settled.

Many of the obstacles which impeded the rapid advance of steamboat navigation were such as were incident to an infant and imperfect state of the art of constructing both boats and engines; while others were inseparable from the condition of the country. In accounting for the length of the earliest voyages, something must be allowed to both these classes of causes, and among the latter may be mentioned the important facts, that the shores of the Ohio and Mississippi were then comparatively unsettled, fuel was not an article of traffic, but was procured from the growing forest by the crews of the boats, and used in its green state; while accidental injuries were repaired with equal inconvenience and delay.

The *General Pike*, built at Cincinnati, in 1818, and intended to ply as a packet between Maysville, Cincinnati, and Louisville, is said to have been the first steamboat constructed on the Western waters for the exclusive convenience of passengers. Her accommodations were ample, her apartments spacious and superbly furnished, and her machinery of superior mechanism. She measured one hundred feet keel, twenty-five feet beam, and drew only three feet three inches water. The length of her cabin was forty feet, the breadth twenty-five feet, in addition to which were fourteen state rooms. The boats previously built had been intended solely for the transportation of merchandise; these objects have subsequently been successfully united.

The *Calhoun*, eighty tons, built at Frankfort, in 1818, the *Expedition*, one hundred and twenty tons, and the *Independence*, fifty tons —the two last built at Pittsburgh—were constructed for the exploration of the Missouri river, in what was popularly termed the Yellow Stone Expedition, projected by Mr. Calhoun, while Secretary of War. The *Independence* was the first steamboat that ascended the powerful current of the Missouri.

The *Post Boy*, two hundred tons, built at New Albany, by Captain Shreve and others,

in 1819, was intended for the conveyance of the mail between Louisville and New Orleans, under an act of Congress, passed in March, 1819. This was the first attempt on the Western waters to carry the mail in steamboats.

The *Western Engineer* was built near Pittsburgh, in 1818, under the direction of Major S. H. Long, of the United States topographical engineers, for the expedition of discovery to the sources of the Missouri, and the Rocky Mountains, which was afterwards so honorably accomplished by himself and his companions. This boat ascended as high as the Council Bluffs, about six hundred and fifty miles above St. Louis, and was the first steamboat that reached that point.

THE ENGLISH PRAIRIE

GEORGE FLOWER

Associated with Morris Birkbeck in establishing an English colony in Illinois was George Flower, a prosperous brewer and farmer of Hertford. Flower came to America in 1816 to look over land on the frontier. After a summer in the West and a winter as a guest of Thomas Jefferson at Monticello, Flower met Birkbeck and his party in Richmond and the colonists headed west. Beyond the Wabash River they inquired the way to the Boltenhouse Prairie, named for an English settler who had built a cabin at its edge. Flower later recalled: "Bruised by the brushwood and exhausted by the extreme heat we almost despaired, when a small cabin and a low fence greeted our eyes. A few steps more and a beautiful prairie suddenly opened to our view. At first we only received the impression of its general beauty. With longer gaze, all of its distinctive features were revealed, lying in profound repose under the warm light of an afternoon's summer sun."

This became the site of the colony which was established a year later. The following narrative, from Flower's History of the English Settlement in Edwards County, Illinois, *tells how it fared in the first season.*

FOR a moment let us glance at the situation of these settlers, a thousand miles inland, at the heels of the retreating Indians. A forest from the Atlantic shore behind them, but thinly settled with small villages, far apart from each other. To the west, one vast uninhabited wilderness of prairie, interspersed with

timber, extending two thousand miles to the Pacific Ocean. Excepting St. Louis, on the Mississippi, then a small place, and Kaskaskia, yet smaller, there were no inhabitants west of us. About the same time, one or two small American settlements were forming a few miles east of the Mississippi, as we were planting ourselves a few miles west of the Wabash. The first member of Congress had to ride an intervening space of a hundred and fifty miles of wilderness between the little settlements of his constituents, lying in the west and east of the State. There were no roads on land, no steam-boats on the waters. The road, so-called, leading to Vandalia (then composed of about a dozen log-houses), was made by one man on horse-back following in the track of another, every rider making the way a little easier to find, until you came to some slush, or swampy place, where all trace was lost, and you got through as others had done, by guessing at the direction, often riding at hazard for miles until you stumbled on the track again. And of these blind traces there were but three or four in the southern half of the State. No roads were worked, no watercourses bridged. Before getting to Vandalia, there was a low piece of timbered bottom-land, wet and swampy, and often covered with water, through which every traveler had to make his way as he best could, often at the risk of his life. Such was the state of the country. No man could feel sure that he was within the limits of the State, but from knowing that he was west of the Wabash and east of the Mississippi. We had some difficulties, peculiar to ourselves, as a foreign people. The Americans by pushing onward and onward for almost two generations, had a training in handling the ax and opening farms, and, from experience, bestowing their labor in the most appropriate manner, which we, from our inexperience, often did not. Fresh from an old country, teeming with the conveniences of civilized life, at once in a wilderness with all our inexperience, our losses were large from misplaced labor. Many were discouraged, and some returned, but the mass of the settlers stayed, and, by gradual experience, corrected their first errors, thus overcoming difficulties which had wellnigh overcome them. The future success of the Settlement was obtained by individual toil and industry. Of the first inconveniences and sufferings, my family had its full share.

The summer had been very hot and latterly wet. Thunder showers of daily occurrence sent mosquitoes in swarms. My cabin, recently built, of course, of green logs, un-

furnished, with rank vegetation growing all around it and up to its very sides, was in its situation and in itself a sufficient cause of disease. My shepherd and his family came, bringing a few choice sheep and an English high-bred cow. His whole family, in a few days, all fell sick, lying in a small cabin, just built, about a hundred yards from my own. Mr. White, carpenter, from London, wife, and two children, occupied a two-horse wagon and a soldier's tent. There was no house for them; they all fell sick. My two sons were speedily taken with fever and ague, to us then a new disease. Miss Fordham, who shared our cabin, was attacked with the same disease. My constitution, strong and good, yielding from exposure to heat and rain, took another form of disease. Boils and irritable sores broke out on both my legs, from knee to ankle, incapacitating me, for a time, from walking. Thus we were situated for two or three weeks, without the slightest assistance from any source, or supplies other than from my own wagons, as they slowly arrived from Shawneetown, giving us sufficient bedding with flour and bacon. All the other merchandise and furniture did but add to our present embarrassment, in attempts to protect them from the weather, and in endeavoring to dry what was wet.

We were carried through this period of trial by the unremitting labor and self-sacrifice of my wife. She alone prepared all our food and bedding, and attended to the wants of the sick and the suffering by night and day. To all this was added a fatigue that a strong man might have shrunk from, in bringing water from that distant well. Sustained in her unremitting labors by unbounded devotion to her family, and a high sense of duty to all within her reach, her spirit and her power seemed to rise above the manifold trials by which she was surrounded. And thus we were saved from probable death or certain dispersion. The incessant labor of the mother told on the infant at the breast; it sickened and died. With returning health we worked our way unaided through our difficulties. To our former friends and those that sustained them in withholding the slightest assistance in our hour of trial, is it strange that we should ac-

Prairie scene, Indiana, engraved by E. Teel after the painting by George Winter.
Courtesy Indiana Historical Society Library

cept the separation, and feel in our hearts that it must be forever?

The buildings necessary to secure our horses and our goods, now daily arriving, were built by the backwoodsmen of whom I have before spoken, among them was my old friend Birk. These men worked well in the morning, slackened toward noon, as the drams of whisky (which they would not work without) told upon them, and, toward evening, indulged in imprecations, brawls, and rough-and-tumble fights.

Emigrants were continually flowing in. They first visited Mr. Birkbeck, who had but small accommodations; they came to me, who, at that time, had still less. At this stage, we were experiencing many of the inconveniences of a population in the wilderness, in advance of necessary food and shelter. Do as you will, if you are the very first in the wilderness, there are many inconveniences, privations, hardships, and sufferings that can not be avoided. My own family, one day, were so close run for provisions, that a dish of the tenderest buds and shoots of the hazle was our only resort.

Mr. Lawrence and Mr. Trimmer, who led the first shipload, made their settlement in the

Village Prairie, a beautiful and extensive prairie, so-called from the Piankeshaw Indians, there formerly located. It was situated about three miles due north of my cabin in the Boltenhouse Prairie, the intervening space covered by timber and underbrush, untouched by the hand of man. Emigrants kept coming in, some on foot, some on horseback, and some in wagons. Some sought employment, and took up with such labor as they could find. Others struck out and made small beginnings for themselves. Some, with feelings of petulence, went farther and fared worse; others dropped back into the towns and settlements in Indiana. At first, I had as much as I could do to build a few cabins for the workmen I then employed, and in erecting a large farmyard, a hundred feet square, enclosed by log-buildings, two stories high; also in building for my father's family a house of considerable size, and appointed with somewhat more of comforts than is generally found in new settlements, to be ready for their reception on the following summer. I had as yet done nothing in erecting buildings for the public in general, as there had been no time. One evening, Mr. Lawrence, Mr. Ronalds, and, I think, Mr. Fordham, called at my cabin, and, after their horses were cared for and supper over, we discussed the measures that should be taken to form some village or town, as a centre for those useful arts necessary to agriculture. Every person wanted the services of a carpenter and blacksmith. But every farmer could not build workshops at his own door.

Daylight ceased, darkness followed. We had no candles, nor any means of making artificial light. On a pallet, mattress, or blanket, each one took to his couch, and carried on the discussion. After much talk, we decided that what we did do should be done in order, and with a view to the future settlement, as well as our own present convenience. The tract of forest lying between Mr. Lawrence's settlement in the Village Prairie, on its southern border, and mine at the north of the Boltenhouse Prairie, was about three-and-a-half miles through. Somewhere in the centre of this tract of woodland seemed to be the place. To the right of this spot, eastward, lay, about a mile distant, several prairies running north and south for many miles, and others east and west to the Bonpas Creek, from three to five miles distant. North-eastward from Mr. Lawrence's cabin, prairies of every form and size continued on indefinitely. About two miles west, and beyond Wanborough, were numerous small and fertile prairies, extending to the Little Wabash, from six to ten miles distant. On the south was my own beautiful prairie. Thus the spot for our town in a central situation was decided upon. Now for a name. We were long at fault. At last we did what almost all emigrants do, pitched on a name that had its association with the land of our birth. Albion was then and there located, built, and peopled in imagination. We dropped off, one by one, to sleep, to confirm in dreams the wanderings of our waking fancies.

TINKERVILLE IN THE SWAMP

CAROLINE KIRKLAND

The urbane and cultivated Mrs. Caroline Stansbury Kirkland went West in 1835, when her husband took charge of the newly organized Detroit Female Seminary. At this time steamboats were bringing to Detroit a thousand emigrants a day, and even an educator could not escape the land fever. William Kirkland bought eight hundred acres of forest and swampland sixty miles northwest of Detroit and turned from running a seminary to founding a settlement deep in the Michigan woods.

In their new town of Pinckney, Mrs. Kirkland wrote her fresh and frank record of frontier life: A New Home—Who'll Follow? With its realistic reporting of pioneer experiences and its sharply focused characterizations, the book won a large readership both in America and abroad. It became, as Edgar Allan Poe observed, an "undoubted sensation."

After five years in their backwoods settlement, the Kirklands returned to New York.

This selection comprises most of Chapters 21 and 22 of A New Home.

TINKERVILLE was originally one of the many speculations of the enterprising Mr. Mazard, and it differed from most of his landed property, in having been purchased at second hand. This fact was often mentioned in his proffers of sale, as a reason why the tract could not be afforded *quite* so low as was his general practice. He omitted to state, that he bought of a person who, having purchased at the land-office without viewing, was so entirely discouraged when he saw the woody swamp in which he was to pitch his tent, that he was glad to sell out to our speculator at a large discount, and try elsewhere on the old and sound principle of "look before you leap." The tract contained, as Mr. Mazard's advertisement fairly set forth, "almost every variety of land;" and as he did not say which kind predominated, nobody could complain if imagination played tricks, as is sometimes the case in land-purchases.

An old gentleman of some property in Massachusetts became the fortunate owner of the emblazoned chart, which Mr. Mazard had caused to set forth the advantages of his choice location. There were canals and rail-roads, with boats and cars at full speed. There was a steam-mill, a wind-mill or two; for even a land-shark did not dare to put a stream where there was scarce running water for the cattle; and a state-road, which had at least been talked of, and a court-house and other county buildings, "all very grand;" for, as the spot was not more than ten miles from the centre of the county, it might some day become the county-seat. Besides all this, there was a large and elegantly-decorated space for the name of the happy purchaser, if he chose thus to dignify his future capital.

Mr. Tinker was easily persuaded that the cherished surname of his ancestors would blend most musically with the modern and very genteel termination in which so many of our western villages glory; so Tinkerville was appointed to fill the trump of fame and the blank on the chart; and Mr. Mazard furnished with full powers, took out the charter, staked out the streets, where he could get at them, and peddled out the lots, and laid out the money, all very much to his own satisfaction; Mr. Tinker rejoicing that he had happened to obtain so "enterprising" an agent.

We were not informed what were the internal sensations of the lot-holders, when they brought their families, and came to take possession of their various "stands for business." They were wise men; and having no money to carry them back, they set about making the best of what they could find. And it is to be doubted whether Mr. Mazard's multifarious avocations permitted him to visit Tinkerville after the settlers began to come in. Many of them expressed themselves quite satisfied that there was an abundance of water there to duck a land-shark, if they could catch him near it; and Mr. Mazard was a wise man too.

While the little settlement was gradually increasing, and a store had been, as we were told, added to its many advantages and attractions, we heard that the padrone of Tinkerville had sold out; but whether from the fear that the income from his Michigan property would scarce become tangible before his great grandson's time, or whether some Bangor Mr. Mazard had offered him a tempting bargain nearer home, remains to us unknown. It was enough for Montacute to discover that the new owners were "enterprising men." This put us all upon the alert.

The Tinkervillians, who were obliged to come to us for grinding until their wind-mills could be erected, talked much of a new hotel, a school-house, and a tannery; all which, they averred, were "going up" immediately. They turned up their noses at our squint-eyed "Montacute house," expressing themselves certain of getting the county honors, and ended by trying to entice away our blacksmith. But our Mr. Porter, who "had a soul above buttons," scorned their arts, and would none of their counsel. Mr. Simeon Jenkins did, I fear, favorably incline to their side; but on its being whispered to him that Montacute had determined upon employing a singing-master next winter; he informed the ambassadors, who were no doubt spies in disguise, that he would never be so selfish as to prefer his own interest to the public good. No one thought of analyzing so patriotic a sentiment, or it might have been doubted whether Mr. Jenkins sacrificed so much in remaining to exercise his many trades, where there were twice as many people to profit by them as he would find at Tinkerville.

Mrs. Rivers and I had long been planning a ride on horseback; and when the good stars were in conjunction, so that two horses and two saddles were to be had at one time, we determined to wend our resolute way as far as Tinkerville, to judge for ourselves of the state of the enemy's preparations. We set out soon after breakfast in high style; my Eclipse being Mr. Jenkins's "old Governor," seventeen last grass; and my fair companion's a twenty-dollar Indian pony, age undecided—men's saddles of course, for the settlement boasts no other as yet; and, by way of luxury, a large long-woolled sheepskin strapped over each.

We jogged on charmingly, now through woods cool and moist as the grotto of Undine, and carpeted everywhere with strawberry vines and thousands of flowers; now across strips of open land where you could look through the straight-stemmed and scattered groves for miles on each side. A marsh or two were to be passed, so said our most minute directions, and then we should come to the trail through deep woods, which would lead us in a short time to the emerging glories of our boastful neighbor.

We found the marshes, without diffi-culty, and soon afterwards the trail, and D'Orsay's joyous bark, as he ran far before us, told that he had made some discovery. "Deer, perhaps," said I. It was only an Indian, and when I stopped and tried to inquire whether we were in the right track, he could not be made to understand but gave the usual assenting grunt and passed on.

When I turned to speak to my companion she was so ashy pale that I feared she must fall from her horse.

"What *is* the matter, my dearest madam!" said I, going as near her as I could coax old Governor.

"The Indian! the Indian!" was all she could utter. I was terribly puzzled. It had never occurred to me that the Indians would naturally be objects of terror to a young lady who had scarcely ever seen one; and I knew we should probably meet dozens of them in the course of our short ride.

I said all I could, and she tried her best to seem courageous, and, after she had rallied her spirits a little, we proceeded, thinking the end of our journey could not be distant, especially as we saw several log-houses at intervals which we supposed were the outskirts of Tinkerville.

But we were disappointed in this; for the road led through a marsh, and then through woods again, and such tangled woods, that I began to fear, in my secret soul, that we had wandered far from our track, betrayed by D'Orsay's frolics.

I was at length constrained to hint to my pale companion my misgivings, and to propose a return to the nearest log hut for information. Without a word she wheeled her shaggy pony, and, in a few minutes, we found ourselves at the bars belonging to the last log-house we had passed.

A wretched looking woman was washing at the door.

"Can you tell us which is the road to Tinkerville?"

"Well, I guess you can't miss it if you follow your own tracks. It a'n't long since you came through it. That big stump is the middle of the public square."

WISCONSIN BOYHOOD

JOHN MUIR

*In the later 1840's, with famine in Ireland and revolution in Germany, im-
migrants thronged the river and lake boats for the frontier states. Wisconsin,
which allowed aliens to vote after a year's residence, was a strong magnet; the
port of Milwaukee received three thousand newcomers in a single week.*

*One of that company arrived in America in 1849 as a boy of eleven, a youth
looking wide-eyed at the vast new world. He grew up in interior Wisconsin,
breaking wild land and wondering about the wilderness at the end of the furrow.
To young John Muir the whole country was enthralling. A few years later he
walked from Lake Michigan to the Gulf of Mexico, studying the flora of the
Mississippi basin. Then he turned to the Far West, to explore the mountain ranges
from Mexico to Alaska. Eventually he sat with Congressional commissions for
the creating of the national parks and forests. A boy from Scotland left his mark
upon America.*

*The following account, beginning with the voyage from Glasgow, is taken
from two chapters of John Muir's ardent* Story of My Boyhood and Youth.

AS we neared the shore of the great new
land, with what eager wonder we watched
the whales and dolphins and porpoises and sea-
birds, and made the good-natured sailors teach
us their names and tell us stories about them!

There were quite a large number of emigrants aboard, many of them newly married
couples, and the advantages of the different
parts of the New World they expected to
settle in were often discussed. My father
started with the intention of going to the
backwoods of Upper Canada. Before the end
of the voyage, however, he was persuaded
that the States offered superior advantages,
especially Wisconsin and Michigan, where
the land was said to be as good as in Canada
and far more easily brought under cultivation; for in Canada the woods were so close
and heavy that a man might wear out his
life in getting a few acres cleared of trees and
stumps. So he changed his mind and concluded to go to one of the Western States.

On our wavering westward way a grain-
dealer in Buffalo told father that most of the
wheat he handled came from Wisconsin; and
this influential information finally determined

my father's choice. At Milwaukee a farmer
who had come in from the country near Fort
Winnebago with a load of wheat agreed to
haul us and our formidable load of stuff to a
little town called Kingston for thirty dollars.
On that hundred-mile journey, just after the
spring thaw, the roads over the prairies were
heavy and miry, causing no end of lamenta-
tion, for we often got stuck in the mud, and
the poor farmer sadly declared that never,
never again would he be tempted to try to
haul such a cruel, heart-breaking, wagon-
breaking, horse-killing load, no, not for a
hundred dollars. In leaving Scotland, father,
like many other home-seekers, burdened himself with far too much luggage, as if all
America were still a wilderness in which little
or nothing could be bought. One of his big
iron-bound boxes must have weighed about
four hundred pounds, for it contained an old-
fashioned beam-scales with a complete set of
cast-iron counterweights, two of them fifty-
six pounds each, a twenty-eight, and so on
down to a single pound. Also a lot of iron
wedges, carpenter's tools, and so forth, and
at Buffalo, as if on the very edge of the

wilderness, he gladly added to his burden a big cast-iron stove with pots and pans, provisions enough for a long siege, and a scythe and cumbersome cradle for cutting wheat, all of which he succeeded in landing in the primeval Wisconsin woods.

A land-agent at Kingston gave father a note to a farmer by the name of Alexander Gray, who lived on the border of the settled part of the country, knew the section-lines, and would probably help him to find a good place for a farm. So father went away to spy out the land, and in the mean time left us children in Kingston in a rented room. It took us less than an hour to get acquainted with some of the boys in the village; we challenged them to wrestle, run races, climb trees, etc., and in a day or two we felt at home, carefree and happy, notwithstanding our family was so widely divided. When father returned he told us that he had found fine land for a farm in sunny open woods on the side of a lake, and that a team of three yoke of oxen with a big wagon was coming to haul us to Mr. Gray's place.

We enjoyed the strange ten-mile ride through the woods very much, wondering how the great oxen could be so strong and wise and tame as to pull so heavy a load with no other harness than a chain and a crooked piece of wood on their necks, and how they could sway so obediently to right and left past roadside trees and stumps when the driver said *haw* and *gee*. At Mr. Gray's house, father again left us for a few days to build a shanty on the quarter-section he had selected four or five miles to the westward. In the mean while we enjoyed our freedom as usual, wandering in the fields and meadows, looking at the trees and flowers, snakes and birds and squirrels. With the help of the nearest neighbors the little shanty was built in less than a day after the rough bur-oak logs for the walls and the white-oak boards for the floor and roof were got together.

To this charming hut, in the sunny woods, overlooking a flowery glacier meadow and a lake rimmed with white water-lilies, we were hauled by an ox-team across trackless carex swamps and low rolling hills sparsely dotted with round-headed oaks. Just as we

arrived at the shanty, before we had time to look at it or the scenery about it, David and I jumped down in a hurry off the load of household goods, for we had discovered a blue jay's nest, and in a minute or so we were up the tree beside it, feasting our eyes on the beautiful green eggs and beautiful birds,—our first memorable discovery. The handsome birds had not seen Scotch boys before and made a desperate screaming as if we were robbers like themselves; though we left the eggs untouched, feeling that we were already beginning to get rich, and wondering how many more nests we should find in the grand sunny woods. Then we ran along the brow of the hill that the shanty stood on, and down to the meadow, searching the trees and grass tufts and bushes, and soon discovered a bluebird's and a woodpecker's nest, and began an acquaintance with the frogs and snakes and turtles in the creeks and springs.

This sudden plash into pure wildness— baptism in Nature's warm heart—how utterly happy it made us! Nature streaming into us, wooingly teaching her wonderful glowing lessons, so unlike the dismal grammar ashes and cinders so long thrashed into us. Here without knowing it we still were at school; every wild lesson a love lesson, not whipped but charmed into us. Oh, that glorious Wisconsin wilderness! Everything new and pure in the very prime of the spring when Nature's pulses were beating highest and mysteriously keeping time with our own! Young hearts, young leaves, flowers, animals, the winds and the streams and the sparkling lake, all wildly, gladly rejoicing together! . . .

It was a great memorable day when the first flock of passenger pigeons came to our farm, calling to mind the story we had read about them when we were at school in Scotland. Of all God's feathered people that sailed the Wisconsin sky, no other bird seemed to us so wonderful. The beautiful wanderers flew like the winds in flocks of millions from climate to climate in accord with the weather, finding their food—acorns, beechnuts, pine-nuts, cranberries, strawberries, huckleberries, juniper berries, hackberries, buckwheat, rice, wheat, oats, corn—in fields and forests thousands of miles apart. I have seen flocks streaming south in the fall so large that they were flowing over from horizon to horizon in an almost continuous stream all day long, at the rate of forty or fifty miles an hour, like a mighty river in the sky, widening, contracting, descending like falls and cataracts, and rising suddenly here and there in huge ragged masses like high-plashing spray. How wonderful the distances they flew in a day—in a year—in a lifetime! They arrived in Wisconsin in the spring just after the sun had cleared away the snow, and alighted in the woods to feed on the fallen acorns that they had missed the previous autumn. A comparatively small flock swept thousands of acres perfectly clean of acorns in a few minutes, by moving straight ahead with a broad front. All got their share, for the rear constantly became the van by flying over the flock and alighting in front, the entire flock constantly changing from rear to front, revolving something like a wheel with a low buzzing wing roar that could be heard a long way off. In summer they feasted on wheat and oats and were easily approached as they rested on the trees along the sides of the field after a good full meal, displaying beautiful iridescent colors as they moved their necks backward and forward when we went very near them. Every shotgun was aimed at them and everybody feasted on pigeon pies, and not a few of the settlers feasted also on the beauty of the wonderful birds. The breast of the male is a fine rosy red, the lower part of the neck behind and along the sides changing from the red of the breast to gold, emerald green and rich crimson. The general color of the upper parts is grayish blue, the under parts white. The extreme length of the bird is about seventeen inches; the finely modeled slender tail about eight inches, and extent of wings twenty-four inches. The females are scarcely less beautiful. "Oh, what bonnie, bonnie birds!" we exclaimed over the first that fell into our hands. "Oh, what colors! Look at their breasts, bonnie as roses, and at their necks aglow wi' every color juist like the wonderfu' wood ducks. Oh, the bonnie, bonnie creatures, they beat a'! Where did they a' come fra, and where are they a' gan? It's awfu' like a sin to kill them!" To this some smug, practical old

sinner would remark: "Aye, it's a peety, as ye say, to kill the bonnie things, but they were made to be killed, and sent for us to eat as the quails were sent to God's chosen people, the Israelites, when they were starving in the desert ayont the Red Sea. And I must confess that meat was never put up in neater, handsomer-painted packages."

In the New England and Canada woods beechnuts were their best and most abundant food, farther north, cranberries and huckleberries. After everything was cleaned up in the north and winter was coming on, they went south for rice, corn, acorns, haws, wild grapes, crab-apples, sparkle-berries, etc. They seemed to require more than half of the continent for feeding-grounds, moving from one table to another, field to field, forest to forest, finding something ripe and wholesome all the year round. In going south in the fine Indian-summer weather they flew high and followed one another, though the head of the flock might be hundreds of miles in advance. But against head winds they took advantage of the inequalities of the ground, flying comparatively low. All followed the leader's ups and downs over hill and dale though far out of sight, never hesitating at any turn of the way, vertical or horizontal that the leaders had taken, though the largest flocks stretched across several States, and belts of different kinds of weather.

There were no roosting- or breeding-places near our farm, and I never saw any of them until long after the great flocks were exterminated. I therefore quote, from Audubon's and Pokagon's vivid descriptions.

"Toward evening," Audubon says, "they depart for the roosting-place, which may be hundreds of miles distant. One on the banks of Green River, Kentucky, was over three miles wide and forty long."

"My first view of it," says the great naturalist, "was about a fortnight after it had been chosen by the birds, and I arrived there nearly two hours before sunset. Few pigeons were then to be seen, but a great many persons with horses and wagons and armed with guns, long poles, sulphur pots, pine pitch torches, etc., had already established encampments on the borders. Two farmers had driven

Life on the frontier: The first crude cabin *(above)* and *(below)* the land cleared for farming.

Life on the frontier: The farm developed *(above)* and *(below)* the family homestead on a large tract.

upwards of three hundred hogs a distance of more than a hundred miles to be fattened on slaughtered pigeons. Here and there the people employed in plucking and salting what had already been secured were sitting in the midst of piles of birds. Dung several inches thick covered the ground. Many trees two feet in diameter were broken off at no great distance from the ground, and the branches of many of the tallest and largest had given way, as if the forest had been swept by a tornado.

"Not a pigeon had arrived at sundown. Suddenly a general cry arose—'Here they come!' The noise they made, though still distant, reminded me of a hard gale at sea passing through the rigging of a close-reefed ship. Thousands were soon knocked down by the pole-men. The birds continued to pour in. The fires were lighted and a magnificent as well as terrifying sight presented itself. The pigeons pouring in alighted everywhere, one above another, until solid masses were formed on the branches all around. Here and there the perches gave way with a crash, and falling destroyed hundreds beneath, forcing down the dense groups with which every stick was loaded; a scene of uproar and conflict. I found it useless to speak or even to shout to those persons nearest me. Even the reports of the guns were seldom heard, and I was made aware of the firing only by seeing the shooters reloading. None dared venture within the line of devastation. The hogs had been penned up in due time, the picking up of the dead and wounded being left for the next morning's employment. The pigeons were constantly coming in and it was after midnight before I perceived a decrease in the number of those that arrived. The uproar continued all night, and anxious to know how far the sound reached I sent off a man who, returning two hours after, informed me that he had heard it distinctly three miles distant.

"Toward daylight the noise in some measure subsided; long before objects were distinguishable the pigeons began to move off in a direction quite different from that in which they had arrived the evening before, and at sunrise all that were able to fly had disappeared. The howling of the wolves now reached our ears, and the foxes, lynxes, cougars, bears, coons, opossums, and polecats were seen sneaking off, while eagles and hawks of different species, accompanied by a crowd of vultures, came to supplant them and enjoy a share of the spoil.

"Then the authors of all this devastation began their entry amongst the dead, the dying and mangled. The pigeons were picked up and piled in heaps until each had as many as they could possibly dispose of, when the hogs were let loose to feed on the remainder.

"The breeding-places are selected with reference to abundance of food, and countless myriads resort to them. At this period the note of the pigeon is coo coo coo, like that of the domestic species but much shorter. They caress by billing, and during incubation the male supplies the female with food. As the young grow, the tyrant of creation appears to disturb the peaceful scene, armed with axes to chop down the squab-laden trees, and the abomination of desolation and destruction produced far surpasses even that of the roosting places."

Pokagon, an educated Indian writer, says: "I saw one nesting-place in Wisconsin one hundred miles long and from three to ten miles wide. Every tree, some of them quite low and scrubby, had from one to fifty nests on each. Some of the nests overflow from the oaks to the hemlock and pine woods. When the pigeon hunters attack the breeding-places they sometimes cut the timber from thousands of acres. Millions are caught in nets with salt or grain for bait, and schooners, sometimes loaded down with the birds, are taken to New York where they are sold for a cent apiece."

YOUNG LINCOLN'S ILLINOIS

JOHN G. NICOLAY AND JOHN HAY

John Nicolay was born in an old city of Bavaria and John Hay was born in backwoods Indiana, but their names were to be linked in the writing of the definitive (ten-volume) life of Abraham Lincoln. Nicolay attended school in Cincinnati and then went to Illinois where he met Lincoln. Hay studied law in Springfield, next door to the office of Lincoln and Herndon. When Lincoln was elected to the presidency he took the two young men to Washington as personal secretaries. In 1875 they began work on their great biography of Lincoln, from the first volume of which the following selection is taken.

THE Lincolns arrived in Illinois just in time to entitle themselves to be called pioneers. When, in after years, associations of "Old Settlers" began to be formed in Central Illinois, the qualification for membership agreed upon by common consent was a residence in the country before "the winter of the deep snow." This was in 1830-31, a season of such extraordinary severity that it has formed for half a century a recognized date in the middle counties of Illinois, among those to whom in those days diaries and journals were unknown. The snowfall began in the Christmas holidays and continued until the snow was three feet deep on level ground. Then came a cold rain, freezing as it fell, until a thick crust of ice gathered over the snow. The weather became intensely cold, the mercury sinking to twelve degrees below zero, Farenheit, and remaining there for two weeks. The storm came on with such suddenness that all who were abroad had great trouble in reaching their homes, and many perished. One man relates that he and a friend or two were out in a hunting party with an ox-team. They had collected a wagon-load of game and were on their way home when the storm struck them. After they had gone four miles they were compelled to abandon their wagon; the snow fell in heavy masses "as if thrown from a scoop-shovel"; arriving within two miles of their habitation, they were forced to trust to the instinct of their animals, and reached home hanging to the tails of their steers. Not all were so fortunate. Some were found weeks afterwards in the snow-drifts, their flesh gnawed by famished wolves; and the fate of others was unknown until the late spring sunshine revealed their resting-places. To those who escaped, the winter was tedious and terrible. It is hard for us to understand the isolation to which such weather condemned the pioneer. For weeks they remained in their cabins hoping for some mitigation of the frost. When at last they were driven out by the fear of famine, the labor of establishing communications was enormous. They finally made roads by "wallowing through the snow," as an Illinois historian expresses it, and going patiently over the same track until the snow was trampled hard and rounded like a turnpike. These roads lasted far into the spring, when the snow had melted from the plains, and wound for miles like threads of silver over the rich black loam of the prairies. After that winter game was never again so plentiful in the State. Much still remained, of course, but it never recovered entirely from the rigors of that season and the stupid enterprise of the pioneer hunters, who, when they came out of their snow-beleaguered cabins, began chasing and killing the starved deer by herds. It was easy work; the crust of the snow was strong enough to bear the weight of men and dogs, but the slender hoofs of the deer would after a few bounds pierce the treacherous surface.

This destructive slaughter went on until the game grew too lean to be worth the killing. All sorts of wild animals grew scarce from that winter. Old settlers say that the slow cowardly breed of prairie wolves, which used to be caught and killed as readily as sheep, disappeared about that time and none but the fleeter and stronger survived.

Only once since then has nature shown such extravagant severity in Illinois, and that was on a day in the winter of 1836, known to Illinoisans as "the sudden change." At noon on the 20th of December, after a warm and rainy morning, the ground being covered with mud and slush, the temperature fell instantly forty degrees. A man riding into Springfield for a marriage license says a roaring and crackling wind came upon him and the rain-drops dripping from his bridle-reins and beard changed in a second into jingling icicles. He rode hastily into the town and arrived in a few minutes at his destination; but his clothes were frozen like sheet iron, and man and saddle had to be taken into the house together to be thawed apart. Geese and chickens were caught by the feet and wings and frozen to the wet ground. A drove of a thousand hogs, which were being driven to St. Louis, rushed together for warmth, and became piled in a great heap. Those inside smothered and those outside froze, and the ghastly pyramid remained there on the prairie for weeks: the drovers barely escaped with their lives. Men killed their horses, disemboweled them, and crept into the cavity of their bodies to escape the murderous wind.

The pioneer period of Illinois was ending as Thomas Lincoln and his tall boy drove their ox-team over the Indiana line. The population of the State had grown to 157,447. It still clung to the wooded borders of the water-courses; scattered settlements were to be found all along the Mississippi and its affluents, from where Cairo struggled for life in the swamps of the Ohio to the bustling and busy mining camps which the recent discovery of lead had brought to Galena. A line of villages from Alton to Peoria dotted the woodland which the Illinois River had stretched, like a green baldric, diagonally across the bosom of the State. Then there were

long reaches of wilderness before you came to Fort Dearborn, where there was nothing as yet to give promise of that miraculous growth which was soon to make Chicago a proverb to the world. There were a few settlements in the fertile region called the Military Tract; the southern part of the State was getting itself settled here and there. People were coming in freely to the Sangamon country. But a grassy solitude stretched from Galena to Chicago, and the upper half of the State was generally a wilderness. The earlier emigrants, principally of the poorer class of Southern farmers, shunned the prairies with something of a superstitious dread. They preferred to pass the first years of their occupation in the wasteful and laborious work of clearing a patch of timber for corn, rather than enter upon those rich savannas which were ready to break into fertility at the slightest provocation of culture. Even so late as 1835, writes J. F. Speed, "no one dreamed the prairies would ever be occupied." It was thought they would be used perpetually as grazing-fields for stock. For years the long processions of "movers" wound over those fertile and neglected plains, taking no hint of the wealth suggested by the rank luxuriance of vegetable growth around them, the carpet of brilliant flowers spread over the verdant knolls, the strong, succulent grass that waved in the breeze, full of warm and vital odor, as high as the waist of a man. In after years, when the emigration from the Northern and Eastern States began to pour in, the prairies were rapidly taken up, and the relative growth and importance of the two sections of the State were immediately reversed. Governor Ford, writing about 1847, attributes this result to the fact that the best class of Southern people were slow to emigrate to a State where they could not take their slaves; while the settlers from the North, not being debarred by the State Constitution from bringing their property with them, were of a different class. "The northern part of the State was settled in the first instance by wealthy farmers, enterprising merchants, millers, and manufacturers. They made farms, built mills, churches, school-houses, towns, and cities, and constructed roads and bridges as if by magic;

so that although the settlements in the southern part of the State are from twenty to fifty years in advance on the score of age, yet are they ten years behind in point of wealth and all the appliances of a higher civilization."

At the time which we are specially considering, however, the few inhabitants of the south and the center were principally from what came afterwards to be called the border slave States. They were mostly a simple, neighborly, unambitious people, contented with their condition, living upon plain fare, and knowing not much of anything better. Luxury was, of course, unknown; even wealth, if it existed, could procure few of the comforts of refined life. There was little or no money in circulation. Exchanges were effected by the most primitive forms of barter, and each family had to rely chiefly upon itself for the means of living. The neighbors would lend a hand in building a cabin for a new-comer; after that he must in most cases shift for himself. Many a man arriving from an old community, and imperfectly appreciating the necessities of pioneer life, has found suddenly, on the approach of winter, that he must learn to makes shoes or go barefoot. The furniture of their houses was made with an axe from the trees of the forest. Their clothing was all made at home. The buckskin days were over to a great extent, though an occasional hunting-shirt and pair of moccasins were still seen. But flax and hemp had begun to be cultivated, and as the wolves were killed off the sheep-folds increased, and garments resembling those of civilization were spun and woven, and cut and sewed, by the women of the family. When a man had a suit of jeans colored with butternut-dye, and his wife a dress of linsey, they could appear with the best at a wedding or a quilting frolic. The superfluous could not have been said to exist in a community where men made their own buttons, where women dug roots in the woods to make their tea with, where many children never saw a stick of candy until after they were grown. The only sweetmeats known were those a skillful cook could compose from the honey plundered from the hollow oaks where the wild bees had stored it. Yet there was withal a kind of rude plenty; the woods swarmed with game, and after swine began to be raised, there was the bacon and hoe-cake which any south-western farmer will say is good enough for a king. The greatest privation was the lack of steel implements. His axe was as precious to the pioneer as his sword to the knight errant. Governor John Reynolds speaks of the panic felt in his father's family when the axe was dropped into a stream. A battered piece of tin was carefully saved and smoothed, and made into a grater for green corn.

They had their own amusements, of course; no form of society is without them, from the anthropoid apes to the Jockey Club. As to the grosser and ruder shapes taken by the diversions of the pioneers, we will let Mr. Herndon speak—their contemporary annalist and ardent panegyrist: "These men could shave a horse's mane and tail, paint, disfigure, and offer it for sale to the owner. They could hoop up in a hogshead a drunken man, they themselves being drunk, put in and nail fast the head, and roll the man down hill a hundred feet or more. They could run down a lean and hungry wild pig, catch it, heat a ten-plate stove furnace hot, and putting in the pig, could cook it, they dancing the while a merry jig." Wild oats of this kind seem hardly compatible with a harvest of civilization, but it is contended that such of these roysterers as survived their stormy beginnings became decent and serious citizens. Indeed, Mr. Herndon insists that even in their hot youth they showed the promise of goodness and piety. "They attended church, heard the sermon, wept and prayed, shouted, got up and fought an hour, and then went back to prayer, just as the spirit moved them." The camp-meeting may be said, with no irreverent intention, to have been their principal means of intellectual excitement. The circuit preachers were for a long time the only circulating medium of thought and emotion that kept the isolated settlements from utter spiritual stagnation. They were men of great physical and moral endurance, absolutely devoted to their work, which they pursued in the face of every hardship and discouragement. Their circuits were frequently so great in extent that they were forced to be constantly on the route; what reading they did was done in the saddle. They received perhaps fifty dollars from the missionary fund and half as much more from their congregations, paid for the most part in necessaries of life. Their oratory was suited to their longitude, and was principally addressed to the emotions of their hearers. It was often very effective, producing shouts and groans and genuflections among the audience at large, and terrible convulsions among the more nervous and excitable. We hear sometimes of a whole congregation prostrated as by a hurricane, flinging their limbs about in furious contortions, with wild outcries. To this day some of the survivors of that period insist that it was the spirit of the Almighty, and nothing less, that thus manifested itself. The minister, however, did not always share in the delirium of his hearers. Governor Reynolds tells us of a preacher in Sangamon County, who, before his sermon, had set a wolf-trap in view from his pulpit. In the midst of his exhortations his keen eyes saw the distant trap collapse, and he continued in the same intonation with which he had been preaching, "Mind the text, brethren, till I go kill that wolf!" With all the failings and eccentricities of this singular class of men, they did a great deal of good, and are entitled to especial credit among those who conquered the wilderness. The emotions they excited did not all die away in the shouts and contortions of the meeting. Not a few of the cabins in the clearings were the abode of a fervent religion and an austere morality. Many a traveler, approaching a rude hut in the woods in the gathering twilight, distrusting the gaunt and silent family who gave him an unsmiling welcome, the bare interior, the rifles and knives conspicuously displayed, has felt his fears vanish when he sat down to supper, and the master of the house, in a few fervent words, invoked the blessing of heaven on the meal.

There was very little social intercourse; a visit was a serious matter, involving the expenditure of days of travel. It was the custom among families, when the longing for the sight of kindred faces was too strong to withstand, to move in a body to the distant settlement where their relatives lived and re-main with them for months at a time. The claims of consanguinity were more regarded than now. Almost the only festivities were those that accompanied weddings, and these were, of course, of a primitive kind. The perils and adventures through which the young pioneers went to obtain their brides furnish forth thousands of tales by Western firesides. Instead of taking the rosy daughter of a neighbor, the enterprising bachelor would often go back to Kentucky, and pass through as many adventures in bringing his wife home as a returning crusader would meet between Beirut and Vienna. If she was a young woman who respected herself, the household gear she would insist on bringing would entail an Iliad of embarrassments. An old farmer of Sangamon County still talks of a feather-bed weighing fifty-four pounds with which his wife made him swim six rivers under penalty of desertion.

It was not always easy to find a competent authority to perform the ceremony. A justice in McLean County lived by the bank of a river, and his services were sometimes required by impatient lovers on the other bank when the waters were too torrential to cross. In such cases, being a conscientious man, he always insisted that they should ride into the stream far enough for him to discern their features, holding torches to their faces by night and by storm. The wooing of those days was prompt and practical. There was no time for the gradual approaches of an idler and more conventional age. It is related of one Stout, one of the legendary Nimrods of Illinois, who was well and frequently married, that he had one unfailing formula of courtship. He always promised the ladies whose hearts he was besieging that "they should live in the timber where they could pick up their own firewood."

Theft was almost unknown; property, being so hard to get, was jealously guarded, as we have already noticed in speaking of the settlement of Kentucky. The pioneers of Illinois brought with them the same rigid notions of honesty which their environment maintained. A man in Macoupin County left his wagon, loaded with corn, stuck in the prairie mud for two weeks near a frequented road. When he returned he found some of his corn gone, but there was money enough tied in the sacks to pay for what was taken. Men carrying bags of silver from the towns of Illinois to St. Louis rather made a display of it, as it enhanced their own importance, and there was no fear of robbery. There were of course no locks on the cabin doors, and the early merchants sometimes left their stores unprotected for days together when they went to the nearest city to replenish their stock. Of course there were rare exceptions to this rule, but a single theft alarmed and excited a whole neighborhood. When a crime was traced home, the family of the criminal were generally obliged to remove.

There were still, even so late as the time to which we are referring, two alien elements in the population of the State—the French and the Indians. The French settlements about Kaskaskia retained much of their national character, and the pioneers from the South who visited them or settled among them never ceased to wonder at their gayety, their peaceable industry and enterprise, and their domestic affection, which they did not care to dissemble and conceal like their shy and reticent neighbors. It was a daily spectacle, which never lost its strangeness for the Tennesseeans and Kentuckians, to see the Frenchman returning from his work greeted by his wife and children with embraces of welcome "at the gate of his door-yard, and in view of all the villagers." The natural and kindly fraternization of the Frenchmen with the Indians was also a cause of wonder to the Americans. The friendly intercourse between them, and their occasional intermarriages, seemed little short of monstrous to the ferocious exclusiveness of the Anglo-Saxon. The Indians in the central part of Illinois cut very little figure in the reminiscences of the pioneers; they occupied much the same relation to them as the tramp to the housewife of to-day. The Winnebago war in 1827 and the Black Hawk war in 1831 disturbed only the northern portion of the State. A few scattered and vagrant lodges of Pottawatomies and Kickapoos were all the pioneers of Sangamon and the neighboring counties ever met. They were spared the heroic struggle of the advance-guard of civilization in other States. A woman was sometimes alarmed by a visit from a drunken savage; poultry and pigs occasionally disappeared when they were in the neighborhood; but life was not darkened by the constant menace of massacre. A few years earlier, indeed, the relations of the two races had been more strained, as may be inferred from an act passed by the territorial Legislature in 1814, offering a reward of fifty dollars to any citizen or ranger who should kill or take any depredating Indian. As only two dollars was paid for killing a wolf, it is easy to see how the pioneers regarded the forest folk in point of relative noxiousness. But ten years later a handful only of the Kickapoos remained in Sangamon County, the specter of the vanished people. A chief named Machina came one day to a family who were clearing a piece of timber, and issued an order of eviction in these words: "Too much come white man. T'other side Sangamon." He threw a handful of dried leaves in the air to show how he would scatter the pale faces, but he never fulfilled his threats further than to come in occasionally and ask for a drink of whisky. That such trivial details are still related, only shows how barren of incident was the life of these obscure founders of a great empire. Any subject of conversation, any cause of sensation, was a godsend. When Vannoy murdered his wife in Springfield, whole families put on their best clothes and drove fifty miles through bottomless mud and swollen rivers to see him hanged.

It is curious to see how naturally in such a state of things the fabric of political society developed itself from its germ. The county of Sangamon was called by an act of the Legislature in 1821 out of a verdant solitude of more than a million acres, inhabited by a few families. An election for county commissioners was ordered; three men were chosen; they came together at the cabin of John Kelly, at Spring Creek. He was a roving bachelor from North Carolina, devoted to the chase, who had built this hut three years before on the margin of a green-bordered rivulet, where the deer passed by in hundreds, going in the morning from the shady banks of the Sangamon to feed on the rich green grass of the prairie, and returning in the twilight. He was so delighted with this hunters' paradise that he sent for his brothers to join him. They came and brought their friends, and so it happened that in this immense county, several thousand square miles in extent, the settlement of John Kelly at Spring Creek was the only place where there was shelter for the commissioners; thus it became the temporary county-seat, duly described in the official report of the commissioners as "a certain point in the prairie near John Kelly's field, on the waters of Spring Creek, at a stake marked Z and D (the initials of the commissioners), to be the temporary seat of justice for said county; and we do further agree that the said county-seat be called and known by the name of Springfield." In this manner the future capital received that hackneyed title, when the distinctive and musical name of Sangamon was ready to their hands. The same day they agreed with John Kelly to build them a court-house, for which they paid him forty-two dollars and fifty cents. In twenty-four days the house was built—one room of rough logs, the jury retiring to any sequestered glade they fancied for their deliberation. They next ordered the building of a jail, which cost just twice as much money as the court-house. Constables and overseers of the poor were appointed, and all the machinery of government prepared for the population which was hourly expected. It was taken for granted that malefactors would come and the constables have employment; and the poor they would have always with them, when once they began to arrive. This was only a temporary arrangement, but when, a year or two later, the time came to fix upon a permanent seat of justice for the county, the resources of the Spring Creek men were equal to the emergency. When the commissioners came to decide on the relative merits of Springfield and another site a few miles away, they led them through brake, through brier, by mud knee-deep and by water-courses so exasperating that the wearied and baffled officials declared they would seek no further, and Springfield became the county-seat for all time; and greater destinies were in store for it through means not wholly dissimilar. Nature had made it merely a pleasant hunting-ground;

the craft and the industry of its first settlers made it a capital.

The courts which were held in these log huts were as rude as might be expected; yet there is evidence that although there was no superfluity of law or of learning, justice was substantially administered. The lawyers came mostly from Kentucky, though an occasional New Englander confronted and lived down the general prejudice against his region and obtained preferment. The profits of the profession were inconceivably small. One early State's Attorney describes his first circuit as a tour of shifts and privations not unlike the wanderings of a mendicant friar. In his first county he received a fee of five dollars for prosecuting the parties to a sanguinary affray. In the next he was equally successful, but barely escaped drowning in Spoon River. In the third there were but two families at the county-seat, and no cases on the docket. Thence he journeyed across a trackless prairie sixty miles, and at Quincy had one case and gained five dollars. In Pike County our much-enduring jurist took no cash, but found a generous sheriff who entertained him without charge. "He was one of nature's noblemen, from Massachusetts," writes the grateful prosecutor. The lawyers in what was called good practice earned less than a street-sweeper to-day. It is related that the famous Stephen A. Douglas once traveled from Springfield to Bloomington and made an extravagant speech, and having gained his case received a fee of five dollars. In such a state of things it was not to be wondered at that the technicalities of law were held in somewhat less veneration than what the pioneer regarded as the essential claims of justice. The infirmities of the jury system gave them less annoyance than they give us. Governor Ford mentions a case where a gang of horse-thieves succeeded in placing one of their confederates upon a jury which was to try them; but he was soon brought to reason by his eleven colleagues making preparations to hang him to the rafters of the jury room. The judges were less hampered by the limitations of their legal lore than by their fears of a loss of popularity as a result of too definite charges in civil suits, or too great severity in criminal cases. They grew very dexterous in avoiding any commitment as to the legal or moral bearings of the questions brought before them. They generally refused to sum up, or to comment upon evidence; when asked by the counsel to give instructions they would say, "Why, gentlemen, the jury understand this case as well as you or I. They will do justice between the parties." One famous judge, who was afterwards governor, when sentencing a murderer, impressed it upon his mind, and wished him to inform his friends, that it was the jury and not the judge who had found him guilty, and then asked him on what day he would like to be hanged. It is needless to say that the bench and bar were not all of this class. There were even at that early day lawyers, and not a few, who had already won reputation in the older States, and whose names are still honored in the profession. Cook, McLean, Edwards, Kane, Thomas, Reynolds, and others, the earliest lawyers of the State, have hardly been since surpassed for learning and ability.

In a community where the principal men were lawyers, where there was as yet little commerce, and industrial enterprise was unknown, it was natural that one of the chief interests of life should be the pursuit of politics. The young State swarmed with politicians; they could be found chewing and whittling at every cross-roads inn; they were busy at every horse-race, arranging their plans and extending their acquaintance; around the burgoo-pot of the hunting party they discussed measures and candidates; they even invaded the camp-meeting and did not disdain the pulpit as a tribune. Of course there was no such thing as organization in the pioneer days. Men were voted for to a great extent independently of partisan questions affecting the nation at large, and in this way the higher offices of the State were filled for many years by men whose personal character compelled the respect and esteem of the citizens. The year 1826 is generally taken as the date which witnessed the change from personal to partisan politics, though several years more elapsed before the rule of conventions came in, which put an end to individual candidacy. In that year, Daniel Pope Cook, who had long represented the State in Congress with singular

ability and purity, was defeated by Governor Joseph Duncan, the candidate of the Jackson men, on account of the vote given by Cook which elected John Quincy Adams to the Presidency. The bitter intolerance of the Jackson party naturally caused their opponents to organize against them, and there were two parties in the State from that time forward. The change in political methods was inevitable, and it is idle to deplore it; but the former system gave the better men in the new State a power and prominence which they have never since enjoyed. Such men as Governor Ninian Edwards, who came with the prestige of a distinguished family connection, a large fortune, a good education, and a distinction of manners and of dress—ruffles, gold buttons, and fair-topped boots—which would hardly have been pardoned a few years later; and Governor Edward Coles, who had been private secretary to Madison, and was familiar with the courts of Europe, a man as notable for his gentleness of manners as for his nobility of nature, could never have come so readily and easily to the head of the government after the machine of the caucus had been perfected. Real ability then imposed itself with more authority upon the ignorant and unpretending politicians from the back timber; so that it is remarked by those who study the early statutes of Illinois that they are far better drawn up, and better edited, than those of a later period, when illiterate tricksters, conscious of the party strength behind them, insisted on shaping legislation according to their own fancy. The men of cultivation wielded an influence in the Legislature entirely out of proportion to their numbers, as the ruder sort of pioneers were naturally in a large majority. The type of a not uncommon class in Illinois tradition was a member from the South who could neither read nor write, and whose apparently ironical patronymic was Grammar. When first elected he had never worn anything except leather; but regarding his tattered buckskin as unfit for the garb of a lawgiver, he and his sons gathered hazel-nuts enough to barter at the nearest store for a few yards of blue strouding such as the Indians used for breech-clouts. When he came home with his purchase and had called together the women of the settlement to make his clothes, it was found that there was only material enough for a very short coat and a long pair of leggings, and thus attired he went to Kaskaskia, the territorial capital. Uncouth as was his appearance, he had in him the raw material of a politician. He invented a system—which was afterwards adopted by many whose breeches were more fashionably cut—of voting against every measure which was proposed. It it failed, the responsibility was broadly shared; if it passed and was popular, no one would care who voted against it; if it passed and did not meet the favor of the people, John Grammar could vaunt his foresight. Between the men like Coles and the men like Grammar there was a wide interval, and the average was about what the people of the State deserved and could appreciate. A legislator was as likely to suffer for doing right as for doing wrong. Governor Ford, in his admirable sketch of the early history of the State, mentions two acts of the Legislature, both of them proper and beneficial, as unequaled in their destructive influence upon the great folks of the State. One was a bill for a loan to meet the honest obligations of the commonwealth, commonly called "the Wiggins loan"; and the other was a law to prevent bulls of inferior size and breed from running at large. This latter set loose all the winds of popular fury: it was cruel, it was aristocratic; it was in the interest of rich men and pampered foreign bulls; and it ended the career of many an aspiring politician in a blast of democratic indignation and scorn. The politician who relied upon immediate and constant contact with the people certainly earned all the emoluments of office he received. His successes were hardly purchased by laborious affability. "A friend of mine," says Ford, "once informed me that he intended to be a candidate for the Legislature, but would not declare himself until just before the election, and assigned as a reason that it was so very hard to be clever for a long time at once." Before the caucus had eliminated the individual initiative, there was much more of personal feeling in elections. A vote against a man had something of offense in it, and sometimes stirred up a defeated candidate to heroic vengeance. In 1827 the Legislature elected a

State treasurer after an exciting contest, and before the members had left the house the unsuccessful aspirant came in and soundly thrashed, one after the other, four of the representatives who had voted against him. Such energy was sure to meet its reward, and he was soon after made clerk of the Circuit Court. It is related by old citizens of Menard County, as a circumstance greatly to the credit of Abraham Lincoln, that when he was a candidate for the Legislature a man who wanted his vote for another place walked to the polls with him and ostentatiously voted for him, hoping to receive his vote in return. Lincoln voted against him, and the act was much admired by those who saw it.

One noticeable fact is observed in relation to the politicians of the day—their careers were generally brief. Superannuation came early. In the latter part of the last century and the first half of this, men were called old whom we should regard as in the prime of life. When the friends of Washington were first pressing the Presidency upon him in 1788, he urged his "advanced age" as an imperative reason for declining it: he was fifty-six years old. When Ninian Edwards was a candidate for Governor of Illinois in 1826, he was only fifty-one, and yet he considered it necessary in his published addresses to refer to the charge that he was too old for the place, and, while admitting the fact that he was no longer young, to urge in extenuation that there are some old things,—like old whisky, old bacon, and old friends,—which are not without their merits. Even so late as 1848, we find a remarkable letter from Mr. Lincoln, who was then in Congress, bearing upon the same point. His partner, William H. Herndon, had written him a letter, complaining that the old men in Sangamon County were unwilling to let the young ones have any opportunity to distinguish themselves. To this Lincoln answered in his usual tone of grave kindness: "The subject of your letter is exceedingly painful to me; and I cannot but think there is some mistake in your impression of the motives of the old men. I suppose I am now one of the old men, and I declare on my veracity, which I think is good with you, that nothing could afford me more satisfaction than to learn that you and others of my young friends at home were doing battle in the contest and endearing themselves to the people and taking a stand far above any I have ever been able to reach in their admiration. I cannot conceive that other old men feel differently. Of course, I cannot demonstrate what I say; but I was young once, and I am sure I was never ungenerously thrust back."

The man who thus counseled petulant youth with the experienced calmness of age was thirty-nine years old. A state of society where one could at that age call himself or be called by others an old man, is proved by that fact alone to be one of wearing hardships and early decay of the vital powers. The survivors of the pioneers stoutly insist upon the contrary view. "It was a glorious life," says one old patriarch; "men would fight for the love of it, and then shake hands and be friends; there is nothing like it now." Another says, "I never enjoy my breakfast now as I used to, when I got up and ran down a deer before I could have anything to eat." But they see the past through a rosy mist of memory, transfigured by the eternal magic of youth. The sober fact is that the life was a hard one, with few rational pleasures, few wholesome appliances. The strong ones lived, and some even attained great length of years; but to the many age came early and was full of infirmity and pain. If we could go back to what our forefathers endured in clearing the Western wilderness, we could then better appreciate our obligations to them. It is detracting from the honor which is their due to say that their lives had much of happiness or comfort, or were in any respect preferable to our own.

RIDING THE SANGAMON CIRCUIT

PETER CARTWRIGHT

The circuit riders were rugged men who smelled of wood smoke and saddle leather and talked of the power of the Holy Ghost. Before the church was established in new regions these mud-stained preachers ranged the country, bringing the word of God to lonely and brutish people. They followed settlements to the farthest claims, threading forests, swimming rivers, crossing waist-deep swamps and snow-swept prairies. They preached in squatters' camps and stump-filled clearings, where no church bell had ever rung. The wilderness was their parish.

The best remembered of them was Peter Cartwright, who rode wild circuits from the Appalachians to the Mississippi. For fifty years he followed the frontier, bringing worship to the wilderness. The following account, from his Autobiography, recalls his first season in Illinois.

The circuit riders had no theological training but a liberal education in personal hardship and crude human nature. Wrote a Methodist colleague of Cartwright's, the nearly blind William Henry Milburn: "The terms of tuition in Brush College and Swamp University are high, the course of study hard, the examinations frequent and severe, but the schooling is capital."

SANGAMON County was not only a newly-settled country, but embraced a large region. It was the most northern and the only northern county organized in the state. It had been settled by a few hardy and enterprising pioneers but a few years before. Just north of us was an unbroken Indian country, and the Indians would come in by scores and camp on the Sangamon River bottom, and hunt and live there through the winter. Their frequent visits to our cabins created sometimes great alarm among the women and children. They were a very degraded and demoralized people, and the white people were very much to blame in dealing out the fire-water so freely among them. But the whites kept advancing further and further into their country, and the Indians kept constantly receding and melting away before their rapid march, until they are now mostly removed west of the Mississippi, the great Father of Waters.

The Sangamon Circuit had been formed about three years when I came to it. Brother J. Sims, I think, formed the circuit. Brother Rice followed, and J. Miller, of one of the Indiana conferences, traveled it in 1823-4. The circuit was in what is called the Illinois District, Samuel H. Thompson presiding elder. I found about two hundred and sixty members in society. The circuit embraced all the scattered settlements in the above-named county, together with parts of Morgan and M'Lean counties. We were almost entirely without ferries, bridges, or roads. My mode of traveling, with a few exceptions, was to go from point to point of timber, through the high grass of the prairie. My circuit extended to Blooming Grove in M'Lean County, near where the City of Bloomington now stands. A few fine Methodist families had settled in this grove; some local preachers from Sangamon Circuit first visited them; then Jesse Walker, who was appointed missionary to the Indians in and about Fort Clark and up the Illinois River toward Lake Michigan. I took it into the Sangamon Circuit, and, in conjunction with Brother Walker, appointed a sacramental meeting at the house of Brother Hendricks, he and his wife being excellent members of the Church, and he was appointed class-leader. Brother Hendricks has long since gone to his reward, while Sister Hendricks still lingers among us a shining example of Christian piety.

An incident occurred at this sacramental meeting worthy of note: The ordinance of baptism was desired by some, and some parents wanted their children baptized, and the brethren desired me to preach on or explain the nature and design of Christian baptism. I did so on the Sabbath. There was present a New Light preacher, who had settled in the grove,

and was a very great stickler for immersion, as the only proper mode. That afternoon there arose a dark cloud, and presently the rain fell in torrents, and continued almost all night; nearly the whole face of the earth was covered with water; the streams rose suddenly and overflowed their banks. A little brook near the house rose so rapidly that it swept away the spring house and some of the fences. Next morning I was riding up the grove to see an old acquaintance. I met Mr. Roads, my New Light preacher, and said "Good morning, sir."

"Good morning," he replied.

Said I, "We have had a tremendous rain."

"Yes, sir," said he; "the Lord sent that rain to convince you of your error."

"Ah!" said I, "what error?"

"Why, about baptism. The Lord sent this flood to convince you that much water was necessary."

"Very good, sir," said I; "and he in like manner sent this flood to convince you of your error."

"What error?" said he.

"Why," said I, "to show you that water comes by pouring and not by immersion."

The preacher got into this mad fit because I had satisfied one of his daughters that immersion was not the proper mode of baptism, and she had joined the Methodists; and I am told that this flood to this day is called "Cartwright's Flood" by way of eminence; and though it rained hard, and my New Light preacher preached hard against us, yet he made little or no impression, but finally evaporated and left for parts unknown. His New Light went out because there was "no oil in the vessel."

I had an appointment in a settlement in a certain brother's cabin. He had a first-rate wife and several interesting daughters; and I will not forget to say, had some three hundred dollars hoarded up to enter land. For the thin settlement we had a good congregation. The meeting closed, and there was but one chair in the house, and that was called the preacher's chair. The bottom was weak and worn out, and one of the upright back pieces was broken off. We had a hewed puncheon for a table, with four holes in it, and four straight sticks put in for legs. The hearth was made of earth,

Above: Peter Cartwright, Methodist preacher and circuit rider. Courtesy Illinois State Historical Society   Below: A camp meeting. Courtesy Ohio Historical Society

and in the center of it was a deep hole, worn by sweeping. Around this hole the women had to cook, which was exceedingly inconvenient, for they had no kitchen. When we came to the table there were wooden trenchers for plates, sharp-pointed pieces of cane for forks, and tin cups for cups and saucers. There was but one knife besides a butcher's knife, and that had the handle off. Four forks were driven down between the puncheons into the ground; for bedsteads, cross poles or side poles put in those forks, and clapboards laid crosswise for cords. The old sister kept up a constant apology, and made many excuses. Now, if the brother had been really poor, I could have excused everything; but, knowing he had money hoarded up, I thought it my duty to speak to him on the subject. I was at first a little careful, so I commenced by praising his good-looking daughters, and noticed what a good cook his wife was if she had any chance. "Now, brother," said I, "do fill up this hole in the hearth, and go to town and get you a set of chairs, knives and forks, cups and saucers, and get you a couple of plain bedsteads and bedcords. Give your wife and daughters a chance. These girls, sir, are smart enough to marry well, if you will fix them up a little." I saw in a moment the women were on my side, and I felt safe. The old brother said he had seen proud preachers before, and that he knew I was proud the moment he saw me with my broadcloth coat on, and he did not thank me for meddling with his affairs.

"Brother," said I, "you have been a member of the Church a long time, and you ought to know that the Discipline of our Church makes it the duty of a circuit preacher to recommend cleanliness and decency everywhere; and, moreover, if there was nothing of this kind in the Discipline at all, my good feelings toward you and your family, prompt me to urge these things on you; and you ought to attend to them for your own comfort, and the great comfort of your family."

The old sister and daughters joined with me in all I said.

"Brother," said I, "you have two fine boys here, and they will help you do up things in a little better style; and I tell you, if you don't do it by the time I come round in four weeks,

I shall move preaching from your cabin somewhere else."

The old brother told me I could move preaching, for if I was too proud to put up with his fare, he did not want me about him. I went on, but left another appointment, and when I came on to it, I tell you things were done up about right. The females had taken my lecture to the old brother for a text, and they had preached successfully to him, for the hole in the hearth was filled up, two new bedsteads were on hand, six new split-bottomed chairs were procured, a new set of knives and forks, cups and saucers, and plates, were all on hand. The women met me very pleasantly, and the old brother himself looked better than usual; and besides all this, the women all had new calico dresses, and looked very neat. We had a good congregation, a good meeting, and things went on very pleasantly with me and the whole family during the two years that I rode the circuit. And better than all this, nearly all the children obtained religion and joined the Church, and those of them who still live, I number among my fast friends.

On Horse Creek we had an appointment, and a good society; old Brother Joseph Dixon was class-leader and steward. I think he was one of the best stewards I ever saw. The country was new; our little market was at St. Louis, distant one hundred miles or more; and some of the people had to go sixty miles for their grinding and bread-stuff; and this country was generally settled with poor, but very kind people; money was very scarce, and what little there was, was generally kept close to enter lands when our Congress should order sales; almost universally we were settled on Congress or government lands. In this condition of affairs, the support of a traveling preacher was exceedingly small. The first year I traveled the Sangamon Circuit with a wife and six children, I received forty dollars all told; the second year I received sixty. This was considered a great improvement in our financial affairs. I state these things that the reader may see the extreme difficulties our early preachers had to contend with. The round before each quarterly meeting, Brother Dixon, the steward, would take his horse and accompany the preacher, and after preaching, and the class had met, he would rise and call on the Church for their aid in supporting the Gospel. He invariably made it a rule to see that every member of his own class paid something every quarter to support the Gospel, and if there were any too poor to pay, he would pay for them.

Brother D. had been a real back-woodsman, a frontier settler, a great hunter and trapper to take furs. Among other early and enterprising trappers, he prepared himself for a hunting and trapping expedition up the Missouri River and its tributaries, which at that early day was an unbroken Indian country, and many of them hostile to the whites. He made himself a canoe or dug-out, to ascend the rivers, laid in his traps, ammunition, and all the necessary fixtures for such a trip, and he and two other partners slowly ascended the Missouri. After ascending this stream for hundreds of miles, and escaping many dangerous ambuscades of the Indians, winter came on with great severity. They dug in the ground and buried their furs and skins at different points, to keep them from being stolen by the Indians. They then dug a deep hole on the sunny side of a hill, gathered their winter meat and fuel, their leaves and grass, and carried them into the hole, and took up their winter quarters. The snows were very deep, the weather intensely cold; but they wintered in comparative safety till returning spring, which they hailed with transports of joy. They were robbed several times by the Indians, had several battles with them, and killed two or three of them. The next fall his partners fell out with him, bought a canoe of the Indians, left him alone, descended the river, dug up their furs, and returned home. Dixon fortunately secured most of the ammunition they had on hand. He again found a dreaded winter approaching. He resorted to the former winter's experiment, and dug his cave in the side of a steep hill, laid up his winter provisions, and took up his winter quarters all alone. In this perilous condition, his eyes became inflamed, and were very much affected from constant gazing on the almost perpetual snows around him, until, such was their diseased state, he could not see anything. Here he was utterly helpless and hopeless. He began to reflect on his dreadful condition, while he felt nothing but certain death, and realized himself to be a great sinner and unprepared to die. For the first time in his life, almost, he kneeled down and asked God for mercy and deliverance from this awful condition. Then and there he promised God if he would spare and deliver him, he would from that solemn moment serve him faithfully the rest of his life. This promise, he told me, he had faithfully kept; and there is not in my mind a single doubt but he kept his covenant till he was safely housed in heaven.

When he made this covenant with God in his desperate condition, all of a sudden there was a strong impression made on his mind that if he would take the inside bark of a certain tree that stood a few steps from the mouth of his earthly habitation, and beat it up, soft and fine, soak it in water, and wash his eyes with it, he would soon recover his sight. He groped his way to the tree, got the bark, prepared it as impressed, bathed his eyes, bound some of this bark to them, and laid down and slept, not knowing whether it was day or night. When he awoke his eyes felt easy; the inflammation was evidently subsiding, and in a short time his sight began to return, and soon was entirely restored. When he gained confidence in his restoration to sight he fell on his knees to return thanks to God; a sweet and heavenly peace run all through his soul, and he then and there, all alone, shouted aloud the high praises of God. He then felt that God had forgiven his sins, blessed his soul, restored his sight, and that he ought to praise and give glory to his holy name.

When the weather opened for trapping he said he had astonishing good luck; took a great amount of the very best furs; and collecting them, began to descend the river. He had an Indian village to pass on the bank of the river, and as they were a deceitful, sly, bad tribe of Indians, he determined to keep his canoe as far from their shore as possible. They made many friendly signs for him to stop, so he concluded to land and trade a little with them. He had his rifle well loaded, and was a very strong man. When his canoe struck the bank a large, stout Indian jumped into it, and others were following. He, accordingly, shoved off, when one on the bank raised his rifle and aimed to shoot him. As quick as thought Dixon jerked the Indian that was in the canoe between him and the other that raised his rifle; the gun fired, and lodged its contents in the heart of the large Indian in the canoe, who fell overboard dead. Dixon paddled with all speed down the river, and escaped being robbed or killed. When he returned to St. Louis he sold his furs for several thousand dollars, and returned to his family, after having been absent nearly three years. He then packed up, moved to Horse Creek, in Sangamon County, took preaching into his cabin, joined the Methodist Episcopal Church, and continued to be a faithful member, leader, and steward for many years. His children mostly grew up, married, and left him; his most excellent wife at length died, witnessing a good confession; his youngest son he named Missouri, in memory of his conversion on the trapping expedition up that turbid stream, and also to keep fresh in his recollection the solemn vow he had made in his perilous condition. After the death of his wife he lingered a few years, and then died in peace, at his daughter's, in Morgan County.

It may be gratifying to some to see what has grown out of what was within the bounds of the old Sangamon Circuit in 1824-5. There is Beardstown Station, Virginia Circuit, Havana Circuit, Delavan Mission, East and West Charges in Bloomington, Randolph's Grove Circuit, Waynesville Circuit, Mount Pleasant Circuit, Clinton, Honey Creek, Mount Pulaski, Decatur Station and Circuit, Taylorsville, Sulphur Spring, Virden Island Grove, and Springfield Station. Thus the old hive has sent forth twenty swarms, and still retains its old name, *Sangamon*. Perhaps this circuit has retained its first name longer than any circuit in the state or conference. At the close of my second year I returned four hundred members, being an increase, in two years, of one hundred and sixty. At our Conference in Charlestown, Indiana, August 25, 1825, Bishop M'Kendree attended and presided; and I was reappointed to Sangamon Circuit. At the time of this conference I was taken down with a violent attack of bilious fever. Three friendly doctors attended me. They succeeded in stopping the

fever. My doctor advised me to travel homeward slowly, and only a few miles a day, till I gained strength, and to take good care of myself. Some of the preachers secured a preacher acquainted with the country through which I had to pass, to go with and take care of me, for I was very feeble. This preacher was under marriage contract, and the day set for the ceremony, but I knew it not. The first day we rode twenty-eight miles. I urged him to stop long before we did. But no; he knew of a Judge Somebody, a fine Methodist, and a good place, etc.; he lived in the west end of a little town. As we passed the tavern I urged the preacher again to stop; but no, he rode up to the judge's, told my name and condition, but he would not take us in. There was present a kind-hearted man, who, on learning my condition, took me home with him and treated me well. Next morning we started on, and when we got into another little town, having rode that day twenty miles, I begged my preacher to let me stop. "O no, no," said he; "there is a fine place three miles down here; we must get there." At that moment I saw a doctor who had been a traveling preacher in Kentucky, and I knew him and called to him, and begged him to take me somewhere that I could rest. I then told my preacher guide to move on and move off, for certainly I would not travel with him a step further. So he left, and the doctor took me home with him, and treated me kindly. On Sunday morning he took me a few miles up the country, on Honey Creek, to a campmeeting that was in progress. Here I tarried and rested a while. I was aiming to cross the Wabash, and get to J. W. M'Reynold's, near Paris.

The day I left the camp-meeting my fever returned, just while I was crossing Honey Creek Prairie. It seemed to me I should die for want of water, there being no house on the road. I was immensely sick, and the day was intensely warm. At length I found a little green bush that afforded a small shade. Here I laid down to die. I saw a house a little way off, over a field, but was unable to get to it. In a few minutes a lady rode up to me, and although I had not seen her for twenty years, I instantly knew her, and she recognized me, and after a few minutes she rode off briskly after help.

In a little time there came a man and buggy, and a small boy. The boy mounted my horse. The man helped me into the buggy, and drove up to his house, and took me in, and placed me on a bed between two doors, where I had a free circulation of air. This was the house where the lady lived. The man was her husband. They took all possible care of me till I got a little better, then I started, and got safe to Brother M'Reynold's. And now I had the Grand Prairie to cross, ninety miles through. To go alone seemed out of the question, and Brother Mac's family was not in a situation for him safely to leave, and carry me in a carriage through; but he said he would go, as I must not go alone.

We arranged to start next morning early; and just as we were about leaving, I saw a carriage with a span of horses drive up to the steps with three persons, and who should they be but Brother and Sister Springer, my neighbors, and my wife, who had heard of my sickness, and had come to convey me home.

A bed was placed in the carriage, and we started. There was but one house for eighty miles across this Grand Prairie, and no water but a few ponds. I thought that these two days that we were crossing, I should surely die for the want of good water. I drank freely of these ponds, and it made me very sick every time; and I threw off great quantities of bile, and this, perhaps, saved my life. After all my fever abated, I gradually grew better, and finally recovered my wonted health.

We had a glorious camp-meeting this year on what was called Waters' Camp Ground, on Spring Creek, six miles west of Springfield. It lasted five days and nights. Over forty professed religion, and joined the Church; and the circuit generally was in a healthy condition.

The country this year settled up very rapidly, and improvements went up equally as rapid in almost every direction.

A YEAR AT EDENSBURGH

MAJOR WALTER WILKEY

For forty years the western country had an exciting press. From journalists, settlers and travelers came a flood of books about the great migration and the land of promise between the Ohio River and the Lakes. In the chorus of affirmation some dissident voices were barely heard.

One of the dissenters was Major Walter Wilkey of Maine. His anti-emigration tract, embellished with some wry cartoons, took a notably dim view of frontier life. Like Dickens' caustic account of "Eden" in Martin Chuzzlewit, *it reported on a year's residence at "Edensburgh," Illinois. Its title page informed the reader that "a more humoursome and interesting 'Traveller's Guide to the West' was never before published, and by which it will be perceived that the famous Maine-Pine-Swamp Speculation has been completely out-done!"*

The following account is from Major Wilkey's breezy burlesque Western Immigration, *published in 1839.*

YES, fellow traveller, I have been to Illinois, and as good luck would have it, after a twelve months miserable half starved residence in that famous and thriving "city of Edensburgh," (so called,) the Major has, with a whole skin, (but with precious little flesh, I assure you) providentially escaped; and is thus far back again to his good old native state of Maine—"and what (do you ask) has your year's residence in that highly extolled country produced you?" Just what you might, by occular demonstration, suppose, honest friend—a broken down waggon!—a broken winded horse!—a broken hearted wife! —a broken legged dog;—and, what is still more to be lamented, the irreparable broken constitutions of my three Fever and Ague sons, Jonathan, Jerry and Joe!—ah, the Major by sad experience can now truly say to you, and to every other son of New England—

Who have a *good home*, and don't *realize* it,
"A trip to the *West*" will teach you to *prize* it.

Nor ought he on the present occasion fail to say to those quizical dogs, those sharp shooters and mischievous scribling Editors of the South—forbear! and no longer ridicule and make sport of our much talked about "Maine-Pine-Swamp-Forest Speculation!" (in which the Major is said to have taken so distinguished a part,) for never could there be experienced just such another confounded take-in, as has been practised upon Major Walter Wilkey, of Mooseboro'! whom, be it remembered, (had he been present,) Queen Victoria's loyal subjects, the Nova Scotians, the boast of Aroostook, could in no way have intimidated, yet, notwithstanding, the Major is obliged to confess (and that to his rotten shame,) that one of those Connecticut-*City*-making-speculating-Illinois-land Jobbers, has for once out-Majored him; and left him without a single laurel to his brow!—and pray (let me ask,) who would not like him, have supposed his fortune made at once, to be offered for a Farm "good for little or nothing," a "first rate Illinois Farm, of 300 acres, producing 400 bushels to an acre!" and, withal, the goodly number of "twenty valuable house lots in EDENSBURGH!" and (as was represented to him) one of the most delightful, prosperous and thriving CITIES in the West, which (in a commercial point of view,) promised soon to equal, if not out-rival the cities of New-York and Philadelphia! and like the former, already boasting of her public

Squares!—her Parks!—her Parade Grounds!— her 'Change!—Broadway—Wall—Washington —Pearl — Franklin — Grand — Commercial and other streets.

Howsomever, a tom-fool as I have been, there is a *leetle* consolation left for the Major, yet; for it is a right-down-uncontradictable fact, that he was for a long time powder-proof against the ten thousand reports in circulation, from Kittery to Mooseboro', of the "increasing wealth and population of the far-famed West," until, as bad luck would have it, he was beset by one of those leetle-too-slick-Yankee-land-jobbing-Gull-Catchers! a second "Simon Swap," who proved himself as smart in the manufacture of new Cities in the West, as that of wooden bowls, combs, clocks, pork hams, and nutmegs in the East! and who first introduced himself among us as "Squire Samuel Soaper," and the better to effect his object, finding fault with and underrating almost everything that could be considered the produce of Mooseboro'!—the "barrenness of the soil!" "impurity of the water!" "infectious air!" "sour crabbed fruit!" "blasted corn!" "watery potatoes" "distempered cattle!" and "scabby sheep!" and, what was a leetle too *personal*, and withal, a right-down-wilful *lie*— "the puny, half-starved-Job-like-appearance of our own dear *selves*, the *Mooseites!*" not forgetting at the same time, to draw wonderful comparisons, and to extol to the skies, the abundant and luxuriant produce of the West! —"pure air!" "sweet water!" "*healthy* climate!" (mark that, fellow traveller) "fertile and easy cultivation of the prairies!" "extensive and *self-sown* wheat fields!" and (what was wonderful indeed) always free and accessable to innumerable droves of well fatted *wild Hogs!* ripe for the slaughter, and so exceedingly kind and accommodating to Maine emigrants, as to approach their barn-yards once a week (not to be *fed*, but lo,) to be *butchered!*" Indeed there was nothing of that country's produce which the "Squire" did not most extravagantly boast, the Fever and Ague excepted, about which he was as mum as a toad-fish! although the whole country so abounded therewith, that had seven-eighths been *barrelled* and *exported* to other parts of the world, there would have remained enough

Anti-emigration cartoon from Wilkey, *Western Emigration*

in all conscience, to have set half New-England into the *shivers!*

Having thus described a *few* of the advantages and good qualities of the West, this honest (soft) Soaper very modestly observed, that "for the *accommodation* of some of his eastern *friends* (as was once said by another of the *family*, who offered to exchange *new* feathers for *old*, bushel for bushel,) he had a good first rate Illinois Farm, of 300 acres, (producing 400 bushels to an acre) and a few *very* valuable house lots, in the thriving City of EDENSBURGH, that he would exchange for one or two *inferior* farms in Maine!" and with saying which, drew from the pocket of his pantaloons (carefully enveloped in parchment,) a "*Platt*" as he termed it, of his "famous thriving *City!*"—here it is, fellow traveller, and the Major will wage that a better *Gull Nett* was never before woven by one of the most skillful artists in the country!—good, bad or indifferent. Fags, the Major was most *napingly* caught therein, neck and heels, boots and spurs, soul and body! and from which (as the fly once said to the spider) he found it a leetle-

desperately-difficult-to-disentangle-himself!

It was at this period, fellow traveller, that Major Wilkey possessed, clear of debt, as good a Farm of 250 acres, as Mooseboro' could boast of—producing quite enough of the necessaries of life for the subsistence of his family, then composed of six souls, self, wife, three remarkable smart and healthy boys, and Ceaser, an old faithful family black—and all as happy and contented as need be, until the arrival among us of that crafty speculator; that kind and obliging *swapper*, of *new* Farms for *old!* and on whose representation of the advantages and enjoyments of a *City* life, Mrs. Wilkey and the boys became so elated that the temptation was, I must confess (to speak grammatically) bordering a mighty deal on *irresistibility!* Howsomever, not to be too hasty to close with the stranger, the Major begged that his family might be indulged with the privilege of one night to *dream* about it (Mrs. Wilkey with the "Platt" under her pillow!) and if the dream of but one should be considered in any way propitious, the bargain should be closed the ensuing morning, and the deed signed, sealed and delivered without further delay—which not being objected to on the part of 'Squire Soaper, my family retired early to bed, with a determination, (asleep or awake) to dream of nothing but about the contemplated exchange! and, as a *dream* was thus not only to determine the fate of the old homestead, but probably that of the Major and his family, *forever*, sometime before the break of day, all were up and prepared to relate, and to hear related, each other's dreams; —the lot falling first on *me*, I found it no difficult task to tell all I *dreamed*, for I assured my family, that whether it could be considered a dream or not, I could not for the life of me "sleep a wink" the whole night, for thinking of the new "Farm of 300 acres, and the 400 bushels to an acre!"—Mrs. Wilkey's turn came next, who with equal confidence declared that she "positively dreamed, (but whether *asleep or awake*, she could not tell,) that she had a full and clear view of 'Edensburgh,' and while taking a delightful promenade down Broadway, was met by her three boys, Jonathan, Jerry, and Joe, garbed in the style of *gentlemen* (with black fox-tail whiskers) and just from their commercial and mercantile business!"—Never could mortal beings be more elated and transported with joy, than were the boys on hearing the relation of their mother's dream, which they declared accorded exactly with their own—as they had not ceased to dream night and day, asleep or awake, that they were all three destined to be great men in "Edensburgh!"

Mrs. Wilkey as well as the rest of the family, (with one exception) now without hesitation, expressed her belief that the *exchange* would be a wise and judicious one—from this opinion, however, old *Ceaze*, dissented—having been reared from his infancy upon the *homestead*, he felt too much attached thereto, to behold it thus dreamed, or rather fooled away, and remain silent—" 'Pend on't, Massa Major, (said he) as de say be, one bird in de hand is ten times better den a whole flock of 'um in de *bushes!*" and, in truth, fellow traveller, I have by bitter experience, since found out to my sorrow that the prognostication of old Ceaze was correct—Mrs. Wilkey and the boys were, however, of quite a different opinion, and being so overjoyed at the thoughts of exchanging a country for a city life, that they became impatient for an immediate reference to the "Platt," and a selection of the twenty undisposed of house lots that had been kindly offered in part payment for the premises—in this selection it may be well for me to remark, friend, that the Major had nothing to do, his mind being at that moment too much engaged (to the exclusion of every thing of minor importance) how and in what manner, he could improve his new farm (producing 400 bushels to an acre) to the best advantage—whether to devote a part or the whole, to the cultivation of peas, beans, or parsnips!—the choice of lots was therefore left wholly and totally to Mrs. Wilkey and the boys,—the first choice falling to the mother, she selected four of the most pleasant and centrally situated in *Broadway*, near *Pearl;* intending that on each should be erected a splendid mansion, one for the Major and self, and one for each of the three boys,—the next choice devolving on Jonathan, and taking it for granted that he would ultimately become an exporter and importer of domestic and foreign goods, he selected all the unoccupied lots on "Commercial-street!" while Jerry selected five of the best on " 'Change!" and Josey the same number between "College!" and "State House Squares!"—each being thus supplied to his mind, and the "Platt" about to be returned to the "Squire," old Ceaze, (who until that moment had remained in a state of sullen silence,) now put in his claim, for at least the choice of one lot—for "what (said he,) you tink old neger goen do to *muse*, and *ploy* hesef, in *Hellinoy*, (as you call 'um)— where de grain *sow*, *reap*, and *trash* hesef!— and de hog *feed*, *fatten* and *kill* hesef?"—the argument of the impertinent black prevailed, and a lot was granted him from the number selected by Jonathan, in "Commercial-street" as Cease said "he should like 'um bess near low water mark, where he could muse 'umsef *'casionally* digging *clam!*"

The exchange being now amicably and finally agreed on, the deeds were filled by the 'Squire (who had a pocket full of them) and were presented to self and wife, for our signatures! which I must confess, fellow traveller, on the reflection that we were about to sign away our patrimonial portions, and to quit-claim forever our right and title to the old homestead, produced for the moment, sensations similar (probably) to those of two wretched condemned criminals, when about to sign (by compulsion) their death warrants! —but it was too late now to repent, the papers were signed, sealed and delivered, and 'Squire *Soaper* put into possession of the premises!— and, the next thing to be done, was to commence forthwith, preparations for a remove, in quest of, and to take possession of our newly acquired Farm, and the "twenty valuable unoccupied house lots!" I had still remaining, a tolerable good draught horse, and an old farm waggon, (which providentially I had not *dreamed* away) and into which were deposited a few of the most useful articles of kitchen furniture, which it was supposed would be most wanted when we should reach our journey's end; and on the top a small vacancy was left, to be occupied by my family. Thus prepared, after a farewell shake of hands with my neighbors, we bid (on my part and no doubt on that of Ceaze) a melancholy adieu to Mooseboro'! . . .

Since we left Michigan, our spirits had been occasionally cheered by the appearance of a hovel or rather, a few unhewn logs piled one upon another, like a Dutch hog-pen, (to serve for the habitation of one or more newly arrived *emigrants:* and no sooner was such a shelter erected, than the inmates, like their neighbors, hung out their shingle and commenced keeping tavern!) but, on this day we had been travelling from sunrise until near sunset, and although in some instances through better wooded groves, yet without the discovery of any thing that had the appearance of inhabitants! Before dark, however, better luck attended us, it was when about to come to the conclusion that we would proceed no further in that direction, that a small log hut (and apparently one of the cheapest and of meanest construction) presented itself to view, with the usual appendage suspended from a pole erected in front, a strip of oak board three inches in width containing the word *Hotel!*—judging from the external appearance of the wretched hovel, that if inhabited at all,

it could not be by any one able to give us the sought for information, yet, as to make the usual inquiry could do us no harm, the Major alone approached for that purpose; and although all was still as death, and not a human being to be seen or heard therein, after one or two heavy thumps at the door with the heel of his boot, accompanied with as many "ho, the house!" the landlady (for such she proved to be) raised and appeared at the window— between whom and myself a conversation like the following immediately thereupon ensued:

Landlady.—"Wha! well traveller—and what is wanting?—entertainment I 'spose!"

Major.—"Can you tell us, good lady, whether you ever heard of such a place in these parts, (or, any other part of the world,) as 'Edensburgh?' and if so, where and in what part of the world it may be found?"

Landlady.—"Wha! why, luck stranger! why, yes you! and you may depend on't as s-a-r-t-i-n-l-y as-you-live, that aunt *Kasiah* tells the *truth*, that you are now no where else upon earth but in Edensburgh City!—you are come from the east, man, I guess, and may I be so bold as to ax you your name?"

Major.—"Well, aged mother, when I left home, my name was 'Major Walter Wilkey of Mooseboro'' but there is I think but precious little of the Major left now! (Ceaze (aside) "I take my oaf ob dat!")—and have come with my family a great way from down east, as purchasers in and actual settlers of the 'populous and thriving City of Edensburgh!'—and, now, madam (joking aside) will you, in pity to us, inform us whether you ever heard of such a 'city' in these parts, or no?"

Landlady.—"Wha! unbelieving man, you, as sure as parsnips are parsnips, this here 'city' is Edensburgh—so named but a-three-months-ago by Squire Soaper, the lucky good man who bought the land!"

Major.—(provoked, dismayed and disheartened,) "SOAPER indeed, and a *soft* one, no doubt!—'Edensburgh!' yes, 'as sure as Parsnips are parsnips,' I am now in 'Edensburgh!'— yes, the 'thriving and populous City of Edensburgh'—Hem! well, may be!—but where in the name of *gosh*, woman, are its 'public and private edifices!' its 'increased population!' its 'Park,' 'College,' 'State House,' and other

'Squares!' its 'Broadway,' 'Pearl,' 'Washington,' 'Wall,' 'Grand' and other streets?"

Ceazer (in a low voice)—"Massa Major, wont you juss plese ax missa, where bout *Commershall-treet!*"

The old lady here hastily withdrew from the window, and for my better information, and in confirmation of what she had declared to me, soon returned with the "Platt" that the Squire had left with her—"here (said she) it is, in plain black and white, just as it was staked down by Squire Soaper, (placing her fore finger of the right hand upon the sheet, and drawing it moderately across from right to left, occasionally looking to *me* and then to the "Platt") you now stand Major, (observed she) with one foot in 'Washington street,' and the other in Grand street, your good woman between 'Pearl and Broadway!' your horse in 'State street,' the fore-wheels of your waggon in 'Wall street' and the hind in 'Market street,' and your black man stands in 'Commercial street!' (Ceaze—"gosh! I taught so! and one feet I spec, at low water mark!")—and your dog in College Square!"

Major.—"My Dog in College Square! and there let him remain, until he becomes more wise than his master has proved himself!— hem! this beats the 'Pine-swamp-speculation' all hollow!" and for the first time the Major perceives and believes, that he has been thoroughly soaped by that arch yankee, "Squire Simon Soaper!—and pray tell me, good woman, how long was the Squire himself an inhabitant of 'Edensburgh' as you call it?"

Landlady.—"Just three half days—half a day in making the purchase and staking out the 'City'—half a day in drawing and fixing this here 'Platt,' and another half day (with the assistance of my old man) in logging the house we live in!"

Major.—"Squire Soaper was a Speculator, I suspect, and came into this country with plenty of gold and silver to buy up Government lands?"

Landlady.—"O, no indeed, that he didn't! he came into this country a poor man, as a body may say, (just as one half the yankee emigrants come here) not worth more than five dollars in the world, and that in a few yankee notions, wooden bowls, and pewter spoons, and the like, which he swoped for this township, and which he says as good opportunities offer, he intends to swop away for good cultivated farms down east!"

Major.—"And Landlady, will you now inform me what is the population, or to be better understood, what number of inhabitants 'Edensburgh' now contains?"

Landlady.—"Well, lets me see, (counting her fingers) there is myself and my old man, are *two*, and there is Bridget Bilkey is *three*, Ebednigo Bilkey is *four*, Epaphrosticus Bilkey is *five*, Askwell Bilkey is *six*, Birchee Bilkey is *seven* and Ruthful Bilkey is *eight*, of these, myself and husband are *living* inhabitants, but the Bilkeys (poor souls) are all *dead*, and died with the *Fever* and *Ague* within one week of each other! and lie buried in 'Market Square!' "

Mrs. Wilkey.—"Pray husband, for the *lives* of us, don't stop here; lets go back again!"

Major.—"That won't do now wife, it is a pity that some of us could not have *dreamed* of this before—the Mooseboro' farm is gone and we have now nothing to go back to but poverty and want!"

Ceazer.—"Yes, Massa Major, I did sartinly dream of um, and I tellee you now, we better be off in a twink ob an eye, fore date *Feber-an-atch* gets hole on us, and make jus such havoc wid our family, and den sus-I, de ole lady be count her finger agin, dus: (Ceaze counting his own) dare Major Wilkey, he is one, and Molly Wilkey, his wife, she two, and Ceazer Wilkey, (gau blessee him, good ole soul) he be three, and Jonathan Wilkey, he is four, Jerry Wilkey, he five, and Josey Wilkey, he make six—six *Bilkeys* and six *Wilkeys* all berried out dare, in Markum Square!—qui!"

Here we were, in a peck of trouble, sure enough! My Mooseboro' Farm gone—irrecoverably gone!—more than eleven hundred miles from a single acquaintance (with the exception of my family) and with but one week's provision on hand, or the most distant prospect of obtaining any—and with but just thirteen shillings and sixpence half-penny in my pocket!—my wife sick, dejected and discouraged! the boys disappointed and mortified!— my horse lame and wind-broken!—old Ceaze fretful and saucy!—and *Watch* (the dog) with a leg broken by the wolves, half starved and snapping at swarms of blood-thirsty musque-toes!—nor was this all, my "Farm of 300 acres, producing 400 bushels to an acre!" had been either swallowed up by an earthquake, or in some other way had unaccountably dis-appeared, and could no where be found!—in such a predicament did the Major and family find themselves on the first day of their arrival at "Edensburgh!" and as night approached, and no other shelter but that afforded by the log-house Inn, it was beneath its humble roof that we were compelled to seek lodgings and therein to abide so long as we remained in the country! which the landlady informed us was erected "expressly for the accommodation of travellers!"—that "the price of board was *one dollar* each, per day!" and on enquiry what kind of living we might expect, her reply was "*a variety*," and referred us to the "Bill of Fare!" a board suspended from a log in the corner of the room, on which was chalked—"for Breakfast—*Pork* and *Potatoes!*" "Dinner —*Potatoes* and *Pork!*"— "Supper—*Indian ash Cakes* without *Potatoes!*" and a "tea-cup of *whiskey*, night and morning, as a substitute for tea and coffee"—"this (she said) was allowed to be a charming living in Illinois, where as there was not one of a million of acres under cultivation (and probably would not be for fifty years hence) beef, grain, and every other eatable was despet scarce and high!"—"But why (said I) good woman, where land is rep-resented so exceeding fertile, does not the 'squire devote a part of his purchase to culti-vation?" "Not he indeed, (she replied) he knows (as every other yankee speculator does,) his interest better than that, that it is of ten times more value to *stake* it out into *City* house lots, which brings a fine price in the market at the east! and it is raley true, Mr. Major, that so much is now-a-days done in this here quarter by your eastern land-spec-ulators, in buying and selling, instead of plant-ing and tilling, that at a mile distance one little patch of corn of half an acre, became the prop-erty of seven different owners before it was fit to harvest, and then for the want of fencing, the pesket wolves reaped and ran off with the crop!—and it is a sartin fact, that so little is done to improve and cultivate the soil, that we have mostly to depend on your east-

ern markets for our Beef and other eatables, which I think must make it very scarce and high! with you down easters!" (Ceaze) "Scarce and high! O no Missa, berry plenty and resonble I sure you at de present time, in New-York an Bosson Markets, and so-fort, where you get a pound ob de berry bess shank-bone-steak for two-an-elben pence, and make you present ob de suet into de bargin!"

It was (as I observed) in this wretched hovel (the produce of one half days labour) and with no better food than that mentioned, that the Major and his family were obliged to put up with for the space of one year! going only a little way abroad in the day time, as we had been at night too much serenaded by the wolves to venture out after dark!—the Major ought not however to omit to mention one convenience of which this famous log-house Inn could boast—one candle (at night) was sufficient to illuminate every room therein —the bar-room, parlour, dining hall, sleeping chambers, &c. &c. had been either all knocked into one, or the careless carpenters, (Squire Soaper and the landlady's "old man") had for-gotten to put up the partition logs—this evil however, was remedied (as regarded the sleep-ing rooms) by suspending blankets between males and females of different families—and hence the accommodating old lady said the custom was on the arrival of many strangers, to enquire how many different families there were and to furnish blankets accordingly!— On Mrs. Wilkey's calling for a broom at night that she might sweep the mud from a space sufficient to lie down and attempt to seek re-pose, the landlady declared that "she didn't b'leve there was such an article in all Illinois! —that the prairie mud in their houses was too thick and heavy for corn and birch brooms," but as a substitute which they used, brought her a scrub hoe! My only object in remaining more than one week in the country, was, the hope that some tom-fool (like myself) might possibly happen along and be found willing to give me a sum sufficient for my "Edens-burgh lots" as would defray our expences back to Maine!—but we had passed nearly six months in the country without beholding the faces of more than two or three strangers, and they on their return to New-England—when early one morning Ceaze rushed into the house, (apparently in great fright and nearly out of breath) and begged that I would get my sword in an instant and *Watch* and the boys and follow him! I hastened to the door, and to my great astonishment, found out the cause of Ceaze's affright and alarm! The whole of "Park" place and a part of "Wall-street," was occupied by one hundred or more, of those detestable Sheeps-head-and-pluck-gormandizers, the Swisses! squatting very composedly on their hams, in a circle around a blazing fire, over which were suspended half a dozen iron pots, filled to their brims with their favorite food! and whom, as soon as our landlady saw, she pronounced "*Squatters!*" and begged that if we valued our "building lots," as worth anything that the intruders might be driven off, and that without a moment's delay, as two hours peaceable possession, would entitle them to an indisputable right to the land!

It was at this important crisis that I the second time discovered since leaving Mooseboro', that I had one spark, at least, of *military* spunk remaining!—I seized my old faithful keen-edged *terrifier*, and mustering my forces, (the three boys, *Watch* and Ceaze) made a dash upon them by surprize!

It was the work of a minute—as in less than that time we got them on a retreat, and we in a close and hot pursuit following them down "Wall-street," through "Broadway," up "Pearl-street," in to "Commercial-street," up to their knees in mud! where, while some were (by their gesticulations) begging for quarter, others were exclaiming, "Ilovshephedhanzsmook'therren!"—"go, and be hang'd to you (said I) and cook and eat your fill of your 'sheeps-head-and-smook't-herren!' but blame me if you shall do it on my territories!" "nor on mine in Commarshall-treet!" added Ceaze, shaking his club—in a very short time thereafter, however, we had the satisfaction to see them extricate themselves from their miry condition, and depart with bag and baggage, pots, pot-hooks and trammels, and leave us once more in quiet possession of "Edensburgh!" and where we were permitted to remain in peace and quietness (with the exception of the dis-mal nocturnal howlings of the wolves) for the space of three months longer, when we were visited by another and still heavier judgment! —my boys, (in company with Mr. Van Swinglecome or Stringlecone, our landlord) having gone in search of prairie hens' eggs and ground nuts, as a substitute for potatoes, (of which, as of every other provision, we had become very short,) they were overtaken nine miles from home, or any other human habitation, by a heavy fall of rain, by which they all took shocking colds and which produced in a few days after, that dreadful scourge of the West—the Fever and Ague!— if there was any thing wanting to complete our misery, it was this! the poor boys one hour alternately shaking and shivering as if freezing to death, and crying out for woollen blankets and warming pans!—and the next burning and blistering with fever heat like a roasting goose or turkey on a spit-jack! and their mother (poor woman) being threatened with an attack of the same complaint, the only nurse that could be depended on was Mrs. Van Swinglecome, who acted in the double capacity of nurse and landlady—and the only medicine that she could prescribe, was powerful doses (five times a day) of *pumpkin whiskey* sweetened with *maple molasses*, which when their chills came on, had a powerful effect to warm and quiet them!—a Physician could indeed have been obtained from the distance of twenty-three miles, but as the landlady observed that she understood that he had obtained a knowledge of his skill from the Swisses, there could be but little doubt that "Ilovshephedhanzsmoktharran" would be the principal ingredient of the medicine that he would administer, and be more likely to kill than cure his patients!

In this dreadful condition (fellow traveller) we worried out a two months longer (completing just one year from the day we entered "Edensburgh!") when we having all become either by sickness or starvation reduced to mere shadows of "living skeletons!" we concluded that before death should in some form or other, unite the *Wilkeys* with the *Bilkeys* it would be best, to satisfy demands, to give our landlord a quit-claim deed of our "Edensburgh building lots" and set out on our return back to Maine—and as you perceive, we are thus far on our journey; determined if kind providence permits us to reach the place of our destination, to say to our old friends as well as to every other son of New England

"Who have a *good home* and don't *realize* it,
A trip to the *West* will teach them to *prize* it!"

ON THE UNDERGROUND RAILROAD

H. H. BANCROFT

Hubert Howe Bancroft was a historian who saw the patterns of American destiny in his own family. His great-grandfather lived on two acres of garden land outside the village of Granville, Massachusetts. His grandfather settled a 100-acre farm at Granville, Ohio; he built the first locks on the Ohio Canal and then went on west to Missouri for a land purchase and to California for gold.

Granville, Ohio, was settled by residents of East Granville, Massachusetts. To the frontier they brought a love of learning and a hatred of slavery; their new Granville became a college town and a center of abolitionism, a link in the "underground railroad" by which escaped slaves were carried to Canada. The big barn on Azariah Bancroft's farm was the first meeting place of the Ohio State Anti-Slavery Society.

The following narrative is taken from H. H. Bancroft's Autobiography.

THE most brilliant exploit of my life was performed at the tender age of eleven, when I spent a whole night in driving a two-horse wagon load of runaway slaves on their way from Kentucky and slavery to Canada and freedom—an exploit which was regarded in those days by that community with little less approbation than that bestowed by a fond Apache mother upon the son who brandishes before her his first scalp. The ebony cargo consisted of three men and two women, who had been brought into town the night before by some teamster of kindred mind to my father's, and kept snugly stowed away from prying eyes during the day. About nine o'clock at night the large lumber-box wagon filled with straw was brought out, and the black dissenters from the American constitution, who so lightly esteemed our glorious land of freedom, were packed under the straw, and some blankets and sacks thrown carelessly over them, so that outwardly there might be no significance of the dark and hidden meaning of the load. My careful mother bundled me in coats and scarfs, to keep me from freezing, and with a round of good-bys, given not without some apprehensions for my safety, and with minute instructions, repeated many times lest I should forget them, I climbed to my seat, took the reins, and drove slowly out of town. Once or twice I was hailed by some curious passer-by with "What have you got there?" to which I made answer as in such case had been provided. Just what the answer was I have forgotten, but it partook somewhat of the flavor of my mission, which was more in the direction of the law of God than of the law of man. Without telling an unadulterated Ananias and Sapphira lie, I gave the inquirer no very reliable information; still, most of the people in that vicinity understood well enough what the load meant, and were in sympathy with the shippers. I was much nearer danger when I fell asleep and ran the wagon against a tree near a bank, over which my load narrowly escaped being turned. The fact is, this was the first time in my life I had ever attempted to keep my eyes open all night, and more than once, as my horses jogged along, I was brought to my senses by a jolt, and without any definite idea of the character of the road for some distance back. My freight behaved very well; once fairly out into the country, and into the night, the 'darkies' straightened up, grinned, and appeared to enjoy the performance hugely. During the night they would frequently get out and walk, always taking care to keep carefully covered in passing through a town. About three o'clock in the morning I entered a village and drove up to the house whither I had been directed, roused the inmates, and transferred to them my load. Then I drove back, sleepy but happy.

Once my father's barn was selected as the most available place for holding a grand abolition meeting, the first anniversary of the Ohio State Anti-Slavery society. Rotten eggs flew lively about the heads of the speakers, but they suffered no serious inconvenience from them until after the meeting was over and they had begun their homeward journey. Beyond the precincts of the village they were met by a mob, and although spurring their horses they did not escape until the foul flood had drenched them. Those were happy days, when there was something to suffer for; now that the slavery monster is dead, and the slayers have well-nigh spent their strength kicking the carcass, there is no help for reformers but to run off into woman's rights, free-love, and a new string of petty isms which should put them to the blush after their doughty deeds. There are yet many souls dissatisfied with God's management of things, who feel themshelves ordained to re-create mankind upon a model of their own. Unfortunately the model varies, and instead of one creator we have ten thousand, who turn the world upside down with their whimsical vagaries.

LOG CABIN DAYS

WILLIAM DEAN HOWELLS

Born in 1837 at Martin's Ferry, Ohio, where drovers ferried cattle and hogs across to Pennsylvania, William Dean Howells was the son of a restless frontier editor. Years afterward, in reminiscent books, Howells recalled his boyhood in Hamilton, Ohio, and later seasons near Xenia where the family lived in a log cabin after the failure of a newspaper in Dayton.

Like Mark Twain, Howells was born in a river town and got his schooling in a printing office. Though he lived in Boston and New York throughout the years of his literary life, his mind often returned to the Ohio of his youth. This selection is taken from My Year in a Log Cabin.

OUR cabin stood close upon the road, but behind it broadened a cornfield of eighty acres. They still built log-cabins for dwellings in that region forty years ago, but ours must have been nearly half a century old when we went into it. It had been recently vacated by an old Virginian couple, who had long occupied it, and we decided that it needed some repairs to make it habitable even for a family inured to hardship by dauntless imaginations, and accustomed to retrospective discomforts of every kind.

So before we all came out to it a deputation of adventurers put it in what rude order they could. They glazed the narrow windows, they relaid the rotten floor, they touched (too sketchily, as it afterwards appeared) the broken roof, and they papered the walls of the groundfloor rooms. Perhaps it was my father's love of literature which inspired him to choose newspapers for this purpose; at any rate, he did so, and the effect, as I remember it, was not without its decorative qualities.

He had used a barrel of papers bought at the nearest post-office, where they had been refused by the persons to whom they had been experimentally sent by the publisher, and the whole first page was taken up by a story, which broke off in the middle of a sentence at the foot of the last column, and tantalized us forever with fruitless conjecture as to the fate of the hero and heroine. I really suppose that a cheap wall-paper could have been got for the same money, though it might not have seemed so economical.

I was not sure that the use of the newspapers was not a tributary reminiscence of my father's pioneer life; I cannot remember that it excited any comment in the neighbors, who were frank with their opinions of everything else we did. But it does not greatly matter; the newspapers hid the walls and the stains with which our old Virginian predecessor, who had the habit of chewing tobacco in bed, had ineffaceably streaked the plastering near the head of his couch.

The cabin, rude as it was, was not without its sophistications, its concessions to the spirit of modern luxury. The logs it was built of had not been left rounded, as they grew, but had been squared in a saw-mill, and the crevices between them had not been chinked with moss and daubed with clay in the true pioneer fashion, but had been neatly plastered with mortar, and the chimney, instead of being a structure of clay-covered sticks, was solidly laid in courses of stone.

Within, however, it was all that could be asked for by the most romantic of pioneer families. It was six feet wide and a yard deep, its cavernous maw would easily swallow a back-log eighteen inches through, and we piled in front the sticks of hickory cord-wood as high as we liked. We made a perfect trial of it when we came out to put the cabin in readiness for the family, and when the hickory had dropped into a mass of tinkling, snapping, bristling embers we laid our rashers of bacon and our slices of steak upon them, and tasted with the appetite of tired youth the flavors of the camp and the wildwood in the captured juices.

I suppose it took a day or two to put the improvements which I have mentioned upon the cabin, but I am not certain. At night we laid our mattresses on the sweet new oak plank of the floor, and slept hard—in every sense. Once I remember waking, and seeing the man who was always the youngest of his boys sitting upright on his bed.

"What are you doing?" I asked.

"Oh, resting!" he answered; and that gave us one of the Heaven-blessed laughs with which we could blow away almost any cloud of care or pain.

In due time the whole family took up its abode in the cabin. The household furniture had been brought out and bestowed in its scanty space, the bookcase had been set up, and the unbound books packed in easily accessible barrels.

There yet remained some of our possessions to follow, chief of which was the cow; for in those simple days people kept cows in town, and it fell to me to help my father drive her out to her future home. We got on famously, talking of the wayside things so beautiful in the beautiful autumnal day, all panoplied in the savage splendor of its painted leaves, and of the poems and histories so dear to the boy who limped barefooted by his father's side, with his eye on the cow and his mind on Cervantes and Shakespeare, on—

"The glory that was Greece,
And the grandeur that was Rome."

But the cow was very slow—far slower than the boy's thoughts—and it had fallen night and was already thick dark when we had made the twelve miles, and stood under the white-limbed phantasmal sycamores beside the tail-race of the grist-mill, and questioned how we should get across with our charge. We did not know how deep the water was, but we knew it was very cold, and we would rather not wade it.

The only thing to do seemed to be for

one of us to run up under those sycamores to the saw-mill, cross the head-race there, and come back to receive the cow on the other side of the tail-race. But the boy could not bring himself either to go or stay. I do not know just how it is with a boy's world now, but at that time it was a very dangerous world. It was full of ghosts, for one thing, and it abounded in Indians on the war-path, and amateurs of kidnapping and murder of all sorts.

The kind-hearted father urged, but he would not compel. You cannot well use force with a boy with whom you have been talking literature and philosophy for half a day. We could see the lights in the cabin cheerfully twinkling, and we shouted to those within, but no one heard us. We called and called in vain. Nothing but the cold rush of the tail-race, the dry rustle of the sycamore leaves, and the homesick lowing of the cow replied.

We determined to drive her across, and pursue her with sticks and stones through the darkness beyond, and then run at the top of our speed to the saw-mill, and get back to take her in custody again. We carried out our part of the plan perfectly, but the cow had apparently not entered into it with intelligence or sympathy.

When we reached the tail-race again she was nowhere to be found, and no appeals of "Boss" or "Suky" or "Subose" availed. She must have instantly turned again, and retraced, in the darkness which seemed to have swallowed her up, the weary steps of the day, for she was found in her old home in town the next morning. At any rate, she had abandoned the father to the conversation of his son, for the time being, and the son had nothing to say.

I do not remember now just how it was that we came by the different "animals of the horse kind," as my father humorously called them, which we housed in an old log-stable not far from our cabin. They must have been a temporary supply until a team worthy our new sky-blue wagon could be found.

One of them was a colossal sorrel, inexorably hide-bound, whose barrel, as I believe the horsemen call the body, showed every hoop upon it. He had a feeble, foolish whim-

per of a voice, and we nicknamed him "Baby." His companion was a dun mare, who had what my father at once called an italic foot, in recognition of the emphatic slant at which she carried it when upon her unwilling travels.

Then there was a small, self-opinionated gray pony, which, I think, came from one of the saw-mill hands, and which was of no service conjecturable after this lapse of time. We boys rode him barebacked, and he used to draw a buggy, which he finally ran away with. I suppose we found him useful in the representation of some of the Indian fights which we were always dramatizing, and I dare say he may have served our turn as an Arab charger, when the Moors of Granada made one of their sallies upon the camp of the Spaniards, and discharged their javelins into it— their javelins were the long, admirably straight and slender ironweeds that grew by the river. This menagerie was constantly breaking bounds and wandering off; and I believe that it was chiefly employed in hunting itself up, its different members taking turns in remaining in the pasture or stable, to be ridden after those that had strayed into the woods.

The origin of a large and eloquent flock of geese is lost in an equal obscurity. I recall their possession simply as an accomplished fact, and I associate their desolate cries with the windy dark of rainy November nights, so that they must at least have come into our hands after the horses. They were fenced into a clayey area next the cabin for safe-keeping, where, perpetually waddling about in a majestic disoccupation, they patted the damp ground down to the hardness and smoothness of a brick yard. Throughout the day they conversed tranquilly together, but by night they woke, goose after goose, to send forth a long clarion alarum, blending in a general concert at last, to assure one another of their safety.

We must have intended to pluck them in the spring, but it never came to that. They stole their nests early in March, and entered upon the nurture of their young before we could prevent it; and it would then have been barbarous to pluck these mothers of families.

Some of their nests we found, notably one under the smoke-house, where the adventurous boy who discovered it was attacked in the dark by its owner and bitten in the nose, to the natural gratification of those who had urged him to the enterprise. But he brought away some of the eggs, and had them fried, and I know nothing that conveys a vivider idea of inexhaustible abundance than a fried goose-egg.

V I

Travelers' Tales

ALONG with its corn and wheat, its barrels of pork, flour, cheese, lard and whiskey, the West produced a surprising crop of books. In the first decades of the nineteenth century the world was hungry for news of the American interior, and scores of journalists, scientists and colonizers traveled west to get the story. They turned out a long shelf of Tours, Travels, Journeys, Rambles, Visits, Sketches, Letters, Notes, Recollections, Diaries and Personal Narratives.

The writers were as various and cosmopolitan as the great migration they reported. There were poets and novelists—Bryant, Irving, Emerson, Melville, Margaret Fuller; scientists—Wilson, Audubon, Michaux, Lyell; titled foreigners— Count Bernhard-Karl and the young Duke of Pourtales; reformers like Morris Birkbeck, Francis Wright and Robert Owen; engineers like Elias Fordham and Michel Chevalier; English and Scottish farmers like Shirreff, Fearon, Faux and Flint. They all added to the literature of the young and yeasty land.

Peak years for the literary travelers were the middle 1830's. In those seasons they turned up almost everywhere on the frontier—Mrs. Trollope acidly etching domestic manners in Cincinnati, one-legged Charles Fenno Hoffman riding horseback on a wolf hunt over the frozen Chicago River, the urbane Kirklands exchanging a New York town house for the wilds of Michigan, Harriet Martineau with her ear trumpet raised to catch the oaths and jests in a crossroads tavern, wiry little Anne Royal in her balloon sleeves and poke bonnet reporting with a sharp pen and a scratchy mind, the caustic Captain Basil Hall and the reckless Captain Marryat writing with the irrelevant assurance of veterans of the British Navy.

In the summer of 1833 travelers were so numerous in the West that two of them jostled, unknown to each other, in the same makeshift stage from Detroit to Chicago. One was an earthy Scot from East Lothian, who signed himself Patrick Shirreff, Farmer; he collected seeds of prairie grass and tested soils with vinegar. The other was Charles Joseph Latrobe, English Alpinist and essayist, who tagged frontier Chicago as "this upstart village." Latrobe had been with Washington Irving on a horseback tour of Indian camps beyond the Mississippi. In Chicago he saw government agents handing out treaty money to the Potawatomis and whiskey pedlars promptly relieving drunken Indians of their bounty.

Besides the traveling writers there were painters on tour in the West. In the

1840's they produced on rolls of canvas two miles long "panoramas" of the Mississippi valley. Four of these mammoth paintings were unrolled for overflow audiences in eastern cities and the capitals of Europe. "The river came to me, instead of my going to the river," wrote Longfellow, who made the vicarious voyage in Boston. One of the panoramas ran for twenty months in London and was seen by half a million people.

All the travelers did not see the same things. Robert Owen beheld in the Wabash valley "a new empire of peace and good will to men," while his countryman Allard Welby, touring Indiana with a manservant in a private carriage, found it brutish, primitive and violent. Putting the travelers' tales together makes a picture wonderfully varied and complete.

CROSSING THE PRAIRIE

JOHN JAMES AUDUBON

John James Audubon, born in Spanish Louisiana and educated in France, wandered for more than forty years over the face of America. From 1812 to 1820 he lived at Henderson, Kentucky, on the Ohio River, and ranged afar on the western frontier. In marsh, prairie and forest he made sketches that developed into his Birds of America. *In the 1830's he published in Edinburgh the five volumes of his* Ornithological Biography, *giving the life history of the species he had so ardently painted. To provide variety in these volumes he interspersed his descriptive ornithology with "episodes" from his own wanderings—one of which is this account of a journey across the southern Illinois prairie in 1812.*

ON my return from the Upper Mississippi I found myself obliged to cross one of the wide prairies which, in that portion of the United States, vary the appearance of the country. The weather was fine; all around me was as fresh and blooming as if it had just issued from the bosom of Nature. My knapsack, my gun, and my dog were all I had for baggage and company. But, although well moccasined, I moved slowly along, attracted by the brilliancy of the flowers, and the gambols of the fawns around their dams, to all appearance as thoughtless of danger as I felt myself.

My march was of long duration; I saw the sun sinking below the horizon long before I could perceive any appearance of woodland, and nothing in the shape of man had I met with that day. The track which I followed was only an old Indian trace, and as darkness overshadowed the prairie I felt some desire to reach at least a copse, in which I might lie down to rest. The Night Hawks were skimming over and around me, attracted by the buzzing wings of the beetles which form their food, and the distant howling of wolves gave me some hope that I should soon arrive at the skirts of some woodlands.

I did so, and almost at the same instant, a firelight attracting my eye, I moved towards it, full of confidence that it proceeded from the camp of some wandering Indians. I was

mistaken: I discovered by its glare that it was from the hearth of a small log cabin, and that a tall figure passed and repassed between it and me, as if busily engaged in household arrangements.

I reached the spot, and presenting myself at the door, asked the tall figure, which proved to be a woman, if I might take shelter under her roof for the night. Her voice was gruff, and her attire negligently thrown about her. She answered in the affirmative. I walked in, took a wooden stool, and quietly seated myself by the fire. The next object that attracted my notice was a finely formed young Indian, resting his head between his hands, with his elbows on his knees. A long bow rested against the log wall near him, while a quantity of arrows and two or three Raccoon skins lay at his feet. He moved not; he apparently breathed not. Accustomed to the habits of Indians, and knowing that they pay little attention to the approach of civilized strangers (a circumstance which is some countries is considered as evincing the apathy of their character), I addressed him in French, a language not infrequently partially known to the people in that neighborhood. He raised his head, pointed to one of his eyes with his finger, and gave me a significant glance with the other. His face was covered with blood. The fact was that an hour before this, as he was in the act of discharging an arrow at a Raccoon in the top of a tree, the arrow had split upon the cord, and sprung back with such violence into his right eye as to destroy it forever.

Feeling hungry, I inquired what sort of fare I might expect. Such a thing as a bed was not to be seen, but many large untanned Bear and Buffalo hides lay piled in a corner. I drew a fine time-piece from my breast, and told the woman that it was late, and that I was fatigued. She had espied my watch, the richness of which seemed to operate upon her feelings with electric quickness. She told me there was plenty of venison and jerked buffalo meat, and that on removing the ashes I should find a cake. But my watch had struck her fancy, and her curiosity had to be gratified by an immediate sight of it. I took off the gold chain that secured it, from around my neck, and presented it to her; she was all ecstasy, spoke of its beauty, asked me its value, and put the chain round her brawny neck, saying how happy the possession of such a watch would make her. Thoughtless, and as I fancied myself in so retired a spot secure, I paid little attention to her talk or her movements. I helped my dog to a good supper of venison, and was not long in satisfying the demands of my own appetite.

The Indian rose from his seat, as if in extreme suffering. He passed and repassed me several times, and once pinched me on the side so violently that the pain nearly brought forth an exclamation of anger. I looked at him. His eye met mine, but his look was so forbidding that it struck a chill into the more nervous part of my system. He again seated himself, drew his butcher-knife from its greasy scabbard, examined its edge, as I would do that of a razor suspected dull, replaced it, and again taking his tomahawk from his back, filled the pipe of it with tobacco, and sent me expressive glances, whenever our hostess chanced to have her back towards us.

Never until that moment had my senses been awakened to the danger which I now suspected to be about me. I returned glance for glance to my companion, and rested well assured that, whatever enemies I might have, he was not of their number.

I asked the woman for my watch, wound it up, and under pretence of wishing to see how the weather might probably be on the morrow, took up my gun, and walked out of the cabin. I slipped a ball into each barrel, scraped the edges of my flints, renewed the primings, and returning to the hut gave a favorable report of my observations. I took a few Bear skins, made a pallet of them, and calling my faithful dog to my side, lay down, with my gun close to my body, and in a few minutes was, to all appearance, fast asleep.

A short time had elapsed when some voices were heard, and from the corner of my eye I saw two athletic youths making their entrance, bearing a dead stag on a pole. They disposed of their burden, and asking for whiskey, helped themselves freely to it. Observing me and the wounded Indian, they asked who I was, and why the devil that rascal (meaning the Indian, who, they knew, understood not a word of English) was in the house. The mother—for so she proved to be—bade them speak less loudly, made mention of my watch, and took them to a corner, where a conversation took place, the purport of which it required little shrewdness in me to guess. I tapped my dog gently. He moved his tail, and with indescribable pleasure I saw his fine eyes alternately fixed on me, and raised towards the trio in the corner. I felt that he perceived danger in my situation. The Indian exchanged a last glance with me.

The lads had eaten and drunk themselves into such a condition that I already looked upon them as *hors de combat;* and the frequent visits of the whiskey bottle to the ugly mouth of their dam, I hoped would soon reduce her to a like state. Judge of my astonishment, reader, when I saw this incarnate fiend take a large carving-knife, and go to the grindstone to whet its edge; I saw her pour the water on the turning machine, and watched her working away with the dangerous instrument, until the cold sweat covered every part of my body, in despite of my determination to defend myself to the last. Her task finished, she walked to her reeling sons, and said: 'There, that'll soon settle him! Boys, kill yon —— ——, and then for the watch.'

I turned, cocked my gun-locks silently, touched my faithful companion, and lay ready to start up and shoot the first who might attempt my life. The moment was fast approaching, and that night might have been my last in this world, had not Providence made preparations for my rescue. All was ready. The infernal hag was advancing slowly, probably contemplating the best way of despatching me, whilst her sons should be engaged with the Indian. I was several times on the eve of rising and shooting her on the spot; but she was not to be punished thus. The door was suddenly opened, and there entered two stout travellers, each with a long rifle on his shoulder. I bounced up on my feet, and making them most heartily welcome, told them how well it was for me that they should have arrived at that moment. The tale was told in a minute. The drunken sons were secured, and the woman, in spite of her defence and vociferations, shared the same fate. The Indian fairly danced with joy, and gave us to understand that, as he could not sleep for pain, he would watch over us. You may suppose we slept much less than we talked. The two strangers gave me an account of their once having been themselves in a somewhat similar situation. Day came, fair and rosy, and with it the punishment of our captives.

They were now quite sobered. Their feet were unbound, but their arms were still securely tied. We marched them into the woods off the road, and having used them as Regulators were wont to use such delinquents, we set fire to the cabin, gave all the skins and implements to the young Indian warrior, and proceeded, well pleased, towards the settlements.

During upwards of twenty-five years, when my wanderings extended to all parts of our country, this was the only time at which my life was in danger from my fellow-creatures. Indeed, so little risk do travellers run in the United States that no one born there ever dreams of any to be encountered on the road; and I can only account for this occurrence by supposing that the inhabitants of the cabin were not Americans.

Will you believe, good-natured reader, that not many miles from the place where this adventure happened, and where fifteen years ago, no habitation belonging to civilized man was expected, and very few ever seen, large roads are now laid out, cultivation has converted the woods into fertile fields, taverns have been erected, and much of what we Americans call comfort is to be met with? So fast does improvement proceed in our abundant and free country.

EMIGRANTS IN EDEN

CHARLES DICKENS

Of the many English travelers to the American frontier the most celebrated was Charles Dickens, who passed his thirtieth birthday in the United States. After being feted in the eastern cities he voyaged down the Ohio and up the Mississippi, and he crossed Ohio, from Cincinnati to Sandusky, in a "shake-guts" stage. His American Notes, *which appeared at the end of that year, 1842, charged Americans with crassness and crudeness, but his real diatribe on the frontier was reserved for the sorry tale of* Martin Chuzzlewit.

Dickens had traveled the water routes that brought multitudes to the frontier. He saw bustling settlements and empty townsites; he talked with speculators, land jobbers and eager emigrants. Back in London, in his cheerful study on Devonshire Terrace, he wrote the wry story of Martin Chuzzlewit and his friend Mark Tapley who planned to set up as architects and surveyors on the luring frontier. They chose the town of Eden, the dismal picture of which Dickens drew from his sketchy memory of Cairo, Illinois, at the meeting of the Ohio and the Mississippi.

The following excerpt finds the two Englishmen en route to Eden on an Ohio River steamboat.

AT first they parted with some of their passengers once or twice a day, and took in others to replace them. But by degrees, the towns upon their route became more thinly scattered; and for many hours together they would see no other habitations than the huts of the wood-cutters, where the vessel stopped for fuel. Sky, wood, and water, all the live-long day; and heat that blistered everything it touched.

On they toiled through great solitudes, where the trees upon the banks grew thick and close; and floated in the stream; and held up shrivelled arms from out the river's depths; and slid down from the margin of the land, half growing, half decaying, in the miry water. On through the weary day and melancholy night: beneath the burning sun, and in the mist and vapour of the evening: on, until return appeared impossible, and restoration to their home a miserable dream.

They had now but few people on board, and these few were as flat, as dull, and stagnant, as the vegetation that oppressed their eyes. No sound of cheerfulness or hope was heard; no pleasant talk beguiled the tardy time; no little group made common cause against the dull depression of the scene. But that, at certain periods, they swallowed food together from a common trough, it might have been old Charon's boat, conveying melancholy shades to judgment.

At length they drew near New Thermopylæ; where, that same evening, Mrs. Hominy would disembark. A gleam of comfort sunk into Martin's bosom when she told him this. Mark needed none; but he was not displeased.

It was almost night when they came alongside the landing-place. A steep bank with an hotel, like a barn, on the top of it; a wooden store or two, and a few scattered sheds.

"You sleep here to-night, and go on in the morning, I suppose, ma'am?" said Martin.

"Where should I go on to?" cried the Mother of the Modern Gracchi.

"To New Thermopylæ."

"My! ain't I there?" said Mrs. Hominy.

Martin looked for it all round the darkening panorama; but he couldn't see it, and was obliged to say so.

"Why that's it!" cried Mrs. Hominy, pointing to the sheds just mentioned.

"*That!*" exclaimed Martin.

"Ah! that; and work it which way you will, it whips Eden," said Mrs. Hominy, nodding her head with great expression.

The married Miss Hominy, who had come on board with her husband, gave to this statement her most unqualified support, as did that gentleman also. Martin gratefully declined their invitation to regale himself at their house during the half-hour of the vessel's stay; and having escorted Mrs. Hominy and the red pocket-handkerchief (which was still on active service) safely across the gangway, returned in a thoughtful mood to watch the emigrants as they removed their goods ashore.

Mark, as he stood beside him, glanced in his face from time to time; anxious to discover what effect this dialogue had had upon him, and not unwilling that his hopes should be dashed before they reached their destination, so that the blow he feared, might be broken in its fall. But saving that he sometimes looked up quickly at the poor erections on the hill, he gave him no clue to what was passing in his mind, until they were again upon their way.

"Mark," he said then, "are there really none but ourselves on board this boat who are bound for Eden?"

"None at all, sir. Most of 'em, as you know, have stopped short; and the few that are left are going further on. What matters that? More room there for us, sir."

"Oh, to be sure!" said Martin. "But I was thinking——" And there he paused.

"Yes, sir?" observed Mark.

"How odd it was that the people should

From *Martin Chuzzlewit*: "The thriving city of Eden, as it appeared in fact."

have arranged to try their fortune at a wretched hole like that, for instance, when there is such a much better, and such a very different kind of place, near at hand, as one may say."

He spoke in a tone so very different from his usual confidence, and with such an obvious dread of Mark's reply, that the good-natured fellow was full of pity.

"Why, you know, sir," said Mark, as gently as he could by any means insinuate the observation, "we must guard against being too sanguine. There's no occasion for it, either, because we're determined to make the best of everything, after we know the worst of it. Ain't we, sir?"

Martin looked at him, but answered not a word.

"Even Eden, you know, ain't all built," said Mark.

"In the name of Heaven, man," cried Martin angrily, "don't talk of Eden in the same breath with that place. Are you mad? There—God forgive me!—don't think harshly of me for my temper!"

After that, he turned away, and walked to and fro upon the deck full two hours. Nor did he speak again, except to say "Goodnight," until next day; nor even then upon this subject, but on other topics quite foreign to the purpose.

As they proceeded further on their track, and came more and more towards their journey's end, the monotonous desolation of the scene increased to that degree, that for any redeeming feature it presented to their eyes, they might have entered, in the body, on the grim domains of Giant Despair. A flat morass, bestrewn with fallen timber; a marsh on which the good growth of the earth seemed to have been wrecked and cast away, that from its decomposing ashes vile and ugly things might rise; where the very trees took the aspect of huge weeds, begotten of the slime from which they sprung, by the hot sun that burnt them up; where fatal maladies, seeking whom they might infect, came forth at night, in misty shapes, and creeping out upon the water, hunted them like spectres until day; where even the blessed sun, shining down on festering elements of corruption and disease, became a horror; this was the realm of Hope through which they moved.

At last they stopped. At Eden too. The waters of the Deluge might have left it but a week before: so choked with slime and matted growth was the hideous swamp which bore that name.

There being no depth of water close in shore, they landed from the vessel's boat, with all their goods beside them. There were a few log-houses visible among the dark trees: the best, a cow-shed or a rude stable. But for the wharves, the market-place, the public buildings!

"Here comes an Edener," said Mark. "He'll get us help to carry these things up. Keep a good heart, sir. Hallo there!"

The man advanced toward them through the thickening gloom, very slowly: leaning on a stick. As he drew nearer, they observed that he was pale and worn, and that his anxious eyes were deeply sunken in his head. His dress of homespun blue hung about him in rags; his feet and head were bare. He sat down on a stump half-way, and beckoned them to come to him. When they complied, he put his hand upon his side as if in pain, and while he fetched his breath stared at them, wondering.

"Strangers!" he exclaimed, as soon as he could speak.

"The very same," said Mark. "How are you, sir?"

"I've had the fever very bad," he answered faintly. "I haven't stood upright these many weeks. Those are your notions I see," pointing to their property.

"Yes, sir," said Mark, "they are. You couldn't recommend us some one as would lend a hand to help carry 'em up to the—to the town, could you, sir?"

"My eldest son would do it if he could," replied the man; "but today he has his chill upon him and is lying wrapped up in the blankets. My youngest died last week."

"I'm sorry for it, governor, with all my heart," said Mark, shaking him by the hand. "Don't mind us. Come along with me, and I'll give you an arm back. The goods is safe enough, sir:" to Martin: "there ain't many people about, to make away with 'em. What a comfort that is!"

"No," cried the man. "You must look for such folk here," knocking his stick upon the ground, "or yonder in the bush, towards the north. We've buried most of 'em. The rest have gone away. Them that we have here, don't come out at night."

"The night air ain't quite wholesome, I suppose?" said Mark.

"It's deadly poison," was the settler's answer.

Mark showed no more uneasiness than if it had been commended to him as ambrosia; but he gave the man his arm, and as they went along explained to him the nature of their purchase, and inquired where it lay. Close to his own log-house, he said: so close that he had used their dwelling as a storehouse for some corn: they must excuse it that night, but he would endeavour to get it taken out upon the morrow. He then gave them to understand, as an additional scrap of local chit-chat, that he had buried the last proprietor with his own hands; a piece of information which Mark also received without the least abatement of his equanimity.

In a word, he conducted them to a miserable cabin, rudely constructed of the trunks of trees; the door of which had either fallen down or been carried away long ago; and which was consequently open to the wild landscape and the dark night. Saving for the little store he had mentioned, it was perfectly bare of all furniture; but they had left a chest upon the landing-place, and he gave them a rude torch in lieu of candle. This latter acquisition Mark planted in the earth, and then declaring the mansion "looked quite comfortable," hurried Martin off again to help bring up the chest. And all the way to the landing-place and back, Mark talked incessantly: as if he would infuse into his partner's breast some faint belief that they had arrived under the most auspicious and cheerful of all imaginable circumstances.

But many a man who would have stood within a home dismantled, strong in his passion and design of vengeance, has had the firmness of his nature conquered by the razing of an air-built castle. When the log-hut received them for the second time, Martin lay down upon the ground, and wept aloud.

"Lord love you, sir!" cried Mr. Tapley, in great terror; "Don't do that! Don't do that, sir! Anything but that! It never helped man, woman, or child, over the lowest fence yet, sir, and it never will. Besides its being of no use to you, it's worse than of no use to me, for the least sound of it will knock me flat down. I can't stand up agin it, sir. Anything but that!"

There is no doubt he spoke the truth, for the extraordinary alarm with which he looked at Martin as he paused upon his knees before the chest, in the act of unlocking it, to say these words, sufficiently confirmed him.

"I ask your forgiveness a thousand times, my dear fellow," said Martin. "I couldn't have helped it, if death had been the penalty."

"Ask my forgiveness!" said Mark, with his accustomed cheerfulness, as he proceeded to unpack the chest. "The head partner a asking forgiveness of Co., eh? There must be something wrong in the firm when that happens. I must have the books inspected, and the accounts gone over immediate. Here we are. Everything in its proper place. Here's the salt pork. Here's the biscuit. Here's the whiskey. Uncommon good it smells too. Here's the tin pot. This tin pot's a small fortun' in itself! Here's the blankets. Here's the axe. Who says we ain't got a first-rate fit out? I feel as if I was a cadet gone out to Indy, and my noble father was chairman of the Board of Directors. Now, when I've got some water from the stream afore the door and mixed the grog," cried Mark, running out to suit the action to the word, "there's a supper ready, comprising every delicacy of the season. Here we are, sir, all complete. For what we are going to receive, et cetrer. Lord bless you, sir, it's very like a gipsy party!"

It was impossible not to take heart, in the company of such a man as this. Martin sat upon the ground beside the box; took out his knife; and ate and drank sturdily.

"Now you see," said Mark, when they had made a hearty meal; "with your knife and mine, I sticks this blanket right afore the door, or where, in a state of high civilisation, the door would be. And very neat it looks. Then I stops the aperture below, by putting the chest agin it. And very neat *that* looks. Then there's your blanket, sir. Then here's mine. And what's to hinder our passing a good night?"

For all his light-hearted speaking, it was long before he slept himself. He wrapped his blanket round him, put the axe ready to his hand, and lay across the threshold of the door: too anxious and too watchful to close his eyes. The novelty of their dreary situation, the dread of some rapacious animal or human enemy, the terrible uncertainty of their means of subsistence, the apprehension of death, the immense distance and the hosts of obstacles between themselves and England, were fruitful sources of disquiet in the deep silence of the night. Though Martin would have had him think otherwise, Mark felt that he was waking also, and a prey to the same reflections.

This was almost worse than all, for if he began to brood over their miseries instead of trying to make head against them, there could be little doubt that such a state of mind would powerfully assist the influence of the pestilent climate. Never had the light of day been half so welcome to his eyes, as when awaking from a fitful doze, Mark saw it shining through the blanket in the doorway.

He stole out gently, for his companion was sleeping now; and having refreshed himself by washing in the river, where it flowed before the door, took a rough survey of the settlement. There were not above a score of cabins in the whole; half of these appeared untenanted; all were rotten and decayed. The most tottering, abject, and forlorn among them, was called, with great propriety, the Bank, and National Credit Office. It had some feeble props about it, but was settling deep down in the mud, past all recovery.

Here and there, an effort had been made to clear the land, and something like a field had been marked out, where, among the stumps and ashes of burnt trees, a scanty crop of Indian corn was growing. In some quarters, a snake or zigzag fence had been begun, but in no instance had it been completed; and the fallen logs, half hidden in the soil, lay mouldering away. Three or four meagre dogs, wasted and vexed with hunger; some long-legged pigs, wandering away into the woods in search of food; some children, nearly naked, gazing at him from the huts; were all the living things he saw. A fetid vapour, hot and sickening as the breath of an oven, rose up from the earth, and hung on everything around; and as his foot-prints sunk into the marshy ground, a black ooze started forth to blot them out.

Their own land was mere forest. The trees had grown so thick and close that they shouldered one another out of their places, and the weakest, forced into shapes of strange distortion, languished like cripples. The best were stunted, from the pressure and the want of room; and high about the stems of all, grew long rank grass, dank weeds, and frowzy underwood; not divisible into their separate kinds, but tangled all together in a heap; a jungle deep and dark, with neither earth nor water at its roots, but putrid mat-

ter, formed of the pulpy offal of the two, and of their own corruption.

He went down to the landing-place where they had left their goods last night; and there he found some half-dozen men—wan and forlorn to look at, but ready enough to assist—who helped him to carry them to the log-house. They shook their heads in speaking of the settlement, and had no comfort to give him. Those who had the means of going away, had all deserted it. They who were left, had lost their wives, their children, friends, or brothers there, and suffered much themselves. Most of them were ill then; none were the men they had been once. They frankly offered their assistance and advice, and, leaving him for that time, went sadly off upon their several tasks.

Martin was by this time stirring; but he had greatly changed, even in one night. He was very pale and languid; he spoke of pains and weakness in his limbs, and complained that his sight was dim, and his voice feeble. Increasing in his own briskness as the prospect grew more and more dismal, Mark brought away a door from one of the deserted houses, and fitted it to their own habitation; then went back again for a rude bench he had observed, with which he presently returned in triumph; and having put this piece of furniture outside the house, arranged the notable tin pot and other such moveables upon it, that it might represent a dresser or sideboard. Greatly satisfied with this arrangement, he next rolled their cask of flour into the house, and set it up on end in one corner, where it served for a side-table. No better dining-table could be required than the chest, which he solemnly devoted to that useful service thenceforth. Their blankets, clothes, and the like, he hung on pegs and nails. And lastly, he brought forth a great placard (which Martin in the exultation of his heart had prepared with his own hands at the National Hotel), bearing the inscription, CHUZZLEWIT & CO., ARCHITECTS AND SURVEYORS, which he displayed upon the most conspicuous part of the premises, with as much gravity as if the thriving city of Eden had a real existence, and they expected to be overwhelmed with business.

"These here tools," said Mark, bringing

forward Martin's case of instruments and sticking the compasses upright in a stump before the door, "shall be set out in the open air to show that we come provided. And now, if any gentleman wants a house built, he'd better give his orders, afore we're other ways bespoke."

Considering the intense heat of the weather, this was not a bad morning's work; but without pausing for a moment, though he was streaming at every pore, Mark vanished into the house again, and presently reappeared with a hatchet: intent on performing some impossibilities with that implement.

"Here's a ugly old tree in the way, sir," he observed, "which'll be all the better down. We can build the oven in the afternoon. There never was such a handy spot for clay as Eden is. That's convenient, anyhow."

But Martin gave him no answer. He had sat the whole time with his head upon his hands, gazing at the current as it rolled swiftly by; thinking, perhaps, how fast it moved towards the open sea, the high road to the home he would never behold again.

A GRAND DUKE VISITS UTOPIA

BERNHARD-KARL, DUKE OF SAXE-WEIMAR EISENACH

When the socialistic community of New Harmony was established on the Wabash, it attracted colonists in frock coats and peasant blouses, in stovepipe hats and coonskin caps. Squatters, scholars and reformers, debt-ridden farmers and ragged schoolmasters, they came from every state in the Union and from all the countries of northern Europe. While this polyglot colony was building Utopia in the wilderness, visitors arrived from near and far, curious to see the rational system of society which Robert Owen had launched.

Among the visitors was a German nobleman. From his early years Bernhard-Karl, Duke of Saxe-Weimar Eisenach, had wanted to visit America, to see the country and the people, their condition and institutions, their customs and manners. At last in 1825 he crossed the Atlantic, and in the spring of 1826 he toured the Ohio valley.

One of the shrewdest chapters in his Travels Through North America 1825–6 *recounts the week he spent in New Harmony, when he happened upon Robert Owen himself and became his guest. Besides New Harmony the Grand Duke visited two outlying communities—Number Two, peopled by backwoods families who remembered the frenzy of the camp meetings and were unwilling to give up religion; and Number Three, a colony of English farmers who liked Owen's socialism but objected to the motley cosmopolitanism of his town. He also visited a German hermit who lived on an Indian mound eight miles from the village, shaking his head over Owen's godless community. When he departed, Count Bernhard-Karl had his own doubts about Utopia.*

ON the following morning, 15th of April, we hired a two-horse wagon, to carry us to the village of New Harmony, which is sixteen miles distant from Mount Vernon, and lies on the left shore of the Wabash. The road passed through a hilly country, thickly grown with green-leaved trees. The way was made very bad by former rains, and the most miry places were mended with logs, forming a grievous causeway; over a little stream, called Big creek, we crossed a tolerable wooden bridge. About half way is Springfield, at first made the capital of Posey county, which, however, afterwards was changed to Mount Vernon, as I have mentioned before. In Springfield the county gaol still remains, also a brick court-house, and about ten wooden houses, two of them are taverns. As the road was very bad, and the horses went very slow, I walked at least ten miles, and arrived at New Harmony, before the carriage. As soon as you clear the woods, you have a very handsome view of the place. It lies in a valley, not far from the Wabash. The woody and low banks of this river, were at present, in the neighbourhood of New Harmony, overflowed. From the roots of trees still remaining, it was visible, that this country had been covered with wood but a short time back.

In fact, it is but eleven years since Mr. Rapp with his society, after they had disposed of Harmony in Pennsylvania, moved here, and felled the first tree to found New Harmony in a country inhabited only by wolves, Indians, bears, rattlesnakes, &c. The hills immediately next to the place, are already cleared of timber of the larger kind; they are converted into vineyards, and partly into orchards. Farther off are meadows and fields to the right, and to the left fruit and vegetable gardens, carefully enclosed by palisades. New Harmony itself, has broad unpaved streets, in which good brick houses appear alternately, with framed cabins and log houses: the streets are regular, running at right angles. We took up our quarters in the only tavern there, belonging to the community; it was passable.

Rapp's society, called from their former residence, the Harmonites, consisted of Wurtemburgers. Their early history is known, and perhaps, when I visit this society from Pittsburgh in their new establishment, "Economy," I may find an opportunity to say more concerning them. Rapp sold New Harmony in the year 1825, to the Englishman, Robert Owen, and left there with his people on the 5th of May, to go up the Ohio to Economy. Mr. Owen was originally engaged in manufactures, and possessed a large cotton factory at New Lanark, on the Falls of Clyde, ten miles from Glasgow in Scotland, where he had, by the

adoption of a new system of education and formation of character, changed a collection of one thousand rude labourers into a community of industrious beings. His system, and his ideas upon the situation of human society, as well as the improvements that are capable of being made, he has divulged in a series of essays, which are collected, and appear in print under the name of a new view of society. They conclude with the project of a constitution for a community formed on his system.

Mr. Owen is an enemy to all sects, the spirit of which has generated so much evil under the imposing name of religion. He allows each person liberty to believe in what he may consider to be good; so that a pure Deism is the peculiar religion of his adherents. On this account he was very obnoxious to the prevailing sects in Great Britain, and accordingly his system could not extend itself there. He was therefore induced to turn his attention to the United States, and particularly to the western part of the Union, where, as he says, there is less hypocrisy of religion prevailing than to the east. He then purchased New Harmony from Mr. Rapp, and commenced his establishment in the month of May last. As he laid the foundation of it entirely on perfect equality and community of property, many enthusiasts in these principles from various parts of the Union joined themselves to him; and also a number of vagabonds and lazy worthless persons, from all parts of the world, that would willingly live well at the public expense, who had drank away the little money, if they brought any at all, at the tavern, and who would not work, but desired to say a great deal. Mr. Owen had gone to England on account of business in the month of July, and during his absence, a complete anarchy had been introduced into the new community. At the end of October he arrived from England at New York on his return, gave lectures there, in Philadelphia, and in Washington, upon his system, made some proselytes in Philadelphia, and came back to New Harmony. He lamented over his people, and brought the situation of anarchy in which they had fallen before their eyes so plainly, with the consequences resulting therefrom, that they invested him with

New Harmony, Indiana, c. 1820. *Courtesy Indiana Historical Society Library*

dictatorial authority for one year.

In the eastern states there is a general dislike to him. It was thought unadvised that he issued a proclamation to the Americans on his last arrival in New York, in which he told them, that among many virtues they possessed great faults, among which he alluded to an ill-directed propensity to religious feelings, and proposed himself as their reformer in this respect. I heard at that time unfavourable expressions from persons in the highest public offices against him; and one of them gave Mr. Owen to understand very

plainly, that he considered his intellects rather deranged. In one family alone, where theory took place of experimental knowledge, did I hear conversation turn to his advantage.

After all this, I came with the utmost expectation to New Harmony, curious to become acquainted with a man of such extraordinary sentiments. In the tavern, I accosted a man very plainly dressed, about fifty years of age, rather of low stature, who entered into a conversation with me, concerning the situation of the place, and the disordered state in which I would find every thing, where all was newly established, &c. When I asked this man how long before Mr. Owen would be there, he announced himself, to my no small surprize, as Mr. Owen, was glad at my visit, and offered himself to show every thing, and explain to me whatever remained without explanation. As the arrangement calculated for Rapp's society was not adapted to his, of course many alterations would naturally be made. All the log houses still standing in the place, he intended to remove, and only brick and framed edifices should be permitted to remain. Also all enclosures about particular gardens, as well as all the enclosures within the place itself, he would take away, and only allow the public highways leading through the settlement to be enclosed. The whole should bear a resemblance to a park, in which the separate houses should be scattered about.

In the first place, Mr. Owen carried me to the quondam church of Rapp's society; a simple wooden building, with a steeple of the same materials, provided with a clock. This church was at present appropriated to joiner's and shoemaker's shops, in which the boys are instructed in these mechanic arts.

Behind the church stands a large brick edifice, built in the form of a cross, and furnished with a species of cupola, the purpose of which is unknown. Rapp, they say, had dreamed three times that this building should be erected, and therefore he had it done; but it is thought, and I believe correctly, that he only did this to keep his society in constant employment, so that they could have no leisure to reflect upon their situation, and dependence upon him. His power over them actually extended so far, that to prevent his society from too great an increase, he forbid the husbands from associating with their wives. I also heard here a report which I had already been apprised of in Germany, that he had himself castrated a son who had transgressed this law, for the sake of example, and that the son had died under the operation. Over one of the entrances of this problematical edifice, stands the date of the year 1822, hewed in stone; under it is a gilt rose, and under this is placed the inscription Micah 4. v. 8. The interior of the house forms a large

hall, in form of a cross, the ceiling is supported by wooden pillars. Mr. Owen has devoted the hall to the purposes of dancing, music, and meetings for philosophical discussions. He told me that he intended to have the ends of the cross, both of the grand saloon as well as those of the hall under the roof, divided off by partitions, so as to use them for school-rooms, for a library, for a cabinet of natural history, of physical objects, &c.

Mr. Owen then conducted me to Rapp's former dwelling, a large, well-built brick house, with two lightning rods. The man of God, it appeared, took especial good care of himself; his house was by far the best in the place, surrounded by a garden, with a flight of stone steps, and the only one furnished with lightning rods. Mr. Owen, on the contrary, contented himself with a small apartment in the same tavern where I lodged. At present, the offices, and the residence of Mr. M'Clure, the associate of Mr. Owen, are in Rapp's house.

Mr. M'Clure is a man distinguished for learning, who has published a geological chart of the United States. He told me that he was in Germany in the year 1802, and also at Weimar, where he had become acquainted with the literati residing there. I was introduced by him to a native of Alsace, of the name of Neef, a rather aged man, who had the superintendence of the boys. Mr. Owen's two eldest sons were also here shown to me, pupils of Fellenberg, who is greatly respected. Afterwards Mr. Owen made me acquainted with Mr. Lewis, secretary of the society, from Virginia, and a relation of the great Washington. He was already pretty far advanced in years, and appeared to have united himself to the society from liberal principles, as far as I could judge from our short conversation. Another acquaintance that I made, was with a Mr. Jennings, from Philadelphia, a young man, who was educated as a clergyman, but had quitted that profession to follow this course of life, and had united himself to Mr. Owen. He intended, nevertheless, to leave this place again, and return back to Philadelphia. Many other members have the same design, and I can hardly believe that this society will have a long duration. Enthusiasm, which abandons its subjects but too soon, as well as the itch for novelty, had contributed much to the formation of this society. In spite of the principles of equality which they recognise, it shocks the feelings of people of education, to live on the same footing with every one indiscriminately, and eat with them at the same table.

The society consisted, as I was informed, of about one thousand members; at a distance of two miles are founded two new communities. Till a general table shall be instituted, according to the fundamental constitution of the society, the members are placed in four boarding-houses, where they must live very frugally. Several of the most turbulent, with an Irishman who wore a long beard, at their head, wished to leave the society immediately to go to Mexico, there to settle themselves, but where their subsistence will be procured with as much difficulty.

In the evening Mr. Owen conducted me to a concert in the non-descript building. Most of the members of the society were present. The orchestra was not numerous, it consisted at first only of one violin, one violoncello, one clarionet and two flutes. Nevertheless the concert was surprisingly good, especially as the musicians have not been together a year. The clarionet player performed particularly well, and afterwards let us hear him on the bugle. Several good male and female vocalists then took a part, they sang among other things a trio accompanied by the clarionet only. Declamation was interspersed among the musical performances, Lord Byron's stanzas to his wife after their separation were extremely well recited. Between the two parts of the concert the music played a march, each gentleman gave a lady his arm, and a promenade took place, resembling a Polonaise with pretty figures, sometimes in two couples, sometimes in four; two ladies in the middle, the gentlemen separated from the ladies, then again all together. The concert closed with a lively cotillion. I was, on the whole, much amused; and Mr. Huygens took an active share in the dancing. This general evening amusement takes place often in the week; besides, on Tuesday, there is a general ball. There is a particular costume adopted for the society. That for the men consists of wide pantaloons buttoned over a boy's jacket, made of light material, without a collar; that of the women of a coat reaching to the knee and pantaloons, such as little girls wear among us. These dresses are not universally adopted, but they have a good appearance. An elderly French lady, who presides over the department of young mothers, and the nursing of all the very small children, stuck by my side during a large portion of the evening, and tormented me with her philosophical views. All the men did not take a share in the dance, i. e. the lower class, but read newspapers, which were scattered over the side-tables.

The public house in which we lived was conducted on account of the society. General Evans was looked for, who was to keep the house; in the mean time it was directed by the physician of the society, Dr. M'Namee, from Vincennes. Among the public buildings I remarked two of which the lower part was strongly built with rough stone, and provided with loopholes. The larger of these was the granary, and it was reasonably thought that Rapp had built this as a defensive redoubt for his own people. At the first period of his establishment in this country he not only had the Indians, but also the rude people known under the general title of backwoodsmen, who not only saw the establishment of such a society with jealous eyes, which they knew would be wealthy in a short time, but also entertained a grudge against Rapp's unnatural rules of chastity.

On the morning of the 14th of April, I strolled about the place to look round me. I visited Mr. Neef, but found his wife only at home, a native of Memmingen, in Swabia. Her husband was in the act of leading the boys out to labour. Military exercises form a part of the instruction of the children. I saw the boys divided into two ranks, and parted into detachments marching to labour, and on the way they performed various wheelings and evolutions. All the boys and girls have a very healthy look, are cheerful and lively, and by no means bashful. The boys labour in the field and garden, and were now occupied with new fencing. The girls learn female employments; they were as little oppressed as the boys with labour and teaching; these happy and interesting children were much more employed in making their youth pass as pleasantly as possible. Madam Neef showed the school-house, in which she dwelt, and in which the places for sleeping were arranged for the boys. Each boy slept on a cot frame, upon a straw bed.

We went next to Rapp's distillery: it will be removed altogether. Mr. Owen has forbidden distilling also, as well as the use of ardent spirits. Notwithstanding this, the Irishmen here find opportunities of getting whiskey and fuddling themselves from the flat boats that stop here, &c. We saw also a dye-house and a mill set in motion by a steam-engine of ten horse-power. The engine was old and not in good order, Mr. Owen said however, he hoped to introduce steam-mills here in time from England. From the mills we went to the vineyard, which was enclosed and kept in very good order. I spoke to an old French vine-dresser here. He assured me that Rapp's people had not understood the art of making wine; that he would in time make more and much better wine, than had been done heretofore. The wine stocks are imported from the Cape of Good Hope, and the wine has an entirely singular and strange taste, which reminds one of the common Spanish wines.

We went again to the quondam church, or workshop for the boys, who are intended for joiners and shoemakers. These boys sleep upon the floor above the church in cribs, three in a row, and thus have their sleeping place and place of instruction close together. We also saw the shops of the shoemakers, tailors and saddlers, also the smiths, of which six were under one roof, and the pottery, in which were two rather large furnaces. A porcelain earth has been discovered on the banks of the Mississippi, in the state of Illinois, not far from St. Louis. Two experienced members of the society, went in that direction, to bring some of the earth to try experiments with, in burning. The greater part of the young girls, whom we chanced to meet at home, we found employed in plaiting straw

hats. I became acquainted with a Madam F——, a native of St. Petersburg. She married an American merchant, settled there, and had the misfortune to lose her husband three days after marriage. She then joined her husband's family in Philadelphia, and as she was somewhat eccentric and sentimental, quickly became enthusiastically attached to Mr. Owen's system. She told me, however, in German, that she found herself egregiously deceived; that the highly vaunted equality was not altogether to her taste; that some of the society were too low, and the table was below all criticism. The good lady appeared to be about to run from one extreme to the other; for she added, that in the summer, she would enter a Shaker establishment near Vincennes.

I renewed acquaintance here with Mr. Say, a distinguished naturalist from Philadelphia, whom I had been introduced to, at the Wistar Party there; unfortunately he had found himself embarrassed in his fortune, and was obliged to come here as a friend of Mr. M'Clure. This gentleman appeared quite comical in the costume of the society, before described, with his hands full of hard lumps and blisters, occasioned by the unusual labour he was obliged to undertake in the garden.

In the evening I went to walk in the streets, and met with several of the ladies of the society, who rested from the labours of the day. Madam F—— was among them, whose complaints of disappointed expectations I had listened to. I feared still more from all that I saw and heard, that the society would have but a brief existence. I accompanied the ladies to a dancing assembly, which was held in the kitchen of one of the boarding-houses. I observed that this was only an hour of instruction to the unpractised in dancing, and that there was some restraint on account of my presence, from politeness I went away, and remained at home the remainder of the evening. About ten o'clock, an alarm of fire was suddenly raised. An old log building used as a wash-house was in flames, immediately the fire-engine kept in a distinct house, was brought and served by persons appointed to that duty. They threw the stream of water through the many apertures of the log-house, and quickly put a stop to the fire. In a quarter of an hour, all was over. Since the houses in the place all stand separately, there is nothing to fear from the extension of fire, unless in a strong wind. The houses, however, are all covered with shingles.

On the 15th of April, I went into the garden back of Rapp's house to see a plate or block of stone, which is remarkable as it bears the impression of two human feet. This piece of stone was hewed out of a rock near St. Louis, and sold to Mr. Rapp. Schoolcraft speaks of it in his travels, and I insert his remarks, as I have found them correct. "The impressions are to all appearance those of a man standing upright, the left foot a little forwards, the heels turned inwards. The distance between the heels by an exact measurement was six and a quarter inches, and thirteen and a half between the extremities of the great toes. By an accurate examination, it however will be ascertained, that they are not the impression of feet, accustomed to the use of European shoes, for the toes are pressed out, and the foot is flat, as is observed in persons who walk barefoot. The probability that they were caused by the pressure of an individual, that belonged to an unknown race of men, ignorant of the art of tanning hides, and that this took place in a much earlier age than the traditions of the present Indians extend to, this probability I say, is strengthened by the extraordinary size of the feet here given. In another respect, the impressions are strikingly natural, since the muscles of the feet are represented with the greatest exactness and truth. This circumstance weakens very much the hypothesis, that they are possibly evidences of the ancient sculpture of a race of men living in the remote ages of this continent. Neither history nor tradition, gives us the slightest information of such a people. For it must be kept in mind, that we have no proof that the people who erected our surprising western tumuli, ever had a knowledge of masonry, even much less of sculpture, or that they had invented the chisel, the knife, or the axe, those excepted made from porphyry, hornstone or obsidian. The medium length of the human male foot can be taken at ten

inches. The length of the foot stamp here described, amounts to ten and a quarter inches, the breadth measured over the toes, in a right angle with the first line is four inches, but the greatest spread of the toes is four and a half inches, which breadth diminishes at the heels to two and a half inches. Directly before these impressions is a well inserted and deep mark, similar to a scroll of which the greatest length is two feet seven inches, and the greatest breadth twelve and a half inches. The rock which contains these interesting traces, is a compact limestone of a bluish-gray colour."

This rock with the unknown impressions are remembered as long as the country about St. Louis has been known, this table is hewn out of a rock, and indeed out of a perpendicular wall of rock.

The garden of Rapp's house was the usual flower-garden of a rich German farmer. In it was a green-house, in which several large fig trees, an orange, and lemon tree stood in the earth. Mr. Owen took me into one of the newly-built houses, in which the married members of the society are to dwell. It consisted of two stories, in each two chambers and two alcoves, with the requisite ventilators. The cellar of the house is to contain a heating apparatus, to heat the whole with warm air. When all shall be thoroughly organized, the members will alternately have the charge of heating the apparatus. Each family will have a chamber and an alcove, which will be sufficient, as the little children will be in a nursery, and the larger at school. They will not require kitchens, as all are to eat in common. The unmarried women will live together, as will also the unmarried men, in the manner of the Moravian brethren.

I had an ample conversation with Mr. Owen, relating to his system, and his expectations. He looks forward to nothing less than to remodel the world entirely; to root out all crime; to abolish all punishments; to create similar views and similar wants, and in this manner to avoid all dissension and warfare. When his system of education shall be brought into connection with the great progress made by mechanics, and which is daily increasing, every man can then, as he thought, provide his smaller necessaries for himself, and trade would cease entirely! I expressed a doubt of the practicability of his system in Europe, and even in the United States. He was too unalterably convinced of the results, to admit the slightest room for doubt. It grieved me to see that Mr. Owen should allow himself to be so infatuated by his passion for universal improvement, as to believe and to say that he is about to reform the whole world; and yet that almost every member of his society, with whom I have conversed apart, acknowledged that he was deceived in his expectations, and expressed their opinion that Mr. Owen had commenced on too grand a scale, and had admitted too many members, without the requisite selection! The territory of the society may contain twenty five thousand acres. The sum of one hundred and twenty thousand dollars was paid to Rapp for this purchase, and for that consideration he also left both his cattle, and a considerable flock of sheep behind.

I went with the elder Doctor M'Namee, to the two new established communities, one of which is called No. 2, or Macluria; the other lately founded, No. 3 No. 2, lies two miles distant from New Harmony, at the entrance of the forest, which will be cleared to make the land fit for cultivation, and consists of nine log houses, first tenanted about four weeks since, by about eighty persons. They are mostly backwoodsmen with their families, who have separated themselves from the community No. 1, in New Harmony, because *no religion* is acknowledged there, and these people wish to hold their prayer meetings undisturbed. The fields in the neighbourhood of this community were of course very new. The community No. 3, consisted of English country people, who formed a new association, as the mixture, or perhaps the cosmopolitism of New Harmony did not suit them; they left the colony planted by Mr. Birkbeck, at English Prairie, about twenty miles hence, on the right bank of the Wabash, after the unfortunate death of that gentleman, and came here. This is a proof that there are two evils that strike at the root of the young societies; one is a sectarian or intolerant spirit;

the other, national prejudice. No. 3, is to be built on a very pretty eminence, as yet there is only a frame building for three families begun.

After we had returned to New Harmony, I went to the orchard on the Mount Vernon road to walk, and beheld, to my great concern, what ravages the frost had committed on the fruit blossoms, the vines must have been completely killed. The orchards planted by Rapp and his society are large and very handsome, containing mostly apple and peach trees, also some pear and cherry trees. One of the gardens is exclusively devoted to flowers, where, in Rapp's time, a labyrinth was constructed of beech tree hedges and flowers, in the middle of which stood a pavilion, covered with the tops of trees.

I afterwards visited Mr. Neef, who is still full of the maxims and principles of the French revolution; captivated with the system of equality; talks of the emancipation of the negroes, and openly proclaims himself an ATHEIST. Such people stand by themselves, and fortunately are so very few in number, that they can do little or no injury.

In the evening there was a general meeting in the large hall, it opened with music. Then one of the members, an English architect of talent, who came to the United States with Mr. Owen, whose confidence he appeared to possess, and was here at the head of the arranging and architectural department, read some extracts from the newspapers, upon which Mr. Owen made a very good commentary; for example, upon the extension and improvement of steam-engines, upon their adaptation to navigation, and the advantages resulting therefrom. He lost himself, however, in his theories, when he expatiated on an article which related to the experiments which had been made with Perkins's steam-gun. During these lectures, I made my observations on the much vaunted equality, as some tatterdemalions stretched themselves on the platform close by Mr. Owen. The better educated members kept themselves together, and took no notice of the others. I remarked also, that the members belonging to the higher class of society had put on the new costume, and made a party by themselves. After the lecture the band played a march, each gentle-man took a lady, and marched with her round the room. Lastly, a cotillion was danced: the ladies were then escorted home, and each retired to his own quarters.

I went early on the following morning, (Sunday,) to the assembly room. The meeting was opened by music. After this Mr. Owen stated a proposition, in the discussion of which he spoke of the advances made by the society, and of the location of a new com-munity at Valley Forge, in Pennsylvania, and another in the state of New York. A classifi-cation of the members was spoken of after-wards. They were separated into three classes, first, of such as undertook to be security for the sums due Mr. Owen and Mr. M'Clure, (that is, for the amount paid to Rapp, and so expended as a pledge to be redeemed by the society,) and who, if desirous to leave the society, must give six months previous notice; secondly, of such as after a notice of fourteen days can depart; and, lastly, of those who are received only on trial.

After this meeting, I paid Mr. M'Clure a visit, and received from him the French papers. Mr. M'Clure is old, childless, was never married, and intends, as is reported, to leave his property to the society. Afterwards I went with Mr. Owen, and some ladies of the society, to walk to the cut-off, as it is called, of the Wabash, where this river has formed a new channel, and an island, which contains more than a hundred acres of the best land; at present, however, inundated by water. There is here a substantial grist-mill, erected by Rapp, which was said to contain a very good set of machinery, but where we could not reach it on account of the water. We went some distance along the river, and then returned through the woods over the hills, which, as it was rather warm, and we could discover no pathway, was very laborious to the ladies, who were uncommonly alarmed at the different snakes we chanced to meet. Most of the serpent species here are harmless, and the children catch them for playthings. The poisonous snakes harbouring about here, are rattlesnakes and copperheads; these, however, diminish rapidly in numbers, for it is a com-mon observation, that the poisonous serpents,

like the Indians and bears, fly before civili-zation. The rattlesnakes have a powerful enemy in the numerous hogs, belonging to the settlers, running about the woods, which are very well skilled in catching them by the neck and devouring them.

In the evening I paid visits to some ladies, and witnessed philosophy and the love of equality put to the severest trial with one of them. She is named Virginia, from Philadel-phia; is very young and pretty, was delicately brought up, and appears to have taken refuge here on account of an unhappy attachment. While she was singing and playing very well on the piano forte, she was told that the milk-ing of the cows was her duty, and that they were waiting unmilked. Almost in tears, she betook herself to this servile employment, deprecating the new social system, and its so much prized equality.

After the cows were milked, in doing which the poor girl was trod on by one, and daubed by another, I joined an aquatic party with the young ladies and some young phil-osophers, in a very good boat upon the inun-dated meadows of the Wabash. The evening was beautiful moonlight, and the air very mild; the beautiful Miss Virginia forgot her *stable* sufferings, and regaled us with her sweet voice. Somewhat later we collected together in the house No. 2, appointed for a school-house, where all the young ladies and gentlemen of *quality* assembled. In spite of the equality so much recommended, this class of persons will not mix with the common sort, and I believe that all the well brought up members are disgusted, and will soon abandon the society. We amused ourselves exceedingly during the whole remainder of the evening, dancing cotillions, reels and waltzes, and with such animation as rendered it quite lively. New figures had been introduced among the cotillions, among which is one called the *new social system*. Several of the ladies made ob-jections to dancing on Sunday; we thought however, that in this sanctuary of philosophy, such prejudices should be utterly discarded, and our arguments, as well as the inclination of the ladies, gained the victory.

On the 17th April, a violent storm arose, which collected such clouds of dust together

Top: Footprints ascribed to the Angel Gabriel at New Harmony. *Courtesy Indiana State Library Middle and bottom:* Theatre ticket and theatre curtain in New Harmony, c. 1826. *Courtesy Indiana Historical Society Library*

that it was hardly possible to remain in the streets, and I remained at home almost all day. I received a visit from a Mr. Von Schott. This person, a Wurtemburger by birth, and a brother of lady Von Mareuil, in Washington, has settled himself seven or eight miles from New Harmony, and lives a real hermit's life, without a servant or assistant of any kind. He was formerly an officer in the Wurtemburg cavalry, took his discharge, and went, from pure enthusiasm, and over-wrought fanaticism, to Greece, to defend their rights. As he there discovered himself to be deceived in his anticipations, he returned to his native country, and delivered himself up to religious superstition. To extricate himself, in his opinion, from this world plunged in wretchedness, he accompanied his sister to the United States, came to Indiana, bought a piece of land from Rapp, by whom he asserted he was imposed upon, and had difficulties to undergo, since he knew nothing of agriculture. He lived in this manner in the midst of the forest with a solitary horse. A cruel accident had befallen him the week before, his stable with his trusty horse was burnt. He appeared to be a well-informed man, and spoke well and rationally, only when he touched upon religious topics, his mind appeared to be somewhat deranged. He declared that he supported all possible privations with the greatest patience, only he felt the want of intercourse with a friend in his solitude.

To-day two companies of the New Harmony militia paraded, with drums beating, and exercised morning and afternoon. They were all in uniform, well armed, and presented an imposing front.

I was invited to dinner in the house, No. 4. Some gentlemen had been out hunting, and had brought home a wild turkey, which must be consumed. This turkey formed the whole dinner. Upon the whole I cannot complain either of an overloaded stomach, or a headache from the wine affecting it, in any way. The living was frugal in the strictest sense, and in nowise pleased the elegant ladies with whom I dined. In the evening I visited Mr. M'Clure and Madam Fretageot, living in the same house. She is a Frenchwoman, who formerly kept a boarding-school in Philadelphia, and is called *mother* by all the young girls here. The handsomest and most polished of the female world here, Miss Lucia Saistare and Miss Virginia, were under her care. The cows were milked this evening when I came in, and therefore we could hear their performance on the piano forte, and their charming voices in peace and quiet. Later in the evening we went to the kitchen of No. 3, where there was a ball. The young ladies of the better class kept themselves in a corner under Madam Fretageot's protection, and formed a little aristocratical club. To prevent all possible partialities, the gentlemen as well as the ladies, drew numbers for the cotillions, and thus apportioned them equitably. Our young ladies turned up their noses apart at the democratic dancers, who often in this way fell to their lot. Although every one was pleased upon the whole, yet they separated at ten o'clock, as it is necessary to rise early here. I accompanied Madam Fretageot and her two pupils home, and passed some time in conversation with Mr. M'Clure on his travels in Europe, which were undertaken with mineralogical views. The architect, Mr. Whitwell, besides showed me to-day the plan of this establishment. I admired particularly the judicious and economical arrangements for warming and ventilating the buildings, as well as the kitchens and laundries. It would indeed be a desirable thing could a building on this plan once be completed, and Mr. Owen hopes that the whole of New Harmony will thus be arranged.

On the following day I received a visit from one of the German patriots who had entered the society, of the name of Schmidt, who wished to have been considered as first lieutenant in the Prussian artillery, at Erfurt. He appeared to have engaged in one of the political conspiracies there, and to have deserted. Mr. Owen brought him from England last autumn as a servant. He was now a member of the society, and had charge of the cattle. His fine visions of freedom seemed to be very much lowered, for he presented himself to me, and his father to Mr. Huygens, to be employed as servants.

Towards evening, an Englishman, a friend of Mr. Owen, Mr. Applegarth, arrived, who had presided over the school in New Lanark, and was to organize one here in all probability. After dinner I went to walk with him in the vineyard and woods. We conversed much concerning the new system, and the consequences which he had reason to expect would result, &c. and we discovered amongst other things, that Mr. Owen must have conceived the rough features of his general system from considering forced services or statutory labour; for the labour imposed upon persons for which they receive no compensation, would apply and operate much more upon them for their lodging, clothing, food, the education and care of their children, &c. so that they would consider their labour in the light of a corveè. We observed several labourers employed in loading bricks upon a cart, and they performed this so tedious and disagreeable task, as a statutory labour imposed on them by circumstances, and this observation led us to the above reflection. I afterwards visited Mr. M'Clure, and entertained myself for an hour with the instructive conversation of this interesting old gentleman. Madam Fretageot, who appears to have considerable influence over Mr. M'Clure, took an animated share in our discourse. In the evening there was a ball in the large assembly room, at which most of the members were present. It lasted only until ten o'clock, in dancing cotillions, and closed with a grand promenade, as before described. There was a particular place marked off by benches for the children to dance in, in the centre of the hall, where they could gambol about without running between the legs of the grown persons.

On the 19th of April, a steam-boat came down the Wabash, bound for Louisville on the Ohio. It stopt opposite Harmony, and sent a boat through the overflow of water to receive passengers. I was at first disposed to embrace the opportunity of leaving this place, but as I heard that the boat was none of the best, I determined rather to remain and go by land to Mount Vernon, to wait for a better steamboat there.

THEATRE ON THE FRONTIER

SOL SMITH

Theatrical history in the West began at Fort Washington, in Cincinnati, in 1801, when a troupe of soldier-actors performed a broadly comic opera, The Poor Soldier, *for an audience of soldiers and settlers. By the 1820's there were two theatres in Cincinnati, and Mrs. Trollope found the playgoers throwing peanuts from the gallery and spitting tobacco on the floors.*

An arresting figure on the frontier stage was Sol Smith of Albany, New York. As a boy of fifteen he worked in harvest fields on Cayuga Lake and was paid six bushels of wheat. He sold the wheat for $7.50 and headed west. At Pittsburgh his money gave out but he worked his way on river craft to Louisville. There he learned the printing trade and joined a Thespian Society. A year later he was in Cincinnati, haunting the new Columbia Street Theatre.

As actor and manager he trouped the country in the years when theatres were spreading over the frontier and the first showboats were plying the rivers. The following excerpt is taken from his racy Sol Smith's Theatrical Apprenticeship, *published in Philadelphia in 1845.*

WHEN the theatre closed for the season (1820) I felt my wandering propensities returning. Without much ceremony of leave-taking, I pushed for the westward again, and, strange as it may seem, I bent my course for Vincennes. Arriving, I found my quondam master had farmed out his printing-office to a Mr. Osborn, with whom I immediately engaged as a compositor. I was kindly received by Mr. and Mrs. Stout—the latter declaring that she liked me all the better for the spirit I had shown in running away! In about a month's time my type-setting was interrupted, and my ideas all thrown into *pi* by the arrival of my old friend, Alexander Drake, with a small company of comedians from St. Louis. They were to play in Vincennes during the summer months. I was four hundred miles from home—the temptation was too great to withstand—I applied—was accepted—and here began my theatrical career.

The company consisted of Messrs. A. Drake, S. Drake, Jun., Palmer Fisher, Douglas, Jones, *Sol. Smith,* and Mesdames Mongin, Fisher, and three or four little female Fishers.

With a company so limited in number, it will be supposed our range of pieces must have been extremely circumscribed; but this was not the case; we grappled at "Pizarro," the "Poor Gentleman," and other equally full plays.

By a lamentable casualty, our number, small as it was, was destined to be reduced. It was a custom with us to bathe in the Wabash river just previous to retiring for the night. Our hotel being on the bank of the river, we undressed in our rooms, and wrapping ourselves in sheets or blankets, we so proceeded to our bath. One morning Douglas was missing—several remembered he had been with us in the water, but none had any recollection of seeing him when we came out. His clothes were found in his room; but there were no signs of his bed having been occupied that night. A search was immediately commenced, and resulted in finding the dead body of our friend two miles below the town!

We had now but four men and two ladies, and, with this number, we played "Pizarro." To those unacquainted with *country theatricals,* the *cast* will be a curiosity:

The showboat *Cotton Blossom*. Courtesy Ohio Historical Society

Pizarro, the Spanish general, Ataliba, king of Quito,	. Mr. S. Drake
Rolla, the Peruvian leader, Las Casas, a Spanish priest,	. . Mr. Fisher
Alonzo, joined with the Peruvians, Orozembo, an old cacique,	. Mr. A. Drake
High Priest of the Sun, Almagro, a Spanish officer, Blind man, Sentinel, Valverde, secretary, Guards,	Mr. Sol. Smith
Peruvian boy, ...	. Miss Fisher
Elvira, Priestess of the Sun,	. . . Mrs. Fisher
Cora, ...	. Mrs. Mongin
Child, ...	. Miss A. Fisher

Thus, Sam Drake, (as Pizarro,) after planning an attack on the unoffending Peruvians while engaged in worship "at their ungodly altars," and assigning his generals (*me*) their "several posts," in the next act is seen (as Ataliba) leading the Indian warriors to battle, declaring that "straight forward will he march, until he sees his people free, or they behold their monarch fall!" He is victorious; and goes to offer up thanks to the gods therefor,—when, Presto! on comes the same man again (as Pizarro) smarting under the stings of defeat!

Fisher (as Las Casas) calls down a curse on the heads of the Spaniards—throws off his cloak; drops his cross; doffs his gray wig, and appears in the next scene as the gallant Rolla, inciting his "brave associates" to deeds of valour! Alexander Drake, as Orozembo, in the first scene gives an excellent character of the youth Alonzo, pronouncing him to be a "nation's benefactor"—he is then stuck under the fifth rib by a Spanish soldier, (that's me again,) and is carried off by his murderer;—he then slips off his shirt and scull-cap, claps on a touch of red paint, and behold! he is the blooming Alonzo, and engaged in a quiet *tête-à-tête* with his Indian spouse!

For my own part, I was the Spanish army entire! but my services were not confined to that party.—Between whiles I had to officiate as High Priest of the Sun—then lose both of my eyes, and feel my way, guided by a little boy, through the heat of the battle, to tell the audience what was going on behind the scenes; afterwards, my sight being restored, and my black cloak dropped, I was placed as a sentinel over Alonzo! Besides, I was obliged to find the sleeping child; fight a blow or two with Rolla; fire off three guns at him while crossing the bridge; beat the alarm drum, and do at least two-thirds of the shouting! Some may think my situation was no sinecure; but being a novice, all *my* exertions were nothing in comparison with those of the Drakes—particularly Sam, who frequently played two or three parts in one play, and, after being killed in the last scene, was obliged *to fall far enough off the stage to play slow music as the curtain descended!*

Our stage was ten feet wide, and eight feet deep. When we played pieces that required bridges and mountains, we had not much room to spare; indeed I might say we were somewhat crowded.

I generally "went on" for what is termed the youthful business; Henry in "Speed the Plough," Henry in the "Magpie and Maid,"

Belville in the "Country Girl," and other characters of a similar grade; but almost always had to "double" them with something else. I recollect going on for Frederick and Stephen Harrowby in the "Poor Gentleman." We played mostly from the Dublin (*doubling*) edition.

The season lasted about eight weeks. The company proceeded to Louisville, and I footed it back to Cincinnati, declining the offers of the Drake family for a permanent engagement, being fearful of the disapprobation of my brothers, who as yet knew nothing of the manner of employing my time in Vincennes. Being partially satisfied with my few weeks' experience as an actor, I now determined to "study the law." I was taken into the justice's office of Daniel Roe, and had the advantage of the books and instruction of Mr. Todd, an excellent lawyer and a worthy man, since dead. Here, and by attending the law lectures of Wm. Greene, Esq., I picked up what little I know of that "intricate science," as it is termed by Sir Walter Scott. Mr. Drake came to Cincinnati, soon after, and opened our Thespian house, under the style of the *Haymarket theatre;* but the concern was unsuccessful, and the company returned to Louisville.

In the winter of 1820, the Columbia street theatre was managed jointly by Mr. Drake and Mr. Collins, the partner of the latter gentleman (Mr. Jones) remaining with the company in the south-western towns. The drama of the "Forty Thieves" was produced with great splendour, and many other novelties were offered; but the season was an unproductive one. The company was indifferent, and the patronage worse than indifferent.

I continued to study the LAW.

"THE FAR WEST"

RALPH WALDO EMERSON

In the spring of 1851 Ralph Waldo Emerson left Concord, Massachusetts, to lecture in the raw academy halls and drafty churches of the frontier. He went by steamboat down the Ohio and then up the Mississippi to the bustling town of Galena, Illinois. Back at home that summer he described the upper Mississippi wilderness to another philosopher, Thomas Carlyle, beside the Thames in London. It seemed to Emerson, as to any traveler who reached the Mississippi, that he had been to the "Far West." That phrase called to mind the current excitement of California, and then he commented on the riches of the Ohio valley, which in time would beggar the bonanza of the Sierras.

Galina, Illinois, in 1851. *Courtesy Illinois State Historical Library*

I HAVE been something of a traveler the last year, and went down the Ohio River to its mouth; walked nine miles into, and nine miles out of, the Mammoth Cave, in Kentucky,—walked or sailed, for we crossed small underground streams,—and lost one day's light; then steamed up the Mississippi, five days to Galena. In the Upper Mississippi, you are always in a lake with many islands. "The Far West" is the right name for these verdant deserts. On the shores, interminable silent forest. If you land there is prairie behind prairie, forest behind forest, sites of nations, no nations. The raw bullion of nature; what we call "moral" value not yet stamped on it.

But in a thousand miles the immense material values will show twenty or fifty Californias; that a good ciphering head will make one where he is. Thus at Pittsburgh, on the Ohio, the Iron City, whither, from want of railroads, few Yankees have penetrated, every acre of land has three or four bottoms; first of rich soil; then nine feet of bituminous coal; a little lower, fourteen feet of coal; then iron, or salt; salt springs, with a valuable oil called petroleum floating on their surface. Yet this acre sells for the price of any tillage acre in Massachusetts; and, in a year, the railroads will reach it, east and west. —I came home by the great Northern Lakes and Niagara.

MAKING A MISSISSIPPI PANORAMA

HENRY LEWIS' JOURNAL OF
A CANOE VOYAGE, 1848

In the middle years of the nineteenth century the Mississippi River was the most dramatic feature of America. With the full tide of western commerce on its waters and the pageant of the frontier along its shores, the river inspired artists like George Catlin and Seth Eastman to paint its varied scenes of wilderness and civilization. Other artists, less disciplined and more expansive, felt its spell. They painted mammoth panoramas, one of them advertised as "four miles long," of the great river. Between 1840 and 1850 six painters recorded the Mississippi in panoramas which were unrolled before rapt audiences, as the valley itself unrolled from the deck of a steamboat.

The most famous of the panoramas was the work of Henry Lewis, an Englishman who came to St. Louis in 1836 and worked as stage carpenter and scene painter in an opera house. In 1848, determined to outdo the existing panoramas of the Mississippi, he went to Fort Snelling, built a floating studio, and voyaged with a journalist companion down the river. On the way Lewis made scores of sketches for the huge panorama—12 feet high and 3,750 feet long—which he painted the following winter.

After showing it to enthusiastic audiences in the American cities, Lewis took his reeled painting to England and the Continent. It was especially popular in Germany. Finally he sold it to an English planter who shipped the panorama to the East Indies. There the record ends.

The Journal of Henry Lewis was edited by Bertha Heilbron and published by the Minnesota Historical Society in 1936. The following selection traces the journey from Fort Snelling to Galena. For all the accuracy of his painting, Lewis did not manage to include a detail that figures emphatically in his narrative— the swarming upper Mississippi mosquitoes.

AFTER waiting some four or five days at St Peters for a fair wind—and the wind being determined not to be fair—we determin'd to start. accordingly every thing being in readiness and attended by an escort of Cap^n Eastman and his family and divers other lookers on besides one passenger a Mr Weld[,] Farmer for the Indi[a]ns at Crow Wing village (of whom more anon) we left our comfortable quarters under the hospitable roof of the Cap^n on Monday afternoon 27 July at 3 o'clock firing a salute at parting in military style, intending to encamp for the night at Little crows village   after a pleasant run altho' the wind was ahead we arriv'd at the village at 8 o'clock

in the evening and here our troubles began—a trouble which altho' it may appear very insignificant at first sight threatens to rob us of half the please [*pleasure*] of our trip, if not half our blood. I mean the musquetoes   I had often heard people talk of clouds of these tormentors and of persons being eaten alive. these I consider'd figurative expressions, but sorry experiance has taught me they are too true. Had we remain'd expos'd to their attacks in the bottom on which we encamp'd that night all that would be left of the chronocle[r] of this journal would have been his skeliton. but fortunately we accepted the hospitality of Mr Weld for which we paid dearly afterwards and got a pretty good nights rest in his house. The men roll'd themselves up in their blankets and lying down in the rank grass with no canopy but the heavens managed somehow to live th[r]o the night. and taking a sketch of the village which contains some 14 or 15 lodges, we started again with a strong head wind our boat swarming with our tormentors, so that it was nothing but slap slap until even an anchorate would have lost his patience.

With all our labour and the current to help us we made but 15 miles this day   I took several sketches after having rigg'd up a bar in our little cabbin, but altogether it was a wretched day and we hail'd with pl[e]asure a beautiful looking spot about ½ past 7 w[h]ere we concluded we would encamp. But oh how appearances in nature as well as man do som[e]times deceive this you would suppose the breading place of all the blooded stock of this most blood thirsty crew. We had hardly landed when we were attacked by hundreds. the fire after it was made attracted thousands and we ate our supper attended by the obsequ[i]ous attentions of millions, until fairly driven into our tent and under our bar where we thought we should have some little peace but bars were no bar to them and we had scarsely got under it when whiz whiz, hum hu[m] you would have thought yourself in a hive of bees. It was dreadful after the fatigue and heat of the day thus to be annoy'd so we determin'd if possible to kill every one in a hive of bees. it was dreadful after the procuring a light we went to work and kill[e]d some hundreds and once more compos'd ourselves but it was no use—in they came again I dont know how, for the bar was perfect, and we got no sleep that night and were fairly driven away without our breakfast, for it was impossible to eat it even if we cook'd it.

After rowing against a head wind for three miles we came upon Red Wings village, beautifully situated on a plateau back'd by a range of beautiful bluffs; the termination of this range forms a bold headland on the river and from its peculiar shape is call'd la Grange (the barn) on the beach under it this bluff there was a fine gravil beach with a breeze blowing from land which seem'd musqueto proff [sic]

and here we took our breakfast surroun[d]ed by some forty as hungry savages as you can well imagine. One of the head men attracted by the smell of the savory fare made a speech in which he highly complimented us and the boat and finished by telling us he was a great man, who liv'd without fear of the Chippeways, and was in fact a great chief. in conclusion he came to the pith of the argument namely that he had a very hungry family at home and finish'd as all indian speeches do finish by begging our last loaf.

As a specimen of the bravery of these Indians I will mention an incident that took place last winter at this village related to me by the Indian farmer. Some indians from a neighbouring village had had some quarrel in a drunken braul but had parted with no other harm than threats and hard words. A short time afterwards one of these indians happen'd to come to this village and whilst seated in one of the Wigwams one of the men with whom he had quarrel'd crept *behind* him and cut his throat. They buried him in ten minutes, but it was suspected that he had been murder'd here and the village hearing that his *brother* was comeing up to take revenge, man, woman and child left the village and cross'd to the other side—and all from one man.

Having finish'd and been gaz'd at to the hearts content of the Indian I prepar'd before leaving to enjoy a view from the summit of La Grange and arming myself with my gun in case of Rattle snakes which are very numerous on this bluff I started I found the views from the top so beautiful that I made a panoramic series of sketches embracing the whole horison, and then we embark'd again on our long and thus far tedious voyage.

after a hard days rowing we cross'd half way thro' lake Pepin and encamp'd July 14th on a beautiful beach which looked as tho' a musqueto or any other annoyance could not dwell there. But we had hardly got our fire made when Whiz, whiz buz buz they came thick as ever until I was fairly constrain'd to eat my supper with my head under a bar—and a funnier set of looking objects perhaps never was seen than we presented each trying with all his might and main to keep off the tormentors. This lake is 25 or 30 miles long with an average width of pe[r]haps 3 miles. it is very subject to sudden storms and squalls, and we heard many ominous prophesies as to whether our little craft could live to pass its dangers, to say nothing of ourselves and we were gravely told to coast along its dangerous shores. I however having a strong and fair wind launch'd boldly on its bosom and steering for the very centre rode on its long swelling waves like a duck Nearing the Lovers Leap or Winonas rock where it is said an Indian maiden disappointed in love committed sucicide, and as the height of this rock has been a matter of a good deal of dispute, I determin'd to measure it and it remains with me to tell the exact height at the base of which love and suicide met. by dint of hard and very dangerous climbing I succeeded at last in reaching the very brink of the precipice and with a long line taken for the purpose I drop'd the other end to my man Franscois below. we found the height to be 126 feet. taking with me as a rememebrance of the spot in the shape of a branch of cedar the parent stem of which might have witness'd the event (supposing cedars have eyes) even if it had happen'd four hundred [years] ago, and after taken [taking] a couple of beautiful views from the summit and seeing like a speck far in the lake below my first officer Robb with the pioneer cutter I de[s]cendend [sic] and again took to the middle of the lake.

The wind held fair for 10 or 12 miles further when it died away after giving a parting puff which drove my hel[m]sman Francois, nearly out of his senses and from his post. I was busy sketching at the time, when I hea[r]d an exclamation Mon Dieu Mon Dieu, we are lost. I flew to the helm lower'd the main sail and bringing her head round again soon put all to rights. We now had to take to our oars and rowing some six miles we came near the foot of the lake which here terminates in a beautiful bay of gravil among which are many beautiful shells and pebbles here are found great numbers of carnelians and agates besides very fine specimens of jasper and field [feld] spar. the rocks arround are principally unstrattified sand stone with large boulders of granite scatter'd at intervals.

Seeing a tent at the further side of this bay about a mile and half to leeward and not having seen Cap^n Robb since morning, I thought it might be him so heaving to I fir'd a gun which was immediately answer'd by my consort I again cross'd the lake and found the cap^n encamped in a spot which combin'd the most exceeding beauty with great utility. It was a scene to be remember'd for a life time; before us stretch'd the Lake for fourteen miles, with its beautifully picturesque shores, and the spot on which our tent was pitched was form'd of the beautiful gravil and sand for which this lake is celebrated. The sun was just setting in the greatest splendour and as he was slowly sinking behind the hills seem'd to linger a mome[n]t as if loth to part with a scene so lovely. We soon had a fire made from the trunk and branches of an old Cedar and sat down right weary and hungry to a good supper of broil'd Ham coffee and lobsters—(think of lobsters on lake Pepin[)]. after making a sketch of our encampment and writing a little in my journal I turn'd in to my tent and slept such sleep as you who dwell in cities seldom know. We made this day only 20 miles owing to head winds and numerous stoppages.

July 14 Got breakfast by daylight and made an early start, the wind high, but fair. The surf running pretty considerable strong from the lake fill'd the bows of our little bark but it could get no further and as to sinking—that was impossible as I had so constructed my boat that it was a perfect life preserver. Therefore when she was bail'd out and her head put before the wind we sail'd away beautifully and the wind holding fair all day we made a fine run to Wabashaw prarie distance 60 miles, and encampd.

I dont know that I have given you a scene in camp and as I have a little spare time I might as well do so now. As soon as the boat lands Fransuois and John pitch our canvass home[,] two things always being consider'd necessary[,] water and a spot where in case of rain it could not run into our tent another important consideration is to find a location where the musquetoes are not in millions Where they are only in thousands is consider'd a good camping ground. Well, the tent being up—the next thing is to make a fire where the wind will carry the smoke towards the door of our tent to keep off the hungry varment, and heat some water to make the coffee. Whilst this is going on I take a stroll with my gun or fishing rod to look for fresh meat and if unsuccessful why we must take a rasher of broil'd ham or dried beef—and the mattrasses being spread in the tent supper is announs'd in due form by striking a knife on the bottom of the frying pan and we sit down a la Turk and take our time to it in true aristocratic style. This performance being over next comes the pipes and then the long chat over the events of the day pass'd and the plans for the coming one & then right well fatigued after setting our night lines we turn in and sleep such sleep as is not even dreamt of beneath city shingles. On the lower end of the prarie on which we were encampt (which you will recollect was the theatre of the stirring events I have related in a preceeding page) were still encampt a company of dragoons, sent to assist in the removal of the Win[n]ebagoes. They were themselves preparing to depart as the last party of the Indians had gone up on the S Boat on her last trip.

July 15   They were landed at Fort Snelling and from thence took up their line of march for their new country—beyond the Crow Wing river some 180 miles further forth [north] Being acquainted with Cap Morgan the gentleman in command as soon as breakfast was finished we struck our tent and dropt down to his encampment where we had a pleasant chat and smoke and when about to start when the steam boat on which he was going to embark his men hove in sight and we must needs stay a little longer as we expected to get at least some papers and see some old friends that we knew were on board. On her arrival our boat became qu[i]te an object of curiosity and many were the visits I had to pay to and from the St Boat to show people our floating curiosity shop, and having linger'd two hours got a batch of late papers, and said farewell we up sail and once more were under way.

Three miles below here we came to Mount Tromp l'eau a large rocky mountain that stands on a small island very pictiresque. Marvellious stories had been told about a lake on its summit full of delicious fish which we found out to be all moonshine (I mean the stories not the lake) as we assended it, and also a much higher hill immediately opposite, from which I took a birds eye view of as grand a scene as ever eye rested upon. Far as the eye could reach could be seen the Missi[ssi]ppi with its thousand islands winding like a stream of silver thro' dense masses of varied green. Mountain o'er mountain rose, forest stretched beyond forest, prairie beyond p[r]arie until the eye sought releif [sic] in the dim purple distance with its broad masses without detail its varied and lengthen'd shadows added a crowning charm to the whole. Yet a feeling of sadness would break over one to think that all this b[e]auty—this adabtation of natures to mans wants was a *solitude*, vast, and lonely, inhabited only by a few bands of indians now fast melting away and the solitary deer and elk. No smoke from the cabin to remind one of home and its comforts no spires, or domes of cities to tell of commerce or its manufactories, no waving fields of grain to contrast with its golden undulations the vast masses of dark green foliage all all was solitude could Zimmerman have stood where I did he would have exclaim'd an[d] been satisfied [let] this be my home. As I looked I felt how hopeless art was to convay the *soul* of such a scene as this and as the poet wishes for the pencil of the artist so did I for the power of discript[i]on to tell of the thousand thoughts fast crowding each other from my mind. But a truce to sentiment here I am with pencil and sketch book ruminating and dreaming when I should be at work so here goes to make the effort if it is only in outline to carry to my friends at home and try and give them some idea of where I have been. There, 'tis done—and now to wake friend Robb who has taken in so much of the poetry of the scene that together with the climb has quite overpower'd him for you must recollect we are five hundred and twenty feet nearer heaven than we were an hour ago on our boat, and I would remark at passing that if the whole road to those delectable regions is as rough as this was it will be a pilgrims progress with a vengeance and an up hill business to boot.

Having order'd the men on starting to

have a cup of coffee for us on our return, we got under way again, and sipping our delicious beverage and enjoying pipes took a view of [the scene] as we floated past of [*sic*] the spot that had cost us so much trouble to ascend. I had forgotten to remark that whilst at the top the steamer dubuque pass'd far below us friend Robb hoisted a blood red handkerchief on the end of an oar he had taken with him to kill rattle snakes and I fir'd a salute of defiance at the passing boat. We are now pulling away again and as the sun set is approaching we began to look out for a camping ground the evening is warm and sultry and I we [*sic*] think we shall catch it certain. therefore as we coasted along if Rob[b] or myself should see a spot we thought would do we would run the boat ashore and try it. Sometimes such an overwhelming army would attack us that we would make the most precipitate and disgraceful retreats for our boat and scratch out into the stream again. We at last discover'd a spot we thought would do at the end of a sand bar and we accordingly encamp'd. but the sentries sounded the cry instantly—fresh meat ashore ready for the charge and we were surrounded and almost carried away. By dint of considerable ingenuity we fix'd a bar on four oars stuck in the sand and defy'd them whilst we took our supper and when once we had them shut out the sensation was delightful to hear and see them in their frantic efforts *rushing madly* at the bar, trying to carry it by storm but a truce to musquetoes I have had enough of them and I presume you have also by this time. after this night they were not so bad. We were encamp'd this evening near the mouth of Black river and we made this day only about 25 miles owing to a head wind and late start and numerous stoppages

July 16th Started early and after taking a sketch of the mouth of Black river proceeded on our way the wind still being ahead but it chang'd about ten o'clock and we made a fine run of it to day of near 50 miles, took a great number of sketches. Prarie la Cross, upper Iowa river, Birds eye view of the celebrated bend call'd Coon slue, with its windings of 14 miles where it does not pass over more the [*than*] 6 miles in a straight line. The view

from the summit of the bluff at the foot of the slue is magnificent but almost impossible to draw, in outline. Just below here we stop'd at Mr Reeds an old hunter and trapper a man that has been in this part of the country some 34 years. We unfortunately found that he was absent at the fort where he had gone to see the payment of the indians he being farmer to Wabashaws band. We antisipated some stirring narratives from this old man, and were much disappointed at not finding him. Here we took a bucket of fine spring water and proceeded on our way.

Soon we came opposite the island made celebrated as the spot where Black Hawk made his last desperate stand and where was fought what is call[e]d the battle of Bad Axe. I immediately went to work and made a true sketch of the spot and near the mouth of the river made our encampment in an old deserted whiskey dealers cabin. This was a most delightful camping ground. the house was in pretty good repair[,] the hugh fire place open'd its hospitable jaws to receive us and soon we had a jolly fire roaring on the hearth. The imagination might here run riot in calling up to ones mind the scenes that had been enacted in this old cabin. The stories of successful hunts, the hair breath scapes, the desperate adventure, the drunken broils and consequent fights with the indians, and a dark tale of blood was hinted at how a half breed woman was murder'd by a drunken husband. but I have not time to tell you of what might have been but of what was and in spite of stories and legends I was soon as fast asleep as tho' I were in some snug little room in St Louis instead of where I was with doors and windows all open to the breeze.

July 17th We made a late start this morning as we had to bake this complicated and difficult opperation I had to take entirely upon myself as our half breeds knew nothing about it. You would have laugh'd to have seen me with my ears tye'd up to keep off the musquetoes an old wollen night cap on my head and, my sleeves roold [*rolled*] up working away kneeding whilst Robb, would be getting ready, the coals, and watching the operation with great interest. Having back'd [*baked*] my loaf I sit down to write first going down to the boat to see all to righ[t]s, hoist my signal lanthorn and set my night lines. The houses here are very scarse, and such articles as fresh milk or beef are out of the question. therefore those travelling as I did must take their coffee without milk and live on salt meat and let the *freshness* of the scenery compensate for other luxuries.

Whi[l]st breakfast was cooking I took a stroll round this old deserted mansion. There were still overgrown with weeds tho' and battling lustily with them for the mastery traces of the little garden and the field. the convolvulus was training up a high wild flower the cultivated golden rod of England, and the pink and marigold tried hard to get a peek of the smiling sun thro' the dark masses of weeds that surrounded them. barly, wheat, and corn, were growing wild all around with an aspect of desolation, and neglect, seen there in the wilderness than [*that*] one can not well describe. it seem'd as tho' man had tried hard to battle with solitude and the forrest but had— had at last to give it up again and seek for more congenial scenes. But we must away again. The Mine-ah-ah lies just below and her little streamer points down stream. A fair wind down the Miss. at this season of the year is not to be lost.

July 18. Struck our tent and silently stole away and on thro' many a varied scene. The picturesque bluffs still continue one which we visited was very high and steep. it is call'd Cap o lange or iron hill. it is cov[er]'d with small pieces of native iron in a tolerably pure state said to have been used by the Indians for spear and arrow heads They might possibly have welded them out into arrow and spear heads as is reported, but I much doubt it with their imperfect implements. On the other side of a small slue which divides this mountain from the one below it South stands the painted rock of the indians this is a very ancient place of worship with them proba[b]ly from its close vicinity to the Iron mountain causing many of them to frequent the spot. The rock is a painted boulder of granite about 3 or 4 feet high

July 19[th] 1848 Encamp'd this evening 3 miles above Prarie du Chaen in a very rich bottom back'd by peculiar bluffs we made a good run this day of 45 miles, and I took a great number of sketches, of the picturesque bluffs as we pass'd them. One bluff owing to its shape we call'd the Alter [*sic*] bluff, for you can see the pulpit the reading desk and the baptismal fount After marking our names on this bluff and giving its name, and after a hearty breakfast from a very fine fish which we found on our night line, we struck tent and hoisted sale for Prarie du Chain distant some 4 or 5 miles. Arriving at an island, overlooking the town I made a careful view of it, and then we row'd up to the town. It is one [of] the oldest if not the oldest town in the West, and its quaint, old, french chateaus and cottages are very picturesque. it was settled originally by traders and trappers from Canada by the way of Lake Michigan and then down [*sic*] Fox river—as early as 1734.

On going up to the printing office which by the by is the Post Office also, I was pleasantly surprise'd at meeting Doc Randall one of the U S. Geological Corps. he had been rob'd by the indians on the head waters of the Des Moin[e]s, by a band of the Sioux call'd the Sis[se]tons. they took two horses from them 3 out of their four blankets (they were not *savages* enou[g]h like some white men to take all) and after braking a very fine revolving rifle and the doc barometer which last was an accident, and after looking with perfect contempt on the doc specimens, and collections of plants they gave him some buffalo meat and told him to go. We pass'd a very pleasant evening together, he telling me of all his adventures and showing me the charts maps and—sections of the whole of that interesting and almost unknown region. He has made many very valuable discoveries on this river both in coal, lead Iron and Gypsum, the latter is very valuable and very rich beginning near the mouth and continueing for 200 miles up. There are also very large and valuable beds of coal on this river which will one day become very valuable as it is no where else found in this part of the country. After stending [*spending*] the night in our tent and taking breakfast with us, we had to part[,] he to proceed to Fort Snelling to refit and I for Galena So wishing him better luck next time we said farewell.

July 20. A fair wind and a clear sky, so after taking another view of the Prarie looking up, we hoisted all sail, determin'd to make Galena by night if the wind held good ran beautifully along 'till we arriv'd at Dubuque, which I took a view of from below call'd here on the E[d]itor of the Dubuque pater [*paper*] and left our names and objects, which he said he would notice. left again and ran splendidly for 4 or 5 hours. We now began to pass many rafts and flats and it was curious to hear them sing out to us—What you got to sell stranger? I would generally answer Elephants turks and Carcassian slaves then there would be a pause and a talking among themselves. We had ma[n]y a pretty little bit of badinage of this kind as we pass'd the shore or rafts. Just below Dubuque is the grave of Dubuque himself on a beautiful eminance near the city he founded. It was formerly made of lead, but the cupidity of some travelling scamps were put to the test and they mutilated and carried away a large portion of it. It has now been repl[a]c'd by one not so valuable in the shape of a substantial stone tomb. We encamp'd this evening at the mouth of Fever River 7 m from Galena. We had a beautiful camping ground but in the hurry of departure I forgot to take a view of it or to leave our names

July 21 Left at 6 o'clock for Galena we had a head wind, and as we had to go up Fever river we congratulated ourselves on the fact that we should have a fine run up. But bad luck attended us from the start this day. I had not a very clear conception which the mouth of Fever river was amongst the many slues that enter the river near its mouth, for you must know it enters the Miss. thro' a series of swamp mouths or bayous. of course I took the wrong one and consequently got slue'd, for after following it up for some 2 or 3 miles we came butt up against the end of it. Robb now got the Fever, for the river I mean, and we retrac'd our steps, or I should say our track, and finally reach'd the genuine river mouth. after a laborious row of 3 hours we got our craft up to the town of Galena and then we were among friends again. Our boat became as great as [*an*] object of curiosity as before and Rob[b] and myself did nothing else that day but walk down with little parties some to look at the boat, some at my drawing, and some to take a chat and a glass with us. I took dinner at the American House with my friend Mr Snyders whom I had met and room'd with at Fort Snelling, and over a bottle of excellent wine I narrated to him my adventures since we parted. A[f]ter many adieus and shaking of hands, we party [*parted*] reluctantly from our kind and hospitable entertainers, One of whom, Mr S. Harris wish'd us to stay with him 2 or 3 weeks. It was now late in the evening and so running down 2 miles below the city we encamp'd for the night. In the night the [Dr.] Franklin pass'd and not seeing us or not caring to extend to us the courtesy of most of the other boats that had pass'd us on this stream, she ran by us with a full head of steam and her swell came near sinking us. but running out of our tent in drawers and stocking feet, I was just in time to save her. I was join'd in Galena by Mr Rogers a gentleman I had been anxiously looking for, to assist me in making sketches.

FARTHEST NORTH

CONSTANCE FENIMORE WOOLSON

A grandniece of Fenimore Cooper, Constance Fenimore Woolson grew up in Cleveland, with summers on Mackinac Island. She visited logging camps, mining towns, and Indian missions in the North. She saw romance in that remote country, with Indian campfires on the shores, iron and copper mines in the

gnarled hills of the Upper Peninsula of Michigan, and black forests framing the icebound straits. Her last fourteen years, before her death in 1894, were spent in England and Italy. "She has a remarkable faculty," Henry James said, "of making the New World seem old." The following scenes are taken from Castle Nowhere, *her volume of Lake-Country Sketches.*

"Surveying Still"

Not many years ago the shore bordering the head of Lake Michigan, the northern curve of that silver sea, was a wilderness unexplored. It is a wilderness still, showing even now on the school-maps nothing save an empty waste of colored paper, generally a pale, cold yellow suitable to the climate, all the way from Point St. Ignace to the iron ports on the Little Bay de Noquet, or Badderknock in lake phraseology, a hundred miles of nothing, according to the map-makers, who, knowing nothing of the region, set it down accordingly, withholding even those long-legged letters, "Chip-pe-was," "Ric-carees," that stretch accommodatingly across so much townless territory farther west. This northern curve is and always has been off the route to anywhere; and mortals, even Indians, prefer as a general rule, when once started, to go somewhere. The earliest Jesuit explorers and the captains of yesterday's schooners had this in common, that they could not, being human, resist a cross-cut; and thus, whether bark canoes of two centuries ago or the high, narrow propellers of today, one and all, coming and going, they veer to the southeast or west, and sail gayly out of sight, leaving this northern curve of ours unvisited and alone. A wilderness still, but not unexplored; for that railroad of the future which is to make of British America a garden of roses, and turn the wild trappers of the Hudson's Bay Company into gently smiling congressmen, has it not sent its missionaries thither, to the astonishment and joy of the beasts that dwell therein? According to tradition, these men surveyed the territory, and then crossed over (those of them at least whom the beasts had spared) to the lower peninsula, where, the pleasing variety of swamps being added to the labyrinth of pines and sand-hills, they soon lost themselves, and to this day have never found

what they lost. As the gleam of a camp-fire is occasionally seen, and now and then a distant shout heard by the hunter passing along the outskirts, it is supposed that they are in there somewhere, surveying still.

"The White Fort"

Up in the northern straits, between blue Lake Huron, with its clear air, and gray Lake Michigan, with its silver fogs, lies the bold island of Mackinac. Clustered along the beach, which runs around its half-moon harbor, are the houses of the old French village, nestling at the foot of the cliff rising behind, crowned with the little white fort, the stars and stripes floating above it against the deep blue sky. Beyond, on all sides, the forest stretches away, cliffs finishing it abruptly, save one slope at the far end of the island, three miles distant, where the British landed in 1812. That is the whole of Mackinac.

The island has a strange sufficiency of its own; it satisfies; all who have lived there feel it. The island has a wild beauty of its own; it fascinates; all who have lived there love it. Among its aromatic cedars, along the aisles of its pine-trees, in the gay company of its maples, there is companionship. On its bald northern cliffs, bathed in sunshine and swept by the pure breeze, there is exhilaration. Many there are, bearing the burden and heat of the day, who look back to the island with the tears that rise but do not fall, the sudden longing despondency that comes occasionally to all, when the tired heart cries out, "O, to escape, to flee away, far, far away, and be at rest!"

In 1856 Fort Mackinac held a major, a captain, three lieutenants, a chaplain, and a surgeon, besides those subordinate officers who wear stripes on their sleeves, and whose rank and duties are mysterious to the uninitiated. The force for this array of commanders was small, less than a company; but what it lacked in quantity it made up in quality, owing to the continual drilling it received.

The days were long at Fort Mackinac; happy thought! drill the men. So when the major had finished, the captain began, and each lieutenant was watching his chance. Much state was kept up also. Whenever the major appeared, "Commanding officer; guard, present arms," was called down the line of men on duty, and the guard hastened to obey, the major acknowledging the salute with stiff precision. By day and by night sentinels paced the walls. True, the walls were crumbling, and the whole force was constantly engaged in propping them up, but none the less did the sentinels pace with dignity. What was it to the captain if, while he sternly inspected the muskets in the block-house, the lieutenant, with a detail of men, was hard at work strengthening its underpinning? None the less did he inspect. The sally-port, mended but imposing; the flag-staff with its fair-weather and storm flags; the frowning iron grating; the sidling white cause-way, constantly falling down and as constantly repaired, which led up to the main entrance; the well-preserved old cannon,—all showed a strict military rule. When the men were not drilling they were propping up the fort, and when they were not propping up the fort they were drilling. In the early days, the days of the first American commanders, military roads had been made through the forest,—roads even now smooth and solid, although trees of a second growth meet overhead. But that was when the fort was young and stood firmly on its legs. In 1856 there was no time for road-making, for when military duty was over there was always more or less mending to keep the whole fortification from sliding down hill into the lake.

On Sunday there was service in the little chapel, an upper room overlooking the inside parade-ground. Here the kindly Episcopal chaplain read the chapters about Balaam and Balak, and always made the same impressive pause after "Let me die the death of the righteous, and let my last end be like his." (Dear old man! he has gone. Would that our last end might indeed be like his!) Not that

the chaplain confined his reading to the Book of Numbers; but as those chapters are appointed for the August Sundays, and as it was in August that the summer visitors came to Mackinac, the little chapel is in many minds associated with the patient Balak, his seven altars, and his seven rams.

There was state and discipline in the fort even on Sundays; bugle-playing marshalled the congregation in, bugle-playing marshalled them out. If the sermon was not finished, so much the worse for the sermon, but it made no difference to the bugle; at a given moment it sounded, and out marched all the soldiers, drowning the poor chaplain's hurrying voice with their tramp down the stairs. The officers attended service in full uniform, sitting erect and dignified in the front seats. We used to smile at the grand air they had, from the stately gray-haired major down to the youngest lieutenant fresh from the Point. But brave hearts were beating under those fine uniforms; and when the great struggle came, one and all died on the field in the front of the battle. Over the grave of the commanding officer is inscribed "Major-General," over the captain's is "Brigadier," and over each young lieutenant is "Colonel." They gained their promotion in death.

"The Apostles"

Toward the western end of Lake Superior there is a group of islands, twenty-three in number, called the "Twelve Apostles." One more and the Apostles might have had two apiece. But although Apostles taken together, officially, as it were, they have personal names of a very different character, such as "Cat," "Eagle," "Bear," "Devil," etc. Whether the Jesuit fathers who first explored this little archipelago had any symbolical ideas connected with these animals we know not, but they were wise enough to appreciate the beauty of the group, and established a little church and Indian college upon the southernmost point of the southernmost island as early as 1680. A village grew slowly into existence on this point,—very slowly, since one hundred and ninety-two years later it was still a village, and less than a village; the Catholic church and adjoining buildings, the house of the Indian agent, and the United States warehouse, stored full at payment time, one store, and the cabins of the fishermen and trappers, comprised the whole. Two miles to the eastward rose a bold promontory, running far out into the bay, and forming the horizon line on that side. Perched upon the edge of this promontory, outlined against the sky, stood a solitary house. The pine forest stopped abruptly behind it, the cliff broke off abruptly in front, and for a long distance up and down the coast there was no beach or landing-place. This spot was "Misery Landing," so called because there was no landing there, not even a miserable one,—at least that was what John Jay said when he first saw the place. The inconsistency pleased him, and forthwith he ordered a cabin built on the edge of the cliff, taking up his abode meanwhile in the village, and systematically investigating the origin of the name. He explored the upper circle, consisting of the Indian agent, the storekeeper, and the priests; but they could tell him nothing. A priest more imaginative than the rest hastily improvised a legend about some miserable sinner, but John refused to accept the obvious fraud. The second circle, consisting of fishermen, voyageurs, and half-breed trappers, knew nothing save the fact that the name belonged to the point before their day. The third circle, consisting of unadulterated Indian, produced the item that the name was given by a white man as long ago as the days of their great-grandfathers. Who the white man was and what his story no one knew, and John was at liberty to imagine anything he pleased. The cabin built, he took possession of his eyrie. It was fortified by a high stockade across the land side; the other three sides were sheer cliffs rising from the deep water. Directly in front of the house, however, a rope-ladder was suspended over the cliff, strongly fastened at the top, but hanging loose at the bottom within two feet of the water; so, in spite of nature's obstacles, he had a landing-place at Misery after all.

VII

Cities in the Morning

WRITING of his travels in the Ohio valley, Dickens referred to certain towns and villages. Then he corrected himself: "I ought to say city; every place is a city here."

If not yet a city, every frontier settlement proposed to become one. An Illinois river town with great expectations changed its name from Stone's Landing to Napoleon. In the same mood Goose Run became the Columbus River, and Spunky Point was renamed Warsaw. To make its future doubly clear a southern Illinois crossroads was named Metropolis City. Some Westerners said that Cairo, at the junction of the Ohio and Mississippi rivers, would surpass Boston and New York.

If there was an art in raising a village into a city it consisted of choosing a location at a meeting of waterways and planting in it some enterprising men. Cincinnati, the one real metropolis of the early West, occupied a strategic site where the Miami River joined the Ohio. The village of Cleveland had a small harbor on Lake Erie, but not until the Ohio Canal was opened into the interior did Cleveland begin to grow. Chicago was incorporated in 1833 with a bare 200 population; four years later it was a city with a fever of speculation for lands on the Illinois and Michigan Canal.

St. Paul, at the head of navigation on the Mississippi, was a natural depot, but the river poured its power over the Falls of St. Anthony until men saw Minneapolis as a site for lumber mills and flour mills. To encourage settlement to South Bend on the St. Joseph River, the first settlers offered free land and a cash bonus to sober tradesmen. They attracted the sober Studebaker brothers who developed a world-famous wagonworks. In 1836 lake ships brought swarms of immigrants to the weedy mouth of the Milwaukee River. Sixty buildings went up in seven months, and in one of them Byron Kilbourn published the town's first newspaper.

As the American economy developed, iron ore came down the lakes and coal came out of the Ohio valley, and both went into blast furnaces in the steel centers of the Midwest. Heavy industry spread westward along the 41st parallel. Buffalo, Erie, Canton, Akron, Cleveland, Lorain, Toledo, Detroit, Chicago, Milwaukee, were in the line of destiny. But no one could read that destiny in the long morning light of 1830. To Shawneetown, Illinois, the old brawling center of the flatboat trade, came some men from the hamlet of Chicago, wanting to borrow $1,000 to get their village out of the mud. The Shawneetown merchants shook their heads; they could not see a future for Chicago.

PITTSBURGH IN 1802

F. A. MICHAUX

The Ohio is a river without a source. It begins, full-fledged, where the muddy Monongahela joins the clear Allegheny, forming America's only interior river that flows westward. There, in colonial times, the French built Fort Duquesne and the British built Fort Pitt, and there Pittsburgh grew up at the meeting of the rivers.

From the height of Grant's Hill, a century and a half ago, it looked like a drowsy settlement. But the wind brought the clatter of hammers from the boatyards and the cries of teamsters on the landing. On the river bank stood gristmills, sawmills, ropewalks, sail lofts, brickyards, breweries, a foundry, an anchor smithy, and the first nail factory in America. A stream of traffic moved in the streets—lumber wagons, brick wagons, farm wagons, movers' wagons, gigs, carts, buckboards, sometimes a string of pack ponies. On the river moved another traffic—arks, skiffs, flatboats, keelboats, carrying men and merchandise to the West.

In 1802 the French naturalist François André Michaux was there, his sharp right eye (the left one had been shot out by a rifle bullet in his youth) taking it all in. He was bound down the Ohio on a scientific tour. Already, at Pittsburgh, his notebook was filling up with the sounds and sights of the new country.

This excerpt is taken from his Travels, *published in London in 1805.*

PITTSBURGH is situated at the conflux of the rivers Monongahela and Alleghany, the uniting of which forms the Ohio. The even soil upon which it is built is not more than forty or fifty acres in extent. It is in the form of an angle, the three sides of which are enclosed either by the bed of the two rivers or by stupendous mountains. The houses are principally brick, they are computed to be about four hundred, most of which are built upon the Monongahela; that side is considered the most commercial part of the town. As a great number of the houses are separated from each other by large spaces, the whole surface of the angle is completely taken up. On the summit of the angle the French built Fort Duquesne, which is now entirely destroyed, and nothing more is seen than the vestige of the ditches that surrounded it. This spot affords the most pleasing view, produced by the perspective of the rivers, overshadowed with forests, and especially the Ohio, which flows in a strait line, and, to appearance, loses itself in space.

The air is very salubrious at Pittsburgh and its environs; intermittent fevers are unknown there, although so common in the southern states, neither are they tormented in the summer with musquitoes. A person may subsist there for one-third of what he pays at Philadelphia. Two printing-offices have been long established there, and, for the amusement of the curious, each publish a newspaper weekly.

Pittsburgh has been long considered by the Americans as the key to the western country. Thence the federal forces were marched against the Indians who opposed the former settlement of the Americans in Kentucky, and on the banks of the Ohio. However, now the Indian nations are repulsed to a considerable distance, and reduced to the impossibility of hurting the most remote settlers in the interior of the states; besides, the western country has acquired a great mass of population, insomuch that there is nothing now at Pittsburgh but a feeble garrison, barracked in a fort belonging to the town, on the banks of the river Allighany.

However, though this town has lost its importance as a military post, it has acquired a still greater one in respect to commerce. It serves as a staple for the different sorts of merchandise that Philadelphia and Baltimore send, in the beginning of spring and autumn, for supplying the states of Ohio, Kentucky, and the settlement of Natches.

The conveyance of merchandise from Philadelphia to Pittsburgh is made in large covered waggons, drawn by four horses two a-breast. The price of carrying goods varies according to the season; but in general it does not exceed six piastres the quintal. They reckon it to be three hundred miles from Philadelphia to Pittsburgh, and the carriers generally make it a journey of from twenty to twenty-four days. The price of conveyance would not be so high as it really is, were it not that the waggons frequently return empty; notwithstanding they sometimes bring back, on their return to Philadelphia or Baltimore, fur skins that come from Illinois or Ginseng, which is very common in that part of Pensylvania.

Pittsburgh is not only the staple of the Philadelphia and Baltimore trade with the western country, but of the numerous settlements that are formed upon the Monongahela and Alleghany. The territorial produce of that part of the country finds an easy and advantageous conveyance by the Ohio and Mississippi. Corn, hams and dried pork are the principal articles sent to New Orleans, whence they are re-exported into the Carribbees. They also export for the consumption of Louisiana, bar-iron, coarse linen, bottles manufactured at Pittsburgh, whiskey, and salt butter. A great part of these provisions come from Redstone, a small commercial town, situated upon the Monongahela, about fifty miles beyond Pittsburgh. All these advantages joined together have, within these ten years, increased tenfold the population and price of articles in the town, and contribute to its improvements, which daily grow more and more rapid.

The major part of the merchants settled at Pittsburgh, or in the environs, are the partners, or else the factors, belonging to the houses at Philadelphia. Their brokers at New Orleans sell, as much as they can, for ready money; or rather, take in exchange cottons, indigo, raw sugar, the produce of Low Louisiana, which they send off by sea to the houses at Philadelphia and Baltimore, and thus cover their first advances. The bargemen return thus by sea to Philadelphia or Baltimore, whence they go by land to Pittsburgh and the environs, where the major part of them generally reside. Although the passage from New Orleans to one of these two ports is twenty or thirty days, and that they have to take a route by land of three hundred miles to return to Pittsburgh, they prefer this way, being not so difficult as the return by land from New Orleans to Pittsburgh, this last distance being fourteen or fifteen hundred miles. However, when the barges are only destined for Limeston, in Kentucky, or for Cincinnati, in the state of Ohio, the bargemen return by land, and by that means take a route of four or five hundred miles.

The navigation of the Ohio and Mississippi is so much improved of late that they can tell almost to a certainty the distance from Pittsburgh to New Orleans, which they compute to be two thousand one hundred miles. The barges in the spring season usually take forty or fifty days to make the passage, which two or three persons in a *pirogue* make in five and-twenty days.

What many, perhaps, are ignorant of in Europe is, that they build large vessels on the Ohio, and at the town of Pittsburgh. One of the principal ship yards is upon the Monongahela, about two hundred fathoms beyond the last houses in the town. The timber they make use of is the white oak, or *quercus alba;* the red oak, or *quercus rubra;* the black oak, or *quercus tinctoria;* a kind of nut tree, or *juglans minima;* the Virginia cherry-tree, or *cerasus Virginia;* and a kind of pine, which they use for masting, as well as for the sides of the vessels which require a slighter wood. The whole of this timber being near at hand, the expense of building is not so great as in the ports of the Atlantic states. The cordage is manufactured at Redstone and Lexinton, where there are two extensive rope-walks, which also supply ships with rigging that are built at Marietta and Louisville. On my journey to Pittsburgh in the month of July 1802, there was a three-mast vessel of two hundred and fifty tons, and a smaller one of ninety, which was on the point of being finished. These ships were to go, in the spring following, to New Orleans, loaded with the produce of the country, after having made a passage of two thousand two hundred miles before they got into the ocean. There is no doubt but they can, by the same rule, build ships two hundred leagues beyond the mouth of the Missouri, fifty from that of the river Illinois, and even in the Mississippi, two hundred beyond the place whence these rivers flow; that is to say, six hundred and fifty leagues from the sea; as their bed in the appointed space is as deep as that of the Ohio at Pittsburgh; in consequence of which it must be a wrong conjecture to suppose that the immense tract of country watered by these rivers cannot be populous enough to execute such undertakings. The rapid population of the three new western states, under less favourable circumstances, proves this assertion to be true. Those states, where thirty years ago there was scarcely three hundred inhabitants, are now computed to contain upwards of a hundred thousand; and although the plantations on the roads are scarcely four miles distant from each other, it is very rare to find one, even among the most flourishing, where one cannot with confidence ask the owner, whence he has emigrated; or, according to the trivial manner of the Americans, "What part of the world do you come from?" as if these immense and fertile regions were to be the asylum common to all the inhabitants of the globe. Now if we consider these astonishing and rapid ameliorations, what ideas must we not form of the height of prosperity to which the western country is rising, and of the recent spring that the commerce, population and culture of the country is taking by uniting Louisiana to the American territory.

The river Monongahela derives its source in Virginia, at the foot of Laurel Mountain, which comprises a part of the chain of the Alleghanies; bending its course toward the west, it runs into Pennsylvania, and before it reaches Alleghany it receives in its current the rivers Chéat and Youghiogheny, which pro-

ceed from the south west. The territory watered by this river is extremely fertile; and the settlements formed upon the banks are not very far apart. It begins to be navigable at Morgan Town, which is composed of about sixty houses, and is situated upon the right, within a hundred miles of its *embouchure*. Of all the little towns built upon the Monongahela, New Geneva and Redstone have the most active commerce. The former has a glass-house in it, the produce of which is exported chiefly into the western country; the latter has shoe and paper manufactories, several flour mills, and contains about five hundred inhabitants. At this town a great number of those who emigrate from the eastern states embark to go into the west. It is also famous for building large boats, called *Kentucky boats*, used in the Kentucky trade; numbers are also built at Elizabeth Town, situated on the same river, about twenty-three miles from Pittsburgh—the *Monongahela Farmer* was launched there, a sailing vessel of two hundred tons.

Alleghany takes its source fifteen or twenty miles from lake Eria; its current is enlarged by the French Creek, and various small rivers of less importance. The Alleghany begins to be navigable within two hundred miles of Pittsburgh. The banks of this river are fertile; the inhabitants who have formed settlements there export, as well as those of Monongahela, the produce of their culture by the way of the Ohio and Mississippi. On the banks of this river they begin to form a few small towns; among the most considerable are Meadville, situated two hundred and thirty miles from Pittsburgh; Franklin, about two hundred; and Freeport, scarcely one; each of which does not contain above forty or fifty houses.

Let the weather be what it will, the stream of the Alleghany is clear and limpid; that of the Monongahela, on the contrary, grows rather muddy with a few days incessant rain in that part of the Alleghany Mountains where it derives its source.

The sugar-maple is very common in every part of Pennsylvania which the Monongahela and Alleghany water. This tree thrives most in cold, wet, and mountainous countries, and its seed is always more abundant when the winter is most severe. The sugar extracted from it is generally very coarse, and is sold, after having been prepared in loaves of six, eight, and ten pounds each, at the rate of seven-pence per pound. The inhabitants manufacture none but for their own use; the greater part of them drink tea and coffee daily, but they use it just as it has passed the first evaporation, and never take the trouble to refine it, on account of the great waste occasioned by the operation. . . .

The Ohio may be, at Pittsburgh, two hundred fathoms broad. The current of this immense and magnificent river inclines at first north west for about twenty miles, then bends gradually west south west. It follows that direction for about the space of five hundred miles; turns thence south west a hundred and sixty miles; then west two hundred and seventy-five; at length runs into the Mississippi in a south-westerly direction, in the latitude of 36 deg. 46 min. about eleven hundred miles from Pittsburgh, and nearly the same distance from Orleans. This river runs so extremely serpentine, that in going down it, you appear following a track directly opposite to the one you mean to take. Its breadth varies from two hundred to a thousand fathoms. The islands that are met with in its current are very numerous. We counted upward of fifty in the space of three hundred and eighty miles. Some contain but a few acres, and others more than a thousand in length. Their banks are very low, and must be subject to inundations. These islands are a great impediment to the navigation in the summer. The sands that the river drives up form, at the head of some of them, a number of little shoals; and in this season of the year the channel is so narrow from the want of water, that the few boats, even of a middling size, that venture to go down, are frequently run aground, and it is with great difficulty that they are got afloat; notwithstanding which there is at all times a sufficiency of water for a skiff or a canoe. As these little boats are very light when they strike upon the sands, it is very easy to push them off into a deeper part. In consequence of this, it is only in the spring and autumn that the Ohio is navigable, at least as far as Limestone,

about a hundred and twenty miles from Pittsburgh. During those two seasons the water rises to such a height, that vessels of three hundred tons, piloted by men who are acquainted with the river, may go down in the greatest safety. The spring season begins at the end of February, and lasts three months; the autumn begins in October, and only lasts till the first of December. In the mean time these two epochs fall sooner or later, as the winter is more or less rainy, or the rivers are a shorter or a longer time thawing. Again, it so happens, that in the course of the summer heavy and incessant rains fall in the Alleghany Mountains, which suddenly swell the Ohio: at that time persons may go down it with the greatest safety; but such circumstances are not always to be depended on.

The banks of the Ohio are high and solid; its current is free from a thousand obstacles that render the navigation of the Mississippi difficult, and often dangerous, when they have not skilful conductors. On the Ohio persons may travel all night without the smallest danger; instead of which, on the Mississippi prudence requires them to stop every evening, at least from the mouth of the Ohio to Naches, a space of nearly seven hundred and fifty miles.

The rapidity of the Ohio's current is extreme in spring; at the same time in this season there is no necessity for rowing. The excessive swiftness it would give, by that means, to the boat would be more dangerous than useful, by turning it out of the current, and running it upon some island or other, where it might get entangled among a heap of dead trees that are half under water, and from which it would be very difficult to extricate them; for which reason they generally go with the current, which is always strong enough to advance with great celerity, and is always more rapid in the middle of the stream. The amazing rapidity of the Ohio has an influence on the shape of the boats that navigate upon it, and that shape is not calculated to accelerate their progress, but to stem the current of the stream. All the boats or barges, whether those in the Kentucky or Mississippi trade, or those which convey the families that go into the eastern or western states, are built in the same manner. They are of a square form, some longer than others; their sides are raised four feet and a half above the water; their length is from fifteen to fifty feet; the two extremities are square, upon one of which is a kind of awning, under which the passengers shelter themselves when it rains. I was alone upon the banks of the Monongahela, when I perceived, at a distance, five or six of these barges, which were going down the river. I could not conceive what these great square boxes were, which, left to the stream, presented alternately their ends, sides, and even their angles. As they advanced, I heard a confused noise, but without distinguishing any thing, on account of their sides being so very high. However, on ascending the banks of the river, I perceived in these barges several families, carrying with them their horses, cows, poultry, waggons, ploughs, harness, beds, instruments of agriculture, in fine, every thing necessary to cultivate the land, and also for domestic use. These people were abandoning themselves to the mercy of the stream, without knowing the place where they should stop, to exercise their industry, and enjoy peaceably the fruit of their labour under one of the best governments that exists in the world.

CINCINNATI IN 1828

FRANCES TROLLOPE

When Mrs. Trollope came to America in 1827 to run a department store, she had no thought of becoming rich and famous as the author of a book. The most important city in the West was Cincinnati, then a bustling frontier town of 20,000, and there she built her fantastic Bazaar with its Moorish windows and Egyptian colonnade. The store, specializing in French finery, failed, but Mrs. Trollope had been making notes on the raw new life around her. When her Domestic Manners of the Americans *was published in 1832, English readers relished its racy picture of American life. In America the book was widely read and angrily denounced. Mark Twain, however, wrote: "She lived three years in this civilization of ours; in the body of it—not on the surface of it, as was the case with most of the foreign tourists of her day. She knew her subject well, and she set it forth fairly and squarely, without any weak ifs and ands and buts. . . . She dealt what the gamblers call a strictly 'square game.' She did not gild us; and neither did she whitewash us."*

The following passages are taken from Chapters 5, 7, and 9.

THOUGH I do not quite sympathise with those who consider Cincinnati as one of the wonders of the earth, I certainly think it a city of extraordinary size and importance, when it is remembered that thirty years ago the aboriginal forest occupied the ground where it stands; and every month appears to extend its limits and its wealth.

Some of the native political economists assert that this rapid conversion of a bear-brake into a prosperous city, is the result of free political institutions; not being very deep in such matters, a more obvious cause suggested itself to me, in the unceasing goad which necessity applies to industry in this country, and in the absence of all resource for the idle. During nearly two years that I resided in Cincinnati, or its neighbourhood, I neither saw a beggar, nor a man of sufficient fortune to permit his ceasing his efforts to increase it; thus every bee in the hive is actively employed in search of that honey of Hybla, vulgarly called money; neither art, science, learning, nor pleasure can seduce them from its pursuit. This unity of purpose, backed by the spirit of enterprise, and joined with an acuteness and total absence of probity, where interest is concerned, which might set canny Yorkshire at defiance, may well go far towards obtaining its purpose.

The low rate of taxation, too, unquestionably permits a more rapid accumulation of individual wealth than with us; but till I had travelled through America, I had no idea how much of the money collected in taxes returns among the people, not only in the purchase of what their industry furnishes, but in the actual enjoyment of what is furnished. Were I an English legislator, instead of sending sedition to the Tower, I would send her to make a tour of the United States. I had a little leaning towards sedition myself when I set out, but before I had half completed my tour I was quite cured. . . .

Perhaps the most advantageous feature in Cincinnati is its market, which, for excellence, abundance, and cheapness can hardly, I should think, be surpassed in any part of the world, if I except the luxury of fruits, which are very inferior to any I have seen in Europe. There are no butchers, fishmongers, or indeed any shops for eatables, except bakeries, as they are called, in the town; every thing must be purchased at market; and to accomplish this, the busy housewife must be stirring betimes, or, 'spite of the abundant supply, she will find her hopes of breakfast, dinner, and supper for the day defeated, the market being pretty well over by eight o'clock.

The beef is excellent, and the highest price when we were there, four cents (about twopence) the pound. The mutton was inferior, and so was veal to the eye, but it ate well, though not very fat; the price was about the same. The poultry was excellent; fowls or full-sized chickens, ready for the table, twelve cents, but much less if bought alive, and not quite fat; turkeys about fifty cents, and geese the same. The Ohio furnishes several sorts of fish, some of them very good, and always to be found cheap and abundant in the market. Eggs, butter, nearly all kinds of vegetables, excellent, and at moderate prices. From June till December tomatoes (the great luxury of the American table in the opinion of most Europeans) may be found in the highest perfection in the market for about sixpence the peck. They have a great variety of beans unknown in England, particularly the lima-bean, the seed of which is dressed like the French harrico; it furnishes a very abundant crop, and is a most delicious vegetable; could it be naturalised with us it would be a valuable acquisition. The Windsor, or broad-bean, will not do well there; Mr. Bullock had them in his garden, where they were cultivated with much care; they grew about a foot high and blossomed, but the pod never ripened. All the fruit I saw exposed for sale in Cincinnati was most miserable. I passed two summers there, but never tasted a peach worth eating. Of apricots and nectarines I saw none; strawberries very small, raspberries much worse; gooseberries very few, and quite uneatable; currants about half the size of ours, and about double the price; grapes too sour for tarts; apples abundant, but very indifferent, none that would be thought good enough for an English table; pears, cherries, and plums most miserably bad. The flowers of these regions were at least equally inferior; whether this proceeds from want of cultivation or from peculiarity of soil I know not, but after leaving Cincinnati, I was told by a gentleman who appeared to understand the subject, that the state of Ohio had no indigenous flowers or fruits. The water-melons, which in that warm climate furnish a delightful refreshment, were abundant and cheap; but all other melons were inferior to those of France, or even of England, when ripened in a common hot-bed.

From the almost total want of pasturage near the city, it is difficult for a stranger to divine how milk is furnished for its supply, but we soon learnt that there are more ways than one of keeping a cow. A large proportion of the families in the town, particularly of the poorer class, have one, though apparently without any accommodation whatever for it. These animals are fed morning and evening at the door of the house, with a good mess of Indian corn, boiled with water; while they eat, they are milked, and when the operation is completed the milk-pail and the meal-tub

Above: Cincinnati in 1835, from a painting by John Casper Wilde. *Courtesy Ohio Historical Society* Below: Cincinnati waterfront, c. 1835, painted by John Casper Wilde. *Courtesy Ohio Historical Society*

retreat into the dwelling, leaving the republican cow to walk away, to take her pleasure on the hills, or in the gutters, as may suit her fancy best. They generally return very regularly to give and take the morning and evening meal; though it more than once happened to us, before we were supplied by a regular milk cart, to have our jug sent home empty, with the sad news that "the cow was not come home, and it was too late to look for her to breakfast now." Once, I remember, the good woman told us that she had overslept herself, and that the cow had come and gone again, "not liking, I expect, to hanker about by herself for nothing, poor thing."

Cincinnati has not many lions to boast, but among them are two museums of natural history; both of these contain many respectable specimens, particularly that of Mr. Dorfeuille, who has, moreover, some highly interesting Indian antiquities. He is a man of taste and science, but a collection formed strictly according to their dictates, would by no means satisfy the western metropolis. The people have a most extravagant passion for wax figures, and the two museums vie with each other in displaying specimens of this barbarous branch of art. As Mr. Dorfeuille cannot trust to his science for attracting the citizens, he has put his ingenuity into requisition, and this has proved to him the surer aid of the two. He has constructed a pandemonium in an upper story of his museum, in which he has congregated all the images of horror that his fertile fancy could devise; dwarfs that by machinery grow into giants before the eyes of the spectator; imps of ebony with eyes of flame; monstrous reptiles devouring youth and beauty; lakes of fire, and mountains of ice; in short, wax, paint and springs have done wonders. "To give the scheme some more effect," he makes it visible only through a grate of massive iron bars, among which are arranged wires connected with an electrical machine in a neighboring chamber; should any daring hand or foot obtrude itself within the bars, it receives a smart shock, that often passes through many of the crowd, and the cause being unknown, the effect is exceedingly comic; terror, astonishment, curiosity, are all set in action, and all contribute to make "Dorfeuille's Hell" one of the most amusing exhibitions imaginable. . . .

It seems hardly fair to quarrel with a place because its staple commodity is not pretty, but I am sure I should have liked Cincinnati much better if the people had not dealt so very largely in hogs. The immense quantity of business done in this line would hardly be believed by those who had not witnessed it. I never saw a newspaper without remarking such advertisements as the following:

"Wanted, immediately, 4,000 fat hogs."

"For sale, 2,000 barrels of prime pork."

But the annoyance came nearer than this; if I determined upon a walk up Main-street, the chances were five hundred to one against my reaching the shady side without brushing by a snout fresh dripping from the kennel; when we had screwed our courage to the enterprise of mounting a certain noble-looking sugar-loaf hill, that promised pure air and a fine view, we found the brook we had to cross, at its foot, red with the stream from a pig slaughter-house; while our noses, instead of meeting "the thyme that loves the green hill's breast," were greeted by odors that I will not describe, and which I heartily hope my readers cannot imagine; our feet, that on leaving the city had expected to press the flowery sod, literally got entangled in pigs' tails and jawbones: and thus the prettiest walk in the neighborhood was interdicted for ever.

One of the sights to stare at in America is that of houses moving from place to place. We were often amused by watching this exhibition of mechanical skill in the streets. They make no difficulty of moving dwellings from one part of the town to another. Those I saw travelling were all of them frame-houses, that is, built wholly of wood, except the chimneys; but it is said that brick buildings are sometimes treated in the same manner. The largest dwelling that I saw in motion was one containing two stories of four rooms each; forty oxen were yoked to it. The first few yards brought down the two stacks of chimneys, but it afterwards went on well. The great difficulties were the first getting it in motion and the stopping exactly in the right place. This locomotive power was extremely convenient at Cincinnati, as the constant improvements going on there made it often desirable to change a wooden dwelling for one of brick; and whenever this happened, we were sure to see the

ex No. 100 of Main-street or the ex No. 55 of Second-street creeping quietly out of town, to take possession of a humble suburban station on the common above it.

BY STEAMBOAT TO DETROIT

CHARLES FENNO HOFFMAN

In the fall of 1833 a one-legged traveler, Charles Fenno Hoffman, limped onto the stagecoaches and steamboats of the West, mingling with speculators, traders, settlers and immigrants. He was a frontier news correspondent, sending back letters to the New York American. *Despite his physical handicap, he rode horseback over the winter country between Detroit and Chicago, and he joined a wolf hunt along the frozen Chicago River. As "the first tourist who has taken a winter view of scenes upon the Indian frontier," he put his observations together in* A Winter in the West *(1835), a travel book notable for its humor, color and human interest. From it the following excerpt is taken.*

Detroit, Michigan, November 25 [1833] I HAD just left the reading-room of the Franklin Hotel, in Cleaveland, and was making myself at home for the rest of the evening, in my own neat chamber, when the sound of a steamboat-bell, about nine o'clock, gave note that one of these vessels, which at this stormy season cannot navigate the lake with any regularity, had touched at Cleaveland on her way to this place. No time was to be lost, and huddling my clothes, &c. into my trunk as quickly as possible, I jumped into a vehicle, waiting at the tavern door, and in a few minutes was upon the quay. Here I witnessed a scene of indescribable confusion. The night was dark and somewhat gusty, and the boat and the wharf were both crowded with boxes, bales, and the effects of emigrants, who were screaming to each other in half as many languages as were spoken at Babel. Lanterns were flashing to and fro along the docks, and hoarse orders and countermands, mingled with the harsh hissing of the steam on every side. At length we pushed from the shore, and escaping in a moment from the head of the mole, stood fairly out into the lake, while the bright beacon of the Cleaveland lighthouse

soon waned in the distance, and was at last lost entirely. I found myself, upon looking around, on board of the fine steamboat "New-York," Captain Fisher, to whose politeness I was much indebted for showing me about the boat before turning in for the night. Taking a lantern in his hand, and tucking my arm under his, he groped about among his motley ship's company like Diogenes looking for an honest man.

Our course first led us through a group of emigrants collected around a stove, mid-ships, where an English mother nursing her infant, a child lying asleep upon a mastiff, and a long-bearded German smoking his meerchaum on the top of a pile of candle-boxes, were the only complete figures I could make out from an indefinite number of heads, arms, and legs lying about in the most whimsical confusion. Passing farther on, we came to two tolerable cabins on either side of the boat just forward of the wheels, both pretty well filled with emigrants, who were here more comfortably bestowed. We next passed the forward bar-room (there being another abaft for cabin-passengers), and finally came to the bow, of which a horse and several dogs had already

Detroit in 1820, with a view of "Walk in the Water." *Courtesy Burton Historical Collection of Detroit Public Library*

been the occupants for so many days,—the New-York having been twice driven into port and delayed by stress of weather,—that it might have been mistaken for either stable or kennel. A noble English blood-hound, the second dog only of that rare breed that I have ever seen, here attracted my attention, and delayed me until I made his acquaintance; which was but a moment, however, for every dog of a generous strain can tell instinctively when a friend of his kind approaches him.

Among others of the canine crew, too, there was a fine spaniel, whose deplorable fate, subsequently, I may as well mention here as elsewhere. The master of poor Dash, it seems, went ashore during the night at Huron, where the boat put in to land way-passengers; and the animal, springing eagerly along a plank at his call, was kicked from his narrow foothold, by some brute of a fellow, into the lake. The night was dark, and the shadow of the high wharf shut out the few lights on shore from the view of the poor animal, while those on board of the boat led him away from the land. He swam after us, yelling most piteously, until

his suffocating cries were lost in the freshening sea, which probably the next morning tossed him a carrion on the shore. Had I witnessed the act of throwing him overboard, I could scarcely have restrained myself from pitching the dastardly perpetrator of the cruelty after the victim of his brutality: for if there be one trait in men which awakens in me indignation amounting almost to loathing of my kind, it is to see human things treating those parts of the animal creation beneath them as if this earth was meant for none of God's creatures but man.

But to return to our travels through this floating castle: We next ascended a steep stairway to the upper deck of all, and I here spent some moments rather amusingly in surveying the furniture of the emigrants with which it was crowded. They differed according to the origin of their owner. The effects of the Yankee were generally limited to a Dearborn wagon, a feather-bed, a saddle and bridle, and some knickknack in the way of a machine for shelling corn, hatchelling flax, or, for aught I know, manufacturing wooden nutmegs for family use. Those of the Englishman are far more numerous; for John Bull, when he wanders from home, would not only, like the roving Trojan, carry his household gods with him into strange lands, but even the fast-anchored isle itself, could he but cut it from its moorings. Whenever, therefore, you see an antique-fashioned looking-glass, a decrepit bureau, and some tenderly-preserved old china, you will probably, upon looking further, have the whole house-keeping array of an honest Briton exposed to your view.

But still further do the Swiss and Germans carry their love of family relics. Mark that quaint-looking wagon which lumbers up a dozen square feet of the deck. You may see a portrait of it among the illuminated letters of a vellum-bound edition of Virgil's Bucolics. It was taken from an Helvetian ancestor that transported Cæsar's baggage into winter-quarters. It might be worth something in a museum, but it has cost five times its value in freight to transport it over the Atlantic. What an indignity it is to overwhelm the triumphal chariot with the beds and ploughs, shovels, saddles, and sideboards, chairs, clocks, and carpets that fill its interior, and to hang those rusty pots and kettles, bakepans, fryingpans, and saucepans, iron candlesticks, old horse-shoes, and broken tobacco-pipes, like trophies of conquest over Time, along its racked and wheezing sides. That short man yonder, with square shoulders and a crooked pipe in his mouth, is the owner; he, with the woollen cap, that is just raising his blue cotton frock to thrust his hand into the fob of his sherrivalleys. That man had probably not the slightest idea of the kind of country he was coming to. His eyes are but now just opening to his new condition; nor will he sacrifice a particle of his useless and expensive trumpery until they are completely open. That man has not yet a thought in common with the people of his new abode around him. He looks, indeed, as if he came from another planet. Visit him on his thriving farm ten years hence, and, except in the single point of language, you will find him (unless he has settled among a nest of his countrymen) at home among his neighbours, and happily conforming to their usages; while

that clean-looking Englishman next to him will still be a stranger in the land.

I subsequently looked into the different cabins and compartments of the boat not yet visited, and had reason to be gratified with the appearance of all; though the steamboat Michigan, which I have since visited at the docks here, puts me completely out of conceit of every part of the New-York, except her captain. The Michigan, machinery and all, was built at Detroit; and without entering into a minute description of it, I may say, that fine as our Atlantic boats are, I do not recollect any on the Atlantic waters, for strength and beauty united, equal to this. A great mistake, however, I think, exists here in building the boats for these waters with cabins on deck, like the river boats. In consequence of such a large part of the hull being above water, they are rendered dangerous during the tremendous gales which sweep Lake Erie, and are often compelled to make a port of safety several times during a passage. The English steamers which ply between Dover and Calais are built like other sea-vessels; and having their machinery below, can consequently keep on their course in a sea where one of ours would live but a few minutes. I was fortunate, considering the stormy season of the year, in having a tolerably smooth passage across the lake, there being but few persons sea-sick on board of the boat, and I happily not included in the number. But it must be very unpleasant, during a heavy blow, to be tossed on the short cobble sea which the light fresh water of these lakes always breaks into beneath the wind.

We passed a number of islands in the morning soon after breakfast; some of them mere rocks, and others several miles in circumference. On one of these, of a few acres in extent, a row-boat, in which a man undertook to transport himself and one or two members of his family to the shore, was wrecked some years since. The father and brother, with a daughter of about twelve years, managed to subsist upon the snakes and snails they found among the rocks, until a passing vessel took them off, after some ten days of suffering.

It was during a shower, shortly after noon, when some low wooded islands on the

American side of the lake, with a tall flag-staff peering above the haze from the little town of Amherstburg on the British shore, indicated that we had entered the mouth of the Detroit River. The wind, which was now beginning to rise into a threatening tempest, compelled us to hug the Canadian shore so closely, that the red-coated sentinel pacing along the barracks above Fort Malden was plainly seen from the boat. The river soon after narrows sufficiently for one to mark with ease the general appearance of its banks, and the different settlements upon their course. Their appearance must be pretty in summer, when fields and woods show to the most advantage. But now, though slightly undulating, with a sudden rise from the river of some fifty or sixty feet, the adjacent country is too low to be strikingly beautiful. Those, however, who admire the Delaware below Trenton, if they can dispense with the handsome seats which ornament its not very clear waters, may find a charm in the gentle banks and transparent tide of the Detroit River.

The city of Detroit itself stands upon an elevated piece of table-land, extending probably for some twenty miles back from the river, and being perfectly unbroken for at least two miles along its margin. Beneath the bluff—for the plain is so high as almost to deserve the name—is a narrow bustling street of about half a mile in length, with the wharves just beyond it; and fifty yards inboard runs a spacious street called Jefferson Avenue, parallel with the lower street and the river; the chief part of the town extends for a mile or two along the latter. The dwelling-houses are generally of wood, but there are a great many stores now building, or already erected, of brick, with stone basements. The brick is generally of an indifferent quality; but the stone, which is brought from Cleaveland, Ohio, is a remarkably fine material for building purposes. It is a kind of yellow freestone, which is easily worked when first taken from the quarry, and hardens subsequently upon exposure to the air. There are at this moment many four-story stores erecting, as well as other substantial buildings, which speak for the flourishing condition of the place.

The want of mechanics is so great, however, that it is difficult as yet to carry on these operations upon the scale common in our Atlantic cities, although the demand for houses in Detroit, it is said, would fully warrant similar outlays of capital. The public buildings are the territorial council-house, situated upon an open piece of ground, designated on an engraved plan of the city as "The Campus Martius," a court-house, academy, and two banks. There are also five churches, a Catholic, an Episcopal, a Presbyterian, Baptist, and Methodist. The Catholic congregation is the largest; their stone church, after remaining several years in an unfinished state, is soon, it is said, to be completed with funds derived from Rome; it will make an imposing appearance when finished. The population of Detroit is, I believe, between three and four thousand —it increases so rapidly, however, that it is difficult to form an estimate. The historical associations, the safety, and commodiousness of the harbour, with its extensive inland commercial advantages, must ever constitute this one of the most interesting and important points in the Union.

LAND SALES IN CHICAGO, 1836

HARRIET MARTINEAU

*Among other surrenders in the Treaty of Greene Ville in 1795 the Indians
ceded to the United States "one piece of land six miles square at the mouth of the
Checagau River, emptying into the southwest end of Lake Michigan where a fort
formerly stood." But after the treaty the tribes remained, and it was their fur trade
that drew the first settlers to Chicago. Fort Dearborn, built in 1803, was burned
by the Indians in 1812 and its garrison was massacred. The fort was rebuilt in
1816 but not until 1830 was a town laid out on the marshy land. In 1832, with
a population of five hundred, the town established a ferry service across the river,
enlarged the log jail and spent twelve dollars on an estray pen for lost animals. So
began the city of Chicago, which soon saw an inrush of merchants and settlers.
The first work on the Illinois and Michigan Canal in 1836 brought a fever
of land speculation.*

*In that hectic season arrived Harriet Martineau of Norwich, England. She
had traveled west by lake boat and stagecoach, and she was glad to stop a while
at Chicago. She found the town raw and bare and far from restful. Tranquillity
lay over the prairies, where a June wind rippled the wild grass like water, but
Chicago was a scene of perpetual clamor and commotion.*

*Miss Martineau was a good traveler despite a handicap. "I labored under one
peculiar disadvantage," she confessed, "I mean my deafness." But she quickly
added: "This does not endanger the accuracy of my information . . . because
I carry a trumpet of remarkable fidelity." She also carried a lively curiosity, an
observant eye, and a zestful, unprejudiced mind.*

Her American travels, ear trumpet in hand, in the 1830's resulted in
A Retrospect of Western Travel *and* Society in America, *from which this
excerpt is taken.*

ON our road to Chicago, the next day,—a road winding in and out among the sand-hills, we were called to alight, and run up a bank to see a wreck. It was the wreck of the Delaware;—the steamer in which it had been a question whether we should not proceed from Niles to Chicago. She had a singular twist in her middle, where she was nearly broken in two. Her passengers stood up to the neck in water, for twenty-four hours before they were taken off; a worse inconvenience than any that we had suffered by coming the other way. The first thing the passengers from the Delaware did, when they had dried and warmed themselves on shore, was to sign a letter to the captain, which appeared in all the neighbouring newspapers, thanking him for the great comfort they had enjoyed on board his vessel. It is to be presumed that they meant previously to their having to stand up to their necks in water.

In the wood which borders the prairie on which Chicago stands, we saw an encampment of United States' troops. Since the rising of the Creeks in Georgia, some months before, there had been apprehensions of an Indian war along the whole frontier. It was believed that a correspondence had taken place among all the tribes, from the Cumanches, who were engaged to fight for the Mexicans in Texas, up to the northern tribes among whom we were going. It was believed that the war-belt was circulating among the Winnebagoes, the war-like tribe who inhabit the western shores of Lake Michigan; and the government had sent troops to Chicago, to keep them in awe. It was of some consequence to us to ascertain the real state of the case; and we were glad to find that alarm was subsiding so fast, that the troops were soon allowed to go where they were more wanted. As soon as they had recovered from the storm which seemed to have incommoded everybody, they broke up their encampment, and departed.

Chicago looks raw and bare, standing on the high prairie above the lake-shore. The houses appeared all insignificant, and run up in various directions, without any principle at all. A friend of mine who resides there had told me that we should find the inns intolerable, at the period of the great land sales, which bring a concourse of speculators to the place. It was even so. The very sight of them was intolerable; and there was not room for our party among them all. I do not know what we should have done, (unless to betake ourselves to the vessels in the harbour,) if our coming had not been foreknown, and most kindly provided for. We were divided between three families, who had the art of removing all our scruples about intruding on perfect strangers. None of us will lose the lively and pleasant associations with the place, which were caused by the hospitalities of its inhabitants.

I never saw a busier place than Chicago was at the time of our arrival. The streets were crowded with land speculators, hurrying from one sale to another. A negro, dressed up in scarlet, bearing a scarlet flag, and riding a white horse with housings of scarlet, announced the times of sale. At every street-corner where he stopped, the crowd flocked round him; and it seemed as if some prevalent mania infected the whole people. The rage for speculation might fairly be so regarded. As the gentlemen of our party walked the streets, store-keepers hailed them from their doors, with offers of farms, and all manner of land-lots, advising them to speculate before the price of land rose higher. A young lawyer, of my acquaintance there, had realised five hundred dollars per day, the five preceding days, by merely making out titles to land. Another friend had realised, in two years, ten times as much money as he had before fixed upon as a competence for life. Of course, this rapid money-making is a merely temporary evil. A bursting of the bubble must come soon. The absurdity of the speculation is so striking, that the wonder is that the fever should have attained such a height as I witnessed. The immediate occasion of the bustle which prevailed, the week we were at Chicago, was the sale of lots, to the value of two millions of dollars, along the course of a projected canal; and of another set, immediately behind these. Persons not intending to game, and not infected with mania, would endeavour to form some reasonable conjecture as to the ultimate value of the lots, by calculating the cost of the canal, the risks from accident, from the possible competition from other places, &c., and, finally, the possible profits, under the most favourable circumstances, within so many years' purchase. Such a calculation would serve as some sort of guide as to the amount of purchase-money to be risked. Whereas, wild land on the banks of a canal, not yet even marked out, was selling at Chicago for more than rich land, well improved, in the finest part of the valley of the Mohawk, on the banks of a canal which is already the medium of an almost inestimable amount of traffic. If sharpers and gamblers were to be the sufferers by the impending crash at Chicago, no one would feel much concerned: but they, unfortunately, are the people who encourage the delusion, in order to profit by it. Many a high-spirited, but inexperienced, young man; many a simple settler, will be ruined for the advantage of knaves.

Others, besides lawyers and speculators by trade, make a fortune in such extraordinary times. A poor man at Chicago had a pre-emption right to some land, for which he paid in the morning one hundred and fifty dollars. In the afternoon, he sold it to a friend of mine for five thousand dollars. A poor Frenchman, married to a squaw, had a suit pending, when I was there, which he was likely to gain, for the right of purchasing some land by the lake for one hundred dollars, which would immediately become worth one million dollars.

There was much gaiety going on at Chicago, as well as business. On the evening of our arrival a fancy fair took place. As I was too much fatigued to go, the ladies sent me a bouquet of prairie flowers. There is some allowable pride in the place about its society. It is a remarkable thing to meet such an assemblage of educated, refined, and wealthy persons as may be found there, living in small, inconvenient houses on the edge of a wild prairie. There is a mixture, of course. I heard of a family of half-breeds setting up a carriage, and wearing fine jewellery. When the present intoxication of prosperity passes away, some of the inhabitants will go back to the eastward; there will be an accession of settlers from the mechanic classes; good houses will have been built for the richer families, and the singularity of the place will subside. It will be like all the other new and thriving lake and river ports of America. Meantime, I am glad to have seen it in its strange early days.

We dined one day with a gentleman who had been Indian agent among the Winnebagoes for some years. He and his lady seem to have had the art of making themselves as absolutely Indian in their sympathies and manners as the welfare of the savages among whom they lived required. They were the only persons I met with who, really knowing the Indians, had any regard for them. The testimony was universal to the good faith, and other virtues of savage life of the unsophisticated Indians; but they were spoken of in a tone of dislike, as well as pity, by all but this family; and they certainly had studied their Indian neighbours very thoroughly. The ladies of Indian agents ought to be women of nerve. Our hostess had slept for weeks with a loaded pistol on each side her pillow, and a dagger under it, when expecting an attack from a hostile tribe. The foe did not, however, come nearer than within a few miles. Her husband's sister was in the massacre when the fort was abandoned, in 1812. Her father and her husband were in the battle, and her mother and young brothers and sisters sat in a boat on the lake near. Out of seventy whites, only seventeen escaped, among whom were her family. She was wounded in the ankle, as she sat on her horse. A painted Indian, in warlike costume, came leaping up to her, and seized her

horse, as she supposed, to murder her. She fought him vigorously, and he bore it without doing her any injury. He spoke, but she could not understand him. Another frightful savage came up, and the two led her horse to the lake, and into it, in spite of her resistance, till the water reached their chins. She concluded that they meant to drown her; but they contented themselves with holding her on her horse till the massacre was over, when they led her out in safety. They were friendly Indians, sent by her husband to guard her. She could not but admire their patience when she found how she had been treating her protectors.

We had the fearful pleasure of seeing various savage dances performed by the Indian agent and his brother, with the accompaniments of complete costume, barbaric music, and whooping. The most intelligible to us was the Discovery Dance, a highly descriptive pantomime. We saw the Indian go out armed for war. We saw him reconnoitre, make signs to his comrades, sleep, warm himself, load his rifle, sharpen his scalping-knife, steal through the grass within rifle-shot of his foes, fire, scalp one of them, and dance, whooping and triumphing. There was a dreadful truth about the whole, and it made our blood run cold. It realised hatred and horror as effectually as Taglioni does love and grace.

We were unexpectedly detained over the Sunday at Chicago; and Dr. F. was requested to preach. Though only two hours' notice was given, a respectable congregation was assembled in the large room of the Lake House; a new hotel then building. Our seats were a few chairs and benches, and planks laid on trestles. The preacher stood behind a rough pine-table, on which a large Bible was placed. I was never present at a more interesting service; and I know that there were others who felt with me.

From Chicago, we made an excursion into the prairies. Our young lawyer-friend threw behind him the five hundred dollars per day which he was making, and went with us. I thought him wise; for there is that to be had in the wilderness which money cannot buy. We drove out of the town at ten o'clock in the morning, too late by two hours; but it was impossible to overcome the introductions

Chicago in 1820. *Courtesy Chicago Historical Society*

to strangers, and the bustle of our preparations, any sooner. Our party consisted of seven, besides the driver. Our vehicle was a wagon with four horses.

We had first to cross the prairie, nine miles wide, on the lake edge of which Chicago stands. This prairie is not usually wet so early in the year; but at this time the water stood almost up to the nave of the wheels: and we crossed it at a walking pace. I saw here, for the first time in the United States, the American primrose. It grew in profusion over the whole prairie, as far as I could see; not so large and fine as in English greenhouses, but graceful and pretty. I now found the truth of what I had read about the difficulty of distinguishing distances on a prairie. The feeling is quite bewildering. A man walking near looks like a Goliath a mile off. I mistook a covered wagon without horses, at a distance of fifty yards, for a white house near the horizon: and so on. We were not sorry to reach the belt of trees, which bounded the swamp we had passed. At a house here, where we stopped to water the horses, and eat dough nuts, we saw a crowd of emigrants; which showed that we had not yet reached the bounds of civilisation. A little further on we came to the river Aux Plaines, spelled on a sign board "Oplain." The ferry here is a monopoly, and the public suffers accordingly. There is only one small flat boat for the service of the concourse of people now pouring into the prairies. Though we happened to arrive nearly first of the crowd of today, we were detained on the bank above an hour;

Chicago in 1840. *Courtesy Illinois State Historical Library*

and then our horses went over at two crossings, and the wagon and ourselves at the third. It was a pretty scene, if we had not been in a hurry; the country wagons and teams in the wood by the side of the quiet clear river; and the oxen swimming over, yoked, with only their patient faces visible above the surface. After crossing, we proceeded briskly till we reached a single house, where, or nowhere, we were to dine. The kind hostess bestirred herself to provide us a good dinner of tea, bread, ham, potatoes, and strawberries, of which a whole pailful, ripe and sweet, had been gathered by the children in the grass round the house, within one hour. While dinner was preparing, we amused ourselves with looking over an excellent small collection of books, belonging to Miss Cynthia, the daughter of the hostess.

I never saw insulation, (not desolation,) to compare with the situation of a settler on a wide prairie. A single house in the middle of Salisbury Plain would be desolate. A single house on a prairie has clumps of trees near it, rich fields about it; and flowers, strawberries, and running water at hand. But when I saw a settler's child tripping out of home-bounds, I had a feeling that it would never get back again. It looked like putting out into Lake Michigan in a canoe. The soil round the dwellings is very rich. It makes no dust, it is so entirely vegetable. It requires merely to be once turned over to produce largely; and, at present, it appears to be inexhaustible. As we proceeded, the scenery became more and more like what all travellers compare it to,—a boundless English park. The grass was wilder, the occasional footpath not so trim, and the single trees less majestic; but no park ever displayed anything equal to the grouping of the trees within the windings of the blue, brimming river Aux Plaines.

THE TWO AKRONS

HERMAN FETZER

Before the age of rubber tires Akron was famous for its sewer-pipe industry and for its match industry which annually used up thirty million feet of white pine lumber. Originally it was a canal town. Its name is Greek, meaning "high place." Akron, on the old Tuscarawas portage, was the highest point on the Ohio and Erie Canal. The town was laid out in 1825 on the eight-mile portage path between the Cuyahoga and Tuscarawas rivers. When canal traffic began in 1827 Akron's future was bright.

Two miles away lay an older settlement, the village of Middlebury, founded by a sea captain from Connecticut who had journeyed by oxcart to the Western Reserve. When the canal was cut through to Cleveland the new Akron took away Middlebury's trade and hostilities began.

Herman Fetzer (1899–1935) ran newspaper columns in Akron and Cleveland. As "Jake Falstaff" he wrote poems and tales redolent of the earth of his native Summit County and marked by the zest, humor and fancy of a folk poet. This narrative is taken from his Centennial History of Akron, *published in 1925.*

NOW opened the most picturesque decade in the history of Akron—the Eventful Thirties.

Picture the situation. Around E. Market st., in the vicinity of Arlington and Case aves., clustered the village of Middlebury, not greatly worried by the upstart growth of its neighbor on the west. At the corner of Main and Exchange sts., was the hamlet of Akron,

Akron in 1853. Courtesy Ohio Historical Society

a canal market which had grown to 400 population with the completion of the Ohio canal from the big river to the big lake. Huddled under the steep bluff of North Hill was the locality known as Dublin—a settlement of Irish workmen.

Taverns were springing up along the canal. Young men, their arms made strong by the swinging of axes, left the clearings in the timber to follow the lure of the canal. The gentlemen of fortune in their fine linens and cambrics sat in the taverns and invited the admiration of more prosaic men and women. Their pockets were full of bogus money made in the hills of Northampton, and mingled with this was the real currency of duped farmers.

One of the residents of Middlebury was a non-practicing doctor of medicine named Eliakim Crosby. He had served in the war of 1812, and in consequence of this loyalty, certain properties he held in Canada were confiscated by the crown. He had deserted, temporarily, the theories of allopathy for those of homeopathy, and eventually had tired completely of the practice of medicine, and had entered on a career of empire-building.

Coming to Middlebury, he bought and for a time operated a plow factory, then a saw mill and then a grist mill. His mind was exalted with visions of fortunes to be made in this virgin manufacturing territory. We have seen him as a representative of Portage county at the meeting called to agitate a canal from Pittsburg to Akron.

"Waterpower" was the motif of his thinking. He had had experience with damming the Little Cuyahoga in his plow plant and his mills. Here was his dream:

He would build a canal which would lead the waters of the Little Cuyahoga from Middlebury to the Ohio canal, at a point several rods north of the northern limits of the new village of Akron. He took into his confidence Gen. Simon Perkins, who owned part of the land which he would have to use, and received encouragement.

Quietly, he began accumulating the riparian rights to the land on both sides of the Little Cuyahoga, and to the right-of-way of his proposed stream.

His plan, if he could carry it out, would provide a fall of 100 feet—an enormous source of power. He would build a city at the most strategic point of this waterway, and this city should be the rival of Middlebury and the new city of Akron. Its name should be Cascade.

The work was not without difficulties. The word of his purchases got abroad, and the farmers who owned land which he had to have held out for prices which were exorbitant for those days. The people of Middlebury and Akron grew suspicious of his movements, and started a counterplot. A syndicate was formed which hired Col. Sebried Dodge (the ruins of whose once fine house are still standing under a wooded hill on the Loyal Oak road) to make surveys for another waterpower project, farther up the stream.

But there was little left after Dr. Crosby had made his plans. He was confident that his project was the best—indeed, the only logical one. When they taunted him with their threats of beating him to the establishment of a new town, he said, "Gentlemen, your scheme won't work, but mine will; and what's more, it will make the grass grow in your streets, and make a goose pasture of your town."

He succeeded. When he saw that the project was big enough for a partner, he took Judge Leicester King of Warren into the proposition, and they two, with Gen. Simon Perkins, proceeded to lay out a town of their own. Its boundaries were these:

North st., Summit st., Oak and Walnut sts., and Quarry, Bowery and W. Center sts. They touched the northern limit of Akron on the last street named, and left a wedge-shaped piece of neutral ground between.

You have heard old-timers refer to downtown Akron as "the gore." If you will look up the word in a dictionary, you will find that it means a triangular piece of land. "The gore," as it was used in Akron, meant the territory between Akron and the new village of Cascade.

Before the canal was complete, work began on a stone mill on part of the site now occupied by the Quaker Oats Co. at Howard and Mill sts. At this point, the new canal was to empty into the Ohio canal. It reached this point by winding around the hill overlooking the fairgrounds, and then flowing down the center of Main st. to a point near Mill, where it turned west to meet the Ohio canal in its present bed. As all old-timers know, the canal is still in this same bed. It flows through a conduit under Main st.

In 1833 both the mill and the canal were finished. The water flowed through the bed as Dr. Crosby had planned it, and furnished ample waterpower. The mill became the most important one in northern Ohio.

Between Mill and Cherry sts. a deep ravine crossed Howard st. This would have to be filled before any building could be done there. So the business center of the new town was not at the same place as its industrial center. Seth Iredell (who was to be the first mayor) built a two-story frame store building at the corner of Howard and Market sts.

His building was the second to be raised in Cascade. Charles W. Howard (for whom the street was named) and Jonathan F. Fenn opened a general store in this building, later selling out to Philander D. Hall and his brother, Lorenzo. For sixty years Hall's store remained at this spot, and the intersection is still known among old-timers as Hall's corners.

A rivalry sprang up. Smug Middlebury, which had relied on its greater age to assure its stability, saw the new town grow formidable; saw it draw business swiftly and surely away from it. Akron, cocksure in its auspicious beginning, saw a strong rival springing up north of it. And the new village, just as confident as any of them, worked from dawn to dusk with a figurative grin on its face and a figurative thumb to its nose.

In its youthful impudence, it discarded the name of Cascade and began calling itself Akron.

This was not to be tolerated by the other Akron. There was great bitterness between the two villages. Middlebury, unable to believe that the upstart villages could do it any permanent harm, sat back and became a spectator to the squabble.

But its main sympathies were with the South-Enders. The overland traffic still flowed through it, and Middlebury directed it to the Exchange street Akron, representing the North-Enders as horse-thieves and cut-throats. Where Buchtel av.—then the Middlebury road—joins Market st., a sign-board was erected, pointing down Buchtel av. toward the South Akron, and bearing the legend, "Akron, One Mile."

The North-Enders at night pointed it down Market st. toward their community. It was changed back and forth several times. Guards were posted. The guards were forced to use physical force to protect the sign. The matter was finally adjusted by having two sign-boards, one pointing to "South Akron" and the other to "North Akron."

THE FLATBOAT TRADE AT DAYTON

HENRY HOWE

Four months after the Treaty of Greene Ville the town of Dayton was laid out at the place where the Mad River flows into the Miami. The land was rich and level, and the Great Miami provided a road to distant markets. In 1799 the villagers loaded a flatboat with grain, pelts, and five hundred venison hams for trade in New Orleans. For thirty years that traffic flowed, linking Dayton with the lower Mississippi. When the Miami and Erie Canal was opened to Toledo, Dayton's trade swung northward and the old flatboat traffic was forgotten.

Henry Howe was a Connecticut Yankee who went West not to take up land but to record frontier history. A long-striding man with a knapsack on his shoulders, he tramped over Ohio in the 1840's, filling his notebooks with the tales of old settlers and his sketchbook with drawings of town squares and country landscapes. In Cincinnati in 1847 he published his Historical Collections of Ohio, *from which this extract is taken.*

THE Great Miami was navigable both above and below Dayton during the great part of the year for keel boats, which were built like canal boats, only slighter and sharper, as well as for flat boats, till about 1820, when the numerous mill-dams that had by that time been erected, obstructed the channel. From that date till 1829, when the canal was opened, freighting south by water, except what was done in flat boats during floods, was almost abandoned. The boats were often loaded with produce taken in exchange for goods, work, or even for lots and houses, for business men, instead of having money to deposit in bank or to invest, were frequently obliged to send cargoes of articles received in place of cash South or North for sale. Cherry and walnut logs were sometimes brought down the river on the flat boats. The flat boatmen sold their boats when they arrived at New Orleans, and, buying a horse, returned home by land. The foundations of many fortunes were laid in this way. Flat boats were made of "green oak plank, fastened by wooden pins to a frame of timber, and caulked with tow or any other pliant substance that could be procured," and were inclosed and roofed with boards. They were only used in descending streams, and floated with the current. Long, sweeping oars fastened at both ends of the boat, worked by men standing on the deck, were employed to keep it in the channel, and in navigating difficult and dangerous places in the river. The first flat boat was launched in the winter of 1799, near McDonald's Creek, by David Lowry. It was loaded in Dayton with grain, pelts and five hundred venison hams, and when the spring freshet raised the river started on the two months' trip to New Orleans. The voyage was safely accomplished.

Fish baskets, of which there is frequent mention in the newspapers of the day, were made by building a dam on the riffles so as to concentrate the water at the middle of the river, where an opening was made into a box constructed of slats and placed at a lower level than the dam. Into this box the fish ran, but were unable to return. A basket of this kind remained on the riffle at the foot of First street as late as 1830.

Paul D. Butler, on the 21st of August, 1809, gives notice in the *Repertory* of his intention to navigate the Miami from Dayton to the mouth of Stony Creek as soon as the season will permit, and forewarns all persons obstructing the navigation by erecting fish

Dayton from the southeast in 1832, drawn by Thomas K. Wharton. *Courtesy New York Public Library*

baskets or any other obstructions, that he is determined to prosecute those who erect them. He and Henry Desbrow soon after proceeded to build two keel boats.

They were built during the winter of 1809-1810 in the street in front of the courthouse, and when finished were moved on rollers up Main street to the river and launched. They ascended the Miami to the *Laramie portage*, which was as far as they could go. Then one of the boats was taken out of the river, and drawn across to the St. Mary's. For some time this boat made regular trips on the Maumee, and the other on the Miami, the portage between them being about

twelve miles across. A freight line which did good business was thus established between Dayton and Lake Erie by way of the Miami, Auglaize and Maumee rivers.

During the last week of March, 1819, eight flat boats and one handsome keel boat loaded here, shoved off for the landing for the markets below, and several flat boats loaded with flour, pork and whiskey also passed down the Miami. This year a second line of keel boats was established for carrying grain and produce up the Miami. At Laramie it was transferred, after a portage across the land intervening between the two rivers, to other boats, and transported down the

Maumee to the rapids, which was the point of transfer from river boats to lake vessels. At the rapids there was a large warehouse for storage of cargoes.

In May, 1819, Daytonians were gratified to see a large keel boat, upwards of seventy feet in length and with twelve tons of merchandise on board, belonging to H. G. Phillips and Messrs. Smith and Eaker, arrive here from Cincinnati. She was the only keel boat that had for a number of years been brought this far up the Miami, as the river between here and its mouth had been much obstructed.

Saturday and Sunday, March 26 and 27, 1825, were unusually exciting days in Dayton among boatmen, millers, distillers, farmers, merchants and teamsters, as a fleet of thirty or more boats that had been embargoed here by low water left their moorings bound for New Orleans. Rain had begun to fall on Wednesday, and continued till Friday, when the river rose. "The people," says the *Watchman*, "flocked to the banks, returning with cheerful countenances, saying, 'The boats will get off.'

"On Saturday all was the busy hum of a seaport; wagons were conveying flour, pork, whiskey, etc., to the different boats strung along the river. Several arrived during the day from the North. On Sunday morning others came down, the water began to fall, and the boats carrying about $40,000 worth of the produce of the country got under way." The whole value of the cargoes that left the Miami above and below Dayton during this freshet was estimated at least $100,000. Some of the boats were stove and the flour damaged, but most of them passed safely to their destination. Twelve boats left here for New Orleans in February, 1827, from Montgomery and Miami Counties, chiefly loaded with flour, pork and whiskey. Their cargoes were worth about $20,000. In February, 1828, the last boat, loaded with produce for New Orleans, left here by the Miami. The next year freight began to be shipped south by canal. As late as 1836, and perhaps a year later, when the canal was opened to Piqua, the line of boats to the north was continued.

CRISIS IN COLUMBUS

J. H. STUDER

Columbus replaced Chillicothe as the capital of Ohio in 1816, when population was moving into the central and northern districts of the state. But its early years were marked by political struggle and natural misfortune. Cholera broke out in 1833, and a third of its three thousand citizens fled to the country. When a new State House was begun in 1838, political rivalry led other towns to agitate for the removal of the state government; for six years work on the building ceased. Not until 1851 was the building assured. Then with convict labor from the penitentiary and a quarry railroad built along Third Street into the State House yard, the capitol rose above the roofs of the town. When the imposing structure was dedicated in 1857, Columbus had a population of 18,000, and its future looked bright.

The following episodes are taken from J. H. Studer's Columbus, Ohio, *published in 1873.*

Columbus, c. 1865. Courtesy Ohio Historical Society

BALLOON ASCENSIONS

THE first balloon ascension from Columbus took place on the 4th of July, 1842. It was made by Mr. Clayton, a celebrated aeronaut of Cincinnati, from the state-house yard, where a large concourse of people had assembled to witness the novel sight. The balloon, it was estimated, rose to a height of two miles. It bore southwardly at first, then eastwardly, and came safely down to the earth about five miles east of Newark.

Nine years afterward, on the 4th of July, 1851, the second balloon ascension was made from the capital city, by the noted John Wise. Pursuant to an engagement with John M. Kinney, Mr. Wise ascended from an inclosure at the corner of Broad and Seventh streets. The ascension was a fine one, and the aeronaut landed, safe and sound, about six miles from his starting point.

These balloon ascensions are mentioned to show that Columbus, in this her fourth decade, was beginning to be regarded by those who provided costly entertainments for the people, as a place with metropolitan curiosity and tastes. . . .

The third balloon ascension from Columbus took place on the 29th of October, 1857, in pursuance of an engagement made by John M. Kinney with M. Godard, a celebrated French aeronaut, to come from Philadelphia and make an ascension on horseback. The ascension on the 29th of October was intended merely as preliminary to the horseback ascension, which was to come off two

days afterward, but which, owing to difficulties in obtaining the requisite supply of gas, did not come off at all. But the preliminary ascension succeeded admirably. It was made from the Capital City Fair Grounds, as Mr. Kinney called his inclosure located near and southeastwardly from the old lunatic asylum. M. Godard was accompanied in the ascent by his brother, and P. W. Huntington and Robert H. Thompson of this city. Three of the company occupied the car, while one of the Godards hung suspended by a rope fifteen or twenty feet below the car, with his head downward, waving a flag as he glided swiftly through the empyrean.

CRUSADE AGAINST COLUMBUS

On the 26th of January, 1838, the legislature passed an act for the erection of a new state-house in the Public Square at Columbus. The corner-stone of the new building was laid on the 4th of July, 1839, and during the season the foundation of the new building was laid to a level with the surface of the ground. The next winter the progress of the work was arrested by one of those singular freaks that large and select bodies of men sometimes cut.

There had been for some time more or less ill feeling on the part of other towns in the central portion of the state toward Columbus as the capital. She was accused of putting on metropolitan airs. An incident occurred in the legislative session of 1839–40 that served to kindle this comparatively latent spark of envy into a flame. This was an investigation by the legislature of certain charges against William B. Lloyd, a member from Cuyahoga county. After the investigation a paper signed by sixty-three citizens of Columbus, principally young men, expressing undiminished confidence in Mr. Lloyd's integrity, appeared in the Columbus *State Journal* of February 17, with the signers' names attached. Many members of the legislature who had voted to censure Lloyd took umbrage at this publication. They denounced it as an unwarrantable intermeddling of the citizens of Columbus with the proceedings of the general assembly. While the excitement was still effervescing, George B. Flood, representative from Licking County, on the day following the obnoxious publication, introduced into the House a bill repealing the act for the erection of a new state-house. It finally passed both branches of the legislature and became a law on the 10th of March. By this action the work on the new state-house was suspended for more than six years.

After the passage of the repealing act, the subject of removing the seat of the state government from Columbus was more earnestly agitated than before. Every conceivable objection was urged against the permanent location of the capital on the banks of the Scioto. The site was said to be the most unhealthy one that could have been selected in the whole state. Besides, it was urged by some that the capital should be nearer the center than Columbus was. For about three years the question of removal was discussed, when, at the session of the legislature in 1842–43, the subject was referred to a committee, who made elaborate majority and minority reports. The majority took the ground that the general assembly could not pass an act for the removal of the seat of government from the location established by a former act, without a violation of the faith of the state. The two reports were principally confined to the discussion of this proposition.

The minority report recommended the adoption of joint resolutions, requesting the governor to issue his proclamation, setting forth that the time had arrived for the permanent establishment of the seat of government, and inviting proposals for its location. These resolutions were adopted by the Senate, on the 6th of March, 1843, by a vote of eighteen to sixteen, but were, the next day, defeated in the House, by a vote of thirty-six to twenty-nine. This seems to have put a final quietus to the agitation about removing the state capital from Columbus.

DESTROYED BY FIRE

The old state-house, after having rendered legislative service for thirty-five years, met an unexpected doom. Early on Sunday morning, February 1, 1852, it was consumed by fire. The fire was first discovered by the watch, on the floor in the center of the Senate chamber. It was nearly extinguished, when it was discovered that the timbers above were on fire. The roof was soon burned through, and the entire belfry was enveloped in flames. The city fire-engineer could not reach the fire with water from his hose. Citizens and strangers, spectators of the scene, came to the conclusion that the venerable edifice, which had in its time been the theater of patriotism and zeal for the public good, as well as of caucusing and "log-rolling," was doomed to inevitable destruction. The belfry, burning brilliantly, cast a lurid light on that Sabbath morning sky. It was said that, as the frame of the belfry swayed to and fro, the clear-toned old bell rang out a parting requiem, and the structure fell with a crash upon the floor of the Senate chamber. Then, the roof gradually falling in, the upper story was soon wrapped in wreathing flames. In vain were strenuous efforts made to confine the fire to the Senate chamber and the upper story. The mass of burning matter was too great to be extinguished with the appliances at hand. The flames soon reached the hall of the House of Representatives, and the entire wood-work of the building was soon consumed. Nothing was to be seen that day, of the pride of Columbus when she was a little "borough," but bare and blackened walls.

THE NEW STATE-HOUSE

The capitol of Ohio [in 1857] stands in the center of the public square, dedicated as its site in the original plat of Columbus. It is a grand and attractive edifice, of great solidity and magnitude, and Doric in its style of architecture. It is admitted to be the most imposing State capitol in the Union. It covers about two acres of ground, and is a bold and noble structure of durable materials and fine proportions. It is built of beautiful gray limestone, obtained from a quarry on the east side of the Scioto river, about three miles from Columbus. . . . The time consumed in building it, after deducting the intervals during which work upon it was suspended, was about fifteen years. . . .

In honor of the opening of the new Capitol of Ohio to legislative and other governmental uses, a superb banquet was given by the citizens of Columbus, on the evening of the 6th of January, 1857, to the members of the general assembly and other State officials, and to visitors from this and other states. All parts of our own state and many of the other states of the Union were represented in the great assemblage gathered in the city on that memorable occasion.

The Cleveland Grays, a fine military company, arrived in the afternoon preceding the festival, and were received by the State Fencibles of Columbus, whose guests they were. The appearance of the two companies, as they paraded the streets together, was the subject of general remark and admiration. During the day the State-house was prepared for the grand banquet and the ceremonies and festivities of the evening. Chairs and furniture were removed from the halls. The rotunda, which had been handsomely arched and beautifully decorated with tri-colored muslin, evergreens, flowers and wreaths, was assigned for the banqueting hall. Tables, bountifully laden, were placed in its eastern half, in a semicircular form.

As evening came on the whole edifice was brilliantly lighted, and crowning all was the illuminated dome, from which the light shone in all directions with rare beauty and effect. At nine o'clock the ceremonies previously arranged began. Rev. Dr. Hoge offered prayer. Alfred Kelley of Columbus, then representing the counties of Franklin and Pickaway in the State Senate, made an address of welcome.

While these exercises were going on in the hall of the House, the Senate chamber was the theater of music and dancing. It was not long before this festivity became general, wherever a space could be cleared for musicians and dancers. Till a late hour at night the capitol was the scene of light, joy, and revelry, while crowds of people of both sexes jostled each other on the stairways and kept thronging through the rotunda, the halls, apartments, and corridors, like the restless waves of old ocean. At one time during the evening the number of people in the building was estimated at eight thousand.

THE BATTLE OF CLEVELAND

CLEVELAND *PLAIN DEALER*

Modern Cleveland, spanning the deep gorge of the Cuyahoga, could not exist without its great viaducts. But in 1840 two rival towns faced each other across the Cuyahoga flats, and a bridge was a cause of warfare. Long after the dispute was past and the West Side rival had become a part of greater Cleveland, the Cleveland Plain Dealer *recalled the Battle of the Bridge.*

WHEN the Connecticut colony received a charter from the English king it was stipulated that its territory extend from ocean to ocean. By reason of this, Connecticut claimed all the region west from her settlements, but gave up all these possessions except the land between the western border of Pennsylvania and the Cuyahoga River and about 800,000 acres west of the Cuyahoga. A company was formed to buy this land and 3,000,000 acres were purchased at 40 cents an acre. Samuel P. Lord contributed $14,092 as a stockholder in the company and his share of the purchased territory included many thousand acres west of the river, beginning at its bank. The purchase was made in 1797, and very soon after the surveyors arrived on the site of Cleveland, headed by Gen. Moses Cleaveland. They left several of their number on the site of the future city when they returned to Connecticut. In 1797, James Kingsbury and family joined the little settlement and took up their abode on the west side of the river, but soon abandoned the locality and moved to what is now Kinsman street, near Kingsbury Run.

Only the Indians inhabited the West Side at that time. The Ottawas and Chippewas had a rendezvous in the woods near what is now the corner of Pearl and Detroit streets. There they held their councils, played their games and performed their dances and other ceremonies. In the Spring of every year they buried their canoes under brushwood and started for the interior on a big hunting expedition. They returned in the Fall well loaded with jerked meats and skins. These were loaded into the canoes preparatory to a trip farther up the lakes to their Winter quarters. Before they made this trip they always sent to the East Side for an abundance of whisky, which was manufactured at a small distillery there, and the "jag" that they deliberately cultivated would have done credit to a more civilized community. The Indians gave up the lands Connecticut claimed and retired still farther west in 1805. The land west of the river was surveyed and it was not many years before settlement began. . . .

The West Side presented a very peculiar appearance in those early days, so different from the present West Side that it is worthy of comment. The river wound through the valley, making many turns as it now does, and skirting its western shore with lowlands, now called the "flats," on which was a light growth of timber. Not a manufacturing establishment was erected there for many years. The present river bed was then a big pond called "Sunfish Pond," on account of the great number of sunfish that might be caught there. The pond seemed to have no connection either with the lake or the river, but was evidently formed by water draining into it through the sand on the lake shore. . . .

To such an extent had the West Side grown in 1836, that the citizens decided that they wanted to be . . . organized into a city. Cleveland also got the city fever about the same time, and it became a question which side would first obtain a charter from the State Legislature. Ohio City men worked shrewdly and managed to beat Cleveland by two days, so that the West Side was actually a city two days before the East Side could claim the same honor. The charter was granted to Ohio City on March 3d, 1836.

The opening of the canal six years before had wrought a great change in both the East and West Sides. Trade increased marvelously and commercial prosperity blessed the people and brought many inhabitants to the two cities. . . .

In 1838, some bright individual conceived the idea of opening "Sunfish Pond" in the old river bed into both the river and lake and using it as a channel for vessels and also building docks there. About forty men with teams were put to work and the passage opened. A small schooner which was on the lake was then pointed into the opening, but the sand filled the passage so rapidly that the men were obliged to help push her into the pond. The passage from the river to the pond is still open. Along the channel thus formed the majority of ore docks have been built, and there thousands of tons of ore are loaded and unloaded every season. As business increased, the channel was from time to time widened.

The effect of increased business was apparent in Ohio City. New houses were being built and the land along the river was being occupied for business purposes. A magnificent hotel, known as The Exchange, was erected at the corner of Main and Center streets in 1834. Some of the old inhabitants who saw it say that it was the finest hotel that Cleveland has ever seen and surpassed anything between Buffalo and Chicago. It was an immense building, handsomely furnished. It was provided with mahogany and cherry furniture, beautifully carved and polished. On the occasion of its opening, the chief citizens of Ohio City enjoyed a lake ride and then banqueted at the hotel. Some of the best families of Ohio City boarded there. After a time the locality became unsuited to reside in, and then the hotel became less and less a public resort and was finally converted into a pail factory, which burned to the ground. In those early days, most of the travel over the river was across the float bridge at the foot of Main street, and this accounts for the business in that locality and the establishment of the hotel.

A great ridge of sand extended along Franklin avenue in those early days. It was nearly a foot deep, but now has been hardened by travel. Up to 1845, squirrel hunting was good west of Kentucky street. Gilman Folsom located a house on Detroit street near Gordon avenue and people wondered why he went so far out into the woods. Detroit street was the chief business street on the bluff, and

it was calculated to make Main street and the surrounding territory the main business and manufacturing part of the town. A very large warehouse business was done in those days and the warehouses were located near Main street. The warehouses were the storage places of vast quantities of wheat, flour, corn, oats, pork, wool, and other provisions. These were brought to Ohio City from the towns and counties to the south and west. During the season when roads were good about 1,200 to 1,500 wagons came into Ohio City laden with provisions of all sorts. The wagons were of the old-fashioned Dutch, top-cover style, and were drawn by oxen and horses. The farmers invested the proceeds of their sales in goods and drove back to their homes. The grain and provisions were loaded into ships and sent to other ports. Great quantities of provisions also came in on the canal.

Ohio City, in 1840, authorized the digging of a branch canal from the old river bed or ship channel to the Cuyahoga river where the head of the canal discharged into the river. Gilman Folsom was given the contract for $28,000 in city bonds. He paid his men 75 cents a day, the usual rate at that time, but they struck for higher wages. The strikers stoned the men who were inclined to work, and it became necessary to call out the militia. This canal drained a large section of the low

The Columbus Street Bridge in Cleveland, 1835. *Courtesy Cleveland Public Library*

THE BATTLE OF CLEVELAND   283

land and gave Ohio City greater advantages, at the same time increasing the rivalry with Cleveland. A permanent bridge was needed at Main street, but Cleveland refused to unite with Ohio City in building it, for the reason that they thought it would add to the prosperity on the western bank of the river. . . .

The very first solid bridge that spanned the Cuyahoga had been erected as a private enterprise in 1836. The population of Cleveland was then about 5,000, while Ohio City could boast of 2,000. John W. Willey and James S. Clark made extensive purchases of land west of the river, near Columbus street. They had commercial interests in Cleveland also, and for two reasons they determined to construct a bridge. One reason was that it would open up their newly acquired lands to trade and population, and divert travel in that direction. The other reason was that the Ohio City people would have opened to them an unobstructed and easily traveled avenue to the East Side, where Willey and Clark would get their business. At this time there was a float bridge, built upon boats, at the foot of Detroit street, and all the travel had been upon this and a ferry boat for pedestrians and vehicles at the foot of Main street.

Ohio City people vigorously opposed the construction of the new bridge, which Willey and Clark undertook at their own expense. Nevertheless the work went on. The objection to it was that people from Brooklyn, Elyria and the surrounding towns would cross the river by the new bridge at Columbus street instead of passing down Pearl street and trading at the stores along that thoroughfare. This meant a decided loss to the West Siders, for hundreds of teams came into the city every year from the south and west, bringing wheat, flour, corn, pork and other provisions. The Ohio City merchants wanted the first choice of these provisions.

When finished, the bridge presented a handsome appearance for those days. It was substantial and was covered the entire length.

Willey and Clark succeeded in carrying out a plan that wrought the West Siders to a high wrath. A resolution was adopted by the council of Cleveland authorizing the removal of the eastern half of the float bridge at Detroit street, this half being the property of Cleveland. In the dead of night the design was accomplished, and Ohio City woke up one bright Summer morn to find only its half of the bridge remaining. The indignation was intense, the feeling bitter. Every West Sider who wanted to cross the river was obliged to go up to Columbus street. . . . The citizens were thoroughly aroused, and their agitation produced a favorable result in the Ohio City council. That body adopted a resolution in which the new bridge was declared to be a public nuisance, and as such it was ordered to be abated. The city marshal swore in some deputies and actually undertook to blow up the bridge. At night, a heavy charge of powder was put under it and exploded. While some damage was done, the result was not up to anticipations. Shortly afterward two immense ditches were dug, one at each end of the structure, thus effectually preventing the crossing of teams.

The citizens then determined to take unto themselves the carrying out of the resolution, and they began to organize for that purpose. Old flintlocks and sabers were rubbed up and preparations made for deeds of heroism. The people of the surrounding towns sympathized with the West Siders, and sent companies to their aid. In all a force of about 1,000 men collected on the day set for the attack on the bridge. They had boldly announced the time for the attack, for they declared that their cause was a just one and would bear the light of day, and they would not work in a cowardly manner under cover of the night, as did the East Siders when the float bridge was cut in twain. Rev. Dr. Picands, pastor of the Presbyterian church, acted as chaplain of the army. When all had assembled he raised his voice, invoking the divine aid in the righteous and just cause. Then the command was given and the march to the scene of the struggle began. . . .

The Clevelanders had not been idle meanwhile. In anticipation of the attack they had made ample preparations to resist it. An old cannon which had been used mainly to add to the noises of many Fourth of July celebrations, was posted on their side of the bridge and was well loaded with death-dealing missiles. A company of militia had also been called out and the men were stationed so as to sweep the bridge with their fire.

On came the West Siders until they arrived at the deep ditch which had been dug at the west end of the bridge to prevent travel. Here they were met by the mayor of Cleveland, who undertook to address them. He was greeted with several volleys of stones and was glad enough to escape to his own side. The bridge had been constructed with "aprons" at either end, which could be lowered or raised at will. When lowered, travel was effectually cut off. The first effort of the West Siders was to lower the "apron" at the east end and in this they succeeded. Behind this they were secure, for the militia could not see where to shoot. Then the task of destroying the structure was begun. Axes and crowbars were applied with a will and planks and timbers were loosened rapidly and thrown into the river. Only a part of the West Side army was actually engaged in this work. The militiamen got upon the bridge and a brief fight ensued. While Russell was busy ripping off a plank, a Clevelander named Jim Crow ran up and was about to plunge a sword into him. Donald Frazier, a big six-foot Scotchman who had served in the British army and was proud of it, stood by Russell, and before Crow could perpetrate the deed he had undertaken, Frazier had him by the collar and was pulling him toward the side of the bridge, bent on throwing him into the stream.

"Hold on, Donald," cried Russell, "we don't want to kill anybody if we can help it."

"But, durn him, he was goin' t' plunge that blade into ye," answered the Scotchman.

It was only after repeated protests that the big Donald released his grip of Crow, but the sword was wrenched from him and thrown into the river. While dredging, only a few years ago, in order to lay the foundations of the new Columbus street bridge, the sword was brought up and is now in the rooms of the Western Reserve Historical Society.

Old Deacon House, father of the present Martin House, who is ex-president of the School Council, took an important part in the warlike proceedings. Putting a file into his pocket, he started across the bridge to where the militia were drawn up. He reeled to and fro just as might a man who had tackled a few drinks of the old-fashioned applejack. The soldiers, perhaps thinking his actions nothing unusual, allowed him to pass. Once across, he staggered about helplessly and gradually made his way to the cannon until he finally brought up against it. In a moment when it was unguarded he slipped the file into the breech and effectually spiked the gun, so that it could not be fired. This was considered a remarkably strategic movement, and brought great praise to the old deacon.

The battle ended after a brief struggle in which one man was seriously wounded. This man was old Deacon Slaght, and a rifle ball had penetrated his nose. He recovered and lived for many years afterward.

The militia was put to inglorious flight and their captain nearly buried in the mud of the ditch. When the West Siders abandoned the bridge it was not so artistic as it had been previously, neither was it quite so useful. In fact, the timbers that remained only gave a slight suggestion of the structure that once spanned the river.

Of course, the Clevelanders were exceedingly wroth at the destruction of the bridge, and they took immediate steps to make the West Siders feel the authority of the law. Warrants were sworn out for the arrest of C. L. Russell and other leaders, on the charge of assault. When he and Hank Whitman next visited Cleveland the officers gave them a hard chase, and Hank was captured. Subsequently Russell was arrested on his own side of the river, but the justice of the peace allowed him to go on his own recognizance, saying that he would send for him when he wanted him, which time never came.

As the higher courts were all on the east side of the river, the Cleveland people decided to have recourse to them, where they thought they were sure of winning a case. Russell was indicted by the grand jury for assault and battery and malicious destruction of property. The accusing witnesses were in court with a big array of legal talent when the case came to trial. After hearing their story the judge announced that the case should never have been taken into court, and had he been interested he would have done exactly as Russell did.

Defeated both in battle and in law, the Cleveland people were brought to terms.

They agreed to restore the float bridge in case the West Siders would not molest the Columbus street bridge when it was repaired. This agreement was carried out and thus ended the bridge war.

THE PROMISE OF MILWAUKEE

MARGARET FULLER

In 1832 the Black Hawk War ended Indian occupancy of southern Wisconsin and opened the country to settlement. Three years later the first families built their cabins at the weedy mouth of the Milwaukee ("Gathering Place") River. Soon land values began to soar, steamboats churned the harbor, and the first rush of immigration thronged the dusty streets beside the river. In 1836 sixty buildings went up in seven months and Byron Kilbourn, recently arrived from New England, established a newspaper to hasten the city's future.

Margaret Fuller is better known as a transcendentalist friend of Emerson and Thoreau and a character in Hawthorne's The Blithedale Romance *than as a western observer. But she made a frontier tour in 1843 and reported it vividly in* A Summer on the Lakes, *from which this passage is taken.*

WISCONSIN, a territory, not yet a state; still, nearer the acorn than we were.

It was very pleasant coming up. These large and elegant boats are so well arranged that every excursion may be a party of pleasure. There are many fair shows to see on the lake and its shores, almost always new and agreeable persons on board, pretty children playing about, ladies singing, (and if not very well, there is room to keep out of the way.) You may see a great deal here of Life, in the London sense, if you know a few people; or if you do not, and have the tact to look about you without seeming to stare.

We came to Milwaukie, where we were to pass a fortnight or more.

This place is most beautifully situated. A little river, with romantic banks, passes up through the town. The bank of the lake is here a bold bluff, eighty feet in height. From its summit, you enjoyed a noble outlook on the lake. A little narrow path wound along the edge of the lake below. I liked this walk much. Above me this high wall of rich earth,

garlanded on its crest with trees, the long ripples of the lake coming up to my feet. Here, standing in the shadow, I could appreciate better its magnificent changes of color, which are the chief beauties of the lake-waters; but these are indescribable.

It was fine to ascend into the lighthouse, above this bluff, and watch from thence the thunder-clouds which so frequently rose over the lake, or the great boats coming in. Approaching the Milwaukie pier, they made a bend, and seemed to do obeisance in the heavy style of some dowager duchess entering a circle she wishes to treat with especial respect.

These boats come in and out every day, and still afford a cause for general excitement. The people swarm down to greet them, to receive and send away their packages and letters. To me they seemed such mighty messengers, to give, by their noble motion, such an idea of the power and fullness of life, that they were worthy to carry despatches from king to king. It must be very pleasant for those who have an active share in carrying on

Milwaukee, c. 1850. *Courtesy State Historical Society of Wisconsin*

the affairs of this great and growing world to see them come in. It must be very pleasant to those who have dearly loved friends at the next station. To those who have neither business nor friends, it sometimes gives a desolating sense of insignificance.

The town promises to be, some time, a fine one, as it is so well situated; and they have good building material—a yellow brick, very pleasing to the eye. It seems to grow before you, and has indeed but just emerged from the thickets of oak and wild roses. A few steps will take you into the thickets, and certainly I never saw so many wild roses, or of so beautiful a red. Of such a color were the first red ones the world ever saw, when, says the legend, Venus flying to the assistance of Adonis, the rosebushes kept catching her

to make her stay, and the drops of blood the thorns drew from her feet, as she tore herself away, fell on the white roses, and turned them this beautiful red. . . .

At Milwaukie, as at Chicago, are many pleasant people, drawn together from all parts of the world. A resident here would find great piquancy in the associations,—those he met having such dissimilar histories and topics. And several persons I saw evidently transplanted from the most refined circles to be met in this country. There are lures enough in the West for people of all kinds;—the enthusiast and the cunning man; the naturalist, and the lover who needs to be rich for the sake of her he loves.

The torrent of emigration swells very strongly towards this place. During the fine weather, the poor refugees arrive daily, in their national dresses, all travel-soiled and worn. The night they pass in rude shantees, in a particular quarter of the town, then walk off into the country—the mothers carrying their infants, the fathers leading the little children by the hand, seeking a home where their hands may maintain them. . . .

Here, on the pier, I see disembarking the Germans, the Norwegians, the Swedes, the Swiss. Who knows how much of old legendary lore, of modern wonder, they have already planted amid the Wisconsin forests? Soon, soon their tales of the origin of things, and the Providence which rules them, will be so mingled with those of the Indian, that the very oak trees will not know them apart,—will not know whether itself be a Runic, a Druid, or a Winnebago oak.

Some seeds of all growths that have ever been known in this world might, no doubt, already be found in these Western wilds, if we had the power to call them to life.

I saw, in the newspaper, that the American Tract Society boasted of their agents' having exchanged, at a Western cabin door, tracts for the Devil on Two Sticks, and then burnt that more entertaining than edifying volume. No wonder, though, they study it there. Could one but have the gift of reading the dreams dreamed by men of such various birth, various history, various mind, it would afford much more extensive amusement than did the chambers of one Spanish city!

Could I but have flown at night through such mental experiences, instead of being shut up in my little bedroom at the Milwaukie boarding house, this chapter would have been worth reading. As it is, let us hasten to a close.

Had I been rich in money, I might have built a house, or set up in business, during my fortnight's stay at Milwaukie, matters move on there at so rapid a rate. But, being only rich in curiosity, I was obliged to walk the streets and pick up what I could in casual intercourse. When I left the street, indeed, and walked on the bluffs, or sat beside the lake in their shadow, my mind was rich in dreams congenial to the scene, some time to be realized, though not by me.

A boat was left, keel up, half on the sand, half in the water, swaying with each swell of the lake. It gave a picturesque grace to that part of the shore, as the only image of inaction —only object of a pensive character to be seen. Near this I sat, to dream my dreams and watch the colors of the lake, changing hourly, till the sun sank. These hours yielded impulses, wove webs, such as life will not again afford.

Returning to the boarding house, which was also a boarding school, we were sure to be greeted by gay laughter.

This school was conducted by two girls of nineteen and seventeen years; their pupils were nearly as old as themselves; the relation seemed very pleasant between them. The only superiority—that of superior knowledge—was sufficient to maintain authority—all the authority that was needed to keep daily life in good order.

In the West, people are not respected merely because they are old in years; people there have not time to keep up appearances in that way; when they cease to have a real advantage in wisdom, knowledge, or enterprise, they must stand back, and let those who are oldest in character "go ahead," however few years they may count. There are no banks of established respectability in which to bury the talent there; no napkin of precedent in which to wrap it. What cannot be made to pass current, is not esteemed coin of the realm.

To the windows of this house, where the daughter of a famous "Indian fighter," i.e. fighter against the Indians, was learning French and the piano, came wild, tawny figures, offering for sale their baskets of berries. The boys now, instead of brandishing the tomahawk, tame their hands to pick raspberries.

Here the evenings were much lightened by the gay chat of one of the party, who, with the excellent practical sense of mature experience, and the kindest heart, united a naïveté and innocence such as I never saw in any other who had walked so long life's tangled path. Like a child, she was everywhere at home, and like a child, received and bestowed entertainment from all places, all persons. I thanked her for making me laugh, as did the sick and poor, whom she was sure to find out in her briefest sojourn in any place, for more substantial aid. Happy are those who never grieve, and so often aid and enliven their fellow men!

This scene, however, I was not sorry to exchange for the much celebrated beauties of the Island of Mackinaw.

INDIANAPOLIS IN 1843

HENRY WARD BEECHER

In 1818 at St. Mary's, Ohio, three Indiana commissioners met a group of Indian chiefs and bought from them the entire central section of Indiana. Surveyors soon divided this "New Purchase" into townships, and settlement began. In this district a site was chosen for the new Hoosier capital; the town was laid out by a young English engineer, Elias Pym Fordham, who had come to America with Morris Birkbeck. In 1824 four farm wagons moved the seat of government from the old State House at Corydon to the new, centrally located capital.

In 1830 the National Road (now US 40) reached Indianapolis from the East. The road was rough and strenuous, but traffic kept coming—big Pennsylvania freight wagons, wiry Maryland ponies drawing "shake-guts" carts, Carolina traps and buckboards, occasionally a roofed shanty on wheels with children peering through a window and smoke sifting from the chimney. The Hoosier population doubled in the 1830's.

After his graduation from Amherst College in 1834, Henry Ward Beecher went West. He enrolled in Lane Theological Seminary in Cincinnati, an institution presided over by his father. In 1839 he became pastor of the Second Presbyterian Church of Indianapolis. He lived in the Hoosier capital for eight years. The following passage is taken from a letter written in 1843. Like pioneers everywhere in the Middle West, the first settlers of Indianapolis attacked the native trees as though they were an enemy. In this letter the eloquent preacher was less concerned with saving souls than with saving trees.

Indianapolis in 1854. *Courtesy Indiana Historical Society Library*

A NUMBER of public-spirited gentlemen have associated, to plant all the private streets in this town with shade trees. We shall select from the ample stock of our own forests, mostly. But it is proposed to put in a number of pear and plum trees—the first being a beautiful shaped tree as well as fruitful, and the plum, it is thought, will be free from the curculio, planted upon a highway. In the three squares upon which stand the State House, Court House, and Governor's House, it is proposed to gather and plant a specimen of all our forest trees.

This reminds me of an incident in our early town history related to me by one of the first settlers. A large circle of nearly four acres was reserved in the center of the town and the native trees, sugar maples, left standing upon it. Under these trees, before churches were built, religious meetings were held in summer, and the prospect was that our town would have an adornment of this little grove which no architecture can bestow. One morning, however, he was attracted thither by the sound of an axe, and found one of the leading lawyers of the place exercising himself, as a preparation for breakfast, in felling one of the largest trees. It was too far cut to be saved. And so good an example could not be lost upon others. One by one those magnificent trees disappeared. Now we have a huge yellow brick building in the center of this circle; about a dozen locusts, with stems half as large as one's wrist, have for the three last years been struggling for life until they seem weary and faint, and so stand still.

The Court House Square, something larger than the former piece of ground, was covered with a noble growth of stately trees, and it was determined to save them. A man was set, however, to thin out the plat, and being left to his own discretion, he felled all the younger trees and left the very old and tall ones standing. As might have been expected, the first wind, finding an easy passage through, uprooted a multitude of trees, and the citizens, to save the rest from a like fate, chopped them down instantly, and happily relieved this square too from unpleasant shade. All is not yet told. At a later day a number of gentlemen procured an order (if I mistake

not) from the county commissioners to plant out the ground with shade trees, and a large number of the locust was set. However, that nothing might break in upon the practice of the county, the jailor's cow was permitted to pasture upon the plat, and in sight of the citizens she proceeded patiently to bark the trees or break them down, until not a single one was left. A gentleman not without a taste for horticulture, from day to day, saw, from his office door, this destruction, as he informed me with great naïvete, as though it were a sin to interfere and save the trees.

Thus in all our towns comes first extermination; then come scorching summer suns, and too late the wish that the trees had been spared; and at last planting begins, and we who live amid the immense forests of a new country—on whose town plat not fifteen years ago grew immense oaks, maples, sycamores, beeches, tulip trees and elms—are planting the short lived locusts (*Robinia pseudo-acacia*) to obtain a speedy shade! I can think of but three forest trees now standing in this town within a space of one mile square—two elms and one buckeye. The same scenes are enacting in every town which springs up at the West. We are gaining meadows, and corn bottoms, and green hillsides, and town plats, by an utter extermination of the forest. Here and there an Indian may be found lingering around the old possessions of his nation, as if to mourn their loss, and to remind us of his ancestors; but of the forest, it is almost true that not a single tree is left to recall to our minds the glory of its fellows. Indeed, I have thought that those who were obliged to clear farms or timber land, imbibe the same feelings toward trees which the pioneers have toward the Indians—as things to be destroyed, of course. This devastation of our forests the political economist regards as a blunder, and says it is an unthrifty practice; but one who looks upon trees almost as if they had souls, witnesses this needless extermination with some feelings which cannot be expressed in the pound and penny language of the mere economist. I think it is Michaux who pronounces the full-grown elm to be the most magnificent production of the vegetable kingdom. Is not an old, and tall, and broad, and healthy tree nobler to the eye than any temple or cathedral? The wonder of a century's growth ends in an hour by some man who never for one single moment thinks of the majesty or beauty of his victim—who only thinks how soonest to get it down, and burned up, and out of the way of the plough.

TROUBLES IN TOLEDO

J. W. SCOTT

Toledo got a late start. Its first settlers, who had come to the mouth of the Maumee after the Treaty of Greene Ville, fled at the outbreak of the War of 1812. In 1817 the Indians ceded their remaining lands in the district and a new settlement began. A bubbling land speculation burst in the 1830's. The region was swampy, early lake vessels bypassed the Maumee entrance on their way to Detroit, and the "Toledo War," 1835–36, a dispute over the Ohio-Michigan boundary, held back the future. At last, in 1837 Toledo became an incorporated city, embracing several rival villages near the Maumee mouth. In the 1840's two canals, the Wabash and Erie and the Miami and Erie, linked the Maumee with the Ohio River, and Toledo's expectations grew.

The following narrative is taken from the reminiscences of an early editor of the city's oldest newspaper, the Toledo Blade.

Toledo in 1876. Courtesy Ohio Historical Society

IN 1828, while residing in Columbia, South Carolina, my thoughts were directed to future seats of commerce to grow up in the great central plain of North America. My conclusion was, that the great city of the nation, and, probably, of the world, would grow up in that plain; and that, on the harbor at the west end of Lake Erie, would grow up a great mart, possibly the largest, probably the second largest, and, certainly, not below the third in rank. The period for the consummation of the superiority of central, over Atlantic cities, was thought to be either the year 1900, or about 100 years from that time—say, 1928—

and, for the supremacy of some central city over any other of the world, by the year 2000 of our era. The largest commercial points in what was then called *"the West,"* were Cincinnati (numbering some 8,000), Pittsburg, Louisville and St. Louis—all smaller than Cincinnati. The idea of an interior mart becoming larger than New York, or New Orleans, was deemed, by persons to whom I stated these opinions, nothing short of the most absurd that could be suggested; and I found no man disposed to give it the least hospitality. Allowing the rate of progress which our population had made to be continued 100 years, the truth of my opinion seemed perfectly demonstrable, and I thought I did make a complete demonstration of it. But I did not satisfy another mind, or make a single convert, for many years.

In the fall of 1830, I removed to Ohio, and, during the year 1832, I published, in a small monthly sheet printed at Norwalk, at my expense, called "The Ohio and Michigan Register and Emigrants' Guide," an article in which I undertook to prove that Cincinnati, or some other city of the great valley, would, in A.D. 1900, be larger than New York, and, by the year A.D. 2000, be larger than any other city of the world.

About 1838, or 1839, I published in the Hesperian magazine, a monthly published in Columbus and Cincinnati, by Gallagher & Curry, a series of papers on internal improvements and interior cities, in which I amplified on my previous article. Previous to this time, to wit: in June, 1832, I visited the country at the mouth of the Maumee. My residence was then, temporarily, at Florence, then in Huron, now in Erie county, Ohio. Although I had for years held in high estimation some indefinite good place for a city on the harbor formed by the entrance of the Maumee into the lake, I had not taken the trouble to visit it, until I read in the *National Intelligencer*, an article from the pen of Major Benjamin F. Stickney, in which it was stated that "the plan of a town—indeed of a city—had been laid out by some enterprising gentlemen from the State of New York," and setting forth the advantages of its position. This called up the desire to see the site of a city that might one day be great; and I accordingly mounted my horse, and,

passing through Milan, then one of the largest places in Northern Ohio, Lower Sandusky (now Fremont, and then a place of some promise, and some 300 or 400 people), and thence along the thirty-one miles of road through the swamp to Perrysburg, thence crossing, by ford, the Maumee, above the old town of the same name, I, with some difficulty, found my way along the Monroe turnpike, and thence from Section 16, T. 3, U. S. R., by a rude path through the openings and woods to the mouth of Swan Creek, and thence down along the river bank, mostly through the forest, to the new town of Vistula; and below to the residence of Major Stickney.

A few board shanties had been put up on Summit street, near Lagrange, and some men were at work grading down what is now the foot of Lagrange street, preparing a wharf for the landing of vessels. At the gate of the brick house now standing—but soon to go the way of all others of the olden time—I overtook Major Stickney and Samuel Allen (known as Captain Allen), the Major's associate in laying out the new town. The Major received my address in his own courteous, grave manner, and Mr. Allen in that prompt business style, and with an air that might have become one of the solid men of Boston, accustomed to shake State street by his stately tread. I told them my errand was to see where the mighty city site of the Maumee should be, and to write about it—perhaps to make some purchase, if I should be satisfied that this was the right spot. Mr. Allen kept, as a boarding house, temporarily, the residence of the Major for the accommodation of the persons coming to settle or purchase in the new plat, or in the neighborhood. There I domiciled myself for a few days to look about.

Mrs. Allen, a Quaker lady, exhibited remarkable talent and tact in pleasing those of her guests who might forward the growth of the city in embryo. In appearance and address, she was no less remarkable than her husband. He was rather short, thick set, straight, and with a quick, firm movement, like one born to lead. No one could be better fitted to lead a forlorn hope in battle, or in city building. His benevolence was high, his organ of hope large, and his caution small, with a back head of sufficient capacity for ample motive power.

Major Stickney, as having had more to do with this city and region, and as a character not less marked, I design to describe more fully hereafter.

FEBRUARY 18, 1857. — The foregoing, written in Toledo over thirteen years ago, and with the intention of regular continuation, has just been looked over; and I now, near Castleton, New York, resume the narrative.

When these notes were commenced, Toledo was a city, to be sure, on paper, and by act of incorporation; but according to an estimate carefully made, the entire population out of the city, on which its commerce depended, did not exceed 200 families of farmers. There were probably living, within the limits, about 2,000 people—many of them holding on with a view to the business that was expected to flow in on the completion of the Wabash and Erie, and the Miami and Erie Canals, then being constructed. Now the population is not less than 12,000, with abundance of business for a good support to all who are willing to work. I now resume the narrative.

On my way to the new "Vistula," I had passed through Perrysburg and Maumee—small, but, as it seemed to me, beautifully situated hamlets, at the head of navigation on the Maumee river, and each claiming to be the best position for the chief town. The principal men were fur traders, or, as they were more generally designated, Indian traders; and their expectation of future greatness was quite limited. The commerce, by lake, of these places, was carried on by two schooners, named "Eagle" and "Guerriere," of about 60 tons burthen, and commanded by two brothers named David and James Wilkinson,—hardy, bluff, and strong-minded men, whose position as friends or enemies no one could long doubt. The principal owner was John Hollister, of Perrysburg, from Pittsfield, Massachusetts, an Indian trader and man of mark, one of nature's noblemen, whose influence was felt in the councils of the State, and in the commercial struggle for the supremacy between the towns at the foot of the rapids, and the new city below.

The Indian trade, in furs and the fisheries, with corn growing on the bottom lands, constituted the business on which these hamlets relied for support; and, with few exceptions, the inhabitants failed to anticipate any considerable change from that condition. There was one man, however, then living in Perrysburg, familiarly known as Judge Rice—Ambrose Rice—who, in native sagacity and foresight, seemed to me, and seems now to me, to have been before any man I have ever known. I afterwards became intimate with him; and, though I have had familiar intercourse with several men who have the position, in public estimation, among the greatest men of our country, I have not known one with so penetrating a judgment, or so clear an intellect. Nor, in moral truthfulness, and stern integrity, was he less distinguished. His position was that of County Surveyor, and agent to select lands for purchasers. His usual habits were secluded, and he spent very little time in conversation. Except on business, he conversed with very few persons, and the community looked upon him as very odd, especially as he usually avoided the society of ladies—being a confirmed bachelor.

The few days at Major Stickney's were spent in looking about and coming to an opinion as to the relative advantages of a city site of the places eight miles above, and the present position of Toledo. What is now partially built over, and laid out into streets,—being nearly all in a wild state,—seemed a wide extent of land admitting room for a choice of location for several towns. The two tracts, Nos. 1 and 2, of the 12 miles square reservation, which embraced the mouth of Swan Creek, had been selected as the best point, and purchased at the sale of the reserve lands in 1817, by Major William Oliver and associates. But, as the adjoining lands, for several years after, were still in possession of the Indians, who were then the sole tenants of all the northwest quarter of Ohio, except a few reservations; and, as the collapse of the credit currency of the country occurred soon after, this effort to start a city at the west end of Lake Erie, proved abortive.

After being taken up the river as far as Delaware flats (where she got aground), by the little steamer "Pioneer," which had been chartered by Stickney and Allen to run between Sandusky City and their "Vistula;" and turning over in my mind the advantages relatively to each other, of the up-river and down-river claimants, I decided that the down-river had the preponderance of advantages, and that the best position for the centre of the down-river town, was just below the entrance of Swan Creek into the river. At this point, there was then a log warehouse, and rude wharf, nearly rotten. Believing in the high destiny of the future city, wherever it should be, and having brought my mind to a satisfactory state as to its precise location, I became anxious to have an interest in it. My means were quite limited, so that it was necessary to make the most of my opportunity to buy in the right place.

The only possible chance that I found, was a very wild and rude piece of ground, then possessed by Dr. Sutphen, being the S. W. fr. ¼ of sec. 36, T. 9 S. R. 7 E., embracing with it a small piece of sec. 35. Of this, I bargained for seventy acres, at $12 per acre. I also wrote to Major Oliver, who resided in Cincinnati, offering to become part owner of his tracts, and to become agent for their management. When my letter reached the Major, there was an applicant with him, having the same object in view, Dr. D. O. Comstock, who bought one-fourth of tracts 1 and 2, and, with his brother, S. B. Comstock, became agent of what was called the Port Lawrence Company —owning river tracts 1 and 2.

At the time I bought the seventy acres, I could have bought the whole fractional quarter of eighty-six acres, by giving $15 per acre for what remained; but, as I thought the part bought was worth more by the acre than what was left, I declined to buy. Having, as I thought, got a fair chance to participate in the advantages of the future rapid growth of a great city, I embarked with my horse on the steamer "Pioneer," for Sandusky City, elated with high hopes of future profit from my purchase. On the steamer I fell in with a man who had just come from the west shore of Lake Michigan, where he had pre-empted, or rather bought the pre-emption of an 80-acre lot at the mouth of the Milwaukee river. This was the first time I had heard the name. I think the land had cost him $6 per acre; and,

as he could hardly spare so much money as it had cost, he offered to let me in as joint purchaser, I think, but am not certain, at the cost price. I declined, telling him that he would do better to make the new town of Vistula the theatre of speculation, as it might, and probably would, become a considerable city before settlements to any extent would reach as far west as Milwaukee.

On my return to Florence, I told my wife, and one or two other persons, that the seventy acres I had bought would, in twenty years, be worth $20,000. They laughed at my sanguine calculation, and they would have been still more merry, if they had been told the real extent of my hopes. In 1852, the twenty years had passed. Toledo then possessed a population of over five thousand, and the seventy acres, if I had owned it all, in one piece, would probably have been marketable at something near, but not much over, twenty thousand dollars. I had, however, in 1835, about three years after the purchase, sold an undivided half of the tract for six thousand dollars, to Edward Bissell, then the largest owner of property in what was then the united village of Toledo—Vistula and Port Lawrence having yielded their separate existence, and become one.

In 1835, commenced that memorable speculation in wild lands, and wild cities, which culminated in 1836. The whole Maumee valley was filled with eastern fortune-hunters. Congress and State lands were raced-for entry, and the shores of the river from Fort Wayne to the Maumee Bay, were alive with city-builders. From the foot of the rapids to the bay, land was all considered necessary for three-story brick blocks; and, after the canal was located on the north side, all the shore from Waterville to Manhattan was held as city property. Jackson's specie circular soon brought their airy fabric into ruin, which was completed by the failure of the United States Bank of Pennsylvania, in 1839.

Under the auspices of Bissell and his associates, Toledo had been pushed forward to be a considerable place—numbering, at one time, probably, over fifteen hundred inhabitants. Most of the buildings of any note, had been erected by the speculative owners, and when money ceased to flow west for investment, and men, from devoting themselves to speculation, turned their attention to earning their daily bread, Toledo was a young city in the wilderness, with high expectations, but with nothing, or next to nothing, to live upon. The great body of lands which surrounded it, had been entered for speculation; so that, up to the time of the canal being completed to Toledo, in 1843, there were not over 200 families out of the city, which resorted to it as their principal place of trade. These families, too, were but little advanced in farming operations; and many of them too deeply in debt to have much means to buy even necessaries. This estimate of the number of families out of Toledo, who could be relied upon to do their business with its citizens, was made by me in 1844, when I was editor of the Toledo *Blade*. At that time, those best informed as to the advantages of the place to become a large commercial town, anticipated a more rapid growth than has been realized. The canal, though a noble channel for commerce, passes through a country with rich and great agricultural capabilities, but out of the tract of the best class of migrating farmers. It has for this and other reasons, had very partial development.

In 1844, Toledo was little more than the dead carcass of speculation. Its previous existence had been abnormal, but its condition was worse than negative. It had acquired a widespread and almost universally-believed character for insalubrity. It would, in its first settlement, have been noted, to some extent, for the severity of its malarial fevers, if it had

been settled by industrious and moral people, having the means to provide comfortable habitations, and healthy food. A large portion of its first inhabitants, though intelligent enough, were not possessed of the means or habits to preserve health, in a new and rich soil. Much sickness and distress, therefore, were suffered. When, therefore, after the canal began to give it a business worth naming, its reputation for sickliness had become such as to divert from it, to other western cities, most of the enterprising business men, who flocked thither from the old States and Europe. Its rivals—and almost all the towns on Lake Erie considered themselves such—were very industrious in giving, and keeping alive, the bad name which it had, in its speculative existence, to some extent, deserved. Other causes conspired to turn the tide of population from the wooded region about Toledo to the prairies beyond Michigan. The most powerful of these was the interest which existed in Buffalo and Oswego, through which, up to 1853, nearly all the immigration flowed, to carry passengers and freight as far as possible, in their steamers and other vessels. Concurring in this, was the interest exerted by speculators in prairie lands, to give to emigrating families in Europe, and especially in Germany, such information of the advantages of the country west of Lake Michigan, as turned the tide almost entirely through that channel. This tide and its reaction built up, in a very short time, the considerable cities of Milwaukee and Chicago. The position of the latter has always seemed to me one of very great commercial power, second, perhaps, to none other of the great plain.

TWIN CITIES IN THE MAKING

LAURENCE OLIPHANT

In the 1830's two rude settlements huddled on the banks of the upper Mississippi. Pig's Eye was a steamboat landing with a busy grogshop. St. Anthony was a mill town, using a waterfall to grind grain and saw lumber. Hence the old saying: "Minneapolis was conceived in water power, St. Paul was born in whisky."

By the 1850's both towns were growing like magic. With the rising tide of immigration they would soon become the twin cities of the North.

In 1854 Laurence Oliphant, far-ranging British traveler and Superintendent of Indian Affairs in Canada, made a journey through Minnesota—"a portion of North America hitherto but little visited." His observations were first published in Blackwood's Magazine *in Edinburgh. In 1855, while in Constantinople, he put them together in* Minnesota and the Far West, *from which the following pages are taken.*

St. Anthony Falls on the Mississippi at Minneapolis, 1869. Courtesy State Historical Society of Wisconsin

THERE was no little curiosity excited in the quiet and remote town of St Anthony, as the unusual procession passed through it, of a bark canoe in a waggon, followed by two voyageurs and four Englishmen; and when we stopped for a moment at the hotel and entered the bar, the billiard-players in the adjoining room, and the loafers of the neighbourhood, crowded inquisitively round to discover the origin of the visit. When they heard the route we had taken from Superior, we were overwhelmed with inquiries as to the nature of the country, the character of the pines on the Upper Mississippi, and its advantages generally as a district in which to settle; for most of the inhabitants of these western towns are anxious to hold land beyond them, so as to profit by the advance of civilisation, and are ever seeking information from explorers, who, if they are personally interested, give the public no more of their experience and observation than they can help, until they have established their own claims in an indisputable manner, and then their descriptions are of course framed so as to induce emigration to flow in the desired direction as freely as possible. As we were quite uninterested,

we were also quite impartial, and gave a true account, which, however, was most probably not believed. St Anthony is a cheerful, pretty place, clean and well built, containing about 2500 inhabitants. A great rivalry exists between it and St Paul; the former owing its prosperity to the conveniences it derives for timber operations from the magnificent water-power —the latter from its position at the head of Mississippi navigation. It is, indeed, possible to navigate the river to this point with a smaller class of boats; but it is doubtful whether those employed below St Paul will ever be able to reach it, or whether it would be desirable that they should do so. The distance is about fourteen miles, but the actual northing is not more than two, while the stages perform the journey overland in less than an hour, the distance not exceeding eight miles. St Anthony is already a curious mixture of a manufacturing town and a watering-place. The extreme beauty of the scenery in the neighbourhood, the attractions of the Falls themselves, and the comfortable and civilised aspect of the town, are beginning to render it a fashionable summer resort, and picturesque villas are springing up on all available sites; but upon the bank of the river saw-mills, foundries, shingle-machines, lath-factories, &c., keep up an incessant hubbub—delightful music to the white man, who recognises in the plashing of water, and the roar of steam, and the ring of a thousand hammers, the potent agency which is to regenerate a magnificent country, and to enrich himself—but the harshest sounds that ever fell upon the ear of the Indian, for they remind him of the great change through which he has already passed, and proclaim his inevitable destiny in loud unfaltering tones.

The first dwelling-house was only erected in this city in the autumn of 1847, and Mrs Ard Godfrey claims the honour of having given birth to the first of the fair daughters of St Anthony. There are now numerous manufactories, shops, newspaper offices, and young ladies; four organised churches—Presbyterian, Baptist, Episcopalian, and Methodist; while the importance of the place has been much increased by its having been selected as the location for the university of Minnesota; the Act providing "that the proceeds of all lands that may hereafter be granted by the United States to the territory, for the support of a university, shall be, and remain, a perpetual fund, to be called the 'University Fund,' the interest of which shall be appropriated to the support of a university." This university was opened in 1851, and already contains about a hundred pupils. Indeed, Minnesota seems determined to be in advance of the age, for two sections in every township have been appropriated for the support of common schools, no other State having previously obtained more than one section in each township for such a purpose.

At the foot of the Falls the voyageurs launched the canoe and prepared lunch, while we explored the neighbourhood and sketched the Falls. They are only twenty feet in height; but the scenery does not derive its interest from their grandeur, but from the perfect grouping of rock and wood and water on a magnificent scale. The Mississippi is upwards of six hundred yards wide above the Falls. These are quite perpendicular, and the water drops in beautiful single sheets on either side of a huge mass of white sandstone, of a pyramidal form, which splits the stream. The

rapids below extend for several hundred yards, and are very broad, divided into various channels by precipitous islands of sandstone, gigantic blocks of which are strewn in grotesque confusion at the base of lofty walls of stratification of dazzling whiteness. These fantastically-shaped islands are thickly wooded, and birch and maple cling with desperate tenacity to nooks and crannies in the perpendicular cliffs. The banks of the river are of a character similar to the islands in its stream; and there is a picturesque old mill upon the opposite side, the first that was built here, which has just arrived at such a stage of decay as to add an additional charm to the scene. The white houses of St Anthony are almost hidden by the thick foliage of the left bank.

We could scarcely bear to tear ourselves away from so lovely a spot, after only two hours spent in exploring its beauties; but we had fourteen miles still before us to St Paul, and the sun was already getting low in the heavens; so we paddled gently on, or sometimes rested on our oars, and, letting our canoe float down the stream between perpendicular cliffs, gave ourselves up to the enervating influences of the balmy evening air, and lay back in quiet contemplation of most magnificent scenery possessing all the charms of novelty, and the advantages of being visited under the most favourable, though certainly somewhat unusual circumstances.

The stream was broad and sluggish, and the fish rose so freely in every direction, and exhibited themselves so temptingly as they jumped and glittered in the sunshine, that our indefatigable fishing companion destroyed his own peace of mind, and kept continually hooking his friends, in unsuccessful attempts to delude his prey with gaudy-coloured flies; but he could only boast of one rise, and that was known to himself alone, so we voted that the tranquil enjoyments of the evening ought not to be disturbed by such restless proceedings; and prohibiting all distracting ejaculations of surprise or delight, made Le Fève chant the melodious song of the voyageur, and watched the thin blue clouds of the fragrant pure leaf of Virginia circling in the air. There was one reach inexpressibly beautiful, where a stream issues from beneath thick foliage, and leaps a perpendicular cliff seventy or eighty feet high. It takes its rise in Lake Minnetonka, twelve miles distant, to the fertile shores of which many immigrants have already been attracted, and, passing through the romantically situated Lake Calhoun, terminates thus abruptly its brief existence. A little below it, a lofty wall of white sandstone, about two hundred feet in height, seems to bar the passage of the river; and the loop-holed walls of Fort Snelling appear to totter upon the brink of the dizzy precipice, but the stars and stripes flaunt bravely above them, and are as little likely to be moved as the rock on which they are planted. Passing round the base of this promontory, we find ourselves opposite the debouchure of the most important tributary of the Upper Mississippi. Here the Minnesota, or St Peter's River, pours in its deep, quiet volume, after a long course through a district which has been described as the Italy of the north-west—the "Undine region" of Nicollet. The river is navigable for many miles, and opens up a country concerning which we can obtain and impart more full information when we arrive at St Paul. Meantime there is the city of Mendota, situated upon an island at the confluence of the two rivers—a less rapidly progressive place than is usual in these parts, having suffered from those obstructive tendencies which characterise war-departments generally, and in consequence of which the large military reserve attached to Fort Snelling, upon which it is situated, has only recently been available for practical purposes. Mendota possesses great advantages of position, and was for long a trading-post of the American Fur Company. Five miles lower down, upon a lofty bluff overhanging the Mississippi, stands the city of St Paul—its handsome houses and churches crowning the heights, and a fleet of steam-boats moored at their base. Slipping unassumingly behind one of these white ungainly river-monsters, we hauled up our picturesque little bark, and, shouldering our packs for the last time, ascended the long staircase which led up the cliff, and found ourselves in the main street of the capital of Minnesota. . . .

St. Paul is perhaps the best specimen to be found in the States, of a town still in its infancy with a great destiny before it. Its progress hitherto has been equalled only by Chicago. In 1847 a few trading huts, rejoicing under the sobriquet of Pig's Eye—a name still retained by some rapids just below the town—marked the site of the present city; and it occurred to some of the French traders and Yankee squatters upon the unpre-empted land in the neighbourhood, to mark out what is called in the States a town plat, without apparently any anticipation of the important results which were ultimately to attend their speculation; indeed, they were somewhat old-fashioned in their notions, and laid out their plat in what one of the present citizens, in his account of the first years of St Paul, calls "little skewdangular lots, about as large as a stingy card of gingerbread broke in two diagonally." The consequence was, that for the first two years there was very little temptation to put anything upon the said lots; but in 1849 some celebrated go-ahead speculators took up the thing, one of whom, Henry M. Rice, is now pushing on Superior as he did St Paul, when he was in company with John R. Irving, with whom he "bought in." At this time there were half-a-dozen log-huts, a hotel, a couple of stores, a log Catholic chapel, and about 150 inhabitants—a community which was worthy of being represented by the press; and, accordingly, Colonel James M. Goodhue arrived in the same year to start a paper, which he intended to call "The Epistle of St Paul." The good people there, however, had discrimination enough to object to the name, and so he called it the *Minnesota Pioneer*, in one of the articles of which he gives an amusing description of his finding himself, on a raw, cloudy day in April '49, in a forlorn condition, at the bottom of the cliff, surrounded by his press, types, and printing apparatus, with no shed to put them in, or acquaintance in the place. A Yankee editor is not to be discouraged by trifles; so he got a room "on" Third Street, "as open as a corn-rick," from which airy tenement his first number issued, "in the presence of Mr Lull, Mr Cavileer, Mr Neill, and perhaps Major Murphy." After that he got a lot in what he supposed would be the middle of the town, having "calculated that the two ends would probably unite there," and building a dwelling-house, lived in it through the next year, without having it lathed or plastered. Such was the origin of St Paul, and such the commencement of the *Pioneer*, which, in the language of the editor, has "advocated Minnesota, morality, and religion, from the beginning." In the recent death of this gentleman, St Paul has sustained a great loss; and if he had been as successful in his advocacy of the two latter principles as of that of the territory, Minnesota would be a terrestrial paradise; for it began to shoot ahead thenceforward with a vengeance. There are now four daily, four weekly, and two tri-weekly papers, which is pretty well for a Far West town only five years old, and more than Manchester and Liverpool put together. There are four or five hotels, and at least half-a-dozen handsome churches, with tall spires pointing heavenward, and sundry meeting-houses, and a population of seven or eight thousand to go to them, and good streets with side-walks, and lofty brick warehouses, and stores, and shops, as well supplied as any in the Union; and "an academy of the highest grade for young ladies;" and wharves at which upwards of three hundred steamers arrive annually, bringing new settlers to this favoured land, and carrying away its produce to the south and east. The navigation of the river is closed during the four winter months, or from November to March. As the resources of Minnesota are developed, the trade upon the river must continue to increase. The saw-mills of St Anthony, St Paul, and Stillwater will supply countless feet of timber for the States further south; its prairies will furnish live stock *ad libitum;* and its cereal produce will, according to Colonel Goodhue, hold its own with the most favoured states. That gentleman thus compares its capabilities in this respect with its principal rival, Illinois: "We will give Illinois May the start, and Minnesota shall come out ahead. Don't care what the crop is—any grain, any root—anything from a castor bean, or an apple or pear tree, or a pumpkin, to a sweet potato or a tobacco plant. Why, sucker, do you know you have frosts two weeks earlier in Illinois than we do here? It is a fact! We will show these people *sights* who come up here in May,

and go shivering back home, saying that Minnesota is 'too cold for *craps.'*" And so on in the same strain with regard to cattle. In addition to all this, there is the Indian trade, which is certainly diminishing, but still forms a large share of the business done in St Paul. During our stay there, we frequented constantly the shops of some of the traders, and overhauled moccasins embroidered with porcupine quills; tobacco-pouches ornamented with beads; tomahawks, pipes, and all the appurtenances of Indian life which these men pick up from Sioux or Chippeway warriors, and sell as curiosities, with histories attached to certain articles, alleged to have been bought from famous chiefs, which may or may not be true, but in consideration of which extra charge is made. At all events, I am prepared to assert against all comers, on the authority of a most respectable citizen from whom I bought them, that a pipe now in my possession, and which bore the traces of recent use, together with a very frowsy old tobacco-pouch, did really belong to the most celebrated war-chief and extensive scalp-taker among the Sioux, popularly called "Medicine Bottle," but whose Indian name is Wah-kan-o-jan-jan, which is an unconscionable amount of gibberish for the word *light*, which it literally signifies.

These shops have their agents up the country, who supply the Indians with ammunition, blankets, guns, &c., in advance, and at a considerable profit, in anticipation of the price at which they purchase their furs and peltries from them. The young men of the tribes, however, very often come into the town to trade, and a party of Chippeways had been in St Paul about three weeks before our visit, who had afterwards gone out upon the war-path. Some Sioux, however, discovered their trail upon the St Peter's River, between Fort Ridgley and Traverse des Sioux, and having lain in ambush till their enemies were in the act of fording the stream, rushed upon them, and took fifteen scalps. Some of the victims were women and children; the Chippeways are the only tribe who take their families with them on the war path.

We hired a light waggon one afternoon, and drove about the country near St Paul, in search of trout streams and pretty scenery. We were not happy in lighting upon the former, but there was ample to gratify us so far as the latter was concerned. St Paul is generally the prominent feature in every view, and its noble position justly entitles it to this distinction. I scarcely ever remember to have seen anything more lovely than the sunset, as we stood upon a newly-raised terrace near an unfinished Elizabethan villa, which an evidently prosperous citizen was erecting upon a hill, and which commanded a noble view of the town, with the deep broad river sweeping past lofty cliffs, and the woodland country stretching away to distant hills bathed in tints of richest purple.

The most striking characteristic of the environs of St Paul, however, is the utter wildness of the surrounding country. In whatever direction you ascend the hills which encircle the town, with the exception of the busy, gay-looking city, all is gloomy forest or solitary prairie; and there can be no stronger testimony to the rapid growth of the place, than the fact that the country in the immediate vicinity is still in a state of savage nature. No doubt a few years will work a marvellous change here too; but the most interesting element of the scenery will be destroyed when this wonderful combination of civilisation and barbarism has disappeared.

WILDCAT MONEY, TOWNSITE FRAUD

GEORGE BYRON MERRICK

While western settlements were growing into cities, speculators were busy plotting towns on paper and selling land titles in cities that had no present existence and a doubtful future. The most ambitious of townsite promoters was Ignatius Donnelly who advertised his nonexistent Nininger as the "future metropolis of the Mississippi." In Philadelphia he published a newspaper with NININGER CITY, MINNESOTA TERRITORY *on its dateline. A running head across the page expressed both his confidence and his classical learning. "Dost thou know how to play the fiddle?" "No," answered Themistocles, "but I understand the art of raising a little village into a great city."*

When the promise of Nininger City ended in the panic of 1857, Donnelly turned to politics. Two years later, at twenty-eight, he was lieutenant governor of Minnesota, and for eight years in the sixties he served as a member of Congress.

George Byron Merrick was the Mark Twain of the upper Mississippi. After an apprenticeship as a printer, he began his river career. He was pantry boy, "cub" engineer, mud-clerk, and eventually pilot on the storied boats of the upper river. In his later years he wrote Old Times on the Upper Mississippi, *from which the following chapter is taken.*

BOTH of these specimens of natural history were bred, nurtured, and let loose in countless numbers to prey upon the people in the early days that witnessed the opening of the Northwestern territories to settlement. The wild-cat dollars waxed fat upon the blood and brawn of the settlers who had already arrived; wildcat town-sites found ready victims in the thousands of Eastern people who desired to better their fortunes, and who lent ready ears to the golden tales of unscrupulous promoters, that told of wonderful cities in the West, whose only reality was that blazoned in the prospectuses scattered broadcast through the East.

The younger generation, whose only acquaintance with the circulating symbols of wealth that we call "money", is confined to the decades since the close of the War of Secession, can have no idea of the laxity of banking laws of the fifties, in the Northwestern states and territories, nor of the instability of the so-called "money" that comprised nine-tenths of the medium of exchange then in use in the West. Nowadays, a bank bill stands for its face value in gold, if it be a National Bank issue. If a state bank—and bills of this sort are comparatively few in these days—they are also guaranteed, in a measure, by the laws of the state in which the bank is situated. In the days of which I am writing, and especially in the unsettled and troublesome times just before the war (from 1856 to 1862), the money that was handled on the river in the prosecution of business, except of course the small proportion of gold that was still in circulation, had little or no backing, either by federal or state enactments.

A man went into an embryo city, consisting in that day of two or three thousand town lots, and from fifty to a hundred inhabitants, with an iron box costing twenty-five dollars. In this box he had ten, twenty, or thirty thousand "dollars" in new bank bills purporting to have been issued from two, three, or four banks doing business in other equally large, populous, and growing cities, situated elsewhere in Wisconsin, or preferably in Illinois, Indiana, or Michigan. How did he become possessed of all this wealth? Was it the savings of years? The iron box was, perhaps; perhaps he got trusted for that. The money was not usually the savings of any time at all; it was simply printed to order.

Five or six persons desirous of benefitting their fellow men by assisting them in opening their farms and "moving their crops", would get together in Chicago, Cincinnati, or St. Louis, wherever there was an establishment capable of engraving and printing bank bills—and not very elegant or artistic printing was required, or desired. These men propose to start as many banks, in as many "cities" in the West. They have money enough, each of them, to buy a safe, an iron box into which any carpenter could bore with an ordinary brace and bit, and enough over to pay for the printing of twenty thousand dollars' worth of bills in denominations of one, two, five and ten dollars. The printing finished, each man would sign his own bills as president, and one of the others would add the final touch of authenticity by signing a fictitious name to the same bills as cashier. Then it was "money".

But it would have been overloading the credulity of even the most gullible denizens of his adopted city to ask them to accept his own bills as legal tender; so a swap was made all around, and when the requisite amount of shuffling was completed, each man had his twenty thousand dollars in bills on four or five banks, but none of his own issue. There was a double incentive in this transaction: first, it inspired the utmost confidence in the minds of the men who were to borrow this money. How could this banker who had come among them for their good, have acquired this money by any other than legitimate transactions? If it were bills on his own bank that he proposed to put into circulation, there might be some question as to their guaranty; but he could not get this money by merely going to the printing office and ordering it, as he might in case of bills on his own institution. It certainly must be good money. Secondly, by distributing his bills in as many different localities as possible, the chances of its never being presented for redemption were greatly multiplied; it might be burned, or lost overboard, or worn out, in which case he would be just so much ahead, and no questions asked.

The foregoing may be a somewhat fanciful statement of the way in which the bankers proceeded, but in essence it is a true picture. They may not have all met in Chicago, or anywhere else, to perfect these arrangements, but the arrangements were all perfected practically as stated: "You put my bills into circulation, and I will put out yours; and in each case the exchange will greatly assist each and all of us in hoodwinking our victims into the belief that it is money, and not merely printed paper which we are offering them".

Equipped with these goods, and with a

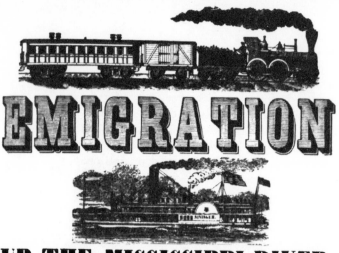

EMIGRATION

UP THE MISSISSIPPI RIVER.

The attention of Emigrants and the Public generally, is called to the now rapidly improving

TERRITORY OF MINNESOTA,

Containing a population of 150,000. and goes into the Union as a State during the present year. According to an act of Congress passed last February, the State is munificently endowed with Lands for Public Schools and State Universities, also granting five per cent. on all sales of U. S. Lands for Internal Improvements. On the 3d March, 1857, grants of Land from Congress was made to the leading Trunk Railroads in Minnesota, so that in a short time the trip from New Orleans to any part of the State will be made in from two and a half to three days. The

CITY OF NININGER,

Situated on the Mississippi River, 35 miles below St. Paul, is now a prominent point for a large Commercial Town, being backed by an extensive Agricultural, Grazing and Farming Country; has fine streams in the interior, well adapted for Milling in all its branches; and Manufacturing **WATER POWER** to any extent.

Mr. JOHN NININGER, (a Gentleman of large means, ideas and liberality, speaking the various languages,) is the principal Proprietor of **Nininger.** He laid it out on such principles as to encourage all **MECHANICS**, Merchants, or Professions of all kinds, on the same equality and footing; the consequence is, the place has gone ahead with such rapidity that it is now an established City, and will annually double in population for years to come.

Persons arriving by Ship or otherwise, can be transferred without expense to Steamers going to Saint Louis; or stop at Cairo, and take Railroad to Dunleith (on the Mississippi). Steamboats leave Saint Louis and Dunleith daily for **NININGER**, and make the trip from Dunleith in 36 to 48 hours.

NOTICES.

1. All Railroads and Steamboats giving this card a conspicuous place, or *gratuitous insertion* in their cards, AIDS THE EMIGRANT and forwards their own interest.

2. For authentic documents, reliable information, and all particulars in regard to Occupations, Wages, Preëmpting Lands (in neighborhood). Lumber, Price of Lots, Expenses, &c., apply to

THOMAS B. WINSTON, 27 Camp street, New Orleans.
ROBERT CAMPBELL, St. Louis.
JOSEPH B. FORBES, Dunleith.

charter from the state in which he proposed to operate—a charter granted for the asking, and no questions raised—the banker transports himself and his box of money to his chosen field of operations. The newspaper which has already been located in the new city heralds the coming of Mr. Rothschild, our new banker, more or less definitely hinting at the great wealth lying behind the coming financier. A bank building is rented, a sign hung out, and he begins to loan his money at five per cent per month on the partially-improved farms of his neighbors, or the house and lot of his "city" friends. He is a liberal man, and if it is not convenient for you to pay the interest as it accrues, he will let it stand—but he does not forget to compound it every month.

The result is inevitable. The debt mounts up with a rapidity that paralyzes the borrower, and in the end a foreclosure adds farm and improvements to the growing assets of the banker. Within a very few years he is the owner of eight or ten of the best farms in the county, and perhaps half a dozen houses and lots in the village, and all with the investment of less than a hundred dollars invested in printing, and an iron box, and without the expenditure of an ounce of energy or a legitimate day's work. And the victims break up and start anew for the still farther West, to take new farms, to be engulfed in the maws of other sharks. One may not greatly pity the men themselves, for men are born to work and suffer; but the women! God pity them. Worn, tired, broken-hearted, they must leave that which is dearest to them in all the world, their homes, and fare forth again into the wilderness, to toil and suffer, and at last, blessed release, to die. . . .

And the bankers? They were counted honest. If by any chance one of their bills came to hand and was presented for payment at the home counter, it was promptly redeemed, sometimes in gold or silver, but oftener with another bill on some other bank belonging to the syndicate. I personally knew some of these bankers. Some of them were freebooters without conscience and without shame. Under color of law, they robbed the settlers of their lands and improvements, and defied public opinion. Others put on a cloak of righteousness; they were leaders in the love-feasts and pillars in the church; and they also had their neighbors' lands and improvements. Their descendants are rich and respected to-day in the communities where their fathers plied their iniquitous trade; and these rule where their fathers robbed.

As a clerk on the river, I had some experience in handling the wild-cat money. At Dunleith, before starting on the up-river trip, we were handed by the secretary of the company, a *Thompson's Bank Note Detector*, and with it a list of the bills that we might accept in payment for freight or passage. We were also given a list of those that we might not accept at all; and still another list upon which we might speculate, at values running from twenty-five to seventy-five per cent of their face denominations. Thus equipped we started upstream, and the trouble started with us. At McGregor we put off a lot of freight, and were tendered money. We consulted our lists and cast into outer darkness that which had upon it the anathema of Mr. Jones, the secretary. We accepted all on the list of the elect, and compromised upon enough more to balance our freight account. The agent at McGregor had a list of his own which partly coincided with ours but in general disagreed. In the meantime another boat of our line had arrived from up river, and we get from her clerk fifteen or twenty lists of bills which would be taken or rejected at as many landings above. This helps somewhat, as we see our way clear to get rid of some of our twenty-five per cent stuff at par in exchange for cord wood or stores on the upper river, and we sort our stock out into packages which are reported current at each landing. We also see an opportunity to swap at Dunleith some bills which are not current there at all, but which are taken at par at Prescott or Stillwater, for other bills which they do not want but which will be taken at the company's office at Dunleith in settlement of our trip.

It required a long head to figure it out. Mine was long enough, but unfortunately it had the same dimensions both ways, and was not to be depended upon in these finer transactions. Mr. Hargus labored with the problem, studying lists until he came nigh to the point of insanity, with the result that when we "cashed in" on our return it was usually found that we had from five hundred to a thousand dollars that was not acceptable. This we kept, and the boat was debited with the amount on the company's books. On the next trip we would usually be able to work off some of this stuff. At the end of one season I recollect that we had some two thousand dollars, face estimate, of this paper on hand, which the treasurer would not accept, for the banks on which the bills were drawn had gone out of existence.

The town-site industry was on the same plane of deception and robbery as the banking frauds, but it found its victims "back East", instead of close at hand. Being Easterners, who had been educated to suppose that integrity and honesty were the basis of all business confidence, and themselves practiced these old-fashioned virtues, they all too readily accepted the assurances of the land-sharks, and invested their money without seeing the property which was so glowingly described in the prospectuses sent out by the Western promoters. The result was, that they were "taken in and done for" by the hundreds of town-site sharks who were operating all along the river, between Dunleith and St. Paul. I shall refer to but one of which I had personal knowledge, and to another described to me by Captain Russell Blakeley.

The city of Nininger, as delineated on the large and beautifully-engraved and printed maps issued by Ingenuous Doemly, was a well-built metropolis capable of containing ten thousand people. As delineated, it had a magnificent court house, this city being the county seat of Dakota County, Minnesota. Four or five church spires sprang a hundred feet each into the atmosphere. It had stores and warehouses, crowded with merchandise, and scores of drays and draymen were working with feverish energy to keep the levee clear of the freight being landed from half a dozen well-known steamboats belonging to the Minnesota Packet Company or the St. Louis & St. Paul Packet Company. An imposing brick structure with cut stone trimmings, four stories high, housed the plant of the Nininger *Daily Bugle*.

This last-mentioned feature of the prospectus was the only one that had the remotest semblance of foundation in fact. There certainly was a *Daily Bugle*, issued once a week, or once in two or three weeks, depending upon the energy of the printer and his "devil", who jointly set the type, and the assiduity of the editors who furnished them with copy. This paper was printed upon the first power press that ever threw off a printed sheet in the Territory of Minnesota. It was a good press, and the paper printed upon it was a monument to the shrewdness and ingenuity of the honorable proprietor of the Nininger town-site. The sheet was filled with a wealth of local advertising—drygoods, groceries, hardware, millinery, shoe stores, blacksmith shops—every class of business found in a large and prosperous city, was represented in those columns. But every name and every business was fictitious, coined in the fertile brain of this chief of all promoters. It was enough to deceive the very elect—and it did. When the Eastern man read that there were six or eight lots, lying just west of Smith & Jones's drygoods store, on West Prairie Street, that could be had at a thousand dollars per lot if taken quickly, and that they were well worth twice that money on account of the advantageous situation, they were snapped up as a toad snaps flies on a summer day.

The paper was filled with local reading matter, describing the rush at the opening of the latest emporium; that Brown had gone East to purchase his spring stock; that Mrs. Newbody entertained at her beautiful new residence on Park Avenue, and gave the names of fifty of her guests. The whole thing was the plan of a Napoleonic mind, being carried out to the minutest detail with painstaking care by a staff of able workers, with the result that the whole prairie for two miles back from the river was sold out at the rate of ten thousand dollars an acre or upwards, and that before the proprietor had himself perfected his legal rights to the land which he was thus retailing.

Henry Lindergreen, the printer who did the mechanical work on the Nininger paper, was a chum of mine, we having set type in the same "alley" elsewhere, and that winter I went up to Nininger to help him out. The four-story brick block of the wood-cuts shrunk into a little frame building, the sides of which were made of inch boards set up on end and battened on the outside. Inside, it was further reinforced with tarred paper; and while I was there a pail of water ten feet from a red-hot stove, froze solid in a night, and the three printers had all they could do to feed the fire fast enough to keep themselves from freezing also, with the mercury down to forty degrees below zero. The editor who, in the absence of the promoter himself, in the East disposing of lots, was hired to improvise facts for the columns of this veracious sheet, lived in St. Paul, and sent his copy down to Hastings, as there was no postoffice at Nininger.

If the editor or the proprietor had been found at Nininger in the following spring when the dupes began to appear, one or two of the jack oaks with which the city lots were plentifully clothed, would have borne a larger fruit than acorns. Even the printer who set the type, was forced to flee for his life.

One of the boldest-faced swindles I ever heard of, was the so-called Rolling Stone colony. In the spring of 1852, some three or four hundred people, chiefly from New York city, came to seek their purchased lands in Rolling Stone. They brought with them beautiful maps and bird's-eye views of the place, showing a large greenhouse, lecture hall, and library. Each colonist was to have a house lot in town and a farm in the neighboring country. The colony had been formed by one William Haddock, and none of the members had the faintest shadow of experience in farming. Boarding steamers at Galena, they expected to be put off at the Rolling Stone levee, for the views represented large houses, a hotel, a big warehouse, and a fine dock. But the steamboat officers had never heard of such a place. Careful questioning, however, seemed to locate the site three miles above Wabasha Prairie, on land then belonging to the Sioux Indians. As they insisted on landing, they were put off at the log cabin of one John Johnson, the only white man within ten miles. They made sod houses for themselves, or dug shelter burrows in the river banks; sickness came; many died during the summer and autumn; and when winter set in the place was abandoned. The people suffered severely, and the story of Rolling Stone makes a sad chapter in the early history of Minnesota.

While the craze was on, some made fortunes, while thousands of trusting men and women lost the savings of years. After the fever of speculation had burned itself out, the actual builders of the commonwealth came in and subdued the land. Nininger and Rolling Stone are still on the map, and that is about all there is of them—a name. La Crosse, Winona, St. Paul and Minneapolis have superseded them, and the population, wealth, and commerce of these are greater in reality than were the airy figments of the brain which they have supplanted.

VIII

West Becomes Midwest

THE first West began at the edge of pioneer Boston and Philadelphia, where Indian trails led into the forest. It was pushed back to the Alleghenies by the time of the Revolution, and then to the Mississippi. The West of the Ohio and Illinois countries was a land of danger and promise, like the Rocky Mountain West after the Civil War. One writer considered that the "Wild West" began at the Wabash, and Emerson traveling up the Mississippi in 1851 thought himself in the "Far West." In 1813 in London young Lord Byron heard that his poems were added to the Coonskin Library (a collection of books bought by trading coonskins) in Athens County, Ohio. He wrote in his diary: "These are the first tidings that sound like fame to my ears—to be read on the banks of the Ohio." It was like being read today on the Yukon or the Zambezi.

But change came quickly. Canals, roads and railroads brought remote places near, the forest gave way to farms, the wild prairie became vast fields of grain. Wilderness remained north of the 44th parallel, where a vast pine, spruce and hemlock forest covered the northern counties of Michigan and Wisconsin. But after the Civil War, in a generation of epic and wasteful labor, the North Woods became a stumpland. In those years lumber schooners whitened the lakes and huge log rafts floated down the Mississippi. The northern forests built the towns and cities of the midlands.

By that time the Old Northwest was no longer a frontier but a region through which new migrations passed on their way to new country. T. S. Eliot, having grown up beside the river at St. Louis, wrote of the Mississippi:

> I think that the river
> Is a strong brown god—sullen, untamed and intractible;
> Patient to some degree, at first recognized as a frontier;
> Useful, untrustworthy, as a conveyor of commerce;
> Then only a problem confronting the builders of bridges.

The Ohio fever was over by 1840, when Ohio sent a President to the White House, and the new goals of migration were Kansas, Texas and Oregon. In 1832 George Catlin, on his way to Indian country beyond the Missouri, stopped in

Cincinnati. "Our town," a citizen told him, "has passed the days of its most rapid growth. It is not far enough west." In 1837 a schoolmaster in the Miami valley wrote to a friend in Pennsylvania: "The great rage even here is to sell out and go West." The early West had become the Midwest, "a young empire," wrote Lyman Beecher on his arrival from Boston, "rushing up to giant manhood with a rapidity and power never before witnessed below the sun."

TIPPECANOE AND TYLER TOO

LAFAYETTE *FREE PRESS*, JUNE 4, 1840

In 1820 the Ohio valley was an outlying country; a generation later it had become a central and determining region. By 1840 the log cabin was not a dwelling but a political symbol, and in the campaign of that year the newly evolved Midwest showed the nation its political energy and power.

As presidential nominee the Whig party chose old William Henry Harrison, who twenty-nine years before had fought the Indians at Tippecanoe. That name became a slogan, and a great rally was held on the nearly forgotten battleground along the Wabash outside the town of Lafayette.

Plans began in Indianapolis where a Whig editor called for a gathering of the Boys of Indiana. "Every man with his wagon, and horses or ox team, horseback or with his knapsack, with his week's provisions, be up and ready to march to Tippecanoe." The idea spread like prairie fire, and delegations came from as far away as the eastern seaboard and the Territory of Iowa. Wrote a Baltimore reporter on the scene in Indiana: "Every avenue leading toward the battleground was filled with wagons, loaded with delegates, horsemen and foot passengers, wending their way to this proud spot for our American arms—and when all were assembled, such a multitude has never been beheld in the interior of the United States; the number cannot with any approximation to certainty be ascertained— it is variously guessed at from 40,000 to 50,000. All agree that there were FIFTEEN ACRES OF MEN *besides from 3,000 to 6,000 females, and the encampment might not inappropriately be compared to Darius' vast encampment preparatory to his descent upon Greece."*

The following account of the monster rally was reprinted from the Lafayette Free Press *by Niles' National Register for June 27, 1840.*

THE great gathering at Tippecanoe came and is past—but the echo of its thunder is still reverberating along the shore of the bountiful Wabash—over the beautiful hills and valleys and the verdant prairies of the great west. The fires of enthusiasm, fanned to a flame at the altar of liberty on that Bunker Hill of the west, will spread abroad in the whole length and breadth of this glorious land of the brave and free, kindling as onward it moves, fresh fires upon other new and living altars, at the shrine of which hosts of freemen will offer up the best fruits of their patriot hearts. Thousands have greeted thousands,—the north has mingled voices with the south;—the east has had free conference with the west—and the patriot spirit which brought them here has received a new accession of zeal for the contest. But who shall describe the tremendous outpouring of the people? What mortal pen can give the faintest sketch of its proceedings? —what pencil delineate its glowing enthusiasm? To be known it must have been seen— to be appreciated it must have been heard.

It would but feebly convey an idea of its vastness, to say that such a multitudinous gathering never before assembled in Indiana; aye, or in the west. And when we consider what brought them here, and the distance many of them overcame, with the almost impassable state of the roads, and the incessant rains, which preceded it, we do not hesitate to pronounce it one of the greatest assemblies ever convened for civic purposes on this side of the broad Atlantic. Before noon of the 28th, thousands upon thousands had arrived at and passed through our town greeted by shouts of welcome at every turn. On the evening of that day, there were two thousand three hundred wagons encamped in the vicinity of the battle ground; and by noon of the 29th, the number was swelled to three thousand two hundred, which were counted,—and the number of persons in attendance on Friday, could not have been less than thirty thousand.

The morning of Thursday gave promise of a fair day, and at an early hour all the thoroughfares leading to Lafayette, were filled with processions on foot and horseback; in wagons and carts; in canoes and in cabins, all flocking to the battle field of Tippecanoe. Five steamboats had arrived at our wharves, crowded with passengers from the towns on the Ohio and the Wabash, while the roar of artillery and the crash of the muskets mingled the shouts and huzzas of the multitude, as they marched with colors unfurled and banners waving in the breeze. In the afternoon however, the rain again poured down in torrents; but onward came the processions in unfaltering array, filled with enthusiasm, and were greeted by hundreds as they passed through our town and proceeded on their way to the battle ground; nor did they cease coming until long after dark. Late in the afternoon of that day, the rain, which had been falling at intervals for the last five days, abated and the sun shone forth. In the evening a number of these persons who remained in Lafayette, assembled at the Presbyterian church, and listened to most eloquent speeches from Messrs. C. B. Smith and H. S. Lane, two of the Harrison candidates for electors in this state, and Mr. James Brooks, editor of the New York Express.

Friday, the 29th, was a bright and glorious day. At an early hour a procession of delegates was formed upon the northern road leading past the battle ground, which presented a most imposing array of the hardy yeomanry of the land—and several fine military companies of volunteers from different parts of the state. . . . The whole proceedings throughout, at proper intervals, were enlivened by excellent music, by bands from Evansville,

Vincennes, Terre Haute, Crawfordsville, Richmond and other places. Every county in the state was, we believe, represented, although the people of many counties did not send delegates, but generously resolved to come themselves. . . .

During a recess for dinner, the old soldiers, survivors of the battle of Tippecanoe, met at one of the cabins, and after an interchange of kindly regard and mingling once more in social converse, passed several resolutions expressive of their feelings on this occasion, and of their undiminished confidence in their old commander.

While the soldiers who fought at Tippecanoe were assembled at one of the cabins, the soldiers of the late war with Great Britain, who were present, assembled to the number of thirty or forty in an adjoining cabin, and passed resolutions unanimously approving of the battle ground of Tippecanoe, and giving it the preference over any place they had seen in the country, as an encampment to resist a night attack from Indians. Several of them had held commissions in the regular army of the United States, and had served, some in the northern, some in the southern, and others in the western divisions of our army. Their testimony, known and appreciated as they are in the different sections of our state, ought forever to silence the tongue of slander, in her busy misrepresentations of that battle field. The proceedings were signed by each one of them, in his own name, with the addition of the division of the army to which he belonged.

The convention met again in the afternoon, when judge William Polke, a soldier under Wayne, and also a soldier at Tippecanoe, introduced to the president, and through him to the convention, the surviving soldiers of the battle, then present: several of whom, as they appeared upon the stand, made short addresses, and testified anew to the bravery and ability of their old commander. The scene was affecting in the extreme, and caused gushing tears to flow over many a time furrowed cheek. There was a large concourse of ladies present upon the occasion, who, while their presence gave animation to the scene, served in a great measure to repress

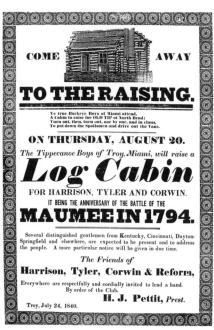

the more enthusiastic outbreakings of excitement. . . .

In the evening there was a handsome display of fireworks, besides several very able and eloquent speeches. Whilst a portion of the convention was witnessing the exhibition of fireworks near the lower point of the battle ground, and a vast concourse gathered at the cabins, listening to the speeches, a splendid aurora appeared at the northwest, and after varying its form for some time, shot across the heavens, forming a galaxy, like one continued stream of light, from horizon to horizon. The edges were perfectly straight, and the width apparently but very few feet. In this form it rested over the cabin for several minutes, exciting the wonder and admiration of the audience; the oldest of whom had never witnessed a similar phenomenon. After the first feelings of awe and admiration had subsided, the crowd hailed it as a sign hung out in the clouds to cheer them on in the glorious work of reform, and like the bow of hope to Noah, it was greeted as a token that their efforts should be crowned with success, and the flood of corruption, which had desolated the land, should cease.

On the morning of Saturday, the convention assembled again and listened to most eloquent speeches from gentlemen who had not before been heard. Votes of thanks to the president and other officers of the convention were passed, and general McCarty made a few very happy and appropriate remarks, which drew forth fresh bursts of applause. . . .

There could not have been less than a thousand to twelve hundred persons in attendance from other states:—we saw badges from Tennessee—from Kentucky—from Massachusetts—from Michigan—from Ohio—from Missouri—from Illinois, and from the territory of Iowa.

The order of the convention was admirable for so large a concourse, and its harmony was never equalled in any large promiscuous assembly. There was no rioting; no disorder; and not a single accident occurred to sadden the feelings or dampen the enthusiasm of the occasion. The convention adjourned in the afternoon of Saturday, and the delegates and visitors departed for their homes well satisfied with the proceedings, and happy in having had an opportunity of seeing with their own eyes that memorable spot, not surpassed in interest and loveliness in the whole regions of the beautiful west;—of hearing with their own ears the testimony of the brave spirits who fought and conquered there.

Thousands upon thousands whose minds had been prejudiced by the false representations of that honored spot, and the slanders so widely circulated against the hero who commanded the gallant spirits, who upon its bosom withstood the deadly shock of the Indian's fiercest assault, have seen and can judge for themselves. They go home satisfied and disabused of their prejudices, and will relate to their neighbors, their friends and their families what they have seen and heard, and will reiterate their own observations upon its beauty and its fitness for an encampment, to resist an attack from Indians. They will glory in having lain upon the same field, where lay Harrison and his brave associates on the night previous to that bloody conflict: and many who were themselves well satisfied before, will be prepared to give the testimony of eye-witnesses to its fitness for the purposes for which it was selected on that occasion.

CANAL DAYS

WILLIAM DEAN HOWELLS

In the spring of 1890 William Dean Howells sat in his Boston study looking out at the new-leafed trees on Commonwealth Avenue. But what he saw was a southern Ohio town, with dusty streets, a curving river, and a series of canal locks letting the barges through. His memory went back to Hamilton, Ohio, on the Great Miami, in the 1840's. All that boyhood world was exciting, the canalboats and the land auctions, the stagecoach horns and the cries of the hog drovers, the bonfires and torchlight parades on election nights. There were memories enough to fill a glimmering and nostalgic book. So he wrote A Boy's Town, *from which this sketch is taken.*

THE canal came from Lake Erie, two hundred miles to the northward, and joined the Ohio River twenty miles south of the Boy's Town. For a time my boy's father was collector of tolls on it, but even when he was old enough to understand that his father held this State office (the canal belonged to the State) because he had been such a good Whig, and published the Whig newspaper, he could not grasp the notion of the distance which the canal-boats came out of and went into. He saw them come and he saw them go; he did not ask whence or whither; his wonder, if he had any about them, did not go beyond the second lock. It was hard enough to get it to the head of the Basin, which left the canal half a mile or so to the eastward, and stretched down into the town, a sheet of smooth water, fifteen or twenty feet deep, and a hundred wide; his sense ached with the effort of conceiving of the other side of it. The Basin was bordered on either side near the end by pork-houses, where the pork was cut up and packed, and then lay in long rows of barrels on the banks, with other long rows of salt-barrels, and yet other long rows of whiskey-barrels; cooper-shops, where the barrels were made, alternated with the pork-houses. The boats brought the salt and carried away the pork and whiskey; but the boy's practical knowledge of them was that they lay there for the boys to dive off of when they went in swimming, and to fish under. The water made a soft tuck-tucking at the sterns of the boat, and you could catch sunfish, if you were the right kind of a boy, or the wrong kind; the luck seemed to go a good deal with boys who were not good for much else. Some of the boats were open their whole length, with a little cabin at the stern, and these pretended to be for carrying wood and stone, but really again were for the use of the boys after a hard rain, when they held a good deal of water, and you

could pole yourself up and down on the loose planks in them. The boys formed the notion at times that some of these boats were abandoned by their owners, and they were apt to be surprised by their sudden return. A feeling of transgression was mixed up with the joys of this kind of navigation; perhaps some of the boys were forbidden it. No limit was placed on their swimming in the Basin, except that of the law which prohibited it in the daytime, as the Basin was quite in the heart of the town. In the warm summer nights of that southerly latitude, the water swarmed with laughing, shouting, screaming boys, who plunged from the banks and rioted in the delicious water, diving and ducking, flying and following, safe in the art of swimming which all of them knew. They turned somersaults from the decks of the canal-boats; some of the boys could turn double somersaults, and one boy got so far as to turn a somersault and a half; it was long before the time of electric lighting, but when he struck the water there came a flash that seemed to illumine the universe.

I am afraid that the Young People will think I am telling them too much about swimming. But in the Boy's Town the boys really led a kind of amphibious life, and as long as the long summer lasted they were almost as much in the water as on the land. The Basin, however, unlike the river, had a winter as well as a summer climate, and one of the very first things that my boy could remember was being on the ice there, when a young man caught him up into his arms, and skated off with him almost as far away as the canal. He remembered the fearful joy of the adventure, and the pride, too; for he had somehow the notion that this young fellow was handsome and fine, and did him an honor by his notice— so soon does some dim notion of worldly splendor turn us into snobs! The next thing

Head of the Miami Canal, Dayton, 1831, drawn by Thomas K. Wharton. *Courtesy New York Public Library and Ohio Historical Society*

was his own attempt at skating, when he was set down from the bank by his brother, full of a vainglorious confidence in his powers, and appeared instantly to strike on the top of his head. Afterwards he learned to skate, but he did not know when, any more than he knew just the moment of learning to read or to swim. He became passionately fond of skating, and kept at it all day long when there was ice for it, which was not often in those soft winters. They made a very little ice go a long way in the Boy's Town; and began to use it for skating as soon as there was a glazing of it on the Basin. None of them ever got drowned there; though a boy would often start from one bank and go flying to the other, trusting his speed to save him, while the thin sheet sank and swayed, but never actually broke under him. Usually the ice was not thick enough to have a fire built on it; and it must have been on ice which was just strong enough to bear that my boy skated all one bitter afternoon at Old River, without a fire to warm by. At first his feet were very cold, and then they gradually felt less cold, and at last he did not feel them at all. He thought this very nice, and he told one of the big boys.

"Why, your feet are frozen!" said the big boy, and he dragged off my boy's skates, and the little one ran all the long mile home, crazed with terror, and not knowing what moment his feet might drop off there in the road. His mother plunged them in a bowl of ice-cold water, and then rubbed them with flannel, and so thawed them out; but that could not save him from the pain of their coming to: it was intense, and there must have been a time afterwards when he did not use his feet.

His skates themselves were of a sort that I am afraid boys would smile at nowadays. When you went to get a pair of skates forty or fifty years ago, you did not make your choice between a Barney & Berry and an Acme, which fastened on with the turn of a screw or the twist of a clamp. You found an assortment of big and little sizes of solid wood bodies with guttered blades turning up in front with a sharp point, or perhaps curling over above the toe. In this case they sometimes ended in an acorn; if this acorn was of brass, it transfigured the boy who wore that skate; he might have been otherwise all rags and patches, but the brass acorn made him splendid from head to foot. When you had bought your skates, you took them to a carpenter, and stood awe-strickenly about while he pierced the wood with strap-holes; or else you managed to bore them through with a hot iron yourself. Then you took them to a saddler, and got him to make straps for them; that is, if you were rich, and your father let you have a quarter to pay for the job. If not, you put strings through, and tied your skates on. They were always coming off, or getting crosswise of your foot, or feeble-mindedly slumping down on one side of the wood; but it did not matter, if you had a fire on the ice, fed with old barrels and boards and cooper's shavings, and could sit round it with your skates on, and talk and tell stories, between your flights and races afar; and come whizzing back to it from the frozen distance, and glide, with one foot lifted, almost among the embers.

Beyond the pork-houses, and up farther towards the canal, there were some houses under the Basin banks. They were good places for the fever-and-ague which people had in those days without knowing it was malaria, or suffering it to interfere much with the pleasure and business of life; but they seemed to my boy bowers of delight, especially one where there was a bear, chained to a weeping-willow, and another where there was a fish-pond with gold-fish in it. He expected this bear to get loose and eat him, but that could not spoil his pleasure in seeing the bear stand on his hind-legs and open his red mouth, as I have seen bears do when you wound them up by a keyhole in the side. In fact, a toy bear is very much like a real bear, and safer to have round. The boys were always wanting to go and look at this bear, but he was not so exciting as the daily arrival of the Dayton packet. To my boy's young vision this craft was of such incomparable lightness and grace as no yacht of Mr. Burgess's could rival. When she came in of a summer evening her deck was thronged with people, and the captain stood with his right foot on the spring-catch that held the tow-rope. The water curled away on either side of her sharp prow, that cut its way onward at the full rate of five miles an hour, and the team came swinging down the tow-path at a gallant trot, the driver sitting the hindmost horse of three, and cracking his long-lashed whip with loud explosions, as he whirled its snaky spirals in the air. All the boys in town were there, meekly proud to be ordered out of his way, to break and fly before his volleyed oaths and far before his horses' feet; and suddenly the captain pressed his foot on the spring and released the tow-rope. The driver kept on to the stable with unslackened speed, and the line followed him, swishing and skating over the water, while the steersman put his helm hard aport, and the packet rounded to, and swam softly and slowly up to her moorings. No steamer arrives from Europe now with such thrilling majesty.

The canal-boatmen were all an heroic race, and the boys humbly hoped that some day, if they proved worthy, they might grow up to be drivers; not indeed packet-drivers; they were not so conceited as that; but freight-boat drivers, of two horses, perhaps, but gladly of one. High or low, the drivers had a great deal of leisure, which commended their calling to the boyish fancy; and my boy saw them, with a longing to speak to them, even to approach them, never satisfied, while they amused the long summer afternoon in the shade of the tavern by a game of skill peculiar to them. They put a tack into a whiplash, and then, whirling it round and round, drove it to the head in a target marked out on the weather-boarding. Some of them had a perfect aim; and in fact it was a very pretty feat, and well worth seeing.

Another feat, which the pioneers of the region had probably learned from the Indians, was throwing the axe. The thrower caught the axe by the end of the helve, and with a dextrous twirl sent it flying through the air, and struck its edge into whatever object he aimed at—usually a tree. Two of the Basin loafers were brothers, and they were always quarrelling and often fighting. One was of the unhappy fraternity of town-drunkards, and somehow the boys thought him a finer fellow than the other, whom somehow they considered "mean," and they were always of his side in their controversies. One afternoon these brothers quarrelled a long time, and then the sober brother retired to the doorway of a pork-house, where he stood, probably brooding upon his injuries, when the drunkard, who had remained near the tavern, suddenly caught up an axe and flung it; the boys saw it sail across the corner of the Basin, and strike in the door just above his brother's head. This one did not lose an instant; while the axe still quivered in the wood, he hurled himself upon the drunkard, and did that justice on him which he would not ask from the law, perhaps because it was a family affair; perhaps because those wretched men were no more under the law than the boys were.

I do not mean that there was no law for the boys, for it was manifest to their terror in two officers whom they knew as constables, and who may have reigned one after another, or together, with full power of life and death over them, as they felt; but who in a community mainly so peaceful acted upon Dogberry's advice, and made and meddled with rogues as little as they could. From time to time it was known among the boys that you would be taken up if you went in swimming inside of the corporation line, and for a while they would be careful to keep beyond it; but this could not last; they were soon back in the old places, and I suppose no arrests were ever really made. They did, indeed, hear once that Old Griffin, as they called him, caught a certain boy in the river before dark, and carried him up through the town to his own home naked. Of course no such thing ever happened; but the boys believed it, and it froze my boy's soul with fear; all the more because this constable was a cabinet-maker and made coffins; from his father's printing-office the boy could hear the long slide of his plane over the wood,

and he could smell the varnish on the boards.

I dare say Old Griffin was a kindly man enough, and not very old; and I suppose that the other constable, as known to his family and friends, was not at all the gloomy headsman he appeared to the boys. When he became constable (they had not the least notion how a man became constable) they heard that his rule was to be marked by unwonted severity against the crime of going in swimming inside the corporation line, and so they kept strictly to the letter of the law. But one day some of them found themselves in the water beyond the First Lock, when the constable appeared on the tow-path, suddenly, as if he and his horse had come up out of the ground. He told them that he had got them now, and he ordered them to come along with him; he remained there amusing himself with their tears, their prayers, and then vanished again. Heaven knows how they lived through it; but they must have got safely home in the usual way, and life must have gone on as before. No doubt the man did not realize the torture he put them to; but it was a cruel thing; and I never have any patience with people who exaggerate a child's offence to it, and make it feel itself a wicked criminal for some little act of scarcely any consequence. If we elders stand here in the place of the Heavenly Father towards those younger children of His, He will not hold us guiltless when we obscure for them the important difference between a great and a small misdeed, or wring their souls, fear-clouded as they always are, with a sense of perdition for no real sin.

FIRST TRAIN ON THE PRAIRIE

DANIEL HARMON BRUSH

In 1821 young Daniel Harmon Brush hitched up a farm wagon in Vermont and started for the western frontier. He became a leading attorney in southern Illinois and the foremost citizen of Carbondale, a town which owed its future to the railroad.

In 1850 Congress granted the State of Illinois 2,595,000 acres to aid in construction of a railroad. The next year the state legislature turned over these *lands to the Illinois Central Rail-Road Company, which offered them for sale at $5 to $25 an acre, with five years to pay. A prospectus issued by the Company in 1855 stated that "Illinois is known throughout the United States as the Garden State of America. . . . Almost the whole state is natural meadow. . . . It will produce, with less labor, as large a crop as any farm in the Eastern or Middle States valued at $100 to $150 an acre. . . . For further information apply personally or by letter in English, French or German." Letters from prairie settlers testifying to the riches of the railroad lands followed.*

The railroad reached Carbondale in the summer of 1854. Years later Daniel Brush recalled in his Growing Up With Southern Illinois *how the first train came through.*

WORK on the road was being prosecuted vigorously from the south, and strong efforts were made to have the track laid from Cairo to Carbondale so that the first engine and cars might make a trip to the latter point on July 4, 1854. This design was announced two or three weeks before the Fourth and the leading citizens of Carbondale determined to have not only a patriotic demonstration because of the glorious Fourth, but also a jubilation over the arrival of the shrieking locomotive in the village.

We concluded to invite everybody within reach to be present on the joyful day. The inhabitants of the place were not numerous, but all were willing to work and resolved to make a splurge that should astonish not only the natives, but strangers and railroaders also. It was announced that a free dinner would be furnished to all, and our people took hold with a will to make the promise good. The women baked the bread and cakes, cooked the poultry and other food, and made the coffee and tea. The men killed and barbecued the beeves, the sheep, and the swine. Farmers close around contributed vegetables and other things they had to spare. For a week before the day almost every house was made a bake shop and all out-doors was in commotion. The railroaders were spacing the ties and spiking down the iron bars, while occasionally the scream of the fiery demon was heard in his approaches from the south. I had completed the freight house for the Company, but it was still under my control. It was fresh and sweet with the odor of green-cut lumber, and by putting shelves in the corners and along the ends excellent storing places for cooked food

were made, while the body of the building afforded space for tables of plank from end to end 100 or more feet in length, arranged so that 500 persons could be seated at one time.

We had sent invitations to Cairo, to Jonesboro and Anna and Murphysboro. On the morning of the Fourth all was in readiness for the train to run up to the north line of the square and work on the road was suspended for the day. Early in the forenoon wagons with whole families in each and the household dogs following, with persons on horseback and on foot, began to arrive. They came from all the country round—men, women, children and dogs—and kept coming until at least two thousand were on the ground, most of whom had never seen a railroad or an engine or a car.

About noon the rumble of the train was heard, then came the shrill cry of the steam whistle, and soon the locomotive and cars slowed up and came to a stop opposite the freight house. The wonder-struck people shouted, some in terror and all in surprise. The horses cavorted and tried to break away. The dogs howled and with tails tucked between their legs stood not upon the order of their going, making hasty strides towards tall timber. The horses, scared and trembling, were mostly held in with bit and bridle, and the startled multitude, perceiving that no one was hurt, soon quieted down. A Fourth of July oration was pronounced in a grove near the station under a Union banner that I had purchased for the occasion, and the first one, I think, ever hoisted in the county.

I did not hear the speeches as I was busy inside the building, where the tables were

Above: Railway construction on the prairie. Courtesy Illinois State Historical Library
Below: Land sale poster. Courtesy Illinois Central Railway

ILLINOIS CENTRAL RAILROAD COMPANY
OFFER FOR SALE
ONE MILLION ACRES OF SUPERIOR FARMING LANDS,
IN FARMS OF
40, 80 & 160 acres and upwards at from $8 to $12 per acre.
THESE LANDS ARE
NOT SURPASSED BY ANY IN THE WORLD.
THEY LIE ALONG
THE WHOLE LINE OF THE CENTRAL ILLINOIS RAILROAD.
For Sale on LONG CREDIT, SHORT CREDIT and for CASH, they are situated near TOWNS, VILLAGES, SCHOOLS and CHURCHES.

being prepared for the dinner to be served and where the women were busy and the carvers were at work, my business being headman and waiter-in-chief. A corps of young men had been selected to wait on the tables, and I drilled them for an hour or so in their duties and allotted each one his theater of action so that conflict and confusion should be avoided. We kept the house closed and allowed no one inside but the workers until all was ready for the eaters, which was at about one o'clock. Then I sent out for special visitors that had come from a distance on the cars and desired to get away early, but the hungry crowd had massed around the building, and particularly in front of the large sliding doors in the center of its sides, so it was impossible to open them without a crush, to the discomfiture of everything like order in the admission of our guests. So we had to introduce such as were compelled to leave early by a private entrance at one end. Afterwards we opened one of the side doors and allowed enough outsiders to enter to fill up the tables, when we closed the doors, announcing to those who were still outside that we had plenty of food for all and requesting them to be patient.

They were, and no such body of hungry people, in my judgment, ever behaved better or more sensibly than they. The first that were admitted fared no better than the last. As soon as one tableful was satisfied they left in good order, the dishes were cleansed, the tables reset, enough of those in waiting were admitted to refill the seats, and the process was continued until all had partaken, and a great abundance of food as good as the best was left. All the workers on the Railroad in attendance—and there were a good many—all the natives of the surrounding country that came—and there was a multitude —as also all the citizens then here, probably 500 or more—in all, probably 2,500 to 3,000 souls, were fed and no word of discord was heard nor any disturbance made. The good fruits of our prohibition of tippling shops was gloriously manifested, there being no drunkenness and no disorderly conduct on the ground during the day.

I had laid in a lot of skyrockets, Roman candles, torpedoes, firecrackers, magic wheels, wriggling serpents, etc., and had announced that when night came a display of fireworks would be made, and invited all who desired to remain and see the sight. There was a light shower in the forenoon, enough to lay the dust and to cool the hot air. Consequently it was very pleasant in the after part of the day, and many remained to view the exhibition, probably not one in a hundred of them ever having seen anything of the sort before. Before touching off my pyrotechnics I caused those present to take positions about the freight house, as the best place to view the show. When they had done so, I placed some boxes for a rostrum near my storehouse, several hundred feet west of the freight house, from which to start the fiery missiles. The box containing the store of serpents, etc., was deposited on the ground beside my platform, so as to have the articles handy. Inadvertently, the lid of the box was left off, and the serpents and wheels and rockets and all the wonderful things to make up the show were exposed to any mishap that might occur.

I commenced by sending up rockets and got along finely until a contrary one was ignited. It fizzed and fluttered, and instead of ascending into outer darkness, as a well behaved skyrocket should have done, it gyrated around sometimes up a little and again down, and finally ended its course by tumbling, fire-end foremost, right into the open box containing the residue of my works. The fuses took fire, and then the fun started in earnest. Fortunately the heads of the projectiles were pointed away from the assemblage, westwardly up the main street, which had been cut out and pretty well cleaned of brush some distance up the hill. A number of canines were prowling in the rear of my position, anxious and expectant. The sparks of fire emitted from the fallen rocket had done their work, the serpents began to hiss and up the street they started squirming and jumping this way and that and seeming to sight the dogs took after them up the hill and into the bushes, wriggling streaks of fire—the scared brutes howling with fright and putting in their best licks to get out of the way. The magic wheels rolled and tumbled, the Roman candles shot forth the best they could, the crackers all popped at once, and the torpedoes with loud reports exploded.

The scene was highly animated and exciting while it lasted, and brought forth yells of delight from the beholders. Chagrined and abashed, I said but little. Soon, however, perceiving that most of the persons present considered the denouement legitimate, and as designed, I let the matter go without explanation. The last heard of the frightened curs was the lingering sounds of their agonized howling, dimly and faintly sounding in the distance as they ran. They may be running and yelling yet, for aught I know. And thus ended the first celebration of the Glorious Fourth of July in Carbondale, with all the participants except the dogs pleased and happy. The crowd dispersed, rejoicing and jubilant, contented with the past and sanguine of prosperity in the future, with a whoop for Carbondale and a hurrah for Illinois, and its first big railroad. The "Good Time" seemed close at hand.

LAND OF THE CROOKED TREE

U. P. HEDRICK

Long before summer visitors found the northern shores of Lake Michigan, French missionaries camped under a distorted tree on a bluff overlooking Little Traverse Bay. They called the country "L'Arbre Croche," and the name survived.

The region remained empty and mysterious until after the Civil War. Then timber cruisers came, tramping the winter woods when the creeks were frozen and the swamps were hard. Behind them came the logging crews, and the great lumber industry began. The Old Northwest had become the Midwest, and the northern forests were turned into building material to erect its countless towns and cities.

Dr. U. P. Hedrick, one of America's foremost horticulturalists, spent a memorable boyhood in that new country. He arrived there in 1874, the year when the wilderness was first opened to private sale and settlement. The following selection is the first chapter of his reminiscent The Land of the Crooked Tree.

IT was the year of 1874. We were on the steamboat *Menominee* in the northern part of Lake Michigan, having left Detroit four days before. Three small children were squabbling at a tiny cabin window for the right to see what was outside. I claimed the right, since my brother, two years older, belonged in another cabin with Father, and our sister, two years younger, was not tall enough to see out of the porthole.

From the tiny window through which I looked, across a mile of billowing whitecaps, a forest floated before my eyes. It was without length or breadth, light and dark green, dropping down a long, high, rolling slope from lazy clouds to snowlike drifts of sand where land and water met. I had never before seen trees or hills.

We had been living in Iowa, where my sister and I were born. Our birthplace was a log cabin that stood on the steep bank of a creek running through the rich black earth of our farm. The land for miles about was as flat as a millpond, except for the steep banks of the creek, up and down which wagons loaded with corn spilled off bushels on autumn days when they crossed the bridge, my big sisters picking up the ears for the cabin cookstove.

I do not know whence came the logs for our solid little log house. In the country round about there was only one tree; all the others, one of my sisters told me, had been cut to build houses. The lone tree belonged to my Uncle John Simpson.

Now, as I stood in the cabin on the *Menominee*, peering with drowsy eyes at a real forest, fear seized me. The wilderness, distant though it was, stirred my imagination as did childhood's nightmares. The dark shadows in the forest took on the semblance of monstrous animals, an endless procession of them. I expected a sudden leap of some wild beast or the war whoop of Indians, who I knew lived in the land to which we were going. In vain I looked for a house, a road, a cultivated field. There were none; the forest began and ended in caves of pitchy blackness.

I asked my mother: 'Are there Indians in those woods? . . . Do white people live in the forest? . . . Can children climb the hills? . . . Can I find my way among so many trees? . . . Are there wild animals there?'

To stop the flow of questions, my mother, who, I suspect, shared in some degree my fears, drew me from the porthole and hurried me into my clothes. My brother was called to take me on deck to my father.

We found Father far up in the bow of the boat talking to a man we had seen the day before, and by whom we had been charmed. Father told us that the man's name was St. Leger; that he was a Frenchman; that he had often been in Little Traverse, the town to which we were going; that he could talk to Indians in their own language; that he had been a trapper; and that he had had many fights with Indians.

The Frenchman was remarkable in appearance. He was tall and straight, wore his jet-black hair long, and had coal-black chin whiskers. His cheeks were purplish-red, his teeth white and even, his eyes black and sharp under heavy eyebrows. He wore a suit with stripes like a zebra and was crowned with a broad-brimmed black hat that made his red face look even redder. St. Leger took us in hand to give us a lesson in the geography of the region bordering the eastern shore of upper Lake Michigan, the country he called in broken English 'my lan'.'

Far off to our right was a long, broken, blue line of islands. On the end of one of them, to our rear, was a flashing light. St. Leger said

it was Big Beaver Light, and that the one directly behind us was Ile aux Galets, which, he said, 'de Yankee call "Skillagalee." ' Behind Skillagalee was Waugashance, and directly ahead was Charlevoix Light. The mainland the French had long ago named L'Arbre Croche.

The musical names, Big Beaver, Skillagalee, Waugashance, Charlevoix, L'Arbre Croche, sang in my ears. With such names the country to which we were going must be a land of enchantment. Besides, there must be white men to take care of the lighthouses. With the knowledge that there were men of our color about, and with the brightness of the mounting sun, I forgot the terrors of the forest.

As the lesson in geography came to an end, the *Menominee*'s captain came up, and, after speaking to Father, turned to St. Leger and asked him whether he had been up to any of his tricks.

St. Leger began feeling in his pockets and looking at his hands.

'Som'body 'ave rob' me!'

Suddenly his hand flashed to the little pocket in my jacket, and out came a gold watch and a huge chain.

'Ha! ma gol' wa'ch!'

Again his hand flashed, this time to my brother's pocket, and out came a fat pocketbook.

'Ha! ma mon'y! . . . Now ma ring, ma gol' ring!'

Seizing me by nose and chin, he opened my mouth and pulled out an enormous gold ring set with a big stone.

Had I not seen smiles on the faces of the captain and Father, and so sensed some sort of joke, I should have jumped overboard in embarrassment.

The breakfast bell was ringing, there was a smell of cooking in the air, and our family were glad enough to make for the dining room for breakfast. As we ate, Father tried to enlighten his sons on the mysteries of sleight-of-hand tricks.

Breakfast over and the family again on deck, we heard a jangling church bell seemingly out of the black wilderness. Then there came in view on the near shore a sparse clear-

Above: Lumberjacks in the woods in the Muskegon River Valley. Courtesy F. Jacobi
Below: The beginning of the drive. Courtesy Grand Rapids Museum

Above: Lake Michigan lumber schooners, 1890. Courtesy Curran Russell   Below:
Prescott Mill in Tawas City, 1890. Courtesy Michigan Historical Commission

ing and a cluster of shabby cabins. In the center of the wretched hamlet was a church with a steeple belfry surmounted by a shining cross. Mother must have been sore at heart as she looked at the little village, since she knew our future home was to be but a few miles away. Much as she had disliked Iowa, no doubt she would gladly have turned and gone back to the prairie with its grasshoppers and cyclones.

St. Leger again joined us and told us the whites called the hamlet we were looking at 'Middle Village,' but to the Indians it was 'L'Arbre Croche, or w'at you say, Crooked Tree.' Then he told us, in his soft broken English that I shall not attempt to reproduce, how the region came to have so curious a name:

'There is where the big crooked tree stood, high up on that hill. When the French priests, the first white people to come this way, paddled their canoes along this shore, they saw there a very big pine tree. Its body was perfect, but its branches were bent and crooked. The tree stood all alone against the sky and could be seen far out in the lake, so that the priests, who had hard work finding names for all the parts of this new land, called the place "L'Arbre Croche." The tree was once perfect, the trunk thicker and the top higher than those of any other pine round about. Then an unhappy accident befell the great tree. An Indian chief, a famous warrior and hunter, stronger than any other man that ever lived, was climbing the bluff with his canoe on his shoulder. When he came under the big pine tree, one of its branches caught the canoe and gave him a nasty fall. Rising in his wrath, the chief struck the trunk and twisted the branches of the pine. The branches were ever after awry.'

Our boat was now turning from the open waters into a spacious harbor formed by a long arrowhead of land jutting a mile into the lake. On the tip of the point was a huge cross of hewn timber. St. Leger told us this cross was a guide to sailors, and then whimsically added:

'Ze *croix* is ev'ryw'ere an' for all leeving t'ings abo't here, as you can see; even ze feesh swim in its shadow.'

Sure enough, a school of herring was jogging slowly by in the shadow of the cross.

The *Menominee* headed straight for the single wharf in the town. Her voice, that of a bull magnified a thousand times, bellowed three long blasts to send notice of her coming miles away into the forest. As we came slowly to dock the eyes of our family scanned the place that was to be our home and the people on the wharf who were to be our neighbors.

The autumn before, Father had visited this northern wilderness to spy out the land. On the dock stood several men he had met on his visit: Blackbird, an Indian chief, postmaster and government agent; Father Zorn, the village priest; Queen Margaret Boyd, sister to Blackbird; Bell, the real-estate agent who had sold my father his land; and Joutel, a half-breed, who had been Father's guide. There were many others of lesser note—sailors, timber buyers, homesteaders, half-breeds, and Indians.

Before the gangplank could be shoved from the *Menominee* to the wharf, several men had leaped aboard; and Joutel, who had recognized Father, came at once to our family group.

'B'jou! B'jou!' he said in a hearty voice.

Strange words, but not unexpected, since Father had told us that *bon jour* was the greeting of northern Indians. Joutel grabbed the bags and led the way through the crowd to the shore, talking with strange oaths.

To Father, he said: 'Joseph! Jesus! Mary! God A'mity! I'm glad to see you.'

Then to Mother: 'Ma gosh! I lak seein' you.'

As I write, I sniff the ghosts of the scents that came to our nostrils on that June morning as Joutel took us ashore. There were the smells of a dozen essences strange to those familiar only with the odors of a farm: the fishy smell of the lake; the ancient smell of the decaying wharf; the pungent tang of tanbark and newly cut lumber; the tarry exhalations of fishnets drying on the shore; the smell of a fire of driftwood; the effluvium of putrid fish offal; the exquisite perfume of some minty weed crushed by our feet.

The waters that touch the shores of the Land of the Crooked Tree have as their seaward boundary a line drawn from the point of one to that of the other of two well-marked capes, Waugashance and Charlevoix. From point to point it was some forty miles. The boundary line on the water can be seen as a bright thread of blue, the *ba-esk-ko-be* of the Indians, the horizon of the whites. The shore itself measures more than twice forty miles, because it is broken by bays and coves. The southern boundary is marked by a nearly circular bay some five or six miles in diameter, called La Petite Traverse to distinguish it from La Grande Traverse, a larger bay a half-day's sail southward.

Sometimes this shore is bordered and bottomed with glistening boulders, rocks, and pebbles of many colors. The forest, always of several species of evergreens and white birches, comes down to the water. Sometimes the shore and bottom are of glistening yellow sand, of which there is a windblown waste of drifting dunes supporting a curious dune-land flora. Always the lake is kept in its basin by a high bluff, which in places is lapped by the water; but mostly bluff and water are separated by dunes or swamps. Every mile or two, brooks or little rivers ripple and gurgle through the sands or roar down the bluffs and over the rocks from the tangles of the forest.

Until long after the beginning of the nineteenth century, these waters and the great lake of which they are a part had been a solitary sea on which were seen only the canoes of traders, trappers, and Indians. Jesuit missionaries first saw the country three centuries ago and gave it the name L'Arbre Croche, as St. Leger had told us, from a large crooked tree standing prominently on a high bluff overlooking Lake Michigan. Priests, explorers, trappers, fishermen, and Indians long knew this land as the home of the Ottawa and Chippewa before whites were allowed to own any piece of it.

When, in 1874, Washington permitted whites to 'take up' land from the government as homesteads and to buy it from Indian owners, there was a rush of farmers, lumbermen, fishermen, pigeon trappers, and summer resorters to settle the new country. Now the horizon marked one of the world's great travel routes. Men from the Atlantic seaboard had discovered the Middle West and now were building western states and cities. Steamships crowded with passengers were hourly passing to and fro. Fleets of sailing ships, rich with wealth from western farms or eastern factories, sailed across the sea between our capes. Steam, as yet, could not compete with wind.

Travel by land had but recently reached the forests of the Land of the Crooked Tree. A trail led north and south from the old town to which we had come, but it was almost impassable in summer, and in winter only travelers on snowshoes could make use of it. To the people of the town, the world beyond was 'outside'; its people, 'outsiders.'

This was the land to which my father was bringing his family.

UNLOCKING THE NORTH

STEWART H. HOLBROOK

In 1835, because of a geographical dispute over Ohio's northwestern boundary, Ohio and Michigan became adversaries in the "Toledo War." Both states laid claim to Toledo and the mouth of the Maumee River, and Michigan militiamen marched into the moot district. After two work horses and some hogs had been killed in shooting forays, the United States Congress intervened, giving Ohio the disputed strip and compensating Michigan with an area of 9,000 square miles beyond the Straits of Mackinac.

At that time the Upper Peninsula was an utter wilderness, which Michigan reluctantly accepted. Ten years later its riches began to appear. In the rough hills and valleys, even under the lakes and swamps of the north, lay vast formations of iron ore; and out the long cape of Keweenaw ran mile-deep veins of copper.

Stewart H. Holbrook has written many books on the American past, with special interest in the country's natural resources and the men who found and exploited them. The following selection is the second chapter of his Iron Brew.

LATE in the afternoon of September 19, 1844, the region just south of Lake Superior ceased to be a howling wilderness. At that hour the needle of a magnetic compass held by William A. Burt dipped and jittered furiously. Then, it quivered with uncertainty a moment and, like a man lost in the woods and gone wholly mad, it darted west and east and south, describing wild arcs, pointing nowhere for long.

Burt was amazed. By comparing the magnetic needle with his solar compass, which continued to point soberly to the poles, he could tell exactly how wildly the needle was performing. Burt and the rest of his survey party had seen needles dip and dodge before, but never anything like this. When the arrow registered a variation of 87 degrees, or almost a quarter of a circle, old Burt could contain himself no longer.

"Boys," he said, "look around and see what you can find."

The boys looked around, and without any trouble they found a score of outcroppings of ore that appeared to be almost pure iron. There it was, hard, black ore in abundance, seemingly an entire hill, almost a mountain of it.

Old Burt didn't give a whoop for iron, but he was immensely proud and pleased. "Look where you'd be if it wasn't for my solar compass," he shouted over and over like a parrot. "Look where you'd be. Why, you wouldn't know where in thunder you were!" The solar compass was his own invention, and now the old gentleman stalked around on the hill, whacking at stones with the blunt end of his ax, cackling his triumph.

The surveyors judged from the wild needle that magnetite ore must be present in large quantities, but none of them was interested in ore. None carried away a sample. They were making a survey of Michigan's Upper Peninsula for the United States Government, and they were tending to business. At the moment their compass started jumping so weirdly, they were running the east line of Township 47 N, Range 27 W, which was to become a part of Marquette County.

Such was the time and the place. What had been until then a howling wilderness indeed, was about to enter its time as a howling region of wild-eyed men seeking copper and iron.

But nothing happened immediately. Burt and his party completed their survey and made the usual accurate and quite dull report, merely noting the "existence of large iron bodies."

Before Burt's party there had been others. Farther east and some two hundred years before, the explorer Champlain had been amazed at the gift of a friendly Indian. It was a piece of copper "a foot long, very handsome and quite pure." This metal had come, so the red man said, from some vague country to the west, a land near Gitche Gumee, the Big-Sea-Water that awaited a New England poet to make its name famous.

French voyageurs ranged across and upward through the Great Lakes to the last and greatest of them, trading for furs. Père Marquette came to found a mision near the wondrous rapids that tumbled so hurriedly out of Gitche Gumee. Other great men came to do this or that and to leave their names secure—LaSalle, Hennepin, Joliet. Some of them heard tales of mysterious lands where stood mountains of mysterious metals—mysterious, and quite useless to the red men. But the early palefaces seemed not interested; they wanted to wish a new and wholly unsuitable kind of God onto the red men and to get the red men's furs. John Jacob Astor didn't worry much about God, but he got a good many of the furs.

For two hundred years this Michigan was

a very bloody ground. French and English fought for it, while the Indians fought both. Then the Colonials fought the British. When the smoke of 1812 had blown away Michigan was discovered to be a part of the new Republic.

The new Republic had considerable trouble in setting the boundaries of Michigan. When the Territory was forming a government in preparation to being admitted to the Union, Michigan wanted within its borders a strip of land around the southwestern bend of Lake Erie. Ohio claimed, and got it. To appease Michigan, Congress with a grand gesture handed it a large hunk of uninhabited and unknown land above the Straits of Mackinac—away, as one local statesman put it, to hell and gone.

Michigan wanted none of this so-called Upper Peninsula. Its officials fought its being saddled on them. Not even deer and bear could live there, they said. They shouted to Congress that this was barren land. It had not a great deal of timber. Grain would not grow there. The place was too close to the Great Cold Lake.

Like it or no, Michigan got the peninsula.

For the next few years the busy new state paid no attention to its upper portion. Then, by some marvel of persuasion, young Douglass Houghton, a geologist who had been giving lectures to a culture-hungry Detroit, got the Michigan legislature of farmers and lumbermen to grant him a little money. He proposed to investigate this upper and well damned peninsula and see what was there. The money soon petered out. Houghton went to Washington, talked Congress into starting a geological survey of all wild lands in the United States, and returned to Michigan to begin the work.

Sometimes with an Indian or two, often alone, Houghton cruised the south shore of the Great Cold Lake, a vast inland sea, lying so remote from all else. He followed the rivers to their sources. He chipped rocks. He observed temperatures and elevations. He even noted the flora and fauna. Everywhere he went in this silent country he mapped and charted. It was well he did. One bitter Octo-

ber night the sinister brooding of Superior whipped to sudden fury and wrecked Douglass Houghton's small Mackinac boat. His notes were saved on the spot, but the lake kept his body for seven months more.

Houghton had written his reports in guarded language. He had foreseen what might happen and had tried to minimize his findings. He wanted no rush of madmen to this northern solitude. But he was an honest man and he had to set down what he had found: an almost incalculable wealth of copper.

What Houghton feared happened soon after his reports were made public. It was a stampede of prospectors seeking copper on the tiny Keweenaw finger that thrusts out into Lake Superior. The rush was sudden and frantic. Men stormed up through the Soo rapids from Lake Huron, pushing small steamboats ahead of them on rollers. Others came by canoe and in bateaux. Hundreds of them came, swinging their picks wildly at every rock, assured that somewhere was a mountain of purest copper. Nobody thought of iron nor looked for it.

The stampede ebbed as quickly as it had flowed. Thousands of men staked their claims to copper, and many of them starved or froze in the climate of the Great Cold Lake's winter. Some went mad in the clouds of the brief summer's gnats and wandered off into the woods, gibbering of copper mountains, to be eaten at their leisure by billions of flies and mosquitoes.

And some, true enough, found copper. There was plenty of copper. The prospectors had not stopped to realize that finding copper and mining it are two different things. Nearly all of them, who survived at all, went back down through the Soo with their boots and clothes in tatters and nothing in their clothes. The great copper rush was over. Companies formed in Boston would come in good season to do the mining and make the money.

It was at this copper-rush period that William Burt's compass pointed four ways at once and started what was to be the rush for iron.

Surveyor Burt's reports made note of the probability of large bodies of iron ore. Philo

M. Everett of Jackson, in lower Michigan, who thought he wanted to own a copper mine and had gone looking for one, heard of Burt's findings. Everett also came in contact with an Indian chief who claimed to know where there was an entire mountain of strange rock.

This Indian labored under the name of Madjigijig, or sometimes Marji Gesick, in paleface spelling. He told Everett that the queer mountain was of black and blue and red and many colors. Everett asked to see it. The chief replied that the mountain was strictly Bad Medicine, filled with countless devils and spirits of one kind and another.

Whether or not Marji Gesick, the Chippewa, had any inkling of the value of this mountain to the palefaces isn't known. In any case, he grunted and muttered—which was hemming and hawing—until Everett offered to give the chief a part of the value of the find, if find it were.

Old Marji Gesick led Everett and his party to a spot on high land near the present city of Negaunee. It was rough, broken ground, with outcroppings of rock all over its surface. The chief, doubtless sweating from fear of Bad Medicine, directed Everett to a huge pine tree lying flat on the ground. He wouldn't approach the windfall himself.

"Catch um there," said Marji Gesick, pointing.

Everett went over to look. Exposed under the big roots was a broad expanse of black ore—heavy magnetic stuff that caused Everett's pocket compass to dip and flutter. It was a June day in 1845, six months after Burt had surveyed along this very hill.

One may be sure that Marji Gesick got none of the money that came from the heavy rock. Nor did Everett. Millions of dollars were dug out of the rough hill, and years later Charlotte, Marji Gesick's daughter, sued for a share. More years passed while Charlotte's case wound its interminable way through the maze of paleface chicanery called courts. She got less than her father did; *he* got his name put on a pretty marker, but by that time he was dead and didn't care.

Whether it is gold or copper or lowly iron ore, there would seem to be little use in trying to keep secret the news of its finding. The news escapes like quicksilver. Everett and his party managed to hold their tongues until they obtained possession of the land on Jackson Mountain, as the property was called; and then the word got out that the whole of Michigan's unwanted Upper Peninsula was one range of solid iron hills.

There were no telegraph lines, but news of the find spread through the wilderness as though the birds had carried it. By the time it had emerged from the wild lands, the iron hills were said to be mountains, each at least a mile high and all of purest iron. The Great Cold Lake, lying there so vast and silent, was rimmed with a collar of iron—iron a mile high, a mile deep and nobody knew how wide. . . . It was a picture to stir the minds of restless men in far places.

Presently there was another traffic jam at the Soo rapids, as men of Buffalo and New York and Cleveland and Boston worked their boats up through the boiling white water or carried them around in a costly portage. It was tough going, this Soo that connected Lake Huron with the Great Cold One.

The young state of Michigan already had looked at the rapids of the St. Mary's River and had asked the Federal Government for permission to build a ship canal through the military reservation there. Congress laughed at the idea and no less than Henry Clay, a very great man, stood up to damn it. "It is," he said, referring to the need for a canal, "it is a work beyond the remotest settlement of the United States, if not the moon." Clay liked the city of Washington, and he didn't get around much.

Charles T. Harvey got around a lot more than Clay did. He was a traveling salesman for the Fairbankses, who made scales in faraway St. Johnsbury, Vermont, and he had been sent West to establish agencies for the Fairbanks products in the new state. While recovering from an attack of typhoid at Sault Ste. Marie, young Harvey spent several weeks in the newly discovered iron district. The wealth being uncovered there, at Jackson Mountain and elsewhere, fascinated him. Here was ore without end, he thought. But how would it be taken to the furnaces of Ohio and

Pennsylvania? They were a thousand miles off. There were no railroads, nor likely to be. There was water, sailing water as far as the Soo—and water beyond the Soo. The Soo had only rapids.

Harvey's lively imagination conjured up a canal around the dangerous rapids, with locks, big locks that could raise and lower the largest boats to sail the Lakes. In spite of Henry Clay, Congress finally granted permission to build the canal, and Harvey, with the sponsorship of the Fairbankses and others, undertook the job of organizing a group to build the canal for Michigan.

Harvey was not quite twenty-five years old. He had the rare qualities of engineering skill and what is called promotional ability. He also had the powerful backing of the Fairbanks family and other men of substance. In a surprisingly short time he had formed a contracting company. He himself took charge of the digging and construction.

It was a titanic job in its day. Harvey's capitalist backers were in New York or even farther east; it required six weeks for an exchange of letters. Nearest telegraph station was at Detroit, 450 miles away. Nearest machine shop was on Saginaw Bay, half as far. Every stick of blasting powder had to come from Delaware, a good thousand miles.

There was not sufficient labor at Sault Ste. Marie to dig a well, to say nothing of a canal 5,700 feet long. Harvey sent agents to board ships before they docked in Boston and New York and grab off what immigrant labor they could, paying fare to the Soo, and doubtless telling whoppers of lies about the opportunities to get rich by digging the Soo Canal.

Harvey's agents managed to get the labor. Starting with a crew of four hundred, he soon had two thousand men on the job. All drilling was by hand, and there was a pile of it to be done, done through rock that was flinty long before history began.

During the short days of winter, which was five months of the year, there was a bare eight hours of sunlight. The temperature hovered around zero much of the time, with sudden drops to as low as 35 degrees below zero. At the head of every runway for wheelbarrows, Harvey stationed a man to watch the workmen and to rub with snow the faces of any who gave sign of frostbite.

January winds roared down off the Great Cold Lake, bringing blizzards that piled snow higher than the bunkhouses and sleet that stung like birdshot. They had winters up there on the Soo. Refrigeration was assured, and every cook in the outfit was furnished with an ax; when he wanted more meat he went out into the shed and hacked it off the sides of beeves that were frozen hard as plank.

Young Harvey was no desk engineer. He faced the winds and the cold and drove his men to the limit. Then, during the last few months of the work, an epidemic of cholera broke out. Men died like flies and were buried as discreetly as possible and late at night in an effort to keep the gang from knowing the dread disease was upon them. Although more than two hundred died within a few weeks and were buried furtively here and there in the woods, not a day was lost by the main crew.

It was a hard and cruel two years of labor and pain and death. Only one strike marked it. The grumbling of hard-driven workmen flared up one day, and a thousand of them paraded the camp, demanding more pay. Harvey met them head on. He shut down the cookhouses at once and placed armed guards at the doors. No work, no grub. The strikers lost two meals and suddenly decided to return to their drilling. There was to be no monkey business on this job. Harvey's driving frenzy continued until the day he opened a sluice gate to let water from the Great Cold Lake flow into the completed locks, and thence into Huron.

Meanwhile, in the rough hills along Superior's south shore, one hundred and fifty miles west of Harvey's new locks, an army of miners, many of them out of Cornwall by way of Pennsylvania, were digging a big hole in Jackson Mountain. Scores of other men were roaming the hills, looking for outcroppings to tell them where to dig for iron that would match the wealth coming out of Jackson. They found it, too, at places soon to be known as the Cleveland, the Winthrop, the Humboldt, the Argyle, and a hundred others.

The Jackson and Cleveland mines were the first. Both were eight miles from Gitche Gumee water, so the Cornish miners loaded the ore into sleighs and Canuck-Frenchmen drove and cursed double teams down dangerous grades to the shore. A little later, over an elegant plank road, the ore went by mule team the twelve long miles to Marquette, destined to be the first great ore shipping port in the United States.

On the 14th of August, 1855, the brig *Columbia*, Judson Wells, master, stood out from Marquette with a hundred tons of rich black ore on her deck. On the 17th she passed without trouble through the new Soo locks and canal, while a blacksmith fired an anvil-cannon and half the men at the Soo were reported to be drunker than so many fiddlers' bitches. If they weren't, they should have been, for the *Columbia* was the first ship to pass down the locks with ore. The Great Cold Lake had ceased to be remote and the Marquette Range had come into being.

Incidentally, a traveling salesman for weighing scales had built what was to be the most important commercial canal in the world, not excepting the Suez and the Panama.

DISASTER IN THE WOODS

JOSEPHINE SAWYER

Logging methods in the northern woods left huge areas covered with slashings, dry as tinder. A spark from a locomotive or a stab of lightning could start a blaze that might sweep the county.

The fearsome fall of 1871 was a season of fires, of the great Chicago fire and vast forest fires that seared four counties along the Oconto and Peshtigo rivers in Wisconsin and burned swaths across the whole state of Michigan. The summer of 1871 was a hot, hazy season, with fires smoldering in cutover sections and miles of slash smoking beside newly completed railroad lines. As autumn came on, the swamps baked dry. September passed without a drop of moisture, and then came the terrible first week of October.

A fresh wind fanned smoldering areas into hungry flame. The heat of fire developed a racing wind. Overnight, fire was raging in a dozen regions. The worst disaster struck at the sawmill town of Peshtigo on the north shore of Green Bay; seven hundred people died in the burning streets or drowned in the river. At neighboring Menominee men toiled in the lurid midnight, digging a firebreak along the Birch Creek road, and women stood waist-deep in the river while sparks and embers hissed around them. The following eyewitness narrative, reprinted from Volume 16 of the Michigan History Magazine, *has the artless drama of actuality.*

THE summer of 1871 was hot and dry. There were frequent forest fires in various parts of the northern states and for weeks before the big fire of October 7 and 8, the smoke hung so heavy that the sun looked like a ball of fire most of the time.

Just when and where the fires started, no one can say, but the woods and swamps between Oconto and Peshtigo had burned at intervals, controlled only by occasional rains. These fires were supposed to have caught from the camp fires of the laborers who were building the Chicago and Northwestern railroad track through to Escanaba that year. The culmination began the evening of October 7.

I think every one had a feeling of uneasiness and premonition for weeks. To my people, our first alarm came in this way. At that time my father (E. S. Ingalls) had a water mill on Little River, about five miles from Menominee. He owned much timber there. The place is occupied by farms now, the Sawyer-Goodman having most of it. October 7 being Sunday, most of the crew had come down town, leaving the boarding-house keeper, his wife and two children and about ten men there. The bookkeeper, Mr. Merrill, had spent the day at our home. About 6:30 P.M. my brother Fred put the team on a light wagon and accompanied by my younger brother, sister and myself, started to take him back. After passing Frenchtown, we noticed an occasional log burning beside the road. Mr. Merrill told us to go back; he would walk the remaining mile and a half. There was already a roaring in the air and the sky was lighted up over towards Peshtigo. The smell of smoke was strong before we were half way back. The roaring became loud and the wind came in fierce hot gusts which fanned the smouldering logs into flames. Often a standing tree took fire. Our horses needed no urging on their way home. Afterward, Mr. Merrill told us his experience.

It took him some time to make his way over the logging road to the mill, for the whirling wind had carried the fire to one side and over Marinette, and struck the mill and surrounding forest. All the buildings were on fire when he got there. He hastily got the books from the office, and taking the cook's baby, ran with the rest of the people to the river. He buried the books in the earth on the river bank. The cattle and horses had been turned loose though one ox fell and was burned on the river bank. Each person had grabbed a pail or something to hold water, and carried it with him. Mr. Merrill said the heat was so intense that the instant they rose out of the water, their clothes caught fire and when they inverted wooden buckets of water over their heads, the bottoms of the buckets would catch fire.

As an example of the fierce heat, he told how a bottle on the edge of the bank melted and ran with a hiss into the water near him.

One freak of the fire that occurred there we kept at my home as a souvenir. A large iron bean pot stood beside the cook house door. As the hot blast struck, one half of this melted like lead; the other half remained intact. Late the next day, my brother-in-law got a team as far as Frenchtown. From there he had to walk the rest of the way to the mill over fallen timber and hot ashes. He found the people all alive but blind from smoke and heat and badly blistered, especially the eighteen months old baby, which could only be held under water a few minutes at a time. He roped them together, so he could guide them, and so carrying the children, and sometimes the woman, they all stumbled along, helping each other as best they could, often falling over burnt logs, or burning their feet in hot ashes till they reached Frenchtown. We kept them at our house for two weeks, feeding them like children, until their eyes recovered. The woman and baby died two or three months later.

As I have said, the whirling wind carried the fire, now high, now low. Marinette, directly in its path, escaped. Only the brush and low growth around the town caught fire, though it kept men busy to control it. Menekaunee was caught in one of the whirls of fire. My remembrance is that everything burned, even fences, walks and the sawdust covered streets. The fierce hot wind carried burning shingles a mile and more out into the bay and set fire to sails of ships. Where the fire struck, it was so sudden and fierce that everything caught at once. In one house a woman was in confinement, with the upper part of the house burning, the doctor and neighbor woman attending her. As soon as the child was born, she was lifted mattress and all and put into a sawdust cart, not a minute too soon, and carried to safety. Menominee, like Marinette was rimmed with fire, and Birch Creek, a settlement of about forty families was entirely burned. The loss of life in this farming village was in proportion to numbers as appalling as at Peshtigo. Several families were entirely wiped out. Most of them lost one or two members. The survivors found safety in root cellars, holes in the ground or in Birch Creek.

DISASTER IN THE WOODS   **329**

Two girl survivors came to Menominee in 1878. I took my horse and buckboard and we went to visit near their old home farm and spent the day wandering through the growth of poplar and firewood that always follow a woods fire. The tree trunks were still lying all in one direction like mown hay. These girls told me there were nine in their family. When the fire struck, the father and mother each took a small child and all ran to reach the creek if possible. These little girls, ten and eleven years old, soon began to stumble and fall. The father suddenly threw them both into the water and mud under roots of an overturned tree, telling them to crouch down and stay there until he came for them. They alone survived in that family.

Our first excitement at home came just after we had returned from Little River mill, about 9:30 probably. There was a fierce gust of wind and a crash, and Belle Stephenson, (Mrs. Joseph Fleshiem) who had been spending the day in Marinette, came running in and told us that their buggy had been blown over into a brush heap, just across the road. (My home was where the Spies Public Library now stands, and the brush heap was on a vacant lot occupied in late years by the Walter Hicks home.) Belle also told us that it was reported in Marinette that Peshtigo was burning and that Marinette would likely burn also, as trees were already burning on the edge of town. Everything seemed to happen all at once after that. The sky south and west was a blaze of light. The fierce hot whirling wind rose and fell, bringing flame to new spots, sometimes rising and leaving a spot of green timber untouched.

Soon people began to drift down from Frenchtown. They said "the jack pines back of the village are burning". We had lived there when we first came to Menominee (1862) and knew many of these people. They camped in our back yard near the bay. I do not know how many there were. I heard my mother say she counted eight little babies in her bed at one time, and children were asleep all over the house. I knew we gave bread and coffee to forty or more the next morning. Their homes did not burn and they went back. There were constant alarms. Gil-

more's mill down on the point where the Hoskins-Morainville plant is now, had caught from the Menekaunee blaze and was burning. Houses kept catching fire. The women and girls pumped water and the men carried wet blankets and covered roofs. This was a common method. Main street, sawdust covered, of course, kept blazing up in spots and we ran with buckets or pitchers, or anything to stop the spread. I met the late Joseph Fleshhiem in one of these sorties, though I did not know it till long after. He had just come off a steamer and was walking up the street, wondering just what he had got into, when a girl came running towards him with a bedroom water pitcher and watering can and said: "The shavings under that porch are on fire. Crawl under and put them out." He crawled while I ran to the bay for more water. The house was that of George Horvath, on one of the Victory Park lots.

Suddenly the swamp which stretched from Ogden Avenue to the river, and was covered with willows and dry grass, (Kirby street was swamp then) was on fire. The only good road, crossing the swamp was Pengilly street, leading to the mills. The older men and women worked along the edge, the women carrying water, the men throwing up fresh earth. The younger folks pumped and carried water also. There was but one good well on the side of the street where the Lloyd store is now, at the Saxon place, later known as the H. P. Bird place. We pumped it dry twice before morning. It was hot exhausting work. The young boys would lie down a few minutes at a time to rest, then go on—our dresses and shoes were scorched and burned.

There were many amusing incidents, amusing afterwards, that is. I saw George Horvath, who owned the biggest dry goods store in town, and was building the new house before mentioned, walking up and down Main street carrying a small gilt mirror in one hand a blanket over one shoulder. The blanket was folded at first, but later trailed behind him in the dust. A clerk told me afterward that he found the store standing open with all lamps burning.

Mr. Phillip Lowenstein had just brought

Victims of the Peshtigo forest fire, 1871. *Courtesy State Historical Society of Wisconsin*

his bride to Menominee. He had a liquor store on Main street. His clerk found him about half way between his house and store, carefully burying a hammer and a lighted lantern in the ground. Theriault, the beloved old fiddler of our dancing days had a store also. He buried several cases of cigars and oysters in the sand on the beach, then took his "little fid" and walked up and down the street the rest of the night. I regret to record that some of the boys found the buried cases. Theriault never did.

My father's law partner, just recently from down east, had his room over Parmenter's store, just south of the Richard House on Main street. He hastily packed his valuables in his bag, ran swiftly down stairs and threw it into a passing farm wagon. He then came up to my father's house with nothing on his mind apparently. Our neighbors across the street had a valued clock. They hastily dug a hole in the yard and put it in. All holes look alike when covered with sand. They could never afford another

clock and came to our house "for the time" for years after. The clock is under the Lloyd store somewhere. Most people buried their valuables on the 8th.

One of the big lake steamers had come in about midnight and tied up at Jones dock. Among other things it brought the furniture for Mr. E. L. Parmenter's beautiful new home on what is now called State street, (The home of F. J. Trudell). About two A.M. I was standing on guard at our gate the others having gone where they were needed more. It was so light from the glare in the sky that I could read a newspaper easily. I saw Charlie Fairchild coming up the street with a load of furniture and called out, "Why take it to the house? The hills are all on fire back of Kirby Creek." He answered, "Well, they'll get the insurance if it's in the house but not if it's in the boat." He told me the boat was being held at the dock for women and children if needed. Some of them fled to it early in the night. It was said that some men wrapped themselves in women's clothes and hid in the boat, but were discovered by Oscar Saxon, the town's official teamster and a strict conformist to methodist ideals. It is said that he used strong language as well as the toe of his boot on such cowards. I am sure his lapse of language was forgiven, for his provocation was great. Had worse come to worst, the boat would have burned at her moorings, for the water in the bay lowered two feet or more under the fierce wind and heat and the boat was fast aground when they tried to move next day.

My brother Charles Ingalls had personal proof of the lowering of the water in the bay. He was getting out cedar posts on my father's Haycreek farm, which ran from the Magnus Relson farm clear through to the bay, joining John Quimby's land at Poplar Point. It included the marsh and site of the Daley mill. The house was on what was known afterward as the Crawford farm and still stands, I think. Charlie had a lumber ship anchored off the point and a crew of twelve or fifteen men. Sunday morning (October 7) most of them had come up town. Seven people were left at the farm, including the farm keepers daughter, who had remained to get meals for the men. When the fire struck the forest and out-buildings, the cattle and horses were turned loose, except one team which Charlie had kept hoping to get to town or to shore. Charlie begged the men to get into the wagon, but four of them hastily threw some planks over a hole in the ground and crawled in. Someone spoke of the girl. Charlie looked for her and found her in her bed, with the clothes drawn over her head. He grabbed her, quilt and all and chucked her into the hole as he started for the shore, for the road was already cut off by flame. One of the men in the hole begged him to write their names on a piece of paper and fasten it on a stump near the hole. Charlie headed for water with one man with him. The team needed no urging. When a hot gust would come, the cattle and horses running ahead would throw themselves down and bury their noses in the sand for a minute or two. The loss of animal life was terrible that night. Several deer, wolves and bear were on the edge of the farm yard in the morning. Live

rabbits ran into the hole with the men and the girl. By some freak of wind, the house did not burn, though barns, fences and surrounding woods, all did. Charlie said the horses ran into the water until it reached the wagon box. He and the men lay down and went to sleep in the wagon and were awakened when the returning water covered them in the morning.

Many of the incidents relating to the burning of Peshtigo were told me by the late Mrs. Isaac Stephenson of Marinette. She was a young girl living with her parents and brother at that time. She said: "The whole town seemed to be on fire all at once." People ran madly to the river. Some sought refuge in cisterns or wells and were smothered there. Nine members of one family were found in their well. Some lingered to save treasured belongings and died in homes. Like most of the people, Mrs. Stephenson with her brother started for the river. She told him (Tom Burns) to go back and help his father and mother. She could go alone. She had not run more than two blocks before she fell exhausted, and would have burned there had not R. M. Hunt, engineer in charge of construction for the C. & N. W. railroad company come along and picked her up and carried her to the river. The scene was terrible. Men were fighting off the crazed horses and cattle to keep them from trampling women and children under water. Their clothes caught fire as they worked.

Mrs. Stephenson told me that she personally knew of seven confinements which took place during the night. Men laid their coats in the mud and ooze at the foot of the bank for the unfortunate women to lie on, and while women were doing what they could for the sufferers, the men carried water and poured over them. Several of the women died, and only three of the babies lived, so far as she knew. So the night passed in terror, pain and grief. In the morning there was nothing but desolation, no food or shelter for hours. They ate potatoes which were baked in the ground.

Among the incidents I knew about personally was this one. A young Frenchman, Joe Martel, running to the river, saw a little baby lying in the road. He picked it up, carried it into the water and took care of it as well as he could. In the morning the women helped him, but all had their own to care for. The child belonged to a niece of Governor Fairchild of Wisconsin. The father and mother died. Governor Fairchild provided for the child, also for the young man. One incident was related to us by Judge Fred Bartels of Peshtigo. When the fire struck the town, he started for Marinette with his horse and buckboard. On the seat with him was the sister of F. J. Trudel. She had recently married and gone to Peshtigo to live. Her husband and another man sat on the back of the buckboard. There was a wall of fire on each side of them and the horse ran of its own accord. Suddenly the two men fell off. The young wife tried to jump off but Mr. Bartels held her. He couldn't stop, for that would have meant death to all.

At the beginning of the fire, a small lumber train which ran to Peshtigo harbor took as many as it could carry down to the harbor. They were safe and soon in communication with outside towns. The trainmen tried to get back for another load, but could not.

Of course, people in near-by towns were not idle. Men from Marinette and Menominee forced their way through burning logs and hot ashes and brought the sufferers to Marinette. Barracks had been hastily built to house them. Governor Fairchild had sent Dr. B. T. Phillips up to take charge. The women of the towns were volunteer nurses. We in Menominee helped. We had the Birch Creek refugees and outlying farmers to look after also. From far and near, food and clothing poured in. It continued coming for months.

I asked Mrs. Stephenson once, when I was in her room, where she got such an oddly shaped white petticoat as she was putting on. She said: "Well, when I got to Green Bay, I didn't have a gown to put on, but I was immediately given thirteen white petticoats. This is one of them."

After the fire destroyed Birch Creek, it leaped over about ten miles of green forest and burned the beautiful beech forest near what we call Greenwoods. Several days after the fire, I went with some friends to try and locate some of their relatives who lived there. I had spent some weeks with them before the fire. We could not get beyond Birch Creek. It was strange to see those great forest trees lying row after row as though cut with a scythe, their tops pointing towards the north. The trunks of some of these great trees still lie in the birch grove beyond Birch Creek.

The fire burned so deeply into the peat bogs near Cedar River that it was still burning a year later. At times, during the first winter after, smoke came up through the snow. The fire got a good start early in the evening of the 7th of October (1871), but the height of its fury and destruction came the morning of the 8th between one and five A.M. approximately.

CHICAGO IN ASHES

HORACE WHITE

Chicago in 1871 was a wooden city, with fifty-six miles of wooden-block pavement and 651 miles of wooden sidewalk. There were thirteen miles of wooden docks along the river, twenty-four wooden bridges, seventeen huge wooden grain elevators, acres of lumberyards, hundreds of wooden mills and factories, thousands of stables. Fires were frequent, and there was but one pumping station—roofed with wood—in the city.

On the evening of the 8th of October, 1871, fire broke out in a stable near the river. The next day the world learned that Chicago was in ashes.

Horace White was editor of the Chicago Tribune *at the time of the fire. The following account, which appeared in the Cincinnati* Commercial, *was written by Editor White to accompany his acknowledgment of printing equipment sent by Editor Murat Halstead from Cincinnati.*

AS a slight acknowledgment of your thoughtful kindness in forwarding to us, without orders, a complete outfit of type and cases, when you heard that we had been burned out, I send you a hastily written sketch of what I saw at the Great Fire. . . .

The history of the Great Fire in Chicago, which rises to the dignity of a national event, cannot be written until each witness, who makes any record whatever, shall have told what he saw. Nobody could see it all—no more than one man could see the whole of the Battle of Gettysburg. It was too vast, too swift, too full of smoke, too full of danger, for anybody to see it all. My experience derives its only public importance from the fact that what I did, substantially, a hundred thousand others did or attempted—that is, saved, or sought to save, their lives and enough of their wearing-apparel to face the sky in. As you have printed in your columns a map of the burned district, I will remark that my starting-point was at my residence, No. 148 Michigan Avenue, between Monroe and Adams streets.

What I saw at the Great Fire embraces nothing more heartrending than the destruction of property. I saw no human beings burned or suffocated in flame and smoke, though there were many. My brother early in the fray stumbled over the bodies of two dead men near the corner of La Salle and Adams streets. My wife saw the body of a dead boy in our own dooryard as she was taking leave of our home. How it got there we know not. Probably it was brought there as to a place of safety, the bearers leaving and forgetting it, or themselves getting fast in some inextricable throng of fugitives. I saw no mothers with new-born babes hurried into the street and carried miles through the night air by the light of burning houses. I have a friend whose wife gave birth to a child within one hour of the time when the flames of Sunday night reddened the sky. Her home was in the North Division, which was swept clean of some ten thousand houses. This suffering lady was taken downstairs with her infant, and carried one mile to a place of supposed safety. She had not been there an hour when she was taken out a second time and carried a mile and a half westward. Blessed be God that she still lives and that the young child breathes sweetly on her bosom!

I had retired to rest, though not to sleep [Sunday, October 8], when the great bell struck the alarm; but fires had been so frequent of late, and had been so speedily extinguished, that I did not deem it worth while to get up and look at it, or even to count the strokes of the bell to learn where it was. The bell paused for fifteen minutes before giving the general alarm, which distinguishes a great fire from a small one. When it sounded the general alarm I rose and looked out. There was a great light to the southwest of my residence, but no greater than I had frequently seen in that quarter, where vast piles of pine lumber have been stored all the time I have lived in Chicago, some eighteen years. But it was not pine lumber that was burning this time. It was a row of wooden tenements in the South Division of the city in which a few days ago were standing whole rows of the most costly buildings which it hath entered into the hearts of architects to conceive. I watched the increasing light a few moments. Red tongues of light began to shoot upward; my family were all aroused by this time, and I dressed myself for the purpose of going to the *Tribune* office to write something about the catastrophe. Once out upon the street, the magnitude of the fire was suddenly disclosed to me.

The dogs of hell were upon the housetops of La Salle and Wells streets, just south of Adams, bounding from one to another. The fire was moving northward like ocean surf on a sand beach. It had already traveled an eighth of a mile and was far beyond control. A column of flame would shoot up from a burning building, catch the force of the wind, and strike the next one, which in turn would perform the same direful office for its neighbor. It was simply indescribable in its terrible grandeur. Vice and crime had got the first scorching. The district where the fire got its first firm foothold was the Alsatia of Chicago. Fleeing before it was a crowd of blear-eyed, drunken, and diseased wretches, male and female, half naked, ghastly, with painted cheeks, cursing and uttering ribald jests as they drifted along.

I went to the *Tribune* office, ascended to the editorial rooms, took the only inflammable thing there, a kerosene lamp, and carried it to the basement, where I emptied the oil into the sewer. This was scarcely done when I perceived the flames breaking out of the roof of the Court-house, the old nucleus of which, in the centre of the edifice, was not constructed of fireproof material, as the new wings had been. As the flames had leaped a vacant space of nearly two hundred feet to get at this roof, it was evident that most of the business portion of the city must go down; but I did not reflect that the city Water Works, with their four great pumping engines, were in a straight line with the fire and wind. Nor did I know then that this priceless machinery was covered by a wooden roof. The flames were driving thither with demon precision.

What happened at the *Tribune* Building has already been told in your columns. We saw the tall buildings on the opposite sides of the two streets melt down in a few moments without scorching ours. The heat broke the plate-glass windows in the lower stories, but not in the upper ones. After the fire in our neighborhood had spent its force, the editorial and composing rooms did not even smell of smoke. Several of our brave fellows who had been up all night had gone to sleep on the lounges, while others were at the sink washing their faces, supposing that all danger to us had passed. So I supposed, and in this belief went home to breakfast. The smoke to the northward was so dense that we could not see the

North Division, where sixty thousand people were flying in mortal terror before the flames. The immense store of Field, Leiter & Co. I observed to be under a shower of water from their own fire-apparatus, and since the First National Bank, a fireproof building, protected it on one corner, I concluded that the progress of the flames in that direction was stopped, as the *Tribune* Building had stopped it where we were. Here, at least, I thought was a saving of twenty millions of property, including the Great Central Depot and the two grain elevators adjoining, effected by two or three buildings which had been erected with a view to such an emergency. The Post-office and Custom-house building (also fireproof according to public rumor) had stopped the flames a little farther to the southwest, although the interior of that structure was burning. A straight line drawn northeast from the Post-office would nearly touch the *Tribune*, First National Bank, Field, Leiter & Co.'s store, and the Illinois Central Railroad land department, another fireproof. Everything east of that line seemed perfectly safe, and with this feeling I went home to breakfast.

With some little difficulty we reached our house, and in less time than we ever set out on a journey before, we dragged seven trunks, four bundles, four valises, two baskets, and one hamper of provisions into the street and piled them on the wagon. The fire was still more than a quarter of a mile distant, and the wind, which was increasing in violence, was driving it not exactly in our direction. The low wooden houses were nearly all gone, and after that the fire must make progress, if at all, against brick and stone. Several churches of massive architecture were between us and harm, and the great Palmer House had not been reached, and might not be if the firemen, who had now got their hose into the lake, could work efficiently in the ever-increasing jam of fugitives.

My wife thought we should have time to take another load; my brother thought so; we all thought so. We had not given due credit either to the savage strength of the fire or the firm pack on Michigan Avenue. Leaving my brother to get the family safely out if I did

THE CITY OF CHICAGO

CHICAGO IN FLAMES

Proclamation.

WHEREAS in the Providence of God, to whose will we humbly submit, a terrible calamity has befallen our city, which demands of us our best efforts for the preservation of order, and the relief of the suffering;

BE IT KNOWN that the faith and credit of the city of Chicago is hereby pledged for the necessary expenses for the relief of the suffering. Public order will be preserved. The Police and Special Police now being appointed, will be responsible for the maintenance of the peace and the protection of property. All officers and men of the Fire Department and Health Department will act as Special Policemen without further notice. The Mayor and Controller will give vouchers for all supplies furnished by the different relief Committees. The head-quarters of the City Government will be at the Congregational Church corner of West Washington and Ann sts. All persons are warned against any acts tending to endanger property. All persons caught in any depredation will be immediately arrested.

With the help of God order and peace and private property shall be preserved. The City Government and committees of citizens pledge themselves to the community to protect them, and prepare the way for a restoration of public and private welfare.

It is believed the fire has spent its force, and all will soon be well.

R. B. MASON, Mayor.

GEO. TAYLOR, Comptroller,
By R. B. MASON.

CHARLES C. P. HOLDEN,
President Common Council.

T. B. BROWN,
President Board of Police.

Chicago, October 9th, 1871.

not return in time, and to pile the most valuable portion of my library into the drawers and bureaus and tables ready for moving, I seized a bird-cage containing a talented green parrot, and mounted the seat with the driver. For one square southward from the corner of Monroe Street we made pretty fair progress. The dust was so thick that we could not see the distance of a whole square ahead. It came, not in clouds, but in a steady storm of sand, the particles impinging against our faces like needle-points. Pretty soon we came to a dead halt. We could move neither forward, nor backward, nor sidewise. The gorge had caught fast somewhere. Yet everybody was good-natured and polite. If I should say I didn't hear on oath all the way down Michigan Avenue, there are probably some mule-drivers in Cincinnati who would say it was a lie. But I did not. The only quarrelsome person I saw was a German laborer (a noted exception to his race), who was protesting that he had lost everything, and that he would not get out of the middle of the road although he was on foot. He became very obstreperous on this point, and commenced beating the head of my horse with his fist. My driver was preparing to knock him down with the butt-end of his whip, when two men seized the insolent Teuton and dragged him to the water's edge, where it is to be hoped he was ducked.

By getting into the park, we succeeded in advancing two squares without impediment, and might have gone farther had we not come upon an excavation which the public authorities had recently made. This drove us back to the Avenue, where another battering-ram made a gap for us at the intersection of Van Buren Street, the north end of Michigan Terrace. Here the gorge seemed impassable. The difficulty proceeded from teams entering Michigan Avenue from cross-streets. Extempore policemen stationed themselves at the crossings, and helped as well as they could, but we were half an hour in passing the Terrace. From this imposing row of residences the millionaires were dragging their trunks and their bundles, and yet there was no panic, no frenzy, no boisterousness, but only the haste which the situation authorized.

There was real danger to life all along the street, but nobody realized it, because the park was ample to hold all the people. None of us asked or thought what would become of those nearest the water if the smoke, and cinders should drive the whole crowd down to the shore, or if the vast bazaar of luggage should itself take fire, as some of it afterwards did. Fortunately for those in the street, there was a limit to the number of teams available in that quarter of the city. The contributions from the cross-streets grew less; and we soon began to move on a walk without interruption. Arriving at Eldridge Court, I turned into Wabash Avenue, where the crowd was thinner. Arriving at the house of a friend, who was on the windward side of the fire, I tumbled off my load and started back to get another.

Half way down Michigan Avenue, which was now perceptibly easier to move in, I discovered my family on the sidewalk, with their arms full of light household effects. My wife told me that the house was already burned, that the flames burst out ready-made in the rear hall before she knew that the roof had been scorched, and that one of the servants, who had disobeyed orders in her eagerness to save some article, had got singed, though not burned, in coming out. My wife and mother, and all the rest were begrimed with dirt and smoke, like blackamoors—everybody was. The "bloated aristocrats" all along the street, who supposed they had lost both home and fortune at one sweep, were a sorry but not despairing congregation. They had saved their lives at all events, and they knew that many of their fellow-creatures must have lost theirs.

I saw a great many kindly acts done as we moved along. The poor helped the rich, and the rich helped the poor (if anybody could be called rich at such a time) to get on with their loads. I heard of cartmen demanding one hundred and fifty dollars (in hand, of course) for carrying a single load. Very likely it was so, but those cases did not come under my own notice. It did come under my notice that some cartmen worked for whatever the sufferers felt able to pay, and one I knew worked with alacrity for nothing. It takes all sorts of people to make a great fire.

I had paid and discharged my driver after extorting his solemn promise to come back and move me again if the wind should shift to the north—in which event everybody knew that the whole South Division, for a distance of four miles, must perish. We soon arrived at the house of the kind friend on Wabash Avenue, where our trunks and bundles had been deposited. This was south of the line of fire, but this did not satisfy anybody, since we had all seen how resolutely the flames had gone transversely across the direction of the wind. Then came a story from down the street that Sheridan was going to blow up the Wabash Avenue Methodist Church on the corner of Harrison Street. We observed a general scattering away of people from that neighborhood. I was nearly four squares south of the locality, and thought that the missiles wouldn't come so far. We awaited the explosion, but it did not come. By and by we picked up courage to go around two or three blocks and see whether the church had fallen down of its own accord. We perceived that two or three houses in the rear of the edifice had been leveled to the ground, that the church itself was standing, and that the fire was out, in that quarter at least; also, that the line of Harrison Street marked the southern limits of the devastation.

The wind continued to blow fiercely from the southwest, and has not ceased to this hour (Saturday, October 14). But it was liable to change. If it chopped around to the north, the burning embers would be blown back upon the South Division. If it veered to the east, they would be blown into the West Division, though the river afforded rather better protection there. Then we should have nothing to do but to keep ahead of the flames and get down as fast as possible to the open prairie, and there spend the night houseless and supperless—and what of the morrow? A full hundred thousand of us. And if we were spared, and the West Division were driven out upon their prairie (a hundred and fifty thousand according to the Federal census), how would the multitude be fed? If there could be anything more awful than what we had already gone through, it would be what we would certainly go through if the wind should change; for with the embers of this great fire flying about, and no water to

fight them, we knew there was not gunpowder enough in Illinois to stop the inevitable conflagration. But this was not all. A well authenticated rumor came up to the city that the prairie was on fire south of Hyde Park, the largest of the southern suburbs.

The grass was as dry as tinder, and so were the leaves in Cottage Grove, a piece of timber several miles square, containing hundreds of residences of the better class, some of them of palatial dimensions. A fire on the prairie, communicating itself to the grove, might cut off the retreat of the one hundred thousand people in the South Division; might invade the South Division itself, and come up under the impulsion of that fierce wind, and where should we all be then? There were three or four bridges leading to the West Division, the only possible avenues of escape—but what were these among so many? And what if the "Commune" should go to work and start incendiary fires while all was yet in confusion? These fiends were improving the daylight by plundering along the street. Before dark the whole male population of the city was organized by spontaneous impulse into a night patrol, with pallid determination to put every incendiary to instant death.

About 5 P. M. I applied to a friend on Wabash Avenue for the use of a team to convey my family and chattels to the southern suburbs, about four miles distant, where my brother happened to own a small cottage, which, up to the present time, nobody could be induced to occupy and pay rent for. My friend replied that his work-teams were engaged hauling water for people to drink. Here was another thing I had not thought of—a great city with no water to drink. Plenty in the lake, to be sure, but none in the city mains or the connecting pipes. Fortunately the extreme western limits were provided with a number of artesian wells, bored for manufacturing establishments. Then there was the river—the horrible, black, stinking river of a few weeks ago, which has since become clear enough for fish to live in, by reason of the deepening of the canal, which draws to the Mississippi a perpetual flow of pure water from Lake Michigan. With the city Pumping Works stopped, the sewers no longer discharged themselves into the river. So this might be used; and it was. Twenty-four hours had not passed before tens of thousands of people were drinking the water of Chicago River, with no unpleasant taste or effects.

The work-teams of my friend being engaged in hauling water for people who could not get any from the wells or the river or lake, he placed at my disposal his carriage, horses, and coachman, whom he directed to take me and the ladies to any place we desired to reach. While we were talking, he hailed another gentleman on the street, who owned a large stevedore wagon, and asked him to convey my trunks, etc., to Cottage Grove Avenue, near Forty-third Street, to which request an immediate and most gracious assent was given. And thus we started again, our hostess pressing a mattress upon us from her store. All the streets leading southward were yet filled with fugitives. Where they all found shelter that night, I know not; but every house seemed to be opened to anybody who desired to enter.

Arrived at our home about dusk; we found in it, as we expected, a cold reception, there being neither stove nor grate, nor fireplace, nor fuel, nor light therein. But I will not dwell upon these things. We really did not mind them, for when we thought of the thousands of men, women, and tender babes huddled together in Lincoln Park, seven miles to the north of us, with no prospect of food, exposed to rain, if it should come, with no canopy but the driving smoke of their homes, we thought how little we had suffered and how much we should be thankful for. How one feels at a particular time depends much upon how he sees others enjoy themselves. All the eight-hour strikers are possessed of more comfort and leisure than we have, but we do not notice anything of it at all. We have secured a stove, and there are plenty of trees around us, and the axe is mightier than the pen to get one's breakfast ready now.

The prairie fire southwest of Hyde Park we found to have been a veritable fact, but it had been put out by diligent effort. The ditches cut for drainage in that region during the last two or three years render it very difficult for a fire to spread far. Yet I revolved in my mind a plan of escape in case the fire should break

out afresh, surmount the ditches, and get into the grove which surrounded us. I judged that a fire could be discerned from our window fully five miles away, and that before it could reach us we could get upon the new South Park Boulevard, two hundred feet wide, the western side of which has no timber to burn. A mere prairie fire coming up to this graveled driveway would go out, and we should suffer nothing worse than a little smoke. I learned the next day that some of the people on the lake shore east of us constructed rafts and gathered a few household effects in convenient places, to be launched whenever the fire should make its appearance on the prairie. It turned out, from the experience of the North Division groves, that these oak woods would not have burned in any case, the timber containing too much moisture. But we did not then know that.

There was no sleep for us until we heard the welcome sound of rain against our windows. How our hearts did rise in thankfulness to heaven for that rain! We thought the poor people in Lincoln Park would rather have the rain on their heads than know that Chicago was exposed to the horror of total conflagration. The wind blew with increasing violence, till our frame house trembled in every rafter. We did not know but it would go over, yet if it would only rain we would stand our ground, for we had no furniture to be broken by an overturned house, or to break our bones rolling about the floor. Now and then we looked at the red sky to the north, and satisfied ourselves that the rest of Chicago was not burning. This gave us comfort, but not sleep.

Details of what I saw might be spun out to the crack of doom, but I must draw it to a close. There will, of course, be much curiosity, to know why the fireproof buildings succumbed. . . .

It is ascertained that no stone ever used in the business part of a city is worth a farthing in such a fire. Brick is the only thing which comes out whole, and is ready to try it again. But it is not fair to say that an absolutely fireproof building cannot be erected. I think it can be. At all events, the architects of the world should come here and study. . . .

And what shall I say of the Christ-like charity that has overwhelmed us in our misfortune? All the tears that have been shed in Chicago, except those which have flowed for the dead and maimed, have been called to our eyes by reading that in this great city and that little town, and yonder hamlet, and across the lakes in Canada, and down among our late enemies of the South, and beyond the mountains in Utah and California, and over the water in England, and on the Continent, God's people were working and giving to save us our affliction. I cannot even write of it, for my eyes fill whenever I think of it.

On Wednesday morning the *Tribune* came out with a half sheet containing among other things a notice that an intelligence office had been opened for lost people to report to, and for those who had lost their friends to inquire at. On the following morning we printed two columns of personal items from this intelligence office. Perhaps you have copied them, but I send you a few taken at random:

Mrs. Bush is at 40 Arnold Street. She lost her baby.

Peter Grace lost wife and children; Church, Carpenter and Washington streets.

Mrs. Tinney lost little girl six years old, Katie, Harrison House.

James Glass lost little boy, Arthur Glass, 342 Hubbard Street.

A little girl, cannot speak her name, at Desplaines Hotel.

The wife and child of Rev. W. A. Jones are missing.

Henry Schneider, baby, in blue poland waist, red skirt, has white hair.

Many of these lost babies were doubtless found; many of these separated families brought together again. What meetings there must have been! But many others have gone over the river, to be found of God, and delivered to their mothers' arms in mansions not made with hands, eternal in the heavens.

THE GREAT STEAMBOAT FIRE

CINCINNATI *ENQUIRER*

Disasters were common in the steamboat trade. In 1817 the pioneer Zebulon M. Pike churned up to St. Louis, the first steam vessel on the upper Mississippi. By 1840 the Pike number eight and the Ben Franklin number seven were calling at St. Louis; all their predecessors had been burned, wrecked or exploded. But the trade kept growing until railroads webbed the Midwest after the Civil War. Even then the steamboatmen held on, carrying mixed cargo from Pittsburgh to New Orleans and from scores of points on the Ohio, Mississippi, Tennessee, Cumberland and lesser rivers.

Meanwhile the fleets were diminishing, as the long list of disasters grew. The year 1872 was a grim time for steamboatmen. In a single month at Cincinnati fifteen big boats were lost—nine of them crushed by ice and six charred by flames on a lurid midnight. These were all old vessels, and there would be no new ones built to take their place. The big white boats were going.

March 7, 1872

THE Public Landing, from the foot of Broadway to the wharfboat at the foot of Main street, was last night the scene of one of the most terrific conflagrations that has visited our city in many years past. A sight like that of six of our magnificent Ohio River steamboats on fire at the same time, and presenting a continuous wall of flame for a distance of two blocks, though grand in the extreme, is

Cincinnati public landing, c. 1850. *Courtesy Ohio Historical Society*

happily an unusual one, and one which while it drew thither ten thousand curious sight seers there is scarce one of the number that would wish to have repeated.

About a quarter after twelve o'clock, one of the policemen on the landing noticed flames coming up through the boiler deck of the St. Charles, a magnificent side-wheel steamer in the Wheeling and Pittsburg trade, which arrived at the wharf day before yesterday. By some blunder the fire alarm was not turned in promptly, and before the Department was notified of the existence of the fire fully fifteen minutes had elapsed, and the fate of the boat was sealed. Indeed so fiercely did the flames burn in the combustible material of the boat, that the officers barely had time to escape, some of them being compelled to leave their clothes on the vessel. Among them the mate of the vessel had to walk off in his stocking feet, there not being time for him to put on his boots.

By the time an alarm had been turned in from the box at the foot of Broadway every part of the boat was in flames, and their reflection was visible from every part of the city. The engines, however, were not slow to answer the summons, when it was once turned in, and in the course of ten minutes there were two relays of them on the landing, and a score of streams were playing on the line of burning boats.

Lying alongside and just above the St. Charles was the Argosy, a New Orleans boat

that had been loading for that city and intermediate points all yesterday and had taken on about two-thirds of her cargo. She was the next to take fire. As soon as the flames were communicated to her the intensity of the fire appeared to double. In addition to other merchandise stored in her hold there were two hundred barrels of whisky and the same amount of pork, and they both burned with extraordinary fierceness. In a few minutes she was enveloped in a sheet of flames as completely as the St. Charles.

Below the St. Charles lay the Kate Robinson, a Tennessee River boat that was advertised to go out tonight. She had taken on most of her cargo and had her crew on board. Several of the crew made narrow escapes in getting off the boat. Among these was the chambermaid, who, finding herself surrounded by flames, with no other chance of escape, boldly jumped into the river and was presently rescued by a gallant roustabout. The boat burned literally to the water's edge, and then careened over and sunk into the river.

Lying just above the Argosy was the Major Anderson, a magnificent side-wheel boat in the Pittsburg trade. She had arrived at the wharf only a day or two ago, and her owners intended to lay her up until a rise in the river took place. She took fire almost immediately after the Argosy, and the flames found the filagree work in her elegant cabins and the other combustible material under her construction choice food. She burned perhaps fifteen or twenty minutes, when her chimneys fell with a loud crash. Soon after the entire hull burned to the river and she was in ruins.

The Abeona was the next in order, though her taking fire may be said to be simultaneous with one or two of the others. She lay at the foot of Main street, just below the Kate Robinson. She had just come in from the Tennessee River, and had the greater part of her cargo still on board. Her fires had not yet gone out and her steam-gauge showed that she had forty pounds of steam, though that was not enough to turn her wheel, and she was totally lost.

Lying just above the Anderson was the Champion, just loaded for Red River. Hose from the fire engines were carried aboard of her and her side next the burning vessel was deluged with water. For some time they were able to keep the flames at bay, but finally the texas and part of the cabin took fire. The firemen however, were finally able to put out the fire before she was more than seriously damaged, and when the fire was over she lay at the landing, the only one of the six vessels that had been saved.

The R. W. Skillinger, lying at the foot of Broadway, and next above the Champion, was towed into the stream by the Newport ferry, Cincinnati Belle, after which Captain Air had come down and taken command and dropped down below the suspension bridge out of danger in a few minutes. The Robert Burns and Mary Miller were also fortunate enough to get out of danger by cutting their cables and drifting away with the current. The Bodmann was tied up just below the Cincinnati and New Orleans wharf-boat; in a perilous situation had not the flames, which fiercely attacked the wharf-boat, been subdued.

The St. Charles

The boat on which the fire originated, was a regular Pittsburg and Cincinnati packet. She had laid up at the wharf on account of the low water above, and was partially loaded. She was a side-wheel steamer, and was worth about $25,000. She was owned by Captain Joseph Smith, of this city, and parties in Pittsburg.

She was insured for $15,000 in the Andes, Western and other Companies of this city, the insurance having been recently transferred from Pittsburg Companies to this city. She had only about thirty tons of freight on board.

The Argosy

The next boat lying above, was a stern-wheel steamer, and run in the Cincinnati and New Orleans trade, her principal trade being towing barges of hay for her owners from Vevay, Indiana. She came here always and loaded with freight. At the time of her destruction she had about 150 tons of freight on board, consisting, in part, of 200 barrels whisky, 200 barrels pork, a large lot of furniture, soap, candles and starch. Captain Schenck estimates her cargo at $60,000. The Argosy was valued at $8,000, and was owned by Captain Schenck and son of Vevay, Indiana. She was commanded by Captain A. J. Schenck. No insurance.

The Major Anderson

Lay next to the Argosy. She was a side-wheel steamer, and a regular Cincinnati and Wheeling packet. She was owned by Captain John K. Booth, of this city, and the Wheeling and Parkersburg Packet Company, the majority of her owners residing in Wheeling. She was valued at $17,000, and insured for $12,000 in the American, Eureka and Burnet Insurance Company of this city. She was also laid up on account of low water, and had no cargo on board. She was commanded by Captain Chas. Muhlman, with Ed. Muhlman as Clerk.

The Champion

Next above the Major Anderson, was a stern-wheel steamer, and was loading for her second trip to Red River. She was about one-third loaded. The engines stayed the fire before she was totally destroyed, but the greatest part of her upper works were burned off. Considerable freight on the Champion, we presume, will be saved. She was owned by Captain John A. Williamson, of Newport, and Captain I. G. Isham, of this city. She was valued at $12,000, on which there was no insurance. The Champion was commanded by Captain Lon Bryson. The loss on cargo can not be estimated.

The R. W. Skillinger

Was next above the Champion, but was towed

away by the Newport ferry-boat Cincinnati Belle.

The Kate Robinson
Lay next below the St. Charles. She was loading for the Tennessee River, and was to have left today. She was about half loaded, and had, perhaps, 150 tons freight on board. She belonged to the Tennessee River Line, and was owned by Captain John A. Williamson of Newport, and Captain I. G. Isham, of this city. She was valued at $12,000, on which there was no insurance. She was commanded by Captain John A. Patterson.

The Abeona
Lay below the St. Charles. She was a stern-wheeler of about the same capacity as the Kate Robinson, and belonged to the Tennessee River Line. She had just arrived with a full load, and had about forty pounds steam on hand at the time, but not enough to turn her wheel. She was almost entirely burned, with the greater part of her cargo. She was owned by Captain John A. Williamson, of Newport, and Captain I. G. Isham of this city. No insurance.

The Cincinnati and New Orleans Wharf-Boat
Was in great danger of conflagration from the steamer Abeona, which steamer lay next the upper end of the wharf-boat. The flames communicated to the roof of the wharf-boat and had made considerable progress before the fire-engines got an opportunity to play upon it. They were soon extinguished, however, by a deluge of water from four sets of hose.

The Charles Rodmann
Lay outside the wharf-boat, but was dropped below out of danger.

The Robert Burns
Also lay outside the wharf-boat, and dropped down to safe quarters.

The Mary Miller
Lay next below, but was out of danger.

At Two O'clock
A keg of powder in the forecastle of the Kate Robinson exploded, with a heavy report that shook the shores and vibrated the air so that a lantern in the hands of the Argosy's watchman was broken. It seemed a signal that the worst was over, for from that moment the limits of the destruction became determinate, and the fireman's duty became work instead of battle. Many bales of cotton on the landing, and, in some instances, other freight, took fire from the fierce heat and sparks, but we do not estimate the loss from this cause as very heavy.

As we go to press the heavens above the scene of disaster still glow with the brightness of an ordinary conflagration, but the dreadful grandeur of the scene, as compared with the half hour when the river and shores were lit with the vivid glare which only a great Western "steamboat fire" can throw over a land and water scape, has lessened, and all but those whose duties or whose misfortunes hold them to the scene are retiring from the carnival of ruin.

March 8, 1872
We have but few additional particulars to give of the great steamboat conflagration from the very full report published in the *Enquirer* yesterday. The six steamers—the Abeona, Kate Robinson, St. Charles, Argosy, Major Anderson, and Champion—all burned to the water's edge and sunk. But little remains of any of the boats. They all lie with their bows on shore, and present a dreary sight, with their blackened and burned timbers, and nothing remains but a mass of ruins. The Champion was entirely destroyed aft of the boiler-deck, and lies sunk with the rest. Her chimneys are still standing. A small portion of the larboard cabin-guard of the Abeona is also left. But little remains but the machinery, which will all be removed, and in due course of time, perhaps, do service again.

While the six boats have been totally destroyed, the loss will not reach $100,000, yet the same steamers could not be replaced for double that sum. The steamers burned were all old, and have served their owners faithfully.

Rumors of the loss of life were still floating around yesterday, but such, we are happy to state, are without foundation. We were assured by the officers of the different steamers that all their crews were safe and had been accounted for. While there were many narrow escapes, there was no serious injury to any one. Captain T. J. Russell, of the St. Charles, had his right hand pretty badly burned, and was compelled to swim for his life, as did one or two others.

RIOT IN HAYMARKET SQUARE

APPLETON'S ANNUAL ENCYCLOPEDIA, 1886

In the spring of 1886 a drab district in Chicago became a name, heard round the world, for class conflict and violence. On May the first, striking for an eight-hour workday, thousands of laborers paralyzed the industry and transportation of the city. Tension culminated in the mass meeting at Haymarket Square four days later.

Many contemporary reports of the Haymarket Affair took violent sides, a few for and more against the labor agitators. From Appleton's Annual Encyclopedia *comes this mainly objective narrative.*

THE Anarchist riot in Chicago of Tuesday, May 4, 1886, may be said to have begun in the eight-hour movement on the previous Saturday, or, more properly, in the attack on Monday, May 3, upon the McCormick reaper-works. The labor agitation throughout the country in the spring was more violent in Chicago than elsewhere.

On Saturday, May 1, 40,000 laborers struck work and demanded a reduction of time from ten to eight hours. Chicago on that day presented a peculiar appearance. In the manufacturing districts the six and seven o'clock whistles were not heard. The usual hurrying crowds of workmen were not seen, and the streets did not contain half the number of trucks commonly in use. During the morning, however, several processions composed of the strikers were formed in the streets. Peaceable furniture-workers and mill-hands paraded, displaying American and German flags and banners, giving praise to the firms that had conceded the eight-hour day. A procession of 10,000 lumbermen, in front of which a man carried a red flag, visited several places and held meetings at which highly incendiary speeches were made. The discontented freight handlers, to the number of

nearly 1,000, marched around the depots and persuaded their fellow-workmen to join them. The freight-handlers of the Chicago, Burlington, and Quincy, and the Chicago and Alton Railroads, to the number of 300, had a brief meeting and marched to the Wabash freight-houses, where they persuaded eighty-five of the Wabash men to join them. The procession swelled and, with great cheers but no disorder, moved from station to station, everywhere urging men to join, who seemed unable to resist. The result was that every railroad in the city was crippled. All the freight-houses were closed and barred as for a prolonged state of siege, and all the industries of the city were paralyzed, for nothing could be delivered.

These proceedings had here and there a threatening appearance. The freight-handlers who went to work were protected by guards with drawn revolvers. One of the processions was headed by a stout German, who carried a big wooden sword, which he had evidently fashioned with his own hands. Several of them marched like soldiers, their correct movements being cheered by the crowds on the sidewalk. These last had no doubt profited by instructions received at meetings such as were afterward described at the trial of the Anarchists.

Police and rioters at point-blank range in Haymarket Square. *Courtesy Illinois State Historical Library*

It was observed by the detectives among the crowds of Germans, Bohemians, and Poles, that their talk was highly incendiary; but there was nothing to indicate such bloody results as followed. Many of the workmen appeared ready to accept reasonable terms from their employers, and did not wish to insist upon getting ten hours' pay for eight hours' work. But the demands of other laborers, particularly the lumbermen, were extreme.

On Monday a great crowd of strikers, mostly lumbermen, inflamed by incendiary speeches, gathered about the McCormick works. Their quarrel with the workmen there was, that they were supposed not to have insisted upon the time-reduction. About half of McCormick's workmen were dissuaded or intimidated by them from going to work; but the other half, about 700, went to work as usual. During the day the company adopted the eight-hour time, and gave the men a half-

holiday. The McCormick workmen, on coming out from their building, were attacked by the crowd with stones, and the men ran away or retreated into the building, the strikers meanwhile breaking a great many of the McCormick windows. The company's guard of a dozen men fired their revolvers into the air, hoping to frighten the strikers, who laughed at these demonstrations. The crowd had begun battering down the doors with crowbars, when a patrol wagon filled with policemen, dashed into the midst of the strikers, who threw stones and bricks at the officers. The officers alighted and drew their revolvers; but the mob kept on throwing missiles, the police dodging them as best they could. At length the crowd, great numbers of whom appeared to be armed, drew their revolvers and fired on the police, and the police returned the fire. The strikers being bad marksmen, none of the police were hurt; but about a dozen of the mob were wounded. On the arrival of re-enforcements, the police dispersed the crowd.

On that evening and the next day a hand-bill, printed in German and English, called upon the workingmen to meet at the corner of Des Plaines and Randolph Streets, on Tuesday evening, the 4th. "Good speakers," it was promised "will be present to denounce the latest atrocious act of the police, the shooting of our fellow-workmen yesterday afternoon."

At Des Plaines Street, Randolph Street, which runs east and west, widens out into a plaza, called the Old Haymarket, about 2,900 feet long by 150 feet wide. The crowd gathered just off the northeastern corner of this plaza in Randolph Street, 100 feet north of Des Plaines Street. About 1,400 men, including many who had been most active in the riot of the previous day, responded to the invitation. Half of these were driven away by a rain-storm, while those who remained were addressed from a wagon by August Spies, editor of the "Arbeiter-Zeitung," and by the Anarchist, A. B. Parsons. These speeches were rather mild; but Fielden, an Englishman, mounted the wagon and made an extremely violent speech of twenty minutes' duration.

Meanwhile 200 police, under Captains Bonfield and Ward, were in readiness at the station in Des Plaines Street, less than 300 feet south of the wagon. When the tenor of Fielden's speech was known at the station, it was decided by the two captains that, in order to avoid a serious riot, it would be best to disperse the crowd. Accordingly 170 men drawn up in line were marched up Des Plaines Street, and when the police were within a few steps of the wagon, Captain Ward ordered the crowd to disperse. Fielden got down from the wagon, saying, "We are peaceable."

At this moment a bomb with a lighted fuse attached was thrown from a crowd of men standing in an alley directly opposite the wagon. It struck the ground among the police, exploded, and worked terrible destruction among them. Numbers of them were wounded, officer Deegan dying almost immediately. The crowd then opened a destructive fire upon the police, sixty of whom were wounded by the bomb and the shooting, of whom seven died. The officers then charged the mob, firing revolvers among them and killing and wounding a large number.

The trial of the persons charged with conspiring to throw the bomb began on the 15th of July, twenty-one days having been consumed in getting a jury. Spies, Parsons, Fischer, Fielden, Engel, Schwab, Lingg, and Neebe were the persons arraigned. Early in the trial Judge Gary gave a decision that greatly facilitated the conviction of the prisoners. His decision was that, that it is not necessary that the members of a conspiracy should have agreed to commit a murder at any particular time to constitute them accessories before the fact; that if murder has been agreed upon, and the time or manner of the crime has not been settled, the conspirators are nevertheless, when the killing has been done, guilty of murder.

The evidence against the prisoners produced at the trial was mostly supplied by Anarchist informers, by detectives, the police, and the reporters. One of the informers, Waller, a Swiss, had been a member of the Lehr und Wehr Verein. This organization, as its name indicates, is a society for exercise and instruction in arms. It was incorporated under the laws of the State in 1875 by thirty German and Bohemian Socialists, and now includes 300 or 400 members, most of whom have seen service in foreign armies. They have been practicing military exercises to prepare themselves for conflicts with the authorities.

Waller testified that he presided at a meeting of the society at Grief's saloon, the usual place of meeting, on Monday night, the 3d. He had seen in the "Arbeiter-Zeitung" the letter "T" and "Come on Monday," which was the signal that there was to be a meeting. Fischer and Engel were present at this meeting. Circulars headed "Revenge!" were issued. The shooting of men at McCormick's was discussed. Engel introduced a resolution regarding what should be done in case there should be a conflict between the strikers and the police. In this case it was resolved that there should be meetings to aid the strikers. The word "Ruhe" (rest) was to be the signal for such meetings. The manner of fighting was also talked over. Engel suggested that a bomb should be thrown into the police-stations; and it was agreed that the mob should use bombs, fire-arms, or any other means of destruction, if they were attacked by the police. The society was to be represented by a committee at the Haymarket meeting. The question upon these measures was put to the meeting by Engel. Waller said that he had himself attended the Haymarket meeting, armed with a dynamite bomb.

Early in 1885 several of the largest property-owners in Chicago had employed Pinkerton's agency to make an investigation as to the real purposes of the Anarchists. One of Pinkerton's men, A. C. Jansen, testified that he was a member of the American branch of the International Workingmen's Association, and belonged to the armed section of that force. He had joined the organization with a view of finding out its objects. He attended all the meetings from February, 1885, till January, 1886, and was present at two meetings of the armed section. At one of these, Spies advised the shooting of a police-officer who had been accused of a serious charge, but had been acquitted on the testimony of his brother officers. Fielden referred to the dedication of the new Board of Trade, with this suggestion: "What a splendid opportunity there would be for some bold fellow, next Tuesday evening, to make capitalists tremble by blowing up the building and all there is in it!"

At one of the meetings, a man armed with a long sword, dressed in a blue blouse and wearing a slouched hat, requested all present to fall in line. The detective and two others stepped forward. On the drill-master's demanding that he should be vouched for, the detective was at a loss what to do; but, to his great relief, Parsons volunteered to be his sponsor. The drill-master invited those present to inspect two tin boxes containing some improved dynamite bombs. At one of the meetings Parsons was elected lieutenant and proposed an attack on the First Regiment armory. In case of a conflict with the authorities, the International Rifles were to act with the Lehr und Wehr Verein. It will be seen that this evidence convicted Spies, Parsons, Fielden, and Engel of conspiracy. The same witnesses,

and others, gave more evidence of a similar character.

It was further proved that dynamite bombs were in the possession of several of the accused. Dynamite was found in Spies's desk at the "Arbeiter-Zeitung" office, and in the cellar of Engel's house. Evidence was given that the article in the "Arbeiter-Zeitung," headed "Blood," was in the handwriting of Schwab, who was an associate of Spies upon that paper. Concerning Fielden, an officer testified that at the approach of the police at the Haymarket, he exclaimed: "Here come the blood-hounds! You do your duty, and I'll do mine!" He said that, just as Capt. Ward was ordering the crowd to disperse, Fielden got down from the wagon and, saying, "We are peaceful," drew his revolver and fired point-blank at Bonfield, Ward, and the other officers. It was at this moment that the bomb exploded.

The evidence against Lingg was given by the informer, Seliger, a member of a Socialist group and recording secretary of the Carpenters' Union. The bombs were made in Seliger's house, under the supervision of Lingg. Seliger said he did not work at his trade on Tuesday. Lingg came on that day. He had previously told Lingg that he wished to have the bombs taken away from his house. In reply, Lingg told him to work diligently, and the bombs would be taken away that afternoon. Seliger went to work, drilling holes in the shells and filling them. Lingg went to a meeting, came back about one o'clock, and complained that Seliger had not worked hard enough; and, when Seliger replied that he had no pleasure in the work, Lingg said that they would have to work harder in the afternoon. He said the bombs were to be used that evening, and ought to be completed; they would make good "fodder" for the capitalists.

In the evening Lingg and Seliger carried the trunk containing the bombs away from the house. They were met by Socialists, who opened the trunk and helped themselves to bombs. As they passed the Larrabee Street police-station, Lingg said it would be a beautiful thing to throw in a bomb. Then a patrol wagon approached, and Lingg said that would be a good opportunity. When Seliger said he thought not, Lingg became much excited and asked for a light from his cigar. Seliger lighted a match, taking time about it, so as to give the wagon time to pass. Lingg wanted to follow the wagon. Lingg showed the witness a copy of the "Arbeiter-Zeitung," containing the word "Ruhe," and said it was a signal for a meeting of armed Socialists on the west side. The two then went to a saloon where there were several other Socialists, one of whom said to Lingg, "You are the cause of it all." They were then told of the Haymarket affair. Lingg said nothing at the moment, but on the way home said that even now he was scolded and gibed at for the work he had done, and that his brothers in the cause did not appreciate him. They hid their bombs under the sidewalk.

Evidence was produced connecting Spies, Schwab, and Fischer with the throwing of the bomb. A witness testified that just before the explosion he saw Spies hand a package to Schnaubelt, the missing Anarchist, who threw the bomb. He was walking in Randolph Street when the Haymarket meeting was assembling. He was near the wagon, when he saw Spies and Schwab pass into the alley. He heard the words "pistols" and "police" used by them, and heard one of them ask the other whether "one would be enough." They came out of the alley and went westward along Randolph Street, when they were presently joined by a third man, whom the witness recognized from a photograph as Schnaubelt. The three then turned and started toward the Haymarket, the witness following them closely. He saw Spies hand Schnaubelt something, which the latter put into his pocket. A moment later he heard Schwab say, "Now if they come, give it to them!" and Spies reply, "I don't think we can, for they won't give us a chance to-night."

Another witness, Gilmer, testified that when Fielden was speaking, he was standing at the mouth of the alley near the wagon. He saw a man descend from the wagon and join a group of four or five persons standing in the alley. At that moment some one cried, "The police are coming!" Then the man who had left the wagon and joined the group in the alley, lighted a match and placed it against something held in the hand of one of the group, whereupon a fuse began to sizzle, and then immediately the bomb was thrown. The witness recognized a picture of Schnaubelt as that of the thrower of the bomb. He recognized Spies as the man that left the wagon and lighted the fuse, and Fischer as a member of the group.

Fischer was arrested at the "Arbeiter-Zeitung" office. He was armed with a revolver and a long knife. It was shown that he had written the words at the head of the Anarchist circulars, "Workingmen, arm yourselves and appear in full force!" Neebe distributed the "Revenge" circulars.

The defense endeavored to set up a new theory regarding the throwing of the bomb. It was, that the bomb did not come from the group in the alley near the wagon, but arose thirty feet south of the wagon, and was hurled through the air in a northwesterly direction, and therefore in a manner toward the speakers' wagon. Testimony was adduced to show that Spies and Schwab did not go into the alley previous to the opening of the meeting. Witnesses were examined to prove that it was the police who began the shooting after the explosion, and not the Anarchists; but these witnesses were usually shown, on cross-examination, to have been members of Anarchist or Socialist organizations. The defense also impeached the veracity of Gilmer, the witness who swore to seeing Spies light the fuse of the bomb. Several of the defendants were placed upon the stand to testify in their own behalf.

Judge Gary made an elaborate charge to the jury, in which he repeated the instruction to which allusion has already been made. He said that if any one of the defendants attempted to overthrow the law by force, and threw the bomb, then the defendants who were in the conspiracy were guilty of murder. If there was a conspiracy, and the defendants were party to it, they were guilty of murder, although the date of the culmination of the conspiracy had not been fixed. The impracticableness of the aims of the defendants was immaterial. He said that the jury might bring in a verdict of manslaughter in the case of any one or of all of the prisoners.

The jury retired after the judge's charge,

and, on the next morning, August 20, gave in their verdict, which was as follows: "We, the jury, find the defendants—August Spies, Michael Schwab, Samuel Fielden, Albert R. Parsons, Adolph Fischer, George Engel, and Louis Lingg—guilty of murder, in the manner and form charged in the indictment, and fix the penalty at imprisonment for fifteen years." The verdict was cheered by the crowd outside the court-house, and was received with great satisfaction by the people of Chicago.

Perhaps the defendants were not all of them the cruel wretches they appeared. They had been for a long time, in their meetings and newspapers, advocating the use of dynamite. Their newspapers referred to it as "this powerful agent of civilization"; and not only did these organs recommend its use in general terms, but they offered practical suggestions regarding the best methods of manufacturing it, as the following extract from one of them will show: "Dynamite is the stuff, and don't you forget it! Enough of it to fill your vest-pocket has power to do more for the wage-slaves of this country than a bushel-basket full of ballots. Fill a piece of gas-pipe with good stuff, plug up the ends, insert a fuse and cap, touch it off, and introduce it among a lot of rich loafers, and there will be a cheerful scattering of unemployed capitalists that will be felt for some time."

They have been long talking in this way, but when the thing has at last been done, and real murders have been committed, they seem to be rather taken aback. Vanity has probably had quite as much to do with their actions as malice or a sense of oppression. It has been said by some one that the attraction of assassination to the poor man is that, when armed with this instrument, he may at least not be despised. When Engel's wife visited him in prison, and chided him for having placed himself in such a position, he wept and said: "I am cursed with eloquence. Louise Michel suffered for a cause. She is a woman. I am a man, and will stand it like a man." When the extract about dynamite, above quoted, was read in court, the prisoners seemed to be greatly amused by the wit of it. Their theatrical and impudent behavior during the trial no doubt bore against them. Certainly the feeling against them in Chicago was very strong. The sufferings of the brave policemen had evidently touched the popular heart.

The prosecution at one time during the trial introduced in evidence a coat, showing many rents, which had been worn by a policeman whom the bomb had wounded in a number of places. The defense asserted that the purpose of introducing the coat was to affect the jury, to which the State's attorney replied that, if he had really wished to move the jury, he would have brought the officer and exhibited his wounds. The prosecution was ably conducted. The result of this trial seems to show that a campaign of dynamite, on the part of the discontented classes, can not be waged with much prospect of success.

WORLD'S FAIR ON THE PRAIRIE

EDGAR LEE MASTERS

Twenty years after the great fire, Chicago was a city of a million people, ready to celebrate the 400th anniversary of the discovery of America with the most lavish exposition ever held. In January, 1891, a group of engineers, architects and artists tramped the desolate lake shore at Jackson Park. The eastern men said it couldn't be done, but Chicago went ahead. Steelworkers, stonemasons, carpenters, architects, painters, sculptors, worked in rain and snow, in mud and dust, amid a forest of derricks and cranes, among smoking engines and hissing boilers. At the formal opening in May, 1893, half a million people marveled at the

White City, the stately Court of Honor and the Grand Basin. Soon Chicago was talked about on five continents.

Above the Midway Plaisance rose an enormous Ferris Wheel (now in the Prater amusement park in Vienna), carrying 1,300 people high above the Exposition grounds. From the crest of the circle they looked over the vast web of Chicago and the endless inland prairie.

Edgar Lee Masters (1869–1950) grew up on that prairie. A boyhood in the Spoon River country gave him the scene and the people he would later portray in the haunting poems of Spoon River Anthology. *At the time of the World's Fair he was a young lawyer in Chicago, discovering the power, brutality and aspiration of the prairie city.*

A SUMMER came on of such clear skies and moderate heat, for the most part, that the Fair was prospered by nature as if by a special dispensation. The city itself was like Monte Carlo. Within a stone's throw of the city hall the most brilliantly equipped gambling houses kept open door without being disturbed. Roulette and stud poker, chuck-a-luck and piquette flourished in gilded rooms. Zealots and reformers were always able to lay an effectual hand of moral severity upon gambling in Chicago when a ribbon clerk from one of the stores or an employee of the gas company embezzled money and lost it in these halls of chance. But this was no summer for such dramatizations; and Harry Varnell's place and others rode high and immune. The city with its vast crowds all summer long was a holiday scene. The most celebrated artists of the world appeared at the crowded theaters. The night life was one of unending joy, as often till dawn the crowds moved about the business district laughing and talking, feasting and drinking and playing. Carriages drove through the streets and out on the boulevards with their occupants singing "After the Ball." They roamed the ways of the Fair itself under the full moon, and under none, and down the Midway where the sound of the cannibal drum maintained a rhythmic booming, as the people talked and laughed. The streets of Cairo, the Irish Village, and a dozen other unique exhibitions on the Midway added to the glad noises of the festival, as their barkers stood at the doors and welcomed visitors. Natives of Siam, of India, of China, of the Isles, dressed in their own costumes, pigtailed, turbaned, robed in motley, mingled with the throngs. Tall Russians from the steppes of Siberia, dwarfs from Africa, every species of people from all parts of the earth could be seen on the Midway. James J. Corbett, the wonder of the day for having defeated Sullivan, had an exhibition room where he punched the bag and demonstrated the agility and skill with which he had overcome the unconquerable boy from Boston. Here, too, were restaurants serving every variety of food, and orchestras and musical companies from every land which swelled the rejoicing sounds of people at play with viols and horns, with bagpipes and drums, with flutes and flagelets, with Chinese and Italian guitars. At Old Vienna, one of the famous restaurants of the Midway, an Hungarian orchestra played ecstatically all summer long, seeming to turn sparkling Burgundy to music. Though the Midway and the Fair grounds were in Hyde Park which, under an old charter was a prohibition district, beer and wine and spirits, French, Italian, German, Japanese, Chinese, and barbarian drink flowed freely without any hindrance. This was true of the neighborhood outside the fences of the Fair. Both situations were well policed and there was order; but for the time the prohibitionist and the theologian could do nothing but walk along with a wry face and lament the anarchy of Chicago. This was the carnival side of the Fair.

But farther on toward the Lake were Machinery Hall and the other great buildings with their unexampled exhibits. There was the Court of Honor, an inexhaustible dream of beauty; there were the buildings of all the various nations, and of all the states of the Union, each with its own special exhibit. The

German Building by the Lake was an impressive Gothic which contained a monster globe of the earth. All the galleries of the world had sent their most priceless pictures to the Palace of Art, and there amid a richness almost equal to that of the Louvre thousands of people walked and looked at works of art of which they had heard all their lives and never expected to see. There were many ways to get about the vast grounds. Wheel chairs and toy railroads and camels served the crowds; and there were the gondolas to carry passengers around the lagoons by day and by night as the gondolieri sang their songs, even as they sang them in Venice. If a visitor tired of art and machinery, he could return to the Midway and enter the Congress of Beauties; or see the dark-haired women from Egypt do the *dance du ventre* as they did it in the cafés of Cairo. Or to get a full view of the whole Fair he could enter one of the cars of the Ferris Wheel, and as it turned with a clink and a grinding sound, rise to a great height and look over the Court of Honor to the east of the Macmonies Fountain and Lake; or west where he could see the rising towers of the University of Chicago and Washington Park beyond. All that summer Buffalo Bill ran his Wild West show in the Coliseum on Sixty-third Street, where the Indians enacted the attack that once was made on the stage coaches; and where a dervish whirled about for the better part of an hour on a high platform, and the band played the "Cow Boy March."

The Illinois Central, running what were called cattle cars, carried vast thousands to the Fair at a speed which was terrifying. But no accident occurred. The Alley L had its share of the passenger traffic, and with a less dangerous service. Carriages and cabs did their part. On state occasions, and sometimes on ordinary days, Mayor Harrison appeared riding his charger, and responding with lifted hat to the acclaims of the people. He was a happy man; and it may be that he thought that Kentucky had been adequately recognized in the circumstance that he was the mayor, and that Mrs. Potter Palmer, whose father was from Kentucky, was President of the Board of Lady Managers of the Fair. Nothing was omitted this summer to please the taste of a cosmopolitan gathering. Pugilism and wrestling may have been more or less banned; but a dubious character from New Orleans built a huge arena at Robey, Indiana, just over the Illinois line, where contests of skill and endurance, as he euphemistically called them, were conducted all that summer, giving satisfaction to the epigonous descendants of the ancient Roman nature. Long trains of cattle cars on the Illinois Central took the crowds there, and brought them back to the city. Day by day the attendance at the Fair increased, in spite of mutterings over the land that hard times were coming. On October ninth, when the anniversary of the Fire was celebrated and called Chicago Day, 761,942 people entered the gates of the Fair, and congested the vast space of Jackson Park. No panic occurred and no accidents of moment; but many felt concerned as they pushed their way along with difficulty, and realized that the weight and strength of thousands of human beings could surge this way or that and instantly crush to death masses of that incredible concourse.

Two World's Fairs in Chicago, 1893 and 1933. Courtesy Chicago Historical Society

IX

Interpreters

A FAVORITE book in the early years of the Ohio valley, when books were far between, was *Gulliver's Travels*. "The Indians," recalled Simon Kenton after the West was won, "never made but two settlements in Kentucky—one at Slate Creek and one at a place called Lul-bel-grud." And Daniel Boone explained in a garbled way where that garbled name came from. "I encamped on Red River with five other men," he said, "and we had with us for our amusement the 'History of Samuel Gulliver's Travels,' whence he gave an account of his young master Glumdelick, careing [*sic*] him on a market day for a show to a town called Lelbegrad. A young man of our camp called Alexander Neely told us that he had been that day to Lulbegrad and had killed two Broddigings in their capital."

When Neely killed the two Indians on Lulbegrad Creek, the Ohio valley was as strange as the lands of Gulliver's four voyages. All its dimensions were impressive, and the giant lands of the Brobdingnags was a ready comparison. Its rivers were broad and deep. Its northern lake was as vast as a sea. From Pennsylvania the land unrolled over rough hills to unmeasured tracts of level country. And the Great Forest covered it like a rug, threaded by the paths of Indians and trampled at the salt licks by the big game animals.

Now the strangeness and wildness are gone. It is tame: you know what lies over the horizon for a hundred miles. It is productive: each section has its fame for corn or wheat or soybeans, for hogs or cattle; each city has its product—machine tools, rubber tires, plate glass, cash registers. It is so typical that its people have little awareness of particularity. In other places a newsman asks a foreign visitor, "What is your impression of Boston?—of New York?—of Texas?—of California?" Here he asks, "What do you think of America?"

It is a uniform, widespread, open country, a land without barriers. In winter when wind and frost have made transparent the scattered woods you can look far off on all sides till the ringed horizon touches the upcurving sky. This is a glacial land, ironed out ages ago by vast sheets of creeping ice. It remains rich and always accessible, a country without mystery, with nothing hidden, nothing denied. The towns straggle out into cornfields, the cities push into the open country with their cemeteries, subdivisions and airports. It is an unfinished country, and a society that has not settled into permanence.

The character of a region is best defined in its literature, while the very books it produces help to create that character. The character of the Midwest is less definite than that of other parts of America; it is elusive, unemphatic, largely unself-conscious, and it is not everywhere the same. Indiana has a Hoosier tradition, provincial, neighborly, full of local memory and local satisfaction. It would be easy to tell from this literature that of all the midland states Indiana had the fewest European immigrants and the greatest access of population from the South. Wisconsin is separated from Indiana by but fifty miles of Lake Michigan shore line, yet the difference is startling. With a great influx of foreign-born and with its more strenuous climate, Wisconsin has been politically aggressive and intellectually restless. These two states offer the greatest contrast within the region, which has the many contrasts of a land half agricultural and half industrial and a society half urban and half rural.

When the sociologists Robert and Helen Lynd sought a typical American community, they found it halfway across the Midwest, near the center of the nation's population. And having described their town in one book they found that another was needed. Its title, *Middletown in Transition*, indicates that the story is still unfolding.

LOCAL HISTORY

CHARLES ALLAN SMART

After several years of editorial work and teaching in the East, Charles Allan Smart retired to an ancestral farm near the old town of Chillicothe in southern Ohio. He lived there during the depression years of the 1930's and wrote the widely read R.F.D. *(1938), from which the following passage is taken.*

I USED to smile at local history; it seemed appropriate only for country parsons and retired editors and professors. Here I have discovered my error. I have not yet had enough time and energy to learn more than what is common knowledge of our local history, but I have learned enough to know that its study need not be an escape; it can enrich and clarify the present.

Our county historical society is led by young people and by a few older people who are notably young in spirit. They have put on historical exhibits, and a parade that were both accurate and imaginative, and they are now building up a museum. My wife has been active, and our hired man and I have helped her to collect and return furniture. I must confess that this side of it leaves me rather cold; I am much more interested in migrations, buildings, old letters, and personalities.

The major trouble with local history is the difficulty in relating it to the history of the region, and of the country as a whole. Whenever I can see such connections, my interest is tripled. The doubtful fact that such-and-such a chair is "more than a hundred years old" doesn't interest me a whit, but if I can find out where it was made, and how it happened to get this far west, and no farther, I feel as though I were getting somewhere. There seem to be good general histories of the westward migrations, and plenty of local histories, if you can find them, but little in between. I can find out, if I want, what building stood on the northeast corner of Paint and Second Streets in 1838, say, but I shall find it extremely difficult to find out exactly what

part this region played in the conquest of the West and in the growth of the nation. Another thing I want is an index to the newly-completed Dictionary of American Biography, made on geographical lines, so that I could read all the biographies of people who were active in this region.

The easiest and pleasantest way to study local history is to look up all the old buildings, and what is known about them. One wouldn't perhaps select southern Ohio as a field for the historical study of architecture, but one winter a professor gave a lecture here that was an eye-opener to me. Climate, tradition, migrations, economic elements, materials, local and imported workmen, pattern books and original ideas—all enter into the human stories waiting to be uncovered in hundreds of old private and public buildings within a couple of hundred miles of where I sit. Like most Easterners, I was provincial and smug. For all I know, there may be wealths of architecture, interesting historically and aesthetically, in such unlikely places as, say, South Dakota and Idaho.

Every time I go to our grocer to buy a loaf of bread, a pound of cheese, and some cans of dog food, that most humdrum of experiences is enlightened by the fact that I go to an old building on the site of a log cabin used by one of the early legislatures of the Northwest Territory. I can't drive up to our other farm at Bellbridge without seeing a burial mound made so long ago as to make Père Lachaise seem almost as new as a cemetery in the Bronx. When I feel a momentary nostalgia

LOCAL HISTORY 357

Top: Shanty boat on the Miami and Erie Canal. Courtesy Anthony Wayne Pkwy Bd
Middle: Klage's ice outfit, mostly canallers on the Miami and Erie Canal. Courtesy Ohio
Historical Society   Bottom: Early mining in the Mahoning Iron Mine, Hibbing, Minnesota.

Top: Cutting out grindstones near Marietta, Ohio. *Courtesy Ohio Historical Society*
Middle: Voting booths in Cleveland, 1890. *Courtesy Ohio Historical Society*   Bottom:
Cleveland Hay Market, 1890, at the east end of Central Viaduct. *Courtesy Ohio
Historical Society*

for France, or use a French word or two, and therefore seem affected, I like to remember that this region was first explored by Frenchmen, and that less than two hundred years ago it was the property of the King of France.

I like to imagine what this country looked like, then, and before, when it had not yet received all these blessings of civilization; or even in the time of my grandfather, who rode and drove horses, and who received and shipped much of his freight on canal-boats. I don't really like to, because I don't enjoy thinking of men as a vicious and depraved breed of animals, who can waste a countryside like a disease. I much prefer to look forward to a time when men can say, We nearly ruined this paradise but now it is restored and protected; it is invaded only for good farms and gardens, for clean, sunny houses and factories that are appropriate, and for inconspicuous, efficient tools.

Only then, perhaps, shall we have the face, as well as the time and energy, to study local history.

PORTAGE, WISCONSIN

ZONA GALE

Born, reared and educated in Portage, Wisconsin, Zona Gale (1874–1938) spent a few years in New York and then returned to her native scene, which provided the background for her short stories, plays and novels. In love with small-town life, she belonged to a town of exceptional grace and tradition. At Portage, the old carrying place between the Fox and Wisconsin rivers, the French explorers had passed on their way to the Mississippi. Here in 1828 was built Fort Winnebago, across from the old Agency House where Juliette Kinzie, author of Wau-Bun, *lived with her husband, the Portage Indian Agent. In the woods of Portage County John Muir spent his ardent boyhood. A generation later Frederick Jackson Turner, pre-eminent historian of the American frontier, grew up in the town between two rivers, one flowing toward the St. Lawrence, the other to the Gulf of Mexico.*

The following selection is taken from Zona Gale's book of essays, Portage, Wisconsin, *published in 1928.*

ON one bank of a river it should lie— the town that one means when one says "small town." Homes should border the bank, small lawns, sloping to lilacs and willows. The current would be lazy and preoccupied, with leisure for eddies, and daily it would bear old dried trees, dislodged from the upstream rocks before the first energy of the water had dissolved into meditation. On the opposite shore would be a feathery second growth of maples and hickory-trees, looking as if they must shelter white temples, but really only covering the Bridge farm chicken coops. Beyond would be hills, neatly buttonhole-stitched against a flat horizon, usually gray, sometimes violet, and on occasion ripe pink and yellow, like a cut peach.

On such a scene our back doors and windows look out, as folk occupying box seats. All the older houses have kitchens at the back, with wash-boilers and clothes-reels and wood-piles; but the newer houses have verandas, green shuttered; and "landscape" windows, scrim curtained, as becomes a home which has just discovered that the back door should be the front. The newest houses have a sun parlor, as if they had always had a "view" and had known it. Only we are particular about terms. For lately a woman from the East, a visitor in the town, paused before a "landscape window" and cried: "Oh what a beautiful vista!" And we told it to one another for days. "Vista!"

All we who live on the river sympathize with those who live remote from it. But many of these others once sympathized with us—("That freezing south wind sweeping across on you. Back street, anyway. Not much of any travel on it.") And if we pointed out that we liked the occasional launches, plying our non-navigable stream, their alert exhausts, their faded colors, and the ancient row-boats which put off at dusk to stretch unlawful nets near the sand-bar; they said: "Well, you always do make the best of things, anyway." But of late, or since we ride in cars, we all know what a "view" is, and now they say: "You were lucky to have a lot here on the river. How did you come to do that?" And we say that it just happened.

The streets stretch away from us in three directions, and they are bordered by trees. We know that it was Judge Guppey and Mr. Turner who urged upon the town these trees, and that in the common council of those days there was a terrible battle before the planting was done. A woman of seventy, whose home is under those ancient elms, recently rocked on her little porch and observed that her husband was in the common council which voted in the trees. "You must be very proud of that," her visitor said, and she answered with composure and a face unchanging: "Yes. Yes, I am . . . My husband opposed it at the time . . ."

Portage, Wisconsin. It seems strange that the majority of the people in the United States have never heard of it. Here it is, with its memories, its traditions, and its settings, and not even the people who pass by on its seventeen through trains daily ever note its name. There is about this circumstance something as piercing as in the look of the visiting-card of a stranger, now dead; or of a nameless photograph on the floor of the attic; or in Milton's line, "The pilot of some small night-foundered skiff."

But we have our revenges. For one midnight I stood at the station and thrilled to see roll on to our tracks a long, sealed train of Pullmans, in whose windows were cards, bearing the two magic words:

Ballet Russe.

For me all Broadway and the metropolitan stage came burning to the West. Those fairy feet so close to our brick platform. . . . And while I looked and marveled, as engines were being changed, one of the station men came by and said: "Some theatrical troupe or other." . . .

The word "mother" has a correspondence in nature, beyond the individual and beyond the possessive. This word appears to signify some spiritual condition which is to the macrocosm what mother is to the human atom. Maternity is less a relationship than an extra-physical force, to which shocking violence has been done by children—through sentimentality, and by mothers—through monarchy.

In this wise it is that, to one born and bred there, a town may be less a place than a force, less a force than a fragrance. Particularly is this true of a small town, as one can be more moved by a puppy of one's own than by anybody else's lion. And the two words "Portage, Wisconsin" have become for me mesmerized, as have certain words of power in which orientals and others find potency, words which through immemorial repetition by the devout have become charged. So these two words, having been written down by me thousands of times, are for me charged words, and do something which the words "Vienna," "Paris," "Pasadena," and "Calcutta" cannot accomplish; for such words I have not entered upon, nor have they created in me their current.

There is more to this condition than we suppose. May it not be that one born and bred in a town, and rooted there by ties, by houses in which one has lived, by childhood, by first school, and by a grave—may it not be that such an one does actually see that town heightened, drawn through into deeper perception, adjusted to contacts not only of the eye and the memory, but of other and far more sensitive cells and powers?

I have looked out on the Wisconsin River

flowing at the foot of our lawn, at the Caledonia hills carving the sky-line, and have wondered if these are as beautiful as I believe them to be, and how a stranger would regard these. And now I wonder whether there is here involved a consideration not of emotion, not of the group soul—but rather of a new physics intimating that love-association does actually unveil properties and perhaps surfaces unknown to the sense of the casual passer-by.

GOOD-BYE WISCONSIN

GLENWAY WESCOTT

In 1924, in his twenty-third year, Glenway Wescott said good-bye to Wisconsin, leaving for southern France where he found a life congenial to his tastes and temperament. His early fiction, The Grandmothers *(1927) and* Good-Bye Wisconsin *(1928), gives an expatriate's view of the Midwest. "How much sweeter to come and go than to stay; that by way of judgment on Wisconsin." But his rejection is mixed with regret. In this account of a temporary homecoming we see a mind moving between Wisconsin and Europe in the winter dusk. It is a muted, half-homesick recollection of things past.*

HOMEWARD bound at last, north from Milwaukee on Christmas Eve. The red-towered station looks very German. But the stern, tattered, tall twilight is American; little by little it will change the German faces; and all that in the near future we can hope for, or fear, is resemblance. There used to be a saintly Scotchwoman in the waiting room to keep country girls from getting into trouble. In the train-shed the crowd surges against a high picket fence, sways in one piece like a boxcarful of cattle: a mixed population, returning to maternal arms, infant arms, arms in love. As the train moves north a blizzard comes south.

My life of the rest of the year being left behind, being buried beneath new impressions, trampled underfoot by resurrected ones, passing through and out of my head, bit by bit . . . The stiff carnations of the Mediterranean are in bloom. Never live in Paris: everyone there has done some harm to everyone else; the heart must be kept in fashion, there was the influence of Henry James, so it is no longer elegant to quarrel; they go on dining together, a malicious intimacy with a lump in its throat. In mid-Atlantic, a short rainbow alongside of the ship with both feet in the sea. Never live in New York either: a town in which "it is as essential to wear one's heart on one's sleeve as one's tongue in one's cheek." New York is halfway between the south of France and Wisconsin, always halfway between any two such places; that is its importance . . .

The train jerks, because the cars are of steel, I suppose. Oranges and green plush. The heat of a Turkish bath into which, through opening doors, through double windowpanes, the awful wind penetrates; nature and a comfort-loving race between them have made this the worst climate in the world. Somewhere up ahead everyone's Christmas tree, squat and dazzling.

A wild-looking youngster asks if anyone has seen his wife and baby. An old man watches over a girl as lovely as a film star. She wears in her hat a tied ostrich plume which looks as if long tresses of hair had grown on a stem; no other woman in the car is unfashionably dressed. She is a half-wit, and keeps eating sandwiches with the impressive ferocity of a monkey, clutching them with both hands. Here and there, students on their way home from college. Middle-class young men in France are less fine physically. Heads almost uniformly well-proportioned; the relaxed look that experts in dissimulation have when they are alone. Either they are blush-pink or they have that translucent dead-leaf skin, without yellowness, without whiteness, which seems peculiar to America and is said to be increasingly common, a result of American air, of the way of life and the climate. The mad girl has it, too.

Throbbing on the rails, the train begins running downhill, which means, I remember from childhood, that we have passed a town called Marblehead. That name and the mature schoolboys make me think of Greece—many-headed, marble-headed. France is its heir, eldest son in this generation of nations. I am jealous of every national glory. Not that I expect my country to become a poets' colony, a sculptors', architects', and moralists' colony. There were all sorts of Greeks . . . Heads of all complexions, even in the sculptured stone: ruddy and ivory and the very vivid brown—as if red rose-leaves had been tanned and made into a leather—which some of my friends, visiting the Mediterranean beaches, find objectionable and others do their best to acquire.

I have to change trains. The snowstorm is over, or we have passed through it. I share a corner of what is called a milk-train with a lot of baggage and two young workmen. One seems unhealthy: large hands bright with chemicals. The other has that look of sheepish melancholy which I frivolously associate with socialism. They engage in conversation about their jobs and each other's relatives which they know by name; their fathers are farmers; the yellow-handed one works in a tannery in Fond du Lac, the other is an iron-worker in a Milwaukee foundry. They speak a mixture of several kinds of English—Swedish, German, Polish, Irish—immigrants' children of the second generation having inherited accents from all their parents at once, all the accents. They keep looking at my cigarette-lighter, my gloves, my tight black cap, a Basque *beret*.

The tanner: "Where d'ya work in Mulwauky?"

"I came up from Chicago."

"Yuh got some folks here?"

"My father and mother live in Claron. He was a farmer until he moved to town."

A pause, without embarrassment on their parts. The ironworker: "Wha' d'ya work at'n Chicago?"

"I don't work in Chicago. I've been in New York." I see myself retreating right round the world . . .

So I offer them cigarettes; they look at the mark; and out of timidity I open Thomas Mann's *Hochstapler Krull*. If this were Europe I could have told them that I was a writer, which would have been the end of it. One day years ago when I was wearing a rather pretentious black cape, I tipped a porter in a Munich railway station. "Thank you kindly, Herr poet," he said.

The train is making up for lost time. I know, I say to myself, what the country is like beyond the syncopated noise, the shaken light-bulbs, outside the sooty windows in the dark. The state with a beautiful name—glaciers once having made of it their pasture—is an anthology, a collection of all the kinds of landscape, perfect examples side by side. Ranges of hills strung from the great lake to the Mississippi River in long, lustrous necklaces, one above another from the northern throat of the state until well below its waist. Peacock lakes of bronze weeds and vivid water, with steep shores; four or five of them to be seen at a time from certain hilltops. Fertility and wilderness in rapid succession along powdery highways: classic meadows where the cattle seem to walk and eat in their sleep, sandy slopes full of foxes, ledges where there are still rattlesnakes. Sad forests full of springs; the springs have a feverish breath. There are metallic plants which burn your hands if you touch them. All summer the horizon trembles, hypnotically flickering over the full grain, the taffeta corn, and the labor in them of dark, overclothed men, singing women, awe-stricken children. These say nothing; their motionless jaws give an account of their self-pity, dignity, and endurance. Sheet-lightning at night, and they sleep in the grass, in hammocks, on folded blankets on the floor—the beds are too hot. They get up and work with strange, ardent motions and the obstinacies of ghosts in the heat; there is wealth in it. In the sky mocking marble palaces, an Eldorado of sterile cloud. Not sterile—for down fall large black-and-blue rains, tied with electric ribbons; they never seem to be doing much good, but the crops are saved . . .

Thus, neglecting the masterpiece which I keep in my hand to prevent the workmen from asking questions but not uninfluenced by its mood of shameless, summery confession —in which the true nature of Herr Krull is almost obscured by the bright light shed on every detail—I think of the land outside the train window as one of perpetual summer. Then the door swings open; the blown cold pounds on the nape of my neck; in spite of the coal-gas, the tobacco, the oranges, the opium-sweetness of warm bodies, I imagine that I can smell snow.

For in reality this is a sort of winter resort for storms from the North Pole; now all the half-tropic vegetation, the flesh and the fruitfulness, stripped and lying quite still, are theirs. You seem to be on a lofty plateau, and you can see with your own eyes that the world is convex. The villages are almost as lonely as the farms. It is like Russia with vodka prohibited and no stationary peasantry—strictly speaking, with none at all. The soul hibernates in the cold body; your feet ache for months at a time. I remember, at church, in my childhood, prayers that were visible, white and tenuous, and moustaches covered with frost through which the slow, discouraging hymn made its way. A good many men get drunk a great deal of the time in spite of everything. Once a month the new moon sets out like the crooked knife of a fairy story in search of a heart to bury itself in. This is the dying-season for old men and women. When the moon is full, over the crusted snow, men go rabbit-hunting . . .

The train stops at a junction and makes its presence known; with another lowing, female sound, another train replies. I have a vague remembrance of that junction, those two deep voices. I ask, and am told that we are coming into Claron.

Out of the dark run forward my young father, my small mother. Across the town in an automobile, no distance at all; home, the new house, a home in a town. On the small square of property close-pressed by other houses, collies with no more herds to tend; the color of pheasants with ruffled plumage, under the arc-light, against the snow-banks. Up the icy steps; a tumult in the doorway; energetic kisses which smell good, smell of health and warm wool; my brother, my sisters. Their courtesy a little affected but with burning eyes, breaking down repeatedly in the stress of the exuberance which they have in common, the stress of joy or disappointment, pride, contention, yearning. This is the wild fountain of friendliness. Sometimes it occurs to me that I ought to play the Ancient Mariner, but I am evidently always to be wedding guest.

There are chocolates and fruit; I remember the annual basket of grapes which my father used to bring from the state fair when we were children, a wooden basket with a wire handle and pale, elongated California grapes—each of us ate his share grape by grape, there were so few. The floors are waxed; carpets like everyone else's have taken the place of the rag rugs accumulated by my grandmothers. That fruitful, severe farmhouse of childhood, it seemed to have an immortal soul and now seems to have borne a physical resemblance to my mother—a house so cold at this time of the year that every vessel which held water had a lip of crystal. Here there is a bathroom. Progress, I think sleepily. The king is dead, long live the king; deprivation is dead . . . I rejoice, but regret some of his poetry. Fortunately, progress has not gone far enough here to deprive me of a cold bed, of the drug of zero weather, the barbaric luxury of frost, in my nostrils all night long.

Early in the morning I go out to look at the town. It is like any other not too new or too large or too small in the state—or perhaps in any state not too far east or west. Main Street down the middle—beef-red brick and faded clapboards; it is lamentably impressive. The new banks, I must admit, are of lighter brick and adorned with brief, reasonably Roman pillars. The churches have an atheistic look and must have been very cheap to build. Dry-goods stores remarkably full of luxury; drug stores which sell everything (at a glance everything seems made of paper) the most expensive cameras and the cheapest books; a windowful of superb apples. Apples are wealth in midwinter; in fact it is all wealth, though it resembles the meanest poverty. Branching off Main Street at right angles, up small hills and down gentle slopes, the other streets: short but spacious avenues, noble trees over the snowbanks, lawns under them. Actually it is one lawn, there being no hedges or fences or walls (during the burning summers, no privacy). The houses are variations on one house, a sort of palatial cottage; principally wood, you can see into most of them and through some, and they do not seem to rest solidly on the ground; the difference between them and a tent is precisely that between moving every generation and moving every month . . .

Where the houses leave off lugubrious poetry begins: never-painted landscape, chiaroscuro of twigs and snow. Framed by a puerile architecture, a patchwork of advertisements, a frieze of restless and almost beautiful men and women. The country, there it lies, a fitful and mysterious source—nothing more. The source of the sunrises, the bad weather, and the food, and of certain books already a little out of date. For the country, in the old sense of the word, has ceased to exist. Wisconsin farmers are no longer rustics; they have become provincials. The former ardent, hungry, tongue-tied life with its mingling of Greek tragedy and idyll has come to an end. Labor for the men, labor-pains for the women, elementary passions like gusts of storm moving unembarrassed in empty hearts, strong minds empty from birth until death of everything but the images of fowls in the rain, lonesome barns in the yellow sunshine—all over and done with. Now, by telephones, the radio, and automobiles, the farms have been turned into a sort of spacious, uncrystallized suburb around towns like Claron; and between the town and the suburbs the contact is close. Now hired men, for example, have the privilege of being in love with Miss Garbo, whose troubling face I find on a bright poster.

Here are the humble-looking churches, half of whose faithful are farmers; many variations, both in appearance and in doctrine, on one church. I attend an elaborate pageant of the Nativity. All of the congregation's tapestries and many of its best bed-sheets; rented crowns and curtains, silly angels painted on a backdrop of sky; footlights and spotlights worthy of an assembly of radio fans. A gaunt little girl in gilt and muslin represents the Angel of History; she plays theatrically, has a very modern body and a cropped honey-colored head, and even her solemnity suggests profane shows in the East. Other all too Western muses. An adolescent chokes on his words, as indeed the original shepherd probably did. One of the Wise Men has forgotten to take off his horn-rimmed spectacles. The Babe in the manger is electricity, which is moving and seems true. It is all moving and true. But as the collection-boxes on long handles are passed, rather too plaintive an appeal for generosity is made; one would suppose that there were niggardly church-goers. And a kindly deacon improvises this prayer:

"Dear Father, we thank Thee that we live in a day when men are given to enjoy many things that they never had before. Especially women—I think women's lives have been made easy and lifted out of the darkness, thanks to the right interpretation of Thy Scriptures. And dear Father, we hear at present a great deal of talk against Thy church. It has its limitations, we know, but it has done a wonderful work for mankind. And what have they found to take its place? Until another institution comes along which can do that work better, let us be faithful to it. Bless us in the name of the Son who, as we have seen, was born unto us this day. Amen." I realize that it is not blasphemous, for it is only rhetorically addressed to God, not meant to be heard in heaven but overheard in this town. Thus the religion of Calvin, holding its own in society at all costs, is helping itself cease to be a religion at all, the little churches becoming—oh, let us say, clubs. . . .

And what of sensual pleasure (call it love) in this town? Out of sight, fraught with dangers up to a certain age, subject to ridicule or worse thereafter. Boyish passion, that of Daphnis and Cherubino alike—its joys are restricted to Latin countries; its pains flourish anywhere. Women who live alone, in these

Above: Congestion at Sault Ste. Marie, 1900. Below: Sight-seeing car in Cleveland, 1910. Courtesy Ohio Historical Society   Below, right: A ride, c. 1909. Courtesy Ohio Historical Society

translucent houses, are easily chaperoned by their neighbors; most people never hear of adultery except when there is a murder trial; there are only one or two charmless loose women, who fulfil their destiny, furthermore, under a cloud of specific suspicions; which leaves, for the vicious or the exasperated, girls of the poorest families, hired girls: obscure nights in motor-cars which are like rudderless boats, a handful of touches, farewells charged with resentment, finally an unpleasant reputation among other men. Americans like what is public, feel cheated by what some other races especially enjoy, the illicit; they dislike obliging their relatives to defend them; they dislike danger. To the young man with ambition enough to matter, premature marriage is the worst of dangers. It means earning a living by whatever is at hand; beggars of jobs cannot experiment, ought not to be far-sighted or fastidious. It means Wisconsin forever, with never any wholesome dissipation of a thousand chimeras—travels, ambitions, curiosities. That illusion should come to grief is the first step toward contentment; early marriage keeps as many hopes as are left intact, embalms them in a safe irreality, and keeps the young husband too young at heart. And almost any girl may spring, under the feet of a beau who suits her, any sort of man-trap. In general the young men mind this danger as well as the others. But fright is a strong stimulant; after dark there is a vibrant atmosphere of pleasure—worried, adored, and left to its meager resources. Fever takes the wheel of the autos. In the round of sufficient amusements, a more or less alert suspicion of their sweethearts and themselves; they must keep their self-control, must keep their bodies safe and sound, must keep from proposing. Under the soft maples, nervous teasing and erotic songs whistled and shrubs jetting their moist flowers and a lump in every throat. Syncopated bewilderment on the dance-floors; the music melts their hands and knees, but nothing is any easier. In the motion-picture theaters, thanks to the disastrous and vacillating ease in Miss Garbo's face—more fever.

A modest theater, shaped like a garage; but it is the imagination's chapel in this town, the small temple dedicated to licentiousness, aspiration, ideals. On the brick wall, on easels on the sidewalk, samples of what it has to offer: the abnormally large and liquid eyes of a beauty; the ridicule and pity of ill-fitting shoes; distant crystal and iron seas; foreign luxury, fashion shows, garden parties white with diamonds and swans. Every plot is founded on restlessness and good luck; every film is a documentary film, fantastic only in relation to its subject—realistically true to the imaginations to which it is addressed. There they all flock to see, not really a world brought to their door, but themselves in every foreign and domestic disguise; themselves as they might be, convincingly photographed where they are not—the variable bodies of other Narcissuses on other mesmerizing streams. And in the dark and pleasant silence, unreasonable music smooths their troubled foreheads. What might be a stimulant is another narcotic. Their restlessness is merely played upon, to pass the time—played upon and just enough, from day to day, appeased. Meanwhile the time does pass. . . .

How much sweeter to come and go than to stay; that by way of judgment upon Wisconsin. The dark red railway station reminds me of Germany, the dim country into which the polished tracks lead away, of Russia—that is, of a place I have never seen. The orchards on the horizon look like black crêpe; there is a little lacquer sunset; useless and uselessly somber things, vainglory of God. Just as a child finds omens all about, I feel glad that I have never written a line for which there is any earthly use. Above the sunset the evening star blazes away superfluously, Mars or Venus in a sky composed of frost—though there is fighting only once a lifetime and, I suppose, less love-making than anywhere else in the world . . .

The train scarcely leaves the dim roofs and yellow windows behind before I feel my imagination beginning to be drawn away elsewhere, to several places irrelevant to each other at once; it is as if half the world were made of magnets. I fight against these charms and suspiciously close Gide's *Les Nourritures Terrestres*, which I had begun to read; my life of the rest of the year will get under way all too soon. Two young women across the aisle try to discover what my book is; theirs is a novel about Helen of Troy. They are workingwomen; I know because I hear them talking about a raise of their wages; but they are as arrogant and delicate as if they were kept. At present the West is a women's world; their bright minds make up its heart. But men's hearts suffer, in 1927, a strangely intellectual ferment . . .

I change trains, and throbbing on the rails the engine climbs up toward the town called Marblehead, which starts the same train of thought as before. It is the Greeks and Romans and the traditions preserved in Europe by the translators of Plutarch and by Montaigne and Goethe which, if one is an American, exasperate the imagination. Traditions of the conduct of life with death in mind . . . Few Americans are reasonable enough even to demand of seventy years their entire sweetness; the fame of too few will outlast, anywhere except in heaven, their mortal bodies. For various reasons we are, in 1927, the dominant nation in the world; there are, nevertheless, in 1927, more Frenchmen than Americans whose lives are to be memorable. (For Lindbergh and Isadora Duncan God be praised . . .) But I believe that American youngsters are equal in force, elasticity, beauty, and other natural gifts to the Greeks. In the fourth university year, let us say; not much longer. Something happens to them; the flower turns out to be seedless. Now all the causes, the mysterious stamens, are undergoing subtle transformations, perhaps for the better, perhaps not. It is a grave situation; and I believe that in the near future descriptive writing about average American destinies must inevitably be that of a reporter, an analyst, a diagnostician.

What may be called honest portrayal of a period of transition, of spiritual circumstances changing for an entire race, requires a fastidious realism, minute notation of events in their exact order, and the special sobriety of doctors or of witnesses at a trial. The more such an author has in common with his characters the better; typical trivialities surpass in significance the noblest feelings; an immediate report is more valuable than reminiscences. The rest is lyricism: the hero's shameless ode

in praise of his own fortune or, even in the great, dim, half-attentive courtyard of the Mississippi Valley, a sort of serenade . . .

For fiction may combine in various proportions poetry and journalism. Poetry dispenses with chronology; it offers object or emotion as an end in itself during one moment which is assumed to be eternal, or under conditions as unfluctuating as those of the golden age; it must have some sort of immutability as a foundation. So I decide that the novelist who is or wishes to be anything of a poet will avoid such problems as, for example, Wisconsin is now likely to suggest; and will try to contribute to the appetites which make themselves felt there rather than to portray the confusion in which they arise. And no judicious novelist, however prosaic, will strive to outdistance life; he will choose problems which only seem insoluble, which in some corner of society, on some small illustrative scale, have been solved. The future of American civilization is a genuine riddle. The riddle of a sphinx with the perfect face of a movie star, with a dead-leaf complexion which is the result of this climate, our heating system, our habits . . .

Over many little bridges the train makes a soft thunder. A piece of moon has come up. In front of it a grove of naked trees, a flat expanse of dreary silver tarnished by weed-tops thrusting through it, a broken-looking house, a town, a living but icy river, rapidly give place to each other; as in the foreground of a writer's attention possible subjects for a book vary and shift before that waxing, waning, one-sided radiance which is his own spirit and about which alone he has no choice.

An English friend of mine once took to visit her father in the country a young American painter of some note. A year or two later he had an exhibition in Paris; she told the aging gentleman about it and asked if he remembered the American. "Ah yes, yes. That was the young man who didn't know where he was born. I thought it very curious."

"Now what made you think that, father? You misunderstood. He was born in the Middle West."

"But that's just it! I asked him, and that

is precisely what he said—all he could tell me."

That, I believe, is a parable. A place which has no fixed boundaries, no particular history; inhabited by no one race; always exhausted by its rich output of food, men, and manufactured articles; loyal to none of its many creeds, prohibitions, fads, hypocrisies; now letting itself be governed, now ungovernable . . . The Middle West is nowhere; an abstract nowhere. However earnestly writers proud of being natives of it may endeavor to give it form and character, it remains out of focus, amorphous, and a mystery.

ARRIVAL IN CHICAGO

FRANK LLOYD WRIGHT

Frank Lloyd Wright was born of Welsh parents at Richland Center, Wisconsin, in 1869. From an uncompleted course of study at the University of Wisconsin he arrived in Chicago, hopeful and penniless, in 1887. As a young draftsman in the raw new city he found himself surrounded by chaos and confusion. But he knew certain things. He loved the prairie as a great simplicity. And he had a vision of a dwelling that would "associate with the ground and become natural to the prairie site." In 1894 he began independent practice at Oak Park, on the edge of Chicago. The rest of his long life is architectural history. Consistent with his first conception of the "prairie house," he became the foremost American exponent of an organic architecture based on the integration of form, function, setting and materials.

The following selection is taken from the 1943 edition of his outspoken Autobiography.

CHICAGO, Wells Street Station: Six o'clock in late spring, 1887. Drizzling. Sputtering white arc-light in the station and in the streets, dazzling and ugly. I had never seen electric lights before.

Crowds. Impersonal. Intent on seeing nothing.

Somehow I didn't like to ask anyone anything. Followed the crowd. Drifted south to the Wells Street Bridge over the Chicago River. The mysterious dark of the river with dim masts, hulks and funnels hung with lights half-smothered in gloom—reflected in black beneath. I stopped to see, holding myself close against the iron rail to avoid the blind, hurrying by.

I wondered where Chicago was—if it was near. Suddenly the clanging of a bell. The crowd began to run. I wondered why: found myself alone and realized why in time to get off, but stayed on as the bridge swung out with me into the channel and a tug, puffing clouds of steam, came pushing along below pulling an enormous iron grain boat, towing it slowly through the gap. Stood there studying the river-sights in the drizzling rain until the bridge followed after and closed to open the street again. Later, I never crossed the river without being charmed by somber beauty.

Wondered where to go for the night. But again if I thought to ask anyone, there was only the brutal, hurrying crowd trying hard not to see.

Drifted south. This must be Chicago now. So cold, black, blue-white and wet. The horrid blue-white glare of arc-lights was over everything. Shivering. Hungry. Went into an eating place near Randolph Street and parted with seventy cents, ten per cent of my entire

State Street, Chicago, 1890. *Courtesy Illinois State Historical Library*

capital. As I ate, I was sure of one thing, never would I go near Uncle Jenkin Lloyd-Jones nor ask his help nor use his name.

Got into the street again to find it colder, raining harder. Drifted south and turned left, shivering now in front of the Chicago Opera House on Washington Street, the flood of hard lights made the unseeing faces of the crowd in the drizzle, livid—ghastly. Under a great canopy that made a shelter from the rain were enormous posters—"Sieba"—Extravaganza by David Henderson, Grand Corps de Ballet. And there the dancers were, life-size almost, out on the sidewalk, holding their color in spite of the glare.

The doors were just open and a dollar let me go in to wait nearly an hour for the show to begin, where it was dry and warm. During that waiting . . . went back to the home by the lake—to see Mother, Jennie and Maginel . . . wondered what they would feel when they knew I had gone for good . . . never to come back? But they were all coming to me in Chicago. There must be clean, quiet "home" places in Chicago. Near the lake, maybe. I wondered if they were anxious about me, hardly realizing I wouldn't be missed until tomorrow night. Saw Mother's sad eyes and pale face as she sat quietly—waiting. She seemed always waiting now. A pang of homesickness already, but the orchestra filed out from under the stage.

Tuning up began, always exciting. Then the florid overture. I knew it wasn't good music—good music was not so sentimental (my father's term of contempt)—but I was glad to hear it. The Henderson Extravaganzas in those days were not unduly extravagant. This one took the roof off an unsophisticated mind.

Went out after all was over, drifting with the crowd to Wabash Avenue. Cottage Grove Avenue cable cars were running there. My first sight of the cable car. So, curious, I got on the grip-car beside the gripman and tried to figure it all out, going south in the process until the car stopped, and "All out!" That car was going to the barn.

Got on one coming out headed north now. Not sleepy nor tired. Half-resentful because compelled to read the signs pressing on the eyes everywhere. They claimed your eyes for this, that, and everything beside. They lined the car above the windows. They lined the way, pushing, crowding and playing all manner of tricks on the victim's eye. Tried to stop looking at them. Unfairly compelled to look again. In self-defense kept on reading until reading got to be torture.

There were glaring signs on the glass shop-fronts against the lights inside, sharp signs in the glare of the sputtering arc-lamps outside. Hurrah signs. Stop signs. Come-on-in signs. Hello signs set out before the blazing windows on the sidewalks. Flat fences lettered both sides, man-high, were hanging out across above the sidewalks and lit by electric lamps. Coming from extravaganza, here was the beginning of phantasmagoria.

Supersensitive eyes were fixed by harsh dissonance and recovered themselves: reasoned and fought for freedom. Compelled again—until the procession of saloons, food shops, barber shops, eating houses, saloons, restaurants, groceries, laundries—and saloons, saloons, tailors, dry goods, candy shops, bakeries and saloons became chaos in a wilderness of Italian, German, Irish, Polack, Greek, English, Swedish, French, Chinese and Spanish names in letters that began to come off and get about, interlace and stick and climb and swing again.

Demoralization of the eye began: names obliterating everything. Names and what they would do for you or with you or to you for your money. Shutting your eyes didn't end it, for then you heard them louder than you saw them. They would begin to mix with absurd effect and you need take nothing to get the effect of another extravaganza. Letters this time. Another ballet, of A. B. C. D. E. F. G., L. M. N. O. P., X. Y and Z., the premiere-danseuse intervening in fantastic dances.

Got to bed at the Brigg's House north on Randolph Street, wrapped a sheet around myself—it seemed awfully like a winding sheet as I caught sight of it in the mirror—and slept. A human item—insignificant but big with interior faith and a great hope. In what? I could not have told you. Asleep in Chicago. And Chicago murderously actual.

Next day I began on Chicago.

My hand in my pocket after breakfast, I could feel sure of three silver dollars and a dime. Took the city directory and made a list of architects, choosing names I had heard in Conover's office or names that sounded interesting. All only names to me and missed the names of all names important to me. The name of the architect of my uncle's new church, "All Souls," I knew by heart—J. L. Silsbee, Lakeside Building, Clark Street, Chicago. But I wasn't going there. Tramped through street after street now seeing Chicago above the sign-belt.

And where was the architecture of the great city—the "Eternal City of the West"? Where was it? Hiding behind these shameless signs? A vacant block would come by. Then the enormous billboards planted there stood up grandly, had it all their own way, obliterating everything in nothing. That was better. Chicago! Immense gridiron of noisy streets. Dirty . . . Heavy traffic crossing both ways at once, managing somehow: torrential noise.

A stupid thing, that gridiron: cross-currents of horses, trucks, street cars grinding on hard rails mingling with streams of human beings in seeming confusion and clamor. But habit was in the movement making it expert, and so safe enough. Dreary—dim—smoked. Smoked dim and smoking. A wide, desolate, vacant strip ran along the waterfront over which the Illinois Central trains puffed, shrieked and ground incessantly, cutting the city off from the lake.

Terrible, this grinding and piling up of blind forces. If there was logic here who could grasp it?

To stop and think in the midst of this would be to give way to terror. The gray, soiled river with its mist of steam and smoke, was the only beauty. And that smelled to heaven.

PRAIRIE TOWN

CARL SANDBURG

Galesburg, Illinois, was settled in 1837 by a high-minded company from New York State who planned to found a theological seminary. Two colleges, Knox and Lombard, were established there, and the town also became an important railroad center. It was the scene of a famous Lincoln-Douglas debate in 1859.

After the Civil War Galesburg attracted a steady stream of immigration. August Sandburg, a Swedish immigrant, worked on a railroad construction gang and in the railroad blacksmith shops. His son became a leading American poet and a prize-winning biographer of Abraham Lincoln. The following sketch of his native town is taken from Carl Sandburg's autobiography, Always the Young Strangers.

THIS small town of Galesburg, as I look back at it, was a piece of the American Republic. Breeds and blood strains that figure in history were there for me, as a boy, to see and hear in their faces and their ways of talking and acting. People from New England and their children owned much of the town and set the main tone in politics, churches, schools and colleges. I heard Yankee old-timers and how they talked "through the nose." Up from Kentucky and Tennessee had come English and Scotch-Irish breeds who were mostly Democrats in favor of the saloons and farther back in favor of Stephen A. Douglas as against Lincoln.

Many Swedes had become voters and a power in politics and business. Their Republican leader for years was a banker, Moses O. Williamson, known as "Mose." He was on the Illinois State Committee of the Republican Party, and if you wanted a state or Federal office the word was "See Mose."

And the Irish? I had Irish schoolteachers and playmates. I would stand still in the Q. yards to watch the switchman, Tom Carmody,

walk. He was a prize-winning dancer and his way of walking had a music to it. Tom Beckum, the happiest drinking man in town, I can never forget, nor Mark Connelly, a Q. shopman. At parties, sociables, picnics, political rallies, among the shopmen, or in a cigar store, Mark, the young Irishman, would give his Swedish dialect stories. He was as good as any Swede at imitating a green Swede. One of his stories that us kids learned ran:

"Goliatt vas a grate beeg fallow, femteen [fifteen] feet high. Dawveed vas a leetle fallow, he hawrdly come up to de knees of Goliatt. Goliatt, he say, 'Dawveed, I goin' to keel you an' eat you.' An' Dawveed, he anta been scared. Dawveed he go to de crick an' he peek heem five stones. An' he put a stone in hees sleeng an' he trow it at Goliatt. An' vat you tink? De stone he trow hit Goliatt right in de stomach an' knock all his brains out!"

The Irish liked it. The Swedes liked it. The "pure Americans" laughed till their ribs shook. Frank Pollock, of one of the native-born American families, at parties and concerts gave imitations of green Swedes. Like Connelly he was a born comedian, though he ended later as a grand-opera tenor. I didn't notice Swedes being sore about these imitations of green Swedes. Along with other young Swedes I did some imitating myself. I had been among the Irish enough so that I picked up their brogue. At times in later years I would drop into the Irish brogue not knowing I was talking it, and I have been taken for one of the Irish. Their brogue and the Swedish accent are the only ones I can put on and be taken for the real thing.

There were names us kids liked to use. We liked them mostly because they sounded funny. A Jew was a "sheeny." The Irish were "micks." A Swede was a "snorky." A Yankee was a "skinflint." The Germans were "Dutch." The Italians were "dagoes." A Negro was a "nigger" or a "smoke." I heard Irish boys say of themselves, "Us micks" and Negroes speak of themselves as "Us niggers," and one Swede boy to another, "Hello, snork." When you hated and wanted to be mean you said, "goddam mick" or "goddam nigger." We believed that the "sheenies" on the quiet might be calling us "snorkies" and calling the Irish "micks" and that would be all right with us because that's what we were. But if they called us "goddam snorkies" or "goddam micks" then we would look for bricks to heave.

Two German Jews, Sol Frolich and Henry Gardt, owned the Union Hotel and bar, and the biggest saloon in that part of Illinois, the White Elephant on Boone's Avenue, next door south of Main Street. Gardt was the quiet one of the two, a smallish man with a black mustache. People said he did the thinking and his partner the talking. Sol Frolich was tall and bald, one of the breeziest laughing men in town. He could mix in any bunch of men with his thick and comical German accent and his sense of fun and fellowship, and they would listen to him. Being in the liquor business, Frolich and Gardt were up to their ears in politics but their foot tracks were not easy to find. Somehow I can't remember any scandal that was raised about them unless it would be that the Reverend W. H. Geistweit mentioned from his pulpit that the White Elephant had been open after midnight. They were strict about not selling liquor to minors and

no women allowed at the bars and no gambling in their places. Many people had a way of laughing when they mentioned "Frolich and Gardt," maybe with a wink of the eye, as though they might more than once have stepped up to the most elegant bar in town at the Union Hotel or into the big barroom of the White Elephant that sold more drinks to more men than any other saloon in town. Frolich and Gardt gave Galesburg color and fun.

The Gumbiner pawnshop, the only one in town, what else was there like it? Where else were there so many different watches to look at—gold, silver, and nickel watches, big old-fashioned "turnips" too big for a vest pocket, a Waltham or two pawned by railroad engineers? But we heard an engineer say the Walthams came "from pickpockets a thousand miles away" and "No engineer would hock his Waltham unless he was drunk and wanted to get drunker." Here at Gumbiner's we saw gold, silver, and brass watch chains, silk and satin watch fobs, big hunting knives and small penknives, pocketknives we wished we had the money to buy, brass knucks and slung shots you could knock a man senseless with, shotguns and rifles and old squirrel guns, Colt's revolvers and the old-time one-shot pocket pistol. And when it came to fifes, flutes, flageolets, clarinets, ocarinas (here I bought my fifteen-cent ocarina, my "sweet potato"), fiddles, accordions, concertinas, banjoes, and guitars plan and fancy, there was no place like Gumbiner's. Nor was there any auctioneer like the slicker at Gumbiner's. His tongue and throat never went back on him. He seemed to wind himself up and then let go on his spiel and he didn't have to stop to oil himself. We were thankful the Gumbiner Jews had come to Galesburg.

Finest of the Jews, said everybody, was Max J. Mack of the men's clothing firm, Jacobi & Mack. Every year a few days after New Year's their front windows would blaze with red price tags and they would have page spreads in the newspapers about their "Annual Red Tag Sale." You couldn't get away from it. They made you want to buy a new suit of clothes.

Max J. Mack for many years was elected

alderman from his ward. He was regular at city-council meetings, had his head in all the facts and figures of city business, watched every ordinance, and if a deal was crooked or wasteful he would vote against it and tell why without insulting anybody. The plainest people could go to him with a complaint or a question and he would give them his time as if they had a perfect right to it. He had a warm heart for all people, and when he said, "I'm for what's good for the city of Galesburg and its people," he wasn't just one more blab-mouth politician. There came a time when Mart tried for several years to get Max J. Mack nominated for mayor, but the Boss couldn't see it. So a Swede failed at giving Galesburg a Jew for mayor.

Among the Negroes I had friends. Morning after morning at the Q. depot I would see "Tip" Murray with his shoeblacking kit hung by a strap from one shoulder. Passengers getting off trains would hear him, "Shine 'em up —a nickel a shine." Tip and I talked baseball, how the big leagues were doing, and what Galesburg might do in the Three-Eye League (Illinois, Indiana, and Iowa). Tip was lean and wiry and could pitch a good game. I could connect with his outcurve but he nearly always fooled me when he put a drop on it. He had his days, he told me, when nobody wanted a shine, other days when he made a couple of nickels, and circus days, holidays, and "big days," when the score ran up to fifteen or twenty nickels.

While I was in short pants I would meet the King brothers from Pine Street. They were shorter than I and lighter weight, but the older one would shine his eyes at me and say, "You want to fight?" I could see he would like to fight me if I was willing, a "snork" and a "smoke" bloodying each other's noses. He didn't holler it nor make a face at me. He said it kind of soft as if he was listening to hear himself say, "You want to fight?" I told him I wasn't looking for a fight and we went on our ways without another word. I figured that Willy King had been saying to himself, "Am I scared to fight a white boy?" And then to make sure he wasn't scared, he puts it to the first white boy he meets, "You want to fight?"

Often walking along South Street a Negro would come in sight and some boy would be sure to say, "There's Double-headed Bill." He was of medium size and build, had a good face, and an extra-big head. You couldn't say he was a freak of nature. He just happened to have a head that was bigger than most people had though you had to look twice to notice it. You didn't draw back from looking at him like when you saw the double-headed calf at the county fair. It was a well-shaped head he had, good to look at even if it was extra-big. But someone had hung on him the nickname "Double-headed Bill" and us kids thought it smart to be saying it.

"Nigger" Duke lived in the Q. yards and shops. He found warm corners for sleeping in the winter, and anywhere would do for him in summer. His meals came out of leftovers in the dinner buckets of shopmen and the wicker baskets of trainmen and enginemen. His legs were two short stubs. He had many years back gone to sleep in a boxcar in zero weather, and the doctors had to saw off his legs a little below the hips. On the bottoms of these stumps he had leather pads. He took short steps and walked himself where he pleased around the Q. yards. Going to the Seventh Ward school we saw him many times near the machine shop or at the Peoria tracks flag shanty. He was thick-chested, a heavy man with fine straight shoulders, a well-shaped head and face. His teeth were white and even, and when he smiled or broke into a laugh from his black-skin face, it was like promises and flowers. He had a greeting, a smile, or a laugh for everyone he met. I heard him say, "We've all got our jobs and my job is to chase away the blues." His voice was high and clear and words tumbled fast from him.

From the Swedes in the shops he had learned to talk Swedish and liked gabbing with the Swedes. There were Swedes hunted him out in the Q. yards to hear a crippled black man talking like any good Swede. We were told in our school days that Nigger Duke happened to be at the Q. depot once when a train loaded with green Swedes fresh from Sweden came in, headed for Nebraska. Nigger Duke lifted himself to a car platform and walked along the aisles of the cars talking

Swedish and telling the newcomers, "After a while when you have been in this country as long as I have you'll turn black like I am." His Swedish was perfect and his white teeth glistened and his laugh rippled as he told this to Swedes who had never heard a black man speaking Swedish. Some laughed at him. Others looked sober and then gloomy, for they half believed him. And it was told there were women on the train who broke into tears and sobbed.

In later years Mart said that Susan Allen, a Negro woman who did cleaning at his house, claimed it was her husband John Allen who got on the train and had the Swedes worried about turning black. I think something like it must have happened though I believe most of the Swedes on the train took it as a good joke. I could see a certain kind of tough Swede saying, "So we're going to change to black, are we? All right, let it come. It'll be fun watching it happen."

I didn't hear what became of Nigger Duke. I can't forget him and wouldn't try to. He was made to laugh through life, to laugh at life, and to bring others to laughing with him. He was a strong man. There were railroad men who said that when he would be gone from the Q. yards a few days or a week he was away with Negro women who enjoyed him—and this could have been just talk. The railroad men were proud of him and said no other railroad had anything like him. And the Swedes were proud of him because he could talk to them in a language the Americans and the Irish hadn't learned. He could say, "*Hur mår du i dag?*" (How are you today?) like a blessing with promises and flowers.

The Negro voters expected and were given two city jobs. There was always one Negro policeman in uniform. And a Negro drove the police patrol wagon.

One Negro had a bad name in the hobo world. His name was Richardson and he was the night policeman for the Q. in the yards. His club had been bloody many a time from beating the head of a hobo. I talked with hoboes who showed scars on their heads where they said the scalp was broken by Richardson's club. The word for him among the hoboes was "that goddam nigger bull in the Galesburg yards." Why the head men of the Q. railroad kept him on duty year after year I didn't hear. Galesburg was a division point and it could have been there were gangs stealing from the cars. Or there may have been hoboes who had ganged up on Richardson and given him a beating and he was hitting back at any and all hoboes. Anyhow he made a name for himself as a terror to those who tried to ride railroad trains without buying tickets.

I first heard German spoken when I played with Mickey Artz in his front yard on Brooks Street. His mother didn't like the way we had run over her flower garden. What she told him was plenty. It was all in German but he heard it and we went to the street to play catch. She reminded me of Grimm's fairy stories and such sentences as, "Hans' wife became enraged and she threatened to cut his head off."

The Italians came late but they pushed their carts and cried their bananas and oranges over every street in town. Before they came by carloads there were two well-known Italians. Father Costa was the priest at the Corpus Christi Church at Kellogg and South streets near the center of town. He was a short, thin-lipped man, with deep small black eyes. I would come near speaking to him on the street but his little black eyes would fix me and I didn't let out a peep. Father Tonelli had the other Catholic church, St. Patrick's, a mile away, off in the Fifth Ward among the Irish. He was handsome, like picture-book Italians. To him I would say a good-morning and he would smile back a good-morning worth at least a dime on a rainy day.

Frenchy Juneau and his father were the only French I knew. I didn't get to know any Poles, Bohemians, Slovaks, Russians, Hungarians, Spanish, Portuguese, Mexicans, South Americans, or Filipinos. I did stop in to watch our two Chinamen ironing and wrapping laundry two doors south of the fire department on Prairie Street. They wore black blouses. Their heads were shaved, and running down from the crown of the head two or three feet was a braided pigtail of hair. They talked singsong up and down to each other, maybe saying, "He's a funny little brat come in to look at us." Through their window I saw them early mornings and late at night ironing, starching, wrapping bundles, and marking the bundles with Chinese letters in big black crayon. They made me think about the human race and how different some parts of it are from others.

Often in the 1890's I would get to thinking about what a young prairie town Galesburg was—nearly twenty thousand people, and they had all come in fifty years. Before that it was empty rolling prairie. And I would ask: Why did they come? Why couldn't they get along where they had started from? Was Galesburg any different from the many other towns, some bigger and some smaller? Did I know America, the United States, because of what I knew about Galesburg? In Sweden all the people in a town were Swedes, in England they were all English, and in Ireland all Irish. But here in Galesburg we had a few from everywhere and there had even been cases of Swedish Lutherans marrying Irish Catholic girls—and what was to come of it all? It didn't bother me nor keep me awake nights but I couldn't help thinking about it and asking: What is this America I am a part of, where I will soon be a full citizen and a voter? All of us are living under the American flag, the Stars and Stripes—what does it mean? Men have died for it—why? When they say it is a free country, they mean free for what and free for whom, and what is freedom?

I said I would listen and read and ask and maybe I would learn. By guessing and hoping and reaching out I might get a hold on some of the answers. Those questions in those words may not have run through my mind yet they ran in my blood. Dark and tangled they were to run in my blood for many years. To some of the questions I would across the years get only half-answers, mystery answers.

TIN LIZZIE

Into his naturalistic fiction John Dos Passos introduced a number of brief, impressionistic biographies, selected because of their bearing upon modern American life. No single career has had more impact upon twentieth-century America than that of Henry Ford, the Michigan farm boy who put the nation on wheels. The irony of Henry Ford's life, the contradiction between his antiquarianism and his assembly line, is brought out in this compressed biography. It is taken from The Big Money *(1937).*

"MR. FORD *the automobileer,*" the feature-writer wrote in 1900,

"*Mr. Ford the automobileer began by giving his steed three or four sharp jerks with the lever at the righthand side of the seat; that is, he pulled the lever up and down sharply in order, as he said, to mix air with gasoline and drive the charge into the exploding cylinder. . . . Mr. Ford slipped a small electric switch handle and there followed a puff, puff, puff. . . . The puffing of the machine assumed a higher key. She was flying along about eight miles an hour. The ruts in the road were deep, but the machine certainly went with a dreamlike smoothness. There was none of the bumping common even to a streetcar. . . . By this time the boulevard had been reached, and the automobileer, letting a lever fall a little, let her out. Whiz! She picked up speed with infinite rapidity. As she ran on there was a clattering behind, the new noise of the automobile.*

For twenty years or more,
ever since he'd left his father's farm when

TIN LIZZIE   **377**

he was sixteen to get a job in a Detroit machineshop, Henry Ford had been nuts about machinery. First it was watches, then he designed a steamtractor, then he built a horseless carriage with an engine adapted from the Otto gasengine he'd read about in *The World of Science*, then a mechanical buggy with a onecylinder fourcycle motor, that would run forward but not back;

at last, in ninetyeight, he felt he was far enough along to risk throwing up his job with the Detroit Edison Company, where he'd worked his way up from night fireman to chief engineer, to put all his time into working on a new gasoline engine,

(in the late eighties he'd met Edison at a meeting of electriclight employees in Atlantic City. He'd gone up to Edison after Edison had delivered an address and asked him if he thought gasoline was practical as a motor fuel. Edison had said yes. If Edison said it, it was true. Edison was the great admiration of Henry Ford's life);

and in driving his mechanical buggy, sitting there at the lever jauntily dressed in a tightbuttoned jacket and a high collar and a derby hat, back and forth over the level illpaved streets of Detroit,

scaring the big brewery horses and the skinny trotting horses and the sleekrumped pacers with the motor's loud explosions,

looking for men scatterbrained enough to invest money in a factory for building automobiles.

He was the eldest son of an Irish immigrant who during the Civil War had married the daughter of a prosperous Pennsylvania Dutch farmer and settled down to farming near Dearborn in Wayne County, Michigan;

like plenty of other Americans, young Henry grew up hating the endless sogging through the mud about the chores, the hauling and pitching manure, the kerosene lamps to clean, the irk and sweat and solitude of the farm.

He was a slender, active youngster, a good skater, clever with his hands; what he liked was to tend the machinery and let the others do the heavy work. His mother had told him not to drink, smoke, gamble or go into debt, and he never did.

When he was in his early twenties his father tried to get him back from Detroit, where he was working as mechanic and repairman for the Drydock Engine Company that built engines for steamboats, by giving him forty acres of land.

Young Henry built himself an uptodate square white dwellinghouse with a false mansard roof and married and settled down on the farm,

but he let the hired men do the farming;

he bought himself a buzzsaw and rented a stationary engine and cut the timber off the woodlots.

He was a thrifty young man who never drank or smoked or gambled or coveted his neighbor's wife, but he couldn't stand living on the farm.

He moved to Detroit, and in the brick barn behind his house tinkered for years in his spare time with a mechanical buggy that would be light enough to run over the clayey wagonroads of Wayne County, Michigan.

By 1900 he had a practicable car to promote.

He was forty years old before the Ford Motor Company was started and production began to move.

Speed was the first thing the early automobile manufacturers went after. Races advertised the makes of cars.

Henry Ford himself hung up several records at the track at Grosse Pointe and on the ice on Lake St. Clair. In his 999 he did the mile in thirtynine and fourfifths seconds.

But it had always been his custom to hire others to do the heavy work. The speed he was busy with was speed in production, the records were records in efficient output. He hired Barney Oldfield, a stunt bicyclerider

from Salt Lake City, to do the racing for him.

Henry Ford had ideas about other things than the designing of motors, carburetors, magnetos, jigs and fixtures, punches and dies; he had ideas about sales,

that the big money was in economical quantity production, quick turnover, cheap interchangeable easilyreplaced standardized parts;

it wasn't until 1909, after years of arguing with his partners, that Ford put out the first Model T.

Henry Ford was right.

That season he sold more than ten thousand tin lizzies, ten years later he was selling almost a million a year.

In these years the Taylor Plan was stirring up plantmanagers and manufacturers all over the country. Efficiency was the word. The same ingenuity that went into improving the performance of a machine could go into improving the performance of the workmen producing the machine.

In 1913 they established the assemblyline at Ford's. That season the profits were something like twentyfive million dollars, but they had trouble in keeping the men on the job, machinists didn't seem to like it at Ford's.

Henry Ford had ideas about other things than production.

He was the largest automobile manufacturer in the world; he paid high wages; maybe if the steady workers thought they were getting a cut (a very small cut) in the profits, it would give trained men an inducement to stick to their jobs,

wellpaid workers might save enough money to buy a tin lizzie; the first day Ford's announced that cleancut properlymarried American workers who wanted jobs had a chance to make five bucks a day (of course it turned out that there were strings to it; always there were strings to it)

such an enormous crowd waited outside the Highland Park plant

all through the zero January night

that there was a riot when the gates were opened; cops broke heads, jobhunters threw bricks; property, Henry Ford's own property, was destroyed. The company dicks had to turn on the firehose to beat back the crowd.

The American Plan; automotive prosperity seeping down from above; it turned out there were strings to it.
But that five dollars a day
paid to good, clean American workmen
who didn't drink or smoke cigarettes or read or think,
and who didn't commit adultery
and whose wives didn't take in boarders,
made America once more the Yukon of the sweated workers of the world;
made all the tin lizzies and the automotive age, and incidentally,
made Henry Ford the automobileer, the admirer of Edison, the birdlover,
the great American of his time.

But Henry Ford had ideas about other things besides assemblylines and the livinghabits of his employees. He was full of ideas. Instead of going to the city to make his fortune, here was a country boy who'd made his fortune by bringing the city out to the farm. The precepts he'd learned out of McGuffey's Reader, his mother's prejudices and preconceptions, he had preserved clean and unworn as freshprinted bills in the safe in a bank.

He wanted people to know about his ideas, so he bought the *Dearborn Independent* and started a campaign against cigarettesmoking.

When war broke out in Europe, he had ideas about that too. (Suspicion of armymen and soldiering were part of the midwest farm tradition, like thrift, stickativeness. temperance and sharp practice in money matters.) Any intelligent American mechanic could see that if the Europeans hadn't been a lot of ignorant underpaid foreigners who drank, smoked, were loose about women and wasteful in their methods of production, the war could never have happened.

When Rosika Schwimmer broke through the stockade of secretaries and servicemen who surrounded Henry Ford and suggested to him that he could stop the war,
he said sure they'd hire a ship and go over

and get the boys out of the trenches by Christmas.

He hired a steamboat, the *Oscar II*, and filled it up with pacifists and socialworkers,
to go over to explain to the princelings of Europe
that what they were doing was vicious and silly.
It wasn't his fault that Poor Richard's commonsense no longer rules the world and that most of the pacifists were nuts,
goofy with headlines.
When William Jennings Bryan went over to Hoboken to see him off, somebody handed William Jennings Bryan a squirrel in a cage; William Jennings Bryan made a speech with the squirrel under his arm. Henry Ford threw American Beauty roses to the crowd. The band played *I Didn't Raise My Boy to Be a Soldier*. Practical jokers let loose more squirrels. An eloping couple was married by a platoon of ministers in the saloon, and Mr. Zero, the flophouse humanitarian, who reached the dock too late to sail,
dove into the North River and swam after the boat.
The *Oscar II* was described as a floating Chautauqua; Henry Ford said it felt like a middlewestern village, but by the time they reached Christiansand in Norway, the reporters had kidded him so that he had gotten cold feet and gone to bed. The world was too crazy outside of Wayne County, Michigan. Mrs. Ford and the management sent an Episcopal dean after him who brought him home under wraps,
and the pacifists had to speechify without him.

Two years later Ford's was manufacturing munitions, Eagle boats; Henry Ford was planning oneman tanks, and oneman submarines like the one tried out in the Revolutionary War. He announced to the press that he'd turn over his war profits to the government,
but there's no record that he ever did.

One thing he brought back from his trip was the Protocols of the Elders of Zion.

He started a campaign to enlighten the world in the *Dearborn Independent;* the Jews were why the world wasn't like Wayne County, Michigan, in the old horse and buggy days;

the Jews had started the war, Bolshevism, Darwinism, Marxism, Nietzsche, short skirts and lipstick. They were behind Wall Street and the international bankers, and the white-slave traffic and the movies and the Supreme Court and ragtime and the illegal liquor business.

Henry Ford denounced the Jews and ran for senator and sued the *Chicago Tribune* for libel,

and was the laughingstock of the kept metropolitan press;

but when the metropolitan bankers tried to horn in on his business

he thoroughly outsmarted them.

In 1918 he had borrowed on notes to buy out his minority stockholders for the picayune sum of seventyfive million dollars.

In February, 1920, he needed cash to pay off some of these notes that were coming due. A banker is supposed to have called on him and offered him every facility if the bankers' representative could be made a member of the board of directors. Henry Ford handed the banker his hat,

and went about raising the money in his own way:

he shipped every car and part he had in his plant to his dealers and demanded immediate cash payment. Let the other fellow do the borrowing had always been a cardinal principle. He shut down production and canceled all orders from the supplyfirms. Many dealers were ruined, many supplyfirms failed, but when he reopened his plant,

he owned it absolutely,

the way a man owns an unmortgaged farm with the taxes paid up.

In 1922 there started the Ford boom for President (high wages, waterpower, industry scattered to the small towns) that was skilfully pricked behind the scenes

by another crackerbarrel philosopher, Calvin Coolidge;

but in 1922 Henry Ford sold one million three hundred and thirtytwo thousand two hundred and nine tin lizzies; he was the richest man in the world.

Good roads had followed the narrow ruts made in the mud by the Model T. The great automotive boom was on. At Ford's production was improving all the time; less waste, more spotters, strawbosses, stoolpigeons (fifteen minutes for lunch, three minutes to go to the toilet, the Taylorized speedup everywhere, reach under, adjust washer, screw down bolt, shove in cotterpin, reachunder, adjustwasher, screwdown bolt, reachunderadjustscrewdownreachunderadjust until every ounce of life was sucked off into production and at night the workmen went home grey shaking husks).

Ford owned every detail of the process from the ore in the hills until the car rolled off the end of the assemblyline under its own power, the plants were rationalized to the last tenthousandth of an inch as measured by the Johansen scale;

in 1926 the production cycle was reduced to eightyone hours from the ore in the mine to the finished salable car proceeding under its own power,

but the Model T was obsolete.

New Era prosperity and the American Plan

(there were strings to it, always there were strings to it)

had killed Tin Lizzie.

Ford's was just one of many automobile plants.

When the stockmarket bubble burst,

Mr. Ford the crackerbarrel philosopher said jubilantly,

"I told you so.

Serves you right for gambling and getting in debt.

The country is sound."

But when the country on cracked shoes, in frayed trousers, belts tightened over hollow bellies,

idle hands cracked and chapped with the cold of that coldest March day of 1932,

started marching from Detroit to Dearborn, asking for work and the American Plan, all they could think of at Ford's was machine-guns.

The country was sound, but they mowed the marchers down.

They shot four of them dead.

Henry Ford as an old man
is a passionate antiquarian,
(lives besieged on his father's farm embedded in an estate of thousands of millionaire acres, protected by an army of servicemen, secretaries, secret agents, dicks under orders of an English exprizefighter,
always afraid of the feet in broken shoes on the roads, afraid the gangs will kidnap his grandchildren,
that a crank will shoot him,
that Change and the idle hands out of work will break through the gates and the high fences;
protected by a private army against
the new America of starved children and hollow bellies and cracked shoes stamping on souplines,
that has swallowed up the old thrifty farmlands

of Wayne County, Michigan,
as if they had never been).
Henry Ford as an old man
is a passionate antiquarian.

He rebuilt his father's farmhouse and put it back exactly in the state he remembered it in as a boy. He built a village of museums for buggies, sleighs, coaches, old plows, water-wheels, obsolete models of motorcars. He scoured the country for fiddlers to play old-fashioned squaredances.

Even old taverns he bought and put back into their original shape, as well as Thomas Edison's early laboratories.

When he bought the Wayside Inn near Sudbury, Massachusetts, he had the new highway where the newmodel cars roared and slithered and hissed oilily past *(the new noise of the automobile)*,

moved away from the door,
put back the old bad road,
so that everything might be
the way it used to be,
in the days of horses and buggies.

WHAT IS OHIO?

HARLAN HATCHER

A century ago it was said that if an Ohio town built a Congregational Church and founded a college, it was certainly of New England origin; if it had a Presbyterian Church and a distillery it was settled by Virginians. The Virginians loved land; they made Ohio a green and fruitful commonwealth. The Yankees were traders, merchants, manufacturers; they filled the state with the throb of industry. And more diversity was coming. Fresh from Europe poured a living stream—the English, German, Irish, Italian, Baltic and Slavic peoples. Young Herman Melville, watching the emigrant ships in Liverpool with their polyglot company bound for the American midlands, said, "You cannot spill a drop of American blood without spilling the blood of the world."

With all this diversity Ohio is not easy to summarize, and instead of offering a definition the following essay asks a question about it. Harlan Hatcher, born in Ohio in 1898, attended the Ohio State University and later became a member of its faculty. In the 1930's he served as director of the Federal Writers Project in Ohio and began the writing of fiction and popular history with a Midwest setting. Since 1951 he has been president of the University of Michigan. This selection is the concluding chapter of The Buckeye Country, *which was published in 1940.*

I HAVE known Ohio people all my life. For the last two decades I have spent a lot of time contemplating us and our ways to see if we do have any characteristics that are singular to Ohio. I am not sure that we do. We have a peculiar way of pronouncing the name of the State. It is not what you might expect if you have heard the riddle we Ohioans learn on our grandfather's knee: "What is round on each end and high in the middle?" It sounds more like two quick Indian grunts—Uh-hia—with a tomahawk stroke on the *i*. It is hard for a New York man to say, and an Englishman simply can't manage it. I once spent an evening in London trying to teach the fine points of the word to one of His Majesty's subjects. But the next day he still rolled it out O-i-o, with full value to the *O's*. Our speech in general is good, standard, countryman's northern with erect *r's* and virile rather than grammatical verb forms. After a hard day of spring plowing in Highland County, a man is all wore out. And his team, flecked white with salty sweat, probably had drinked at the creek on the way home to supper.

You will seldom hear Ohio people mention the State as though it were the crown and jewel of the Republic. We leave that form of local pride to our neighbors across the Ohio and the Great Miami Rivers. I never in my life heard a Buckeye get into his voice that quiver of ecstasy that is second nature to a Corncracker when he mentions his bluegrass and his mountains and his folks. In fact I never heard an Ohioan say much about his State one way or another. Ohio is a stalwart leader in the nation, wealthy, powerful, self-assured, and we proceed quietly from this assumption without troubling to be vocal about it.

That doesn't mean that Ohioans do not love their State. When they leave it for other parts they miss it and take proper steps to keep green their memories. I notice this all through the states to the west where successive waves of Ohio's young generations went to take up land. In Iowa and Nebraska, Ohio men cherish the home place of their grandfathers back in the East, in Ohio, and speak affectionately of their mother State. And in New York, as well as in Chicago, the Ohio Society is the largest and most active of all the state organizations. When I go among these groups I get a new insight into the strong but reticent bond of State patriotism that holds the hearts of Ohioans close to the land between Lake Erie and the Ohio. I remember how oddly pleased we were one autumn when we were living in Massachusetts to find in the door of our car parked at Sudbury a greeting from some fellow citizen on a blank check of a Cadiz bank—Clark Gable's home town. We never saw the greeter, but we knew how he felt about it. And when Fanny Hurst's mother came all the way back from Missouri to her old homestead at Hamilton just to have her baby born to greatness on the sacred soil, she was only doing a little more boldly what genuine Ohioans all do in one way and another.

We have around seven million people in Ohio now. They live in every imaginable kind of community. They are sprawled all over big, amorphous Cleveland, from the new Federal Houses down near the spot on the Cuyahoga where Moses Cleaveland landed, back along the industrial flats, out through the slums, and on and on and on to swanky Shaker Heights where the rich have turned into a landscaped private reflecting basin for their mansions the mill ponds of the ancient communal group of farmers that gave the heights above the lake its pleasant name. They live in homogeneous groups according to nationality in the big cities. They live in the smoke-screened Mahoning Valley, crowded in steel workers' houses in the grimy flats of Youngstown, or scattered in the big castles of Little Steel on great estates on the hills. They swarm in the rubber capital at Akron, or retire into seclusion behind masses of shrubbery on vast lawns on the hills above the Cuyahoga gorge. They live modestly and unobtrusively in the old towns with stable industries like Chillicothe, Zanesville,

Coshocton and Mansfield. They go their quiet ways in semirural towns like Marietta, Hillsboro, and Mechanicsburg. They are congested in the Basin at Cincinnati, exposed to floods in the decaying streets along the river, and at ease on the hills in mansions reached by roads so carefully screened off at the entrance that you can pass by without dreaming that the beshrubbed pilasters are not on somebody's private yard. They live in more little towns and villages than the people of any other state: Somerset and New Lexington on their hills, Hudson and Streetsboro around the green, old canal villages and National Road towns, and at crossroads centers with a filling-station, grain elevator, and a general store. They live in fine country houses on the big highways and in little shacks reached only by a mud lane easement across a neighbor's farm. They live on huge collectivist-sized farms in the fat valleys, and on submarginal and even abandoned lands in the hilly southeast. And the one thing typically Ohio about all this is its extremity and diversity.

In fact the variety surpasses the belief of our citizens who have not poked around in the quiet corners of our State. The typical Ohio towns are, of course, commonplace knowledge. But colorful cities like Cincinnati have exhilarating little communities tucked away in the hollows that back up from the Basin. And scattered around over the State are the most surprising and unexpected oddities. In western Ohio you come upon villages like New Bremen and Minster—German settlements gathered around a cathedral whose spires are thrust up starkly above the flat plain and visible for miles as you drive past the thrifty farms each with a mailbox bearing good, mouthfilling German names. If you stop at the local eating place and dance hall you may be refreshed with beer, gooseliver, and pumpernickel all made in the village. There are also still a few French villages and cemeteries over there with French names fading above the abandoned harness shops, and clock-maker shops, carved on the stones, and still bright on the rural mailboxes. These communities seem at first sight as alien to the Ohio plains as those Connecticut fishing villages set down in the Western Reserve.

In contrast to these spick-and-span communities are the strange little pockets in the hill regions to the south completely unknown to most Ohioans. They lie up grass-grown dirt roads that look like ancient Indian trails where they are visited only by the census taker and the sheriff if at all. Here on the edge of the big state forests, screened by woods and underbrush, they eke out an existence by poaching on these forbidden preserves for small game, by cooking up astonishing pot mixtures, including savory morsels of rattlesnakes (don't be incredulous; you may buy canned rattlesnake now at fashionable grocery stores), by raising thin patches of corn and hogs, by making moonshine and weaving beautiful baskets from strips of white-oak bark.

In the Ross, Pike, Highland County region the people are a picturesque mingling of Shawnee Indians, whose ancestors escaped the reservations and took refuge here; of Negroes whose forefathers fled from slavery across the Ohio to these isolated hollows; and of poor whites, many with jail records, who have found refuge in the hills. They have all the individuality common to such groups. The copper-colored ones wear bandannas on their heads; many of them in the winter wrap their legs in coffee sacks to keep off the cold. Imbecility and witchcraft are common. And in a cemetery there, a writing friend of mine, who is doing a novel about this region, saw the grave of a man beside the grave of his amputated leg which he had mournfully buried in a pine box many years before.

We call the attractive section north of Granville the Welsh Hills because the Welsh followed the New Englanders there and thriftily took over the section. The region around Jackson might have had the same name for the same reasons because Welsh communities are thick; they date back to the era of the salt works and the booming charcoal furnaces of a century ago. To this day they keep some of their best customs—including their singing festivals.

And so the communities go, all round the State, if you are interested in searching them out.

As soon as you have crossed from Ohio

over into Pennsylvania and find yourself among those trim fields and meadows on the hills, those homelike stone and brick houses by their enormous red barns with the mystic insignia above the doors or in the gables, or when you cross the Ohio River and find yourself among the tobacco patches, the pastures with their horseponds, the rows of limestone fences, and the strange feel of leisure about the white houses and the Negro quarters; you know at once that these are not Ohio, even if you can't be sure just what in Ohio corresponds to these things. Perhaps it is the urban and national cross-roads character of Ohio that makes it seem less individual than these states.

For Ohio is known among statisticians as the index state of the nation; if you want to know the national average for almost any item like the proportion of doctors to the population (about one to eight hundred) or like savings or insurance or number of automobiles or college graduates—just look at the figures for Ohio and in most cases they will be the same as for the nation at large. Ohioans do more things, more often, in more places than most of their neighbors. They rush around a good deal, buying, selling, making things, raising things, very restless and active. They worry more about getting the children educated, married, and well placed. They worry more about paying their taxes, and their preacher (some of them), about keeping the schools open, the busses running, the fire departments staffed, the garbage collected, the roads repaired, the poor fed, and their governments—all of them, including WPA—going and reasonably efficient and not too scandalously dishonest. They don't have any genius for the fine art of just settin' like the Kentuckians, nor the passion for order and neatness like the Pennsylvanians. They don't like to be bothered too much about reforms in their antiquated and even disgraceful prisons, especially that ancient and over-crowded rat trap by the Scioto in Columbus where all those prisoners got burned to death a decade ago; nor their hospitals for their public charges. They are modest and unimaginative in supporting their fine structure of universities. But they get by,

at least, and in these human respects differ little from other democratic Americans.

On the other hand we do go in heavily for literacy and for libraries. I have already lingered over the zealous efforts of our forefathers to get books in circulation in the first frontier settlements. The good Thomas Ewing and the farmers around Belpre would (perhaps do) take great satisfaction in our present library system. For we now have two hundred and sixty-seven tax supported libraries in our State—not counting our college and private collections; and we have more than a score of bookmobiles: carefully designed book trucks that take books to rural doors all over Ohio just like the U. S. Mail or the bread delivery. They circulate more than a million and a half books a year with this handy system. Our active State Library serves the citizens in outlying sections throughout Ohio in astonishing fashion with its traveling libraries and its individual loans. We have six of the leading thirty-six public libraries as listed in the *World Almanac*, and that worthy compendium somehow overlooked the Columbus libraries. It is a man's own fault if he is ignorant or bored in the State of Ohio.

In more personal matters we seem to people south of the Ohio a little stiff and reserved toward strangers, as though we lived in the midst of the Grand Central Station instead of the hospitable West. We seem to be sizing them up rather coolly before we take them by the hand and offer them bread and a chair. They find this frank and unsmiling skepticism somewhat disconcerting, and they even speak of it as our "A-hi-a manners," though people who come among us from Wisconsin and Minnesota or from down East, feel that they have arrived in the warm South. This complaint against our reserved manner was made by the earlier travelers who unanimously noted down in their journals our lack of interest in them—all, that is, except Charles Dickens whom we annoyed even more by a too active curiosity about him and his party.

The fact of the apparent frigidity is certain—on the surface. I can discover only a few localities in Ohio where the tradition of visiting back and forth, characteristic of Kentucky, is carried on. The front door is closed, the front shades drawn, and there is no invitation to leisure or merriment. But these appearances may easily deceive you. Katharine Brush wrote home to Massachusetts from East Liverpool, Ohio, where she lived for several years in the early twenties, "You simply never saw such friendly people. Compared with stand-offish New Englanders, they're simply wonderful." Of course that was before they had accused her of shoplifting, as she tells so cheerfully in the Ohio sections of her autobiography, *This Is On Me*. And another and more conservative New Englander, Mary Ellen Chase, not only enjoyed Ohio more than any of the forty-eight states in which she lectured because "So many people in Ohio have been friendly to me," but also surprisingly enough to foreigners, for its "inimitable art colony of cooks," and because it is "the one state in the Union which has given me neither a chicken patty nor vanilla ice-cream with chocolate sauce to eat."

Miss Chase was luckier on the whole than I have been, but Ohio can be like that. I have enjoyed few experiences more than a threshing day, dinner and supper, on Ohio farms; or sheep-shearing time; or, especially in southern Ohio, apple time, when there was laughter and the general sense of good living in the big kitchen and around the barn. Even rural Ohioans are less constrained during these rituals, and become human enough to suit the Kentuckians from the first tier of hill counties east of the Bluegrass. I think Ohio may have got too much of its general tone from those tight-lipped and stiff-necked New Englanders who poured into the State, and for a century held a costly monopoly on our schools and pulpits. I am not sure but that we Ohioans as a people are still a little scared of these stern Puritan ghosts and let them censor our natural gifts for the art of gentle living.

Our people are always much in the news and they are probably even a little above the national average in fame for their works. We offer everything beginning with the "Desire Under The Elms" theme of the mother down

Xenia way who murdered her children because, she said, "he didn't like them"; and when he learned what she had done he said, "I guess I'll go to the store and get some butter." Our papers, as you might expect, carry a goodly number of these acts of diversified men.

But over in Dayton are three big airports and many landing fields, vast green meadows crisscrossed with concrete runways by day, huge rectangular necklaces of red beads by night, to remind us of two young Dayton boys, Wilbur and Orville Wright, bicycle repairmen and jacks of all trades, who tinkered with flying machines in their shop and in a nearby pasture field, and flew for the first time a practical airplane on the sands at Kittyhawk, North Carolina, a week before Christmas, 1903.

Up in the center of the Firelands in Milan, a little village of 678 souls (Norwalk long ago stole from it the county-seat and bigness), is the birthplace of Thomas Alva Edison. The little cottage of red brick under big trees at the north end of the town looks across the valley down which, when Edison was born, went huge quantities of grain by canal to the lake in boats made at this serene and leisurely village. And we could fill up a very big book even with such brief reminders of Ohio men, not otherwise mentioned here, who are known to the nation—John D. Rockefeller, Tom Corwin, the Van Sweringens, "Golden Rule" Johnson, Charles F. Kettering, Daniel Frohman, Cass Gilbert, Kenesaw Mountain Landis, Clarence Darrow, Lowell Thomas, et cetera, et cetera. For the pattern of diversity with which we began as settlements continues to this day in all its forms.

We even have a high quota of oddities. Ever since the first pioneering days, eccentric people have been wont to appear from time to time among us. We had the "Leatherwood God," one of many religious fanatics, who became a legend—not a very happy one, to be sure, even when treated by William Dean Howells. He appeared miraculously from nowhere in the midst of a camp-meeting over near Salesville in 1828, and interrupted the sermonic oratory by shouting the word "Salvation." This startled the people no less than his claim that he was God Almighty, and was about to bring to earth the New Jerusalem. He gathered bands of followers, and grew strong; but when he failed to perform the miracle of making a seamless garment, he was driven into hiding and then out of the State by the unbelievers.

Over around Clark County a legend is growing up about the Hermit of Mad River who lived for nearly forty years in a cabin built in a tree eighty feet above the ground and reached by tortuous ladders. He became a learned man, and an artist, whose mode of life and accomplishments, as well as his odd appearance, brought visitors from everywhere to his tree. Another of equal proportions centers around the religious hermit of Hewitt's Cave along the Scioto Trail, who, like King David, and Prince Hamlet, feigned insanity to gain protection, and roamed the hills of Ross County. An inscription at the cave reads: "William Hewitt, the Hermit, occupied this cave for fourteen years while all was wilderness around him. He died in 1834, aged 70 years." On a hill in Muskingum County lives a naturally gifted and self-taught sculptor, an undertaker by profession, who in his spare moments has carved the native outcropping stone on his place into rather Egyptian-limbed statues, fascinating in their crude vigor, of Presidents, celebrities, animals and other subjects, and set them up around the brow of the ridge for all who come to see. This cheerful oddity overlooking the valley and other rows of hills is now known as Baughman's Park.

One of the most diverting of our eccentrics lived and, in his fashion, practised herb medicine in Dayton, where he advertised himself as "the discoverer of a cure for consumption, bronchitis, catarrh, and big neck," and asked pay in proportion to cure—no cure, no pay; half cure, half pay; work well done, full pay. He lived alone in stinking surroundings on the main street of the town between the hospital and the medical center, and on the route of the funeral processions. And when a cortège passed by on its way to the cemetery the doctor dressed up, put on a silk hat, and stood on the street with a placard sign for all to see: "Not my patient."

We have had scores of these interesting fellows, and they, too, are Ohio, along with Grant, Mad Ann Bailey, Sherman, and Harry Micajah Daugherty.

Our farm and manufacturing products are as varied as our men. We grow almost everything there is in Ohio. We have vineyards on the lake; we have sugar-beet fields; we have great onion swamps, and tobacco patches; we have acres of gardens under glass near the cities, and big wheat fields and corn lands, and hay meadows, and orchards. We have nurseries everywhere. We have a peony festival at Van Wert in the northwest, and we have maple groves that yield even better syrup than Vermont itself produces. The abundant fat flocks and herds, the brood mares and colts, the pigs and chickens, ducks and geese, turkeys and guinea fowl, thick on the farms, give life and color to the countryside everywhere. And one does not have to be either sentimental or provincially Ohioan to be inspired at the big State Fair held in Columbus late each August by the sight of farm boys exhibiting their pure-bred sheep, their cows, horses, and hogs; and farm women arranging for display their prize fruits, corn, garden stuff, and handiwork; all giving some insight into the stability and pride and variety of life in rural Ohio.

For that life is probably more satisfactory than ever before in the history of the State. Something important happens to 4H boys and girls who grow prize corn, care for a personal pet farm animal, who raise a disowned lamb, and cart it in for exhibit at the County Fair. Few Ohio farms are far from paved roads and a fair-sized town. There are summer camps for the women, cooperative live-stock markets for the men, and fine big community-center township schools for all. I have dedicated some of these buildings, and have been at their commencements, and still I marvel at the way the local women serve meals in the gymnasium from the school kitchen, and the way the people flock in to the movies and the doings at these schools. All this, too, is Ohio.

We make almost everything ever heard tell of in this State. I once thought of setting down a bald list of Ohio products beginning, say, with aircraft, aluminum ware, automotive manufacturing, books, boating, playing cards, cans, carriages, cranes, and on down through drugs, elevators, fire engines, fiberglass and glass building blocks, harness, leather, and lithographing equipment, to radios, railroad cars and engines, soap, watches, and yeast. But I soon found that the list would grow tedious long before I had made a good start on the ramifications of aircraft alone, to say nothing of ambulances, hearses, trailers, pots, pans, paper, roller bearings, safety razors, fertilizer, bolts, baseballs, and golf clubs. We even manufacture bees, in a manner of speaking, sell them by the package like raisins, and ship queens to all parts of the world. Ohio had the first silk factory in the United States; it was set up at Mount Pleasant in 1841. Its owners bought silkworm eggs in France, hatched them in sheds, fed them on twenty-five acres of mulberry trees, wove silk on a "drawboy loom," took first prize at the Crystal Palace Exposition in London in 1851, and, they say, made a waistcoat of "Buckeye Burr" (light buff) which Henry Clay delighted to wear. You may see samples of this Ohio silk in our Museum at Columbus. The good poet Longfellow at a Cambridge dinner in 1849 served Ohio champagne made at Cincinnati from Catawba grapes grown on the river bluffs there by Nicholas Longworth. Whatever men can want, Ohio can make—and probably does.

It is quite possible that all these facts leave us as far afield as when we started on our search for what is singularly Ohio in Ohio. Perhaps, as the social scientists say, we are only a national average, a convenient yard stick, typical in all things, singular in nothing. But we Ohioans know that there is an illusive something more ("and how much it is"), the subtle X that colors our politics and religion; that gives tone to our big cities, and our country acres; that emanates from the college campuses and university halls; that broods over the hills of the Muskingum valley and over the lake shore and the plains; and we call it simply Ohio. It is a unity in all this diversity. Putnam, Cutler, Worthington, Kilburn, Symmes, Cleaveland might recognize it if they visited us today, and they would approve of much of it. Cuming and Flint would support Anderson's loving satire, and still be happily surprised at the adult into which the crude child who annoyed them has grown. Of course even we are not wholly satisfied with ourselves and our State, and we mourn its scars and its weaknesses. But we lament only in the spirit of divine Odysseus:

> Tho' much is taken, much abides; and tho'
> We are not now that strength which in old days
> Moved earth and heaven, that which we are, we are,—
> One equal temper of heroic hearts,
> Made weak by time and fate, but strong in will
> To strive, to seek, to find, and not to yield.

INDIANA, HER SOIL AND LIGHT

THEODORE DREISER

Early Midwest settlements were said to be made up of Yankee, Hoosier, Yorker, Yahoo, Buckskin, Buckeye, Chegoe, Sucker. These hearty names identified Americans of various backgrounds who had come into new regions. Of all the nicknames, "Hoosier" has become the most expressive and the most cherished. Its origin is vague. Three thin inferences suggest that it came from: 1) the Anglo-Saxon hoo, *meaning a rustic person; 2) the pioneer's wary greeting to newcomers, "Who's yer?"; 3) an early canal foreman named Samuel Hoosier who preferred to hire workmen from the Indiana side of the Ohio River. None of these derivations has the humanity that the term acquired as it passed into the American speech.*

It is implicit in the name that the Hoosier has a warm feeling for his state. Even Theodore Dreiser (1871–1945), with his dark, deterministic vision of the modern, competitive America, turned tender and wistful when he wrote, in 1923, this essay on the temperament of Indiana.

THERE is about it a charm which I shall not be able to express, I know, but which is of its soil and sky and water—those bucolic streams and lakes which so charm those who see them. And where else will one find such beech and sugar groves, so stately and still and serene—the seeming abodes of spirits and elves that are both friendly and content? Rains come infrequently and then only in deluging showers. Corn and wheat and hay and melons flourish throughout the State. Spring comes early. Autumn lingers pleasingly into November. The winters are not, in the main, severe. Yet deep, delicious snows fall. And a dry cold in the northern portion makes sleighing and skating a delight. The many lakes and streams afford ample opportunity for house-boats, lakeside cottages, and bungalows as well as canoeing and fishing and idling and dreaming. In the beech and sugar groves are many turtledoves. The bluejay and the scarlet tanager flash and cry. Hawks and buzzards and even eagles, betimes, soar high in the air. Under the eaves of your cottage are sure to be wrens and bluebirds. Your chimneys are certain to shelter a covey of martins. And to your porches will cling the trumpet vine, purple clematis, and wistaria. From the orchard and woodlot of your farm will sound the rusty squeak of the guinea hen and the more pleasing cry of the peacock, "calling for rain."

One should not conclude from this, of course, that the State is without manufacture, or that, size for size, its cities and towns are not as interesting as those of other States. To me they are more so. There is something in the very air that sustains them that is of the substance of charm. What it is I cannot say. You will find it suggested in the poems of Riley and the stories of Tarkington, a kind of wistfulness that is the natural accompaniment of the dreams of unsophistication. To be sure the State is lacking in urban centers of great size which somehow, regardless of character, manage to focus the interest of the outside world. Apart from Indianapolis, a city of three hundred thousand, there is no other of even a third of its size within its borders. Evansville, on the Ohio, and at the extreme southwest corner of the State, has possibly eighty thousand. Ft. Wayne, in the northern portion of the State, the same. Terre Haute, the most forthright of its several manufacturing centers, had, until recently at least, a population of seventy thousand. And because of the character of its manufactories which relate to steel and coal it is looked upon by many who are not a part of it as grimy. Its smaller cities such as Gary, Hammond, South Bend, Kokomo, Richmond, Muncie, and several others literally resound with manufacture, being centers for steel, packing, automobiles, engineering supplies, farm machinery, and so forth. Yet contrasted with the neighboring States of Ohio, Michigan, and Illinois—in particular the latter's northern portion—it pales as a center of manufacture. Ohio can boast quite ten centers to its one. In passing from any of these States into Indiana one is reminded of the difference between Holland and Germany or France, the one with its canals, its windmills, and level fields, dotted with simple homes, the other with its plethora of cities and factories and, in the old days, its ever-present army. The one is idyllic, the other almost disturbingly real and irritatingly energetic.

Yet to my way of thinking the State is to be congratulated rather than not upon this limited commercial equipment. Not all of our national domain needs to be commercial, I trust, however much we may wish it. A few such pastoral areas might prove an advantage. Besides, as I have indicated, there is running through the mood of the State something which those who are most intimate with it are pleased to denominate "homey" or "folksy" —a general geniality and sociability. And with this I agree. The automobile and the phonograph, plus the dancing which the latter inspires, have added so much to the color of the small town and the farm in these days. Or, if it be the lone cottage, far from any town, with neither automobile nor phonograph, then the harmonica and the accordion are found to be in service. And one may sing and dance to those. Is it the light, or the soil, or what?

In this connection the church life of Indiana, as well as its moral taboos, have always interested me. Morality one might well assume by now, as well as all important social regulations, are best and most understandingly based upon and regulated by the Golden Rule. Beyond that, among the intelligent, restrictions and compulsions are few. Neither theory nor dogma nor ritual nor custom nor creed are disturbingly binding. Yet in my native State, and despite the steady growth in scientific knowledge, devotion to denominational liturgy and dogma appears to be unmodified. Go where you will, into any city or town you choose, and there will be not one but four or five or six or more churches of the ultra sectarian type and each with a lusty and *convinced* following. Nowhere, considering the sizes of the various cities and towns and hamlets, will you see larger or more attractive edifices of this character. And not infrequently the Bible school attachments or additions are almost as impressive as the churches themselves. In short, sectarian religion appears to flourish mightily. It is the most vigorous and binding of all local social activities. The affairs of the church are not only spiritually but socially of the utmost importance. Nearly everyone belongs to one or another of the various denominations and the rivalry between the several sects is not infrequently keen, especially in the smaller places. And in the main, and despite all science, they are still imperialistic in their claim

to revelation and devotion. Religious innovations are taboo. Even modern liberalizing theologic tendencies, though sanctioned by a stray soul here and there, are not in the main either understood or approved of. To this day in many orthodox quarters the youths of the hour are still discouraged from attending the State or any other university on the ground that they are "hotbeds of infidelity and irreligion." And the local press, running true to form, as it does everywhere, editorially sustains this contention.

And yet, as the world knows, Indiana has its "genius belt" geographically deliminated even, as "south of a line running east and west through Crawfordsville." And, locally at least, and until recently there was no hesitation in stamping the decidedly successful literary and art products of the State as the effusions of genius. Well, there's neither good nor ill but thinking makes it so. Certainly the State may well be proud of George Ade and Booth Tarkington and William M. Chase, the artist, to say nothing of those distinguished elders James Whitcomb Riley and General Lew Wallace, the author of "Ben Hur." Whether as much may be said for some others still remains to be seen. Certainly from the point of view of current popularity they have nothing to complain of. And as for posterity, well, posterity pays no grocer's bills. There are many aspiring writers who would gladly change place with George Barr McCutcheon or Charles Major, who wrote "When Knighthood Was in Flower."

Yet apart from these the State is not without a few personalities whose names will awaken responsive and other than literary thought beyond its borders—William Henry Harrison, the "Indian fighter" and quondam President, for instance, and Thomas B. Hendricks, once a Vice-President. Also Oliver P. Morton, an efficient early Governor; John Hay, diplomat, author, and cabinet officer of his day; and John Clark Ridpath, the historian. As a true and loyal Hoosier I suppose I should add that James B. Eads, the distinguished engineer, once lived in Brookville, Indiana, that Robert Owen founded his human brotherhood experiment at New Harmony, in Posey County, that Henry Ward Beecher was once pastor of the Second Presbyterian Church of Indianapolis, and that Abraham Lincoln is supposed to have studied those few books and caught that elusive something that later gave character and beauty to his utterances somewhere in a log cabin in Spencer County.

But beyond these, what? Well, beyond an agreeable and respectable and kindly social world in which to be and pass one's brief and changeful days, what more is needed? Trusts? There are several in active operation, ye tin-plate and ye steel trust, for instance; the former organized at Kokomo, Indiana, the latter in full and dictatorial swing at Gary and Hammond, where only so recently as July, 1919, a number of very respectable employees on strike were promptly and in true liberty fashion shot to death upon the streets of Hammond, their crime being, apparently, opposition to insufficient wages and certain (as they seem to have assumed) unsatisfactory piece-work conditions. The moral entanglements resulting from this method of adjusting labor difficulties are before the courts of Indiana at this very time. Large industries? Indianapolis, Kokomo, and South Bend are assumed to be automobile manufacturing centers of the greatest import, nationally and internationally speaking. The steel interests of Gary, Hammond, and Terre Haute are assumed, not only locally but nationally, to be second to none in America. Indianapolis has not one but several enormous packing plants. The underlying coal-beds of southwestern Indiana—especially about Terre Haute—are listed as among the important resources of the Central West. The melon- and fruit-bearing powers of the climate and soil of that same area have brought about not only specialization and intensive cultivation but a trade-mark which is of the greatest value. In addition the State has scenic wonders such as the caves about Wyandotte and such natural scenery and curative springs as have given rise to French Lick, West Baden, Mud Lavia, The Glades, and all the delightful lake life that characterizes its northern half.

But perhaps, after all, this is not the type of thing that should be registered of Indiana. Despite a long and happy intimacy with it, it is entirely possible that I have not even suggested or have entirely missed its truer spiritual significance as we are wont to say of so much that is but deeply human. Going south through Indiana once with a friend and fellow Hoosier, we two fell into a solemn and almost esoteric, I might say, discussion of the State and its significance, intellectually, emotionally, and otherwise. Previous to what I am about to set down I had been pointing out a number of things—not only those that have always appealed to me, the poetic and folksy charm of the State and its inhabitants—but also a number of other things that rather irritated me, its social devotion to dogmatic religion, for one thing, its rather pharisaical restfulness in its assumed enlightenment and knowledge of what is true and important to the world at large, its political somnolence as suggested by its profound and unchanging devotion to the two ancient and utterly platitudinous parties. With all of this he most solemnly agreed. Then, having done so, entered not so much upon a defense as an interpretation of the State which I will here set down as best I can.

"You should go sometime to an automobile speed contest such as is held annually at the Speedway at Indianapolis, as I have often, year after year; in fact, since it was first built. There, just when the first real summer days begin to take on that wonderful light that characterizes them out here—a kind of luminous silence that suggests growing corn and ripening wheat and quails whistling in the meadows over by the woods, you will find assembled thousands from this and other countries, with their cars and at times their foreign tongues, individuals interested in speed or fame or the development of the automobile. And this might cause you to feel, as it has me, that as rural as it all is, at times Indiana is quite as much of a center and more so even, than places which, by reason of larger populations, set themselves up as such. As I say, I have been there often, and getting a bit tired of watching the cars have gone over into the woods inside the course and lain down on the grass on my back.

"There, about me, would be the same familiar things I have always known and loved since I was a boy here, but that getting out into the world for a time had made me think that I had forgotten, though I hadn't—the sugar and hickory and beech trees, the little cool breezes that come up in the middle of the day and cool the face and hands for a moment, and rustle the leaves—the same fine blue sky that I used to look up into when a boy. But circling around me continuously, just the same, to the south and the north and the east and the west, where were the banks of the track beyond the woods, were these scores of cars from all parts of the world, with their thunder and dust, the thunder and dust of an international conflict. Then I would get up and look to the south along the immense grandstand that was there and would see, flying in this Indiana sunlight, the flags of all the great nations, Italy and England, France and Belgium, Holland and Germany, Austria and Spain. And it came to me then that the spirit that had been instrumental for some reason in distinguishing this particular State from its sister States, as it unquestionably has been distinguished, was and still is, I think, effective. It has won for Indiana a freedom from isolation and mere locality which is world-wide. It has accomplished here, on this quiet Hoosier soil, a very vital contact with universal thought."

"Universal thought is a pretty large thing to connect up with, F———," I contended genially. "And this is all very flattering to dear old Indiana, but do you really believe yourself? It seems to me that, if anything, the State is a little bit sluggish, intellectually and otherwise. Or, if it isn't that, exactly, then certainly there is an element of self-complacency that permits the largest percentage of its population to rest content in the most retarding forms of political, religious, and social fol de rol. They are all, or nearly all, out here, good and unregenerate Democrats or Republicans, as they have been for, lo! these seventy years, now—come next Wednesday. Nearly all belong to one or another of the twenty-seven sure-cure sects of Protestantism. And they are nearly all most heartily responsive to any -ism which is advertised to solve all the troubles of the world, including those of our own dear nation. I call your attention to the history of the Millerites of southeast Indiana, with their certain date for the ending of the world and their serious and complete preparation for the

same; the Spiritualists and free lovers who fixed themselves in northwestern Indiana, about Valparaiso, if I am not mistaken, and Mormon fashion ruled all others out; the something of soil magnetism which drew Robert Owen from Scotland to New Harmony and there produced that other attempt at solving all the ills to which the flesh is heir. Don't forget that the Dunkards—that curious variation of Mennonism—took root out here and flourished mightily for years, and exists to this day, as you know. Also the reformed Quakers. And now I hear that Christian Science and a Christianized form of Spiritualism are almost topmost in the matter of growth and the enthusiasm of their followers. I have no quarrel with any faith as a means to private mental blessedness. But you were speaking of universal and creative thought. Just how do you explain this?"

"Well, I can and I can't," was his rather enigmatic reply. "This is a most peculiar State. It may not be so dynamic nor yet so creative, sociologically, as it is fecund of things which relate to the spirit—or perhaps I had better say to poetry and the interpretative arts. How else do you explain William M. Chase, born here in Brookville, I believe, General Lew Wallace, James Whitcomb Riley, Edward Eggleston and his 'Hoosier Schoolmaster,' Booth Tarkington, George Ade, John Clark Ridpath, Roswell Smith, who founded the *Century Magazine*, and then Lincoln studying and dreaming down in Spencer County? All accidents? I wonder. In fact I am inclined to think that there is much more to soil and light in so far as temperament and genius are concerned than we have any idea of as yet. There may be, and personally I am inclined to think there is, a magnetic and also generative something appertaining to soil and light which is not unrelated to the electro-magnetic field of science in which so much takes place. I look upon them as potent and psycho-genetic even, capable of producing and actually productive of new and strange and valuable things in the way of human temperament. Take little Holland, for instance, and its amazing school of great painters. And Greece, with its unrivaled burst of genius. Or Italy, with its understanding of the arts. Or, England, with its genius for governing. There is something about the soil and light of certain regions that makes not only for individuality in the land but in the people of the land."

"For instance," he continued, "I insist that the Hoosier is different mentally and spiritually to the average American. He is softer, less sophisticated, more poetic and romantic. He dreams a lot. He likes to play in simple ways. He is not as grasping as some other Americans and some other nationalities. That may be due to the fact that he is not as practical, being as poetic and good natured as he is. If he be poor and uneducated he likes to fish and play an accordion or sing. If he is better schooled he likes to read, write verse, maybe, or books, and dream. In a crude way, perhaps, he has the temperament of the artist, and so I still look to Indiana, or its children, at least, to do great things, artistically. And all this I lay to the soil and light. Why? I don't know. I just guess that they have something to do with it.

"Nothing else explains to me Edward Eggleston and his turning to letters at that early time and in the region from which he hailed—the extreme southeastern part of Indiana. Or General Lew Wallace writing 'Ben Hur' there in Crawfordsville, under a beech tree. Neither will anything else explain to me why the first automobile this side of France was built right here at Kokomo, and almost at the same time that the first one was perfected in France. Nor why the first automobile course, after Brooklands, England, was built here at Indianapolis—not near New York or Chicago, as one might have expected, perhaps. Or why an adventurer like La Salle should come canoeing up the Maumee and the St. Joseph into this particular region. The French, who first had this territory, chose to fortify at Terre Haute and Vincennes. Why? They might just as well have fortified at other points beyond the present State borders.

"What I am trying to get at is this: Via such a soil and such light as is here coöperating you have a temperament more sensitive to the resource above mentioned. In the case of those who wandered in here, like La Salle and Lincoln, you have sensitives affected by the conditions here. Their dreams or aspirations were here strengthened. This is a region not unlike those which produce gold or fleet horses or oranges or adventurers. There are such regions. They are different. And I look upon Indiana as one such."

"Bravo!" I applauded. "Very flattering to dear old Indiana, to say the least, and as an honest native, and moved by self-interest, I hereby subscribe. But—" And then I went back to the churches, the hard-headed conventionalities, the fact that the "inventor" of the first automobile here was accused of robbing the French of their patents, that Robert Owen was a canny Scot who saw to it that he never lost a dollar in his idealistic enterprise but held the whole town of New Harmony and all that thereunto appertained in fee simple, so that when the idea proved groundless he was able to shoo all his assembled theorists off the place and sell it for what it would bring. But my friend was not in the last abashed. He reproached me with being incurably materialistic and clung to his soil and light theory, which, I may as well admit, appeals to me very much. His final rebuke to materialism was that human nature in toto is nothing but a manifestation of forces which unavoidably assume opposite phases, which same we label good or evil, but which really are found to be supplementing each other in any manifestation which can be labeled life. So you may see how far Indiana with its temperament carried us.

But admiring and even revering the State as my native heath I am perfectly willing to admit all of his claims and even more of such as may be in its favor.

ILLINOIS, PRAIRIE PROVINCE

DONALD CULROSS PEATTIE

Illinois was the first great grassland that American frontiersmen found. It was a land unlike anything in Europe, and no English word could fit it. The French prairie *meant meadow; their word took on a new spaciousness and wildness, with a touch of wonder, when it was attached to the grasslands that began beyond the Wabash. And where did the prairie end? Charles Fenno Hoffman on horseback in 1834 came suddenly to Door Prairie in northern Indiana. "It forms a door," he wrote, "opening upon an arm of the Grand Prairie, which runs through the states of Indiana and Illinois and extends afterward, if I mistake not, to the base of the Rocky Mountains." He was not mistaken. Illinois is but the beginning of the prairie grasses and the marching plain.*

Since his boyhood in northern Illinois half a century ago, Donald Culross Peattie has lived in distant parts of America and the world. But he never forgot the arching sky of Illinois and the wind-swept prairie. The state is shaped like an arrowhead, and after all the inrush of people, from old Shawneetown on the river to Chicago on the Seaway, it retains a clean, raw strength, uncorrupted still. Illinois is core America, he felt—heartland.

The following selection, a kind of prairie reverie, is taken from A Prairie Grove *(1938), which has been called a compound of natural and American history.*

OF the prairie province they say that the seas made it. Its bones are of coral, of diatoms, and protean microscopic animals. A little later, in the course of millennia that cannot be reckoned, the fishes made it. And then, when the bed of the sea was uplifted and it became dry land, rain fell on it, and the tropical club mosses grew in the marshes tall as trees. When the Carboniferous wind blew in their awkward branches, the golden spores were piled like snowdrifts in the peat. So were the coal measures laid down, and sometimes a fern leaf, broken by an amphibian foot, fell in the ooze to leave its imprint fossil there. Students go down into mines now to look for those superscriptions of past time. A fireman, flinging coal into the engine's firebox, burns them away, in the hot prairie night, and the train tears off more miles.

The seas came back, and the continent uneasily shouldered them off again. Each time the great waters came and went they laid down the deep layers of death, out of which life was born. It took all of that—all that growth and dying and time measured off by the millions of years of planetary revolution around the sun—to make the Indian corn grow so tall and taste so like an August day.

In the age of man come the glaciers. They say the glaciers came and went four times. The interval of years between the third and fourth was longer than the years elapsed since the last one. In Greenland, around the polar sea, the ice is still waiting to come back. It hangs on the sides of the Rockies; even in the Berkshires there are snow holes where the ice does not melt all summer. Lower the average temperature only a little, increase the precipitation, tamper a trifle with the small but vital carbon-dioxide content of the air, and the ice might come again, sagging outward under its own weight, bulging southward, finding all ready for it—short summers, long winters.

The glaciers blocked the drainage into lakes and swamps. They made the five Great Lakes, the greatest reservoirs of pure fresh water in the world. They made old lakes now vanished, whose faint shore lines strewn with shell and gravel and clean sand are smothered now in the height of the prairie grasses.

For when a glacier leaves the field, it drops its scourings as it shrinks. That is where we got the boulders of Canada granite lying on the soft black velvet of our loam. My people mounted to the stirrup from such boulders, hauled to lie beneath the shady trees before the farmhouse door.

When their work was done, the glaciers had changed the life of this country. The elephant, the camel and the horse, or their ancient prototypes, were gone. So were the ferns and cycads, but the face of the land was covered swiftly, with harsh sedges in the swamps, high grasses on the upland, and a few old indomitable types of trees—the nut trees, the catkinbearing trees, oak and hickory, cottonwood and beech and birch and elm. Add ash and linden and a low thorn forest of the stone fruits, hawthorn and crab, plum and chokecherry. The grass and the trees went to war, and they are still fighting for the land. No one knows why the forest suddenly stops, cleft away, vertical might giving place to limitless breadth. So the first explorers found it; so, the Indian said, was it always.

There are many wise guesses about the prairie. They say that grass grows best where most of the rain falls in summer. They say that if you make a map of the area having the most violent changes of temperature, it coincides precisely with the lay of the temperate savanna. Some think that the Indians held back the forest with fire, those fires laid to drive the game to the kill.

Of all things that live and grow upon this earth, grass is the most important. It feeds the world. Its hollow stems, its sheathing leaves and chaffy flowers, above all its unique freight of grain, describe only grass, and perhaps the sedges. These are the marsh cousins of the grasses, but they are useless, harsh, withdrawn and cryptic. Grass is generous, swift-springing, candid-growing, full of motion and sound and light. From the first oak openings of Ohio and Kentucky till it washed to the foot of the Rockies, grass ocean filled the space under the sky. Steppe meadow, buffalo country, wide wilderness, where a man could call and call but there was nothing to send back an echo.

Root touched root across this empire. The harsh edged leaves locked fingers, and the thoughtless west wind bore the pollen to the feathery purple stigmas of the husk-cupped flowers. In the jointed culms were water and salts, in the herbage was strength for the grazing herds, in the starch-filled seeds harvest for the mice. To the small rodents grass was forest. To the bison it was life certain underneath their hooves. Here the cock prairie chicken strutted before his wives, here in trust the lark sparrow laid her clutch of little eggs scrawled on the end with the illegible brown rune of her species, and the rattlers had a care for their frail spines when the elk walked by, terrible in branch and rut.

You may have seen Nebraska prairie, but that is low grass, bunch grass, a scattered, a semidesertic formation. You may have seen meadows, full of timothy and bluegrass, orchard grass and daisies. Those are introduced species; those are tamed Old World immigrants. The aboriginal high-grass prairie is nearly gone now. And it was something else.

It grew taller than a certain traveler who has left us his notes, taller than this man when he sat in his saddle. It grew so thick it flung the plowshares up when they came to break it. When it burned, they say, it filled the sky with its smoke, the smoke blew through the forest belt, and when the Dakotah were rounding up the game, the Ottawa in the woods of Michigan smelt that great hunt in the air.

But we have come to subdue the grasses, to conquer the empire of locked roots. The furrows lie even and open now, in spring and fall. The geometry of fields rules the landscape. It is a land turned to use, and I do not say it is not a good use, but some purity is gone. For the fallowed field does not grow up again to prairie. Thistles and burdock come up instead; we have the tares with our wheat, and nothing wholly wild is left.

But after long hunting I have found, upon the edge of my island grove, one slim paring of forgotten virgin prairie. I knew it first because the thistles had stopped stabbing at my knees, and there was nothing here so gentle as daisies. It was not tall as the banished high grass, but it was unsullied by a single foreign weed. Between field and field of grain, it grew with a varied flourish; close set, coarse-stemmed, the rank flowers sprang amid the whistling grasses. Nothing grew there because it was useful; it was itself, complete, sufficient, claiming the land by the most ancient of rights.

I sat down there and looked away from the farms. I lay down and looked up at the sky. I felt this most uncorrupted earth beneath me, and all its cleanly, raw, hard strength. I knew the prairie was once all thus, and I tried to remember how that must have been. There would have been no feeling of fences around me, but only forest and grass, grass and forest, and rivers winding through. Even now was left to me that baked rosin odor of the compass plants; I saw the irritable tribal toil of the ants in their enormous mound, and in my ears the crackling of the locusts' wings and the distant anger of the crows were like primordial Amerind language.

What had happened on this natural stage?

There are histories to tell me that, eyewitnesses who wrote in languages I understand. But on this turf and in the grove behind me the red men had a camp and a portage. That portage, to them but one of thousands, was, by the great accident that predestines any pattern we may see, directly in the road of history. Men of my own race had to come here. They were searching a passage to the China Seas, they were bringing the totem of a pale Manitou. Or they were men with lesser aims and common hungers, bringing only their right to grow where they stood and fling their seeds where they had cleared.

The bell of the church a mile north on the road rang down the fields. It is a good sound, even to unbelievers, but it broke some dream. So I stood up, the grass rising no higher than my knees. You are not so tall today, you prairie, as we are, and we shall never make you grow again, except in our thoughts.

THE REAL MICHIGAN

BRUCE CATTON

No other of the diverse United States contains the contrasts of Michigan, a name which means both industry and wilderness. At one end it is Hiawatha country, at the other it is the land of Henry Ford.

The differences between northern and southern Michigan are emphasized by the six-mile gulf of blue water at the Straits of Mackinac. Since 1958 a soaring bridge has spanned the straits, but the difference remains. It is farther from Ironwood and Ontanagon to Detroit than from Detroit to New York, and in spirit the two Michigans are more distant still. Yet they are linked together in the modern economy. The assembly lines and superhighways of Detroit rest upon the iron ore in the primordial North Country. Michigan is a land of paradox.

Bruce Catton, editor of American Heritage *and a ranking American historian, frankly prefers his native Michigan of the northern woods and waters to the industrial complex that has spread out from Detroit. This memorable essay appeared in* Holiday *in 1957.*

MICHIGAN is perhaps the strangest state in the Union, a place where the past, the present and the future are all tied up together in a hard knot. It is the 20th Century incarnate, and if you look closely you can also see the twenty-first coming in; but it is also the 19th Century, the backward glance and the authentic feel and taste of a day that is gone forever. It killed the past and it is the past; it is the skyscraper, the mass-production line and the frantic rush into what the machine will some day make of all of us, and at the same time it is golden sand, blue water, green pine trees on empty hills, and a wind that comes down from the cold spaces, scented with the forests that were butchered by hard-handed men in checked flannel shirts and floppy pants. It is the North Country wedded to the force that destroyed it.

You enter Michigan, mostly, by way of Detroit, which is something special. It is a profound weight on the land; an enormous city, with great skyscrapers taking the light from Canada, automobile factories and used-car lots scattered across the flat prairies, enough business strewn along the Detroit River to make a Russian's eyes pop; and in the old days, which lasted until World War II, you came into Detroit, usually, by steamboat, which was an experience in itself.

The boats came up from the Lake Erie ports, Cleveland and Buffalo and Sandusky, and they gave a theatrical touch to the whole business. Lake Erie is beautiful and shallow and treacherous, with a capacity for whipping up unexpected storms that would bother any mariner who ever lived, although mostly it is pleasant enough; and the old side-wheelers came paddling down its length, usually in the middle of the night—it was nice sleeping, in a snug stateroom on one of those boats, with an air-conditioned wind coming in at the open porthole, and the wash of the paddle wheels beating a quiet rhythm in the darkness—and in the morning the boat came up the Detroit River, and the factories and pumping stations on the bank suddenly made you realize that man had taken over Nature and was trying to make something out of it. Then, a little after breakfast time, the boat docked along the Detroit water front, and no city in America offered a more thrilling or exciting entrance.

The boats are mostly gone, and this is really Detroit's fault. Detroit did not exactly invent the automobile, but it picked the thing up when it was nothing better than a costly and unreliable toy for the rich and made it a necessity for everybody in America, and the automobile—getting slightly out of hand—

killed the Great Lakes passenger boats, except for a few cruise ships. You come into Detroit nowadays in your own car, or perhaps by train, and the old impact is gone. The place dawns on you gradually now; it used to hit you between the eyes, with the early light slanting in from beyond Ontario. But even now Detroit clamors at you, arrogantly, with all the confidence that comes to men who know they are really in charge of things and who don't mind enjoying the feeling, and there is something overwhelming about it all.

For here is a foretaste of what the machine is doing to us. Here men picked up the Industrial Revolution and swung it; this place, with its infinite genius for making any sort of contrivance men have ever dreamed of, and making it more cheaply and better than anyone else, is the doorway to the future. Everything goes in a rush, everybody is busy—and the place is big and sprawling and grimy and pulsing with life. Here is where we are going, make no mistake about it, and the big financial centers down East can say what they like and be hanged. Detroit sets the pace because this is where the muscle and the knowledge are; and if you don't think the future belongs to America, you should come here and breathe the air for a while.

Detroit makes its bow to the past, of course. It has such a place as Greenfield Village, in Dearborn, and here the past that Detroit killed forever—the past of wayside inns, one-man machine shops, quiet country villages snuggling by the route of stagecoaches, and rural dancers moving to the wheezy tunes scraped out by self-taught fiddlers—is preserved like a fly in amber, and it is very much worth visiting. But this, after all, is only a gesture. Detroit has been taking us away from that for half a century, and if it shows you Greenfield Village it also shows you the machine-age pace which turned everything Dearborn has on exhibit into museum pieces. Dearborn houses both this fragment of the past and also the Ford Motor Company, which did as much as any one organism could do to put the past in its place.

Detroit's streets come in like the spokes of a wheel, the other half of the wheel having been cut off by the Detroit River. Because the pace has been uneven there are vast skyscrapers standing beside parking lots, with rummy old brick buildings from the Civil War era snuggling up against twenty-story hotels and elongated office buildings; burlesque theaters and sleazy secondhand-book stores rub elbows with the most up-to-date, chromium-and-cutstone buildings that America can build, and the river drifts by, down in front, bearing the iron ore and coal and petroleum on which modern America is built; and whether you like it or not you can feel the hard pulse of America beating up and down these automobile-clogged streets.

Some years ago a civic-minded booster dreamed up the phrase, "dynamic Detroit," to express the essence of this city. He hit it off perfectly. Detroit is dynamic. Here is where they call the tune, and it is not a tune the Greenfield Village fiddlers ever quite managed to express.

But Detroit, after all, is not really Michigan. Its industrial empire spraddles over a good part of the state, to be sure—with Flint, and Pontiac, and Jackson and Lansing and Grand Rapids and all the rest—but the tremendous industrial nexus centered here is only half of the story. The other half is something very different—old times, the breath of by-gone days and memories that went out of date before the men who remembered them were old—and as a man born out of his proper time I love this other Michigan a good deal more than I love Detroit.

The map of the Lower Peninsula of Michigan is shaped like a fat old-fashioned mitten—a left-hand mitten, placed palm down, with a bulky thumb sticking out into the cold blue of Lake Huron. Detroit is down in the lower right-hand margin, below where the thumb begins, and the great industrial network lies across the lower part of the state; across the upper part of the wrist. But if you will take the map, and draw a line from Bay City—at the bottom of the gap between the bulbous thumb and the rest of the hand—straight west across the state, you will have cut Michigan into its two distinctive parts. Everything below the line is 20th Century; everything above it is North Country—old, half empty, touched by the cold winds that

drift down from the Arctic, with trees and sand and crystal-clear water and drowsy small towns as its distinguishing marks. It is a country that will put its seal on you if you are not careful, because it offers a lonely beauty and an escape from almost everything Detroit stands for.

The present falls away, when you go up into this part of the state. Suppose you drive up from Detroit, along U.S. Route 10; it goes through places like Flint and Saginaw and Midland, any one of which would be world-famous if it were in some other country—and then, suddenly, it takes you into the empty cutover land, where ghost towns cluster by the road, where the rivers flow cold and clear past hills that furnished lumber for half the world a generation or two ago, where cabins nestle down by quiet lakes and where the air drifts straight through you as if nobody had ever soiled it with smoke or grime or gas fumes. From here on north there are not so many farms, the soil is very sandy, excellent for growing pine trees, not often so good for growing anything else, and if it amuses you to count abandoned farms (unpainted shacks going peacefully to ruin amid fields nobody has tilled for a quarter century or more) you can make quite a list in an afternoon's drive. The road leads you out of ambition into peace and contentment; the deceptive light of an eternal summer afternoon lies on the rolling country; the unnumerable lakes glitter brightly blue in the fading light, and when you stop your car and listen you hear a blessed quiet.

This part of the state must have been quite a sight, a hundred years ago. Over an area of better than 25,000 square miles there was a magnificent forest—great pines, mostly, with a healthy sprinkling of hardwoods like maples and beeches—like nothing you can find in America today. From lake to lake and for 250 miles from north to south there was an eternal green twilight, with open spaces where the lakes and rivers were; twilight, with the wind forever making an unobtrusive noise in the branches overhead, brown matted needles and leaves underfoot—everything just about as it was shortly after the last ice age.

There is one tiny fragment of it left. If you will go to the little town of Kalkaska, in the northwest part of the state's Lower Peninsula, and drive thirty miles or so to the east, you will reach Hartwick Pines State Park; and here, running down to the bank of the Au Sable River, is an eighty-five-acre tract of virgin timber, the last that remains, preserved for tourists. You leave your car by the park-administration building and suddenly you are in the middle of it, with trees rising 150 feet overhead, and a shaded coolness all about that is proof against the summer's worst heat wave. Walking through it is not unlike walking through a cathedral. It has that effect on people. It is even more moving in the dead of winter, with the big trees coming up out of a white silence that is all but absolute; the trouble is that then you have to use skis or snowshoes to get there.

Anyway, Michigan a century ago was one magnificent forest, and even as recently as the Civil War it had hardly been touched. But then the lumberjacks went to work, and they shaved the countryside the way a razor shaves a man's chin. Where there had been wilderness, boom lumber towns sprang up, with rickety railroad lines threading their way back into the hills. In the springtime, every stream was clogged with logs, with lumberjacks scampering across the treacherous shifting carpet with peavy and cant hook, mounds of sawdust rising beside the busy mills, and a mill town with 1200 inhabitants normally supported from twelve to twenty saloons. Michigan voted for prohibition before the Federal prohibition amendment went into effect in 1920, and anyone who remembers what those saloons did to small-town life can easily understand why. For a time Saginaw was the greatest lumber city in the world, then Muskegon had the title, and then some other place; fresh-cut boards were stacked in endless piles by the railroad sidings or the lakeside wharves . . . and then, all of a sudden, it was all over. The lumber was gone, the mills were dismantled, the booming cities and towns lapsed into drowsiness, store-fronts were boarded up—and the razor which had done all of this shaving had left a stubble of stumps like a frowsy three-day beard across thousands of square miles. Some towns died entirely, some

almost died, and the endless whine of the gang saws became quiet forever.

All of which put its mark on a whole generation of people. Here was a region half the size of Ireland which, after only fifty years of history, suddenly found itself at a dead end. A society began to decay before it had matured. Towns dwindled and died before the eyes of the very men who had founded them. Boys who grew to manhood in these dying towns moved off to the city, leaving behind the old folks and the girls—half a century ago it was not so simple for an untrained girl to make a place for herself in a far-off city, and thousands upon thousands of these girls were condemned to lives of unwanted loneliness. They were strong and healthy and they had dreams and high hopes, and these came to very little because life had shoved them off into a side alley, since marriage was just about the only career a girl could hope for in those days. The human cost of a dying boom can be pretty high.

So they killed the infinite forest, once and for all. But there was still the land itself, rolling in vast gentle waves under a clear blue sky; there were the hundreds and hundreds of lakes, blue and cold and sparkling with imitation whitecaps; there was the great stretch of sand, putting a golden border on the water; there were the rivers, so clear you could count bits of gravel ten feet deep, so cold they turned your feet numb if you tried to wade; and there was the air, filtered by its eternal drift down from the ultimate edge of icy nowhere, fresh enough to revive a Peruvian mummy, odorous with the scent of jack pines.

All of this adds up to an earthly paradise for people from the hot cities who want to get away from asphalt and noise and muggy heat when they have a chance and touch base with Mother Nature; and today the tourist trade is the second industry in the entire state, topped only by the exalted automobile industry itself. This place where the wilderness used to be may indeed be the North Country, but it is only a hop-skip-and-jump from enormous centers of population. From Detroit or Chicago, it is a handy one-day drive to any spot in the Lower Peninsula, but at the end of the drive you feel that you have left the city and all of its works in another world.

So the old lumber area has had a rebirth, and the air of defeat and decline has vanished. This change has gone hand in hand with others. For one thing, the trees are coming back; huge state and national forests lie across vast stretches of empty land. In addition, there is a belt of cherry and peach orchards twenty miles wide and 200 miles long down the western side of the state. In spring, when the blossoms are out, the rolling hillsides near Lake Michigan offer a spectacle of breath-taking beauty, and many a town that used to live on its sawmills now lives on its cannery-and-packing plant. Every spring they have a big "cherry festival" at Traverse City—a bright, bustling little city which has made full recovery from the death of the lumber boom—and a pretty girl is named Cherry Queen; her function, usually, in addition to posing for photographs, is to take a cherry pie to Washington and present it to the President. This makes a nice trip for the girl, nets the President a first-rate pie, and presumably makes everybody happy.

But under everything there is this strange, beautiful, lonely land itself, this land of blue sky and clear water, where puff-ball clouds drift lazily overhead, trailing pleasant shadows over water and forest and bright little towns as if nobody ever had to be in a hurry about anything and time had come to a standstill just because what is here and now is too pleasant to leave. This is good country to come from and it is even better to go back to. It is a land of memories and also a land of escape; a place where you can be utterly idle in more pleasant ways than any other place I know.

I was born in Michigan and I grew up there, and not long ago I went back to see what it is like today. I came in through the industrial network in the lower right-hand corner of the state, and after a while I was driving northwest on U.S. Route 10—a fine road which goes for many miles at a stretch without touching a town, and which cannot in any case touch a real, full-dress city because in all of Michigan, north of that east-west line from Bay City, there is not a single place with as many as 20,000 permanent residents.

Beyond Clare, which calls itself the gateway to the northland, I turned right on M 115 which goes on past pleasant little lakes dotted with summer cottages, past a sprinkling of drowsy farms, and past uncounted miles of unused land. Yet a road, after all, takes you where you yourself are going, and not where the road goes, and what you see depends mostly on what's inside of you; and when you go back to re-explore your own country you are likely to find memories and dreams all mixed up with solid reality. I was heading for my own particular corner of the state, where I spent my boyhood, because I wanted to see what the years had done to it; and if in the end I learned more about what the years had done to me—well, that is what usually happens when you go on a pilgrimage.

My own land is mostly Benzie County, which has fewer inhabitants now than it had half a century ago but which has lost its old backwoods isolation and is a homey, friendly sort of country. There is a tiny town with the improbable name of Benzonia, which was founded by some eager folk from Oberlin College just before the Civil War when all of this land was new. The air was so clear and good that they wanted a name that would tell about it, so they dipped into their erudition and came up with a Latin-Greek hybrid which means, roughly, fragrant air. They built a little college, and for fifty years it struggled along, graduating eight or ten people a year; then it was turned into a preparatory school, and my father was principal of it when I was a boy, and just after World War I there was no longer any need for this school because the state's high schools had improved and it quietly died. Nothing is left of it now except a brick building which has been turned into a village community house, but the little town drowses under the long sunlight, with a special flavor that other little towns don't have, touched by the memory of the old-timers who wanted to bring education to the lumber country.

Every man makes his own state—or maybe his state makes him; it is hard to be certain about such things. But you grow up with something on your mind, and it comes out of the place where you were born and reared, and you never can get away from it no matter where you go. And if you go back, long afterward, to the place you knew when you were young, you see it through eyes that were specially conditioned; you cannot be objective about it; you try to write about your background and find that you are really writing about yourself.

I remember, forty years ago, a January night when the thermometer registered five below and there was a brilliant full moon, and I went to the front door, late at night, to lock up. I stood in the doorway for a moment looking out at the moonlit landscape, the little grove of trees across the street and the three feet of snow that covered everything. There is not in all America today anything quite as still and quiet as a Michigan small town could be, late on a moon-swept night, in January, in the days before World War I. Nobody in all the earth was making a sound, nothing was moving, there was only the white snow, the black trees, the blue shadows lying on the whiteness, and the big moon in a cloudless sky; and to stand there and look out at it was, inexplicably, to be in touch with the Infinite—and, somehow, the Infinite was good, it was lonely and friendly, it meant something you did not have to be afraid of if you understood it. So Michigan means that to me—along with much else—and coldness and loneliness and shattering loveliness go hand in hand, so that while you will always be awed and abashed when you come up against the Infinite you do not really need to be afraid. And maybe that is a fairly good idea to get and take with you.

I can remember another night, in summertime, much earlier, when a rather small boy my family took me across Lake Michigan on a steamboat from Milwaukee. It was dark and cool and windy, and we came out of the river and out past the breakwater, and the steamer began to rise and fall on the waves of the big lake. For a small child it was quite scary—nothing but water and the dark, with big waves coming in from nowhere and making foaming noises under the bow, and the Michigan shore seemed an unimaginable distance away and the dark sea ahead was what all adventurers have always seen when they pitted themselves against the great emptiness and its wonder and peril, and life itself is an enormous gamble played by people who are eager and frightened at the same time, with nothingness before and above and the chance of a dawn-swept landfall in the morning lying there, insubstantial and improbably beyond the night, as the possible reward. That is really the truth of it, and that too is good to know.

I am well aware, of course, that, as the world's seas go, Lake Michigan is not really a very large body of water. To cross it by steamer is to spend no more than half a dozen hours afloat, and when the trip is over you have reached only the state of Michigan, which actually is as prosaic a bit of land as you can find. Yet the thoughts of a small boy can be lonely, frightening and touched with unfathomable wonder, and the borders of an unattainable land can glimmer, insubstantial but genuine, over the most matter-of-fact horizon. What you owe the land where you were born and reared is something you can never quite pin down; but if that land can stir dreams and fears and the hints of a completely illogical but convincing promise, you are that much ahead of the game. For what you think and feel when you are very small never quite leaves you, and if it always lures you on to something that the visible landscape does not quite make explicit you are immeasurably the gainer.

All of this means very little, probably, by any rational scheme of things. Yet somehow it is part of the color and the flavor which this strange, light-struck, improbable country gave to me when I was too young to know any better, and it has had its own queer effect on everything I have thought or done ever since. So I bring it in here, along with the pine trees and the cold winds and the everlasting golden sands, to try to explain why I like to go back to Michigan. I am probably trying to recapture something unattainable, but that does not matter; so long as the feel and the gleam of it still lie on the edge of my subconscious it is real, for me, and the only value in any dream consists in the fact that you have to keep pursuing it even though you know that you can never quite reach it. If the real Michigan keeps getting overlaid with the Michigan I thought I saw in the old days, I can only say that I am that much better off—for what I thought I saw then was worth a lifetime's quest.

There is plenty to see up here. Half a mile from this hilltop village is one of America's loveliest lakes—Crystal Lake, named with an utter literalness; it is so clear you can see the bottom where it is twenty feet deep—nine miles long by three miles wide, with wooded hills all around and a fringe of pleasant summer cottages along its sandy shores.

Crystal Lake itself will always be something special for me, because it symbolizes an emotion that goes beyond time and space. When I was very small the minister of the one church in my town of Benzonia took some months off, and—by dint of what patient frugality I do not know: the pastor of a country church at that time earned precious little money—made a trip to the Holy Land. When he returned he made his report, and of it I remember just one thing. The magical Sea of Galilee, he said, the sea where our Lord walked and taught and performed miracles, was just about the size and shape of our Crystal Lake. To be sure, the hills which bordered Galilee were dun-colored, barren of trees, a bleak and impoverished landscape; while our hills, green as the heart of a maple leaf, were ringed with clear water, set about with pleasant little towns, cool and pleasant, inviting people to linger on their long journey from one mystery to another. But the resemblance was there, and the lake in which I caught diminutive perch was very like the lake on which Peter tried to walk dry-shod; and for some reason my life is richer because a saintlike little pastor, half a century ago, saw Galilee through innocent eyes which could interpret any lake in terms of Michigan's pine trees and green open valleys. I have never been to Palestine, but somehow I have seen the Sea of Galilee, and the Word that was preached by that Near-Eastern sea has a special sound for me.

Over the range of hills at the western end of my Crystal Lake there is Lake Michigan itself, and where a little river cuts a channel through the high bluffs there is Frankfort, a summer-resort town and a busy little seaport

as well. The Ann Arbor Railroad has its terminus here, with a fleet of car ferries that carry whole freight trains across Lake Michigan, and these big black steamers come and go at all hours of the day and night, 365 days a year. In the winter when the big lake is full of ice these boats often have quite a time of it, but they are sturdy icebreakers and they hack their way through regardless, although they sometimes make port with their upper works encased in ice.

From Frankfort you swing up toward Traverse City on route M 22, which cuts up across what is known as the Leelenau Peninsula. Once this was lumber country and now it is cherry country, but mostly it is a region for summer vacationers. Every little town has its lake (Glen Lake, which lies back of Sleeping Bear Point, is a show place) and there are other lakes with no towns at all, locked in by ice and snow for four or five months of the year.

Sleeping Bear Point is an enormous sand dune, five miles long by 500 feet high, jutting out into Lake Michigan. A road of sorts leads to the top, but your car would stall in the deep, fine sand, so you go to the town of Glen Haven and take passage in one of the special low-gear cars with oversized, half-inflated tires, which waddle through the sand as if they were made for it. On the crest there is nothing at all to see but this golden empty ridge and the great blue plain of Lake Michigan far below, with white surf curling on the beach at the foot of the bluff, yet it is one of the finest sights in the Middle West. There is no noise except the lake wind ruffling the spare trees: there is just nothing except a feeling of infinite space and brightness, and utter freedom from the smoke and the rush and the racket of ordinary 20th Century life.

The country north of Traverse City is high and open, with Lake Michigan nearly always in view off to the left, and the little towns and villages along the way reflect the past in a curious manner. First there was the lumber era, in which today's sleepy hamlet was a rip-roaring little city with a solid mile of sawmills along the water front. Then, when the lumber was gone, there was the early summer-resort trade: passenger boats coming up from Chicago or around from Detroit; imposing but flimsy frame hotels, all veranda and white pillars, overlooking every beach; Pullman cars unloading a new consignment of vacationers at the railroad depot every morning . . . and after a while the automobiles came and killed boat lines, passenger trains and most of the hotels, so that these towns which had made one readjustment had to make another. The result is odd. Every town contains echoes of those two vanished eras, and seems to be looking back regretfully to the past; and yet most of them are brighter and more hopeful than they ever were before, the old feeling of backwoods isolation is gone, the people who live here are having a better time of it than ever before and the general level of prosperity is higher and more stable. Yet the feeling of the past does linger, so that in this area which has hardly been settled more than a century there are haunting echoes of antiquity.

Your memory can play queer tricks on you. At Charlevoix I drove east, skirting the south shore of beautiful Lake Charlevoix to reach Boyne City. Boyne City was perhaps the last lumber boom town in the Lower Peninsula. We lived there, for a year or so, when I was about six years old, and it was a lively place then. There were four immense sawmills along the lake front, and a big "chemical plant"—I suppose it was a place where they extracted turpentine and other by-products from the pines—and there was even a blast furnace, although what it may have been doing there I have never been able to understand. Anyway, Boyne City was bustling and exciting, and our back yard ran down to the Boyne River, where the log drives came down in the spring. To my six-year-old eyes that river was immense; it was, I realized, probably smaller than the Mississippi, but it was fascinating, wide, turbulent, somehow menacing—a dangerous river which easily could (and, two or three times, very nearly did) drown a small boy who incautiously tried to play on its treacherous carpet of moving logs. So I returned to the old back yard and took another look at the river—and realized that either the river had shrunk or I had stretched considerably. The river is charming—gentle, crystal-clear, friendly, no more hostile than a brook.

Along the lake front there is an uncommonly pleasant park, where the sawmills used to be. A rusted remnant of the old blast furnace still survives, but everything else seems to be gone; and this is not the exciting town where I used to live, it is just a bright, friendly little community where old memories are held in suspension in the sunlight.

Another of my favorite towns in this part of the state is Petoskey, where I was born. No man ever breaks completely away from his birthplace; you carry the mark of your home town with you. I remember it as a sleepy sort of place, built on a spectacular side hill that slants up steeply from the cold blue of Little Traverse Bay, with funny little tourist-bait shops at the bottom where Indian wares and other trinkets were offered for sale to the "summer people." These shops always smelled pleasantly of birch bark—there were baskets, and toy canoes, and other contrivances—and to this day the odor of birch bark takes me back to tiny stores which must have gone out of existence a whole generation ago.

Petoskey has grown up to date and prosperous. It is no longer a lumber center, and the great trains of flatcars piled high with pine logs no longer go rumbling past what used to be the Grand Rapids & Indiana depot, and the sprawling summer hotels I remember so well are not there any more; but because the hill is so high and because so much of the big lake lies open at the foot of the hill Petoskey gives you what so much of this part of Michigan always gives—the strange feeling that you are at an immense altitude, on some sort of ridge where you can look down on half of the Middle West and where the wind that never quite dies down has come to you without touching anything at all along the way from wherever it is that winds are born.

Even though it always speaks of the past, and seems to look back toward it in a dreamy sort of way, most of this part of Michigan has no particular history. But when you go north from Petoskey you step far back into legend and the distant past. Things were going on here nearly three centuries ago. At Mackinaw City, at the very tip of Michigan's Lower Peninsula, and an hour's easy drive from Petoskey, there is a lake-front park with a rebuilt stockade which marks the site of one of early America's most significant strong points—Fort Michilimackinac. Here, around 1681, missionaries and fur traders and French soldiers and a scattering of just plain adventurers built an outpost of French civilization in a spot which was more remote and isolated than any spot on earth can be today.

After the French left Canada the British took over, and in 1763 Pontiac's painted warriors broke in, seized stockade and fort, and massacred the British garrison. Then the fort was abandoned, to be rebuilt on Mackinac Island, which lies in the center of the straits. The Americans took it over after the Revolution, and the British recaptured it in the War of 1812, and then it was returned to American possession again. Now it stands empty, a tourists' show place, looking out at the unending procession of freighters that cruise slowly past on their way to and from the lower lakes.

Mackinac Island is a delightful spot, and it is unusual in two ways. In the first place, although it is spelled Mackinac it is, for some incomprehensible reason, pronounced Mackinaw; and in the second place it is the one spot in the whole state of Michigan—one of the very few spots in all the United States— where you never see an automobile. Automobiles are not allowed on the island, and to come to this place, with its hotels and boardinghouses and curio shops lining the quiet streets, and the old-fashioned horse-drawn surreys leisurely wheeling their way in and out, is to step straight back into the Victorian era. To get about the island you walk, or ride behind a horse, or get on a bicycle. More so that any other place in the state, this is a refuge from the present.

Big changes are coming to Upper Michigan and the symbol of their approach is the stupendous five-mile-long bridge across the straits. . . . The Upper Peninsula is an immense finger of land running 300 miles from west to east, with cold, steely-blue Lake Superior, the largest lake in the world, lying all along its northern flank. Eighty-five per cent of this area is forested and lumbering is still going on, the Marquette iron range still turns out iron ore, and some copper is still being mined; but comparatively speaking the Upper Peninsula

is almost empty, with fewer than 300,000 inhabitants. . . .

Marquette is the metropolis of the Upper Peninsula. It is a solid industrial town, with red ore from the great ridges behind it coming down to the docks in red hopper cars, and if it is not the most lovely city in the United States it occupies one of the nation's most beautiful sites. The south shore of Lake Superior curves in and out, along here, with deep bays and jutting, pine-crowned headlands; the old primeval rock breaks through the crust of the land to remind you that this is the backbone of the continent, where rocks so ancient they even lack fossils lie bare under the long summer sunlight, grim and lonely and desolate. Just at sunset, from east of Marquette, you can see the city with the opaque blue panel of Lake Superior silent in front of it and a flaming red sky behind it, lying in the evening stillness like a dream of the city that never was; it is transfigured, a strange light lies on its towers and parapets, and this place that for so long was a Mecca for Cornish miners (the roadside stands still peddle Cornish pasties instead of hot dogs, and very good they are too) becomes an unattainable no-place out of fable, dropping long dark shadows on a silent cold sea.

If you are well-advised, you will head west from Marquette for the copper country. Do it, if possible, early in October when the lonely road will take you through forests aflame with scarlet and gold and bronze, and a wild, doomed beauty that belongs beyond the farthest edge of the world lies on all the landscape; the touch of everlasting winter is in the air and yet for an hour or so the sunlight is still warm, and nothing you will ever see will move you more or linger with you longer. You come out, at last, onto the long spine of the Keweenaw Peninsula—an outcrop of rock and wild trees, reaching far up into Lake Superior, perhaps the oldest land in the new world. The copper mines which caused men to come here in the first place go deep under the lake—some of the shafts go down for more than a mile. You get the feeling of a land that has been passed by, a hard, forbidding and strangely charming bit of country that had a short hectic history and does not especially want any more; and all about is the cold steely blue of the greatest of lakes, and the picturesque little settlements that manage to be both friendly and forsaken at the same moment.

It would be possible, of course, to drive on, noting the points of interest in the Upper Peninsula, mentioning the more unusual towns —like Eagle Harbor, one of the most completely beautiful villages I ever expect to see, with two long headlands enclosing a quiet strip of water and the great angry lake piling destructive surging waves against the rocks outside—but my state is half reality and half the dim, enchanted memories of a long-lost boyhood, and anyway I did not live in the entire state of Michigan, I knew only selected parts of it, and these parts stay in my memory and call back unforgettable things which were born of the cold emptiness and the inviting, menacing beauty of this North Country.

They are Upper Michigan, the part that lies north of the automobile belt, the doomed, bewitched country which presently will surrender to the Mackinac bridge and to the superhighway and which, ultimately, will undoubtedly become just another part of the sprawling, industrialized Middle West. But while today's light lasts it is still a land apart; there is a pleasantly melancholy flavor of a lost past to it, and although men murdered the forests with a passionate ferocity the forests somehow still live and put their strange touch on the countryside. There are cool shadows under the trees and a timeless peace lies on the cutover tracts and the fields where the young second growth is hiding the stumps.

It is a strange country: lonely enough, even in summer, and cold as the far side of the moon when winter comes, with the far-off hills rising pale blue from the frozen white landscape. It offers a chance to draw a deep breath, to turn around and look back at the traveled path, to stand on a high hill and be alone with the fresh air and the sunlight. It is wood and water, golden sand and blue lakes, emptiness and memories and the sort of isolation which it is hard for a city man to come by, these days. All in all, it is quite a state.

GHOSTS IN WISCONSIN

WILLIAM ELLERY LEONARD

Born in New Jersey and educated in Massachusetts and Germany, William Ellery Leonard (1876–1944) spent a long teaching and writing career at the University of Wisconsin. Personal experience is recounted in his sonnet sequence, Two Lives *(1922), as well as in his autobiography,* The Locomotive-God *(1927). The following essay, published in the* Wisconsin Magazine of History *in 1923, offers a panoramic view of the Wisconsin past and present.*

WISCONSIN, lopped from Michigan as a territory in 1836 to become a state twelve years later, shares in the story of the discovery and the settlement and in the qualities and activities of her population much in common with the whole North Middle West. Yet Wisconsin possesses an individuality, both historical and social, more organic than the little red line of the map. Geography has had profoundly to do with her becoming; in her, the regional characteristics of man find the most indubitable and emphatic expression; and, moreover, once organized as a state, she began instinctively, like many other state units, to create personality, as must any group, however artificial or accidental at first, when it makes its laws together under one dome in the spiritual center, and sends its youth to one schoolhouse on a neighboring hill.

But the story of man here, between the

majestic castellated bluffs of the upper Mississippi and the stern iron and copper bearing rocks of Superior's wave eaten shores, is not one story but three. There have been three human occupations of this rolling terrain of sunny swale and drumlins, with its innumerous rivers winding between the wild rice marshes, or the now perishing forests, or the shadowy scarps and dalles, with its thousand glacial lakes in the northern pineries or the midland oak openings, and with its wide driftless area, once surrounded but never traversed by the ice sheet, where today the unstriated old Cambrian sandstone stands weathered and carved into mesas and giant toadstools. But no man, from first to last, ever settled on the mountains of Wisconsin, for the primeval ranges were beveled down to that peneplain underlying the Cambrian long before the trilobite or protozoan—though sometimes in the jagged cloud banks, white on afternoon horizons of early autumn, one may fancy he sees their tremendous ghosts.

The three occupations of this ancient land have been three independent efforts of man to light his fire and to sing his song. And, though only the third, with its hosts of inpouring exiles and seekers, constitutes the epic of the settlement, of the building of our cities and the state, nevertheless, the occupation of the red man invited the Frenchman, and the Frenchman pioneered the thoroughfares thither for the aftercomers and their household gods. The aborigines (Fox, Menominee, Winnebago, and other tribes finally huddled between the fierce Dakota on the west and the fierce inland ranging Iroquois from the east) have left to none of our states more reminders of a vanished folk culture: the Indian names of so many rivers, lakes, and hills; the trails whose grass-grown depressions may still be traced down the groves; the stone celts and spear points and the copper knives and needles dug up by fresh-water beaches or along the ploughed fields; the chipping sites under primeval oak trees; the corn hills; and above all, the hundreds of earthworks, both conical barrows over the bones of unknown chiefs, and those totemic animal effigies that lie on their gigantic sides asleep on so many low hilltops and green declivities, by the waters of ancient villages. The native tribes—long since, as white men's hunters, for a pittance of glass beads, iron hatchets, and whisky, debauched in their handicrafts and agriculture—have been exterminated or deported (like some of the Winnebago to Nebraska), or live sordidly on the northern reservations, putting on, with the encouragement of white anthropologists, now and then the tarnished relics of ancestral costumes for ritual dance and religious festival, doing odd jobs at lumbering or berry picking, or occasionally, up to fifteen years ago at least, coming down in little bands as far as Madison to trap the muskrat in their fathers' streams and lakes. An alien stock, the Christian Oneida, brought by American philanthropic enterprise from New York, are almost the only well kempt, prosperous Indian citizens about Wisconsin—farmers and business men and good Episcopalians in a community of their own. Our people, largely through the activities of the Archeological Society and the Historical Museum at Madison, in coöperation with the state legislature, have begun to develop both a scientific curiosity and a memorial piety touching their red predecessors, which sometimes unite, by one of those minor ironies of history, present-day Germans, Norwegians, Saxons, Celts, and Slavs in little excavation parties or local site marking ceremonials.

In the softened grays and purples of the twilight atmosphere, when the distant roads and the barns are blurred in the lowlands and the crows are flying to the copses, the outlook from many a height over valley and lake and river, especially if the moon is bulging up, is peculiarly aboriginal in these parts: I have never so had the feeling of the ghosts of Indian days in any landscape as in Wisconsin. Nicolet, in his Chinese damask robe, with his seven Hurons around him, discharging thunder and lightning from pistols in both hands, as he stands on Wisconsin's landfall by his beached canoe at the foot of the bluffs up in Green Bay, before the naked and awestruck autochthons, seems a more haunting presence than John Smith, Miles Standish, or Massasoit. He came, you remember, up the Ottawa, having heard of the "People of the Sea" (so the Hurons called the Winnebago), thinking to open trade relations, on behalf of Champlain and the Hundred Associates, with Orientals on the Pacific, and took possession forever in the name of the King of France. This was in 1634.

Freedom to trade, not freedom to worship God or to manage one's own politics, was the impulse to the first white occupation, as freedom to plant one's own corn was, on the whole, the impulse to the second. As the years went by after Marquette with Jolliet in 1673 paddled down the Great Lakes and across the state, and entered the Father of Waters—"with a joy I cannot express"—the Fox-Wisconsin Portage became the determinant of the human affairs of a province and of an empire. Here the basin of the St. Lawrence, represented by the upper currents of Fox River, may glimpse beyond a mile or so of marshy plain, alive with blackbirds and meadow larks, the Wisconsin powerfully flowing off toward the Mississippi; here the Atlantic touches the Gulf of Mexico. Kept open only by long wars with the natives, the Fox-Wisconsin waterway established and sustained the fur trade, which was the economic life of the old régime in Wisconsin, no less than in Canada. Linking far-away Quebec with far-away New Orleans, it was the indirect occasion of much of the strategy of the conflict with Great Britain—fundamentally over the control of the fur trade—that cost France her power in North America; and it continued to affect man's trafficking in some measure—Congress appropriated millions of dollars for its improvement—until the age of steel rails. Without it, neither France nor Britain might have come to Wisconsin any more than to Minnesota.

The trading posts left their names to modern cities and towns—Prairie du Chien, La Crosse, Eau Claire, Trempealeau; and the descendants of the habitants—the blacksmiths, carpenters, farmers, and retired traders—who squatted around them, give today a sprinkling of French to the polyglot roll call of legislature and college class room. But the bark chapels and the log crosses of the "Black Gowns" soon rotted away or were burnt by hands still heathen, leaving only the names of a coastal island and a river town or so, the silver ostensorium of Perrot still bearing the date 1686, and the *Jesuit Relations*—those faith-ful reports to their masters in France of lands and waters seen, aborigines baptized, and hungers survived. And La Salle's *Griffon*, the first boat besides dugout or war canoe launched upon the Great Lakes, lies sunk, mast and sail, somewhere off Door Peninsula, with all its peltries. In pathetic contrast to southern Louisiana, the old French world vanished here, even more completely than the Roman world vanished from Britain; not, however, because it withdrew or was exterminated, for Frenchmen were still about, swapping produce and yarns with Britisher and Yankee; but because it was too tenuous, migratory, and scattered, too lacking in urban life, to maintain for long its individuality over against the dominantly Germanic invaders. One hears French today only among the French-Indian half-breeds of the reservations or in the recent villages of the Walloons.

The British domination lasted with cheerful impudence, in spite of the Treaty of Paris of 1783 and the Jay Treaty of 1795, till the close of the War of 1812, with entire satisfaction to the French, who had indeed actively sided with England against the hated "Bostonnais" in the Revolution. The fur trade continued to march on, integrated now with the huge English enterprise of the Far North; but another business, at first only an adjunct of the fur trade, was pressing hard upon it, with a sinister and prophetic face.

The French, having early discovered the Indians scratching for lead in the southwest corner, began to pay a price per pound that bullets should be more abundant; and the savages scratched more busily. With better guns and bigger shovels, as destined lords of all mines—coal, gold, and diamond—our Anglo-Saxons drove out the aborigines and the shallow burrows were deepened. By Uncle Sam's garrison days of the thirties, a riffraff of adventurers from the border states was rushing in, as it was later to rush to the gold of California and the silver of Colorado; and the earliest European immigration of what I call the settlement was invited by the lead mines, first and last—some seven thousand Cornishmen, and these a sturdy stock. Great bateaux of twenty-oar power carried the lead down the Mississippi to New Orleans, long years before the Civil War definitively deflected Wisconsin's southern trade connections eastward; or the ox teams would drag it overland to the lake ports. By the fifties, for several reasons entirely economic, it declined, to be only partially revived in recent years. Abandoned diggings are now among the pious ruins of Wisconsin, along with the sleepy or abandoned villages that sprung up on the water fronts in the reign of King Lumber, the third dynasty of Big Business hereabouts, with its devastation of the northern pineries and hardwoods, and for a generation its log rafts on eight rivers.

Meantime the settlement was steadily going on. The planters of grain and the milkers of cows were coming from all the world, who were to vindicate the barn against trading post, burrow, and lumber shack. Even the mill for paper and the factory for chairs, windowframes, steam cookers, textiles, underwear, farm machinery, leather goods, automobiles, or the brewery for fresh-water pop were not to prevail against it. Though there is a great playground developing in the wooded and watered northern counties, and though there is an increasingly busy manufacturing strip along the southern Michigan shore, in the cities of Racine, Kenosha, Milwaukee, and Sheboygan, Wisconsin is primarily an agricultural state, thanks to her level and fertile glaciated soil and to the practical hardihood of the vast majority of her settlers, who have been ambitious only of a homestead and acres. Wheat led first; but now, with a start perhaps from the Swiss immigrants and certainly with the scientific coöperation of the University, it's butter and cheese: we are the buttery, cheesery, creamery of the United States. But the barn would vindicate itself only when the land was cleared and ploughed, and the cattle pastured; and all this took time and many people.

The story of the settlement begins with the Black Hawk War. The newspaper correspondents, lacking much martial material about the precipitate retreat of the brave but broken Sauk leader, with his murdered tribesmen and women and children, sent east such detailed and alluring accounts of the country itself that it may not be a fancy to credit them with a part in the foundation of the state.

Whatever the origin of the rumor, pioneering families were soon en route: from New York and New England down the Great Lakes or the Ohio, and from the southeast by the old Wilderness Road of Daniel Boone. It is these who began to supply that contribution of native American stock and enterprise, politically and economically dominant in territorial days, and still a good third in numbers and perhaps more than a third in power. The rest is new life out of old Europe. The admission of Wisconsin to statehood coincides historically and symbolically in date with famines, with economic unrest, and with political revolutions on the Continent. Here were broad spaces and easy laws of citizenship—opportunity for bread and votes, a chance to build a house and a commonwealth. The European printing presses spread the news, assisted by promoters on the ground. The boats filled with folk. The Germans came, Carl Schurz among them, with their pastors, Catholic and Protestant. The boats filled with folk. The sons of the Vikings came, with Christ instead of Thor, migrating as they had done to Iceland and Greenland in neighborhood groups of a hundred or so. The boats filled with folk. Now it was five hundred from a famished Swiss canton, whose government had paid for transportation and for the land which is now New Glarus. Letters went back to the old home and more boats were filled. The Dutch came too. And the Irish. And the Scotch, one family bringing a son named John Muir. And the Welsh. And the Belgians. And the Bohemians. But read the Books of the Chronicles—the *Collections* of the Wisconsin Historical Society, under the editorship of Draper, long dead, and of the late Reuben Thwaites; for the state from within a decade of its statehood has been zealously collecting and recording its origins. There are villages of Icelandic fishermen on Washington Island off Door Peninsula; and even in the last twenty years colonies of Finns have settled on the Superior shore, already influencing the state by their intelligent coöperative methods. Though Poles and Italians are to be found mainly in districts of the factory cities, and though scattered Greeks sell candy or black boots, and Russian Jews collect junk or make pants to help their boys to the

University, and a few Cantonese Chinamen, now shorn of their pig-tails, launder collars and cuffs, most of the non-English speaking immigrants, especially in the big years of the settlement, tended to found their own little communities, and have conserved to this day something of native speech or customs—as sometimes the Angelus or a wayside shrine, sometimes wooden shoes, sometimes an outlandish stew or pie. But the achieving of a common action on a common soil, and the sharing of a common stake in a settled as opposed to a roving life, seem to have united them as good Wisconsinians. Often, too, there was intermingling of stocks, by marriage—or socially, as when a stray Norwegian would be assisted, not only by Norse, but by Irish and German and Anglo-American neighbors, in building his cabin, with its clay or puncheon floor, its one window of greased sheepskin, and its broad bowlder-based chimney that narrowed against the outer side-wall to a square flue of interlaced and mud plastered sticks. If there be any "foreigners" still unbaptized in the Jordan of the New Faith, their home-born schoolma'ams will catch them, who so often go back to their home townspeople after graduating from the University or one of the several state (or county) normal schools, and tactfully carry the good news of Americanism, single negatives, toothbrushes, and operations for adenoids. But there has been little effort to uproot the joy and the pride in the traditions and customs of the several racial strains; and very few feel that the republic is in danger because a high-school class song in the vernacular has, say, a Scandinavian chorus. To be sure, there is, I believe, a well-to-do league in Milwaukee founded since the war to combat, with pamphlets and bibliographies, the menace of socialism, about which most of our citizens are, however, quite as innocent of serious knowledge as the league itself; but there has been no state legislation in Wisconsin outlawing foreign languages, as in more vigilant Iowa and Nebraska. The voluntary participation of such diverse races in the creative energies of the commonwealth is witnessed by the names in *Blue Book*, in University catalogue, and in the lists of bar, bench, and legislature. Down at the capitol the other day I dropped in on one of the numerous commissions—on a Dutchman, an Irishman, a Norwegian, and an Englishman, all four engaged upon the state taxes. Governor Blaine, old American Scotch-Irish on his father's side, is the son of a Norwegian mother who came to America only seven years before he was born.

But the war record of these Germans, Scandinavians, and other foreigners? In the Civil War 'a Wisconsin regiment was worth a battalion' went the saying in the tents of the generals; and Old Abe, the trained eagle, who perched on the standard-beam going into battle and whirled screaming overhead when the cannon began booming or the charge was on, was a symbol famous all over the North, still recalled at Grand Army encampments, though his stuffed body was burned up in the capitol fire years ago. In the World War, though the compulsory service here as elsewhere renders it impracticable to draw patriotic conclusions from the muster, Wisconsin's voluntary coöperation in the cause at home and abroad was eager and efficient; and there was a noticeable state pride in the fact that so many of originally so diverse races were united in an American enterprise. Wisconsin reacted as all other states in those tense and raucous days, though illustrating perhaps more strikingly than some states with more homogeneous population, the commonalty to all mankind of the more elemental feelings and instincts—the common responsiveness to the war cry, the common susceptibility to mobilization of opinion and emotion. Most so-called pro-Germans in the beginning were the broken-hearted, torn, abused, and frightened citizens of later emigrations, trying often with a higher ethos than the crowd to do their civic duty. Their racial sympathies in 1914–16 had sharpened their eyesight to the real policies of the Allies, albeit they failed often enough to see the real policies of the German government. That minority in Wisconsin that was unconvinced grew every day smaller with the educational program of federal government and state university; and the skeptical or intransigent group that remained in the end is to be distinguished less by the kind of racial stock than by the kind of vision. It is, for instance, unnecessary to attribute the position of Wisconsin's senior Senator to anything but his own vision of affairs—historical, economic, diplomatic.

Far more significant for the fusion of races into one American commonwealth than the recent war records, is Wisconsin's achievement in public welfare: patriotism of one sort is largely a mob emotion; true citizenship is a life. A new technique of service and control has developed from the days when lumber and steel rails corrupted state politics, and Governor La Follette among other vital reforms succeeded in replacing the caucus with the direct primary. It is not socialism, but what its protagonists have called an adventure in democracy. In working to equalize opportunities, to protect the laboring class, to make capital realize its social obligations and public utilities serve the public, to protect natural resources—forests, waters, and metals—to bring health, books, and schooling to all, to develop the broad highways for all—in such matters, Wisconsin, in her legislation by her delegated citizenry and its execution by her delegated experts—the various state commissions—has many aims not unlike the socialist conception of a commonwealth. But in economic principle it is building merely toward a more just and efficient working of the familiar old order—better conditions for a thriving state where production is carried on for profit, not for use, and where competition rather than coöperation rules factories, farms, and markets. Yet coöperative organizations, especially agricultural, are scattered through the state and protected by legislation; and now and then a suspiciously socialistic measure, like compulsory teachers' insurance (from which a University faculty, fervently hostile to socialism, will profit nicely), gets itself written into the statutes. How the University specialists have been called in to assist the law makers; how Frank Hutchins and Charles McCarthy, both gone from us, developed the Legislative Reference Library; how the late President Van Hise gave no little reality to his dream of a university that should serve all the people of the state—a center for the distribution, even to farm and factory hand and convict, of the long results of the sciences and the arts—all

this was in the magazines a decade ago. Our progressive legislation had survived ten years of relatively mild reaction, when the candidate of the Non-Partisan League and the La Follette forces was inaugurated as governor in 1921, and democracy celebrated its triumph by a ball, without white kids, swallow-tails, or decolleté, among the balusters, pilasters, and piers of Italian, Norwegian, or Greek marble, under the dome of the new capitol—the white granite pile erected, it would seem for all time, under the Progressive régime.

Various efforts have been made to "explain Wisconsin." It was usually taken for granted before the war that several of our public welfare devices were the faithful experiments of borrowing for a democracy the efficient technique of bureaucratic Germany, under encouragement by the German element in the state. Much, however, is due to ideas that popped into the heads of the natives. There is a set in Wisconsin toward civic affairs, a concern for the state's welfare, that is in a degree traced by some to the University training under men like Ely and Commons, and especially to John Bascom, president when elder men here were boys in college classes. This spirit communicates itself to the incomers; the Irishman McCarthy himself, a chief enthusiast and spokesman for the "Wisconsin Idea," came in from Rhode Island, a graduate from Brown. These men get their notions, talk them over, work them out, and obtain interested sponsors at the capitol or the University. There is little noise, fuss, or exaltation. They are quiet, simple-mannered citizens, but far-sighted, energetic, practical schemers for one or another special civic program. Aside from La Follette, Van Hise, McCarthy, and Chief Justice John Winslow, few would probably be called original or powerful personalities; yet it is they, many of them almost unknown by name even in the state, who best illustrate the kind of leadership that has made the modern Wisconsin. And the public servants—inheritors and conservers of a recent tradition—go about their duties, whether Progressive or Stalwart or Democrat, as naïvely honest as some state officers and their ilk of a former day were naïvely dishonest. The state capitol was building through four administrations, and without, I am told, one penny to graft. The judiciary has not thwarted the Progressive urge; and citizens will quote you with pride the words of the late Chief Justice John Winslow in a supreme court decision: "When an eighteenth century constitution forms the charter of liberty of a twentieth century government, must its general provisions be construed and interpreted by an eighteenth century mind surrounded by eighteenth century conditions and ideals?" The University, with a faculty composed of native born, of Easterners and Westerners, of Canadians and a few Europeans, though today apparently more conservative than the state administration, has been from its beginning in the year the state itself began, true, in spite of brief interregnums of reaction and timidity, in the main true to the bronze tablet on Bascom Hall, just behind the statue of Lincoln on the hill: "Whatever may be the limitations which trammel inquiry elsewhere, we believe that the great State University of Wisconsin should ever encourage that continual and fearless sifting and winnowing by which alone the truth can be found."

But—but it is a commonplace, of course, that the state of Wisconsin, like all the Middle West, is in the finer things of civilization by and large still crude in sentiment and achievement, still imperfectly organized in effort. She has had from the beginning of her statehood her men and women of broad and cultivated tastes, also concerned for the public welfare in things of the spirit; but they have seldom hit on a technique of leadership. Thus uncouthness, knowing not itself but glowing with its adventure in democracy, blunders monotonously into a self-expression, which is scarcely the expression of what the best of us hereabouts can do. Not altogether in jest might one propose a state commission for overlooking, say, the English in the guide books to our famous places (the Dalles, Devils Lake, Madison herself of the Four Lakes) and on the signs before the animal cages of our zoölogical gardens, and for hanging the perpetrators of at least one memorial arch and several public buildings. And though we have a library among the greatest in the land, culture is still subordinate to agriculture, the stock pavilion houses our commencements, and a remodelled horse barn our department of art.

However—Wisconsin spells a swift and solid achievement in man's economic and social mastery on one quarter-section of this earth, which less than a hundred years ago was largely as primeval as when the southwind and the northing beast and bird bore in the seeds of grass and trees and berries after the ice age. That there is much yet to do before she ripens a rich and regnant Life is in the nature of things. And the state motto is "Forward."

MINNESOTA, THE NORSE STATE

SINCLAIR LEWIS

The great tide of immigration in the second half of the nineteenth century poured into huge and hospitable Minnesota. Certain counties took the color of German, Czech, Polish or Scandinavian settlement. Others were mixed. A twenty-mile circle drawn around Bemidji includes the towns of Naytawash, Fernhill, Gunder, Ebro, LaPorte—five nations and five languages there; in 1910 the mining town of Hibbing contained people of twenty-five nationalities. Though the Scandinavians have been predominant in Minnesota politics, the state is marked by a broad cultural variety. It is natural that the folk stories of the state are dialect stories.

Sinclair Lewis (1885–1951), always restless and on the run, wrote Babbitt *in France,* Arrowsmith *in Italy,* Dodsworth *in Berlin and Naples. But he was a product of the frontier forests and wheat fields, and he remained a man from Minnesota. The following essay on his native state was written in the early 1920's, soon after the publication of* Main Street *and* Babbitt.

ON May 9, 1922, Mr. Henry Lorenz of Pleasantdale, Saskatchewan, milked the cows and fed the horses and received the calls of his next farm neighbors. Obviously he was still young and lively, though it did happen that on May 9 he was one hundred and seventeen years old. When St. Paul, Mendota, and Marine, the first towns in Minnesota, were established, Henry was a man in his mid-thirties —yes, and President Eliot was seven and Uncle Joe Cannon was five. As for Minneapolis, now a city of four hundred thousand people, seventy-five years ago it consisted of one cabin. Before 1837, there were less than three hundred whites and mixed breeds in all this Minnesotan domain of eighty thousand square miles—the size of England and Scotland put together.

It is so incredibly new; it has grown so dizzyingly. Here is a village which during the Civil War was merely a stockade with two or three log stores and a company of infantry, a refuge for the settlers when the Sioux came raiding. During a raid in 1863, a settler was scalped within sight of the stockade.

Now, on the spot where the settler was scalped, is a bungalow farmhouse, with leaded casement windows, with radio and phonograph, and electric lights in house and garage and barns. A hundred blooded cows are milked there by machinery. The farmer goes into town for Kiwanis Club meetings, and last year he drove his Buick to Los Angeles. He is, or was, too prosperous to belong to the Non-partisan League or to vote the Farmer-Labor ticket.

Minnesota is unknown to the Average Easterner, say to a Hartford insurance man or to a New York garment-worker, not so much because it is new as because it is neither Western and violent, nor Eastern and crystallized. Factories and shore hotels are inevitably associated with New Jersey, cowpunchers and buttes with Montana; California is apparent, and Florida and Maine. But Minnesota is un-

placed. I have heard a Yale junior speculate: "Now you take those Minnesota cities—say take Milwaukee, for instance. Why, it must have a couple of hundred thousand population, hasn't it?" (Nor is this fiction. He really said it.)

This would be a composite Eastern impression of Minnesota: a vastness of wind-beaten prairie, flat as a parade ground, wholly given up to wheat-growing save for a fringe of pines at the north and a few market-towns at the south; these steppes inhabited by a few splendid Yankees—one's own sort of people— and by Swedes who always begin sentences with "Vell, Aye tank," who are farmhands, kitchen-maids, and icemen, and who are invariably humorous.

This popular outline bears examination as well as most popular beliefs; quite as well as the concept that Negroes born in Chicago are less courteous than those born in Alabama. Minnesota is not flat. It is far less flat than the province of Quebec. Most of it is prairie, but the prairie rolls and dips and curves; it lures the motorist like the English roads of Broad Highway fiction. Along the skyline the cumulus clouds forever belly and, with our dry air, nothing is more spectacular than the crimson chaos of our sunsets. But our most obvious beauty is the lakes. There are thousands of them—nine or ten thousand—brilliant among suave grain fields or masked by cool birch and maples. On the dozen-mile-wide lakes of the north are summer cottages of the prosperous from Missouri, Illinois, even Texas.

Leagues of the prairie are utterly treeless, except for artificial windbreaks of willows and cottonwoods encircling the farmhouses. Here the German Catholic spire can be seen a dozen miles off, and the smoke of the Soo Line freight two stations away. But from this plains country you come into a northern pine wilderness, "the Big Woods," a land of lumber camps and reservation Indians and lonely tote-roads, kingdom of Paul Bunyan, the mythical hero of the lumberjacks.

The second error is to suppose that Minnesota is entirely a wheat State. It was, at one time, and the Minneapolis flour-mills are still the largest in the world. Not even Castoria is hymned by more billboards than is Minneapolis flour. But today it is Montana and Saskatchewan and the Dakotas which produce most of the wheat for our mills, while the Minnesota farmers, building tall red silos which adorn their barns like the turrets of Picardy, turn increasingly to dairying. We ship beef to London, butter to Philadelphia. The iron from our Mesaba mines is in Alaskan rails and South African bridges, and as to manufacturing, our refrigerators and heat-regulators comfort Park Avenue apartment-houses, while our chief underwear factory would satisfy a Massachusetts Brahmin or even a Chicago advertising-man.

Greatest error of all is to believe that Minnesota is entirely Yankee and Scandinavian, and that the Swedes are helots and somehow ludicrous.

A school principal in New Duluth analyzed his three hundred and thirty children as Slovene, 49; Italian, 47; Serbian, 39; American, 37; Polish, 30; Austrian and Swedish, 22 each; Croatian, 20; colored, 9 (it is instructive to note that he did not include them among the "Americans"); Finnish, 7; Scotch, 6; Slav unspecified, 5; German, French, Bohemian, and Jewish, 4 each; Rumanian, Norwegian, and Canadian, 3 each; Scandinavian, unspecified; Lithuanian, Irish, Ukrainian, and Greek, 2 each; Russian and English, 1 each—60 per cent of them from Southern and Eastern Europe!

Such a Slavification would, of course, be true only of an industrial or mining community, but it does indicate that the whole Mid-Western population may alter as much as has the East. In most of the State there is a predomination of Yankees, Germans, Irish, and all branches of Scandinavians, Icelanders and Danes as well as Swedes and Norwegians. And among all racial misconceptions none is more vigorously absurd than the belief that the Minnesota Scandinavians are, no matter how long they remain here, like the characters of that estimable old stock-company play

"Yon Yonson"—a tribe humorous, inferior, and unassimilable. To generalize, any popular generalization about Scandinavians in America is completely and ingeniously and always wrong.

In Minnesota itself one does not hear (from the superior Yankees whom one questions about that sort of thing) that the Scandinavians are a comic people, but rather that they are surly, that they are Socialistic, that they "won't Americanize." Manufacturers and employing lumbermen speak of their Swedish employees precisely as wealthy Seattleites speak of the Japs, Bostonians of the Irish, Southwesterners of the Mexicans, New Yorkers of the Jews, marine officers of the Haitians, and Mr. Rudyard Kipling of nationalist Hindus—or nationalist Americans. Unconsciously, all of them give away the Inferior Race Theory, which is this: An inferior race is one whose members work for me. They are treacherous, ungrateful, ignorant, lazy, and agitator-ridden, because they ask for higher wages and thus seek to rob me of the dollars which I desire for my wife's frocks and for the charities which glorify me. This inferiority is inherent. Never can they become Good Americans (or English Gentlemen, or High-wellborn Prussians). I know that this is so, because all my university classmates and bridge-partners agree with me.

The truth is that the Scandinavians Americanize only too quickly. They Americanize much more quickly than Americans. For generation after generation there is a remnant of stubborn American abolitionist stock which either supports forlorn causes and in jail sings low ballads in a Harvard accent, or else upholds, like Lodge, an Adams tradition which is as poisonous as communism to a joy in brotherly boosting. So thorough are the Scandinavians about it that in 1963 we shall be hearing Norwegian Trygavasons and Icelandic Gislasons saying of the Montenegrins and Letts: "They're reg'lar hogs about wages, but the worst is, they simply won't Americanize. They won't vote either the Rotary or the Ku Klux ticket. They keep hollering about wanting some kind of a doggone Third Party."

Scandinavians take to American commerce and schooling and journalism as do

Sauk Centre, Minnesota—Sinclair Lewis's "Main Street"—in the '20's and thirty years later. *Wide World Photos*

Scotsmen or Cockneys. Particularly they take to American politics, the good old politics of Harrison and McKinley and Charley Murphy. Usually, they bring nothing new from their own experimental countries. They permit their traditions to be snatched away. True, many of them have labored for the Nonpartisan League, for woman suffrage, for coöperative societies. The late Governor John Johnson of Minnesota seems to have been a man of destiny; had he lived he would probably have been President, and possibly a President of power and originality. But again—there was Senator Knute Nelson, who made McCumber look like a left-wing syndicalist and Judge Gary like François Villon. There is Congressman Steenerson of Minnesota, chairman of the House postal committee. Mr. Steenerson once produced, out of a rich talent matured by a quarter of a century in the House, an immortal sentence. He had been complaining at lunch that the Nonpartisan League had introduced the obscene writings of "this Russian woman, Ellen Key," into the innocent public schools. Someone hinted to the Scandinavian Mr. Steenerson, "But I thought she was a Swede."

MINNESOTA, THE NORSE STATE   **415**

He answered: *"No, the Key woman comes from Finland and the rest of Red Russia, where they nationalize the women."*

Naturally it is the two new Senators, Hendrik Shipstead and Magnus Johnson, who now represent to the world the Scandinavian element in Minnesota. How much they may bring to the cautious respectability of the Senate cannot be predicted but certainly, like John Johnson, they vigorously represent everything that is pioneer, democratic, realistic, *American* in our history.

Good and bad, the Scandinavians monopolize Minnesota politics. Of the last nine governors of the State, including Senatorial-Candidate Preus, six have been Scandinavians. So is Harold Knutson, Republican whip of the House. Scandinavians make up a large proportion of the Minnesota State Legislature, and while in Santa Fé the Mexican legislators speak Spanish, while in Quebec the representatives still debate in French though for generations they have been citizens of a British dominion, in Minnesota the politicians who were born abroad are zealous to speak nothing but Americanese. Thus it is in business and the home. Though a man may not have left Scandinavia till he was twenty, his sons will use the same English, good and bad, as the sons of settlers from Maine, and his daughters will go into music clubs or into cocktail sets, into college or into factories, with the same prejudices and ideals and intonations as girls named Smith and Brewster.

The curious newness of Minnesota has been suggested, but the really astonishing thing is not the newness—it is the oldness, the solid, traditionalized, cotton-wrapped oldness. A study of it would be damaging to the Free and Fluid Young America theory. While parts of the State are still so raw that the villages among the furrows or the dusty pines are but frontier camps, in the cities and in a few of the towns there is as firm a financial oligarchy and almost as definite a social system as London, and this power is behind all Sound Politics, in direct or indirect control of all business. It has its Old Families, who tend to marry only within their set. Anywhere in the world, an Old Family is one which has had wealth for at least thirty years longer than average families

of the same neighborhood. In England, it takes (at most) five generations to absorb "parvenus" and "profiteers" into the gentry, whether they were steel profiteers in the Great War or yet untitled land profiteers under William the Conqueror. In New York it takes three generations—often. In the Middle West it takes one and a half.

No fable is more bracing, or more absurd, than that all the sons and grandsons of the pioneers, in Minnesota or in California, in Arizona or Nebraska, are racy and breezy, unmannerly but intoxicatingly free. The grandchildren of men who in 1862 fought the Minnesota Indians, who dogtrotted a hundred miles over swamp-blurred trails to bear the alarm to the nearest troops—some of them are still clearing the land, but some of them are complaining of the un-English quality of the Orange Pekoe in dainty painty city tea-rooms which stand where three generations ago the Red River fur-carts rested; their chauffeurs await them in Pierce Arrow limousines (special bodies by Kimball, silver fittings from Tiffany); they present Schnitzler and St. John Ervine at their Little Theaters; between rehearsals they chatter of meeting James Joyce in Paris; and always in high-pitched Mayfair laughter they ridicule the Scandinavians and Finns who are trying to shoulder into their sacred, ancient Yankee caste. A good many of their names are German.

Naturally, beneath this Junker class there is a useful, sophisticated, and growing company of doctors, teachers, newspapermen, liberal lawyers, musicians who have given up Munich and Milan for the interest of developing orchestras in the new land. There is a scientific body of farmers. The agricultural school of the huge University of Minnesota is sound and creative. And still more naturally, between Labor and Aristocracy there is an army of the peppy, poker-playing, sales-hustling He-men who are our most characteristic Americans. But even the He-men are not so obvious as they seem. What their future is, no man knows—and no woman dares believe. It is conceivable that, instead of being a menace in their naïve boosting and their fear of the unusual, they may pass only too soon; it is possible that their standardized bathrooms and Overlands will change to an equally standardized and formula-bound culture—yearning Culture, arty Art. We have been hurled from tobacco-chewing to tea-drinking with gasping speed; we may as quickly dash from boosting to a beautiful and languorous death. If it is necessary to be Fabian in politics, to keep the reformers (left wing or rigid right) from making us perfect too rapidly, it is yet more necessary to be a little doubtful about the ardent souls who would sell Culture; and if the Tired Business Man is unlovely and a little dull, at least he is real, and we shall build only on reality.

Small is the ducal set which controls these other classes. It need be but small. In our rapid accumulation of wealth we have been able to create an oligarchy with ease and efficiency, with none of the vulgar risks which sword-girt Norfolks and Percys encountered. This is one of the jests which we have perpetrated. The nimbler among our pioneering grandfathers appropriated to their private uses some thousands of square miles in northern Minnesota, and cut off—or cheerfully lost by forest fire—certain billions of feet of such lumber as will never be seen again. When the lumber was gone, the land seemed worthless. It was good for nothing but agriculture, which is an unromantic occupation, incapable of making millionaires in one generation. The owners had few of them acquired more than a million dollars, and now they could scarcely give their holdings away. Suddenly, on parts of this scraggly land, iron was discovered, iron in preposterous quantities, to be mined in the open pit, as easily as hauling out gravel. Here is the chief supply of the Gary and South Chicago mills. The owners of the land do not mine the ore. They have gracefully leased it—though we are but Westerners, we have our subsidiary of the United States Steel Company. The landowner himself has only to go abroad and sit in beauty like a flower, and every time a steam shovel dips into the ore, a quarter drops into his pocket.

So at last our iron-lumber-flour railroad aristocracy has begun to rival the beef barons of Chicago, the coal lords of Pennsylvania, and the bond princes of New York.

This article is intended to be a secret but flagrant boost. It is meant to increase civic pride and the value of Minnesota real estate. Yet the writer wonders if he will completely satisfy his chambers of commerce. There is a chance that they would prefer a statement of the value of our dairy products, the number of our admirable new school-buildings, the number of motor tourists visiting our lakes, and an account of James J. Hill's encouraging progress from poverty to magnificence. But a skilled press agent knows that this would not be a boost; it would be an admission of commerce-ruled barrenness. The interesting thing in Minnesota is the swift evolution of a complex social system, and, since in two generations we have changed from wilderness to country clubs, the question is what the next two generations will produce. It defies certain answer; it demands a scrupulous speculation free equally from the bland certitudes of chambers of commerce and the sardonic impatience of professional radicals. To a realistic philosopher, the existence of an aristocracy is not (since it does exist) a thing to be bewailed, but to be examined as a fact.

There is one merit not of Minnesota alone but of all the Middle West which must be considered. The rulers of our new land may to the eye seem altogether like the rulers of the East—of New England, New York, Pennsylvania. Both groups are chiefly reverent toward banking, sound Republicanism, the playing of golf and bridge, and the possession of large motors. But whereas the Easterner is content with these symbols and smugly desires nothing else, the Westerner, however golfocentric he may be, is not altogether satisfied; and raucously though he may snortle at his wife's "fool suffrage ideas" and "all this highbrow junk the lecture-hounds spring on you," yet secretly, wistfully he desires a beauty that he does not understand.

As a pendant, to hint that our society has become somewhat involved in the few years since Mr. Henry Lorenz of Saskatchewan was seventy, let me illogically lump a few personal observations of Minnesota:

Here is an ex-professor of history in the State University, an excellent scholar who, retiring after many years of service, cheerfully grows potatoes in a backwoods farm among the northern Minnesota pines, and builds up coöperative selling for all the farmers of his district.

Here is the head of a Minneapolis school for kindergartners, a woman who is summoned all over the country to address teachers' associations. She will not admit candidates for matriculation until she is sure they have a gift for teaching. She does something of the work of a Montessori, with none of the trumpeting and anguish of the dottoressa.

Here is the greatest, or certainly the largest, medical clinic in the world—the Mayo clinic, with over a hundred medical specialists besides the clerks and nurses. It is the supreme court of diagnosis. Though it is situated in a small town, off the through rail routes, it is besieged by patients from Utah and Ontario and New York as much as by Minnesotans. When the famous European doctors come to America, they may look at the Rockefeller Institute, they may stop at Harvard and Rush and Johns Hopkins and the headquarters of the American Medical Association, but certainly they will go on to Rochester. The names of "Charley" and "Will" have something of the familiarity of "R. L. S." and "T. R."

Here is a Chippewa as silent and swart as his grandfather, an active person whom the cavalry used to hunt every open season. The grandson conducts a garage, and he actually understands ignition. His farm among the lowering Norway pines he plows with a tractor.

Here is a new bookshop which is publishing the first English translation of the letters of Abélard. The translator, Henry Bellows, is a Ph.D., an editor, and a colonel of militia.

Here are really glorious buildings: the Minneapolis Art Institute, the State Capitol, the St. Paul Public Library, and Ralph Adams Cram's loveliest church. Here, on the shore of Lake of the Isles, is an Italian palace built by a wheat speculator. Here where five years ago were muddy ruts are perfect cement roads.

Here is a small town, a "typical prairie town," which has just constructed a competent golf course. From this town came a minister to Siam and a professor of history in Columbia.

And here are certain Minnesota authors. You know what Mid-Western authors are—rough fellows but vigorous, ignorant of the classics and of Burgundy, yet close to the heart of humanity. They write about farmyards and wear flannel shirts. Let us confirm this portrait by a sketch of eleven Minnesota authors, most of them born in the State:

Charles Flandrau, author of "Harvard Episodes" and "Viva Mexico," one-time Harvard instructor, now wandering in Spain. Agnes Repplier has called him the swiftest blade among American essayists. Scott Fitzgerald, very much a Minnesotan, yet the father of the Long Island flapper, the prophet of the Ritz, the idol of every Junior League. Alice Ames Winter, recently president of the General Federation of Women's Clubs. Claude Washburn, author of "The Lonely Warrior" and several other novels which, though they are laid in America, imply a European background. He has lived for years now in France and Italy. Margaret Banning, author of "Spellbinders." Thomas Boyd, author of that valiant impression of youth in battle, "Through the Wheat." Grace Flandrau, of "Being Respectable" and other authentically sophisticated novels. Woodward Boyd, whose first novel, "The Love Legend," is a raid on the domestic sentimentalists. Carlton Miles, a dramatic critic who gives Minnesota readers the latest news of the continental stage. He is just back from a European year spent with such men as Shaw, Drinkwater, and the director of La Scala. Brenda Ueland, who lives in Greenwich Village and writes for the *Atlantic Monthly*. Sinclair Lewis, known publicly as a scolding corn-belt realist, but actually (as betrayed by the samite-yclad, Tennyson-and-water verse which he wrote when he was in college) a yearner over what in private life he probably calls "quaint ivied cottages."

Seventy-five years ago—a Chippewa-haunted wilderness. Today—a complex civilization with a future which, stirring or dismaying or both, is altogether unknowable. To understand America, it is merely necessary to understand Minnesota. But to understand Minnesota you must be an historian, an ethnologist, a poet, a cynic, and a graduate prophet all in one.

AMERICAN HUNGER

SHERWOOD ANDERSON

On the march across Ohio in 1813, one of General Harrison's young officers took a liking to a campsite in Sandusky County. Beside his campfire he drove a stake into the ground, and said, "At this spot I shall build my future home, which shall be the nucleus of a thriving town." In 1820 he returned, searched the woods for his weathered stake, and found smoke sifting up from a squatter's cabin. He bought the squatter off with a barrel of whiskey, and took possession. In time a settlement, named Clyde, grew up on his land. A hundred years later Sherwood Anderson portrayed the town in Winesburg, Ohio.

Like Masters' "Spoon River," Anderson's "Winesburg" is a town of outer monotony and inner turmoil, its people driven by vague desires, frustrations, revolts. Anderson saw the half-wild Midwest landscape, the unformed community, the slack, downhill lives of a post-frontier people. Yet at times there came a startled sense of wonder and unrealized opportunity.

All his life Sherwood Anderson (1876–1941) kept asking questions, especially about the Midwest that he knew by bruising contact and brooding reflection. Was it a land of promise, or a land of defeat? He never could decide. But in Tar, *the story of a Midwest childhood, he saw that his native region, careless and wasteful as it was, nurtured its children with a certain hunger and reward.*

OHIO in the spring or summer, race horses trotting on a race track, corn growing in fields, little streams in narrow valleys, men going out in the spring to plow. In the fall, the nuts getting ripe in the woods about an Ohio town. Over in Europe they clean everything up. They have a lot of people and not too much land. When he grew to be a man Tar saw Europe and liked it, but all the time he was there he had an American hunger and it wasn't a Star Spangled Banner hunger either.

What he hungered for was waste places, roominess. He wanted to see weeds growing, neglected old orchards, empty haunted houses.

An old worm fence where the elders and berries grow wild wastes a lot of land a barbed wire fence saves, but it is nice. It's a place for a boy to crawl under and hide for a while. A man, if he is any good, never gets over being a boy.

In the woods about Middle-Western towns in Tar's time, a world of waste places. From the top of the hill where the Mooreheads lived, after Tar got well and began to go to school, you only had to walk across a cornfield and a meadow, where the Shepards kept their cow, to get to the woods along Squirrel Creek. John was selling papers and was pretty busy, so maybe he couldn't go along and Robert was too young.

Jim Moore lived down the road in a white, freshly-painted house and could nearly always get away. The other boys at school called him "Pee-Wee Moore," but Tar didn't. Jim was a year older and was pretty strong, but that wasn't the only reason. Tar and Jim went through the standing corn, they went across the meadow.

If Jim could not go it was all right.

What Tar did when he went alone was

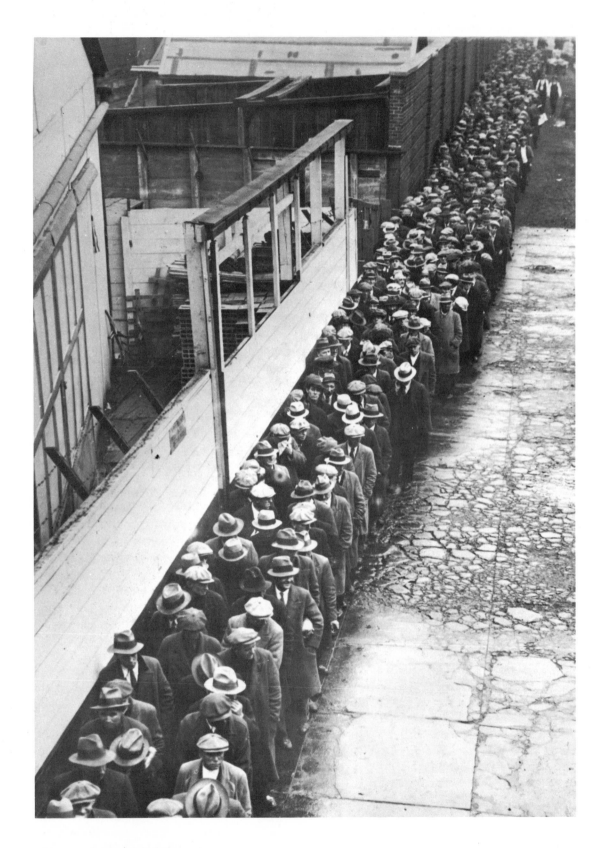

Left: The jobless in the '30's. *Wide World Photo*   Above: Hooverville near the Free
Bridge between Illinois and Missouri, 1931. *Wide World Photo*   Below: The steel
strike in Chicago, 1937. *Wide World Photo*

to imagine things. His imagination made him afraid sometimes, it made him glad and happy sometimes.

The corn, when it grew high, was like a forest down under which there was always a strange soft light. It was hot down under the corn and made Tar sweat. At night his mother made him wash his feet and hands before he went to bed, so he got as dirty as he wanted to. There was nothing saved by keeping clean.

Sometimes he sprawled on the ground and lay for a long time sweating and watching the ants and bugs on the ground under the corn.

Ants, grasshoppers and bugs in general had a world of their own, birds had their world, wild animals and tame animals had their worlds. What does a pig think? Tame ducks in some one's yard are the funniest things in the world. They are scattered around and one of them makes a honking sound and they all begin to run. The back part of a duck wobbles up and down when he runs. Their flat feet go pitter-patter, pitter-patter,

the funniest sound. And then they all get together and there isn't anything special going on. They stand looking at each other. "Well, what were you honking for? What'd you call us for, you fool?"

In the woods along a creek in a wasteful country, logs lie about rotting. There is first a cleared place and then a place so filled with brush and berry bushes, you can't see into it. It makes a good kind of place for rabbits—or snakes.

In a woods like that there are paths everywhere, leading just nowhere. You sit on a log. If there is a rabbit in the pile of brush in front, what do you suppose he is thinking about? He sees you and you can't see him. If there is a man and a woman rabbit, what are they saying to each other? Do you suppose a man rabbit ever gets a little lit up and comes home to sit around bragging to the neighbors about when he was in the army, the neighbors having been only privates while he was a captain? If the man rabbit does that he certainly talks pretty low. You can't hear a word he says.

MIDDLETOWN . . . IN TRANSITION

ROBERT S. LYND
AND HELEN MERRELL LYND

When the Lynds chose a representative American community for social study, it could not be a New England town, a southern town, or a town in the Rocky Mountains. It had to be, they felt, "in that common-denominator of America, the Middle West," near the national center of population, which was then in west central Indiana. They chose the city of Muncie, which they called Middletown. In 1929 appeared their comprehensive study of Middletown, *which was followed eight years later by* Middletown in Transition.

At the Treaty of Greene Ville, which lies behind so much of Midwest history, General Wayne's chief interpreter was Captain William Wells, a white man who had been reared by the Miami Indians. He had married a daughter of Chief Little Turtle and was the father of four black-eyed children. In the allotment of lands one of his daughters was given a 672-acre tract on the White River in Indiana, the former site of a Munsee Indian village. At the time of the St. Mary's Indian Treaty in 1818 this half-breed woman sold her land to a speculator. In 1827 the village of Munseytown was laid out, and settlement began. The name was changed to Muncie in 1845.

The background of the city, its economic growth, and certain of its social attitudes are sketched in these excerpts from Middletown *and its sequel,* Middletown in Transition.

TWO major experiences in Middletown antedate 1890, the date taken as the horizon of this study: the pioneer life of the earlier part of the century, and the gas boom of the end of the eighties which ushered in Middletown's industrial revolution. Both are within the memory of men who still walk the streets of the city.

The first permanent settlement in this county occurred in 1820, and county government was granted in 1827. The memory of one of the oldest citizens, a leading local physician throughout the nineties, reaches back to the eighteen-forties. Within the lifetime of this one man local transportation has changed from virtually the "hoof and sail" methods in use in the time of Homer; grain has ceased to be cut in the state by thrusting the sickle into the ripened grain as in the days of Ruth and threshing done by trampling out by horses on the threshing-floor or by flail; getting a living and making a home have ceased to be conducted under one roof by the majority of the American people; education has ceased to be a luxury accessible only to the few; in his own field of medicine the X-ray, anaesthetics, asepsis, and other developments have tended to make the healing art a science; electricity, the telephone, telegraph, and radio have appeared; and the theory of evolution has shaken the theological cosmogony that had reigned for centuries.

This local physician whose lifetime so nearly spans that of Middletown, the tenth of a family of eleven, was named, with the political fervor of the time, General William Harrison K———. The log farmhouse of his father was ceiled inside without plaster, the walls bare save for three prized pictures of Washington, Jackson, and Clay. All meals were cooked before the great kitchen fireplace, corn pones and "cracklings" and bread being baked in the glare of a large curved reflector set before the open fire. At night the rooms were lighted by the open fire and by tallow dips; there was great excitement later when the first candle mold appeared in the neighborhood. Standard time was unknown; few owned watches, and sun time was good enough during the day, while early and late candle lighting served to distinguish the periods at night. When the fire went out on the family hearth the boy ran to a neighbor's to bring home fire between two boards; it was not until later that the first box of little sticks tipped with sulphur startled the neighborhood.

The homely wisdom of pioneer life prescribed that children be passed through a hole in the trunk of a hollow tree to cure "short growth"; hogs must be slaughtered at certain times of the moon or the bacon would shrink; babies must be weaned at certain times of the zodiac; the "madstone," "a small bone from the heart of a deer," was a valuable antidote for hydrophobia or snake-bite; certain persons "blew the fire out of a burn," arrested hemorrhage or cured erysipelas by uttering mysterious charms; a pan of water under the bed was used to check night sweats; bleeding was the sovereign remedy for fits, loss of consciousness, fever, and many other ills; and "in eruptive fevers, especially measles, where the eruption was delayed, a tea made of sheep's dung, popularly known as 'nanny tea,' was a household remedy."

Social calls were unknown, but all-day visits were the rule, a family going to visit either by horseback, the children seated behind the grown-ups, or in chairs set in the springless farm wagon. Social intercourse performed a highly important service; there were no daily papers in the region, and much news traveled by word of mouth. Nobody came to the home around mealtime who was not urged to take his place at the table—preachers being particularly welcome. Men would talk together for hours on the Providential portent of the great Comet of 1843, or of the time ten years before when the "stars fell." Men and women went miles and spent days in order to hear champions argue disputed political or religious points. People "got religion" and were "awakened to sin" at camp meetings under the vivid exhortation of baptizing preachers. The "Word" wove its influence closely about everyday acts.

Forty years later, in 1885, before gas and wealth spouted from the earth, bringing in their wake a helter-skelter industrial development, Middletown, a placid county-seat of some 6,000 souls, still retained some of the simplicity of this early pioneer life. "On the streets . . . on fair days lawyers, doctors, the officials of the county courts, and the merchants walked about in their shirt sleeves. The house painter went along with his ladder on his shoulder. In the stillness there could be heard the hammers of the carpenters building a new house for the son of a merchant who had married the daughter of a blacksmith." Men in their prime who had grown up under pioneer conditions now controlled the affairs of Middletown. They were occupied with such momentous matters as offering "$200 for the scalp or body of any person in the city caught setting fire to the property of another," or passing regulations in response to complaints about neighborhood cows running through the streets and destroying lawns, or with badly bungling the job of laying the first town sewer.

The thin edge of industry was beginning to appear, though few people thought of the place then as anything but an agricultural county-seat: a bagging plant employed from a hundred to a hundred and fifty people, making bags from the flax grown in the surrounding countryside; a clay tile yard employed some fifteen; a roller-skate "company" in an old barn up an alley, perhaps eight; a feather-duster "factory," five or six; a small foundry, half a dozen; and a planing mill and two flour mills, a few more. It was still for Middletown the age of wood, and a new industry meant a hardwood skewer shop, a barrel-heading shop, or a small wooden pump works.

Such modest ventures in manufacturing as the community exhibited were the tentative responses of small local capital to the thing that was happening to the whole Middle West. The Federal Census reveals a steady move-ment westward of the center of manufacturing; in 1880 it was still in Pennsylvania, but by 1890 it had pushed on until it was eight and one-half miles west of Canton, Ohio. Dry-goods clerks were beginning to spend their evenings perfecting little models of washing-machines, mechanical hair-clippers, can-openers, various power-driven devices. The proprietor of a small Middletown restaurant who led a town band in the evening and "was always neglecting business to tinker around at things" saw a crude cash-register in a saloon in a neighboring city while on a trip there with his band, conceived the idea of a self-adding register, and set to work in the hope of making his fortune. The annual total of patents registered in Washington, which had remained practically constant during the decade of the seventies, jumped in 1890 to roughly double the 1880 figure.

In the state in which Middletown is located, the number of wage-earners increased from 69,508 in 1880 to 110,590 in 1890, and by 1900 was to total 155,956. The capital invested in manufacturing plants in the state doubled between 1880 and 1890 and was almost to double again by 1900.

The quiet life of the town drowsing about its courthouse square with its wooden pump—and iron dippers, punctually renewed every Fourth of July—was beginning to stir to these outside influences. A small Business and Manufacturing Association was formed about 1886 for "the promotion of any and all undertakings calculated to advance the interests, improvements and general welfare of the city."

And then in the fall of '86 came gas.

In 1876 a company boring for coal twelve miles north of the town had plugged up the hole and abandoned the project after boring 600 feet: all they "struck" was a foul odor and a roaring sound deep in the bowels of the earth, and rumor had it that they had invaded "his Satanic Majesty's domain." Nine years later, when natural gas was discovered at other points in the Middle West, the incident of the plugged-up hole north of town was recalled. In October, 1886, there was great local excitement over the plans "to bore for gas or oil or both." In November we read, "The persons employed to bore for oil have this morning 'struck' gas, and everybody is on the way to see for themselves." The roar of the escaping gas is said to have been audible for two miles and the flame when it was "lit up" could be seen in Middletown a dozen miles away.

The boom was on.

The laying of a pipe line to bring the gas into the county-seat began immediately, and new wells were sunk. By the following April a local well was producing 5,000,000 feet daily. New wells multiplied on every hand. In January, 1891, the local paper exclaimed, "We have a new gas well which really does eclipse all others in the [gas] belt. Daily output is nearly 15,000,000 feet, and they worked over thirty hours trying to anchor the flow." No wonder the little town went wild!

Meanwhile, from the spring of '87 on through '91 and '92, the "boomers" were arriving:

"Four vestibule, one dining-room and one baggage special train from Buffalo with 134 of its capitalists came in last night to see for themselves what gas can do and are much pleased. . . . Taken in carriages to all the factories and sites. . . . Grand manufacturing exhibition at the Rink, and a beautiful display of four open street cars." "A trainload of 1,200 from Cincinnati." "Quite a number of New York City capitalists and newspaper men came in from the East last night; three and one-half pages of the ——— Hotel register were covered with their signatures." "American Association for the Advancement of Science visits the city and witnesses the wonders of natural gas; 300 scientists and men of affairs in the party."

Real estate was being turned over with dizzy rapidity. In 1888 a man tried to buy an eight-acre chunk of farm land on the outskirts of town but, shying at the price of $1,600, took only a sixty-day option. Before the sixty-day option expired the eight acres changed hands five times, the final price being $3,200.

Nothing short of the sky seemed an adequate limit to the citizens of Middletown. A contemporary parody runs—

"Tell me not in mournful numbers
That the town is full of gloom,

For the man's a crank who slumbers
In these bursting days of boom."

Optimists predicted a population of 50,000 in five years and even the pessimists allowed only ten years. The general sentiment was that the gas supply was inexhaustible. Some called it "The City of Eternal Gas." The Introduction to the Middletown City Directory announced confidently, "Every forty acres will supply a gas well, and 576 wells can be drilled within . . . [the] corporate limits and suburbs." "The mathematical deduction would be," chanted a "boom book," "that the continuance of this supply would be, at least, one hundred times as long as at Pittsburgh, which would be 700 years." Great flambeaus burned recklessly day and night in the streets and at the wells. When the pipe lines were laid, consumers were charged by the fixture rather than by any system of exact measurement. It was cheaper to leave the gas on and to throw open doors and windows than to expend a match in relighting it.

With the boomers came new industries lured by free fuel and free building sites. The earlier Business and Manufacturing Association awakened to new life in February, 1887, as the "Board of Trade," and concerted efforts were made to "sell the town" to industrial capital. Glass came first. Next were the iron mills—a bridge company, a nail works. A diary for 1888-9 buzzes with rumors of the coming of these new plants:

"Report that another glass factory is coming immediately." "Work progressing on the pulp mill and rubber factory." "A nail works wants to come here from ———." "Considerable talk about a Palace Stock Car Factory." "A boot and shoe factory is coming; building commenced this afternoon."

By the summer of 1890 the local paper speaks of the thriving little "gasopolis" with pardonable pride:

"Two and one-half years ago when natural gas was first discovered [Middletown] was a county-seat of 7,000 inhabitants. . . . It has grown since that time to a busy manufacturing city of 12,000. . . . Over forty factories have located here during that time. . . . There has been $1,500,000 invested in Middletown manufacturing enterprises employing 3,000 men. . . . Over thirty gas wells have been drilled in and around the city, every one of which is good. . . ."

The first boom of '87 and '88 was the spontaneous, unorganized rush to a new El Dorado. When the earlier boom was renewed in '91 it was engineered by the Eastern land syndicate and carried forward by the local boosters' association, the Citizens' Enterprise Company, organized in August, 1891. The last-named organization raised a $200,000 fund to lure new industries with free sites and capital.

Several years later, as abruptly as it had come, the gas departed. By the turn of the century or shortly thereafter, natural gas for manufacturing purposes was virtually a thing of the past in Middletown. But the city had grown by then to 20,000, and, while industry after industry moved away, a substantial foundation had been laid for the industrial life of the city of today.

And yet it is easy, peering back at the little city of 1890 through the spectacles of the present, to see in the dust and clatter of its new industrialism a developed industrial culture that did not exist. Crop reports were still printed on the front page of the leading paper in 1890, and the paper carried a daily column of agricultural suggestions headed "Farm and Garden." Local retail stores were overgrown country stores swaggering under such names as "The Temple of Economy" and "The Beehive Bazaar." The young Goliath, Industry, was still a neighborly sort of fellow. The agricultural predominance in the county-seat was gone, but the diffusion of the new industrial type of culture was as yet largely superficial—only skin-deep. . . .

One went down across the railroad tracks and stood at the gate of the General Motors plant watching the men come off the job in the afternoon: Here was a horde of men heavily on the young side, walking rapidly toward the parking space for employees' cars, laughing and talking in groups of twos and threes about baseball, exclaiming, "Boy! I'm

goin' home and have a steak"; or "What's the weather goin' to do Sunday? We wanta drive up to the lakes." The whole feel of the scene was on the easy, resilient side. Here was no crew of helots or men cowed into furtiveness. Half an hour later, as one walked the tree-shaded streets, one saw these men mowing the lawn, painting the garage, playing "catch" with a small son, and smoking a pipe over the evening paper on the front porch.

Perhaps it was because it was June; part of it undoubtedly was because these men had jobs again after the long layoff; part of it was probably due to the general optimism in the air locally. But something else was undoubtedly present, too, to account for these contradictory elements in these workingmen. Actually, both a deep concern over their insecurity and an almost happy-go-lucky indifference exist together inside the skins of Middletown workers. The very presence of the former probably helps to create the latter as an emotional defense enabling the sequence of big and little incidents of daily living to make a tolerable degree of sense.

But one must go deeper to understand the inertias, the lack of solidarity, the concern with present immediacies, the easy contentments, the happy-go-lucky quality, that baffle labor organizers and make Middletown an industrialists' happy hunting ground. The Middletown workingman is American born of American parents. He lives on a Middle Western farm, has moved in from the farm, or his father's family moved to town from a farm. He is thus close to the network of habits of thought engendered by the isolated, self-contained enterprise of farming. One local worker caught up the resistance of these American farm and ex-farm dwellers to labor-union efforts in the succinct statement: "Shucks! fellows from Selma and De Soto [outlying hamlets] can't be organized." This Middletown worker has not lived in a large city where he lost contact with the earth; even his single-family house has a yard, shade trees, and often flowers. This means that he feels he "belongs" on the earth and in this Middletown culture to an extent not so likely to be true among large-city workers living in impersonal flats off the ground. He has not worked with masses of big-city men, many of them foreign born, where he has lost his personal identity and learned to substitute as symbols of his "belonging" the traditions and ideologies of massed proletarians concerning the "class struggle" and similar amalgamating concepts. He is an individualist in an individualistic culture, and he owns some kind of an auto instead of riding other people's streetcars and buses. He has or he wants a job—being "on the county" is a calamity to him—and he is bent primarily on getting ahead under his own steam and ingenuity, like a "good American," even though he is apparently increasingly in a twilight zone of doubt as to whether he can actually get ahead. In his bleak moments of doubt or of sobering advancing age, there are still his "kids going to high school" to keep up the illusion or reality of progress in his life. He doubts, and he also hopes vaguely—and meanwhile he continues to live. This man, with his feet on the ground, jerked about disconcertingly by "good" and "bad" times, lives in the South Side subculture of similarly placed working people, in which one learns to tolerate, as normal, kinds of discontinuities that would upset his brothers north of the tracks. Like the Eskimos under the Arctic Circle, one learns to stabilize one's life on a chancy plane of circumstances.

To such a man, class solidarity and unionization are emotionally foreign, and when tension and opportunity do mount to the point of inducing him to join a union, he is apt to want quick action, or his union becomes just another thing that bothers him needlessly as he patiently seeks to knit a living out of the scant threads at his command.

The Middletown worker may be licked by the economic order now—and now—and now—in the endless series of each day's immediate issues; but the only generalizations about life that his culture has taught him concern *tomorrow*, and "tomorrow" according to the American formula always means "progress," getting closer to whatever it is that one craves. Save for a few veteran socialists who knew Gene Debs, there is not chronically present in Middletown the type of generalization of living that pulls down tomorrow's hope to the dead level of today's frustrations and finds a permanent cause of labor's stalemate in the man-made elements of a capitalist economy. Like the business class, Middletown labor is prone to recognize its disabilities only when they become especially acute, and to take good and bad alike as "in the nature of things," and more due to the inscrutabilities of the cosmic order than to man-generated causes. In the absence of a hard-bitten, tenaciously held system of rationalizations of labor's place in a capitalist economy, Middletown labor in characteristic American fashion lacks any driving sense of class consciousness. It has no dynamic symbols for itself as *over against* the business class; but it has been taught by press, by school, by church, and by tradition to accept, as its own, watered versions of the official business-class symbols. The investigator sensed in the sore, defeated South Side of 1935 more doubts, more sense of being "permanently licked" as a group, of the emptiness of business-class hopes *for them*, a little more feeling of being a permanent group apart, than he sensed in 1925. But all these doubts and incipient tendencies to class consciousness must operate in the face of the strong, clear note of hope so conspicuous in the culture.

THE BIG ADVENTURE

GRAHAM HUTTON

Some of the most acute interpretations of America have come from foreign observers. Graham Hutton, English author and journalist, was a recent visitor to the United States who looked closely and reflected on what he saw. As an official of the British Ministry of Information he spent six years in the Middle West. "The longer I lived there," he observed, "the more I became convinced that the Midwest and its people were largely unknown, widely misinterpreted, and greatly misunderstood."

So he wrote Midwest At Noon *(1946), from which comes this significant summary of the energies and aspirations that enliven the American heartland.*

MOVEMENT made the Midwest, and the Midwest made movement. Perhaps no political revolution ever made as much difference to a country as the revolution in transport made to America. Because of its vast interior this was only natural. As the war of the Revolution and its aftermath sent the pioneers into the Midwest, so the age of steam, with its railroads and steamships, developed it. The result was a miracle.

The natural trend of trade, communications, and ideas, for over two centuries until the early decades of the American Union, was along a north-south line, in either direction. This held colonial society in one mold, one pattern, whether of the New England kind or of the South.

But within one generation after the Midwest was safely acquired, roads were built to aid the pioneers and settlers, and canals were dug to link the rivers or lakes on the east and the west of the Appalachian ranges. At the same time the steamship and railroad were first introduced. The Midwest was bound to become linked with the seaboard, but with which section: North or South? At this beginning of east-west development few midwesterners and few easterners saw as far ahead as the leading southerners, who were quick to sense not only a danger to their profits but also to their dominating political position in House and Senate. The development of the Midwest meant new states, which in turn meant more senators and representatives. How, and with whom, would they vote? And for what?

The first means of locomotion by land into, and inside, the Midwest between 1785 and 1825 were as primitive as any in human history: shanks' mare, oxcart, horses, solid wooden wheels or rollers, and the sled. The latter was not, as its name implies for Europeans, a winter vehicle. It was the equivalent on land of the flatboat on the rivers of the Midwest, and it was necessary because in the dense and matted undergrowth and close-packed forests of the region it was often impracticable for the pioneers to use even rudimentary wheels: wheels are no good until there are fairly clear tracks, and they sink or cut into the ground. The sled was used in summer more than in winter, for in the winters of the Midwest none moved if he could help it; and the phrases "tough sledding" and "hard sledding," which are still used many times daily in Midwest conversation, stem from the pioneers and do not refer to easy sliding over snow.

The primitive trackways, unimaginably befouled in winter and in the thaw or rains, radiated from the great riverways of the region. These waterways were the first roads, and along them the first settlements were made. The sites of great Midwest cities today were first located at fords, portages, and narrows, or where the shortest overland trackway hit the river: Detroit, Green Bay, Portage, Prairie du Chien, La Crosse, Chicago, Peoria, Joliet, Vincennes, St. Louis, Kansas City, Cincinnati, Dubuque, Rock Island, and many another. The rivers flow down to the Mississippi, draining from what used to be the northern ice cap. They form one great drainage basin. They run inward from the foothills of the Rockies on the west, and from the slight spurs of high land surrounding the Great Lakes, and a little way inland from their southern and western shores, on the east. Terre Haute, Highland, Akron, and many placenames including "falls" or "bluffs" mark these spurs. The pioneers had only to strike these lesser or greater tributaries of the Great River and they had an easy, if tedious and meandering, means of locomotion from north and east toward the west and south and eventually right down to New Orleans and the Gulf. These rivers are mighty. The Illinois at Peoria is far wider than the Danube at Budapest.

These routes were all, in the final analysis, north-south. They made the Old Midwest look mainly southward. They strengthened the influence of the southern pioneers who first came into the Midwest. They made it natural that the first Midwest should align itself with Andrew Jackson, himself a pioneer in Tennessee.

The life, traffic, and traffickers on these rivers fill volumes of Midwest folklore, history, fact, fiction, and travelers' tales. Incidentally, someone should explain why freshwater sailors and watermen have always been so quarrelsome, loud-mouthed, and foulmouthed. The bargee in Britain enjoys the same reputation or position in folklore as the Midwest watermen and Mike Fink. Yet it is hard to find such legendary salt-water sailors. Many of the self-assertive, pompous, braggart, quarrelsome, argumentative, and extremely exaggerating characteristics of midwesterners, as testified in American and other visitors' books and as still observable in modified forms today, derive from this river epoch. It was a rough, tough, chip-on-the-shoulder, coat-trailing period.

But it was short lived. The steamboats which only began to ply regularly on the rivers in the 1830's—and incidentally for the first time to chug *upstream* with bulky return cargoes from the South—were themselves to become extinct within four decades as their land cousin, the railroad, carried all before him. The steamboats, however, did begin a revolution in moods and influences in the Midwest. The Hudson-Erie Canal was opened in 1825, carrying freight to and from New York by the navigable Hudson and then through the Mohawk River Valley to Buffalo and so into Lake Erie. The steamboats linked the Great Lakes with this new east-west route —the first east-west route for goods and persons in any bulk—and immeasurably cut down both the time which was required before the 1830's to reach the heart of the Midwest and the cost of getting to or from it. Much more important, however, the canal and the steamboats were the first elements in a long chain of causes, finished by the first railroads, which also followed the water-level routes. These causes very quickly — amazingly quickly — forced an east-west pattern of trade and thought upon the Midwest and weaned it from its former north-south outlook. In the 1840's the British traveler in the interior, Mackay, not only prophesied the abolition of slavery or the end of the Union. He also said that the mere existence of the Mississippi Basin, the Midwest, would prevent any permanent separation of North and South, for the Midwest could not permit the mouth of the Mississippi and its long, level, inland valley to fall under the control of a foreign government.

New Englanders flocked as emigrants by the new route into the Midwest and largely took over the task of breaking the prairies or building up the first midwestern factories and industries and financial institutions. Eastern cities and their capitalists also vied with each other, and even with British capitalists, over the building of Midwest railroads; and, as the first modern communications and factory industries were taken into a Midwest that was eager for them, the products and trade of that Midwest necessarily became directed and "keyed" to the commerce of the East—which in turn was intimately and long connected with the trading needs of Europe, especially Britain. This was the influence which led the

Above: The Pit at the Chicago Board of Trade. *Wide World Photo*   Below: Steel mills on the Cuyahoga at Cleveland. *Courtesy Ohio Historical Society*   Right: Main spans of the Mackinac Bridge from the southwest. *Photo by H. D. Ellis, courtesy Mackinac Bridge Authority*

Midwest to farm not only for America but for countries overseas; and it led to the rapid settlement and development of the prairies. By the same token, it laid the farmers open to the movements of world prices; whereas the tariffs of Clay's "American system" and of the new Republican party insulated the manufacturers, at the Midwest farmers' expense, from the world prices of manufactures.

When Midwest communications were dependent on waterways, settlements could not be located too far from them. The vast spaces or forests between rivers were slow in being cleared and settled. That is why, to this day, the Old Midwest is still more discernible along the rivers, and within a day's walk or ride of their banks, than it is on the prairie, where water is more scarce and the rivers farther away. This Old Midwest was settled, therefore, by reference not to the best soil but to the best land available within these distances of the rivers or lakes. So the coming of the railroads caused a revolution in agriculture, too, as well as in the mere settlement, peopling, and industrialization of the region. The railroads could run anywhere provided, as was true of the prairies, the contours were not too steep and the forests, tall grasses, and undergrowth could be cleared and swamps drained. The most populated settlements then in existence were, of course, those located at the junctions or crossings of waterways; and, wherever these could be easily reached over gently rolling forested or flat prairie country, the first railroads either spring from them or toward them, whereas the building of highways across such country would have been unnecessary and impossible. Accordingly, the first locomotive bells rang the knell of the great primeval Midwest forests as well as that of the six-foot grasses of the prairie; they were a voice in the wilderness preparing a path for the automobile and highway. . . .

Two developments, directly due to geography and transport, had a particular influence on the nature of the Midwest. The first was the discovery and working of the iron-ore deposits in North Michigan and northern Minnesota on the rim of the Great Lakes shortly after the Civil War. Feeder railroads quickly took this ore to the ships, and the new

Soo (Sault Ste Marie) Locks—which now carry more traffic in eight months than the Suez and Panama canals combined carry in a full year—passed the ships along the Lakes to lakeside iron and steel works which otherwise would not exist: Hammond, Gary, and Indiana Harbor in Chicagoland; the Detroit district; Toledo, Cleveland, and many other parts on the Ohio shore of Lake Erie. It then went by rail or water to the Pittsburgh-Youngstown steel area between Ohio and Pennsylvania; and to Buffalo in New York State. Railroads bring the coking coal from the Appalachian or West Virginian coal fields up to the Lakes for transshipment as a return cargo or direct to the iron and steel mills by rail. This peculiar interaction of natural resources and transport routes along the Great Lakes and their hinterland—of iron ore, coal, stone, lumber, and wheat—was of crucial importance in the extension and location of American cities and heavy industries along that narrow hinterland, from Buffalo in the Empire State to Duluth in Minnesota. It contracted an industrial marriage with the new railroads and steamships. Of this natural union of steel and water, coal and steam, was born the industrial revolution of the Midwest after 1860.

The second factor was the differential freight rates of the railroads, which favored the Midwest. Almost but not altogether by chance, the Midwest region became the national hub of the railroad network. Anyone in Chicago can go by train to New York, Washington, New Orleans, Houston, or Denver in the Rocky Mountains overnight—that is, from 750 to over 1,000 miles between about four in the afternoon and nine the next morning. Similarly, within the Midwest region—north of the Ohio River, west of the Appalachians, and east of the Great Plains—the great cities grew great by virtue of their rail connections with the lesser areas around them, which they served as a metropolis, and over which a minor rail network was spread. Coupling these networks with the transcontinental routes and the shipping on the Lakes, the Midwest could scarcely help becoming the region in which the shortest average rail-hauls led either to the biggest retail markets or to the sources of the necessary materials of industry; and most frequently the freight trains bringing the raw materials for one industry were able to return taking finished products to market. Few were the "return empties." This resulted in that simultaneous, mutual, and complementary development of midwestern agriculture and industry, and of midwestern and eastern industry with southern borderland coal and northern ores. Today, and for a long time past, it has made Ohio, Indiana, or Illinois the best center for a factory making consumers' goods and has made the bulk of America's retail market lie east of the Mississippi and north of the Ohio. Most graphically can this be seen in the steady march, decade by decade, of the center of the United States population from east of the Appalachians to Illinois.

One final influence of transport in the development of the region must be mentioned. It is the automobile, which killed the old horse and buggy and necessitated those paved highways which, from the air, make the interior of America look like the unending aftermath of a ticker-tape celebration. Before 1918 the highways were, at their rarest and best, macadam and, at their most frequent and worst, just plain dirt roads—mud in the rains and dust in summer, comfortable for horses and barefoot boys and for nobody else. The cheap automobile after 1912, the truck and trailer, were a boon to the Midwest. To the farmers they meant, first, cheap tractors, pumps, and light engines to save labor and time on the farm. They meant transport which could effectively compete with the disliked and distrusted railroads on the shorter hauls. They meant bringing the regional town or city into what would have been termed mere riding distance before. They meant an evening-up of land values, since land near rail heads up until this time commanded a higher price. They meant a welcome diminution of dependence on weather, bad roads, and horses and wagons. They meant frequent and larger meetings of farmers over a wider area. And they meant the possibility of more mixed farming for the nearest city or large town.

To the urban dwellers they meant nothing less than a social revolution which powerfully affected manners, vacations, sports, health, crime, sexual morality, the solidarity of the family, the natural Midwest insularity of outlook, and the keeping of the Sabbath. They sent unwanted farm labor and farmers' sons to the cities and towns. They gave a powerful impetus to the industrialists' desire to quit the highly taxed centers of cities, since now each worker could afford to go to and fro in his own car on cheap gasoline. Therewith they aggravated the problems of the cities.

The internal combustion engines and the highways they necessitated set the seal on that final *internal* development of the Midwest which the railroads had really begun. Automobiles virtually obliterated its remaining unsettled, uncleared, but cultivable spaces. They gave the well-to-do Midwest city dwellers their first practical possibility of acquiring farms. Hundreds of thousands, having begun life on them, had nostalgically but vainly ached to own or retire to them. These farms could now lie as far as a hundred or two hundred miles from the owner's, or part-owner's, urban workplace and yet be visited and superintended each week end. From each Midwest city, too, the big distributing, wholesale, retail, and mail-order firms could now extend their radius of activity—delivering by truck and trailer, knocking out the characteristic village stores and sometimes the village itself, increasing their own size and turnover and influence on the manufacturer, spreading the gospel of standardized products to the rural population, reducing costs of production and increasing profits and dividends—though not always reducing the cost to consumers, who regretted the passing of the crossroads store and its social focus. But the internal combustion engine also brought better roads, the delivery truck, the doctor, the ambulance, and the school bus.

In this way the Midwest in the automobile age became even more of a melting-pot than ever. The city went to the country for pleasure. The country children went to the town, and so to the city, for careers. More cross-fertilization occurred, more crisscrossing of attitudes, ideas, and ideals. The Old Midwest, hitherto insulated in the farmlands, began at last to lose its compactness and its uniformity. The New Midwest of the cities began to have its first serious doubts.

Thus there quickly came about a great transfiguration of the Midwest. In 1860, except for the Irish and many of the Germans, the population of city and town and farmland was almost uniform: it was Anglo-Saxon, Protestant, equalitarian, and, except for Negroes, free of any sign of economic "status" to which a group or class or nationality were, tacitly or avowedly, ascribed. But an economic and social élite quickly developed, and established its social claims, in the cities of the Midwest. (It had always existed in the East.) It was overwhelmingly Protestant, Anglo-Saxon, or early American.

It could not, except in very few cases, notably from the Old South and New England, claim pride of parentage; but it could rightly claim distinctions of achievement, as proved by great wealth. The wealth was made from the rapidly rising real estate values or from producing or purveying the produce or requirements of the region; or from furnishing its utilities and transport: meat, grains, liquor, groceries, hotels, department stores, and railroads. Later came fortunes from steel and machinery and oil. Beneath this apex of the social pyramid in the Midwest came the attendant professions and services; and beneath them came layer after layer of economic functions, many of which were accounted respectable and many not, ending with those the performers of which had to live "on the wrong side of the tracks." These infinite gradations in the pyramid of Midwest society were largely caused by the immigration, which in turn was caused by the increasing complexity due to industrialization. These complications and social gradations multiplied after 1900, and, as industry itself became more delicately complex, they became more rigid.

They differed, however, in two notable particulars from the social pyramids of the East and of industrialized or industrializing countries in Europe. First, and always excepting the Negro, if it was relatively hard for the father to emancipate himself from a lower economic grade and move to a higher, it was still relatively easier for him than anywhere else on earth, and quite easy for his sons and daughters if they were healthy and capable. Secondly, great wealth, however come by,

could break the charmed limits of these grades in Midwest urban society—which it could not always do in Boston or New York or the South and could not do in Europe.

To this second exception there were, in turn, two exceptions: the Negro and the Jew. They could never "break into" society; and the Negro, unlike the Jew, could not even get rich. With exceptions in the Midwest today that could almost be named and counted on the fingers of two hands, the Jewish families—at least, those known to be Jews—settled in defined districts and were "restricted" from refined ones. They are still kept out of the select residential districts and clubs and have therefore established their own. And the Negroes, flocking more into the Midwest than into any other region after each of the three big wars since 1860, have been kept to the lowest social and economic strata of the social pyramid, thereby making the "Negro problem" as acute in Midwest cities as anywhere in America.

What happened to Negro and Jew in the Midwest, however, is only an extreme example of a social process observable all over the Western world, even where there were no Jews or Negroes. It was not due solely to ill-will on the part of the older residents of the Midwest. It can be seen in all the rapidly growing cities of Western countries, in which economic undertakings and functions have tended to become frozen. It is the problem of our civilization: the urban proletariat. It has been the universal accompaniment of rapid industrialization, modern mass-production methods, and the decline of handicrafts and skill. Accordingly, in the Midwest, as elsewhere, it has happened to all the lower-income groups or lesser economic functions in cities, irrespective of race or nationality. No region of the world has been more rapidly transformed, from a primarily agricultural economy with a racially simple and uniform society, to a leading industrial region with a racially complex and highly differentiated society. This transformation has taken place entirely in its cities, leaving the old, pre-1860 Midwest, with its simpler and more uniform patterns of life, religion, and thought, still perceptible on the farmlands.

So the visitor to the Midwest today finds not one people, not a uniform type of midwesterner. He finds, instead—if he is careful, observant, and slow to judgment—many Midwests with many midwesterners inhabiting them. Some of these Midwests, defined only by the characteristics of their people or their economic status and functions, are as much a part of the East, South, or Far West and their cities as they are of the Midwest proper. In the Midwest proper the visitor finds the wealthiest midwesterners now in its big metropolitan cities. They are mainly Anglo-Saxons, Germans, and Jews by origin, owning big businesses and exercising professions, living a life of material privilege and luxury which is as extreme as, if not more so than, that of Manhattan or Los Angeles. He finds the Italian, Greek, Lithuanian, Polish, Hungarian, Czech, and Negro factory worker or service worker at the base of the social and economic pyramid, but still in towns and cities. Between these extremes he finds, still in towns and cities, a vaguer and less rigidly defined middle class of white-collar workers, run-of-the-mill professional workers, artisans, and workers in the distributive trades, transport, and public service, who are of all European national origins.

All these people are the children of the New Midwest which came into being after 1865. The visitor finds this New Midwest revolving in its cities at a dizzy and wearing tempo: vigorous, excited and excitable, mercurial, intemperate, immoderate, blatant, dirty, but with all the blatancy of its vulgar vigor, and all the dirt of its fantastic work and output; irreligious, yet sheltering all conceivable religions; of one nation, yet of all skins and accents and statures; of differences, extremes, contrasts, and paradoxes, yet of a rude equality and a growing uniformity; of great economic and other social distinctions, yet of a growing standardization of reaction, response, and pattern of thought; cynical yet kind; irresponsible yet affectionate; of violent and rash prejudgments, yet avid for new ideas and for learning.

But if our visitor leaves the cities and goes out to the farming lands, beyond the limits of the cities' truck-farming areas, he finds farms and little farm towns which provide the most striking conceivable contrast with what he has just left. Here is the Old Midwest which came into being between 1800 and 1860 and still remains: virile, still mainly Anglo-Saxon and Protestant, speaking mainly with the same accents, quiet, unexcitable, scrupulously honest, devout, clean, sober, hard-working, living at a steady tempo of natural routine, full of an old culture and of much unconscious memory or history, unsophisticated, philosophical, slow to judgment, inflexible when convinced, and far less volatile or mercurial than its counterpart in the cities.

Thus the Midwest reflects in its popular composition today the two great periods of its own making: the era of primary pioneering and agricultural settlement up to 1860 and the era of urban industrialism thereafter. These two Midwest epochs go on living side by side today. The New Midwest of the towns and cities constantly recruits itself, at the lower levels, from the children of the farms and from immigrants and, at the upper levels, from leading professional and businessmen who come to make a better material living in it from other American regions.

In the still existent Old Midwest of the farms, however, there is little new recruitment. There is little social or economic mobility in it. Accordingly, the psychology and way of life of this older, more settled, more solid, rural Midwest bulks smaller every year in the life of the region as a whole. It remains —if observed at all—as a reminder to the city dwellers of the human qualities of the pioneer and settler who prepared a way in the wilderness for the railroads and factories and cities which, to a cynic, seem bent on making it into another kind of wilderness: grime and mean streets, slums and saloons, graft and rackets, mob politics and lawlessness, group tensions and intolerance, social divisions and conflicts of economic interest.

The people, their widely different origins and outlooks, their conflicting religions and pursuits, made the Midwest as we see it today. They also made themselves, the midwesterners, since, however different they were in their origins and whatever they brought in with them, they all had to adapt themselves to the new and growing life of a new and growing region. It was always, and still is, "becoming." It has not yet completely "jelled" into something immutable and irrevocable. Within a setting fixed only by natural boundaries, soil, and climate, everything else was highly mobile and fluid; institutions, governmental systems, ideas, and Midwest society itself were constantly, and are still, in flux—as you would expect of so vast a melting-pot and such vast quantities of different alloys. The easterner, like the European who came still farther from the east, quickly became altered in this fluid society and took on many of its peculiar characteristics. True to its own origin in great natural extremes, and in the hands of men of great extremes, the Midwest in its miraculous development produced extremes far greater than those of any other region.

Nothing perhaps exemplifies the midwesterners today better than a short inquiry into their genealogy. One typical Chicago family of my acquaintance in 1945 carries its family tree directly back through Prairie du Chien, Wisconsin, to French chevaliers in Canada who were in the fur trade under Louis XV; to Czechs from Brünn, under a Hapsburg emperor, who went to farm in Iowa eighty years ago; to Englishmen who came up from Virginia to farm near Peoria in Illinois over a century ago; to Norwegian dairy farmers who settled in Wisconsin seventy years ago; to a Connecticut Yankee merchant who came to Chicago one hundred years ago; and to Scottish Presbyterian industrialists who came down from Canada about seventy years ago. The family today is "on La Salle Street"—bankers and investment brokers. That is the story of the Midwest in the making. It is a story of the hopes, fears, and triumphs of many nations and peoples. It is a story which is still unfolding, still to unfold. It is the story of "an awfully big adventure."

Acknowledgments

IN compiling this anthology of Midwest experience I have had generous assistance from a number of persons and institutions. Dr. James H. Rodabaugh of the Ohio Historical Society helped me with problems of selection, both of historical texts and of illustrations. Dr. Lewis Beeson of the Michigan Historical Commission allowed me to draw upon the large resources of the Michigan archives, where I had the ready help of Miss Geneva Kebler in choosing picture material. Miss Caroline Dunn of the Indiana Historical Society Library located items which have the substance and flavor of Hoosier history, and she saved me from including a spurious account of travel in pioneer Indiana. Mrs. Hazel Hopper and Miss Louise Wood of the Indiana State Library helped me to find picture materials. For further assistance with period illustration I am indebted to Dr. Clyde C. Walton, Miss Margaret Flint and Mr. S. A. Wetherbee of the Illinois State Historical Library, Miss Cheryle M. Hughes of the Iconographic Collections of the Wisconsin State Historical Society, Mr. J. Richard Lawwill of the Anthony Wayne Parkway Board, and Mrs. Elleine H. Stones of the Burton Historical Collection of the Detroit Public Library, Mr. Ivan E. Whitney of the Buffalo Historical Society, and Miss Sue Sahli of the History Department of the Cleveland Public Library. For information and assistance I am grateful to Miss Bertha Heilbron of the Minnesota Historical Society, Mr. Ralph A. Ulveling, director of the Detroit Public Library, Mrs. Edith Reiter of Marietta, Ohio, and Mr. L. S. Dutton and members of the staff of the Miami University Library. For assistance with textual materials I am indebted to members of the staff of the Audio-Visual Services of Miami University.

WALTER HAVIGHURST
Oxford, Ohio

Date Due

Date Due			
3/16/61			
JUN 29 1961			
1/26/63			
MAR 4 1964			
OCT 22 1964			
JUN 17 1980			
FEB. 29 1984			
JN 0 5 1984			
NO 08 '85			
MY 20 '87			
OC 23 '92			

977
H

AUTHOR   3672

Havighurst, Walter
TITLE
Land of the Long Horizons

DATE DUE   BORRO

977
H   3672
Havighurst, Walter
Land of the Long Horizons